THE
IMPERIAL
ANIMAL

THE
IMPERIAL
ANIMAL

LIONEL TIGER & ROBIN FOX

HOLT, RINEHART AND WINSTON

New York   Chicago   San Francisco

ISBN: 0-03-086582-4

Library of Congress Catalog Card Number: 78-155535

First Edition

Designer: Nancy Tausek

Printed in the United States of America

CONTENTS

PREFACE

ALTHOUGH WE ARE finally responsible for what is in this book, we owe many debts to many people. The book has been in its various stages of preparation for a long time, and we have benefited from very numerous contacts with colleagues and friends. We hope that they will know that although we do not mention them by name, we are nonetheless most grateful for their time, talk, and encouragement.

We are happy to acknowledge the research assistance of George Allyn, Usher Fleising, Frances Hopenwasser, Ray Larsen, Gloria Levitas, Nelson Ossorio, and Ann Parker. It is a pleasure to thank Richard and Judy Bergman and Alfonso and Margaret Ortiz for providing us with occasional places to work. It is also a pleasure to thank Merle Williams, the secretary of the Rutgers Department of Anthropology, for her benign efficiency and for her careful management of many of the important details which our work involves. Since 1967 Rutgers University has offered us a decisively constructive situation in which to work; we are especially happy to express our gratitude to Dean Ernest Lynton of Livingston College and Dean Henry Torrey of The Graduate School.

We owe a particular and elaborate debt to Steven M. L. Aronson, whose unusually extensive and energetic help has contributed much to the clarity of our argument. His patience and humor are such that even the final harassed weeks of the procedure of writing a book were bearable, and civilized to boot.

We are indebted to the Rutgers University Research Council for assistance in gathering some of the information used in the book. Fox wishes to thank the National Institute of Mental Health for a Special Fellowship (under the sponsorship of the Department of Psychiatry, Stanford University School of Medicine) during the tenure of which information pertinent to the book was gathered. Tiger gratefully acknowledges the assistance of the Canada Council and the Guggenheim Foundation.

Man is a primate—a member of the same zoological order as the monkeys, apes, and prosimians, and it is with this meaning that we usually use the word "primates." However, we have also used "primates" to mean "primates other than man," or "nonhuman primates." The context will, we hope, make the usage clear.

The numbers in the text indicate references at the end of the book. These references are purely bibliographical: they indicate sources of information, document matters of fact, and suggest further material. They contain no substantive comment on the text, and nonspecialists can ignore them.

The book is the result of a completely cooperative effort. The order of the names on the title page was decided by the flip of a ha'penny.

ROBIN FOX
Princeton, New Jersey

LIONEL TIGER
New York City, New York

February, 1971

INTRODUCTION

THIS MAY BE a time like the early Renaissance. Perceptions of human-
kind grow especially confused; structures of thought splinter apart;
no theory of behavior amply and believably helps us satisfy our deep
curiosity about ourselves. The distemper in universities, the disbelieved
assertions of shrill governors, the virtually total erosion of the force of
religion in intellectual life, the difficulty of sustaining energizing moral
codes through whole communities—in essence, the ambiguous nature
of human encounter—all shine from different bits of the same cracked
mirror in which we view ourselves. Not only are there theoretical issues.
There are also issues of immense practicality and of cumulative intrusion into people's lives: suddenly a new baby represents a menacing
crowded future, a bottle of Burgundy quickly turns to garbage, weapons
boasting the promise of security endanger the genes of born and unborn, the clattering volume of human communication documents with
painful energy the thousand forms and foci of human conflict. In the
age in which masses of humans crowd into cities, the act of joining a
city is an adventure into turmoil, into formidable compromise, into a
crowd of silent mourners for civility. When two hundred people leave
for their holidays, two million people must listen to the screaming jet
that takes them.

But the urgency of the need for change is unmatched by the knowledge we have of how to change, and why, and with what prospect of improving our situation. This book records an effort to confront the intellectual and scientific problem in the context of the real one: how to understand ourselves as a species and how to act on this to ensure our survival. It would be laughable to pretend that solutions to either problem lurk in the pages that follow. But we have tried to identify the problems and provide the kind of information to help us solve them.

The book is a tour of the social system of human beings—the broad and major features of how we live together. The route the tour takes is somewhat unusual—at least for two conventionally trained social scientists—because we look not only to what can be seen with the eyes but also to what René Dubos has called "the biological remembrance of things past." And yet this seems sternly necessary, for our apparently precarious social arrangements rest on an old and profound foundation which it is not only essential to map out carefully but also exciting to wander in. This foundation is not in ruins; it is in our genes.

A note is in order about the small history of this book. The authors met in 1965 at a symposium of the Royal Society, held appropriately enough at the London Zoo. Once the trivial novelty of the conjunction of our names wore off, we became aware of the serious identity of our interests in the role of biology in the process of human social life. An introductory paper appeared in 1966 in *Man: The Journal of the Royal Anthropological Institute.* Its title was "The Zoological Perspective in Social Science," and that perspective continues to define our work. Soon thereafter we contrived to find ourselves in the same university. Our first plan was to prepare a textbook, but it became clear that it was hopeless to write a textbook for a discipline that did not exist.

The discipline did not exist because the natural sciences and the social sciences had split away from each other in the early part of this century; social scientists grew increasingly ignorant about biology, while biologists remained naïve about the complex behavior of human beings. Both of us have been conventional researchers: Fox interested in Irish peasants and Pueblo Indians of New Mexico—their systems of landholding and their patterns of kinship and marriage; Tiger interested in Canadian scientific bureaucracies and in how the Ghanaian Civil Service became an independent arm of an independent government. But the book that follows goes beyond all this to describe the result of an effort to unite as fruitfully as possible the information and theory of social science with the perspective and general insights of biology. We do this as social scientists confident of the explanatory powers of our traditional craft, but as professional anthropologists we want to do something else as well.

Anthropologists have stubbornly maintained—despite the ravages of social Darwinism, biologistic racism, the sanctimony of eugenicists— a kernel of interest in the biology of man's evolution. But anthropologists have always seen this in the context of the rich variety of human cultures—unlike some biologists who have recently with undue innocence leaped from discussion of simple animals to the most complex of all. The leap can be made, but not in ignorance of the details and uniqueness of human social institutions. This yields not only inadequate social science, but bad biology as well. Anthropology is well placed as the point of departure to assimilate information about a species beleaguered by the effect of cultural conflicts and yet tantalized by the ancient vision of human unity and the oneness of life. It has also been a clear and inviting window through which members of one culture see how members of another arrange their lives and prepare their theories. Now that we—all of us—become weary with the exotic because our own lives are alarmingly exotic enough, it seems time to exchange the clear window on others for a new mirror on ourselves. This is controversial, hotly so, because people defend, often bitterly, the vision they have of what the human animal is. This defensiveness is part of the problem.

Tout être vivant est aussi un fossile

—Jacques Monod

1.

BEGINNING
BIOGRAMMAR

WE KNOW OURSELVES surprisingly well. The isolation of the individual is neither final nor merciless. We are none of us truly isolated; we are connected to one another by a web of regularities and by a host of shared, deep-seated certainties. People age, and their behavior changes. Males and females differ; their interaction and their separateness are trying, necessary, and exciting. Confident of these regularities, people seek to define their own special reproductive and erotic lives. Children are noisy and full of needs. Parents confront these needs with an astonishing certainty, and a hard—if superficially sentimental—commitment to a process they themselves started. Powerful people strut, and though the notion of power is as offensive to some as the strutting, there continue to be powerful people who continue to strut. There will always be black limousines; it is only the people in the black limousines who change. There will always be someone hunching in those seats in the same confident, heavy way. Humans need food, and from that need a breadwinner speaks to his fellows with a silent eloquence. A mother with her child makes demands that are universally acceptable to even the most ruthless despot or doctrinaire reformer. That bond is the expression of a wealth of understandings and the assertion of a forceful dictate: babies are important, growth is good; the mother and child are icons for our unspoken statements about the value of living

1

and persisting. In each small circle of people—wherever—there is the same pleasure and involvement in what is represented by the simple notice attached to the gates of palaces: "A child, Prince Henrik Fynn, was born at 9:30. . . ." The fact of birth is its own statement, widely understood.

The purpose of this book is twofold: to describe what is known about the evolution of human behavior, and then to try to show how the consequences of this evolution affect our behavior today. To do this we must draw from zoology, biology, history, and genetics. We must use the sophisticated techniques and many materials of the social sciences—the techniques with which, as social scientists, we are most familiar—to place man in the broad context of the natural world. The real and intellectual pressures forcing us to see ourselves as an endangered species demand an expansion of the vision of the social sciences. They demand a skeptical review of how we explain our political behavior, our economies, our leisure, our forms of education, and the recurring tragedy of war.

As conventionally trained students of human behavior we know we can explain a great deal with the techniques we conventionally use. But not enough. The sciences of behavior have an incomplete concept of what governs and constrains human action. They fail to take seriously enough the possibility that there is an authentic "human nature" —that just as we can define *Homo sapiens* by how he looks, we may be able to define him by the way he acts and by the social structures he sustains.

Viewing man as an endangered species helps us to focus on the most serious failure of social science—the failure to deal with the species as a whole. This is strange when we consider that in dealing with other animals we treat a species as an entity, a whole, a unit of evolutionary history; something that has come into the stream of organic life by a natural process, has adapted or failed to adapt, and, if it has failed, passed out of that stream again into the museums and preserving bottles.

A species often deals itself a bad hand, and we are no exception. But we are unique in that we can understand ourselves as a species. It is to this introspective and yet objective task that we address ourselves.

How do we achieve this understanding? Given a species of butterfly, and faced with the questions What is this species about? How did it get that way? Why does it do the things it does? What are its chances for survival?—how do we set about finding the answers? And will the techniques that will help us find them for our butterflies help us at all when we apply them to so elaborate an animal as man?

Zoologists and evolutionary biologists have led the search for such answers ever since Darwin revolutionized biology with his decisive concept of natural selection.[1] Species are not immutable; new species develop out of old ones; mutations in the genetic material which favor survival are preserved. The end product of such an evolution is, very simply, every contemporary species. Their anatomy and physiology are the result of trial and error and the sifting of genes over countless generations. A species is what it is because of the pattern of successful adaptation built into its genes. It is programmed to grow and develop in a highly specific way, and the program is transmitted from generation to generation in the genetic code. If we know enough, on the one hand, about the contemporary condition of a creature, and, on the other, about its evolutionary history, we will be able to answer the deliberately naïve questions: Why is it like it is? Why does it do what it does?

It is like it is because of the history of its adaptational strategies.[2] It does what it does because this behavior has paid off in the struggle for survival. But there is always the possibility that altered circumstances will make the strategy obsolete and even detrimental. If the obsolete strategy persists, the result is extinction. The adaptational strategies of the human species have clearly been highly successful, but their success seems in danger of backfiring. The circumstances *created* by these adaptational strategies are such that they cannot be *maintained* by them. The analogy with the hydrogen bomb is all too clear: the super weapon is so powerful that, if used, it will destroy everything—including the user.

If we are to begin to understand the impasse we have created for ourselves, we have to look at ourselves as a species—as the end product of a particular path of evolution. We have to look at the form of our bodies and the related structure of our behavior and ask: What is it for? What were the adaptational strategies that produced it? What were the circumstances that caused this particular mode of moving or behaving to be selected? Is the behavior that was selected still appropriate to life today? And if it is not, what can we do about it? We know that the striding walk—a form of locomotion peculiar to our species—was an adaptation to hunting life on the savannas.[3] But how much of our behavior is similarly adapted?

These are not easy questions. It is not even easy to know the right way to set about asking them. A good deal of conventional wisdom both inside and outside the sciences would deny the validity of an essentially biological approach. Nonetheless, man is just one species among all the others. As long as he reigned confident over the others, he could declare his independence of nature and get away with it. Now, when he is faced with his own possible demise, he has to recognize his commonality with the other species in at least this one unavoidable respect: that no species is sacrosanct—either it adapts or it disappears. There is, therefore, only one intellectual route left for a judicious appraisal of our future: coming to terms with the process of our own behavioral evolution in the past.

To this end we must try to discover the regularities of human behavior—of the behavior of man in society—and to understand them in terms of the adaptive significance they have had. Scientists have looked for regularities before and found them, but they have not necessarily put them into an evolutionary context. They have not seen them as end products of our evolutionary history; they have not treated man as a species, but as a conglomerate of diverse populations, nations, cultures. We are less concerned here with the differences than with the overwhelming similarities—what zoologists would call the "species specific" behavioral regularities that characterize all men at all times and that stem from the very nature of the animal species—*Homo sapiens*—we are dealing with.[4] For it is an article of scientific faith among Darwinians that any regularities that characterize a species must exist because of their adaptational significance in the evolution of the species. If we then ask how a species evolved and what the changing circumstances were that it was adapting to, we can begin to understand what on the surface often appears to be a bizarre piece of anatomy or a decidedly odd item of behavior. So, in asking these questions about the social behavior of man, we need whatever help we can get from the evidence of fossils and from the discoveries of social scientists about the uniformities and variations in our social systems.

To add to this explanatory mix the things we have in common with animals is at once to complicate by adding more data and yet to simplify by insisting that certain features of our behavior have already been observed and explained in other species. This is not a matter of seeking attractive analogies between human and animal ways, but of insisting that we are animals still and that things that are true for the rest of nature hold true for us too. In looking at how various species use, for example, complex social arrangements in the struggle for survival, we learn something about the use of society as an adaptive strategy, about its successes and its limitations. If men are men everywhere, so that studying one group of men will reveal something about all men, so animals are animals everywhere, and learning about the adaptational patterns of one species will tell us something about the processes of adaptation in all species. Including our own.

Our point of departure, then, is to treat man as an alien species, one whose behavior is as strange as an unknown foreign language. Faced with an unrecorded language, the linguist assumes very little except that the phonetic patterns can be recorded accurately, that the minimal units of meaning—the phonemes—can be isolated, and that ultimately the grammar of the language can be analyzed. He knows this because, however much the languages of mankind may differ in content, there has to be a regular relationship between the phonemes, morphemes, clauses, and sentences; and if the relationship is regular, then the code can be cracked.

But why this universal regularity? Because we are one species, and our spoken language—our particular and unique form of communication—is a common biological heritage. It is one of the end products of our evolution that demanded its own very complex kind of communication system. But every species has a system of communication that enables the animals to signal to one another their moods and intentions. And in every species it is the totality of the behavior of the animals that constitutes the communication system.[5] Ours is no exception. That we speak grammatically and behave in regular and predictable ways are both outcomes of our common evolutionary history rooted in our biology. A species tends to "enjoy" doing what has been important to its survival: sex and eating are the two most obvious examples. We enjoy both our verbal and our behavioral languages. And this enjoyment is matched by our intense curiosity, our drive to understand what our behavior is saying, our delight in exploring the behavioral biogrammar.

Biogrammar? Each species has a repertoire of signals—postures, gestures, movements—to communicate what the animals feel and what they plan to do. When a young Gelada baboon intrudes into the personal space of an irascible elder, the latter affects what looks to be a huge yawn but what is, on the contrary, a warning display of canine teeth and red gum tissue meant to intimidate the careless youngster.[6] When one herring gull lands on another's territory, the situation instantly becomes ambiguous. Male and female gulls look more or less the same to one another. The intruder may be either a challenging male to be fought, or an enterprising female to be courted. If the newcomer stares head on, it is a signal for a fight; if it wags its head, it is an invitation to seduction.[7] If one of the wives of a Hamadryas baboon strays too far and shows a friendly rump to a roving bachelor, her overlord will chase her and bite her on the neck—a part of her anatomy well enough padded to prevent damage but sensitive enough to remind her that, for better or for worse, she is part of an exclusive mating group.[8] If a human being gives something—real or incorporeal —to another, something will be given back. Even the Spanish beggar gives his blessing in return for alms.[9] A female chimpanzee who has left her band to give birth to a new member does not simply rejoin without ceremony. She approaches the old males of the band with hand outstretched in a begging gesture; the old males touch her palm or stroke the back of her neck; only then will she rejoin the females of the group.[10]

All these examples, taken more or less at random from the behavioral repertoires of various animal species, may vary in complexity as one ascends the scale of evolution. But for any species a set of predictable transactions could be drawn up to show how they interact or occur in sequence, how they can be modified, under what circumstances they will be applied, and, finally, how they help the species survive. The total repertoire of possible behaviors of any species is sometimes called the "biogram."[11] But this is a static list; to understand how the elements in the list are related, we need to know the rules that govern the relationships. For although the language of behavior is readily intelligible to whatever species speaks it, it can seem no more than gibberish to the outsider. A foreign language is an unintelligible stream of noise to a nonspeaker, who, however, armed with a grammar, can begin to make sense of it, to isolate elements, and eventually to put them together and communicate. In short, he learns the rules. In order to understand the language of behavior, we need a comparable set of rules for the biogram—the biogrammar, a relatively small word on which hang all the major questions of social science.

These rules describe the principles on which the language of behavior works, though they offer no certainty as to what individuals are going to do. The actual watchfulness and relative viciousness of the hamadryas male will vary from one to another and from circumstance to circumstance, but the response to provocation will invariably be the neck bite and not something else. The form and content of human gift-giving vary enormously, but behind each of its many manifestations the ground rules of reciprocity operate just as surely as the rules relating subject to predicate lie behind all the rich and unpredictable outpourings of Romance languages. Within the limits set by the rules, there is room for eloquence as well as plain speaking. Even those who like to say how much they hate the crabbiness of perfect grammar must observe its rules. If they did not, their words would fail to make sense to anyone else.

If the rules of language are not observed, verbal communication breaks down, and the result is gibberish; if the rules of behavior for a species are not observed, social communication breaks down, and the result is behavioral gibberish. Most people want—and need—to understand one another. They try, as hard as they can, *not* to talk gibberish. But at the behavioral level, in their own species at least, they seem constantly to verge on breakdown.

In this book we want to search for some of the principles on which behavioral literacy should be based.

To do this we have to discover those elusive ground rules and those elements of human behavior that are the lexicon of social action. Here we run into the controversy that has plagued the social sciences since Darwin first forced on us the recognition of our cousinship with the beast. Can the underlying structure of behavior be *bio*grammatical, rooted in the biology of the species? Can elements of our own behavior be compared with the animal biogrammar?[12]

To a large section of the social-science establishment such a comparison would be anathema—however obvious it may be to the intelligent animal lover. But, again and yet again, man *is* an animal. He has evolved as other animals: he is a vertebrate, a mammal, a member of the order Primates. How, then, can the same principles of analysis that we apply to the study of the animal kingdom at large not be applied to him?

Once upon a time people actually doubted that there was any *physical* continuity between humans and animals.[13] This is astonishing to us now, and yet it appears likely that it will seem equally bizarre in fifty years that many sensible people—even many of the scientists paid and trained to know better—claimed that there was no significant and analyzable continuity between the *behavior* of humans and other animals. It isn't only a view of man that is involved, but rather a whole sense of nature and the process of living things and the system of beings—in other words, a world view which encompasses a man view. The artist Francis Bacon paints decomposing slabs of meat, obscene popes, people whose flesh is already almost part of the air surrounding them; in their state of nature even the envelope of their skin is gapingly open. Bacon's vision is that all animals exchange being with their whole environment; nothing is crisp and particular, everything blends. The digestive guts of a chimpanzee and of a man are both wet and colorful, and both are arenas for the interaction of chemicals and food. If we are related so irrevocably in our very centers, it is going to be hard to argue that we are unrelated at the extensions of those centers—our behavior. The duke and the chimp are fellow citizens in the democracy of nature. What unites them is as important as what divides them. The distinctions which obviously do exist are the more intriguing and important precisely because the duke and the chimp both share the inexorable fact of a common primate, even mammalian history.

In fact, the only way we can understand the exact nature of the distinction between man and animal is by first looking at what they have in common. It has long been held, out of ideology, ignorance, and just plain fear, that man is unique in the animal world, that the difference between him and brute nature is a difference not of degree but of kind. A comforting abyss separates the semidivine human from the dumb brute—no matter that the demigod has the body of a brute. For brutes, so goes the catechism, do not have souls or minds, reason or foresight, wisdom or culture, language or opposable thumbs, fire or any one of a host of attributes that set man "above" nature, exclude biology in favor of culture, and enable him to "triumph" over mere animality.

Man's body is unique; so is his behavior. And in both his body and his behavior the uniqueness represents very special biological adaptations built in by the exacting process of natural selection. The point is not that man has shed or risen above his primate nature, but, simply, that he is a unique primate with a unique primate nature. But every species is unique in its specializations—that is, after all, how we tell them apart; and it is often easier, if they are closely related, to tell them apart by their behavior than by their anatomy and physiology.[14] Behavior is as much a part of the evolutionary process as anatomy. The head-wagging of the herring gull is as essential to its survival and success as its wings are. It is *how the animal performs* that determines its chances of survival. Sexual anatomy is ingeniously adaptive, but it is sexual behavior that determines which characteristics will appear in the next generation; the magnificence of an individual hamadryas baboon's genitalia will not ensure it genetic immortality unless it manages its neck-biting act successfully.

The uniqueness of man's body does not represent a difference in kind between him and his primate cousins. It represents a series of often trying specializations. The most obvious of these is permanent bipedalism.[15] Other primates are able to walk on two legs, but most of the time they do not. Man made this change as he adapted to a hunting life on the hot savannas. His spine straightened, his pelvis narrowed, his ankle bone solidified, his buttocks expanded, his head balanced precariously on top of the spine. The outcome of all this was the striding walk—the most efficient and least fatiguing way to cover long distances.

In the same adaptive context the frontal lobes of the brain grew in both size and complexity; the outcome of this was an increase in intelligence, articulate speech, greater learning capacity, foresight, and the overall ability to process more and more complex data.[16] But the other primates have brains with frontal lobes, too. The other primates have spines and a pelvis, too. They are different because they have specialized differently in response to different evolutionary problems. The gibbon has specialized in long arms and the ability to swing gracefully through the trees; the gorilla in great size and the ability to digest stems and roots; the baboon in quadrupedalism, large canines, and high speed; man in bipedalism, the striding walk, and the enlarged brain.[17]

Even so, these anatomical specializations in a sense have a kind of either/or quality not always found in behavioral differences. Either a primate has a large brain or he does not; either a primate has the striding walk or he does not. The physical differences are thus clear-cut, whereas, with the exception of language, the behavioral differences are not. Everyone except the hardiest fundamentalists understands that bodily continuities exist and are even obvious. But our suspicion is that behavioral continuities are even more obvious. No one saw the anatomical continuity between man and the other primates, because no one looked for it. The feeling that there is a great and unbridgeable gulf between human and animal behavior also has resulted from a failure to look closely and think comparatively. A theoretical blindness about physical structure has been replaced by a theoretical blindness about behavior.

Of course we have cultures, of course we have symbols, of course
we have Beethoven, Stravinsky, and Paul McCartney; clearly, we
are the only species with the Koran, the Bible, the Torah, and the
Communist Manifesto. And of course we boast a plastics industry,
supersonic fighters, remedial-reading courses, custom-made jewelry,
Ferraris, and crêpes suzette. We are the only primates who make
things and then lose them and then dig them up and place them in
museums.

And surely no one has a more complicated (and probably unworkable) educational system in all of nature. No one but a human could
take our kinship systems seriously. We are perhaps the only species that
selects certain especially endowed females for purposes of communal
worship because of their sexual magic. And certainly the only species
that covers those very sexual organs whose energetic exercise we seem
to crave and in which we seem to have a particular if private pride.
Only people plant flowers.

But what can be expected from this kind of animal? We do these
things because these are the things that this animal does. Given an
animal endowed with the biological capacity to produce and attach
itself to symbols, we can confidently predict a range of bizarre outcomes. Endow our hamadryas baboon with the same capacity, and the
simple neck-biting procedure would burgeon into weird, beautiful, or
grotesque variants. In one community the punishment might take the
shape of attaching the errant wife to a painted post by a collar made
of carved ivory fitted with spikes; in another there might be a ceremonial public humiliation in which the chief of the band cut off the
transgressor's hair and branded her neck with a red-hot sword; in yet
another the husband might lead her around the camp in a halter while
the women of his harem sang ribald and satirical songs; in another she
might be hanged by the neck until dead. The only limit to the variety
of punishments would be the limits of the imagination of the species.

The same can be said about the rituals of courtship. Everywhere
in human society this activity is carried on. In some places girls put
hibiscus flowers behind their ears, in others they put on a date's fraternity pin, but everywhere they announce by symbolic devices of one
kind or another that they are in the running and ready to run. The
content of courtship practices may vary a good deal, but the process
itself is universal.

At first glance the bewildering variety of customs suggests that
humans can invent any kind of culture with any kind of processes.

But on closer scrutiny it turns out that while the variations are almost endless, the themes are restricted in number, and are, in all cultures, the fixed points on which the system turns. The story can be told in many different ways, but the plot and the characters remain the same.

Universal processes, however, do not necessarily have universal results, nor do they give birth to identical institutions. This holds true even in the plant world; the same plant going through the same life processes will look totally different at maturity, according to where it was grown and what the history of its growth has been. But it *is* the same plant. In the same way, human culture can flower and wither. But because we are the kind of animal we are, there will be fixed points in the culture's development and routines which are as predictable as the neck bite of the baboon.

We inevitably produce culture, and culture inevitably varies from population to population. Of course, human beings will do human things, and baboons will do baboon things. Dealing with this variation is a problem, because the ideology dies hard that the division between us and the brutes is that brute behavior is passed on genetically, while ours is passed on culturally—by processes of teaching and learning, couched in symbols and particularly in language. This ideology has it that the little baboon is born with a bundle of genes to guide his life down to the last detail, and that, though learning will play some part in his behavior, the use of symbols, foresight, and the application of intelligence will not. He will bite his consort's neck because his genes tell him to, not because his culture has made it a rule. He will collect a harem because the instruction to do so rests in his genetic code, not because polygamy is an invention of his tribe and one of its laws. He will adopt young female infants as prospective brides because this is one of the things baboons cannot help doing, not because child betrothal is encouraged by his religious code.

Not only is this an oversimplified view of animals—particularly of our nearest relatives—but it poses an unreal dichotomy. Here it is useful to employ a term of polite abuse: the "culturalist" view. This assumes that the human infant is a *tabula rasa*—a blank slate—unencumbered with the imperative, instinctive demands that manipulate animals. All the infant has is intelligence—and the capacity to learn anything it is taught. Thus, goes the claim, any culture can write anything it likes on the blank slate, limited only by physiology and the laws of learning discovered by behavioral psychologists. Of course, the culture cannot demand that the infant fly or lay eggs or live underwater. It must reinforce learning properly, through reward and punishment, in order to condition the organism to conform to the mores of the clan, tribe, class, or nation involved. The organism is a receptor and capable of learning anything that is properly fed into it. It will break down only if the conditioning process is ineptly applied. There are, in this view, theoretically no limits to the learning process, and the incredible and arbitrary variety of human cultures testify to this. What is more, in this ideology *all* cultures are invention. They may rest on certain universal needs and emotions but these have little specific effect. It is argued, for example, that the sex need does nothing to explain why some cultures are monogamous and others polygamous. (The fact that whatever the rules, all cultures are adulterous, and that it is the women who get punished, is overlooked.) In this theory, the need for food (or "hunger drive") does not explain the variety of food taboos, nor the need for shelter the incredible variety of human architecture.[18]

At the level of specific content this view is perfectly true. It has been suggested that the existence of a grammar does *not* enable us to predict what people are going to say; it tells us only how they must say it in order to be understood. So the question has to be faced: Are the only rules of human behavior those of learning psychology, or is there something else in human beings that produces regularities that, despite their surface differences, crop up in society after society?

Again, the comparison with language is useful. On the *tabula rasa* principle, all language must be learned by the processes of imitation, reward, and punishment. But modern linguists argue that this is an impossible position to sustain—as any parent will quickly understand. Linguists like Chomsky and psychologists like Lenneberg argue that the capacity for grammatical speech is somehow "in" the brain, as the capacity to walk is somehow "in" the body, and matures as the child matures.[19] The child learns because it has a cerebral *language-acquisition device* that enables it to learn rules for the production of sentences it has never heard before. The device enables it to process data and deduce rules. Most importantly, the rules of child speech are not just poor imitations of adult grammar; they are based on rules of sentence production appropriate to the child's level of maturity.

Thus every child has the capacity for grammatical speech, and is ready to be programmed with whatever specific grammar its culture provides. The specific grammars are many and various, like the cultures in which they are used. There is no "explanation" for why one grammar does what it does, as opposed to any other. Nevertheless the speech patterns of all languages are known to operate on a few basic principles, which linguists have identified. The grammatical patterns may well also be reducible in this way once what Chomsky calls the "deep structures" of all languages are known. Then we can write the "universal grammar," which will tell us the principles on which all particular grammars rest. Even at this point in our understanding, no language exists that a linguist cannot record with the universal phonetic alphabet in the first place and analyze with universally applicable techniques of semantic analysis in the second. This can be done, because, despite the variety of surface grammars, languages are all doing the same job, and in a limited number of ways.

In the same way, *all* the rest of human culture lies in the biology of the species. We have a *culture-acquisition device* constraining us to produce recognizable and analyzable human cultures, just as we must produce recognizable human languages, however varied the local manifestations may be. Just as a child can learn only a language that follows the "normal" rules of grammar for human languages, he can learn only a grammar of behavior that follows the parallel rules of the biogrammar. Of course, in either case, a departure from normal grammar may be tried, but the likelihood is that it will end only in gibberish.

This view of human behavior is very different from that of the culturalists or the behaviorists. It makes the organism an active, searching, and stubborn participant in the learning process, rather than just a receiver; it suggests that the teacher is as moved to teach in a certain way as the pupil is to learn. The slate here is not blank at all; it is doing a lot of its own writing.

If all behavior, including linguistic behavior, is simply the result of cultural conditioning, then the logical conclusion is that if ever a new generation were cut off from tradition, it would be unlikely to invent one again. In this view, human culture does not stem in a direct way from human nature, but is, rather, a precious accumulation of unique skills and knowledge that must be passed on or be lost.

But is it? As far as language is concerned, at least two monarchs in history have had their doubts. Would untutored children speak, they asked? The Egyptian Psamtik I (in the seventh century B.C.) and James IV of Scotland (in the fifteenth century of the Christian era) are both reputed to have tried isolating children at birth and leaving them to grow up without human communication, to see what language, if any, they would speak. Perhaps King James's pious hope that it would be Hebrew may have been somewhat optimistic, but his belief that they could invent a language without ever having been taught one is theoretically justifiable. This invented language, although totally different from any known to us, would be analyzable by linguists on the same basis as any other language, and thus translatable into all known languages.

The experiment can be extended. If our children could survive and breed—still in isolation from any cultural influences—then eventually their descendants would produce a society and culture recognizably human in all its details. But even if its content differed from any we have so far seen, even if it had different gods, devils, and theories, bizarre marriage rules and obsequies, its scheme could be identified by biogrammarians. Its status structure could boast untold absurdities and countless seemingly trivial distinctions. But there would be a status system and it would therefore not be trivial. Perhaps the culture would subject its young to ferocious ceremonies of initiation. But there would be ceremonies, and they would be initiated. It could use or treat schizophrenia in wholly unexpected ways; but a biogrammarian would recognize the type and note it down in his rapidly expanding behavioral lexicon. Such things, and more, would be there because *Homo sapiens* is the kind of animal he is.

And if the feral children-parents, Adam and Eve, could survive and breed despite their isolation from the influences of culture, we can be reasonably sure that they would do a predictable variety of things: they would spawn a society with laws about incest and how and whom to marry; rules about property; habits of taboo and ritual avoidance. They would defer to the supernatural and try to control it in some regular fashion. They too would have their initiations; they would foment courtship ceremonies and fuss elaborately about the adornment of young females. Men would do certain things which excluded women; in some of these all-male associations secrecy would hold the members together as surely as prison walls. Some intriguing form of gambling would probably go on. Weapons and tools would be made. Our biogrammarian would be sure to find the following, too: myths and legends, dancing, psychosis and neurosis, adultery, homosexuality, homicide, suicide, loyalty, desertion, juvenile delinquents, senile fools, and various shrewd practitioners to cure or take advantage of the various ills from which communities and people suffer.

This picture of the behavioral infrastructure of human societies may seem little more than a tridimensional comment about human reality—that we became this way, we are this way, and we will be this way for a long time still: a human is a human is a human. But it is not so simple as that. To understand it we must turn to the new data and theory which permit us to insist on the continuity of human experience over long periods of time, and to assert the real effect of biological control even though the weight of our intellectual history and the aggressive optimism of our progressivist leaders deny us the ambiguous luxury of attributing at least some of what we are to . . . what we are.

Without any exposure to cultural traditions, our isolated tribe would develop very specific and highly complex cultural patterns, and probably very quickly—a matter of a few generations, once they got a language going. And they would do this for the same reason that the baboons produce a baboon social system in captivity —because it is in the beast. Baboons—primates—humans have not only a very general physical capacity to learn, they have a programmed preference to learn some things rather than others, and to learn some things more easily than others.

It is not *instincts* in any old-fashioned sense that are at issue here; initiation ceremonies and male rituals are not "instinctive." They emerge from the biology of an animal programmed to produce them, once it is given the appropriate stimuli. Without these stimuli, there will be no behavior, or only a modified or distorted form of it. The human organism is like a computer that is set up or "wired" in a particular way. It is always in a state of readiness —at successive points in the life cycle—to process certain kinds of information and to produce certain kinds of information. To be sure, the information has to be of a specific type in order to be processed, but its content can vary a great deal. Once the information is received, the computer stores it and goes onto the next task. If the system is confused—if, for example, adult programs are fed to adolescent computers—then the fuses blow and there is risk of breakdown. This analogy pushed to its logical conclusion would yield a bizarre science-fiction world in which computers fed one another information—thus simulating the human condition. Only when they were synchronized would the system run smoothly.

This model of human behavior, although stark, really does differ decisively from that favored by either instinctivists or culturalists. To the instinctivists, behavior resulted simply from the manifestation of innate tendencies like "maternalism," "self-abasement," and "acquisitiveness." The theory failed because it ended up as little more than a list of ever-more-specific human attributes.[20] Culturalists hold that if cultures are similar it is because the same basic "needs," or "functional prerequisites," must be met in them all, and because the laws of "conditioning" are universally applicable.[21]

But an alternative, if more moderate, view may be offered in the biological context: that is, that the human organism is "wired" in a certain way so that it can process and emit information about certain facts of social life such as language and rules about sex, and that, furthermore, it can process this information only at certain times and only in certain ways. The wiring is geared to the life cycle so that at any one moment in a population of *Homo sapiens* there will be individuals with a certain "store" of behavior giving out information at another stage to others who are wired to treat this information in a particular way. The outcome of the interaction of these individuals will be certain "typical" relationships.

There is nothing specific in the genetic code about initiation ceremonies for young males. There are no instructions about circumcision whizzing around the bends of the alpha helix. But neither are male initiation ceremonies pure cultural inventions—results of the free activity of the intellect. They occur because we are biologically wired the way we are. We can predict how older and younger males in a community will relate to one another because of the way their wiring allows them to be programmed and to program them in turn. In postadolescent males the genetic message is one of sinister and often undirected rebelliousness; this threatening information is received by older males, whose steadier hormonal systems go into a reaction and insist on containment. So all societies find ways of taming and using the young men and of forcing them to identify with the system. There is, theoretically, a variety of ways of doing this, but relatively few are used. Not only does it appear that we have to stick to the grammar, but to a relative modesty of vocabulary and expression as well.

Of course, the particular transaction between older and younger males called initiation does not always result in a specific ceremony; but it is always at the very least a process. Young braves are subjected to it; so are graduate students, junior executives, apprentices, novices in religious orders, even outlaw gangs. Of course, the initiation need not always "take": for example, one might argue that some of the difficulty universities throughout the world are having with the simple problem of discipline—let alone the more trying one of actually teaching and discovering—is that as a system of initiation, the university is far too arbitrary, unsatisfying, and undemanding for the young men concerned. No brave would count it a particular honor to triumph in history at Berkeley or Bombay. The challenge is somehow unmanly and the challengers themselves vaguely laughable and inept. It now seems to take a special faith to accept the value of the life of the mind; a good many twenty-year-olds lack the faith and reject the challenge. The university crisis is a good example of feeding the wrong program at the wrong time to the people. Perhaps more explicit, ceremonial, and physical initiation processes would "solve" the problem (though these are clearly unfashionable at present). Perhaps they will not. Nonetheless, we may have to be prepared as a community to consider novel and unexpected ways of reordering our educational practices to accord more faithfully to the biogrammatical dictates, to which—our suggestion is— we have to yield at least a little or endure a lot.[22]

We have confidently asserted that identifiable propensities for behavior are in the wiring. Unless we look to divine intervention, these got there by the same route as they got into the wiring of any other animal: by mutation and natural selection. One of the sturdiest theories in science, widely and agreeably accepted, is that animals vary along a normal curve in a number of respects, and that selection occurs in terms of this curve. Taller giraffes could secure more food and consequently reproduce more and better offspring—which is why they developed long necks. Early turtles with hard backs could survive their enemies by withdrawing behind a shelter of their own; they lived to endow their successors with this specialized characteristic. The broad outlines of the theory, and the process, are clear and indisputable: biological change results from a knowable and known procedure.[23]

This is easily seen when physical characteristics change through selection. More subtle and more exciting is the matter of behavioral evolution, which the science of ethology has forced us to recognize

as a central issue.[24] We can readily see that species can be defined
physically, but as we get better information about how they behave
in natural settings, we begin to see how they can be classified behaviorally. The implication here is important: regularities of behavior
are as predictable and discernible as the color of plumage and the
shape of eggs. But how is this regularity controlled? Why is it
that, while almost anything can happen in principle, only a limited
and specialized set of actions occurs in practice?

Back to the wiring, and back to the new data we have about
genetics and the control of living systems. Though we have known
for many years how genetic systems worked, breaking the genetic
code—the structure of the DNA molecule—allowed a rather hard-
headed species to see with its own eyes how the life of an animal
was controlled by facts of nature as comprehensible as a computer
program.[25] The genetic code *is* a program, and it *is* a way of trans-
mitting a program from generation to generation. DNA is immensely
complex in itself and in what it does, but its overriding work is
carrying from the parents to the offspring a program that includes
behavior as well as body shape, color, and sense of smell. The most
obvious program is the life cycle itself, which is both profoundly
physical and profoundly behavioral at the same time.[26] The cater-
pillar turns into a butterfly in an astonishing display of life-cycling.
The human infant begins to smile at a predictable time, and the boy
soon loses his shrillness and darting lightness and becomes a character
more uncertain, more portentous, more annoying to his elders. He
is, without doubt, a different creature, and all at once subject to
forces even free will and the force of government cannot hold back.
His behavior changes as it is programmed to do. He is wired so
that this will happen, and indeed not only human boys but also
young males in many other primate groups suffer the scorn of their
elders and the uncertainty of a transition from one difficult role to
another. It is as much a behavior as dying. The geneticist J. Z.
Young once defined death as "what happens when there is no longer
a program to repair the program to repair the program to repair the
program . . . etc., etc." It is unnecessary to labor the point that
living involves successful programs and that successful behavioral
programs are as much a result of natural selection as the opposable
thumb and the reproductive differences between men and women.

The unique outcome of the human wiring is human cultural behavior, with its rich symbolic content, its complex social traditions,

and its nongenetic mode of transferring information from one generation to another. But how did the human animal get wired for culture
in the first place? The theory used to be that, for some reason or
other, at some time or other, the human brain expanded to the point
where it was capable of producing first symbols and then culture.[27]
This no longer seems plausible.[28] Our little-brained ape-man ancestors
of two million years ago—with skull spaces no larger than a gorilla's
—were doing cultural things. For a start, they were making tools
of bone and stone.[29] At first glance this may not seem a great leap
forward (after all, the rudiments of toolmaking occur in chimpanzees),[30] but it implies that these creatures were organizing their experience in a manner that was already typically human. They had
diverged from the rest of the primates as surely in this respect as in
the upright stance and the splayed big toe, and this divergence was
a consequence of the momentous transition from vegetarianism to
systematic hunting. It was *after* they started doing cultural things
that the brain grew in size and complexity[31]—for the making of
butchering tools to deal with the proceeds of cooperative hunting
implies foresight and planning, a complex system of cooperation, and
a division of labor that in turn presupposes some fairly advanced
form of communication.[32] Obviously there was a selective advantage
to cultural behavior, as in the clear cases of the hard shell of the
turtle and the neck of the giraffe. There was a premium on an animal
which could learn a lot and learn it quickly and which did not
depend too heavily on direct instructions from the genes for each
item of behavior. Selection favored the smarter animals, and they
in turn bred smarter ones still, whose skills and cunning enabled
them to survive and flourish. But this process constantly created a
new environment for the human animal—an environment of its own
making. Once the animal became dependent for survival on speech,
for example, selection would favor whatever mutations produced
some improvement in the speech organs;[33] if the variable were imagination, selection would operate in the same way. The genetic
qualities that favored scientific activity or associative learning,
"general intelligence" or the ability to inhibit present gratification
in anticipation of future wants, or the propensity to obey rules, would
be subject to selection as much as the muscular qualities that facili-
tated the striding walk.[34]

Obeying rules is important: the animal had not only to do things,
but *not* to do them as well.[35] It was beginning to shed its dependency
on the precarious certainty of instinct, but it still had to get done—

somehow—the jobs that instinct did for other animals. It substituted customs and habits, but these had nonetheless to be obeyed like instincts, and they had to be almost semiautomatic to be successful.[36] Selection, then, clearly favored those creatures with a propensity to obey rules, to feel guilty about breaking them, and, generally, to control their sexual and aggressive tendencies enough to let otherwise recalcitrant individuals form a working society. In a real sense, this yielded citizens more effective for the evolving human social group and its evolving cultural patterns. Selection put into the actual wiring those qualities and propensities that made for a successful social and cultural animal. It left a lot of variety, of course —that is nature's way.

What happened was that culture itself became a selection pressure that favored animals with attributes which served a culture-bearing creature.[37] Man became dependent on cultural modes of surviving: the more capable of cultural behavior he was, the more he prospered. And the result was an animal that is not only the producer of culture but its product as well. It is not surprising that man is driven to produce that which produced him.[38]

In sum: we behave culturally because it is in our nature to behave culturally, because natural selection has produced an animal that has to behave culturally, that has to invent rules, make myths, speak languages, and form men's clubs, in the same way that the hamadryas baboon has to form harems, adopt infants, and bite its wives on the neck.[39]

We fail to appreciate this infrastructure of our cultural behavior because our perspective on ourselves as a species is chronically limited. To most of us a generation is a long time. How many people can grasp with any constructive imagination the period of a life span? To all of us the period of known history is a very long time and fades into indistinction with the advent of civilization. But that five thousand years which is civilization is, in evolutionary terms, as but an evening gone. From the perspective of the evolution of the species, nothing much has happened in that period except an unprecedented rise in population. It is just an episode. Given the right perspective, everything is just an episode. The order of Primates, our order, is a seventy-million-year-old episode in the history of the mammals—itself an episode in the history of the vertebrates, itself an espisode in the history of organic life. The line leading to man probably broke off from the other primates more than twenty million years ago,[40] while indisputable remains of our ape-man ancestor—*Australopithecus*—date back some five and one-half million years.[41] The first upright and big-brained human—*Homo erectus*[42]—is usually credited with about one million years of history. *Homo sapiens* is half a million years old, while the appearance of truly modern man—*Cro-Magnon*—dates from forty or fifty thousand years ago.[43]

This is our time scale for the evolution not only of physique but also of social behavior, emotions, patterns of learning, loving, and hating. Stored in the older parts of the brain are all those codes and messages held over from that ancient time—the heat of the jungle past and the long drag on the Pliocene savannas. Surrounding and coming to terms with this old brain is a new brain forged mostly in the cool-to-icy environment of the Pleistocene and the touch-and-go battle with the snaking ice.[44] And since then? Fire is maybe half a million years old; agriculture at least ten thousand years; large settlements five thousand; elaborate cities three thousand; steam power and industrial explosion a mere two hundred. Nuclear man appeared yesterday.

If we made an hour-long film to represent the history of tool-making man, industrial man would flash by in a few seconds at the end—he would barely be seen. Yet it is only the flashy and tortured complexity of industrial man that is so often taken to be truly human. Or, at best, we use civilized man as our model. But civilized man is an evolutionary afterthought. We remain Upper Paleolithic hunters, fine-honed machines designed for the efficient pursuit of game. Nothing worth noting has happened in our evolutionary history since we left off hunting and took to the fields and the towns—nothing except perhaps a little selection for immunity to epidemics, and probably not even that.[45] "Man the hunter" is not an episode in our distant past: we are still man the hunter, incarcerated, domesticated, polluted, crowded, and bemused.

We have overtaken ourselves with those fantasy structures called civilizations, and with the sheer overpowering growth of our numbers. For most of our hunting past—for ninety-nine percent of our history —the population of the species stayed steady at about one million. With the dawn of agriculture it leaped to one hundred million. Since the advent of industry it has reached 3,700 million, and by the year 2000 it will be 7,000 million. A creature evolved for living in bands of 50 or so cannot but have problems with such a series of population explosions and their organizational consequences. Most of what we take for granted in human nature is in fact an end product of the pathological events attendant on the incarceration of our hunting selves. We are all in this together, treading on one another's toes.

Without a grasp of this perspective we will never understand ourselves or our societies or the sustaining and yet undermining role of our culture-producing brains. We have to make the imaginative and unsettling leap into understanding that *agricultural and industrial civilizations have put nothing into the basic wiring of the human animal.* We are wired for hunting—for the emotions, the excitements, the curiosities, the regularities, the fears, and the social relationships that were needed to survive in the hunting way of life. And we are wired basically on a primate model. This primate wiring was adjusted and readjusted for over seventy million years before we emerged as distinct from the rest of our order. In this perspective even the forebrain is an afterthought. The cerebral cortex struggles with a heritage it did not ask for and has frequently wished aloud it did not have.[46] "What art thou, O Man, when thou art full of lust?" said an anguished prophet. What, when thou art full of compassion, or ambition, or the urge to exchange, or the pleasure in taking risks, or the skill in dealing with associates, or the compulsion to explore, or the need to be talked to?

Ours is a heritage stretching over millions of years of the primate hunting past and capped by a recently acquired symbolizing brain. Yet we are still living inside our own skulls and feeding on our fantasies. When we see how helpless we are to prevent war and civil violence, when we rail against the pollution of our air and rivers, when we find ourselves unable to bridge the gap of understanding between old and young, when we watch our cities fall into greater and grimier decay, when we come up against the seemingly inexorable nature of racial conflict and religious prejudice—when, in short, we look at or hide from the progressively awful spectacle we present to ourselves, we can react only in terms of what our intellect offers us as alibis. We blame the decline of monopoly capitalism, the communist conspiracy, the military-industrial complex, the corruption of the powerful, the permissiveness of parents, the viciousness of the right or the subversiveness of the left, the falling away from God, affluence, imperialism, racism, Marxism, the cult of youth, overpopulation, the shadow of the bomb, and the innate brutality of man.

But in the cold eye of nature we are just another species in trouble. This has happened before, and there were no conspirators to blame then. If a species fails to adapt, it does not survive. It is finally as simple as that. It did the tyrannosaurs no good to blame one another for their failure. They could not adapt to reality, and they became extinct. If and when we are gone, our quarrels about which of us was to blame will merely seem funny—except that there will be nobody there to laugh. We are the first species to hold in its own hands the power to affect consciously its own survival. But this can be achieved only if we know ourselves as a species, and, more important, *sense* ourselves as a species, and, in the last resort, *act* as a species in the interests of the species as a whole.

2.

POLITICAL
NATURE

WE USUALLY THINK of politics as a highly specialized affair involving special people called politicians, an affair that, moreover, touches people at large only when their votes are wanted or their taxes are collected. We harbor a regiment of people called political scientists who carefully inspect what politicians do, and who develop ideas about something called the "political system." But in our earnestness we have forgotten what it is all about, and why, in the first place, we have politics at all.

Analogies are often drawn between human and ant societies.[1] There are, to be sure, striking similarities—such as division of labor, caste system, and domestication of other creatures—but the analogy breaks down at one fundamental point: human societies are political, and ant societies are apolitical. The social order of an ant colony is genetically fixed. Workers are workers, drones drones, queens queens, soldiers soldiers, and so on. Workers cannot usurp power in the colony, because they are genetically programmed to be workers and nothing else. There can be no redistribution of power, of place, and, most importantly, of breeding ability, and therefore of contribution to the genetic pool. This is a critical difference. Politics involves the possibility of changing the distribution of resources in a society—one of which is the control over the future that breeding allows. The political process—the process of redistributing control over resources among the individuals of a group—is, in evolutionary terms, a breeding process. The political system is a breeding system. When we apply the word "lust" to both power and sex, we are nearer the truth than we imagine. In the struggle for reproductive advantage, some do better than others. It is this that changes the distribution of genes in a population and affects its genetic future. This is a world of winners and losers, a world of politics—of the haves and the have-nots, of those who have made it and those who sulk on the sidelines.

God was notably astute in arranging Eden: there was one male and one female and no politics. The question could not arise of who had access to Eve and who had sons and daughters, and who could see in a small living creature a reassuring echo of his own existence. Politics as a process began when the wicked snake competed with Adam for the loyalty of Eve, when innocence was lost because good and evil—that is to say, the possibility of choice—sharply disrupted what promised to become one of the most tedious perfections of all creation. From that time on, the species has been irretrievably concerned with who can marry whom and with the relationship between position, property, and productive copulation.

The result of the reproductive struggle is a social system that is profoundly hierarchical and competitive. And if human politics exhibits a constant tension between the communally valued ideal of equality and the privately valued aim of happy inequality, then this is simply a reflection of our evolutionary history. The imaginative brain —our means of pursuing this equality—developed long after those deeper primate motives devoted to the pursuit of unfair shares and an unequal access to control over genes and privilege. This ancient pursuit, however, had its own set of ground rules, and we are heirs to its inhibitions as much as to its lusts. To compete we must cooperate as well as fight. To dominate we must be merciful as well as ruthless. We must be, in a word, political. Our own political behavior and ideologies should be explored in the context of Aristotle's dictum that man is, *by nature*, a political animal; that he is the only animal with empires, justice, and formalized welfare, but that he remains an animal nevertheless.

Society has been an important weapon in the struggle for survival of many animal species.[2] It is, of course, possible to survive by adopting the solitary life—except for brief mating periods—but it is also something of a dead end. The beginning of society is gregariousness, but that alone is not enough. Fish and birds flock, ungulates wander about in herds, but often they have only the rudiments of society. The individual members respond to one another, not so much as individuals as other members of the flock or herd moving in certain directions and taking up certain space. A herd or flock or school is like a wave in which the members are drops of water: the flock undulates and ripples in response to the attraction of food or the sense of danger, but it is not more than a rudimentary society. A true social system begins to emerge when animals develop contrasting but complementary roles within the group.

The simplest example is the male-female pair. Societies emerge when pairs form constituent units of larger groups and where relations between the pairs—usually spatial or "territorial"—become elaborated. The example is well known of the colonies of birds in which males stake out territories first, then are joined by females, then each pair defends its nest site and its young. In such arrangements, some males do not get territories and some females do not get mates.[3] Those who miss their footing on the merry-go-round of marriage are banished to the peripheries of the society and do not mate. If they die before breeding, their genes will not join the common pool of the species's genes, and future generations will be stamped with the characteristics of their successful rivals. Mutations favorable to the successful acquisition of nest and mates would be selected for. Included in these mutations would be the physiological basis of successful aggression on the one hand and, on the other and just as important, a successful bonding, in this case with the mate. Animals able to drive off rivals and retain females with ease would be at a distinct advantage; the characteristics favoring this, such as size, agility, coloring, aggressiveness, and sex appeal, would be favored reproductively and passed on. This is not a simple matter of aesthetics or animal flirtation: it is a sober business which, alternately in leaps and subtle sifting, changes the course of evolution by producing new species and modifying old ones.

Competition for scarce resources—food, nest sites, mates—is the basis of society and the stuff of politics. But the simple nest-site competition is not very complex; no really ingenious political system can be seen to come out of it. The basic processes, however, are there— competition, inequality, exclusion, bonding. In any competition, someone wins and someone loses; a relationship of dominance and subordination is set up. If the subordinate is excluded, the matter quickly loses its interest as far as the forging of political systems is concerned. But if the dominant and subordinate animals remain in some relationship to each other, and if the dominance and subordination continue to be recognized, and if, further, the subordinate animal is itself dominant over yet another animal, then the rudiments of hierarchy emerge, and a political system now exists.[4] It is a system of inequalities in that those at the top get more than those lower down (including such intangibles as freedom of movement); it is a system of politics in that changes in status can take place—indeed, this is what political systems are about.

This conversion of status into reproduction has an historical aspect; it has always been a way for information about one generation's experience to become part of the reality of the next. It is, in the technical and aesthetic senses, the biological rendering of history. In this context, there is no generation gap, just an inexplicably cumulative and effective bridge whose gatekeeper is none other than the ubiquitous Politics. Hence the political process is not only about the existential business of feeling powerful, being vain, leaving a room in which one's low status is an embarrassment. The very intensity of these status fights masks their implication for the future.

We ourselves have by and large lost sight of the place of politics in the arrangement of our genetic future. We remain caught in the process and seek both power and genetic immortality without trying to formulate the relationship between the process and its consequence, and without caring—if we do figure it out—that the heat of the moment is defined by its effect on the cold facts of the species's future. Only when mating and politics affect major fortunes and conspicuous lineages—as with aristocrats and feuding families or tribes—do we pay explicit attention to genes and power. Otherwise, like the gourmet wholly unconcerned about vitamins, we partake and enjoy. What the human species in particular has become obscures many of these relationships. But in many primate systems the constituents remain, and it is these that must first be isolated and described.

Because there is considerable variety in primate political organization, we can only summarize some of the most general characteristics, those common to a large variety of systems.[5] However, it must always be remembered that man has had a peculiar evolutionary history during which he has evolved features peculiar to him as a species. Because he is a gregarious, terrestrial primate with a history of savanna living, it will help us to look at other terrestrial primates with a similar history and see what adaptations have ensured their success.[6]

One hurdle must be cleared at the outset. It was thought for a long time that the primal social bond that held primate societies together was the constant sexual interest of the members in one another.[7] In many ungulates—the red deer, for example—the sexes mix only during the breeding season, when the powerful stags gather harems of females and defend them. Once the season is over, the stags form an all-male group or become solitary, the females with the young in turn form their own group, and the sexes thus part company. It used to be thought that primates bred all year round. This, it was claimed, was the real difference between them and other mammals, which, like the red deer, formed a total male-female society only during the rutting season.[8]

This theory would have sexual attraction as the basis of politics. Without constant sex there would have been no enduring society whose politics could become a matter of dispute. But this is not so. Many primates that maintain year-round societies do not engage in year-round sexual activity. Thus, a male is not ensured perpetual sexual bliss by being at the top of the primate hierarchy, even though he will indeed be more likely to breed than his inferiors. Which reinforces the point: politics is about genetics, not sex per se. The more powerful animal gets a better chance to perpetuate himself genetically rather than simply a better chance to indulge in sybaritic excesses. This raises a second point: if constant copulation is not the reward, and hence the goal, of power, then power must be attractive in itself. At the risk of seeming anthropomorphic, we can hazard a guess that animals strive for dominance because they want to be dominant. A dominant animal moves more freely, eats better, gets more attention, lives longer, is healthier and less anxious, and generally has a better time than a lowly and peripheral animal. To escape from the gloom of peripherality into the aristocratic confidence of the central hierarchy must be its own reward. The effective outcome of this, aside from the apparent pleasure, is simply that while all males get a chance to copulate, only the more dominant get a chance to breed. This is the point around which the whole social system revolves: who does the breeding?

A typical savanna baboon troop has an average of forty members. How the troop organizes itself can be seen in its spatial arrangements both at rest and on the move, more typically the latter. The group moves about all day foraging for food—mostly grass—and each member fends for himself. At the center of the group are the dominant males—never more than about six adults, however large the troop. Around them cluster the females and the young. Spread out around this central core are the "cadets"—the more junior males who are candidates for the central hierarchy. The peripheral males are confined to the edges of the group; here these animals which have left their mothers and moved to the borders are joined by some older males that have not made the central hierarchy. The males of the central core act as bosses, defenders, policemen, and leaders in a complex set of actions and inter-actions. Within the hierarchy there are coalitions of animals, usually two or three, which, when acting in concert, can outrank any individ-ual, no matter how strong. This system has great advantages to a troop moving across the savanna. The peripheral males—the most expendable—are at the edges, where they are most likely to encounter predators and give the warning. The mothers and young are near the big males. In the event of danger from lions or leopards, for example, the big males will come out and threaten and usually succeed in driving off the foe. A large male baboon with his huge sharp canines is a formidable fighting animal, and even carnivores hesitate to risk wounds that might prove fatal.

A group like this has to be disciplined in order to survive, and this discipline is maintained by the ranking system. For example, the large males will tolerate little quarreling within the group and will quickly stop fights between females and juveniles. Furthermore, the attention of the lower-ranking animals is directed mostly toward the top male. Among the ranking males there is very little fighting over food, space, and females. Once the ranking order has been determined, threats are enough to maintain it: a fierce baring of the canines will put a sub-ordinate in its place very quickly. The ranking pattern therefore tends to be very stable over time. Palace revolutions do occur from time to time, and older males are ousted, but it is remarkable how long a dominant male can hold his position, even when he has grown old and lost his teeth and could easily be defeated by a better-equipped junior. The habit of obedience dies hard. On the other hand, some animals that are individually quite dominant do not seem to have the taste for leadership; some achieve power only to discover they do not like it. They leave the band and become "solitaries." Sometimes they return for brief periods to play among the peripherals, but most of the time they prefer their own company. This often happens to males at the top when for some reason the group gets very large.

In a large group there are subunits of female relatives and their young, which also act in some sense as coalitions. The females have their ranking too, even if it is not as clear and is more volatile than the male hierarchy. These subunits of females—for example, among the baboonlike macaques—can themselves be ranked. The ranking of females is important, since the sons of high-ranking mothers stand a better chance of making it into the hierarchy than do the sons of lowlier females. Perhaps this is because the high-ranking mothers are nearer the dominant males and are able to keep their youngsters with them longer. The sons of the hoi polloi move out to the edge as early as one year after birth, but the aristocrats can stay in the court circle for two or three years. The big males learn to recognize and tolerate them, and they themselves learn that they are born dominant. Their mother can probably outrank even some of the males; the youngster becomes accustomed to seeing animals flee from him; and the emotional tone and confidence of a dominant female are his to share.[9]

The males without this privilege must sit it out at the peripheries, playing their games when young and cautiously testing out their strength as they get older. They will either push into the central hierarchy of their own band, leave and try elsewhere, or die. The death rate among peripheral males at puberty is very high: as many as half their number will never see adulthood. Again we have a weeding-out process favoring not only the strongest but also the most confident, controlled, cunning, and in some ways cooperative males. They must cooperate with other males in many ways; they must pull in the female vote. A top male who is totally unacceptable to the females may not keep his position. He is subject to too much female harassment. And the big males will win female approval only if they indulge and supervise the infants of the community.[10]

The nonhierarchical animals carefully watch their bosses. Rather than sex, this may be the clue to the cohesiveness of primate groups. The lower animals seem to be programmed to pay attention to the dominant animals, who, however, pay little attention to them and gaze off into the middle distance with relative indifference unless challenged or disturbed. Peripherals are so apprehensive they will often abandon the very food they are eating in order to focus all their attention on the dominant males.[11]

Who gets paid attention to can apparently help to change the structure of a troop. Animals display different capacities for dominant behavior—which, like intelligence in humans, is not uniformly distributed through the population. Unusually dominant animals are not necessarily the ones that can win the most fights, but often those that can get the rest to pay attention to them. The dominant animal is by definition the one to whom the rest pay the closest attention. And within limits the group will take an animal at its own evaluation. Thus the dominant animal is the one that behaves most like a dominant animal and can convince the others that it is. This is why a strange animal can often usurp the top position in a group. His novelty value is a great asset in getting attention and also explains why, once dominant, an animal can remain dominant for a long time: it is hard to get attention diverted from it.

How does this affect the female population? What matters in the system is who does the breeding.[12] This is what being top animal means in genetic terms. Females go through a monthly cycle of sexual behavior—the estrous cycle. During and just before menstruation, they are not sexually receptive, and the males are not interested in them. But for a few days in mid-cycle they go into heat—a kind of sexual mania—when they solicit the attention of the males. This solicitation—the presenting of the hindquarters—is aided in some species by spectacular swellings and colorations of the genital areas. While they are actually in heat, the females will be appropriated by a dominant male, who will try to monopolize them. If he is successful, he will be the only one to copulate with them during this period. Since this is their time of ovulation, it follows that he will be the only one to impregnate them.

Before and after this peak of estrus, the dominant male is more or less sexually indifferent and will often let inferior males mount the females. Everyone copulates; only dominants propagate. The genetic composition of the group in the future is heavily determined by the breeding privilege these high-ranking animals exercise. They control not only the present of the group, but its genetic future too.

These are some of the features of baboon and macaque social structure. The social systems of many terrestrial primates do *not* have the concentric structure described here. But whatever the details of the system, certain underlying processes are obvious despite the diversity of surface structures, and can be easily summarized.

The system is based on hierarchy and competition for status, which determine access to resources and the privilege of breeding.

The males dominate the political system, and the older males dominate the younger.

Females can be influential in sending males up the status ladder; and their long-term relationships to one another are critical for the stability of the system.

The dominant males keep order among the females and juveniles; they are nurturers and protectors of the young.

Cooperation among males is essential; coalitions of bonded males act as units in the dominance system.

The whole structure is held together by the attractiveness of the dominants and the attention that is constantly paid them.

Because of this, charismatic individuals can upset the hierarchical structure, and by the same token, retain power.

It will be quickly apparent that these rules apply to human beings as well as to many of the other primates. Of course, there are differences: humans differ from baboons, as chimpanzees differ from gorillas. But the basic biogrammar is there, in which we can recognize many of the syllables of our common behavioral language. The point is that human communities are fundamentally concerned with the same things as other primate communities—surviving, perpetuating the group, defending it, keeping some social order, using the environment reasonably constructively, and just generally muddling through. The woman with a baby or the pasha bidding weary good-bye to a representative of his harem may think they are serving themselves and their own pleasures and vanity. They are, but they are aiding and abetting the species even more directly than themselves: the reason they get pleasure in what they do is that pleasure and survival are linked; our most primitive hedonisms are episodes in nature's scheme for making sure that animals do what is necessary for their survival.

Human political systems are based on hierarchy and competition for status; it remains an ardently sought political ideal to divorce ascribed or inherited status from control over resources. But not only have most states failed to wither away, they have prospered. The encompassing grip grows rather tighter of pettily differentiated hierarchies doling out pettily or even grandly differentiated payments and perquisites. Hierarchies lend coherence to whatever systems of government humans create; competition for status is to social process as sexual attraction is to reproduction. That sex and status are connected should not surprise us: the primate quest for high status seems more pervasive and persuasive in practice than the human quest for equality is in theory. This is not to deny the importance and complexity of political idealism and its effect on the sundry forms of human politics. It is only to suggest that the earlier primate passion for preeminence in terms of which reproduction occurs still underlies and inhibits our political idealism.

But why have any hierarchies at all? To pontificate about original sin would be neither original nor helpful, and the whole effort of blaming unfortunate patterns of social life on some forms of dispensable nastiness would exercise the moral muscles beautifully but provide no answers, and no insights into reality. No matter how hard and how often we rail against them, the affections for difference in status are also part of our primate structure, part of our "primative" reflex to be higher rather than lower. We refine this reflex endlessly; we humiliate others; we are rank-makers and flag-planters. We create a god to whom *we* can be subordinate. So committed are we to the notion of hierarchy that even our mightiest leaders must subserve something or someone. We set about formulating governmental systems that are retained by boundaries of territory or of group. But then we spill over these boundaries and become a highly specialized kind of primate, one who creates out of the stuff of a local hierarchy the basis of an imperial apparatus. By the use of symbol wedded to underlying propensity, we strive to control huge areas of land and large groups of people. That we accomplish and justify this is an ambivalent tribute to our humanness and our brain. That we want to at all is a predictable outcome of our evolution as primates.

No one would affirm the necessity of hierarchies nor be so foolish as to argue that when a man loses his empire he loses his humanity. But it must be understood that the process which gives rise to empire is the very same process that primates engage in simply in order to exist and persist. The hierarchical encounter and the rank order are the cells out of which whole and larger systems are built.

What can be the relationship of hierarchy to such quintessentially human structures as empires, bureaucracies, and ideologically committed political parties? What happened was a change of gear. Our earlier hominid ancestors had lived a simple primate life with a society compounded of the elements we have described. They too roamed the savannas in search of food, but at some point they made a breakthrough: they abandoned total dependence on vegetable food and took to hunting—small game at first, but later bigger and bigger animals and in ever greater quantities.[13] They invented tools and weapons, fire and clothing, and the whole complex of culture. To do this they had, as we saw in Chapter 1, to improve their brains in feedback with their improving skills as hunters and weapon-makers. The improved brain was capable of novel symbolic processes, but it was working on the same material. The symbolic processes enabled the evolving hominid hunters to create political structures that overstepped the boundaries of the troop even as they continued to use the same raw material.

A very simple example serves to illustrate this. When primate groups get too big they split up into two groups, usually of about equal size. There are upper organizational limits to the troop—as we have seen, forty or fifty individuals is just right, as in human hunting groups. The primate groups that split become, in effect, two new breeding groups; if they are still in close proximity, they establish at once a dominance-subordination relationship. But that is the limit of their continuing association.[14]

Human groups also split; it is clear that those of our evolving hunter ancestors did. But their capacity to make symbols would enable them to do several additional things. They could, on the one hand, continue to trace genealogical relationships to one another and remain united as kin, even though they were divided as ecological units. On the other hand, they could share a common name and gather for ritual activities that would be unique to them and bind them as one clan. Often a worship of common ancestors would serve as the operative religious code—a very effective way to maintain continuing identity. In the primate groups the males move around from group to group, but when they leave a particular group they are effectively lost to it. Human hunters—both males and females—can and could move around too, but their identity with members of the parent group would not necessarily be lost, since they would bear a common name and be able at all times to conceptualize their relationships and rights with those of their group of origin. In this way, although ecological considerations as inexorably divide expanding human groups into fragments as they do groups of baboons, symbolic processes can weld them together into clans and tribes. Even among hunters and gatherers who have to be dispersed, as many as between one thousand and five thousand people can be linked by language and kinship and common ritual.[15] In this way, they are able to respond to the symbols rather than only to the persons. To a male baboon of one troop, a male baboon of another is simply another male baboon—and thus a potential threat. The human tribesman, on the other hand, is able to ascertain whether or not the

other male is a member of the same tribe. If he is, is he a member of
the same kinship group? Is he a close or distant kinsman? Is he a
relative to be joked with or avoided, avenged or even murdered? The
human tribesman responds to the man not only as an individual but
as a representative of a category of persons.

Clearly the ability to bind otherwise fragmentable groups gave an
enormous advantage to the humanizing hominids. Their ever-growing
hunter bands became the most effective and efficient predators on the
face of the earth. Their ability to exploit an environment multipled n
times, and very rapidly too. What this uniquely human feature did—
and the point cannot be overstressed—was to reorganize the basic
material of the ancestral primate political system. It added no new
words to the vocabulary of politics. Its contribution was a new way of
organizing the words into more ambitious sentences and paragraphs.
It enabled us to elaborate and categorize, to define and analyze. And,
as culture began to make more and more demands, it enabled us to
think up more and more complex criteria of rank, so that, for example,
eloquence might well be as important as strength, and the great
speaker—for the speaking primate—could be as likely to reach high
office as the great hunter. Territories could be mapped, instead of de-
marcated by physical approach and retreat; relations between neighbors could be formalized by agreements. Internal order could be coded
in rules, laws, and maxims, and enforced not only by the patience of the
strong and the consent of the weak but also by the fact that the agents
of the law are themselves constrained by the rules of the group.

This change can be seen aesthetically, as the longest-running ballet
in history. The choreography of the movements of the animals—man
and prehuman—depends on the same scheme. There is attraction between the animals. They seek one another out, sit with one another,
cluster in coveys, range together, and reproduce. If they are successful,
the groups increase in size, and this very success forces the group to
split, to start the process all over again. Baboons do this, and they
have colonized Africa so extensively that there are now more of them
than people. Humans danced to the same basic choreography: they
moved together, interacted, had babies, grew, and with overpopulation found new continents, new hearths, another human colony. The
rhythm is slow and measured; the individuals move with the stateliness
of creatures knowing that it takes a whole lifetime to live a whole lifetime; the components of their lives are inexorably linked with the
components of the lives of others.

Yet the colonies remained linked. That is the great human invention, the new melody and color in the dance. The groups still cluster together, fondle babies, laugh at jokes, and worry about keeping dry. But a web of symbols and reminiscences called history now binds them. The first human empire was just down the road; our great leap forward was a quiet amble to see the People of Other Village, *and we knew them and could state our connection.* It was an intimate empire, based on our astonishing knack for spacing ourselves out to keep physically healthy at the same time that we bound ourselves together to preserve the richness of our society. We kept both our primate inheritances, body and group, but we found a way of expanding our societies, though our bodies remained substantially the same—except for our heads, which we filled with brain tissue, in good part to keep track of our extended web of people and ideas about people. We became superlative primates; the breeding system that was so effective that we had to colonize also yielded the political skills necessary to make empires of separated groups, make theories of society out of the way we treated with our neighbors, make gods out of what we thought we shared in common, and make primate order out of human symbol.

The transition is subtle, but it can and should be explained. The political process in its evolutionary setting is a breeding process—part of the system of natural and sexual selection. Power equals self-perpetuation—or at least some more throws of the dice, a statistically better chance of contributing disproportionately to the gene pool. When the system of power and perpetuation comes to include not only genes but also material goods and hereditary privileges, the matter becomes much more complicated. We inherit a system in which males strive for dominance; we have seen how this perpetuates their genes; differential access to food, females, and security are the objects of the game. The human innovation is to add to this a conscious striving to perpetuate the nongenetic heritage as an end in itself: power, goods, office, and influence—as well as offspring—become the counters in this new version of the old game.

The crucial aspect of the new politics is the divorce of the ends of the game from its motivations. The deep motives of the participants stem from the system of selection in which they evolved—the hierarchy-dominance-breeding system. But the ends are no longer simply the dominance of the genetic structure of the future, though this has certainly played its part in human politics. In Australian aboriginal societies, for example (and there are many cases just like this), the most successful males collect the most wives and contribute unequally to the gene pool. King Ismail of Morocco (1672–1727) is said to have fathered 1,056 children from "countless" concubines and wives.[16] But as society increased in density and complexity, sexual dominance ceased to be much of a genetic issue. Natural and particularly sexual selection continued and indeed continues to operate, but not primarily through hierarchical politics. Even the *droit de seigneur* did not ensure the overlords a monopoly of genetic power. In fact, the situation soon reversed itself, and the poor and oppressed began to outbreed their masters.

Power became divorced from the control of the genetic future of the population, and fastened instead onto the control of material goods and the symbolic future. The leaders could not ensure that they controlled the future merely by peopling it with their own offspring; they had to ensure that their offspring controlled the future by having the monopoly on wealth and power. The same basic motive power that moved our primate ancestors and hominid forebears flowed into a new political system, but because of the move to symbolic operation, no longer occupied the same niche in the natural order of things. Politics was thus severed from its evolutionary role—with consequences both benign and malignant.

Control over the power and wealth of future generations, however, was, and to a large extent still is, linked to breeding through systems of succession and inheritance. If an aristocratic class controls the system, then the only way to participate in that control is to be or become a member of that class. This "breeding elite" differs from primate breeding elites: it is an elite of the "well bred" or properly fathered which links genes to power in a peculiarly human way. Human societies have the same problems of stability and perpetuation that their nonhuman cousins have. Some kind of aristocratic system is a common human answer to these ancient evolutionary problems. For human society has a conscious concern with continuity and the preservation of stability— not things that seem to actively trouble our primate cousins. The processes that give stability and order to primate groups have already been described; now we should see how the aristocratic principle manifests, supplements, or negates these principles in human society.

By an "aristocratic principle" we mean any system of domination based on hereditary position—what Max Weber would have called a "traditional" system of political domination.[17] Continuity is provided simply and effectively by allowing heirs of aristocrats to be aristocrats in their turn. Since legitimate heirs are a special resource, aristocratic families are usually very careful about their women and the general control over reproductive capacity that women represent. There is no doubt that women have always been important counters in the political game; the fate of empires can turn on the marriages they make and the potential heirs they carry. The aristocratic way assures stability, but at the risk of stagnation, since there is no guarantee that the heir will be competent—a common and vexatious problem of monarchical systems. But aristocracy nonetheless taps some of the basic primate processes. For a start, it is avowedly based on a system of inequalities and often on an exquisitely graded hierarchy. All men may in theory be equal before God in some ultimate sense, and the meek may very well inherit the earth, but in the meantime society is fixed on a rigorously rank-ordered basis. As long as one stays within the system, the only way to achieve power is to make an aristocratic claim to legitimate authority, either by being born noble, by being ennobled, or by managing to sustain a claim to legitimate nobility. Challengers to thrones before Perkin Warbeck and after had to claim that they were the true heirs of some dead and undisputed monarch; Pugachev had to claim that he was in fact Peter III, and most claimants to the English throne had, for some tortuous reason, to prove descent from John of Gaunt.

Yet even within the central hierarchy of an aristocratic system, there is a quite ferocious competition for effective power. The position of king or chief may well be fixed, but the system is rare in which all power effectively resides in one person. It does happen—oriental despots did flourish—but even there the power play among the elite was considerable.[18] The central hierarchy of high aristocrats played power politics among themselves, but at the same time they joined forces to keep at bay any peripheral groups that sought to usurp aristocratic power; and there were always such groups—serfs, burghers, peasants, free knights—harassing the central core. What Disraeli fondly referred to as the "aristocratic settlement" had to be preserved.[19] But inside the boundaries drawn around nobility, the gloves were off. Thus both hierarchy and competition were incorporated into the system. Membership of the central hierarchy was relatively stable, and with this the group as a whole was assured stability and continuity, but the members of the central hierarchy could give expression to the need to strive for dominance and maintain it.

The maintenance of dominance in such a system was based on the one hand on coercion and threat, and on the other on established habits of deference. Effete aristocracies could often last for a long time after their real power had evaporated. They could even continue to exercise great influence, although formally stripped of much of their legitimate authority. Both ethnographers in Africa and historians in Europe have noted that, remarkably, rebels in feudal-type societies rarely challenged the feudal principle itself. Peripherals who moved in to challenge did not want to change the system—merely the personnel who ran it. The impulse is to accept the established hierarchy—which enhances stability and makes matters easy for the dominants, who can maintain their dominance largely by ritual means. Ultimately, of course, there is the threat of force—the primeval canine tooth—but most of the time subordinates will defer to badges of rank and thus to those who wear them.[20]

Babies born to aristocrats are "superior" immediately. Babies born to commoners are what they are and no more. The aristocratic system possesses the distinct advantage—in terms of maintaining formal stability if that is what is wanted—of being able to induct members of the society into the pattern of dominance right from birth. When two men meet after one has known for thirty years he would be king and the other that he was only a commoner, the encounter must reflect a habit hard to break, even with the best intentions in the world. His Royal Highness and Mr. Smith may, in terms of some theory or other, be brothers under their respective skins, but in their habits as animals, one takes precedence *as a person*, and the other defers. Aristocrats are people. They are even primates; perhaps a useful analogy can be drawn with those primates whose birth from a high-ranking mother makes it much more likely that they themselves will become dominant. One animal learns to dominate as another learns to serve. There is no reason to believe, as far as dominance is concerned, that the human primate learns less than baboons; we can be sure that he learns even more. So the duke is more appalled by being crowded—he needs more space, and usually gets or is given it. First-class travel gives you more room to move. And the duke expects not only room, but that people will make room. It is a habit learned young, which dies hard.

Aristocrats know all the primate tricks—particularly those relating to what Michael Chance has called "attention structure." Dominant primates get looked at most; they are the focus of attention, and also the center of the group's social structure. It is not clear—nor does it really matter—which comes first. What matters is that leadership and

visibility are closely linked, and that human attention structures—
while infinitely more complex and symbolic than the other primates'—
nonetheless can be identified and their functions for politics made
clear. Consider the dramaturgy of aristocracy—the forms of address,
the styles of clothing, the seating plans, and the very dining halls
themselves.[21] The architecture is made to impress as much as to shelter,
and to be definitive rather than merely serviceable. The round of life
celebrates the status and pomp of the aristocracy, the more visible the
better. Perhaps it is true that tourists crowd around to peer at Greenwich Village hippies just as avidly as they flow around the rails of
Buckingham Palace. But they go to Greenwich Village and Buckingham Palace for different reasons, and they react differently when the
Queen appears or disappears than when even a queenly hippie girl
makes an entrance or a sign. It is too easy to scorn the tourists at both
places. They are real people who choose to spend their time and energy
this way; it is expensive to gape at foreign palaces. Nonetheless, they
willingly place themselves, in terms of the attention structure, in a
position of subservience, along with autograph hounds and consumers
of gossip columns. It is beside the point to say that this is a good or
bad thing or that aristocracies are better or worse than other systems.
The point is that many of the components of primate systems of hierarchy and deference can be seen in the attention-structure efforts of
aristocrats.

Of course, aristocracies and similar traditional systems of dominance
can be challenged and overthrown like any other political systems. In
the context of our earlier distinction between primate politics, which
have to do with differentiation and acknowledged hierarchy, and
human politics, which have to do with the search for equality and
humane management, we can quickly understand the special attraction
of primate politics for aristocrats.

In other words, aristocracy is more primitive than democracy. This
primitiveness is effective not simply because aristocrats are integrated
into a well-protected and economically overprivileged social class, but
because humans appear to find satisfaction in such an enticing display
of dramaturgy and stability. This deference may be extremely expensive to those who defer. But in the business of being inferior and
superior, we do not begin from scratch, but rather draw on an elaborate
repertoire of already broadly programmed ways of showing those differences of status it seems we are compelled to show. The inflexible
and consistent connection of all this with the way we evolved as a
breeding species confirms our connection with our own prehistory. It

also suggests that, despite our noble wishes, there are limits to how much we can affect our circumstances by our will, and our community by our goodwill.

Despite this, there is a sense in which democratic arrangements are even more "primitive" than aristocratic ones. The primate political system is based on ruthless but ritualized competition for power. Though some systems have some hereditary elements (the advantages gained by the son of a high-ranking mother), it is on the whole true that all young males are thrown into the pool of potential leaders and have to work their way to the top. In primate groups, perhaps the basic feature and certainly the most important is competition for status. This plays a part in aristocracies too, but the very nature of the hereditary principle acts to play it down by defining the over-whelming majority of males as ineligible for the competition. These males may succeed in local status competitions, but it is not the same thing: being best archer or best sackbut player in Walton-on-Thames is a poor substitute for being Lord of the Marches. Aristocracy capital-izes on those primate features that favor long-term stability—the "stability of the dominance hierarchy"—and the principle of a central hierarchy as a focus of attention and cohesion. But it reduces the feature of competition as far as the whole population is concerned. Democratic regimes in effect open up the status competition to greater numbers of people, but they base the competition on a principle of rotating leadership unknown among primates. To some extent, while a dominant primate male cannot hold effective power without the con-sent of the governed, he does not depend on this consent to achieve office. Democratic politicians battle with one another as ruthlessly and with many of the same tricks as their primate counterparts, but ulti-mately they get to the top by getting votes, not by physically defeat-ing their rivals.

It may be instructive for us to look at the voting system as a con-ventionalized, or ritualized, competition. The primate wins his battles and maintains his position chiefly by bluff. He convinces his opponents that it is not worth their while to take him on physically, and they defer. To listen to the speeches of candidates during an election is to believe that the victory of the opposing party will lead to nothing short of national if not cosmic disaster, not to mention the personal misery and poverty of each and every voter. But what happens in-stead? Each side counts heads, and when one side sees that the other has more physical support, it backs down, leaving its opponent the field, but continues to harass it and wait for another opportunity to challenge. Votes are the canine teeth and threat display of democratic politics.

Democratic regimes are faced with the problem of continuity, and usually settle it by having as the focus of the attention structure some person or institution who persists despite changes in the effective leadership. This person or institution can be a constitution, a supreme court that is not elected, a president who is "above" politics, or a constitutional monarch as titular head of state. Political theorists trying endlessly to define the significance of this concept of "head of state" have been given pause by the seeming paradox that the most stable democracies are constitutional monarchies.[22] A student of attention structure would immediately recognize the value of Queen Elizabeth, not as a technical element in the British constitution, but as a persisting focus of national attention who can be venerated while prime ministers are despised. One of the problems with the American presidency is that it confuses these two roles: one must respect the office while possibly despising its holders. There is always a fair chance that the near-half of the population who voted against the victorious candidate may do just that.

Democracies cannot escape dealing with the same primate problems as the aristocracies they overtly disparage and often secretly envy. And despite their egalitarian theories, they often generate very similar structures. In the same way that they intensify the status competition, they stress the attention structure, and here they have a lot of the primate heritage going for them. For example, the dominant male is visible and an object of intense interest and observation. The cohesion of the group depends on this structure of attention. The attention is competed for, and the dominant animal is the one who can get it. He is not born with attention directed toward him—although a high-ranking mother can help to draw some—but has to compete for it either as a rugged individual or in consort with bonded male companions. The democratic politician is in somewhat the same position. If he wants to get to the top, he has to be visible, has to get attention and hold it, in open competition with other politicians. Of course, like his well-born primate cousin, he can start with great advantages. A common explanation for the success of the Kennedys was that the best way to get to the top is to start there. This beautifully illustrates the point that it *is* attention that counts. Whatever his merits as an individual politician, a Kennedy (or a Rockefeller or a Roosevelt) starts with more than his fair share of almost hypnotized attention from the voters. Yet he still has to compete, and is not—as would be the case if this were an aristocracy—handed office on a plate simply because he is his father's son.[23]

We can see that aristocracies, oligarchies, plutocracies, tyrannies, despotisms, democracies, and all other forms of political dominance, despite their obvious overt differences, all work according to the same basic processes. They differ in the way they institutionalize the basic features, and how they emphasize different parts of the primate political biogram. For example, tyrants and despots exploit the virtues of a strong dominant male; but they make the mistake of trying to wipe out the competitive arena so essential to the successful running of a dominance system. Aristocracies see the virtues of the stability of the dominance hierarchy and allow for competition within it. But they make the mistake—by severely restricting entry to the arena—of permanently frustrating the peripherals. The most successful aristocracies, the ones that have survived in even attenuated forms, are those that have freely admitted new members on the one hand, and readily demoted old members on the other. In this way they have avoided becoming castes or closed estates. A familiar example of this process is the British system, in which younger sons did not receive titles, and often married into the bourgeoisie, while wealthy burghers, and recently men of talent, have been admitted to hereditary peerages. An aristocratic-democratic compromise has thus been reached, in which socialist leaders become earls and viscounts, and the younger sons of peers become socialist Members of Parliament.

In theory, the perfect system would be a true democracy, not because it renders all men equal, but because it gives them an equal chance to become unequal. An aristocracy, on the other hand, allows them only an unequal chance to become unequal. Inequality is the goal of both systems, and democratic ideology and theory only become self-defeating when they confuse the democratic process with egalitarianism. Egalitarianism is often the stated goal of democratic idealists; indeed, it is often adopted as a symbolic structure (*Mr.* President, *Comrade* Stalin, *Citizen* Robespierre), but here the possible hiatus between symbol and action is the most glaring—a continuing testimony to the human capacity for self-deception that is at once necessary and disastrous. Necessary because without it there would be no democratic ideals; disastrous when it comes between us and a proper understanding of the limits within which those ideals can operate.

A political society is more than just a system for integrating unequal organisms (although it is that); it is a system that allows organisms to strive for inequality—a system rooted in the evolutionary
process.[24] What true democratic theory advocates is simply that the
basis for this striving should not be arbitrary, that the criteria for
being a competitor should not be fixed at birth by class, sex, or color;
that people should be allowed to dominate other people on their merits
and not on the basis of factors beyond their control.

The ground rules of the political biogrammar become clear: organisms are unequal in their capacity for dominance; they strive to dominate one another; they should have a roughly equal chance to compete
in this process. These are not statements of any particular political
ideology—they are in fact compatible with several; they are statements about the animal and the conditions of its evolution, and any
political system is going to have to face up to them. Most systems
operate this way anyway, even though they may have overt ideologies
to the contrary. If they do not, they are doomed to fail. If a system
denies effective competition, it will frustrate its best talents and
stagnate.

There is another set of ground rules, apparently contradictory, that
have to do with the necessity that rulers be regarded as competent and
merciful. It does a leader no good to be visible and authoritative if
he is always widely regarded as improvident and tyrannical. All
primate leaders must attend to infants and females and successfully
respond to the challenges of both the outside environment and the
social disruptions within the group. This is the least they must do. If a
community permits a total and antisocial incompetent to lead it, it may
not survive to tell the story of its political misjudgment.

Human populations also suffer from the slovenliness, avarice, and
callousness of their leaders. It is small consolation to tell a shanghaied
soldier or a half-starved peon that his splendid warrior king is winning
lands galore from the perfidious enemy or building the world's most
glorious marble palace. It takes judgment on the part of leaders to appear dominant enough to be treated as dominants and yet not affirm
too relentlessly the subdominance of their followers. Everyone always
says that all taxes are too high; yet, for the most part, they are paid,
and whatever dissent there is is restrained and formal.

Nonetheless, there have been occasions when the venality, incompetence, and simple greed of leaders have driven the imperial animal
to the elaborate gamble of revolt, of revolution, of desperate anarchy

made tolerable in the present only by the prospect of a more perfect union of all people when the rottenness is expunged and the inequities balanced back. We can expect revolutionary action or wish from young people—that is an old and honorable part of the political process; old men can be so boring, so rich, so full of the rectitude of their own customs, and the young male primate in particular has little time for them and their works. The exceptional act of revolution which is human specifically involves mature males without power confronting mature males with it. That is bitter, and that is remarkably troubling to communities. It is a military truism that civil wars are the most severe and perplexing of all. And well they might be, for they affirm that the community has failed to find within the common symbolism of its former unity reason enough to stop the killing of opponents once friends if not kin. Civil wars are in this sense just extended revolutions—a coup that failed but an impetus that remained.

No almighty formula could possibly apply to all the problems that arise from uncertainty about competence, hierarchy, authority, tenderness, ruthlessness, and mercy, which in varying proportions compose the biogrammar of the politics of the imperial animal. The most complex judgments come into play in deciding who should be leader, and for how long, and under what circumstances, and why. In principle, the institutions of most societies are supposed to serve the exercise of this judgment, though they often prevent its free emergence and almost always add a baffling rigmarole. As primates we are constantly making political judgments, constantly looking to the center, constantly buzzing around the central hierarchy. This hierarchy too looks outward—through agents of tyranny such as brutal police, secret police, debt collectors, and, *in extremis,* the army. Politicians are intensely sensitive, if only to one another. They may learn of their standing from agents or opinion pollsters or regional advisers, or from actual encounters with their constituents. They must be aware all the time of their problematical link with the people they represent and lead, but upon whom they also depend for their income and sense of mighty place. It is no accident that kings have castles with heavy walls and secret passages, that presidents have conspicuous guards, that a Swiss bank account is as much part of the dictator's kit as his control of contracts and of guns. That leaders are loved or respected or at least equably tolerated is no guarantee that they will be safe.

This brings us to the question of change in political systems. Primate systems do not change basically unless some evolutionary mechanism operates to produce new behavior. But certain processes in primate society give us clues to the seemingly inexplicable and often frightening upheavals that can take place in human groups, and often do. Attention structure is a rule in the grammar of stability. But this is a two-edged weapon, for if attention can be taken away from the dominant animals, then the hierarchy can be changed. On a small scale, every grade-school teacher knows how dangerous is the child in the class whose antics—often of an incredible sophistication—so easily divert the class that the authority of the teacher is strained and often seriously threatened. The same tension and unseemly panic can be seen on a larger scale among political figures of established dominance when a prophet arises from nowhere and begins to draw vast crowds with a doctrine that threatens not only the politicians' persons but also the very system of dominance to which they are committed:[25] this may be a system in which they can rise and fall, but it is also one whose rules they know and play by, and whose familiar rhetoric and pomp they enjoy and crave.

Such disruptive people who claim no authority other than their own vision have been called "charismatic" personalities.[26] Their doctrines are many and various, their inspiration profoundly mystical, as was Christ's, or harshly secular, as was Lenin's. What they have in common is a refusal to work within the established order of dominance, and a recurrent claim to a "higher" good to which they owe their allegiance—the coming of the kingdom of God, the triumph of the proletariat, or whatever. The body social has been pumped full of such injections of idiosyncratic energy, but only the few that "take" always have other things going for them. The process is uniformly the same: the zealots capture the attention of the masses or of a revolutionary elite, and eventually overthrow the established system. This they do ostensibly with ideas, and although ideas can be—and are—important, it is the processes that operate irrespective of ideas or ideologies that concern us here.

It may well be that of all processes of social change, those that depend on the vehicle of a charismatic leader for their effectiveness are in a real sense the most rudimentary. Whether the leader is good or bad, provident or irresponsible, sacred or secular, there seems always to be a ferocity of interaction and personal intensity in his relationship to his followers and in their commitment and response. It is an almost desperately indulgent act—to claim that one has the truth or the only plan or scheme to change the world forever. Such a claimant must be

willing to traffic with his constituency with all his most skillful resources as a political animal. There can be no babbling about constitu-
tions here, nor any memos about conciliation. Just as the archetypal
siren provokes in a host of men the taste of promised love, so the
charismatic leader must promise and offer instantly to his followers
an incontrovertible sense of the drama of his energy, the majesty of his
vision, and their special blast of fortune in joining with him at this
critical time for this critical purpose. Charisma requires for its perpetuation a commitment of people's full time and complete political heat,
and needs nothing more than a touch of indifference to kill it. The ideas
of the leader and the promised land he holds out are important, but
they are to the structure of the social relationships as the tracery is to
a flying buttress.

If the participants in a charismatic drama may not understand
what moves them, neither do social scientists. Max Weber used the
term "charisma" to describe the form of dominance that derived its
legitimacy not from tradition or rationally established legality but
from the personal authority of the leader; he was well aware that he
was dealing with something beyond sociological explanation. Sociologists might be able to explain some of the conditions under which
charismatic figures rose and operated successfully. But they could not
explain the nature or peculiar effectiveness of the leader-follower
bond that was involved. Weber recognized this as a phenomenon that
had passed "imperceptibly into the biological."[27] And we can see why.
What is involved is one of the most basic of all biosocial processes,
one that is rooted in the evolutionary struggle for dominance within a
population. The paying of attention to a dominant animal is both the
basis of political society and the major mode of its dynamics. Millions
of years of biopolitical evolution have programmed the primate to be
ready to pay attention to dominant animals, provided the right cues
are given; the natural variety within their populations has ensured
that individuals with superdominance potential will be thrown up in
each generation. It is as unlikely that all of these will achieve leadership positions as it is that a community will discover all its Ein-
steins—but they remain a pool of threatening potentiality.

A leap of the imagination is necessary to see that the massive events
of political upheaval gather their primitive energy from the same
evolutionary source as sexual ardor. But the power and the passion
of a leader for his followers, and the passion of the followers for the
beloved voice and presence, are of the same stuff as the agony of a

lover for his mistress. Both are products of that blind, persistent struggle for dominance and reproductive advantage that is the primal energy of evolution in the animal world. A beautiful woman who arouses a man's lust, and a religious leader who inspires fanatical devotion, are *both* playing the oldest game of all.

There is an infrastructure to all political activity, which we share in part with the other primates and in part with our species-ancestors. Our politics, like our digestion, have biological components. Though an elaborate and vexatiously variable series of options is open to the political animal, there are certain central points which remain determinable. After all, if history is important, then it must count for something that most of our history was spent in small groups of perhaps thirty to fifty individuals and that presumably our political motivations, responses, and controls are adapted to cope on that scale and with that intimacy. In this context, and for this animal, it becomes an act of political extremism to create bureaucracies. Bureaucracy as a theoretical system, and bureaucracies as undeniable and pervasive realities, constitute both a tribute to our exquisite skill of social organization and a caricature of our capacity to create quiet brittle lunacies in the name of reason.

Large-scale bureaucratic organizations are constantly criticized for their inhumanity and impersonality; they are charged with reducing individuals to numbers, computerizing social relationships, overorganizing their conformity-obsessed members, and eventually producing anomie, ulcers, delinquency, anxiety, and wife-swapping. And yet no other form of organization can cope effectively with the overarching problems of a system that goes beyond the face-to-face.[28] Bureaucracy stands at the opposite pole to charisma, with hereditary systems hovering between. The bureaucrat owes his dominance position to formal qualifications; it is not his person that is deferred to, but his office. This replacement of person with office is, as Weber saw, the major characteristic of formal organization, and as inevitable as it is unprimate and inhuman.[29] Unprimate because primate politics are personal politics; eyeball-to-eyeball politics—literally. There are no primate officeholders, only primate individuals.

The paradox is that in order to survive, the human animal has to employ a mode of social organization that in many ways negates all those features that have brought him into the exalted position of needing such an organization in the first place.

Behavior evolved in a social context marked by intensive relation-ships in hunting communities of thirty to fifty people; we have been hunters for ninety-nine percent of our existence, and it was in this context that our behavior was selected, and to these ends. One com-ponent of this inheritance is our skill in dealing with human relations on a small scale. The housewives' kaffeeklatsche, the poker players' evening out, the gang of adolescent boys, the cabals in the Senate, the PTA, the local Democratic club, the party cell, the men's hut, the office clique—are the small groups in which we excel and find satisfac-tion and fulfillment. But when we move to higher levels of bureaucratic organization we lose our sense of scale and rapidly move out of touch with our own human natures. It is the comparatively new and rela-tively untried organ called the cerebral cortex that makes it possible for us to organize ourselves beyond the intimate. No wonder the fruits of reason are sometimes sour. The big brain with its power of unlimited symbolization puts big organization within our grasp, but in grasping it we lose our grip on just those social processes we are so sensitively equipped to handle. When students seek commitment, relevance, and contact, when workers become alienated, when psychiatrists advocate fulfilling relationships, when we curse Big Government and abhor the impersonality of bureaucracies, we are trying to affirm the value of our skill at intimacy and the heartlessness of those who appear to con-demn us to live and work in dehumanized ways. Our revolt against bureaucracy is really a revolt of nature against antinature, of all our evolutionary skills against a system that is their negation.

The small groups we can handle so well may be trying, but at least the problems they present are not insoluble. But when we go beyond groups of about fifty, we can no longer relate in a face-to-face way; we have to relate to symbols of the group or its parts: Department X, Platoon 6, Division 9. We first respond to the symbols rather than to the occupant of the office, whom we may not know at all as a person and who may know us only as a case in a file. Yet we do respond to the large office, to the quiet and seclusive waiting room, to the execu-tive with the alert chauffeur, to the person with "in-chief" attached to his title. We are willing spectators of the drama of political presenta-tion. The students of Columbia University who sat in its president's office and smoked his cigars were not so much scorning the man himself as they were the circumstances that gave a stranger such apparent in-fluence over their education and their sense of personal well-being. Had they, without knowing his specific place and function, met him in, say, a boutique or a billiards hall, such preemptive antipathy would almost certainly not have marked their encounter. This simple point has its ramifications; how else could the students attack a system than by focusing on the local conditions of the man who led it? And yet how else could a man take a high place in a rich endeavor than by assuming all the symbolic trappings that this and other cultures attach to dignitaries? Officials spend considerable time protecting themselves as persons against those with whom they interact as officeholders. Hence the rule book, and hence the justified charge that systems are more important than the very people to whom the systems are alleged to cater.

And yet we have so far found no other good way to encourage warmly personal relationships in impersonal systems. Sociologists were right to make the important distinction between formal and informal organization; there is a conflict—an elaborate and eventful one. Bureaucracies are inhuman because large-scale rule-abiding organizations require the denial of the quick kinetic primate interpersonality which we crave and which in the web of nonformal encounters we try to re-create. The office party is a revealing event, not simply in its apparent aphrodisiac effect; it is a ritual that makes an ironic statement of the strains of being one kind of officer or another. Here are all these people, full of valences and antipathies, normally controlled by the rules of work and the etiquette of organization; yet the party offers that possibility of reversal which anthropologists describe; the day of the lords of misrule; the day when the king is mocked, when the "officers" serve the "men."[30] But there is an even deeper reversal going on, too: the structure is overturned or mixed up. For a careful, limited few hours bosses are just people, employees just men and women with rights to the same full grasp of a human occasion as anyone else, particularly the bosses.

The office party is a dramatic enough example of a continuous and pervasive process—the process of conflict between the established routines of "bureaucratic politics" and the pressures of "primate politics." One of the central sources of disillusion that political idealists may experience in contemplating political life is the extent to which personal situations—such as friendships, allegiances, kinship ties, even racial, ethnic, and class patterns—appear to govern political and bureaucratic appointments and activity, and seem to intrude into the theoretically ordered impersonal system. We are trying to play politics with the wrong rule book—but we have no alternative.

The frustrations felt by most people who deal with bureaucratic organizations are as real and justified as the criticisms they provoke.

But they stem from deeper causes than are commonly recognized—from the fact that we are trapped in a form of political organization that is contrary to our political natures yet necessary for our social survival. Millions of years ago the ants managed to program such a form of organization into their genes; in consequence, their social systems are infinitely better organized and much more efficient than our own. But, again, ants don't have politics. Man seeks to combine primate politics with insect bureaucracy, to reinvent consciously what the ants evolved genetically. It is no wonder that there is revolt against this unnatural reversal of the natural trend of our behavioral evolution. Why, then, do bureaucracies survive at all? Why do they not constantly fail?

The answer takes us even further into paradox. Bureaucracies certainly negate major principles of primate political behavior. But they also tap deep human motivations, particularly those that have to do with dominance. This gives the players in the bureaucratic game a feeling that the old rule book is still in operation. They are teased into thinking that primate politics are still being played. Senior members of large organizations occupy large personal spaces into which intrusion is forbidden without rituals of submission (such as making an appointment, waiting in the outer office, etc.) that send out strong signals of dominance and attention. Loyalty and orderliness so essential to organizations are aspects of pack hunting.[31] So are the sense of belonging and the hostility to outgroups. So is the sense of hierarchy and competition. Yet formal organization sends out recognizable cues from the repertoire of primate politics at the same time that it denies the participants the right to play the person-to-person game that is what those politics are about.

If bureaucracy were simply a denial of humanity, it would have no success at all. Both its successes and its frustrations lie in the fact that it uses human motives to inhuman ends. That people constantly feel in some deep way *cheated*, and eventually alienated, by this double-bind situation is not surprising. Bureaucracy is an infuriating tease; it may constitute a career, and structure a life, but it is less life-enhancing than many of its members and clients want. Bending its rules is only infidelity, and not emancipation. Bureaucracy has a human face that is too much like a passport photo.

In its conservatism, bureaucracy reflects a general problem of human political systems that it is both trying to confront and hazardous to avoid: how to change, and how much. These are problems that every community has to face—even those communities that give the appearance of not changing, and even those changing so quickly that their members find it hard to root even their own social experience in sufficiently tangible realities to feel continuity from one year or decade to the next. The problem of change is based on a regularity of the species perhaps as predictable and necessary as that there will be some short and some tall, some fat and some thin, some fast and some slow: in every community there will be some who are eager and vitalized when change occurs and others who are cautious and hold on to the present and the past inherent in it. This difference in attitude toward change cuts across class, creed, party, and even age group. It is the difference between the innovator and the conserver, the hearth-watcher and the explorer.

In "Beginning Biogrammar" we saw the importance in human evolution of the development of inhibition and the capacity to obey rules. If culture was to replace instinct, this had to happen. But, like all the other potentialities under discussion—dominance, sexuality, intelligence, etc.—the capacity to obey rules is distributed on the normal curve. There are those so constituted that no amount of socialization will ever turn them into men in gray flannel suits, while there are others who seem to be enveloped in this unlovely material from birth. Of course, training has a great deal to do with the development of a conforming or a rebellious personality. But it is equally clear that all animals are different from birth: some of Pavlov's dogs were very difficult to condition, and most experimenters have encountered the "impossible" rat that just has to be discarded. Strains of easily trainable or recalcitrant animals can be bred.[32] The set of differences is ultimately located in the central nervous systems of the animals.[33] It seems inevitable that there will be more conformists than rebels; this is nature's only sensible strategy, since nature is essentially conservative. Most mutations, whether genetic or cultural, are deleterious. Even those that are favorable are favored because they help to maintain a traditional way of life rather than because they lead to new possibilities. Thus the strong fins of the Devonian lung fish—the first fish to venture onto land—were selected for because they enabled the fish to get back into the water. In some of the fish—those that stayed ashore longer than the others—the fins eventually became legs, and so the land animals were born. But legs were originally devices to keep us fish rather than to turn us into animals.[34] When man substituted custom for instinct, the same pattern continued to apply. There has to be a balance between stability and persistence in social systems. On the one hand there are well-tried customs and institutions, and on the other the need for innovation in changed circumstances. The weight is on the side of persistence—of the wisdom of group experience embodied in those customs that have existed from "time immemorial." Innovation is more readily accepted if it tends to preserve the status quo than if it threatens to disrupt it.

Again, nature has not left this to chance and the vagaries of learning; she has ensured that a majority of us shall be predisposed to conformity and caution through a vigorous incorporation of the rules of the tribe into our own personalities. On the other hand, there are always those who resist socialization to help innovate, rebel, and otherwise buck the system. Most fall by the wayside, but occasionally, when times are propitious, their innovative behavior pays off. They may be radical politicians, bloody-minded intellectuals, criminals, religious maniacs, unconventional artists, military geniuses, visionary poets, reformist priests, revolutionary philosophers, or simply men in the street who have the courage and the need to say no to the gray mass of those-who-follow-the-ways-of-our-fathers.

Philosophers of history as well as sociologists and psychologists have noted this distinction. But in this biological context it becomes a natural process in the fullest sense, inasmuch as it reflects a principle that runs throughout the evolution of organic life, a principle as true for our species as for any other—that a species is essentially conservative but that it must allow for innovation. To strike a balance between these two forces is the quintessential evolutionary challenge. A species that provides for a wide variety of characteristics is clearly better off than one that gambles heavily on a few. The balance, however, has to be in favor of conservation. In a species like ours, heavily dependent on learning and socialization, the balance is struck by providing a large pool of overlearners and a smaller pool of restless, "undersocialized" innovators. This biological polarization lies behind all the great movements of class war, national conflict, and party feuding. It does not necessarily correspond to the "conservative-radical" distinction as it is culturally defined; it cuts across these institutional systems: there are nonconformist conservatives and rigid radicals. But at times in the history of tribes or nations it can crystallize and form the basis for conflict and opposition. This may be one reason for the heat, the acrimony, and the ardor of political encounter—and for the antipathy of rednecks and longhairs to each other.

If a broadly biological process is implied by the fact that there is a predictable quota of radicals and back-looking hard-liners in any group, or even that group dynamics urge such a divergence, then the attitude we can have to political systems becomes somewhat clearer. Absolute dictatorships that depend upon one man for their procedures and goals will probably fail—except by escalating force—in the task of keeping some reasonable social order that provides members some satisfaction and some dignity. And the other extreme, structures in which everyone is required to be a proponent of change, will experience difficulty too. The world is a hard place even for those who wish it otherwise and can present plans to make it better. Neither the perfection of God nor of Stalin, Perón, Napoleon, or Lucky Luciano can totally mask the dynamic realities of change that mark all living systems. Nor can the perfections of the kibbutz, the urban commune, the Scandinavian state, or the wholly permissive classroom solve all problems. There will always be the question of what to do with innovations—once enthusiastically made by admirable predecessors—that are now stultifying and in disharmony with the new realities. And it is not a counsel of despair to say that when hatred and loathing form the only bridge between the judges and the accused, between the pigs and the yippies, between the socialists striving for higher taxes from the rich and the businessmen picking shreds of steak from their teeth after banquets, something is going on more influential and conscribed than any of us can know. It is all part of a complex drama of preservation and repair, flurried by a new sortie in a new direction, by the fear in retreat and the dawning pride of discovery. It is not only a conflict between heart and stone, between wisdom and theory, or an engagement between people who understand and love human potential and those who fear the proneness to folly in a complex species. In another sense it may all be as predictable and banal—and hence glorious in the way the baffling change of seasons is glorious—as that some are tall, some short, some fast, some slow. The importance of this encounter between finders and keepers is an invitation at best for us to indulge both our sympathy and our understanding, without loss of ambition for the species or affection for our friends.

The science of politics should have the preeminence in the scheme of moral sciences that Aristotle gave it, and for the same reason: man is, by nature, a political animal.[35] Our approach is basically different from that of the pre-Darwinian sage. The political process has been offered as *the* basic natural process in its evolutionary role as part of the organization of sexual and natural selection.

Sex and politics are two sides of the same evolutionary coin, but we have lost sight of this both as a species and as theorists of our own behavior. What textbook on sexual behavior treats it as a political process? And what primer of political science recognizes that its subject matter is a derivative of a biological theme as fundamental as the struggle for reproductive success? What politician sees his own compulsive energy as fired by the ancient impulses of sexual competition? What lover sees his amorous pride as part of the necessary comportment of the successful mammalian politician? Our political institutions draw their strength and energy from the motives of the old breeding systems. But they offer very different rewards. It is scarcely surprising that reasonable systems fail because people behave unreasonably.

3.

BOND ISSUE ONE: WOMEN AND CHILDREN FIRST

THE YOUNG MOTHER pushes the empty stroller along the sidewalk while her small child stumbles and lurches ahead, testing, as well as his legs, his ability to move willingly away from his mother's body. She is about five yards behind, and mother and child smile with certainty at each other. He runs ahead another two yards—but perhaps he is too young for that, because a signal of alarm is on his face now. As if on some firm elastic rope tied to her child, the mother moves forward; mother and child now move physically toward each other. They are both keen and vital during this small circumstance. They are both almost intrinsic to each other; they are really part of each other's being. Were they minerals, we'd call them magnetized. Because they're people, we say "They love"; because they are animals, we know they must have this group-of-two, just as to walk we need the use of two legs, and to carry, the use of two arms. It is no accident that mother and child do what they do: it is as highly predictable and as much a feature of the life cycles of both as are puberty and growing old.

Around their campfire on the night before a raid on the enemy, a group of Crow Indians, mostly young males, is engaged in cutting up a sausage. As each brave cuts a piece off the sausage and passes it on to the next man, he recites the names of all his lovers since the last raid. He does this with complete honesty, even though the list may include the wife or daughter of a comrade. There is pain in an older man's eyes as his wife's name is recited more than once, but he makes no move. A young man hears his mistress named and flinches slightly, but he takes his piece of sausage and recites unhesitatingly in his turn. On any other occasion this knowledge would have driven either man to anger and retaliation. But this is the night before a raid. At dawn these men must stand together against their enemies; they must fight together, and possibly die together. So on this evening they reaffirm their bonds as men, asserting that their relationship as warriors in a war party supersedes all others, and in particular their relationship with women. Once a man has recited his list of names, he is free forever from retaliation on that score; the slate is wiped clean. The warrior band is freed from the contamination of sexual jealousy and can go about its essentially male business. War and fighting and the hunt have always been the business of human males, just as the protection of the troop is the business of male primates. Women are always a potential source of disruption to the unity, loyalty, and trust necessary to comrades in arms. Far from belittling the strength and importance of women, this affirms it. It is important enough to everyone to be made the focus of the only ceremony which precedes the day during which men must trust one another or maybe die, and even die despite the forces generated by their certainty and by their collective yearning for a triumph.[1]

In the children's house of a kibbutz surrounded by Israeli desert and stimulated and formed by socialist ideals, a group of boys and girls between seven and ten years of age play together. They learn the skills and facts and theories appropriate to becoming functioning adults in communities committed to prosperity, growth, and egalitarian integrity. Every day they eat together and play the same games and compete and cooperate, and sleep in the same rooms every night. They see their colleagues-in-growth more often than they see their parents; with the cruel and yet implacably positive demand for insight which children can afford, they come to know one another's fears and competence, and to share hilarities and scorn.

The expectation of the "system" and the hope of the adults is that the children will mature sexually and marry formally and raise more children, to enlarge the area that is not desert. This is a reasonable expectation. The sociological "law of propinquity" is that, all other things being equal, young men and women marry young men and women who live nearby rather than far away. This law is followed—except in the kibbutz.[2]

Here there is an antibond: friendship in childhood seems to prohibit love in maturity. The boys and girls who grow up together rarely marry: once they are adult, only a tiny number of them break the routine of general familiarity to enter into intimacy and the attempt to maintain a special sexual valence in the context of general social links. One kind of bond seems, in a surprisingly uniform and profound way, to preclude another. Perhaps familiarity does not really breed contempt—but it does not appear to breed at all. There may be a lesson in this: that it is difficult to have more than one kind of major bond with another person. It is therefore difficult for brothers and sisters to marry; despite the myth of Oedipus, it is difficult for sons to have sexual intercourse with their mothers; despite the current myth of many cultures, it may be difficult for parents also to be lovers. We do know that it appears to be virtually impossible for Israeli boys and girls raised in egalitarian and committed groups to form that smallest-group-of-all which bears children and rears them.

A lovers' quarrel has just ensued. The lovers are alarmed at their own capacity for hostility, and frightened at the ensuing sense of loss. Never had they realized how closely bound they were to each other than when faced with the possibility of breaking the bond. What is worse, they cannot pin down the source of the anger: she says it is his possessiveness, he says it is her coquetry. But they know that it come from something deep that at once draws them inexorably close and yet builds up tensions and fears bound to erupt sooner or later in accusation. But her tears move him to pity, so that he wants to protect her; his bafflement moves her to compassion, so that she wants to comfort him. Soon they apologize, embrace, and laugh. It is an old story. We are spared from further elaboration by the very banality of the event we are describing.

All social acts are patterned. They are as nonrandom as our physical structures. The patterns of social relationships into which they are formed can be predicted and explained. They are major regularities of the species—of any species. They can be called bonds. What dogs feel for their masters is an example of what bonding is about. What parents feel for their children is another example of this bonding; what parents do for their offspring is yet another feature of a process to which humans, like other social animals, are prone. This process of social bonding encompasses the formation and maintenance of certain relationships that appear to be stimulating, easy to learn, and in some cases necessary for the general health of the individuals concerned— to say nothing of the well-being and persistence of whole communities.

Human social life is not anarchic; it is not random; it is not capricious. With which woman or man or workmate or best friend we bond may be capricious, particularly for transients and dwellers in large cities. But that we will bond at all, and within certain definable limits, is no less "part of the wiring" than our bodily structure or our growth patterns. This is both true and a truism; yet perhaps it permits us to build a model of a human society that accommodates both willful choice and biological constraint. It allows us to say that the human being not only will proceed through a definable life cycle but also will engage in social relationships—of foreseeable intensity and meaning— with predictable categories of people of predictable ages. Our behavioral biogrammar underlies not only how we will act but how we will interact and with whom.

Though it is far from our intention here to revive the essentially false image of "society as a physical body," we want now to try to show how our interactions are as nonrandom as the shape of human heads and the rate of people's metabolism. There may be as much variation in behavior as there is variation in the size of physical items and the rate of physical processes: both are subject to similar basic rules. Not only human will and the dictates of social culture, but other regularities too, determine how people live gregariously, with whom, and why.

When the origins of the central political process—in essence the process of sexual selection—were discussed in "Political Nature," the basis of bonding was linked to evolution. A species can get by without much bonding. Flocks and herds and schools of fish are notable for the interchangeability of their members: one individual is by and large substitutable for another, as far as any individual is concerned. Such species can be very successful, but like breeding systems with asexual reproduction, they restrict their options and reduce the amount of variety on which natural selection can work. A true social system, as we saw, begins when animals respond differentially to other members of the species as individuals. They begin to *select* other members for specific kinds of relatively permanent interaction. In many animals this is related to territory. A creature defending its area reacts to other creatures as enemies. It is usually the male who defends the area, but, for reproductive and rearing purposes, he has to be joined at some point by a female. He responds selectively to this female as an individual, not simply as any female of the species. Insofar as their relationship has any degree of stability—either over a breeding season or for life—they can be described as "mates," and we can watch a fundamental bond in action. The mates are closely attached to each other. They drive off intruders, perform ceremonies, rear and protect their young, build nests, feed each other, and indulge in a host of intimate grooming and ritual activities that are not promiscuously shared but exclusive to the bonded pair.

A great deal of their ritual has to do with the tricky problem of reducing potential aggression between them. The male is initially hostile to all intruders. If he is to mate at all, he has to come to terms with his potential female partner. In providing sometimes elaborate ritual behavioral mechanisms for reducing potential aggression, nature has also provided the bases of successful bonding. The ceremonies that initially reduced the chances of a fight between mating couples become the means whereby the mates learn to recognize, tolerate, and finally to prefer each other to all others. As Lorenz points out, the fact that love and hate, passion and aggression, are two sides of the same coin is something built into the very nature of the bonding process. Indeed, it is only when a species is, for example, territorial and aggressive that bonding of this kind can begin.[3] Unless there is something to force the animals apart, there is no reason to evolve complicated means of bringing them together. Unless the conditions of life provoke mistrust, there is no need for ways of ensuring trust. This may reflect a biological principle: that the more highly developed the species, the more likely there is to be a high degree of individualism and aggressiveness, and hence of mistrust, and consequently of bonding. If it is indeed *Homo sapiens* who is the most highly developed, then it stands to reason that all these factors should be maximized in his behavior.

Our first example of the bonding process was the mating, or "pair" bond. But there is an even more fundamental bond that all mammals at least have to respect—the bond between mother and child.[4] Even in those mammalian species without pair bonds, where mating is brief and where the sexes part immediately after the mating season, the association of the young with the mother remains important. This is particularly true in all those species where the young are relatively dependent. Whether or not the pair bond will figure significantly in the social system seems to depend on factors associated with territoriality on the one hand, and the nature of the protection needed for the mother and young on the other. In some cases the mother and children can fend for themselves. The breeding season of the hamster, for example, lasts only about a week. During this time the males invade female burrows and then retire to their own. The mother and babies stay in the maternal burrow during the brief maturation period, after which the young disperse and the process starts all over again. With slower-maturing young this is not so easily arranged. Sometimes, as with wolves, pairs form and rear the young together. But with many ungulates, like the red deer, a group of females with their offspring, led by an older hind, form the ongoing social unit. Males associate with these "harems" only at the rutting period.

The reason behind the invariability of the mother-child bond in mammals—as compared with the extreme variability of the male-female bond—is very simple: suckling.[5] Mammals after all are by definition the animals that suckle their young. With this evolutionary innovation the basis is laid for a greater development of sociality than can be found elsewhere in nature. This in turn follows from the longer period of dependency and immaturity in mammalian young. The young of an animal that mature quickly are fully formed both physically and socially at an early stage. Those that mature slowly have plenty of time to *learn* their sociality and incorporate greater variety into their behavior. As we go up the phylogenetic scale of mammals, we find several trends: life span increases; the gestation period becomes longer; the period of immaturity lengthens; the suckling period is extended; the size of the litter decreases until single births are most common. All these factors conspire to delay the maturity of the young animal as long as possible, to prevent his becoming fully formed too quickly.

In all these matters man is the supermammal. He does not achieve this by somehow overcoming or denying or surpassing his mammalian nature, but by exaggerating it.[6] Of all mammals it is man who capitalizes most on the biological particularities of his order. This means that he exaggerates the *behavioral* characteristics—an increase in learning ability dependent on the greater size and complexity of the brain, an even more pronounced period of mother-child dependency, a greater emotional lability, a more elaborate sexuality, more complex play, more spectacular aggressivity, a greater propensity for bonding, a more extended system of communications, and so on. But all this rests on the bedrock of the mother-child bond, itself a product of the live-birth-and-suckling syndrome that is the defining characteristic of the zoological order to which we belong.

The mammalian mother has to suckle the child so that it can live, flourish, and eventually breed. But again, the higher we mount the scale of mammalian complexity, the more it becomes true that something other than simple feeding is involved in the mother-child relationship—particularly when, as with bottle-feeding, actual suckling is unnecessary. The further we move from the governance of primary instincts into the arena of learned abilities, the more it becomes essential for the slowly growing young animal to get its learning *right*. A great deal of its most important learning occurs early and involves those experiences that will provide the foundations for further learning. Since this is the time when the young will be intensively suckling, nature has no option but to make the mother-child bond the matrix for the basic learning processes of the maturing animal.

Simply on the basis of what we know about the social mammals in general, we can predict that if the mother-child bond does not go right, the unfortunate youngster may never get any of his *other* bonds right. The first instruction in the program says: "Form a close and emotionally satisfying bond with the mother; when completed, move on to form x number of bonds, in the following order." Ultimately the "nonbreeding" bond with the mother has to be transformed into a "breeding" bond with a member of the opposite sex. If the initial instructions are not properly followed, the rest of the program may be jeopardized and emerge in an attenuated or skewed form. At worst the wrongly programmed animal may not be able to breed at all and thus be lost to the gene pool; at best it may breed but put the programming of its own offspring in danger.

Sometimes nature tries to make sure of the bond by relatively mechanical means. These, like all instinctive mechanisms, have the advantage of sureness—but they can also go disastrously awry because of their otherwise advantageous rigidity. The idea of "imprinting" is now firmly established in both the ethological literature and the popular imagination.[7] In some animals (*e.g.*, most species of duck) the young learn quickly and dramatically to associate with the first moving object of a given size and color that they see—or even more generally with any larger object that they encounter at a specific period in their development. They will follow and respond to this object in predictable and specified ways. The "object," of course, is almost always their mother, but if for some reason it is something else, the program is totally and irreversibly confused, and a duckling may become attached to a dog or an ethologist or a scientist's boot. The unfortunate creature accepts this object as of its own "species"; once the animal matures, the inexorably confused program instructs it to mate with the only other member of its "species," with comic and yet pathetic results. Zoo animals, to the distress of zoological societies and breeders, thus fixate on their keepers and fail to breed with their own kind. But this is rare. Usually the creature makes the appropriate fixation, and often this is ensured by such devices as having mother and child isolated for a period immediately after the birth. This is common in mammals and gives time for the bond to be formed exclusively with the mother animal, who will then be followed incessantly, turned to in danger, and generally used as a base providing security for forays into the outside world.

Ethologists, with some accuracy, have established "critical periods" during which various types of imprinting take place in various species. But even if the "learning" involved is not of this rather dramatic and rigid character—as is the case with higher mammals—it is nevertheless like it in that it must take place at certain times and in certain ways, and that its outcome determines to a large extent the future performance of the creature. For example, some infants for some reason may not take easily to food, and some mothers may be unwilling or temperamentally incapable of suckling or otherwise feeding them. As we have noted, these characteristics will simply not reproduce themselves in the gene pool if the infant dies or later cannot breed. And, again, the infant may be permanently damaged in a behavioral sense because it has not learned the first rule of the behavioral biogrammar that allows him or her to go on.

This sounds drastic, and it is. There is a striking similarity between behavioral "malnutrition" and food malnutrition. It is now absolutely clear that children deprived of good food—chiefly the substances contained in milk—when they are very young can never wholly recover. For one thing, their growth rates are adversely affected.[8] This has evident consequences for other features of their development. Also, it has been shown recently that the lack of protein in the newborn's diet inhibits the little body's development of myelin, which is necessary if brain cells are to form in the appropriate sequence.[9] Brain damage results as surely from deprivation in the first weeks and months of life as it does from a concussion later.

Development is also closely tied to social patterns, and there is a close connection between behavior and food—one without the other will not do. There is no point in going into an attractive restaurant staffed with capable and friendly waiters who do not serve food; it is just as unpleasant to eat good food in an environment in which one is harassed and abused. For the infant it is a far more desperate matter. Children in orphanages get the food but not the behavior; infants of loving but poor parents may get the behavior, but they will not get the food.[10] In both cases, if the children live to become adults they will be less effective and more frail than their counterparts who were raised by competent mothers and given suitable food.

Our proposal is that the mother-infant bond precedes all others in time—which is obvious—and is the basis for the development of the other bonds that humans are "programmed" to be likely to have. What is the evidence for a statement both so simple and so portentous of complexities to come?

The maladjusted adult has frequently been traced back to the disturbed child, and the disturbed child to the unloved infant. Psychoanalysts argue among themselves about the most vulnerable period of the mother-child relationship.[11] Some favor a late date, some argue for the first few months, some stress the moment of birth itself with its attendant traumas, while still others look into the darkness of the womb—which does in fact contain a living child capable of psychic upset. In any event, the child *is* born in a very "fetal" state—one of the means of extending its dependency and hence its maturation period. But all agree that basic disturbances in the early stages will adversely affect proper passage through the later ones. Many of these explanations and arguments seem overelaborate. A convergence of work in child psychiatry and the study of animal behavior suggests that something rather simple is behind all this, even if the simplicity is disguised by the jargon term "separation trauma."[12] Nature intended mother and child to be together. It is at once as simple and as profound as that. If they are separated when the bond should be forming, it forms imperfectly, if at all. The child suffers a deep sense of loss and even physical distress. And though the mother may not be clear about what has happened to her, she too may suffer—from feelings of depression and inadequacy.

The mother is totally essential to the well-being of the child. Remove her, and its world collapses. This dependence is based on the suckling tendency of mammals, but it does not wholly hinge on food. It is largely a matter of emotional security, of which food is but a part.

The human mother is a splendid mammal—the epitome of her order. Her physiology is more highly developed for suckling behavior—with permanent breasts, for example—than any of her cousins, except domesticated ungulates bred specially for milk-giving. But more than this, she is, like any other mammal, emotionally programmed to be responsive to the growing child. Her whole physiology from the moment she conceives is changed not only to accommodate the sheer business of parturition but also to cope with this physical extension of her body for years after the event. Animal experiments have shown that the softness and texture of the mother—and even her smell—are more important to the child than simply her milk supply, although without the latter, in most "wild" conditions, it would not live. Primate infants deprived of real mothers will adapt best to mechanical substitutes that are alike in *texture* to their real parent, in preference to those that simply provide milk but no warmth.[13]

Whatever the value of the substitute, the young animal, psychically, is permanently damaged by the separation.[14] The male may never learn to relate to females, with the consequence that his sexual identity will be confused.[15] The female will almost certainly fail in her task as a mother by ignoring her own offspring, as she was ignored herself.[16] Anyone who has seen the grief, the listlessness, the obvious and heart-rending despair of infant monkeys deprived, in an experiment, of maternal care, will echo the sentiments of the man who performed the experiment. He declared: "Thank God we only have to do it once to prove the point."[17]

The point is proved time and time again in human society. Brief separations of mother and child are bad enough, but excessive separations are devastating. Nature is ruthless about this. In the case of some animals, if the mother is not able to find the child immediately at birth, respond to its cries, and above all, lick it from head to foot, she will treat it as a stranger and refuse to suckle it when it is later presented to her.[18] Yet in the name of sanitation we risk tampering with this delicate system by taking babies away from their mothers on the maternity wards moments after they are born. Monkey infants that lose their mothers develop all the characteristics of autistic children, even to the endless rocking and crouching—with little chance of becoming fully functioning adults. Our orphanages and nurseries are full of children wholly or partly so deprived who also rock and grieve and make only painfully insecure adjustments to the adult world.

The practice of taking infants from their mothers during the first

five days of life is an example of the acceptance of hygiene and comfort as of greater importance than the possibility of behavioral disruption—if this is even considered. In some of the most sophisticated
and admirable places on earth—the wards of excellent hospitals—
newborn organisms emerge from their mothers' wombs in a demanding
and exciting process to face a suddenly novel environment containing
unmuted sounds, swirls of unfamiliar air, and the impressive movements of hands and bodies. Often the mother of such a confused and
needy creature is drugged and will sleep for many hours after this
first potential social encounter with her child. The neonate itself may
be somewhat under the influence of her drugs and in any event will be
quickly removed in a plastic basket from her presence to a ward of a
dozen or two similar creatures, many crying, all under high light, and
all handled by skilled nurses—part of whose professional skill must be
that denial of the special treatment which seems to mark how women
treat their own children as opposed to the children of others. The
child will be labeled by a card on its container, and some mothers will
confuse their own child with another, and the more naïve among them
will question their competence as mothers: if they cannot even recognize their child, how can they possibly cope with it?

This plight has to be seen in the context of the improved health of
mothers and infants. It is probably true that there are important
advantages to having the mother rest after the single most trying of
all predictable human actions. The question here is about the effects
of systems—which are perhaps useful for mothers and certainly efficient
for hospitals—on the essential bond between mother and infant.
On theoretical and empirical grounds there is a real and disturbing
possibility that—with effects difficult to measure—some human babies
and their mothers encounter in the act of birth a fact of technology
and custom that may make more uncertain the elaboration of a bond
begun *in utero,* a bond severely interrupted at just that point when
presumably some forceful re-creation of the certainty and strength of
uterine environment is most necessary.

The mother-child bond is the basic instruction in the human bonding
program, and the ground rule of the human biogrammar. If this rule is
not learned, the human may not learn to "speak" behaviorally, just as,
if he does not learn the difference between subject and predicate, he
will never be able to handle the verbal grammar. What he "learns,"
essentially, is the ability to make successful bonds in general. Bonds
depend on feelings, and the mother-deprived child is most commonly

described as "affectless"—lacking the motive power to love or care. It is here that the groundwork for "emotional maturity" is laid: that the child will eventually become an adult capable of the full sexual experience and of complete parental behavior. In general, he learns to be confident in his own ability to explore; he develops self-confidence and security. Young monkeys with mothers will move off to enjoy the pleasures of curiosity, whereas maternally deprived monkeys will be afraid to. Successful bonding in later life depends to a great extent on this tendency to explore. This program of security/exploration is so easily interfered with—especially in "advanced" societies—that a large number of people end up by making only partial adjustments in all these areas, to the detriment of their social relationships.[19]

It is just as important to note that the instructions are also quite precise about the termination of the bond—which begins with the gross physiological act of weaning and ends with the transference of emotional ties onto peers and mates.[20] If the mother ignores the instructions to terminate the bond, the results can be just as disastrous as if the child continues to talk baby talk into adulthood: its chances of communicating effectively with other adults are severely curtailed. "Maternal overprotection"—the continuation into adolescence of the relationship appropriate to childhood—extends the mother-child program to a time when the "child-child" and "child–other-adult" programs should be coming into play.

It is not necessary here to pursue the *content* of the mother-child bond, once it has been established as the basic bond. Whatever else a linguistic system does, it has to have some means of sorting out subject from object. Whatever else a social system does, it has to have some means of ensuring the security of the relationship between mother and infant until at least that point when the infant is independently mobile and able to survive with a reasonable chance of reaching adulthood. There are many and various ways of doing this. Within any animal species they tend to be uniform, but across species, as has been seen, they are very diverse. Within the human species, given the biological adaptation of culture, there is also diversity—but within very narrow limits. And the diversity revolves around this basic dyad as a fixed point in a changing social universe. The languages are exotically different, but the basic grammar is always the same.

The mother-child bond offers a model for other bonded relationships in which humans and other social animals engage. The model implies that social responses of a surprisingly complicated kind involve genetic programming. These patterns, far from reflecting simple "instinctive" needs, are directly social; their stimulus, operation, and consummation depend upon the existence of other members of the species and their actions. This is really the heart of the ethological approach; social interactions reveal the evolutionary history and biology of an animal as much as its digestive processes and means of movement do.

In this context we can reexamine some of the more common human relationships. Perhaps this will clarify the limits of variation and the intricacy of the special process of affiliation that marks us as the particular animal we are. So let us turn to some of the other strategic bonds between members of our species, in order to understand better how these "social organs" have worked in our history and how they are expressed today.

The claim that the mother-child bond is the basic one might appear paradoxical, if not repetitious; after all, it is preceded by sexual intercourse—which implies that the mating bond preceded *it*. But the answer to this is that the mating "bond" may or may *not* have preceded it—it does not have to. A simple act of copulation which need last only ninety seconds is all that is necessary to start the mother-child process.

But a mating bond is convenient to ensure food and protection for the mother and child at a later stage. Protection is what the whole business is about. In other species and many human societies, the mating bond as such is not activated to this end. There are many alternatives. Among deer, as we have seen, a group of self-sufficient females provides this envelope of provision and protection.[21] Even when the "harems" form during the rutting season, the stag does not in any sense control the group—he is preoccupied with repeated copulation on the one hand and driving off rival males on the other. The harem generally responds to the leadership of the old female; once his inseminating function is completed, the male leaves for the rest of the year. Sometimes the mother and young can survive without any help at all—as with the hamster. In other cases a troop organization takes over as the envelope or shell, as with elephants or trooping monkeys. Here the whole group is responsible for the mother-child units within it. All the males and mature childless females surround and protect the nursing mothers. Many bonds are activated in this way, but in none of these cases is the mating bond more than a brief episode.

The bond, once activated, can take a number of forms. With some carnivores, such as wolves, pairs form for life, develop "packs" with the offspring, and enter a cycle of family development.[22] Alternatively, as with hamadryas baboons, "harems" (each male may have four or five females) are collected, which last for a lifetime and not just a rutting season.[23] Among the anthropoid apes there is the unique case of the gibbon, which lives in treetops and defends territories. On each territory a mated pair jointly repels intruders and disperses its young as soon as they are mature.[24] In all these primate groups the mother-child unit is a "constant." What varies is the degree of involvement of the mate. In most cases of pair formation the key determinants are ecological—the unit of male-plus-female (or females) and offspring is the optimum unit for survival. Where these ecological conditions do not hold, a species is unlikely to make much of the mating bond.

What is true across the range of mammalian species is true across different populations of the human species. Because of the brilliant biological adaptation of culture, human societies can create different rules. They can adapt various customs to fit different ecological niches, and need not wait for natural selection to program them genetically. They have to observe a number of grammatical ground rules—one of which has already been explored here—but they can use a variety of languages. Each human population protects and provides for its mother-child units; but whether or not the father stays "home" is another and highly variable matter. The strategy of the father staying home has been commonly adopted because human cultures can capitalize on the powerful motivations aroused by courtship, especially during the volatile and intense period of puberty. These motivations can then be changed into powerful bonding patterns associated with parenthood. The combination can produce a relatively lasting set of bonds that make up what we commonly refer to as the "family."

But it is revealing that societies always seem to find it necessary to surround these "natural" bonds with a host of legal provisions and sanctions to make them stick. This is not the case with many consanguine bonds: people do not have to enter into contractual obligations to be made someone's sister, but they do have to have a "contract" to become someone's husband or wife. It is arguable that without all the legal safeguards a much more fluid mating and family system would prevail; indeed, there are many instances where this is so.

This is a central point. Many social scientists want to maintain that the "family" is in some sense a "natural" unit like the "family" of the gibbon and is based on a similar "pairing-for-life" instinct.[25] When people persistently behave differently, they are accused of failing to live up to their natural obligations, and we speak of breakdown, neuroses, the crisis in the family, etc. Our interpretation is exactly the opposite.[26] What the "family" as a unit does is artificially to cement together, with social conventions and legal rules, one subset of the possible sets of bonds that can be used as the envelope for the mother-child unit.[27] In many senses this parental bond is the most fragile, even if the most common, of such arrangements, since it involves bringing together two people not previously related and predicating the success of their relationship on the relatively temporary emotional ties that flood through them and between them in the courtship stage. Most societies that use mated pairs as the basic units do not dare to leave the necessary stability of the family to the vagaries of adolescent emotion. They "arrange" marriages without regard to such emotion, but with the continuity and stability of the unit in mind.

It is nonsense to assume that the only kind of "parental" bond possible in the human species is between sexual partners. Yes, the mother has to be impregnated, but her impregnator need not be the male who provides the provision and protection for her and her young. There is another bond more fundamental in some ways, and just as logical—the bond between brother and sister. This is an asexual bond that grows up over the years and is in some sense ready-made for the task of parental care. It does not involve the setting up of a new and risky contractual relationship, but can draw on already existing trust and deeply developed obligations. In some human societies, the weight of responsibility for a woman and her children rests with her brothers. Her sex life is separate from her parental role. Usually she has a series of lovers more or less attached to her. To call such systems exceptional is to beg the question: they represent a logical and viable alternative that, while relatively rare, works well in certain circumstances. The mating relationship and the security relationship are simply not allowed to coincide.[28]

In other cases the two types of bond—blood ties and mating ties—may both be partly activated. Some aspects of security can be associated with the mating bond, and so shared with the brother-sister tie.[29] The most common arrangement here is for groups of related women to live together and to depend for some things on their brothers and sons, and for other things on their husbands and sons-in-law. Again the brother-sister tie is permanent and continuous (one cannot divorce a brother), while the husband-wife tie is relatively loose. The ecological factors are uppermost here. It is quite possible for the female households to live without reliable and continuous male support. There is no need for the mating bond to be protected by a weight of sanctions, since intermittent male help will suffice. Men therefore tend to float about between households, and while some marriages can be long-lasting, many are short-lived. This is sometimes described as a system with a "high divorce rate," but this description is very ethnocentric. It is more accurate to see it as a high turnover of mates.

A similar solution involves groups of related females as the envelope, but with no real institution of marriage. "Boyfriends," or whatever they may be called, can meander through the system, but the women can get by without them; they exist to satisfy sexual and emotional needs, and not to protect and provide. Sometimes the women are simply self-sufficient, or sometimes, in good primate style, the society at large assumes the role of protector.[30]

Here the chief function of the mating bond is not to ensure the security of the mother-child unit; it is a natural device for bringing together the healthy young males and females on whose sexual enthusiasm rests the survival of the group. The bond is as much the result of maturation and biological "wiring" as puberty is. It is so strong that virtually all communities create rules to control its incidence; rarely is sexual intercourse completely random and unrelated to measures of social inhibition. In fact, a lot of work goes into keeping pairs apart.

In quite dramatic contrast, most societies create elaborate and formidable rules to keep the pairs together, once they have mated. Far from representing the intrinsic normality of the mating bond, these rules suggest how precarious it really is. The great variety and depth of customs surrounding kinship and marriage are not expressions of an innate and ready tendency to form families: *they are devices to protect the mother-child unit from the potential fragility of the mating bond.*

This is diametrically opposed to the agreeable fantasy that families will live happily ever after if only they will love each other more in some fine romantic fashion. The parental bond is not the mating bond; recalling and evoking the mating bond may embellish and stimulate the parental one, but it is still not the same thing. The traditional Indian scheme reverses this procedure. Marriages are arranged by elders to suit the needs and structures of the overall community. It is possible that the couple may not have met before their elaborate wedding commits them to each other for life. But then the assumption is that for perhaps a year they will do very little, and spend a great deal of time learning about each other both socially and sexually. The elaborate manuals of sexual technique—such as the *Kama Sutra*—which surprise many Euro-Americans by their earnestness and invention, are guides in a situation in which the equivalent of courtship happens *after* the equivalent of mating.[31]

In examining the biogram of primate politics we tried to see how far the human primate was governed by, or transgressed, this set of ground rules. We sought to clarify the relationship between breeding systems and political systems. Here we are considering the primate breeding system in its human manifestation, and accordingly we should outline the rules of the primate breeding biogram.

In itself the primate breeding biogram falls within the mammalian parameters already described, sometimes pushing them to extravagant extremes.[32] But however much variety we find in the politico-breeding systems of the higher primates, certain features are outstanding. For one thing, in direct contrast to the ungulates, both sexes associate the whole year round in relatively closed groups. As we have seen in "Political Nature," this was once attributed to year-round sexual activity, which kept the males interested in the females.

But this is too simple. Even in groups that have marked breeding seasons on the ungulate pattern, the association of the sexes is not sporadic but continuous throughout the year. This is all clearly related to the adaptive functions of the group as a defense mechanism in the struggle for survival—particularly against the more dangerous carnivores. Because they lacked, among other things, the ungulate specializations of speed and large numbers, the primates on the plains had to stick together if their little breeding groups were to survive. The protecting and controlling functions of the males, and the constant attention paid them by the females, are what ensure the heterosexual bond among the savanna monkeys rather than year-round sexual delectation.

In all the higher primates the males and females are sexually intrigued by one another only at certain times.[33] When the female is menstruating or pregnant she is not an object of interest. As she approaches ovulation (the midpoint of her menstrual cycle) and recedes from it, she herself initiates sexual activity by soliciting the attention of males through sexual presentation. Despite the sometimes spectacular genital swellings and colorings that attract male attention, it is certain that her ripeness is judged by smell rather than sight.[34]

In the typical baboon group, the dominant male takes over the ovulating female at peak estrus to form with her what primatologists call a "consort" relationship.[35] For a short period—from a few days to a week—he directs all his attention to her and she to him. They groom each other incessantly, and copulate often. Once the honeymoon is over, she is thrown back into the pool of females. Others may have a chance to mount her, subject, of course, to the whims of the alpha male. She, however, grows less and less interested, gradually ceasing to take part. Thus, for a brief while at her peak of sexual receptivity she is the exclusive "property" of one male; but before and after this she becomes the relatively asexual property of the group at large.

There are variations on this pattern. Baboons in the dry desert, faced with different survival problems, have to be relatively puritanical in their sexual lives.[36] However, chimpanzees in their forest paradise can afford greater sexual freedom. The desert baboons have as the subunit of their large herds the individual "harem." Here each successful male has several females that he has "kidnapped" as infants, then mothered and nurtured, and so "bonded" to himself by a fairly elaborate process. Even so, he has to keep them near him and faithful by administering neck bites when they stray adulterously toward the eager young males on the periphery; and so they soon learn the close limits of their sexual options. It is the female who inevitably gets punished in primate society for her failure to attend exclusively to the sexual needs of her consort. The marauding male is ignored by the irate cuckold. But even the arrogant dominant male will allow an "apprentice" younger male to join the group and eventually succeed him as harem leader. This scheme makes the otherwise brief "consort" relationship into a year-round structure by this spectacular method of attaching females to a particular male or males. It is into these units that herds split up in the dry season. Ecologically this is the most efficient organization for such a harsh and demanding environment. Out of the basic primate biogram emerges thus a "polygamous" unit by means of a particular version of the bonding process. The difference between the two systems, however, is one of emphasis. In some sense, even among the savanna baboons, the females continue all year to "belong" to the alpha male of the group. Since he has ultimate control over their sexual activity, he can allow himself the luxury of tolerating other males around in a way that his desert cousins cannot. The hamadryas baboon in the Ethiopian desert, for example, will tolerate only his apprentice near his females, while his chacma cousin on the plains will tolerate a larger number of subdominant males. The basic program is put to different uses in the two cases, but in both it remains true that the male is only sexually interested, and the female only sexually receptive, at certain points of the cycle.

Defensive measures and ecological pressures are not so prominent among the forest chimpanzee.[37] Once a female goes into heat, the whole band of males will pursue her and copulate with her in turn. The order of copulation may be determined by dominance, but everyone participates. The chimpanzee, we have to conclude, is incurably promiscuous. But here again sexual interest depends on the cycle of the female; it is she who initiates the activity. This is one end of the primate scale of sexual behavior; the consortship of the savanna baboons is yet a stage further toward some kind of assignment of mates; the harems of the desert baboons are the extreme of this process, in which a new bonding mechanism—kidnap-adoption—is utilized to make the consort relationship virtually permanent.

The gibbon must be mentioned here. He alone forms nuclear families, and so is dear to the hearts of those who want to derive Euro-American mating customs from a primate source. But the gibbon never came down from the treetops to which he fatally overadapted with his fantastic brachiation abilities. He is a rather large animal, and in order to survive in his treetop habitat, he had to adopt territorialism; students of gibbon behavior have calculated that a gibbon territory will support only a pair of adults and their young. Thus, the only system open to him is that of pair formation. Once they are mobile, the offspring are ejected from the territory, like young birds from the nest. After this they fend for themselves. There is nothing here to suggest a forerunner of a human situation, as the gibbon is much more like some birds or some of the prosimians than like his ape and monkey cousins who took to the ground.[38]

In all these cases the constant again is the mother-child unit, and all the variable systems are just strategies to protect it. In all of them the female has a cycle of hormonally controlled receptivity that governs male sexual interest in her. In varying degrees, females are attached to males for longer periods, according to the specializations of the species. The intensity of this attachment has to do with the degree of tolerance a male will show toward other males in his personal space. When females are in heat, they will present promiscuously, and the male therefore has to establish his exclusive right to copulate with them. So, along with the female cycle, there are two other factors:

male rights to copulate, which depend on dominance, and the establishment of male rights to exclusive attention for varying periods. But in all cases there remains constant a degree of protection for the results of the copulation: there is always an envelope for the mother-child unit. The primate system differs from the ungulate system in its year-round association of males and females: the protection of the mother-child units is a full-time function of primate males.

There is an important contrast here with pair formation among the carnivores. A number of investigators have stressed the fact that the human primate became carnivorous and his social organization should therefore be compared with that of the pack of hunting carnivores.[39] But what became omnivorous (not carnivorous) was a previously largely vegetarian primate. This was undoubtedly a major shift and did not have a background of millions of years of carnivorous experience built into it. The great cats and the hunting dogs fixed on their specializations earlier and built them into their genes. One of their strategies was classical "pair formation," in which animals at puberty mate for life, sometimes eventually forming packs with their offspring, or sometimes, like the gibbon, sending out their young to fend for themselves. Whatever the ground-dwelling primates did in their transition to hunting and regular meat-eating had to be manufactured out of the primate biogram.

To see what they did in fact do, we have to look at the end result—ourselves. To what extent have we, in the course of our particular evolution as a species, made radical changes in the biogram, and to what extent, in preserving it, have we molded it to suit our particular needs? At least one change has been offered as being fairly spectacular: the estrous cycle of sexual activity has been "lost," and with it the essential dominance of hormonal control over female sexual behavior.[40]

But this can be examined more closely. We are led to believe that the structuring of human sexual behavior is predominantly sociocultural; the fact that sexual activity results in the biological fact of procreation is somehow abstracted from what is an otherwise non-biological business. And also that females are not governed or even indirectly influenced by the estrous cycle, because they do not exhibit the extravagant coloration of the other primates' estrous displays, and because there are no evident human equivalents of the heady quest for intercourse that marks the rhythm of the primate sisterhood. The upshot of this is that the menstrual cycle is purely physiological in effect and utterly nonsocial in implication. This may be so, but if it is, it is curious, since a sensible biological rule is that breeding—which is never left to chance—is always mediated and stimulated by a set of signals and states of readiness that are not left to chance, either.

However, there is suggestive evidence that the menstrual cycle of the human female serves at least some of the functions of the general primate cycle, through the variation and subtlety in the expression of these functions are of a quite different order. (Assuming, that is, that primatologists who study the sexual behavior of their subjects perceive all the features of mating encounters. Of this we cannot be confident— for example, the crucial role of smell in primate sexual attraction has only recently been appreciated for the central mechanism it is.[41] There may be others; the fact that we cannot easily imagine what they could be is neither here nor there, and is chiefly another restatement of the reality that one of the useful things scientists do is find things they did not expect to find, or even look for.) This estimate of the possible importance of the menstrual cycle for the human female de- rives from the general idea that any important bond in the animal world is served by some mechanism that ensures its occurrence and abets its success. But if the courtship or mating pattern is such an important one—and our stubborn breeding proclivities even in an era when children are not an economic asset seem to support this view—there are probably some features of the bond that are like the other primates'.

Undoubtedly, cortical additions and modifications are important and consequential. It is true that human females are permanently able to engage in sexual relations and always susceptible to particular blandishments of circumstance and person. This is how they are able to behave, but it is not clear that this describes how they do behave.

One is tantalized by evidence like the following: if we do not inquire about subjective feelings and urges, but simply count objectively what primatologists refer to with characteristic indelicacy as "copulatory success," we find that human females are more likely to copulate more often at the midpoint of their cycles, when they are ovulating, than at either end of the cycles. There is a slight rise in the frequency of copulation just before the onset of menstruation, and there is a clear peak in mid-cycle. The curious thing is that the curve of human female copulatory success and that of the macaque monkey (for which the most data are available) are identical—a rise toward midpoint, a fall-off, and then a slight rise before the menstrual period begins.

The clustering of copulatory acts at the midpoint of the cycle is equally true, though less well documented, for all other primates.[42] Just as for the other primates, the physical cycle of the human female is accompanied by a behavioral cycle. This cycling is not as obvious in the case of humans—even to the individual women who routinely fail to anticipate cyclical changes in their moods and predispositions. But our prediction is that if we managed to get fair reports of both sexual activity and sexual feelings, we would find that, despite variations in class, culture, climate, and protocol of sexual relationship, there was a central tendency for women to want, and to have, sexual intercourse far more when they are likely to conceive than when they are not. That this might surprise some people is itself surprising. The menstrual cycle is related in part to hormone levels, which we know influence behavior in general and sexual behavior in particular. In normal conditions the production of hormones in the female system is tied to the reproductive cycle. Why, after all, should the existence of sexual hormones be unrelated to the sexual process? What we see in this cyclical business is yet another feature of the general phenomenon that physical processes are related to social ones, and that this is especially so where the sexual interaction is concerned.[43]

A particularly dramatic piece of evidence for this involves that sense of smell so important in the sexual signaling system of primates. Women, it seems, increase by fantastic proportions their ability to detect the odor of musk (and strong odors generally) during ovulation.[44] At this behaviorally intense moment in their cycle, they need, in order to detect its presence, only a small fraction of the amount of musk scent needed at either end of their cycle. That increased sensitivity to odor should correlate with increased sexual excitement makes excellent primatological sense. Not only is the sense of smell affected, but so is clarity of perception. In the three days immediately preceding and following menstrual bleeding, human females display an array of behavioral disturbances.[45] Menstruation is signally influential. No woman needs to be told this, and most men have felt its impact. When her sexual excitability runs down and her body readjusts to prepare for the ejection of the unfertilized eggs, she suffers from considerable perceptual confusion, and fails in tests where she has to discriminate the relevant from the irrelevant.[46] (These tests have been conducted largely by men, who have not so far tried to find out if women are better at discrimination performances when they are ovulating. They should be, in the same way that they are better at detecting certain odors. For at this point they are keyed up to perform one of their essential mammalian female tasks to the best of their ability—getting themselves impregnated, and presumably by males they prefer over others.)

The female's perceptual confusion as she moves toward the turbulent monthly episode is accompanied by a rise in her propensity to accidents,[47] nervous disorder and mental breakdown, criminality,[48] inability to work and concentrate, poor performance in examinations,[49] and a general if relative dislocation of normal routines. It appears that the more sensitive researchers become to these special factors, the more related they turn out to be to more behaviors in general.

Throughout this whole debate on what humans are really like in their sexual bonding behavior and what implications this behavior has for "families," there is a vital non sequitur, a constant tendency to leap from animal *behavior* to human *institutions*. Thus an observer of human behavior can argue that although many marriages, in America for example, fail, most married couples stay together, and that this illustrates the "strength of the pair bond."[50] But it does not necessarily illustrate anything of the kind. In societies without divorce laws, where separation is wholly at the discretion of the individuals involved, separation is much more common than permanence. What the figures for the United States show is that the institution of marriage—a contractual legal institution that binds couples together and allows them to separate only at considerable cost and with considerable trouble and sometimes penalty—can be made to look successful in the purely statistical sense. On the other hand, when we look at what human creatures *do* about their sexual and mating behavior, we may again find that the difference between them and their primate relatives is of degree only.

This is not to underestimate the importance of the male-female bond, ephemeral, buttressed by legal conventions and customs, and secondary to the demands of the mother-infant bond as it is. There is one sense in which it is crushingly important to individuals and central to the mating arrangement of communities. Two individuals formerly capable of sustaining a round of activities and of living in their own skulls and in terms of the needs which they can fulfill for themselves become inordinately and troublingly attached to each other. The ardor of this need is most easily observed in adolescents—but adolescents are not the only ones who bond fully and single-mindedly. At some time or other something happens to nearly everyone so that he focuses all his attention on another person, from whom he in turn demands attention of the same dire and exhausting kind. Every act, every word, every touch, is a marker for the lover's insistence that this encounter is particularly blessed. Shaw once said that "Love consists in overestimating the difference between one woman and another." But perhaps when one makes the personally revolutionary move of becoming attached to another person, one must be convinced that the object of this disruptive act is not only desirable but unique as well.

This is very dramatic, but the encounter itself is dramatic. It has to be. The bond that unites people to breed is altered by the very circumstances and effect of its success—that persons marry and bear young. But the way of uniting them in the first place is so strong and demanding that people want to re-create it. Thus, many try to have a second honeymoon, to relive the "first date" or the first love, or somehow to recapture that mixture of innocence and imperious demand that is agonizing at the time but nonetheless thrilling in anticipation or in memory.

The dilemma is clear enough, especially for adolescents, who have spent extremely important years with their mother and other kin and have estimated their movements in terms of these familiar realities. But now they are sexually mature: there are hormonal storms and physical eruptions, changes in cosmetic and hair pattern; legs suddenly grow too fast and control too slowly. Reputation among peers and little tides of childish fashion were important to them. But they grow out of the home base, out of whatever family structure there was. Now, with considerable speed, boys and girls become males and females; the sexes divide in corners at parties or gatherings, only to engage in the central arena, where the dancing is, in an increasingly fierce and troubling way. It is suddenly very hard to ask parental advice; rumors about the appropriate conduct of sexual-social relationships circulate freely. Young girls become worrisome to their parents. Young males become objectionable to the dominant males, who cannot countenance their emotional storms, their increasingly embarrassing demands for opportunities for drama, heroism, and participation in sexual action. Among baboons at this point the emerging males are as far from the center of the group as they are ever likely to be. They form little groups of two or three, and are bitten by the dominant males as they steal around the females.

This "peripheralization"—this being pushed out to the fringes—is equaled by the new, urgent desire to get to the center, both to be among the dominant males and to have access to the females. Among humans, there is this same interest in the females, the same wariness as in baboons. The human male and female have complex social cues to take, elaborate ritual paraphernalia and notions to carry with them in this little odyssey from one defined system of bonds given by their progenitors to another, which they will have somehow to create for themselves.

Adolescent males suffer confused instructions from the old program: become mature; remain dependent; show affection to girls and hardness to boys; accuse the dominants of being too powerful, yet admire their power; and perhaps begin dimly to shape out some way of reproducing. The job of reproducing is easy and fast and also immensely pleasurable. But reproduction, like justice, must not only be done, it must be seen to be done. Some social analogue of the actual or potential copulation must be established—the fraternity pin, the hibiscus behind the ear, the exchange of love fetishes or food. It is hard to become a sexual adult rather than a nonsexual needy child; the strength of the emotional interactions involved reveals both the intrinsic difficulty of reproductive bonding and its central importance to the persistence of the group and the actual life cycles of its members.

The various "instructions" the pubertal organism receives at this point are among the most complex it will receive in its whole life cycle. The adolescent is being told to go through the painful business of terminating the mother-child bond, and the only slightly less painful process of establishing heterosexual and unisexual bonds outside the immediate circle of kin. The young male is also being instructed to make forays into the male competitive arena, with the double outcome of establishing himself as a potentially successful breeder and a likely candidate for a position in the male hierarchy—two positions that have always been closely related in evolutionary history.

The establishment of the mating bond can be seen as a direct successor to the consort behavior described for the primates. It is clearly unlike the territorial pair-bonding of the gibbon, or the "parent-surrogate" bonding of the hamadryas baboon, although parent-child elements do enter into it in part. In its structure it is much more like the relatively exclusive and very intense consort pairing that characterizes those savanna-dwelling primates, who are perhaps the best evidence so far mustered for the proto-stages of our own sexual evolution, and whose female sexual cycle resembles that of human females.

The heterosexual bond in our prototype primate has two phases. There is the constant year-round association of the males generally with the females generally, and all the noncopulatory elements of protection, control, cooperative care of the young, and grooming that go with it. This is punctuated by periods when females are sexually receptive and the object of competition among the males, with the dominant animal or animals taking priority. While the consort period lasts, the relationship between the animals is relatively exclusive, and their attention is directed almost exclusively to each other. Indeed, this emphasis on selective attention is the most obvious of the consort relationship.

The normal progress of this bonding episode is well established. The female first obtains the attention of the male by *visual* means—the coloring of the genital area. The male follows and inspects, chiefly with his nose. From this develops a *tactile* encounter involving grooming and mounting. Finally, if all these stages go well, there is the consummatory act of copulation. In between copulations there is a great deal of repetition of these stages, particularly grooming. Again the animals pay exclusive attention to each other, the male pausing only to drive off rivals. The period of sexual intensity wanes along with the interest of the male. Finally the female returns to the other females, and the male goes about his normal business, which is largely conducted in terms of his fellow males.

But his relationship with the female does *not* cease with the diminution of his intense sexual interest in her. She is still a female of his breeding group, and still under his control, care, and protection. She is like the wife of a polygamous sultan who, whether she is in favor with her master or an outcast among the eunuchs (males made physiologically peripheral), remains his property. But no primate male ever *provides* for his partners. The element of the parental or protective relationship in the male's bond with the mother-child units should not be overlooked.

In human courtship—the method by which the mating bond is established—much the same features and sequences occur, although they last, in some cases but not always, for a longer period than the maximum time of sexual receptivity.[51] Courtships can be brief and explosive or long and subdued, but they go though a well-established sequence. First the boy sees and is attracted to the girl; he then follows and approaches, and since he is human, uses speech. Tactile communication of a preliminary sort should come next, then copulation itself. In the intervals between copulations there will be repetitions of parts of this sequence, with a good deal of emphasis on tactile and verbal communication.

The bonding period will be characterized by the same qualities of intensive and exclusive attention between the partners that are found in the primates; this is a constant source of amazement and delight to the partners, and of sentimental pleasure or cynical amusement to the onlookers. During this period the male is extremely possessive of the female. He displays her and himself to other males, whose challenges he is ever ready to fight off. This is the "normal" procedure.

It is interesting that all the sexual behavior described as "pathological" involves fixation at one point of this sequence or the omission of various stages.[52] Thus the voyeur is stuck at the visual stage and the frissoneur at the tactile stage; and the rapist leaps literally from the sight to the act without going through the rest of the sequence. It is no surprise that failure to follow the correct program is related to the initial failure of the mother-child bond. Thus the success of the mating bond is in itself dependent on the success of the initial bond and does not automatically emerge as a "pair bond" on the carnivore or bird pattern at puberty. Only the message to try to form such a bond in the appropriate sequence is transmitted at this confusing and exciting time.

Like its primate counterpart, this bond is not necessarily either long-lasting or exclusive. Both longevity and exclusivity are contingent factors. It is true that the bond is usually exclusive for a time, but, as it is highly dependent on novelty for its effectiveness, it can and does very often wane rapidly when the partners seek fresh adventures. Its exclusivity, too, is a problem. Humans find it well within their capacity to bond successfully with more than one partner. This is not promiscuity—although humans can be as promiscuous as chimpanzees if they wish and have the opportunity. It is simply a question of having more than one partner with whom the courtship sequence has been successfully accomplished. Very often it is not only social sanctions, but time, energy, and resources as well that limit the possibilities of multiple bonding, which, however, can and does occur. Thus a male may take on the responsibility for protecting and providing for one mate, or as in polygynous societies, more than one, and these potentially parental duties may keep him around—especially if he is susceptible to legal sanctions. But his interest in novelty is not necessarily any more extinguished than it is in his savanna-monkey counterpart. Nor is his need to express dominance through display of subservient females—a need he will satisfy in fantasy, even if he does not in fact, through fear, devotion, or simple confusion about what he is supposed to be doing.

He will not only express dominance in fantasy but in fact, even if the factual situation excludes the element of sexual intercourse itself. For polygamy has to do with power rather than with sex. An alpha male *controls* his females and thus demonstrates his dominance; his erotic acts are less significant than his political ones. Even our latter-day bureaucratic polygamists can do this by the (theoretically) asexual method of controlling bevies of typists, research assistants, secretaries, nurses, receptionists, and other more or less skilled females. Perhaps the dominant male may hint that his bureaucratic control is also sexual and that the formal relationships which indicate his power as an official are matched by his intimate relations which suggest his power as a male. But this is relatively unimportant. What matters is that dominance is marked by increasingly exclusive control over female services.

Of course, as with all hierarchical relations, there is a symbolic as well as real aspect of the services provided the dominant males. In this context, sexual-political relationships are forms of the more general hierarchical principle—dominant men also have men who work for them, and occasionally dominant females have men working for them. It is enough now to suggest that altering the patterns of sexual dominance may have strange effects on the signaling system so deeply embedded in the wiring of the male-female interactions. It has been found consistently that female workers are more likely to be happy with male than with female bosses. No doubt in good measure they have been explicitly taught to respond in this way, as men have. Nonetheless, the ubiquity of the pattern suggests that the instruction is given to willing learners. That the problem is symbolized in the cliché figure of the "office wife" may belie the closeness of the association between the theoretical impersonality of industry and officialdom and the real intensity of the valences between their male and female workers.[53]

Let us summarize the main issues in our discussion of the male-female bond. There are continuities between the human and primate biograms at several points. Sexual behavior cycles with the female cycle, although less spectacularly; the mating sequence—"consort behavior" is very similar, with intense selective attention as the main feature; there is year-round association of males and females, largely having to do with protection of the young.

Human male-female bonding can capitalize on these features in several ways. It can combine the motivations of consort behavior with those of care and protection, to form a "parental bond," and hence a "family." But because of the potential volatility of the consort relationship, it needs to augment the bond with sanctions; it can separate these functions and allow care and protection to fall, for example, to the consanguine bond, while consort behavior remains purely sexual and companionable and never becomes "parental."

Much of the richness and variety of human kinship, marriage, and family systems depends on the possibilities inherent in this separation of "protective" and sexual functions, which we inherit.

This separation and its consequences are possible precisely because human sexual bonding is *not* like animal pair bonding, but essentially a compound of primate materials adapted to human ends.

Sex and dominance, reproduction and power, are so intimately linked that it is hard to disentangle the one from the other when considering sex in its social as opposed to its purely individual and personal setting.

In this chapter the concern has been more with the mechanisms of the bonds—mother-child and male-female—than with the selection pressures that produced them. The focus is the same for human societies as for primate societies—the male control of females for sex and dominance, and the female use of the males for impregnation and protection. But the purposes of this behavior, and hence its direction and content, become radically changed during the transition to humanity that hunting provoked. It is to this that we must now turn.

4.

BOND ISSUE TWO:
MAN TO MAN

So FAR THESE primatelike patterns have been seen mostly in terms of their importance for individuals. We must now consider the importance of the bonds for the establishment of community, and focus on the all-important breakthrough from breeding systems to kinship systems.[1] The latter utilize our bonding potential to form unique breeding patterns that build on, but depart from, the basic rules of the primate biogrammar. In this context, male-female and mother-child bonds are not the only ones to be considered. There is the crucial set of male-male bonds that underlie politics, defense, the conduct of war, and a host of other activities vital to the broad self-interest of the community; and the set of female-female bonds important in maintaining social coherence.[2] We hope to show how mother-child and male-female bonds relate to male and female bonds. Humans pay great attention to rules of marriage and authority over children—and this can be seen to tie in with the political interactions of males and the notions of propriety and necessity that males contrive. To put it another way, humans retain many of the basic primate breeding and political patterns, but through kinship they incorporate females directly into the central processes of social life very differently from the way primate females are brought in.

That this happens through the exchange of females from one political group to another, in terms of some agreed scheme of reciprocity and commitment, is the very essence of this human innovation.

Among the terrestrial primates a division of labor among adult males, females, and young males already exists. Mature males control and defend the group; the females take care of the next generation; and the young males at the periphery act as guards and watchdogs. Certain key preoccupations provoke interaction between these "blocks" of the social system. The males are interested in the females for sexual purposes; the females look to the males for sexual encounter and for protection; the young males are attracted both to the females and to the advantages that positions in the central hierarchy can bring. The aim of the primate male is to get to the top of the male hierarchy and so control the females for purposes of sexual satisfaction. This applies to the primate male's *own* females—the females of his own group, who may well be his genetic sisters and daughters (though not usually his mother, for reasons that will be explored later). The philosophy of the human primate male, which seems to be slightly, but is in essence profoundly, different, is to get to the top of the male hierarchy and so control the females of his own group in *order to exchange them for females of another group*—thus achieving sexual satisfaction and political advantage. The evolutionary history of this extraordinary sexual revolution can be usefully reconstructed.

The prehuman division of labor was strongly affected by the radical transition to hunting. (Some primates hunt sporadically and in a rudimentary fashion, but hunting is nowhere a systematic way of life.[3]) The real shift that came with hunting, with its injection of animal protein into the primate diet, was the sharing of food. Primates do not share food. Each animal fends for itself. So of the two essential needs of the mother-child group, protection and provision, only protection is provided by the males. Males and females in the primate group even actively compete for food; and when the males do on the odd occasion indulge themselves in the luxury of the flesh of a newborn gazelle, for example, the alpha male either keeps it for himself or at best allows his nearest male bondmates to take a little. But the females are given nothing.

All this changed when the species changed to a semicarnivorous diet. Biologically, it was simply not possible to have the males taking all the animal protein while the females lived on gathered vegetable matter.

The division of labor was thus extended to the securing of food. Males ventured off into the new and exciting sphere of pursuit and killing of game, while females continued gathering in the ancient tradition of their primate forebears. This, if anything, intensified the differences in function between the two sexes, since very different selection pressures were now being brought to bear on them. But it also required that a new kind of relationship be set up, not only between men and women but also between men and men, older men and younger men, old ladies and young wives, and even between mothers and their children. In short, the whole scheme of social relationships had to be revamped—but only on the basis of what was given in the biogrammar. (It must be remembered that this was *not* a carnivore's biogrammar, which makes comparisons with carnivores interesting but dangerous if taken too literally.)

To put it simply, certain aspects of cooperation in the primate biogram could be capitalized on, while certain aspects of competition had to be rechanneled.[4] These were not bred out or in any way eliminated; they were mitigated or turned to advantage. One result was the women continued to cooperate in many established ways. Another was that the close interest in the young of new mothers that draws primate females together could be worked into the basis for cooperative gathering and food preparation. Also, the bonding of males for competition in the hierarchy and protection against predators could be used as the basis for cooperation, collective hunting, and defense. The hierarchy itself could operate as a selective device in producing good hunters and in the training of the young, as well as establishing candidates for leadership.

But it was absolutely necessary to mitigate the extreme competition in the search for food, where each primate foraged for himself at the possible expense of the others. It is often argued that sexual competition had to be eliminated, too. But sexual competition has never been eliminated—only reworked, and reworked to meet the new needs we have been describing. It was food that mattered, not sex.[5]

Under the new circumstances, each "block" of the social system had to develop strategies to get what it wanted out of the other blocks. The women needed sex, protection, and animal protein from the men; the men likewise needed sex, and the gathering and preparation of vegetable foods from the women. They also wanted two of the other products of female labor—daughters to exchange and sons to incorporate eventually into the male group. And so the adolescent boys were caught in the middle.

In theory, there was no obvious reason why these arrangements should not be made on a group basis, with the men as a whole taking from the women, and vice versa. However, this is neither the primate way, nor was it the best strategy for our emerging humans. As far as female needs are concerned, female primates do show preferences in mating, and the dominant males are more attractive to them as year-round objects of attention than their subordinates are. Besides, this would become doubly true when dominant males were likely to be the best hunters and therefore the best source of animal protein needed by them and their growing offspring. A female, or more likely several, would tend to fasten onto a male who was an excellent and guaranteed source of meat—who literally brought home the bacon. The male who could command the services of these females would in turn have an assured supply of vegetable food for himself and his companions in the hunt; he was also, of course, interested in her as a supplier of males for recruitment to his group, and of females for purposes of exchange.

This is a startling development. It has to do with changed conditions of male bonding. The complexities of human social life in the hunting phase required bonded male groups that were much more complex than those found in the vegetarian primates. For a start, a new phenomenon of *cooperation between groups* came into play for the exploitation of larger hunting territories, or at its most negative, for the establishment of "hands-off" treaties between groups on adjacent hunting grounds. Also, cooperation had to be set up between men previously unrelated—in much the same way as the mating bond set up relationships between men and women previously not bonded. *Allies* became necessary in a way that had not existed before. They were partly an insurance against help in times of difficulty, or again, at the negative end of the scale, partners in an agreement to suspend hostilities. The prototypes of the radically new bonds set up in response to these exigencies are the father-in-law–son-in-law bond and the bond between brothers-in-law. It might even be said that the bond between brothers-in-law is to males what the bond between husband and wife is to males and females. It is a contractual bond formed late in life by two previously unbonded individuals. Man and wife exchange services; brothers-in-law exchange women. That men exchange sisters (or daughters—it amounts to the same thing) is a custom enshrined in many human kinship systems. The brothers-in-law are then bound together by certain obligations, which vary from locale to locale but have the same general aim and object already discussed.

Once this principle is extended across groups, a new basis of integrating larger hunting units is formed. This can be stated as a principle: the men of a group will always take their women from one or more other groups, and yield all their own women in return. This makes the various groups *dependent* on each other for women and hence for offspring, and so binds them into a relationship, even if they are hostile. No one can afford to wipe out the people who supply them with wives. This principle of "out marriage" is technically called "exogamy," and is the basis of all human kinship systems. There are various versions of this basic principle, but it is enough to recognize that a new game is being played: "We will give our women to you if you give yours to us." Successful groups could extend alliances and join in a network of dominance relations between groups. Human kinship systems concern the patterns of relationships between individuals and groups brought about by the exchange of women.[6]

This is not a wild reconstruction of our past, but a description of what humans do all the time. Even in Euro-American society the minimal exogamic prohibition is observed: men do not marry their own mothers, sisters, or daughters. They "unload" them onto the marriage market and take other people's sisters and daughters—and less often mothers—in exchange. This exchange is not "direct," as it is in many other societies. But that is simply one way of playing the game. Too, in our society daughters are not usually the bases for alliances—but parents are often very choosy anyway about whom their children marry; it is not long since marriages were arranged with pecuniary, political, and other interests of the families chiefly in mind, and racial and religious interests are still influential.

Our humanized male primate does not stop competing sexually with other males. Nor does he cease to control and dominate females for purposes of dominance display. But given his changed conditions, he changes the nature of the women with whom these games are played: they are no longer his *own* women, but someone else's. What is more, the competitor is a possible ally. The primate male is playing the eternal game of genetic politics when he consorts with, dominates, and inpregnates his sister. The human male plays this basic game, but with a twist—he dominates, controls, and copulates with someone else's sister. But even copulation is not really the issue—it is control. Marriage is one human institution allocating this control over women and offspring, and making it effective. Copulation can go on inside and outside marriage, and does all the time. In man copulatory and political success are usually coincident, but logically separate. Sultans have been known to have hundreds of wives and never to have copulated with any of them; Shaka Zulu had one hundred wives but only one son,[7] while many men have had great and widespread copulatory success without either becoming demagogues or even marrying.

The "blocks" of the social system involve particular categories of members, with fairly predictable relationships between them. Links between the blocks can be drawn, and arrows seen moving back and forth between adult males and females, between females and young, between adolescent males and adult males, and so on. Social traffic can be plotted between the elements in the overall plan. Now let us imagine that we have diagrammed this on a rubber sheet. If we pull the sheet one way, we lengthen the distance between males and females and bring adolescent and adult males very close. Or we can stretch it another way and create a formidable hiatus between the females and males and bring the adolescent males very close to their mothers, sisters, and aunts. There are many possibilities.

But the different blocks always remain in relationship with one another, and each set of links remains essential to the overall picture. Though this is of course crudely oversimplified, it serves to show that we are dealing with a gestalt, a configuration, which may change its shape and dimensions but not its components and their interrelations. In essence this is an analogy from the branch of mathematics, topology, that concerns itself with this very problem and deals in detail with the regularities in the relationships that continue to exist despite the shape of the figure. The rubber sheet can be twisted, tied in knots, stretched over a steel drum, but the diagram remains the same because the points retain their relationship as long as the diagram remains intact. What human cultures do—to extend this analogy a precarious moment more—is stretch, twist, blow up like a balloon, press together, and influence the distances between the points. Yet the points remain and form the constituents of all cultures.[8]

It is still important to recall that these blocks and their relationships have been selected for, which has consequences for how individuals relate to one another—what they want from one another, what they can give to one another, what they can do together, and what they think of themselves in the presence of others. The women will relate to other women differently from the way men relate to other men. What men as individuals want from women will be very different in emphasis from what women as individuals want from men. Since we are concerned here with social structures rather than with personalities, we will concentrate on the consequences for societies of these outcomes of evolution, rather than on their troubling but often strangely satisfying manifestations in individual lives.

Each individual by definition acts idiosyncratically. But at the same time he is acting in some deep sense as a representative of his age and sex group, just as the speaker of a particular language may never say quite the same things in quite the same way as another speaker, but nevertheless represents that language in speaking it. His speech, however idiosyncratic in style, tone, and delivery, is a valid sample of the language at large and can be used as a basis for analyzing its grammar. So every man, when courting a woman for example, is acting out the evolutionary history of his sex: he is not simply one man approaching one woman, but Man approaching Woman. What he wants from her as an individual is in a broad sense what men have become programmed to want from women in general, and vice versa.

There is not necessarily any symmetry in this system of needs. A good deal of what men want from women has to do directly with what men want from one another and therefore with the processes going on in the male "block" of the system. The collection or conquest of women for dominance display again (even if they are only secretaries, typists, or research assistants), is a comment on relationships between men in their hierarchy. It may well serve a woman's purpose to be so used, insofar as she gets the protection and protein she needs for herself and her offspring. But it is not the congruence of common wants between a woman and her mate that produces their relationship. That women want different things from men than men want from women, or that each wants the same thing but for different purposes, must be related to the topology of the total system. To build a system of marriage, for example, on the assumption that male and female wants are totally coincident and basically the same may be charming, but it is very impractical.[9]

This sounds rather glum, at least; and at the most it can suggest that the relationships between people are crassly exploitative and unthinkingly selfish. However, the point here is just the contrary—that when individuals act in terms of the "interests" we have outlined, they are certainly not just being selfish and manipulative. They are, rather, reflecting their own reality as animals and are members of a larger system adapted to the successful survival of the whole group. Some people speak crudely, some eloquently. Some are careful about the effect of their words, others insult people without care. The same is true about individual behavior in the context of the "blocks" we have described. Some men are bold and frank about their exploitation of women, and some women lack any modesty about their success in depriving males of time, funds, energy, protein, or anything else. One measure of the humanity of a particular society is how well it induces people to be aware of these possibilities, and to be careful and even kind in dealing with other people. In extreme cases, the law will be invoked to remind husbands of alimony and wives of the hazards of adultery. Once upon a time, even breach of promise could be a business of the courts. Though civility comes hard, all communities go through some effort to stimulate its existence.

Against the background of this argument, it is logical that optimists will see these relationships as proof of man's potential for good, and pessimists as vindication of the poverty of their hope for man. The logic is really biological, neither good nor bad in itself. In a jet age, it might be "better" if we had wings, or at least some helicopterish knack of getting to airports. But we do not. In an age of nuclear families, it would be better if there was exact identity between male and female needs and expectations, and those of offspring. But there is not. This is neither proof of human degradation nor denial of human possibility, but a serious feature of the moral realities with which all groups must deal, and in terms of which most individual lives are led.

At the beginning of "Bond Issue One" we caught a brief glimpse of Crow Indian warriors ceremoniously affirming their bonds on the night before a raid. Although this ceremony was obviously intended to promote the solidarity of the group, it recognized the element of sexual competition between the men. It simply eliminated this aspect of male-male behavior in the face of the greater danger to follow, and in face of the even greater competition between the men, not as sexual beings, but as warriors. When the raid is over and, it is hoped, successful, the Crow will return to their camp to celebrate. Then the tally will be taken of enemy slain, horses and weapons captured, number of coups counted, and many other subtleties of status which will result in a rearrangement of the hierarchy, of promotions and demotions in the complex ranking system by which the men relate to one another.

The need of the men to cooperate in order to compete, and to exclude women from the bonding complex, which this involves, is projected spectacularly in another Crow ceremony—the annual wife abductions. The Crow had two major warrior "clubs" or "brigades," the Lump- woods and the Foxes. Each year during a set week the men of these clubs were allowed to abduct the wives of men of the opposite group. The rules were simple: a man could go to the tepee of a member of the other group and take that man's wife (or one of his wives if he was a polygamist) only if the wife had been a former lover. The husband was not allowed to make any move to interfere, and the ab- ductor had to be honest. Crow individuals were not indifferent to this event or unmoved by it. Men and their wives were often very devoted to each other; a man's pride could be deeply offended by an abduc- tion, and a woman's otherwise happy marriage ruined. Men tried some- times to hide their wives—or the wives themselves would go off into the hills. But the abductors were expected to be ruthless. Once the wives had been taken, the warriors, dressed in their finery, would parade around the camp singing and boasting, with the women on the backs of their horses. After this event the first war party of the year would take place, because, as the Crow said, the abductions made the men feel very brave and ready to fight.[10]

This, to us, outrageous ceremony, like its more restrained counter- part in the calling out of mistresses' names, illustrates dramatically a very general point: that when men are called upon to act together in an all-male activity, particularly a dangerous one, they may reaffirm their solidarity partly by degrading the male-female bond at the ex- pense of the male-male bond. Faced with extreme danger, they go to extreme lengths. In a less violent and disturbing way they do it all the time. What they are saying is that, in some circumstances, no woman is as important to any man as men are to one another.

Informal friendship may reflect this same thing as well as traditional wars. In North America a bride-to-be is customarily given a party called a "shower" by her female friends and relatives, in which she is presented with gifts that will help her furnish her home and conduct her domestic ceremonies. Towels, fish forks, sheets, glasses, or money represent her female associates' commitment to the mating bond and in turn enmesh her in a web of female-centered obligations that she will perform in her turn, and that will be renewed when the birth of her child stimulates gifts of the new set of properties babies require and mothers perhaps enjoy.

And what do the males do? Something very different. The roughly analogous ceremony that the men undertake is the stag party. This varies according to ethnic group, class, and region. But the essence of the business is that the groom-to-be is given a party by his male friends at which male camaraderie is stressed and the "antifemale tradition" is often invoked. Pornographic films may be shown, strippers may dance—in any case, the potential tenderness between the man and wife is mocked by his friends' provision of squalid entertainment, perceived by them to be manly. In some American modern groups almost as outrageous as the Crow, the groom will be made to have intercourse with a prostitute in view of his friends. No more clear and demanding claim can be made by the men on the love life of the groom, and no more poignant if disagreeable episode can characterize the difference between the shower and the stag. In one the mating bond is supported and the bride given to her new role with helpful and cementing gifts of property. In the other the principle of woman-sex is scorned and the claim of woman on man—however crassly and episodically stated—is reduced to a man's degradation of women's sex, either on a film or on a table in the center of the room, but nonetheless with the curious mystique that some males at least appear to share.

Examples of this kind of behavior could be multiplied indefinitely for society after society throughout space and time. But beneath the lurid surface differences in custom and conceit, certain general principles stand out. The most obvious is that at all times and in all places men form groups from which they exclude women. The male "block," described in our topology of the social system, asserts its exclusivity, assigns to itself certain privileges, undertakes a number of specific tasks, and both promotes and controls competition among its members. In a small society the entire male block may organize itself as one association, but it is more likely that there will be a number of male associations, each with its emblems and secrets, and that they will compete with one another and cooperate against the males of other societies. The groups may be formal or informal, and they range from the regular Friday-night poker party through the totem lodge to the Athenaeum, the College of Cardinals, and the Pentagon.

As has been seen repeatedly in the discussion of behavioral evolution, the basis for male bonding is deeply involved with the history of the species. The need of primate males to bond is clear and evident. The reasons—hierarchical competition, social stability, and defense—are obvious. If we add to this the exigencies of the hunting life and the burden of provisioning that fell to the males in this formative and prolonged phase, the growing selection pressures become paramount in favor of males who could and would successfully bond with their fellows for hunting and defense. The lone male was probably a dead male—at least a male less likely to contribute effectively to the gene pool.

So we have another very basic and diffuse instruction in the program of human behavior—but one that is sex specific. The male-male bond is to the male block of the system what the mother-child is to the female. It is as important and as emotionally charged for its political/aggressive purposes as the male-female bond is for its reproductive purposes. It interferes, often traumatically, with these other bonds: the adult males must take the boys away from their mothers, and must, like the Crow Indians, ensure that the mating bond does not undermine male solidarity.

This notion of male bonds can be rather perplexing, because often it does not seem that anything is happening in them that is directly or even remotely biological. Here is where an analogy with the male-female bond is very useful. In the mating situation, a male responds to a female in a particular way; only a small portion of the time they spend in interaction is specifically sexual—that is, erotic. An evening or two or three, or a month's or year's courtship may be consummated in perhaps an hour's physical encounter. But all that precedes and follows is just as sexual as the contact of skin itself. Sex is a critical aspect of systems of behavior, but much of what goes on in its name is social.

In the other primates the fact of being male or female governs not only reproduction, but other things as well—roles in politics, in defense, in socializing the young, the length of time it takes to become adult; all these complex and nonerotic matters are controlled by the biosocial fact of being male or female. Just as they are with other animals. Give a female rat male sex hormones and she will become aggressive, perform mounting and thrusting like a male, abuse her young, and confuse her nesting work. Give a male the female hormones, and he will tend to act accordingly. The fact that it is just a tiny amount of a single substance that is involved underscores its importance in making a massive difference, and suggests how fundamental is the fact of being male or female. The hormones in this sense are like poison; only a little bit has the major effect of killing an otherwise thriving organism. A simple alteration in hormone balance can effect remarkable change in the round of life. So far as one can tell, the higher up the biological scale one goes, the more important, not less, do these regularities become for the infrastructuring of the individual's action.[11]

Healthy human males respond to healthy human females in predictable, biologically determined, and culturally mediated ways. The nature of this response changes dramatically at puberty. If males respond differently to females at this transitional stage, why not to males also? This is more than a rhetorical question, because there is an answer: they do. And they form groups in which to do it.

But what do they actually *do?* In a great many cases it is not obvious that they *do* anything very much in these groups; they just *are* in them. Membership is its own reward, even if the outcome is only a series of bull sessions and a lot of smoke. Often the group is simply an end in itself and seems to exist to satisfy a need to dress up in elaborate insignia of rank; to organize according to a hierarchy of statuses and complex rules; to eat and drink together; to make noise and parade; to outdo one another and other similarly organized groups in ruthlessly unpragmatic activities; to canvass and initiate new members; to preserve secrecy and enforce loyalty; either to exclude women completely or to admit them only on special occasions (which serves to reinforce their exclusion) ; and above all simply to be together, doing things as a group distinct and distinguished from other groups.

Of course, that is only part of the business—the minimal feature of what happens. Usually something else happens too. The group may plot to take over a government, or it may actually be the government, and meet in friendly and confident camaradie in cabinet chambers or the junta's headquarters. It may be their secrets that are a source of the magical power over young boys changing to manhood. The group may be a soccer team, aware of the stars and the aspirants, wary of the management, eager to reward or bilk the fans, but always in connection with their teammates; even stars need a setting; even poor teams of amateurs will enjoy some sense of their skill alongside the physical incompetents who cheer or harass them. The group may be insurance agents working an area with territories divided between them—in competition but also in cooperation under the umbrella of Head Office with its structure of goals and rewards. The process may be represented by a unit of a police force or an army, and even huge groups must be broken down into small face-to-face ones. We may find executives planning a takeover of a smaller company; then two groups may compete for the faith of shareholders and the proxy votes this means. Or it may be the dark and lucrative secrecy of criminals to which the young are inducted by a bond of fear and threat and increasing commitment to the only culture and skill they have. Or a dozen young priests may enjoy one another's support as they venture into a career of a strangely practical and yet theoretical life of juggling ideas, rules, and people in some forcefully benign routine.

Associating with males energizes and gratifies the members of this legion of groups, and the participants in this variety of cooperative enterprises. It is a way of taking up the time and effort of the young by assimilating them into the schemes of the old. It is also a way of deciding which of the young men will be the leaders of the group in the future; it at least delimits the contenders for this opportunity. What happens in the block of the males is common to all societies— this process of tantalizing them with adult power, instructing them, testing them, thwarting carefully their impetuous drive to dominate everything and everyone right away.

This process offers them seniority in return for consent, and privilege in exchange for waiting around. It is not really very sophisticated— though there are many changes to be rung on this standard theme— and it is certainly easily predictable. It is predictable not only because it is so often observed in such a variety of places. As a process, it reflects what we are, and how we evolved as primates uniquely skilled at gluing symbols onto relationships. This should make us as skeptical about the elimination of this bonding tendency as we would be of seriously curtailing heterosexual activity. If one forbids sex among young people, it does not necessarily disappear; it becomes clandestine —as illegitimacy rates testify. Surrealistic as it may seem, the current fashion for decrying and inhibiting male encounter could result in groups of men meeting as conspiratorially as lovers did under regimes marked by a more familiar puritanism.

Whatever may happen in the future, a striking example of male success in managing these bonds so far is the preeminence males as a sex exert over females in the political life of communities. It would be difficult to avoid the conclusion that at least some differences between the sexes—both physiological and behavioral—are biologically based. Consequently, if some universal form of human activity appears to be dominated by one or the other sex, there is at least a prima-facie case for looking at this dominance as a sex-linked characteristic. Men universally dominate the political arena. Women, as all men know, can exert great influence over the course of political events, but formal organization from tribe to empire is predominantly a male activity.[12]

It is also clearly an activity that taps much that is biologically male in behavior. The male primate dominates the troop and keeps order within its boundaries. He protects it against other troops and predators. He plays politics with his fellow males in which he dominates some, ingratiates himself with others, and most importantly, forms strong alliances with still others. In all this he dominates his females. Females definitely exert influence. It is hard for a leader to be successful if he does not have the confidence of the females, who in a real sense may be said to form the most stable core of the group. When new groups are forming among macaque monkeys, for example, the first nucleus is a group of females and young. But the group will persist over time only if a male (and later other males) attaches himself to it and acts as a focus of attention and source of authority.[13] Among humans, male politicians may depend on the female vote, but the politicians are overwhelmingly male. There have of course been female leaders more outstanding than many of their male counterparts—many queens, for example. Here the principle of hereditary succession is so central that failing a male heir, a female is accepted. But no queen has ever surrounded herself with female advisers, female civil servants, female generals, etc. The Amazons exist only in male fantasy. Even in societies where inheritance and succession are through females rather than males, the men ultimately control the situation. There is no such thing as a matriarchy. If succession is through females, then a man's heir is his sister's son, but such a system gives the sister no more power than it gives a wife in the case where a man's heir is his own son.[14]

Why should this male dominance exist? And why should it exist all over the earth, so regularly and so predictably? One favorite explanation is the conspiracy theory.[15] This view holds that men everywhere contrive to keep women everywhere in subservience and in dismayed if baffled ineffectiveness. The notion is that men are as aware of their interests as a sex as bondholders are of their dependence on strong financial structures. This is, of course, possible. But it is very unlikely. We are talking here about so many different cultures, with so many different kinds of religion, economy, ecology, political structure, tradition, and ways of raising children, that it would be statistically inevitable that a fair number of these different systems would throw up a genuinely female-dominated political system. For it is not a question of being technologically primitive—like the aborigines, whose women are not politicians. Or advanced, like the Americans, whose women are only minutely represented in the councils of high power. Or well-meaning, like the Russians—whose women's place in fact is much less exalted than their place in theory. Or in some Arab countries, where the question hardly arises.[16]

Money seems not to be the variable—for then the richest women in the world, the American ones, would be the most powerful. Nor is ideology, nor is religion. It is indeed possible that there is a conspiracy against women, in which case one must slyly ask: if men all over the world have always been able to keep women subdominant all over the world and under all conditions—perhaps they *are* politically superior to women. Perhaps—in the name of sexual equality—we are proposing to admit into political councils already having trouble enough a group of individuals who have proven by their lack of political success over centuries that they are less competent even than men.

This idea must be rejected at once. Division of labor—odious though it may seem to some who see that all people can and should do all things—does not have to mean difference of status. Sexual difference is not the same thing as sexual inequality. Political equality has nothing to do with the facts that women menstruate and bear children and that men die earlier than women and have heart attacks more. Perhaps the political differences between males and females are of the same order as the reproductive differences—politics, evolution, and reproduction have been seen to be so closely linked. One must look at the whole system of reproduction and selection and ask how individual features of our present pattern may result from an old process. The issue here is not female competence and intelligence—these may well be superior to males'—but female political skills and enthusiasms.[17] The business of politics, absurd as much of its posturing, threat, display, cunning, chicanery, bonhomie, and pomposity, with its almost ludicrous tolerance of boredom, must seem to the intelligent or cynical woman, is a business that requires skills and attitudes that are peculiarly male. What is more, women seem to recognize this. For every woman who claims that politics (or war) is as much her game as any man's, there are a thousand women who would feel much more comfortable with a man at the helm. Women vote for men rather than other women. The theory that this male dominance is the result of centuries of brainwashing runs aground again on the argument used before: what kind of creature is it that will allow itself to be so easily brainwashed? The conspiracy theory in fact takes a very low view of female intelligence and ability.

We have seen how sexual differentiation is rooted in primate political-breeding processes: the dominant males are the focus of attention and hence cohesion; they dominate by overt strength and by ritualized threat and display; they protect and keep order; they compete in a never-ceasing test of their ability to dominate; but they also combine in coalitions to exercise more effective dominance or to forage and explore. The course of human evolution added to this basic pattern all the complexities of the hunting life. Man does not live by bread alone, but how he finds his bread is still important, particularly when it is not bread but meat that mattered, and when the hunting way of life persisted for millions of years.

One of the most important effects of hunting was to widen the gap between males and females as far as behavior was concerned. Men hunted, women did not. This was decisive for a very long time. The new knack of killing animals emphasized the sexual differences that existed before. For if males bonded in order to chatter about politics, discipline the young, and defend the troops, it was even more important that they joined together to leave the camp to hunt animals increasingly large and dangerous as time went on, increasingly huntable only by groups, and only by groups of men. When we recall that the brain doubled in size during this initial hunting period—one of the most astonishing of all transformations of all organs in all of nature—we will see that the selective factors that went into this change must have been rigorous indeed. The early primate pattern of bonding became the new and phenomenally significant pattern of cooperative hunting. Out of this grew our ability to attach to the relatively fragile links between men the grand and demanding structures of empire, of moon shots, of corporations, of systems of irrigation, and of the medieval church.

To females, political procedure must seem hopelessly bizarre and almost frighteningly irrelevant to the simple concerns of constituents, children, and anyone else who wants clean air and an agreeable sense of community, among other things. Politicians are very odd, really, with their rotund phrases and meeting-room rotundas; their committees and their extraordinary protocol, their fear of seeming weak and fearful. Yet the peahen, too, must have her doubts about the sanity or at least sense of the male world when she patiently and resignedly waits for the nth display of male grandeur and aggrandizement—for the strutting, the preening, the seemingly overdone intimidation of rivals, the assertion, the condescension—the whole panoply of male vanity. Yes, she is perhaps bored and cynical as yet another silly male begins to do his male thing. But this male thing has been clearly important for the evolutionary story—the story of breeding, nesting, selective mating, territorial defense, protection of young, ritualization of aggression. These mechanics of selection have operated on the behavior of the males of any species to produce the extravagant but effective results that seem so dear to the male ego and so trivial to female good sense.

Boys will indeed be boys, and males will do their male thing with a curious enjoyment in the sensation of being male and doing what men do—without women. Behind many a successful man there stands the proverbial woman—telling him not to make a fool of himself. But the fooling is in deadly earnest. It is the old business of bluff and threat and convoluted rivalry that is part of male being, and it is ridiculous only when seen out of its evolutionary context. The peacock and the fruit fly may seem lunatic in their mating antics, but the selective advantages of their respective rituals can be easily understood. The rituals of male dominance in politics appear to be as necessary and inevitable as the tail of the peacock or the dance of the fruit fly.

The point here is similar to the one, made before, about aristocracies: neither aristocracies nor male dominance as forms of politics are necessarily the "best" forms in terms of human political ideals. But they have a lot going for them that lies deeper than reason and ideology. Any kind of egalitarian system suffers from a disadvantage. Inequality between men and a division of political function between men and women flow naturally from the nature of the primate that we are. Equality and an equal participation of men and women in the political arena are things that must be energetically striven for. Ultimately, they must be imposed. In both cases we must say "no" to nature— our own human nature. To make women equal participants in the political process, we will have to change the very process itself, which means changing a pattern bred into our behavior over the millennia. It may well be possible, but it will not be easy. And it will certainly not be made easier by pretending that all men really want to be equal or that women are simply men who happen occasionally to take time off to have babies.

It is almost impossible to stress this point too much. If we want to change a system, we must understand it first. It did early engineers no good to protest that the law of gravity reduced their most imaginative cathedrals to dust and clutter. They had to know this law, its relationship to rocks and size, its effect on the realities of structure and design. Ideologists may enthuse about the value of creating political systems that involve women fully and with dignity. But what is more necessary and initially more valuable than their admirable enthusiasm is knowledge of just what it is we are trying to change and what kind of success we may expect. Given the current arrangement of politics in nearly all countries—and women have failed to find their places in these so far—it may be statistically unlikely that anything significant will change unless our consciousness changes first. In other words, we must begin to understand the nature of sexual difference and come to terms with it and operate within it, not against it, and to use it constructively and not deny it in the name of equality. Probably equality can be realized only if men become sufficiently understanding of their own peacock enterprises to accept that they have not actually made provision for full female participation in politics. It is hardly enough simply to solicit the votes of females; this is, after all, just another way of keeping power in the hands of candidates who are nearly always male. For men to understand that they are socially different from females, and how, may induce them more effectively to invite women to genuine colleagueship in the places where power is manipulated. On their part, females may more rapidly and happily achieve political goals by asserting the value of specifically female skills and interests rather than by denying the reality of any differences and insisting that all social tasks are performed in the same way by males and females.[18]

This is the place to explore the chief characteristics of the social relations in the "block" of females. Undoubtedly it is women who have borne most of the effects of changes in human technology. Nearly all females for most of their adult lives in nearly all places throughout virtually all of human history have been involved with childbearing and child-rearing. Nothing less than the very survival of the group in which they lived depended upon their successful gestation and raising of a child until it could manage on its own. Because learning and maturation are so important to humans, this is a long process; indeed, it remains the most time-consuming and labor-intensive of all major human tasks. It is also very difficult to mechanize, and even to bureaucratize in some efficient and personal fashion. This has plainly meant that women have had to spend much time with children, one direct consequence of which is that they have also spent much time with other women—their own friends, and mothers of their children's friends.

There are some general questions about the biogrammar of female bonding that must be answered: What patterns may we have inherited from our history as prehumans? What could we do with this inheritance to bend it to our new conditions and to our new ability to impose will between ourselves and nature? And what social relationships among females would fit, influence, and conflict with the patterns among males, and the relations between males and females that we have some reason to believe actually marked our evolution?

Primate females are intensely interested in newborn infants. Mothers have high status among the other females; so do those who are pregnant; childless females will plead to hold an infant, and, as a favor, they will be allowed to.[19] Among humans the situation becomes more complex, though the basic emotional patterns the primates display seem to persist, in however attenuated and modified form. The new complexity stems from the importance of the child as both a measure and as a property of the kinship structure. The matter of what happens to infants is therefore of considerable concern to the males, and the social career of the child is carefully worked out in the context of the overall pattern of social bonds. The net effect of this concern is to bind females into the social structure in a much more demanding, elaborate, and persistent way than is possible among the nonhuman primates where the cycles of estrus rather than the long-term cycle of life govern how males and females interact.

The act of having a child is thus for the human female not only a new event biologically and emotionally but also a contract with her community—a contract perhaps not always formalized but certainly always palpable. The conditions of motherhood are real: mothers must attend to their children, must not leave them alone, must not injure them, and must give them that care and tutelage thought seemly by their fellow citizens. In return females are offered protection, welfare, tax advantages if they have children, and a generalized claim on the resources of time and property of the dominants—both male and female—of the community. (The responsibility of the community to mothers is relatively clear, though with the development in industrial societies of mechanical forms of welfare, women with children but without male supporters are often treated harshly in relation to the difficulty of their task and the scarcity of their resources.)

We have seen how males bond to help one another gain power, defend groups, and acquire animal protein. Females bond too, but in different ways, for significantly different purposes, and with different results for the overall social structure. To put it as economically as possible, males bond for reasons of macrostructure, females for reasons of microstructure—that is, in general, females occupy themselves with interpersonal matters involving face-to-face encounters and focusing upon subjects that have to do with the bearing, nurturing, and training of the young, and with the establishment and management of dwellings and other immediate surroundings. By contrast, males involve themselves with groups and activities that extend directly to the whole community. Here again the primate biogrammar emerges from a variety of possible patterns. The females are at the center of the group; they are concerned chiefly with what happens there and with their relations to the males and young. The males are at the center too, but only after they have served a period of apprenticeship at the periphery, and in some cases only after, in bands of two or three, they have explored some strange terrain and become accustomed to seeing their local place in terms of its wider setting.

This pattern corresponds with a tediously conventional view of the distinction between what men and women do. The important point remains that throughout selection, as we became human, we retained many of the emphases and predispositions of our primate colleagues. We have already noted how significant it was that, alone among the primates, man divided labor between males and females, and that this division depended on males forming effective and cooperative groups for hunting. Females too formed groups, but were best adapted for groups that did different things, and in a different perspective, and with a different set of challenges and satisfactions. This is quite another thing from saying "a woman's place is in the home." If a woman's place is anywhere at all, it is precisely not in the home but in an arena of great interpersonal activity, a place from which brief excursions for purposes of gathering may be undertaken, and a place in which—because of the kinship breakthrough—the lives of individuals are articulated, structured, and blended in concern and competition with the lives of others.

Our concern at this point is with groups, not individuals, because groups of females seem to do different things from groups of males, and have different ways of doing the different things they do. Of course, individual females can perform as well as individual males, and many males can perform tasks usually taken to be the special province of females. But predictably in a gregarious species, male-male bonds differ from male-female bonds, and female-female bonds differ from both.

What are some of these differences? One of the most characteristic and consequential is that the status of females depends on their mates far more than the other way around, and on their reproductive situation. For example, males very rarely take their wives' names at marriage, and this reflects the reality that social placement normally occurs in terms of the occupational and ritual status of the chief male in the female's life.

Females have more to gain and lose by their marriage arrangements than males do. For all males' remarkable concern with status differences, females are capable of even greater interest in the thrust of a snub and the refinement of a pretension. In a real sense this is because females are more committed to the intimate sphere and more dependent on the implications of their personal encounters for their income and satisfaction than males, who may contrive relatively impersonal items of work or group antagonism on which to focus their energy and concern. It is important not to confuse these differences of emphasis and activity with the evaluation of status and importance. To do so is to devalue that intimate sphere in which all people must live, enjoy, and grow, and to glorify activities—often the prerogative of males—that may be destructive, exploitative, crass, and pointless.

We have already noted the significant phenomenon among some primates that although females formed groups of mother-child units (plus interested childless or pregnant females), the groups were totally unstable unless a male joined them as a focus of attention and an agent of social control. This need not seem strange. The female is primarily concerned with the survival of her own little unit—and rightly so. Insofar as other females may help, they are tolerated, but this is at best a tenuous and short-term toleration. Once the child is old enough to fend for itself, the female is interested in getting herself pregnant again and once again is in competition with the other females as she directs her attention toward the mature males.

The human mother is likewise caught in these two intensive activities —looking after her child and maintaining a relationship with a supportive male. In the first instance other women may be useful; in the second, however, they are a direct threat. Coping with the eternal round of birth, copulation, and child-rearing does not leave any primate mother with much time for the great affairs of state, and this has been the lot of the human mother for virtually our whole history as a species. On the other hand, the male, who is not constrained in this way, can exercise these functions and hold the group together—

particularly as the attention of the females becomes fixed on him as a source to which they can turn for protection and sexual satisfaction. The male, then, is concerned with the whole community of mothers, mates, and children, while the female tends to be more narrowly occupied. Thus she cannot act as focus of cohesion, nor can she effectively form the kinds of bonds males form to achieve those male ends that affect the interests of whole communities.

Both females and males enter into sexual competition with others of their sex, and to some extent their status depends on the outcome, but men have always had something over and above this competition for which they must bond and from which they could derive status, while women have rarely had any other source from which to gain a sense of personal worth and social superiority than their position in the reproductive struggle—measured in terms of their mate and their offspring. Women have had little opportunity or reason (in these terms) to bond or form groups for macrostructural purposes. This, then, is the primate situation, and it has been the basic human situation for most of our history. It can be—and is being—mitigated and changed in ways which allow women greater opportunity for involvement in the macrosystem. But these women carry with them a considerable evolutionary burden which may demand more energy and enthusiasm from them than from men to seek these opportunities, and which makes their task more difficult once they become involved in the intricacies of the program they wish to follow.

In one vital and all but unexplored respect the relationships between females differ from those between men. Young males, human and primate, have in a real sense to go to the peripheries of the group before they regain internal status; the distance they go and the length of time it takes them to get back can be considerable. Young females, on the other hand, except in those countries where their education is deliberately fashioned on the male model (but even to some extent in these), are never "peripheralized" to the same extent. Physically they may never move from their mothers until they marry; their base is always "home." Their peripheralization is metaphorical rather than real, in the sense that between puberty and marriage they have a transitional status. But this is usually brief; on marriage the girl automatically joins the ranks of "married women" with all the status implications this carries and often becomes a mother almost immediately. She does not have to win her way back to the center in the same way as a boy; the transition is not so severe; very few will ever fail to make it. She proves herself in a simple biological way—by being fertile; she continues with tasks that she has already been performing anyway in her mother's household. The affluent and technologically advanced nation that peripheralizes females in the same way that it does males may find (and often does find) itself in some difficulty. It reverses the natural trend, breaks the evolutionary continuity which has insisted on a continuing and close bond between older women and young potential wives. Educated young women in particular find the transition to household chores unbearably difficult and uncongenial, not only because they feel they are wasting their education, but because they have suffered a bond disruption and a minor separation trauma. An adolescent female is just not a substitute adolescent male.

Neither is a mother simply a father who has children. But what about the postmenopausal female? In some sense she is a biological anomaly. What use to a species is a female who can no longer reproduce and who is consuming valuable food that might well go to youngsters, mothers, and warriors? In most species the female life span is the reproductive life span, and no more. It occasionally happens that an older female past childbearing will take on some role. The most spectacular example is in the red deer, where an old hind becomes the leader of the group of hinds. She is their focus of attention, and even when the stag has gathered her little group together as a harem during the rutting season, she remains the leader. The stag does not control the movement of the hinds—he simply focuses on the activities of his male rivals. Otherwise he follows the harem about rather ineffectively. Here the experience and sagacity of the older female are called into play very successfully. But this is in a situation where males do not form the focus of the attention structure.

When they do, what role is there for the older female to play? Clearly her usefulness in the human primate society should lie in the area of economic activity. The demands the dependent human infant makes on the young mother inhibit her contribution. But the old woman can make up for this loss in the labor force. Her knowledge of the terrain—of the roots and berries and grains—is incomparably greater, and she can teach all this to her daughters. If they always had to learn it from scratch, it would be an insufferably inefficient system. She is also a store of knowledge and help on the subject of child-rearing. After all, in primitive conditions not that many women live beyond their reproductive period anyway. Certainly in times of food shortage they are often the first to go—along with female infants.

(The death of the one conserves food supplies; the death of the other prevents an increase in future population.)

With the remarkable increase in the life span of recent years, we are faced with the problem of a vast expansion of the numbers of post-reproductive females. These women may not be integrated into the female world of their daughters made independent by machinery and often callous by social mobility or change in generation life style. But the old women are not really making their way into the man's world, either, where they are, logically at least, most likely to fit, since they are through with the essentially female business of child-rearing. For example, from a simple-minded point of view it remains curious that such females do not take a more active role in formal politics, since of all the groups in the population they have probably the most time and the most money with which to support their effort. What in fact do they do?

One important activity, at least in industrialized communities, which they can undertake successfully and with some contentment, is a set of voluntary activities that support other sections of the community. They may be welfare workers, canvassers, fund-raisers for worthwhile causes. The women who tend toward volunteer work are usually well-off; they have none of the need for a job that poor women, even with husbands, have. It is a comment on the impracticality and anti-feminism of most communities that they are more willing to accommodate their otherwise rigid schedules to suit the free time of volunteer workers than of women who need money as well as want to accomplish something outside their home and in their community.

Of course, this varies considerably in many communities. In the Soviet Union many grandmothers live with their daughters or sons; it is the *babushka* who minds the child while the mother is at work. Even in such a committed and self-consciously revolutionary society, there is nothing approaching an adequate number of day-care centers; as usual, it is to old primate bonds that we turn when we want to take part in even postindustrial activity. In a society like ours, the solution is far more complex, because in part the mother-daughter bond is disrupted by education, by mobility, and by the rapidity of social change which makes the mother seem irrelevant to the practices and ideals of the daughter. Indeed, there is often bleak antipathy between mother and daughter, if only because they share households; perhaps one reason for the declining age at which females marry is that girls cannot abide their mothers and must leave their houses and their implicitly supervised bedrooms. And yet, tragically, psychiatric records tell of many girls who bear children earlier than they openly want them or are married or can afford them, in good part because they want to affirm themselves against their mothers.

Once again, then, we see that the fruits of the industrial revolution were most sour for females; it was they who had their important bond earliest threatened and first broken. In school they lost their mothers' philosophy, and in mobility their presence. In the factory they lost the dependence out of which reciprocity is made. With puberty arriving earlier and earlier—four months sooner every ten years—the transitional period described above was extended at the same time as the demand for schooling and for skills increased the time it took the capacities of their bodies to make themselves manifest in their behavior. And it is even possible that the earlier arrival of puberty is in part the result of competition among younger and younger girls to stimulate men to bear them off and away from home.[20] As bodily changes may affect behavior, so different pressures from behavior may (as with psychosomatic diseases) speed up or slow down bodily processes.

Females bond; but in quantity, quality, direction, purpose and even aesthetic, their bonding processes and procedures differ considerably from those of the male block in direct proportion to the difference in life cycle, life style, and life chance of males and females. Their long-lasting bonds are largely kinship bonds. Outside these, their bonding is more tenuous, more episodic, and less productive of groupings that affect the macrostructure than in the case of the male. But the female bonds are as crucial and heroic as the more political male bonds. If they fail, the system collapses, and no amount of male solidarity will be able to hold it together.

If females have difficulties, so do males. In the subhuman primate troop the saddest character is the peripheral male. At a still tender age he has left his mother to go to the edges of the group. For a while he will be indulged by the older males and will form play groups with his peers, where he will sort out his dominance relationships in play-fighting and rough-and-tumble. But with the approach of sexual maturity, he is placed in the impossible position of being driven to compete with males twice his size to whom he has learned to defer and from whom he can expect no charity.

The so-far neglected block of our social system—the block of adolescent boys—is different from the others in that it involves a transitory status. In some societies the adolescent is classified with the females, and can only be "made" into a man. He shares this problem of self-establishment with his primate cousins. Manhood is not achieved simply by maturing, it must be proved. Among the now familiar Crow this was starkly dramatized. A young man was expected to become a warrior—the only other status in the community was that of woman. If he failed to make it as a warrior, then he had no choice but to accept the only other classification. He put on women's clothes, did women's work, got married, and lived as a *berdache*—a man-woman.

For girls it is different. At first menstruation a young girl in a real sense becomes a woman without further effort. She stays with the women, and begins to take part in women's work. In most parts of the world she marries soon after this—if not before. Initiation ceremonies for girls are really puberty ceremonies, to celebrate *menarche*.[21] For boys, however, the ceremonies are correlated only roughly with puberty, and may occur at any age from seven to twenty or may be stretched over a long period.[22] For a man does not just occur—he has to be made. He has to be incorporated into the block of adult males. He will not be measured by secondary sexual characteristics, but by his performance, his behavior, and his success in doing the male thing in a manner that satisfies the already initiated males of his community. The stakes are high, the mortality rate is high, and the demands for achievement are high. For all the disadvantages that females seem to suffer in the political system, they have this one enormous advantage during the treacherous period of adolescence: the community helps them, and it hinders the males. A girl has only to mature physically to be fully accepted as a woman and to contribute to the next generation; a boy has to go beyond mere physical maturity, and here he may or may not succeed.

The other primates, however, resist such sentimentalization. The young males of the troop would kill their older relatives and take over the coveted central position of attention and power—if they could. And when they can, they do. Ethologists speak of the "ritualization of aggression"—but the aggression has to be ritualized because it is so real. And ritual does not always work. The death rate among four-year-old primate males is high during the breeding season. The ritualization helps only when the order has been established, and then it helps to keep it that way.

Freud acutely observed that the primate situation would become much more tricky with the advent of weapons.[23] The older and more dominant baboon is physically bigger and has longer canines than his challenger. But a young man armed with a spear or club may very well be a match for his older opponent. The whole body of young warriors must always appear as much a potential threat to the older males holding power as they appear a delightful prospect to the young girls awaiting marriage. And the whole thing can be, and often is, soured by the fact that the older males have already used their prerogative to take more than their fair share of the young girls. At one stroke this doubles the frustrations of the young males and makes life more difficult for the polygamous elders. Many human societies echo almost directly the primate horde situation: the older males monopolize the females, use various devices to control the young males and their entry into the hierarchy, and spend a great deal of time ensuring that the juniors do not get a chance to copulate with the younger wives.[24]

The traditional way of dealing with the aggression and frustration of the young male is to direct it outward. The peripheral primate is the first to deal with predators, and the young warriors the first to face the enemy and die. The Crow again show how aggression can be turned to advantage by making the war game into a status race. To get into the male hierarchy, the young brave had to perform certain feats of courage and cunning that could be validated before his elders. His energies were directed outward toward the foe rather than upward toward his own superiors. Furthermore, he had to joust with death if he wanted to become an important male. Universally it is the old men who make the rules, own the teams, promote the boxing matches; it is the young men who leap at barbed wire, concuss one another, and devote more physical energy now than at any other time in their lives to attempts to outdo one another. While possessing females is important to the young males, and is in some sense the whole point of the evolutionary process, it is not necessarily the basic motivating factor. The possession of a female or females can be viewed as one more validation of male status, which is an end in itself, because, once achieved, the women follow anyway. Whatever the advocates of student power do want—and it is not always clear—one thing they plainly do *not* want is access to their professors' wives. But then the whole thing might well be different if their professors had managed to monopolize not only decisions about the curriculum, but the majority of the female undergraduates as well. (Although the now declining *in loco parentis* attitude which sought to control where and when female undergraduates should sleep sought to do just that—in a typically blundering and indirect academic way.)

In every human population, the adolescent and postadolescent males are at once a resource and a threat. The platoon of young soldiers is cheered and even idolized; the teen-age gang is feared and hunted down. The resource has to be used; the threat must be handled—and every human society has evolved fairly elaborate methods to handle it. Overwhelmingly, educational systems have focused their attentions on boys; only rich girls were expected to learn some set of practices, and these were more for the management of their domestic lives than for the conduct of communal affairs or the improvement of their own minds. But the boys were sent on mock hunts, enrolled in equivalents of the Boy Scouts, removed to boarding schools, taken on warring parties, set alongside rabbis to learn their bar-mitzvah songs. They have done their vision quests, been apprenticed to carpenters and thatchers, have been unpaid deckhands on the dangerous fish trawlers of Portugal and Hull. The extension of the educational system recently to include females is nothing less than equitable—an extension of human rights. But it means as well that females have joined a system of long-term oppression, one of the functions of which is to induce young males to spend a long time learning particular practices vaguely related to adult statuses, and committing themselves to the structures of the adult males from which all blessings flow.

Validation rather than education is our real concern here. One of the important features of validation for boys is that they must do it in terms of other boys, even if it is the adult males who set the limits and some of the standards. If men form groups, boys form gangs, and swarm kinetically from place to place full of noise and incipient action. These gangs may be scout troops, platoons, slum war machines, musical bands, rowing teams, fraternities, or groups of mechanically minded semisuicidal malcontents keen to race stripped-down cars in some inconvenient arena to show they can do this better than the driver the next car over. Girls are far less likely to do such things, and they are also far less likely to become involved in criminal activity (except for shoplifting—a new-fashioned form of gathering—and sexual crimes, an old-fashioned form of being exploited in the most apt way they know how). But crime spreads among boys as quickly as a new scheme of haircutting or width of trouser leg—ten times as quickly as among girls, in fact, and with far more implication for the eventual relationship which individuals will have with the basic structures of complex societies like those of Europe and America.

The role of these groups in the lives of the boys who are their members is clear. Hours are spent on streetcorners, in clubhouses, and on sportsfields, anywhere they will be tolerated. The activities of sports heroes and other denizens of their imaginations are catalogued, recalled, and analyzed with accuracy and affection. These feats of memory and analysis would baffle a teacher hopelessly confronting their apathetic response to the pleasures of the calculus and American or European history. Boys do best what they are most interested in—with the consequence that they drop out of school more enthusiastically than girls, though there is in one sense much more at stake for them.

This business of gangs may be troublesome to the elders when it becomes disruptive of the social order to whose perpetuation they are committed. But it is essential nonetheless that the gangs exist, because in them boys learn—just before they finally take the plunge into male adulthood—a set of important skills and enthusiasms: How to be loyal to the group and how to get on with it. How to exercise leadership if they can, and how to be helpful if they cannot. How to identify with the totem or symbol of group and see its interest as the same as their own. How to be willing to spend a lot of time not doing anything but keeping the group going. How, in extreme cases, to be wounded for or die for the collective. How to know the limits of their own privacy. How to "walk tall" because they do not walk alone, and how to be helpful to members they do not really like because they are members, and for no other reason. How to do things they hate, and commit cruelties they would privately abhor. In other words, that there is something called morality which is absolute and yet mediated by the local group. In their gangs they learn the enthusiasm and the careful restriction of enthusiasm that will be necessary when they join the men and have to take orders warmly and in the proper spirit.[25]

But these boys do not simply achieve some abstract status of manhood as a result of their trials and exertions: they achieve membership in specific male organizations. Their initiatory struggles are often in the nature of a test whereby the older males select from the candidates those best fitted for the tasks of the group. The cultural elaborateness of all this can easily blind us to its underlying motivation, which is little different, if different at all, from the motivation of the lowly savanna-monkey juveniles and their irascible but cunning elders. There is, however, one big difference: human juveniles are faced not with one hierarchy but, except in the very simplest societies, with many. Dominance patterns established in youth, in the gang or play group, may not persist into adulthood when the gang is dispersed, and the boys then may become members of many different organizations. There is a switch—or several switches—of hierarchy, and this involves selection. For men take their groups, even if they are essentially recreational groups, very seriously. All men—with a few maverick exceptions—will end up in one group or another. But then comes another human twist: some *groups* rank higher than others. This introduces complications, obviously, in that the skills involved in being in one kind of group are not those prized or needed in another. It does mean that in more complex societies there is more room for more and different types of maleness. But in all these cases, any man's personal status will be mediated by one or more immediate groups with which he identifies. The *processes* of induction, acceptance, validation, promotion, and even personal satisfaction are those basic processes of male bonding that characterized the hunting team, and which even the most sophisticated of contemporary male organizations replicate with primitive skill and atavistic energy.

When the pieces of the jigsaw that we have been laboriously constructing over the last three chapters are put together, a scheme of the human social system emerges to place it squarely within the primate biogram and yet to point up its uniquely human attributes. The major division is into three "blocks"—the male block, the female-with-young block, and the adolescent-male block—exactly as with the basic primate system. The dynamics of the system concern on the one hand the processes going on within each block, and on the other the processes that relate them to one another.

The picture is of a very recognizably primate social system, modified by the evolutionary changes introduced by hunting and the consequent division of labor, which give it its species-specific characteristics. Since it is so basic a pattern, societies strain toward it, however much they may bend and twist the rubber sheet. In many rituals, and in times of great crisis, it asserts itself. The mothers of America have very little to say in a system where boards of senior males select those of their sons best fitted to die for causes which may make sense to some powerful men but often not, in the mothers' eyes, worth the life of even one carefully nursed and proudly reared boy. But the mothers may learn to weep with some reluctant dignity and mellow their sorrow with pride if they truly sense that the sacrifice has indeed been for the safety of the greater collective of which their little familial unit is a part. This is one of their basic services—to provide warriors, who in turn will provide protection. Perhaps one moral of this dismal story is that the men had better fight wars that the women can believe in; otherwise, they may shake the confidence of the female block in the credibility of their protective intent and the competence of their plans. And there is another moral to this story of constant and reiterated tragedy. Boys are taken from the women who have devoted the fresh and hopeful years of their lives to raising them to fight against boys similarly hothoused in some enemy tribe, thus expressing in a clear and brutal way the power of the male block over the others and the irrelevance of tender personal histories to the merciless demands some males make and their lackeys enforce.

If we add to these processes the more general political interactions of attention structure, hierarchy, competitiveness, coalition, ritualization, etc., we begin to see the elements into which all societies dissolve and the dynamics on which they all operate—whatever the actual cultural content that their own particular histories and ecologies conspire to infuse into the system.

There remains one brief and general point to make about the bonding process: one good bond does not deserve another. Or, put more accurately, one good bond precludes another. At the beginning of "Bond Issue One" we said that boys and girls in kibbutzim who are raised in the same group do not marry each other. Our point is that they cannot. A teacher and pupil who are well bonded will find it difficult to become colleagues when the pupil becomes a teacher too. A father and son who have a complex history of support and authority will be tried by the equality necessary to run a business together, and a mother and daughter will be hard put to act otherwise after they have for a long time experienced the particular relationship of motherhood and childhood. Though it amuses the fancy of novelists and may be the fantasy of many brothers and sisters, siblings of similar ages never marry and hardly ever court and mate, except where law—such as among the ill-fated Egyptian royal family—says they can or must.

The kibbutz evidence is nothing less than startling. The kibbutz is a communal form devoted to warm camaraderie, the equality of males and females, and growth of population and resource. Everywhere else men and women tend to marry men and women who have been boys and girls with them in the same place—the simple fact of distance keeps them together. But not on the kibbutz; and not only do they not marry, but they do not even court. In the kibbutz, where so-called "free love" is supposed to prevail, they choose to sleep in separate rooms after adolescence. One good bond seems to inhibit another, and this is why so much of the discourse about incest is misplaced and wrong. Hamlet and Oedipus had genuinely difficult problems—mature females are rarely attracted by young and very subdominant males. (Primate males rarely if ever mate with their mothers anyway.)[26] Sexual feeling may mark the encounters of sons and mothers, but that is because sex is part of any human relationship—we are, after all, males and females always. But a full-fledged sexual unit cannot be formed on this basis; it is so difficult to achieve that it is less a problem in fact than a provocation in fantasy.

More tempestuous is the father-daughter bond. A quick look at the reported cases of incest shows that this is the most common of all incestuous encounters. This is understandable enough, because one enhancing spice of some sexual relationships seems to be a touch of that ritual neck-bite dominance the hamadryas baboon or the ambitious sultan appears to show. Fathers dominate daughters, and only the most insensitive father could deny that one claim his daughters make on his time and concern is a wily female one. Of course, the father-daughter bond is nearly always maintained without the courting and mating process interfering, and without sexual intercourse augmenting social intercourse. The whole issue of incest and its fascination and horror may be nothing so lurid as poets and psychoanalysts seem to imagine, but may hinge on the simple fact that to commit incest one has to disrupt an already established bond and substitute another and often antipathetical one. That humans resist this effort on the one hand and are fascinated by its possibilities—because they are sexual, and humans are fascinated by sex—on the other is inherent in the very nature of bonding.[27]

The exclusion principle may well explain why humans experience difficulty in yet another area. The bond between lovers is sexual and a matter for them only; the bond between parents is nurturant and it is mediated by the demands placed on both by, and the affection of both for, the troublesome infant that is the product of their voluntary labors. To some extent, if they are to be successful parents, they must re-create with each other aspects of their own childhood bonds. But this in turn may act to preclude a relationship that is based on sexual encounter. In other words, does the parent-parent bond exclude—or at least make difficult—the lover-lover or courtship bond? The incidence of marital breakdown in our own culture and the ubiquity of marital infidelity in all cultures—including and perhaps especially the polygamous ones—would suggest that this is so. It is not the only ingredient—male aggrandizement and female boredom contribute their share—but the attempt of many people to re-create the sensuousness and irresponsibility of the courtship phase outside the bounds of legal marriage cannot be dismissed as either sin or pathology. If we are searching for universal characteristics of the species, we can safely say that while no one form of marriage is universal, marital infidelity is universal: all cultures may not be monogamous, but they are all certainly adulterous.

There is nothing inevitable about this in the lives of individuals. Some individuals commit incest with their sisters or daughters, others live lives of model sexual constancy with the mothers and fathers of their children. But in terms of central tendency, most people do not commit incest, most men are unfaithful,[28] and most people who have had a long superordinate-subordinate relationship do not easily convert it to a bond of equality. Bonding is too serious for us promiscuously to transmute one tie of great intensity into its opposite, and then run both together. Love and marriage may go together like a horse and carriage, but the horse has to be broken and yoked, and the carriage pulled.

5.

GIVE
AND TAKE

IT REALLY IS better to give than to receive. The very act of giving is
perhaps the most basic step on the road to truly human social relationships: it implies an obligation to return the gift.[1] It sets up a relationship of indebtedness unknown in the animal world; it creates
networks of indebtedness; vast systems of credit; things offered and
things owed; those to whom we have given and those to whom we must
give; those from whom we may expect and those who may expect
from us in turn. The system of exchange is never in equilibrium; somebody always owes somebody else something. If all debts were canceled,
social relationships would scarcely exist; but they are never all canceled. Of all the social bonds that exist, those between debtor and
creditor are the most characteristically human, and depart furthest
from the basic biogrammar of primate bonding. No monkey was ever
in debt to another monkey. While human society is integrated in
many of the same ways as primate society, it adds this totally new
dimension of exchange and contract—a dimension that cuts across all
the bonding processes and creates a strange world of its own. This
world is not immediately strange to us, because it is our very own
human world of give and take and the sense of obligation. But in
evolutionary terms it is very strange indeed, and from our perspective
we must look at it for what it is: a remarkable adaptation, a unique
adaptive mechanism of one particular species—ours.

118

The adaptation can be phrased like this: all animal populations have ecologies, only human populations have economies. This has been put another way: humans have a sense of "property."[2] This proposal has been challenged by defenders of animal sagacity on the grounds that animals defend territories—and what is more basically "property" than real estate?[3] The analogy of property and territory has been taken very far and used to explain a great deal about human behavior. But most of this analogizing misses the important point: an animal simply *defends* its territory and would never give it up unless forced; humans use property to *exchange* for other property. In other words, they willingly give up their property, provided they get something equivalent (or better) in return. This an animal would never do. No animal would understand for a moment the elaborate exchanges of pieces of the globe that went on after each European war. Human territories certainly have some of the characteristics of animal territories; they both provide food and living and breeding space, as any nation or tribe under attack will readily demonstrate; but no animal territory can have the characteristic of human property—that it can be exchanged.

Here we want to explore the consequences of this particular change of evolutionary gear from being a primate with a simple ecological relationship to the environment, to being one with a complex economy involving the exchange of property among its members. To do this we will have to look again at our evolutionary history. Once more we will have to be concerned with the hunter's round of life: the hunter dividing his kill with his colleagues, his children, and the needy of his group; the male hunter seeking meat while the females gather vegetables; the hunter gambling—working out the odds against him and against a certain tactic; the hunter exchanging women and arranging feasts. This hunter is not just an affliction of our pages; he is a present reality, he is a feature of contemporary reality: our elaborate cities and their often harsh individualism are closer to the environment in which we were selected and in terms of which we became skilled than is the agricultural or pastoral phase of the human story. Not that there are any real animals left to kill. But there are campaigns to be fought, deals to be made; there is a great possible richness of reciprocity. To be close to nature is not necessarily to be close to human nature. It is what we do that is important, not where we do it. It is with whom and why behavior occurs that matter, not the scenery and the smell of trees that surround the encounters. We are what we do. And now we must look at what we do with our resources and our needs, with our self-concerns and our generosity, and how we run the most exciting and elaborate credit system in nature.

Primates do not share. Neither do they exchange. We have already seen how far-reaching are the effects of that most primitive pattern of exchange that involved the men in providing meat and the women in providing vegetable foods.[4] Again, the human breakthrough involves the evolution of the notion of women as property—perhaps the most primitive form of property. The first debt in the world was probably a woman, and the first blank check was most likely the right to any of his daughters, born and unborn, granted by one man to another. The first economy in the world—and for at least a million years the only economy in the world—was a hunting economy. It was in this context that our behavior as exchanging, distributing, and maximizing creatures evolved. The pitifully short time since we invented agriculture (about ten thousand years ago), and the even shorter time since industrialization began in earnest (perhaps two hundred years ago), should not blind us to the reality of our evolutionary heritage. In our economic behavior, as in so much else, we are still Paleolithic hunters.[5]

Economics reflects evolution just as much as politics and sex do. In some ways the discontinuities between ourselves and our primate ancestors are more pronounced in the area of economics than anyplace else. Certainly our sexuality was changed in our struggle to become human, but for sheer physiological reasons it has a direct continuity with primate ancestry. This holds true for politics, too: we have changed the content but retain the processes and motivations. We effectively radicalized our relationship to resources and their production by introducing property, exchange, and the bond of indebtedness.

But if animals do not have property in the same sense as humans do, how did humans come to need it in the first place? It is not enough to say that hunting was involved; wolves hunt, but they do not have a mania for property. It is not simply hunting, but the manner of hunting that counted. Lacking the natural attributes of the carnivore, human hunters needed tools and weapons for the hunt.[6] Human hunting with its toolbase required also a kind of social organization that had to go beyond that of the pack to be successful.[7] Men had to accommodate to one another and to the varied skills they unequally shared, so they made deals. Tools and deals are the bedrock of human economic behavior, and originally and for a long time the deal was clinched with an exchange of females.[8] The web of indebtedness involved the transfer of women, the exchange of services, and the distribution of meat. The first tools on earth were butchering tools. From the clash of stone and flesh, generosity and economy were born.

The hunting way became successful; from being at first simply a supplementary activity, it rapidly came to dominate the whole course of human evolution. Men became dependent on the hunting way of life and evolved to cope with its ever-increasing complexities. Our whole anatomy reflects this development, from our convoluted brain with its powers of speech and association to our striding walk and upright carriage. From the unpromising beginnings of the little man-ape of south Africa we evolved into a very fine hunting machine geared to the nomadic life of the savannas and the relentless, if not swift, pursuit of game. But at the same time, our emotions, our intelligence, and our social skills were evolving to meet the same exigencies.[9]

But in no hunting group was the distribution of skills exactly even. One man might be an excellent tracker but perhaps useless with a spear; another might be extremely brave at the kill but lack the perspicacity to find the prey; another might be unfit altogether for the hunt but skilled in the manufacture of the necessary tools; another might be useless at anything but taking trips into the world of spirits to bring back messages of health and well-being; another might lack specific abilities but be able to plan large-scale activities with a logistical knack. The old would be stores of knowledge, the young reserves of strength, and the whole machinery must be made to work together for the success and survival of the group. There was also competition, for this was still the competitive primate to whom status mattered as much as meat, and for whom meat might well be the route to status. It was also a world in which groups split up and expanded to exploit wider hunting areas, but did not lose touch and remained in a related but competing bond with the original group and the other groups around. Another major source of differentiation was the division of labor between men and women, and the need of each sex for the products and services of the other.

There was a differentiation of skills, a differentiation of groups, and a differentiation of the sexes with regard to economic activity. The outcome of differentiation and competition was the deal. Men as individuals, and groups of men, set up alliances based on the exchange of property. Obligations were thus assumed by the exchanging parties, whether they were a man and his wife, a young man and an older relative, or two groups of hunting men. No one man could ever ensure his own survival: man was never a lone hunter, and he needed allies as insurance. He needed men who were dependent on him, and men on whom he was dependent. The more dependents he had, the more powerful and successful he would be, and the more likely to be the focus of attention and hence deference in the group. Also he would be most likely to accumulate females and thus disproportionately influence the genetics of future generations.[10]

The economy of hunting, therefore, involved bargaining, calculation, the assessment of odds and the taking of risks, insurance, speculation, the making of deals, the controlling of distribution, investment, capital accumulation, debt and obligation, and a series of similar skills that look different from those we are used to exercising ourselves only because the context is so different to start with. But over millennia we evolved as a creature that derived great emotional satisfaction from having and using such skills. If man is nature's great ward boss and her equally great lover, he is also her supreme wheeler and dealer. The deal is a recognition of one's limited strength, one's frailty in the face of larger problems. It is an assertion of community and a denial of the tiny megalomaniacal center-of-the-world which small children cherish and grown-ups occasionally seek to re-create when they are tired, or have tantrums, or become so pathologically convinced of their special virtue that they can no longer deal but can only command.

And of course it is not only men who deal. Women deal too, be they the lady borrowing a cup of sugar, a Ghanaian mammy-trader selling cans of corned beef to a smaller trader in a suburb, the clever suburban mothers marshaling fleets of station wagons full of children to ballfields, dance classes, birthday parties, and Hebrew schools. The poor mother with an absent or unemployed husband will use a friend or relative to mind her children while she works; girls who are courting will share clothes and cooperate to secure the best dates; childless women will be given babies to hold and feel community with, and not only because this relieves a mother or entertains a child. Women will organize extensive parties for fun or "charity"; they manage businesses, nurse patients, and counsel baffled children. They deal a lot to keep things going.

But the big adventures and the dramatic hunts are male. It appears still to be the case that the uncertainty and particular sensitivity of the hunt and its metaphor galvanizes men more than women, and boys more than girls. It is the band of men who play music like warriors, who worry a melody, turn it around, pass it back and forth, hide from it altogether, pair up, split up, combine to chase it, come crashing or singing around, and then drive to some utterly expert and exhausted point of rest when the improvisation is done and when the millisecond mutual awareness has paid off in a satisfaction only an improvising musician can understand as an essential luxury for his being. There are no bands of women who do this, though women as well as men are made still by the noise of instruments and are entangled in the whole wordless enterprise of solving a problem which need not and does not exist and which to the young particularly is more than entertainment. The music is the hunt; the method is the deal. It is something boys learn themselves, outside of or despite their schools, and then bring to such perfection of time and pitch that their elders almost fail to recognize their offspring for all their skill. They do this because they want to, and because their peers want to hear them. In a relatively free age, this is what some young men choose to do. As they play, they exchange constantly: you take a solo, and then I will; let's all ramify the drummer's statement; let's speed up, though the leader will keep the basic beat in his head; let's play till exhaustion. This is an almost pure emotional analogue of the hunt; music is not only the food of love but of predation too.

Not only is the male body adapted for tropical savanna hunting in groups, but much of his emotional life and many of the skills he most enthusiastically cultivates are also related to huntinglike activities. Our hunting legacy is a male creature evolved for certain work and seeking certain satisfactions. He likes to exchange, to solve, to maximize. Our legatee enjoys speculating, competing, and he loves cooperating and even after work goes out for drinks with his colleagues. Predictably, he enjoys feeling prosperous, but there is a critical ambiguity here, because this prosperity cannot consistently and openly contradict the public interest or what it is thought to be. The reason is simple and very important. High status among males is closely related to being the *center of redistributive activity*. The chief must give gifts as well as receive them.[11] The rich man becomes odious if he remains miserly; he is the moral cousin of the beggar who takes without giving. The miser threatens the whole system of social relationships in the same way as the incestuous man. Each one consumes what he owns and does not give it up in return for something else.

Such behavior carried to its logical conclusion would put an end to social relationships, since it would deny the fundamental importance of exchange and reciprocity. In all human economic systems which involve the accumulation of wealth, and hence the existence of wealthy men, the pressures toward and rewards derived from public generosity are universal and obvious. This is not to say that the rich and powerful always see it this way—miserable exploitation is just as universal but it is a perilous enterprise and usually successful only if backed by force.

No one in the hunting band can afford to exploit or expropriate anyone else too consistently. Individual survival is too fragile. An individual who accumulates and does not redistribute would be doomed if the situation were ever reversed. In any case, the hunting band is a face-to-face economy in which one is locked into a system of personal obligations. Accumulation for a hunter is, after a certain point, useless: he cannot consume more meat than he needs or use more weapons than he can handle. The successful hunter therefore has to convert surplus into prestige. In return he will be deferred to and also will be allowed to accumulate the primeval liquid asset—women. This represents the group's collective investment in him, from which it will reap the reward, it hopes, of fine hunters—the first compound interest. There is a mutuality of goals and indebtedness between the big man and his group. The whole point of being powerful and important is the control of distribution; the whole point of accumulation is the eventual sharing; the outcome of this strategy is, at least theoretically, food for all. Thus, in the ideal economy, accumulation and generosity are two sides of the same coin; getting and sharing are virtually one and the same activity.

But being generous is not purely a voluntary, sunny, and spontaneous act. It is a genuine casting of the bread upon the waters in the expectation of a future return. Our ancestors could not have based their evolutionary success on mere casual generosity. As the great French anthropologist Marcel Mauss put it, there is an *obligation* to give, an *obligation* to receive, and an *obligation* to repay.[12] The belief in these obligations is universal in human society, and the man who fails it is either despised or punished; he is admired only in joke and story, where his very deviousness serves to point up the accepted code. It is a rather tight little system based on the economics of tight little groups working seriously at the business of survival. The topology of its motivations is still with us, but as we shall see, the rubber sheeting has been stretched to breaking point by some of the content we have poured into this mold since the development of cities, civilization, and industry.

The main features of the hunting economy can be succinctly described.[13]

The primate base provides for (a) a rudimentary sexual division of labor, (b) foraging by the males, (c) the cooperation of males in the framework of (d) competition between males.

It is small-scale, face-to-face, and personalized.

It is based on a sexual division of work requiring males to hunt and females to gather.

It is based on tool and weapon manufacture.

It is based on a division of skills and the integration of these skills through networks of exchange (of goods, services, and women).

These are networks of alliances and contracts—deals—among men.

It involves foresight, investment, judgment, risk taking—a strong element of gambling.

It involves social relationships based on a credit system of indebtedness and obligation.

It involves a redistributive system operating through the channels of exchange and generosity; exploitation is constrained in the interest of group survival.[14]

It bases status on accumulative skill married to distributive control—again in the interest of the group as a whole.

It is important to see all these factors as integrated into the hunt. They are social, intellectual, and emotional devices that go to make up an efficient hunting economy, in the same way that muscles, joint articulation, eyesight, intelligence, etc., go to make up the efficient hunting body. They are the anatomy and physiology of the hunting body social. It is a system of the savannas and the hunting range, and it is the context of our social, emotional, and intellectual evolution.

Our economic dilemmas are rooted in recent changes. The anguish is relatively sudden, and what stimulates it is now relatively new. Until about twenty-five thousand years ago the number of hominids in the world was as little as 125,000, as many as two or three million.[15] We hunted with lots of space to range in. Our tools improved, as did our language and our skill for organization. Our brains improved to arrange these stimuli and make them useful for our purposes. We became more prosperous and bred more successfully. By about forty thousand years ago our evolution as a species was substantially at the point where it now hovers. Ten thousand years of agriculture, and the density that results from settling near rivers, deltas, and valleys, allowed us to begin to revise some of our tested procedures for raising the young and keeping the adults alive.[16] We domesticated animals and paid them careful attention as symbols of both prosperity and real wealth.[17] Animals entered our lives in a more intimate way than before.[18] They were no longer there just for us to kill, they now accompanied us on our life cycles, and to this day we attach ourselves tenaciously to expensive and inconvenient creatures we call pets, just as in a supermarket system we grow plants and try to embellish ourselves and our houses with trees and flowers.

We speak glibly and easily of the "agricultural revolution" and see it as the great leap forward in human history.[19] Before it was "prehistory"—the dark ages of the savage hunter. Agriculture gave us, the myth persists, a food surplus, settlement, leisure, and the beginnings of the necessary baseline of civilization.[20] But it also gave us two things calculated to put the severest of strains on the fine-honed hunting animal that we were (and still are): it gave us an uncontrollable and alarmingly increasing population density, and it gave us the daily round, the common task, the drudgery of unremitting year-round agricultural toil. It created the peasant, as inhuman a figure as the bureaucrat, and while it ultimately freed a "creative" class that developed writing and all the other appurtenances of the civilized life, it condemned the overwhelming majority of the mushrooming human population to a sedentary and servile existence.[21]

In a very profound, human sense, the agricultural revolution was the great leap backward. It returned the majority of us to the restrictive food-getting state of our primate past: we spent most of the day in food-getting activity, each day and every day, year in and year out. It condemned us to live and depend on small areas of land, and robbed all but the rich of the pleasures and drama of the chase. It let us continue to wheel and deal and make alliances through our females (the peasant raised all this to a fine if petty art), but it did not connect all this to the macrostructures of economic power.[22] It left us, as individuals, no longer contributing to the destiny of the larger group but insecure and at the mercy of those who were able to maintain the predatory life. Finally it created slaves and serfs who were robbed even of restricted territory and autonomy.[23] And it did this in a breathtakingly brief period, a mere ten thousand years. It did it to an animal that had carefully and beautifully prepared itself through millions of years of natural selection to range and gamble, lounge and play, feast and forage—all in pursuit of four-footed protein over wide and varied areas of the earth.

As if this was not enough, the species had to make a second spectacular leap into a yet more complex and difficult economy and an even more explosive rise in numbers. Two hundred years of industrialization have catapulted the species into a situation as different from the agricultural tradition as this was from the hunting way. The rate of population growth increased, the degradation of the environment begun by the domesticators of plants and animals was brought to near completion, and a new kind of creature—the wage laborer—was created, with no analogue in nature and no place in the evolutionary scheme of things.[24] On top of this the rate of social change was accelerated to a point where any sense of continuity from generation to generation —something deep in the hunter's experience—was lost almost completely.[25]

In one sense it is a great compliment to the hunting brain that it had the reserves and capacity that could cope with, and indeed provoke, these revolutions. But this brain is still the old primate brain with the overlay of gray matter wrinkled into self-consciousness by the hunting transformation.

In the same way, we still have the old primate body molded into a hunting machine by the savanna experience. As we have stressed, there has not been time for an agricultural or an industrial brain or body to evolve. The body was not framed for sitting at a desk or crouching all day in a field—as those who do too much of either usually discover to their cost; our emotional needs and satisfactions were not necessarily framed to these ends either. It is usually assumed that, because we are infinitely adaptable, this does not matter. But does it?

At every stage in these overnight developments we both imposed on ourselves severe costs and allowed ourselves some gains. The question is, did the gains ever outweigh the costs? In a strictly biological sense the species prospered. It multiplied and spread and outmaneuvered other species in the struggle for existence. But the costs to individuals were relatively high. And the distortions of social organization that followed may ultimately prove disastrous. To oversimplify: insofar as any new economic system allowed the participants some of the emotional and intellectual satisfactions of the hunt, it represented at least a holding operation; insofar as it denied a majority of the

participants these satisfactions, it represented a definite loss. The
frustrations resulting from the repression of the full expression of the
hunting syndrome lie behind most of the anger and alienation that
have characterized socioeconomic revolt. Marx saw that "alienation"
robbed men of their contact with nature.[26] Contemporary workers are
alienated not only from the fruits of their labor but also from the roots
of their biology. Of course, revolution and revolt are often in the name
of equality and take the color of morality. Clearly the demanding
indulgences of the rich outrage the poor who must make of frugality a
virtue and turn self-denial into self-enhancement. It is plain that the
incompetence of generals and commissars oppresses those who are
forced to flee their clumsiness. The perception of inequity was the basis
of a new dialect for social dialogue—a manner of speaking not commonly heard in many places and often still unclearly understood where
it is most often used.

But perhaps we can go beyond this form of deprivation and callousness to another which is rooted more directly in our technological systems and our new customs of working than it is in our selfishness and
vested disinterest. Economies must not only provide bread (and even
wine), but they must also satisfy the provider: to deny a human enjoyment of work is to a person's behavioral needs as the denial of a
vitamin is to his blood, as movement is to his muscles. We have already
noted that humans invented work. This was so when we placed new
demands on an old creature. We created new milieus to do tasks done
otherwise when all managers were also colleagues, and when there
were no bosses but rather persons with whom one lived in nice proximity, who had a knack for a task that mattered, and who could be
trusted. Not so in agriculture, where the lord might live in Prague or
Bath or Alexandria. And certainly not so in industrial places where
the lord resides in the system, where the manager will move on elsewhere, and where a shiny head-office building will harbor plans to
scatter people as effectively as cavalry, and more tidily. It is a very
different matter for a worker to perform a minute task of a small part
of a larger construction than it is to prepare a hunting song, to run
as swiftly as the others to the scene, to communicate like musicians
about the feeling and pace of the business, and to conclude the matter
with failure or success but at least in familiar company and with the
knowledge that the task was worth the time, and the time was one's
own. Punch a time clock, and it punches back. The animal who invented calendars to assist in religious rituals got lumbered with clocks

whose intimate tacit tyranny is suspended in the most modern places only in playoff games, murder trials, wars, and such genuine crises where an answer is essential or a resolution the only thing worth waiting for.

The agricultural-pastoral phase, while depriving many of much in the way of behavioral satisfaction, did not entirely undermine psychic economy in the interests of material economy. In tribal agricultural systems there is still the small-scale face-to-face involvement, the immediate satisfaction of food needs through one's own labor, the making and unmaking of alliances and deals through the exchange of women, and the pressure toward redistribution. There is ample evidence that chiefs as such emerged simply as redistributive centers in economic systems that became more complex than the simple hunting band.[27] The chief's granaries, say the Bantu, are always open to the people.[28] The grain, cattle, and even wives that he receives as "tribute" eventually find their way back into the system again through the network of alliances and the generosity of feasts and festivals. Many systems remain "mixed" in the sense that some hunting is still done, or at least its analogue in tribal warfare—often highly ritualized—is carried on. There is continuity from generation to generation, and everyone is a part of the system to which he is responsible and which is responsible to him.[29]

The predominantly pastoral tribes have all these features, to which is added the advantage of movement, of nomadism.[30] The productive unit needed for herding has many analogies with the hunting group, even though the relationship to the animal world is radically altered. Again some hunting or some analogues to the hunt are practiced: at least the whole thing operates out of doors and in a context of movement across the country, passing from place to place, experiencing variety and exercising decision. The gardening and horticultural peoples[31] of the Pacific and Melanesia get their subsistence in peasant fashion from little plots of ground, but their activity in the vegetable gardens is simply the background and prelude to exciting and dangerous overseas trading expeditions by small groups of men in outrigger canoes. These expeditions have less to do with real trade than with the exchange of ceremonial objects among fixed "exchange partners" in various islands along fixed routes traveled in a fixed order. The ceremonial nature of these elaborate voyages was puzzling to anthropologists, until they realized that the exchange was an end in itself— that it simply creates and sustains relationships and that, although this is never stressed, it creates the analogue of the hunting expedition for people who live by growing tubers. This is what exchange is all about anyway, and the "useless" sea voyages of the Melanesians with their exchange of shell necklaces and coral beads are almost pure expressions of the principle: it is done for its own sake, for the intrinsic satisfactions that it brings the creature.[32]

The landlocked relatives of the Melanesians in New Guinea also live by pigs and tubers, and manage to find substitutes for the satisfactions of the sea voyages.[33] Elaborate trading parties formed of groups of related "allies" go off on long overland expeditions; here too the ceremony of aggressive trade is important. Head-hunting parties, largely concerned with vengeance and status validation, are similarly composed, and venture, like the Crow Indian war party, on raids into enemy territory. Warfare is highly stylized entertainment and consists largely of dodging enemy spears and demonstrating bravery. But all these things allow for the free play and elaboration of the tendency to exchange, to range, to face risks and dangers with colleagues, to deal, to ally, to compete, to triumph or mourn in concert, and above all to *participate* on the old hunting pattern. Given all this, those hours in the yam gardens may seem less onerous.

In all these cases the element of hunting-by-analogy rests not only on the expedition and the kill, but on the exercise of certain skills developed in the hunting economy. Of these, the business of ceremonial exchange is perhaps the most elusive and yet the most significant. It is almost akin to what ethologists call a "vacuum activity."[34] Birds that have never had a chance to peck at insects, and yet that in nature feed off them, will indulge in pecking activity on the walls of their cages or ceilings of rooms or wherever they are incarcerated. It is simply what they do, and they will do it even in the absence of the appropriate stimulus. Wind up chickens, and they start to peck: wind up human beings, and they start to exchange things. Exchange is in some ways the prime human skill, and in engaging in "pure" exchange we are simply exercising this skill, much as in running for sport we exercise our capacity to move swiftly through space.

Nothing could be further from the arena of action of our ancestral hunters than the factories emitting smoke and producing metals, than the pristine reasonableness of an automated plastics factory, than the perplexingly detailed massiveness of a large insurance firm. But even in these organizations, bits of the human biogrammar must still be audible and rhythms of its expression still apparent. It is now appropriate to look at industrial and postindustrial economies, to see how they reflect or inhibit what we came to be and are, and to raise that traditionally vexing question: Can economies be contrived better to fit people, instead of people being coerced, or tempted, to fit economies?

The division of labor is nothing new in itself.[35] Those who claim that the only complete human being is the one who does all the work necessary for survival himself are creating an unnecessary and improbable economic saint. The essence of exchange is that it deals with temporary deficits and surpluses of either food or weapons or clothes or time or affection or skill—whatever a community deems valuable, and whatever its members need to survive. Thoreau was an interesting character, and his uncontrolled experiment at Walden Pond a cheerful portrayal of the corrupted Rousseauist fantasy about natural man. But it is no more a metaphor for human potential or reality than a ranting mob. It was an extreme and joyful trick, but no lesson about man and no comment on our economies and our love of commerce and exchange. So unsure are we about our daily reality, and so bemused by the power of our theory of what it could be, that we can take with a straight face an ironic hermit's revenge on what he feared was burgeoning sanctimony about the necessity of industrialization. Thoreau was not only a charming metaphysical jester, he was also wrong. He once asked, tellingly, when a telegraph was installed between Boston and Bangor, "But do the people of Boston have anything to say to the people of Bangor?" The question implied that the answer was, "No, not really." In fact, the answer is, yes, they had, or if they had not, they soon found something to telegraph about. The first reality of industrial community is that it is based on the division of labor, which is an ancient good in itself, and the second is that it permits, even if it also compels, people to communicate with one another.

It is true that the division of labor is pushed further in industrial society than in any other. It is true that it is the basis of industrial efficiency, but it may also be true that it is the basis of industrial misery. Marx hated the division of labor, but his alternative was never clear.[36] Durkheim saw its obvious benefits for producing a more organic society with interdependent parts, but he saw, too, how easily it could lapse into anomie.[37] We can all see the devastating results of overspecialization in the Chaplinesque tragedy of the man whose whole working life is spent in turning nut after nut on car after car on the assembly line.[38] But it is not the division of labor in and of itself that produces this misery. We have to blend this ancient organizing principle with something else before we can produce the explosive mixture Marx rightly saw brewing in the grime of nineteenth-century industrial cities. That men should perform specific and allotted tasks, which, taken together, would produce a finished article or achieve a common goal, was neither new nor terrible in human evolution.

But the primitive division of skills in terms of which we evolved took place in the intimate context of the hunting group with all its characteristics. The contrast is not between the totally self-sufficient individual on the one hand, who never existed anyway, and the over-specialized and depersonalized individual on the other. It is between the depersonalized individual, and the specialized individual who is locked into a small group on equal terms with his fellows—who knows that through his network of alliances he can depend on a return from the group for his specialized effort. He is part of the redistributive network, and from the cumulative effects of his group's activities he can expect some reward. No matter how far down the pecking order he is, he is someone's ally through marriage or ceremonial exchange or partnership, and the group is responsible for him. He is not so much closely connected with the product of his *own* labor as he is with the product of the *joint* labors of his group, in a direct and satisfying way. The unalienated man is not the self-sufficient man at all, but the socially sufficient man—and it is this sense of social sufficiency that modern industrial organization endangers.

It does this by removing the mass of individuals from participation in the predatory process and turning them into "tools"—objects of exchange (to be bought and sold) rather than agents of exchange. The agricultural system did the same thing to peasants, but at least it left them something, some control of their lives and their haggling. Industry, like slavery, robbed men of even that. The arbitrary routines of factories with their callously unwholesome environments and the virtual interchangeability of one jobholder for another were symptoms of a new refinement in the elaboration of anomie. Women lost their womanhood, children lost their childhood, men lost their manhood, because machines demanded their time and small manipulations, and because the virtue of the free-enterprise system was such that higher wages and gentler conditions would quickly put an entrepreneur out of competitive business. One had to work because there was no vegetable garden from which to get food, and no hut to spend the night in. And one had to work in the miserable factories, because the system had few alternatives for the masses forced into cities. One sold one's time and one's unskilled labor the way the modern urban American poor in slums sell bottles of their blood, because it is what—or maybe

all—they have to sell. Selling one's labor to the factory was an innovation, a socioeconomic prostitution without even the dubious boon
of physical contact with one's buyer and without even the option to
charm, bargain, or threaten with guilt. The mercenary soldier also sold
his labor. But he saw some fairly immediate results—adventure, the
exercise of predatory skills, and not least, booty and women. The
factory worker had all the disadvantages of the peasant and none of
his advantages. Technically free, he was in effect a wage slave.

What did industry leave, if anything, of the satisfactions inherent
in the hunting animal's life-way? It had one advantage over a true
slave system: technically, at least, it allowed men and women to provide for their families with their own labor. It permitted them a small
feeling of effectiveness, which was, however, so precarious as to rob
it of real meaning. The threat of unemployment became a chronic
feature of the system, over which the individual had no control, and
was a constant reminder of his helplessness.[39] There is no unemployment among hunters. Employment is guaranteed even for slaves.

Like its agriculturally based predecessors, the industrial system
easily turned from redistribution to exploitation. Again, this had the
effect of concentrating predatory activity in the hands of a few; it condemned the majority to a role more like that of the exploited herds of
the pastoralists than that of the participant hunters. Marx's main insight was to see that this exploitation was not the result of human
wickedness, but a property of the system itself. The entrepreneur had
no choice but to exploit his workers, in the same way that the hunters
had no choice but to exploit their particular environment. But the
entrepreneur was not locked into any system of redistributive generosity. Individual spontaneous generosity was always present in the
form of charity, but the hunter's redistributive system never depended
on spontaneity. Even the tribal chief was expected—rather, obliged—
to give back that which he received. This was praised in song and tribal
legend as generosity, but the praise only underlined the obligatory
nature of the giving. There is strong pressure on the wealthy in industrial societies to redistribute their wealth in the form of public and
charitable benefactions—with often very beneficial results. But, as
Marx clearly saw, no number of gestures of goodwill could alter the
nature of the system. His predictions and remedies may have been
wrong, but his analysis was accurate enough. Eventually, and despite
the opposition of economic theorists, governments had to step in and
take over the redistributive functions that the system lacked. Sometimes this change was forced on nations by revolution, sometimes it

came gradually as a result of a series of pressures—workers' movements, the spread of joint-stock ownership, the growth of socialist ideologies, etc.—and it is still going on. But, by whatever means, it had to come.

There is no need to chronicle—or even list—the evils of the industrial revolution, or the built-in weaknesses of capitalist economies, or the necessities of responsible social welfare; they are all well enough known. It is enough here to show how any economic system, like any political system, has to take into account the kind of animal we are and the kind of social relationships with which we were evolved to cope. Our adaptation to the hunting economy predisposed us to expect certain satisfactions and to seek certain goals. Economies that fail to provide for these—be they capitalist, socialist, mixed, slave, peasant, or anything else—will founder as much because they fail to deliver the psychosocial as the material goods. The argument here is exactly the same as that for political systems; of course, economic and political systems cannot easily be separated. Any political system has to take into account the political nature of the animal, and no system could really ignore the fundamental satisfactions that the creature needed from its hierarchies, attention structures, coalitions, etc. Therefore, systems that condemn most of their members to places at the peripheries of power have problems similar to those that condemn often the same majority to positions outside the central networks of exchange, production, and distribution. In each case, the system capitalizes on some aspects of the biogram to the often disastrous exclusion of others.

Economic systems are customarily judged by their productivity and by their capacity for generating wealth and economic growth. But that is only one of the criteria for assessing them: our suggestion is that it is both humane and strategical to view such systems as means of providing not only wealth but also a measure of satisfaction for members and some sense of that mutual aid that may be part of the imperial animal's central orientation to his fellow man. We know enough now about wealth to understand that once some basic standard of food and shelter is provided, humans are enormously inventive about immediately creating new wants, which then become needs for some and luxuries for others. Our concern here is with not the "veterinarian" level of satisfying needs but with the behavioral consequences of economic activity. Some economic arrangements generate more wealth than others, but do they necessarily generate more satisfaction?

One of the basic satisfactions, we have argued, is a sense of participation in predatory activity and the consequent exercise of the skills and enjoyment of the rewards associated with it. Another satisfaction lies in the surety of being a participant in the redistributive system. All economies allow some participants these pleasures, but few economies allow them to all participants.[40] In this sense, welfare becomes neither a graceful display of the mercifulness and humanity of an economy nor a technical means of ensuring the health and consent of employed persons. It becomes, instead, as biological a right as the right to shelter, to basic food, to the protection by some agency against the force of others—as biological as the rights of children to the times and resources of adults. What becomes increasingly clear is the foolishness and cruelty of those who claim, in the name of biology, that the so-called strong must not aid the so-called weak.[41] A more accurate claim, in the name of biology, is that the very opposite is more likely the case. The most democratic communities are those based on the commonality of the human gene pool. Sharing resources to sustain those who carry these various genes is nothing more than prudent— and nothing less than a conservative estimate that there is some good for the species in all people. Who can decide at any point which characteristics are more desirable and which more redundant? The narrow-mindedness of eugenicists and all those who quibble about superior and inferior "stocks" represents a crude distortion of the lesson of population genetics.[42]

A person who *receives* nothing from his community loses an important stimulus of his humanity, and so does a person unable to *contribute* to his fellow citizens. This is not to say that a man will be made desperately unhappy if he cannot extend the benefits of his Swiss bank account to Indian peasants. But if he cannot work among his fellows, if he cannot advise, if he cannot offer his experience as a guide to other people's efforts, if he cannot influence the young or satisfy the old, he is deprived of an exchange as meaningful as speech and a basis of commitment more general than patriotism and more energizing than theories of responsibility. The saddest examples of those who lose this aspect of humanness are the unemployed and the unemployables—those deemed unworthy of employment by their fellows and unable to contrive some tasks for themselves which will earn them money and a dignified place in the community. In societies which use it, money is an important index of personal worth, particularly in the basic sense that one either can earn it or cannot. Welfare money is not the same as worked-for money; there is now ample evidence of the effects on personality of receiving welfare for a long time and of being persistently unable to get worthwhile and enhancing work. It is not simply work itself that is at issue here, but the sense an individual may have of being skilled in some way that will allow him some broadly beneficial effect on his community—even as a Buddhist priest who does nothing but encounter the perplexities of his fellow man, or a retired man who stops traffic at a corner for schoolchildren going home, or a girl reading stories to a blind child.

This is not to say that receiving welfare funds is morally bad. It is to say that the right to give, in terms of the kind of active gregarious animal we are, is just as necessary as the right to receive—which progressive legislation has at last reassured with schemes of welfare. And yet this is not progress at all: it is regress to the interdependence of prehistory and to the articulated and assured communality of hunting humans. The dual claims of a "right to work" and "to each according to his need" are not highly developed moral precepts issuing from advanced progressive thought, but some of the most basic demands of the human organism—the political philosopher's elusive "natural rights." In demanding the right to be allowed to give and to receive and to participate, men are simply demanding the right to be human and to indulge in that basic set of exchanges that so defines them.

These are only baseline provisions—like having arms or legs. It is not only the job and the security that count, but the manner in which the job is done. Again, the economy can either maximize the predatory satisfactions or deny them. Usually it gives full rein only to a few of its participants, and the problem is that these then become predators on the rest. Other men become defined as "environment," to be preyed upon and exploited; here, just as in bureaucracy, people are defined as things, tools, objects—as "labor" or "consumer." The satisfactions for the few, however, can be enormous.

In the capitalist, or free-enterprise, economy the entrepreneur is given free play for his predatory tendencies. His small-farmer cousin may be nearer the soil but the urban businessman is nearer his own biology. Outside the teen-age gang, the outlaw band, or the military platoon, that delight of the theoretical economist's dream of perfect competition, the small firm, is the nearest thing we have today to a hunting group. In many ways we can gain by seeing it side by side with its seeming opposite, the illegal, extrasocietal, violent band of outlaws. This is a predatory group par excellence; it is, then, surely not accidental that it is one of the more enduring sacred cows of the entertainment business. From Robin Hood to Jesse James the story has been the same: the band, while often technically democratic, is in fact based on a powerful principle of dominance, with often a latent and intense dominance struggle as part of the plot. It is composed of males joined together by strong bonds. Females play service roles of one kind or another to the males, and often act as catalysts in the plot, either through their provocation of male rivalry, which disrupts the bonds, or through their perfidy, which destroys the group, or through their weakness, which in turn weakens the group. The group preys on the "environment," which in this case is the lawful society. Most of the tension in the group is caused by disputes and haggling over the division of the "kill" and its ultimate disposition. The men make elaborate deals with each other concerning the division of the spoils. In legend, if not in fact, the group is seen as a redistributive agency which takes from the exploiters (barons, bankers, etc.) and gives to the deserving poor, or at least represents the poor in its attacks on the rich. The band, finally, is nomadic, although usually with a home base, and it follows its prey over a fairly extensive range. It is all very familiar and thrilling. The tension involved in the gambling or risk-taking element is essential to good entertainment.

Because of its graphic and violent nature, the outlaw's life is naturally considered better entertainment value than, say, the success story of a business firm. But in essence the same elements are there, even if no one gets killed during the board meeting. At least there the "kill" is not quite so obvious, but the tender, the contract, the take-over, the franchise, and the account all have the attributes of the predatory goal. Gambling and risk are a first principle: even in the abstruse realms of economic theory, profits are the rewards of risk-taking. The business team is most often all-male. Women, usually seen as disruptive to its enterprise, are there only to serve in some way. Establishing and maintaining a hierarchy of command and authority is central to the business organization. The division of profits, the principle on which this will operate, and the control over this re-distributive activity—even if it is only the declaration of the dividend —are everywhere in evidence. Haggling, wheeling and dealing, and the making of alliances—not uncommonly by marriage, in some cases— are even more important here than among the outlaws. Ceremonial gift-giving is often rife, and used as a way of cementing or promoting alliances—even if only in the form of elaborate entertainment—from the two-martini business lunch to the long weekend at the hunting lodge. Triumph ceremonies, feasts, and elaborate initiation procedures complete the picture.

Though outlaws and small businessmen differ in what they do and what people think of them, there are similar units in their behavior. The maneuver about position, tactics, and the spoils, the estimation of value—and no creature is vainer and more sensitive to his reputation than an outlaw or entrepreneur—and all the elements of risk and success cut across both enterprises. But groups that cohere and take the right risks with the right resources are bound to grow larger. What happens to this pattern of quasi-hunting action under these new circumstances? What do people do for drama and a sense of easy competence when they are just single units of populous endeavors? When the assistant manager of a shoe section in a mediocre department store returns home, does he carry with him any sense of triumph or even self-regard?

Typically, and here the slang expresses a reality, it is the big wheels who deal; the bosses hunt and calculate, risk and fight, threaten and accommodate, run and pause. In the huge corporation, the very word "executive" implies the facts of the matter. The executive *does* things; he is not a worker, he is a different form of person; he is paid by the year, not the hour, because his scope is so great and his plans so complex. The painful fact is, he *is* different. The executive can take a place in the old hunting program, he can make a difference because of what he does, and he can enjoy the complicated and often hazardous decision-making his job demands. His employees, and the employees of his colleague executives, are a class apart. They are to the executive as bullets, horses, and hardtack are to the outlaw—items to be used in the pursuit of goals. He decides their income and fixes how and with whom they will spend their working hours. He can trade them off by selling a company, or purchase the products of their skills by buying one. He can lay them off, fire them, and insist on eating in a different dining room to preserve the thick sense of power the sleek dominant males at the center of the hierarchy create like some electric current and share like some bequest from an unusually discerning providence. He votes himself stock options and gives himself cars and expense accounts on the basic ground that his very being is so important that all comfort must accompany his mighty efforts. His status is affirmed for all to see and mark. Small wonder he trumpets sober praise of this system which seems so sensible to him; it is no surprise that industrial executives in capitalist and communist countries alike feel properly rewarded only by disproportionate rewards. They, after all, are the ones who do the dramatic and hardy things that we value. They execute, they do not work. They may be tools of the system overall, but their satisfactions are qualitatively different from those of the assembly-line workers, and their options always more momentous.

But they are dispensable too. The jobs they fill are so desirable that there are always hundreds aching to occupy the swivel chairs of power. One need only look at the advertising executive earning a vast sum to know his awareness of his precarious grip on this astonishing boon. He must keep hard to the front line all the time, be beautifully groomed and fit, be as contemporary in all things as decency permits, be the effortlessly effective master of the magic words and pictures he wields in sales campaign after sales compaign. Let him lose a large account, and see the sleekness become tighter, the confidence somewhat urgent, the grasp somewhat cautious or more headstrong. He is part of a benign and splendid group, but he was not born to it. It can be taken away from him, with all the money and the trappings. He has to be at the front line all the time, because the prey is fat and delicious. But it is not his own village that helps him hunt the prey, it is some people whom he must constantly impress and who can turn on him should his work be badly fashioned or should he slip twice or antagonize some statesman from a wealthy advertiser. He can get a lot, but having got it, he is then in the frightening position of perhaps losing as much as that, and more, because the future becomes suddenly gray and the terrain rough.[43]

Let us not ache over the adman teetering on the edge of a thousand dollars a week for pocket money. But his dilemma is in this sense only more glorious and dramatic than the same problem his secretary faces or his chauffeur or barber. He can be splendid and return to his home on the hill bearing cruise tickets and hi-fidelity structures. But he faces the same bleak sense of personal finiteness.

In sum: once the hunting-business-outlaw band turns into the large, impersonal organization, the glories and penalties of the predatory way become the province chiefly of the dominants. The majority, whether of the Mafia or General Motors, are condemned, as "workers," to become tools; again, the opportunity to exercise predatory skills is the province of the few. Even so, there are restrictions. Labor unions intervene to limit the freedom of action of executives. In creating unions, workers became effective predators of a kind themselves.

Unions were at first almost outlaw bands. Secret, continually harassed by police, they demanded of their members high dedication and the ability to assume risk and bear unpleasantness in the face of the larger goal of affecting the division of spoils and control of workers' destinies. Early unions allowed workers a stringent dignity. Later on, the same processes of bureaucratization that affect the entrepreneur affected them too, and union leaders became part of a wider group related to government and business, though with a particular mandate from a clear economic interest group.[44]

If unions were one disruptive subsystem, the government was another. It became patently and painfully clear that free enterprise as a system would not ensure adequate distributive justice just as the communist state would not wither away. Accordingly, through the weapon of taxation and the techniques of economics, capitalist governments sought to make some more acceptable allocation of wealth without inhibiting too much these businessmen presumed to create it. In effect, unionization and government intervention in private economic matters are a close approximation of a pattern of redistributive justice that hunters required. For even very cynical governments are aware of the limits of their options. In any system the relationship between politics and economic activity becomes clear at the point at which the following decisions are made: How much do we redistribute? How much goes for new tools and shrines? How much can the major hunters appropriate? What leeway have individuals in deciding how much of what the community produces should be theirs?

The basic economic propensities of the human animal are compatible with various systems in various degrees. Some systems maximize some potentials and ignore others, offer some satisfactions and deny others. What is important is not only how systems create and distribute wealth but also how they allocate the right to *behave* in certain crucial human ways. A Catholic priest, for example, is given food, clothing, and shelter, but denied sex. Some economies provide these staples for their members but deny all or most of them the right to act in ways that are as basic to the organism's "natural" behavior as sex itself.

In theory at least, laissez-faire capitalist economy gives a very full rein to predatory tendencies and those patterns of behavior associated with them. A large number of small competing firms replicates the hunting situation in many respects. This is in human terms, as well as in economic theory, "perfect competition." This pattern is also easily upset, both by its own dynamics and by its tendencies to monopolistic competition on the one hand and polarization of wealth on the other— as Marx saw. The spread of ownership among thousands of shareholders and the rise of managerial elites and their bureaucratic structures can also alter it beyond recognition. All these tendencies combine to rob the majority of a role in the predatory process and make impossible any equitable system of distribution—either of wealth or of satisfying behavior.

The socialist or communist economy, on the other hand, maximizes the redistributive functions—at least in theory—but plays down or eliminates altogether the predatory patterns of its capitalist counterpart. Indeed, this is its moral object. In social welfare, health, education, housing, and employment, the individual (or family) has a rightful claim on the community's resources—a community to which he is also allowed and encouraged to give his labor, with a sense of important participation and symbolic reward for Stakhanovite effort. But this economy is constantly in danger of stagnation, precisely because competition and predatory infighting have been removed. In removing them, the economy has removed a great deal of initiative and innovation and the keenness that provokes efficiency when profit or even survival are at stake. The cautious experiments at feeding competitive "capitalist" mechanisms into otherwise socialized economies reflect a grudging recognition of the problem.[45]

The mixed economy might seem to be the solution. Predatory free enterprise would be allowed, but the government would own the larger service industries (railways, banks, hospitals, etc.) and act through legislation and taxation as a redistributive center. But this raises the problem of finding a reasonable balance among the subsystems; it could well be that such economies would get the worst, rather than the best, of both worlds. If they really proved inefficient, they would end up by frustrating all the behavioral propensities of their members sufficiently to provoke considerable unrest. The problem is the same as for large bureaucratic structures. We were not evolved to cope with organization on this scale, it is almost literally inhuman, however there is no way back; we cannot envisage handling large populations with complex economies in any other way. But we are not here to sit in judgment on economic systems or theories, simply to point out what it is about the evolved behavior of man-the-economizing-animal that such systems and theories have to take into account.

One thing that every system has to take into account is the sexual division of labor. We have maintained elsewhere in this book that the degree and nature of the participation of men and women in the economy is very different. We suggested that this goes back to the evolution of the hunting animal, where male and female were assigned radically different tasks, each essential to the success and survival of the group, and that therefore they were subjected to very different kinds of selection pressure.[46] We can come to the same conclusions about economic as political division of labor, but the details differ insofar as women are of necessity deeply involved in the economy at the same time that they are shut out completely from any political activity. But it can be predicted that in each case men will want to keep them from controlling the system, and women will be unlikely to make effective inroads on any scale into the centers of economic power. The roots of this dilemma are deep in our history. Women did not hunt.

Some of the physical differences between males and females, which are related to different roles during our formative evolution, have already been discussed, but it is necessary here to note some of them briefly in order to root behavior directly in its biological context. These differences are first of all based on clear reproductive distinctions. Female reproductive physiology places simple structural limits on what women can do. They must have wider pelvises than men, because the birth canal must accommodate the infant's large head; therefore they use more energy in locomotion, because their hips swing wider from side to side. In addition, the fat deposits on their buttocks are heavy and use up precious energy. Accordingly, women cannot run as quickly or for as long as men. Of course, there is a normal curve of variation here as elsewhere, and some women will run faster than some men; the curve of variations of the male and female will overlap, but the curves are nonetheless real and significant. This is true also of the ability to throw objects such as balls and spears—a matter obviously relevant to a hunting animal. Furthermore, females adapt less readily than males to changes in temperature—a considerable hazard in hot environments. We now know that there are predictable and disruptive effects on female performance that depend on their menstrual cycles;[47] and it remains an abiding index of male callousness to female realities that rarely are these normal and foreseeable stimuli considered in arranging work and even domestic schedules. (This can become positively inequitable when females are engaged in crucial tests of various kinds. For example, some reports indicate that females achieve some fourteen-percent-lower grades on examination during the premenstrual days, when they are at a considerable disadvantage. Depending on the nature of the examination in question, a woman may be affected for her entire career because she could not demonstrate the ability she normally has. Conversely, if she were to confront this examination at mid-cycle, her performance might be better than usual. In another milieu, the first female Russian astronaut has argued that while women could do the tasks men do, it was still necessary to take the menstrual cycle into account in managing the routines of space flight.[48])

There is a series of other differences of this kind that could be described, but it is clearly more relevant today to focus less upon explicitly physical features of work performance than upon those involving emotional, intellectual, and social skills and enthusiasm. There are, after all, relatively few jobs in industrial societies that demand strength of arm and speed of foot so greedily that females could not meet the needs. Women can and do drive huge trucks and airplanes, operate elaborate machines, and physically cope with the air-conditioned cabins and power-assisted controls of huge cranes and earth movers. There is very little justification for assuming that any job that men now do women could not do too. And vice versa: aside from bearing and suckling children, there is no characteristically women's work that some husky baritone copilot could not do. Our ideas about equality and the right to widespread social participation of men and women all urge us overwhelmingly in the direction of a society in which male and female roles are more or less interchangeable and in which no particular cachet or stigma attaches to men doing what was once women's work, or the other way around.

But the reality falls far short of the ideal. The potentialities are felt only weakly in what actually still goes on. One of the few general rules about human cultures that anthropologists can safely affirm is that in all known societies a distinction is made between "women's work" and "men's work." The inconsistencies in attitudes are plentiful and comical from one society to another; in one place, men will carry water and women will plant yams, while ten villages away the inhabitants will defend with high intensity the obviously correct proposition that women must carry water and men plant yams. So the first point is that even where the distinctions are not especially reasonable or defensible, they are inevitably made. The next general feature of this division of labor by sex is that some jobs are widely thought to be the rightful provinces of males, and others of females. Hunting, the manufacture of weapons, and the construction of boats are almost universally thought to be male, while such tasks as grinding seeds and gathering nuts are reckoned females' work nearly everywhere. This follows understandably from the hunting past.

But what is not easily understandable is the extraordinary persistence of the division of labor by sex in societies with different forms and levels of industrialization, different climates, different histories, and varying notions about the good man, the good woman, and the good life. This must be explained.

We have already indicated how persistent male-female differences both baffled ideologists and violated the laws of chance. There is no particular reason why females must be part of formal politics. But women must work, and they must be part of the economy, any economy. Of course, in broad terms, they always are, to the extent that they do housework, prepare food, mind and socialize children, and attend to the clothing of their family. That this is not regarded as work in the sense that factory labor is, is a conceit of economic analysis, and part, besides, of a general devaluation of intimate (as opposed to public) activity—a devaluation that applies to the do-it-yourself man who contributes nothing to the Gross National Product when he builds himself a bookshelf but pushes it up two hundred dollars when he buys one from a shop. Women have to be in on the economy. But a basic element of the biogrammar here seems to be that they have to be in on only specially defined terms: there appears to be a tendency to define some work as female and some as male, and to maintain the distinction whatever the content and whatever the cost. This is the same principle of male-bond–female-exclusion that, in politics, so rudely circumscribed the female role. In economic matters, since females cannot be excluded totally, at least they can be segregated into some set of specific activities.

But does it go deeper even than this? We argued that the central arena of politics was male because of differences in male and female potentials for successful large-scale competitive bonding. Insofar as the central arena of economic life demands similar organization, we would expect males to dominate it. Where business and industry, or the organization of production consumption and exchange, generally demand cohort activity, it will be male cohorts who will be in evidence. Where control is involved, men will work together and women will be excluded or allowed in only if they agree to play male roles in a male fashion. Women usually lend themselves to this strategy by agreeing that it is not specific female skills that they bring to their roles as executives, and that in simply filling male positions they are substitute males. This attitude strictly delimits female behavior in business.

It also accounts for the pressures against overt sexuality on the job. Seductive arts are disruptive of male cohesion. The outlaw band or the board of directors assumes that they are not part of its normal routines, and women who want seriously to play the power game must leave their false eyelashes at home.

This may seem a facetious point, but it is a point that underlies a very serious truth. False eyelashes are supplements to female court-ship-display behavior. They enhance the "recognition flutter" and coy covering of the dilating pupils in courtship exchanges.[49] As such they are part of the apparatus that aids in promoting and cementing the courtship bond. This is a male-female bond and operates in the arena of sexual competition and eventual mating. It is outside of and inimical to the male-male bond that operates in the politicoeconomic arena for purposes of cohort formation and maintenance in the pursuit of effec-tive defense and predation. This is a point difficult, of course, to prove, yet it seems clear enough: that one serious if tragicomic reason for the difficulty females experience in male work groups is not that males dislike females but rather that the force of their enthusiasm for females can disrupt the work and endanger the integrity of groups of men.

We needn't waste sympathy on men harassed by such enthusiasm for women that they reject them as colleagues and force them into occupa-tional ghettos so the precious male mystique will remain undisturbed. Our suggestion is that it is not malice alone, and not prejudice only, and not just cultural lag and individual fear that stimulate an obvious antifemale inequity. The same pattern emerges both in coun-tries that devalue women and in countries that eagerly support them. The opportunities for women in the economy of the United States have declined over the past sixty years, though the number of women with advanced and technical education has increased enormously.[50] The Israeli experience, both in and out of the kibbutz, is even more dis-couraging to those who looked to their ideology about sexual equality to produce radical social change. And in Russia itself, the first and most important revolutionary society, the position of women has not been improved in any sense commensurate with either the expressed idealism of the community or its willingness to try relatively egali-tarian socioeconomic forms and approaches to the ownership and con-trol of wealth.

So it cannot be a conspiracy of men against women that once swept the world that now—so apparently securely—sets limits to the range of female options to enter the powerful macrostructures of economic life. The evidence against conspiracy comes from too heterogeneous a set of places: females are obviously able to do the tasks men can— that is, when they are given the opportunity; males are unlikely to have deliberately thought up ways of maintaining women in their homes for domestic and sexual convenience and then brainwashed them to accept such an exploitative situation—if exploitative it is. Perhaps, as with some of the other bonds, we are dealing here with a regularity of the biogrammar that has to do with ancient forms of survival that mark us still today. That the thrilling and elaborate innovations of our technology seem to have relatively little effect on the work relationships of men and women attests either to the un-importance of technology—which is foolish—or to the importance of the biogrammar. Though puritans and Calvinists will shrink at the thought, it may be true that social relationships are more important than work encounters, and the apparent rigidity of the sexual division of labor represents both men and women "voting with their feet" for the notion that difference does not necessarily connote inferiority or superiority, and that the division of labor is not necessarily the squalid display of human invidiousness that, for example, racism undoubtedly is. The sexual division of labor has no racial home. The analogy is faulty because sex differences are important biologically and tangible behaviorally, whereas racial ones are unimportant biologically and meaningless behaviorally. The bad analogy confuses policy even more than it confuses people: to avoid the consequences of racism, it is imperative that all people be treated equally, but to avoid the features of the sexual division of labor that many men and women find un-desirable, it may be necessary to treat men and women differently and not deny their real biologies in the name of theoretical equities.

In the same way that sexual intercourse must not only result in offspring but also be enjoyable for its own sake if a mating bond is to "take," so economic activity must not only result in the production of wealth but also provide behavioral satisfactions if people are to realize their humanity. That economies can be dehumanizing is a common-place, but critics of inhuman economic systems have had a hard time locating the truly human element that is at best simply lacking or at worst brutally denied in so many wealth-producing, people-consuming economic machines. The only "psychology" that economists assume is necessary to an understanding of economic man is that he be "rational" —that he can see the difference between the same item at a high price and at a low price, and that he choose the latter as preferable.[51] Economists would undoubtedly hold that the point about economies not providing satisfactions—like Marx's point about their producing alienation—referred to strictly extraeconomic aspects of behavior. But the opposite can be maintained. Economic behavior is as much a part of human nature as sexual behavior: to take away a man's right to exchange, to make deals, to be in debt and to repay, is as damaging as to take away his right to sexual satisfaction. It may even be more damaging, for a man can, after all, relieve his physical sexual tensions himself without help, whereas he cannot make exchanges without a partner. The heart of the argument here is that exchanging is the fundamental human act and that to deny it is indeed to deny humanity.[52]

This is another set of instructions in the wiring of the behavioral repertoire. As with politics and with personal bonds, we can write either compatible or incompatible programs. But we are feeding them not into a void but into an active, demanding organism—an organism demanding to be allowed to behave economically in the way that it has evolved to behave. To revert to the other analogy, certain very specific rules of the human biogrammar can be violated only at the risk of considerable peril. The amount of variety in the spoken language that is possible is very great indeed—as long as the rules are observed. Economic behavioral languages that disobey the rules break down all too blatantly. It seems, in fact, that they are in some ways the most vulnerable. There is considerably greater latitude in the political arrangements we can make without risking gibberish. Perhaps this is because we are still playing primate politics, whereas economies are species-specified—aspects of human behavior deeply implicated in the transition to humanity that took place through the hunting revolution.

The more general points about economic man and human economic systems can be briefly summarized.

The basic and differential feature of human economic systems is property, which differs from animal territory in that it is in its very essence something that can be exchanged.

The exchange of property (real or incorporeal) is the basic act of truly human social relationships.

These social relationships are created through indebtedness as a result of giving (which creates a debt), receiving (which in turn creates an obligation), and of giving back (which fulfills the obligation).

The socioeconomic system is therefore a credit system in which everyone always owes something to someone else. The importance of the giver-receiver, creditor-debtor relationship is often expressed in acts of ceremonial or "pure" exchange.

This basic pattern evolved in a hunting context that molded its content and direction. The basic economic group is the hunting group or its analogue, and basic economic activity is on the predatory model.

In consequence, all the following features figured prominently in the evolution of human economic behavior: cooperation for competition; division of labor; exchange and alliance; participation in risk-taking; a sexual division of function; and a redistributive system. That this begins to apply—however incipiently and inadequately—not only between individuals but also between nations suggests the strength of the pattern of giving, taking, and sharing.

6.

THE
BENIGN
OPPRESSION

EDUCATION HAS ONLY a little to do with the transfer of objective information. Its purpose—and it starts at birth and continues into old age—is to produce acceptable members of the community. It substitutes for instinct the inculcation of fixed habits of thought and action. It is the end product of the trend in mammalian evolution toward a greater use of learning and a longer learning period. It is another illustration of the refractory truth that our uniqueness lies in being more mammalian than the other mammals, not qualitatively different from them. Among all the social mammals, learning becomes very important, since instinct cannot cope with the complexities of social life. The instructions in the genes become more general and open-ended; they consist more and more of instructions to *learn* rather than simply instructions to *perform*.[1] In this evolution the growing cortex has two crucial functions: it provides for greater memory storage, and it promotes ease of self-control or inhibition.[2] Thus impulses come under the control of thought, of hindsight and foresight, of knowledge, of the process of deferred gratification—the knowledge that giving up immediate pleasure may lead to greater pleasure in the future. The advantage in flexibility of such a system is obvious, but it has its costs. If the learning is ineffective, there is no instinct to take over automatically. The more prolonged and complicated the learning process, the more likely things are to go wrong, because there are more choice points and thus more opportunity for wrong choices. To compensate, the learning process has to do something very curious: it has to instill into the organism patterns of behavior that are, in their effects, the same as instincts. They must be general in the population, relatively unmodifiable, and relatively automatic in their functioning. Loosely we call these patterns habits, and inculcating them is what most education is about.[3]

This transfer from instinct to learning—a transfer to a different kind of wiring system—has gone further in man than in any other mammal. In primate socialization there is little in the way of teaching. Most primate learning consists of picking up behavior patterns and information through play, observation, and imitation. Among some carnivores it seems that the deliberate inculcation of behavior is at work when the young are "taught" hunting.[4] This may be an interesting clue in examining the shift of emphasis, not only from instinct to learning, but within the process of learning itself, from learning to teaching. Onto the primate learning patterns were grafted the new urgencies resulting from the transition to hunting. Society became more complex: knowledge was accumulated, and social control began to involve processes more subtle than gestures of threat and appeasement.

Ultimately, a thing unheard of in nature was invented to take care of the programming of the human young—the teacher. The amount of information that the young human has to store in order to deal with the complexities and absurdities of civilized society is such that the species can no longer depend on simply picking it up during the normal processes of living. Nor is the average adult able to carry enough of this information to pass it on to his own children.

A specialist class of teachers is needed. Children are taken away from their "natural" learning environments and put into specially constructed, highly artificial environments. These are devoted solely to the instilling of knowledge and habits more or less related to the children's futures as members of the community.

But even where there are no formal schools, no paid teachers, and no packs of students, there is still education.[5] A broad notion of education must be used here, not just one that rests on printed curricula and fifteen minutes for recess. Every human gets educated, though not all go to school. A baby whose parent dangles a mobile in front of its eyes is learning coordination and delight in objects. The small child jumping, at first timidly, from a medium-high fence, is learning something about gravity and his skill in dealing with his falling body. The young fisherman sharing a beer with his elders in a seashore bar is learning, if indirectly, how to heed the tides. A middle-aged man talking with an old man can apprehend what the state of being old is, how it represents itself in experience, and how it can be sensibly encountered. Every time we see a movie, stare at a new cut of coat, fiddle with the parts of a simple gadget, try to cook a favorite food in a novel way, we are learning, educating ourselves, and being educated. For most of us the limits on what we can learn, if we have the time and will, are so far away from our present skills and knowledge that we need have no fear of running out of subjects. We are not just plastic animals, we are also porous. Not only do we try to learn about what we already know, but we also try to find out what we do not know. We have recently come to honor scientists who prove to us how imperfect our grasp is of where we live and why we do what we do. If we are imperial animals, part of the empire we claim and adorn is in our own heads. Whether we are having fun with making riddles and doing crosswords for no other reason than just doing them, or puzzling about the architecture of Assyria and the structure of the gene, we are probing and handling our environment.

We are all active participants in the learning process, and not simply the passive learning machines of the behaviorists that can be "trained" only by processes of reward and punishment. Education involves our whole beings, not just our intellectual forebrain processes. These latter provide for rational learning in the same way that they provide for rationality in economic decision-making. The argument here is the same as for economics: to concentrate solely on these rational processes is to ignore the satisfactions and conditions under which either educational or economic rationality operates effectively. The forebrain can certainly handle the formalities of learning mathematics, but if the teaching of mathematics is done in a way that obstructs the normal motivations of curiosity in the young human primate, then no amount of formal rationality can repair this deprivation. It is an unbalanced diet lacking in vital behavioral vitamins; only too often we see the results in "learning failures," "behavioral problems," "learning blocks," and "dropouts."[6] The process of creating a desirable "whole man" and "whole woman"—one ideal of most formal educational systems—itself involves the whole person. To ignore this is as foolish as to ignore the health of a dancer in allocating ballet roles, or to assume that only the fingers and the feet constitute the pianist. The tedious and traditional conflict between "instinct" and "learning" is fruitless and beside the point. If anything, we have a propensity to learn, as higher animals do. And we also have a propensity to teach. These combine to make the teacher-student relationship a potentially very satisfying one. That it often is not may very well mean that the context is wrong, that the rewards are too removed from the encounter, and that what is primarily a social relationship has become a technical transaction between organisms insufficiently comparable to make exchange agreeable or even possible.

Criticism of formal educational systems is commonplace, and there is no need to add to the catalog of complaints.[7] Everyone knows that the patient is sick, but the diagnoses are as numerous as the doctors, and some of the proposed cures more disturbing than the illness. Here we want to locate, if we can, the basic biogrammar of the system of education. Then we can look at educative processes in human society to see how they either conform to or distort this grammar, and if they conform to it, whether they put it to eloquent or clumsy use.

What are the basic instructions of the educational biogrammar for the human primate? Like all other behavior systems, it has two layers—the underlying primate layer, and the additions and modifications that hunting brought in its wake.

Primates want to live as much as humans do, and living involves them in many of the complications it presents to us. Yet primates learn how to get on, what to eat and where, with whom to fight and to whom to show respect, how to play and how to threaten. They learn the social prelude to mating. Primate mothers are more skilled with their second infant than with their first. It requires no particular imagination to see how many of their simple underlying forms of social life are cousins to our own; it is clear now that they learn this social formality, and that *they want to do so.* That young monkeys learn things and want to learn things is just as predictable as that they get hungry and that after they eat, they digest. They are fortunate in that they have solved the problem of relevance in education: monkey see, monkey do—and what he does do is pertinent to surviving and to being sociable. Not for a monkey the puzzling business of deciding the relevance of algebra to being a good field-hockey player, and the importance of the names of presidents and kings for decorating the gymnasium for a dance. Monkeys are spared the cynical gap between sanctimonious visions of how our societies are supposed to work and the ghetto children's emergent understanding that the numbers man and the cop both violate the version of truth so confidently asserted by teachers and elders and by official spokesmen of mythic culture. This violation recurs in human community after human community; cynicism is an extra dimension of human educational systems. For primates there is no such highly evolved feature of growing up. All the dimensions are plain, and all the characters are there in front of the face. Learning is an emotionally rich enterprise, part of a lively network of encounters and retreats. It may now be useful to spell out what and how our cousins learn at "school."

It is too simple to say that they learn by imitation. Of course they do, but their imitating is embedded in a network of social relationships. In the earliest part of its life the young primate learns primarily about its relationship to its mother. It literally clings to her. As long as the mother-child bond is firmly established, the young animal will begin to explore in ever-widening circles, always returning when frightened in any way. Once it has learned the basic lesson that its mother is there at all times to be turned to, it will begin to unleash its curiosity on the social and physical environment. What it learns at this stage is a basic security and confidence, without which its motivation to explore is severely impaired.[8] This underscores the importance of the mother-child bond. It is not only emotional maturity that is affected by the bond, but the capacity to learn in general. Bold exploration and mischievous curiosity,[9] the desire to manipulate and investigate the environment—none of these will successfully mature if the young animal lacks a sense of security. It will go out into the world—physically and intellectually—only if it has somewhere to come back to in case of emergency, or just plain fright.[10]

This sense of security is a kind of overdrive, a facilitating mechanism that stimulates a wide range of activities necessary to the learning process. The lack of it at best inhibits, and at worst cripples, the whole range of learning behaviors. It may very well, for example, inhibit the animal's capacity to play and thus cut it off from the most important of all learning experiences.

Play: schooltime is divided into work and play periods; our lives are divided unhappily and unevenly between work and play. We speak of "schoolwork," but the compound word "schoolplay" would appear simply ridiculous. Learning has become identified with working, and children plow through the assigned pages in their "workbooks" with the same glum persistance as the peasant behind his oxen. No other primate would make or understand this distinction. The first transition the young primate makes is from his mother to his peers. But before this he has started to become playful.[11] He romps around his mother and possibly his older siblings, and he bothers the big males, who tolerate him in a way that would never be tolerated from his older brothers. After he has found his feet, his playfulness with his peers increases, and becomes intense. Playing becomes a full-time activity. Games of hide-and-seek and follow-the-leader teach the young animal to use the terrain, to maneuver through the trees, to develop skills in discriminating between objects, and above all to relate to his fellows through a knowledge of his own strengths and weaknesses. In all this "play" he is learning through active participation. No one teaches him anything; at best, adults will chastise and sometimes divert or control in a mild way, but they do not instruct. If he is bothering the big males too much, the mother chimpanzee will grab him and lead him away. In a savanna baboon troop the group of playmates is always watched by a big male, to provide protection (and unintentionally a sense of security), but also to break up quarrels if they become too rough. A mother chimpanzee will "termite" (use prepared twigs to pick ants out of anthills) while her infant climbs all over her, watches at ridiculously close quarters, and hinders her efforts with his clowning. She takes little or no notice. But he will taste the ants and observe the performance and imitate it many times until he is himself an expert with the peeled twigs.[12]

But mostly he is learning role-playing. He is learning what dominance and submission mean, when and whom to groom, when and how to try his strength and exercise restraint. He is storing up incredible amounts of information, but not as a passive learner. Perhaps the most important thing of all is that he is *moving about*. The pleasure he has learned to take in the widening range of things he can do well with his body is wedded to the social actions that are features of his particular and unique "personality" and place him in his community. His high-energy output is matched by a high-information input; he constantly trades energy for information. He is not a receptor only, but a seeker-out, a seemingly inexhaustible investigator. He actively solicits and provokes stimuli. And, most significantly, this play-learning gives him enjoyment, pleasure in doing and risking within the framework of security provided by his mother in the first instance, and by the social organization of his troop under the control of the big males in the second.

For the growing primate, learning is inseparable not only from playing but also from living—from what he himself can see as relevant to what he does. No little primate has to sit down and relate the bad deeds of Henry VIII to the realities of his own existence. There is an immediate feedback from what he learns to what he does, since he learns through doing, and doing is the same as being, as existing in society and through society and for society. Thus in his rough-and-tumble play with the originally democratic play group, he gradually learns to sort out those he can beat from those he cannot; he learns how to appease those stronger than himself whom he has provoked too much; he learns how to threaten those less tough than himself who assert themselves too much; he learns the limits of his own capacity to control and to cajole; he learns how to associate with peers to achieve joint ends. All this learning is of immediate and continuing relevance, since it is with these peers that he may spend his whole life.[13]

It is in the context of the whole life cycle that learning has to be seen. We have already discussed the importance of the mother-infant bond. From the Harlows' experiments with isolated and badly mothered infants, we know that once a rhesus macaque has been deprived of affection and even physical contact, no amount of subsequent experience can totally reverse the traumatic effects.[14] Not only does learning take place all the time, but it appears to be rather predictably phased; there may be "critical periods" as relevant to other activities as early mothering is to adult sexuality.[15]

We gain a graphic sense of this phasing process by focusing on the differences between males and females. Though, among the other primates, this varies between species, broadly speaking, males take almost twice as long to assume adult roles as females do. For one thing, they must grow more, because they may end up twice the size of females. And for another, there is the possibility that the skills that they must learn take longer to acquire and that the selection process in which they find themselves is more drawn out than among females. This is a sociological feature of the same order as differences in rates of maturation. Among savanna baboons, for example, by the age of three and one-half the females are already involved in the estrous cycle and may bear their first infant shortly thereafter. At that time the males are still part of subadult male groups, playing increasingly rough games (though from the start males play more roughly and aggressively than females), and—most significantly—moving to the outskirts of the group. Now, at this roughly adolescent stage, they become unsettling to the dominant males, who attack them if they approach too closely. The annoyance expressed by the dominants at their very existence seems as uncritical and self-righteous as that of some suburban principals commenting on the preposterous hair and habits of some of their young men. These young baboon males then circle the troop; their next task is somehow to work their way back in by maintaining their useful truculence and energy while at the same time slowly making themselves acceptable enough to the dominant males to be able to join a coalition and take over the breeding and the power.

But this takes a long time and is dangerous. We have noted that mortality rates in primate groups are far higher among young males than females; one estimate is that as many as eighty percent are killed before adulthood. But if the task of the male is more difficult to learn than the task of the female, the individual male is less important than the individual female. Only a few males are necessary to breed with a large number of females and even to defend the group. While they are in the vulnerable stage, they also serve as the sentries for the group and its unwitting first line of defense against predators and other dangers. They serve their time as the draftees of their group. If they are clever and lucky, they return to take advantage of what they have learned and what they have endured, and of their now more formidable appearance and demeanor.

It is quicker and easier for the females. They do not have to leave the central area at all, and they do not. It is the males who form the roving bands moving from troop to troop; the females lose their infancy, gain their childhood, and pass through their adolescence all within the same physical space. This may be because the adult males do not resent them as they do the young males, but it may also be that there is less need for them to learn outside the area where the infants and the senior females are. For this is where their life contingencies will be worked out—in their encounter with the dominant males, who will fertilize them; with the other females, who will help them with their infants; and with the infants themselves, whose behavior they can mark and with whom they can themselves learn the skills and confidence a successful mother requires.

Why we think this is also true for the human primate will become clearer when we consider the transition to a hunting economy in these terms. For the moment it is essential to remember that we retain some primate characteristics in our bodies and central nervous systems. Before moving on to humans once more, let us very quickly summarize these characteristics.

The potential for efficiency and efficacy is maximized when the animal is secure and confident. This security enables it to explore and exploit its natural curiosity.

Playfulness is the basis of successful learning. Participation and sheer movement are important, and the animal learns best when it is actively seeking stimulation rather than receiving it passively.

Guidance and tolerance rather than positive instruction characterize the role of the adult in the learning process.

The learning is immediately relevant to the social existence of the learner.

The most important skill learned is how to play social roles.

There is a marked difference between the learning histories of males and those of females. The male pattern is more complex and demanding, and the female more circumscribed spacially.

Most of a young animal's learning is done with its peers, which, in the male case at least, introduces tension and competitiveness even if the animals are playful.

There are critical periods in the learning process when certain kinds of information should be acquired; failure to do so may impair future performance.

This or something very like it was the educational system we had to work with when we made the leap into hunting. What did we have to add to or subtract from the scheme to adapt our learning patterns to the hunting way? A number of specific things; for example, with the advent of home bases and camps we had to teach our young not to foul their nests, which is their natural inclination. Toilet training, as every psychoanalyst and every baby will testify, is a traumatic imposition on the organism. But this is too specific, here, where we want to explore some of the more general consequences.

We must recapitulate a little. The hunting transition coincided, and not accidentally, with the rapid growth of the neocortex. This is itself related to the need for greater storage of information and greater inhibition. The consequence for education was that sheer instruction became more important. It was a long time before this became specialized instruction, but the careful chipping of flint arrowheads, the preparation of poisons to smear on the points, the dressing of hides, and many other skills obviously required something other than trial-and-error learning. The same was true of social skills. The "manners and customs" that accumulated after the development of language, the values and traditions by which the early humans lived, their rules of descent, marriage, property, and exchange, all had to be learned and stored as a result of fairly direct instruction. In some areas, such as the learning of spells, myths, shamanistic techniques, art, etc., the instruction definitely took on the character of "teaching" as we understand it. Even so, the greater part of the process of learning continued to be through play—hunting play, house play, sex play, and through active participation in the life of the band.[16]

The greatest responsibility to be instructed fell on the postpubescent males during their initiation into adulthood. They were still, despite their languages and decorations, the same young primates who were bucking for the central hierarchy. The same motives were—and are—present in both the young men and their elders, but they had to be handled differently if the young men were to be channeled into the tribe as useful members. We have already examined the bonding aspects; here we must look at the consequences for education. The elders could no longer rely on their physical weight to keep the young men in check, but they could rely on the weight of tradition. Without a knowledge of the traditions of the group, a man was as helpless as a lower animal that by some genetic quirk had failed to acquire its proper instincts. Without a knowledge of male secrets and male rituals and taboos, a boy could not be a man. This was the trick. One could not simply *become* a man, one had to *know how* to become a man. The first schools, in the technical sense, were initiation schools. Their overt function was to pass on knowledge and to "make men"; their covert function was to preserve the ascendancy of the elders. These functions allied knowledge and power in the process of ensuring safety and seeking food. Without this contribution, the hunting primate stood in danger of losing his characteristic knack, and was in danger of having to poke at ants and grub for roots once more.

Initiation procedures vary, but there are some standard elements. The initiates are separated from the women and kept in seclusion. They are hazed and humiliated by their elders. They undergo ordeals of endurance and tests of manly skills. They are often physically mutilated, and quite commonly and significantly the mutilation is of the genitals—circumcision, superincision, subincision (the slitting of the urethra), or all three. They are compelled to learn masses of arcane wisdom, as well as the proper conduct of ritual and the proper cherishing of myths and traditions of the group. They often indulge in homosexual practices. Finally, they are sometimes ritually slain and brought back to life as "men." Isolation, endurance, testing, mutilation, and the internalization of tribal wisdom in some form or other crop up in society after society as each in its peculiar way copes with the problem of tapping and controlling the ambivalent energy of the initiate.[17]

While all this may seem to the civilized reader a little excessive, one has to remember that at this period these young men are secreting some ten to thirty times more testosterone than they did as boys.[18] (Girls only double their level, and from a lower base to begin with.) This hormone is what changes boys into men. It is closely connected with heightened levels of aggression as well as of sexuality. Very suddenly, yesterday's boys receive massive doses of this powerful stimulant. Suddenly they are the most energetic and aggressive members of the community. But they have not had time to learn how to cope with this infusion of novel and stormy information from the ancient areas of the brain. One strategy involves forcing them to exercise the inhibiting functions of the newer brain by learning restraint on the one hand and by storing large amounts of information on the other. That the information may well be largely "useless" in some objective sense is neither here nor there; many of the "physical" things they learn are not very useful either. What it does is to make them use their forebrains rather than act out the more devastating instructions from the lower brain. These latter can then be controlled and channeled to the advantage of the community.

Female initiation is of relatively minor importance,[19] which illustrates another consequence of the great shift: the differences already present in primates between male and female socialization are accentuated by adaptation to the hunting pattern. While it appears that physical differences between males and females diminished—such as in size, teeth formation, and coloring—there was a critically important increase in the distinction between what men had to do and what women had to do, and hence in what they had to learn. There is much evidence from an enormous range of human societies that female initiations, compared with male, are gentle, often focused on mating, less likely to require long and difficult isolation, and less caught up with the business of acquiring and producing bits of information and sets of cultural lore. We can conclude also that the female ceremonies were far less oppressive and less provocative of consternation, hysteria, and simple excitement. With the females, the old primate program is quite reliable: they will first come to maturity, and perhaps indulge in some premarital sex play with what appears to be a "programmed" adolescent sterility that protects them against having infants when they are themselves too inexperienced as persons. Then they will marry, or take part in whatever organization of breeding their community has. Once they have an infant, they will assume full adult status and be rewarded accordingly.

Of course, there is a great deal they must learn—how to deal with themselves, with other females, with males, with infants and children. They learn skills involved with the management of households, and in many places with the conduct of some public business such as trading. But they do not have to be *controlled* in the same way as males. They appear to get less from the process of maturation, but they also give less insofar as they run less risk of death or mutilation, are less prone to attacks of anxiety and neurosis, and by and large, are assured that they will be able to achieve a fit and proper adult role by producing a child. They will compete for males—compete certainly in the exercise of the skills they know and the arts of decoration they employ. But unless there is a great preponderance of females—and there may be in warlike communities that do not also practice female infanticide—they are assured on purely statistical grounds that they will become the powerful females they observed as children, and continued to observe in the intimate arena of their adolescence. For the males, though, the statistics are unpropitious; there are not that many splendid posts; there are too many young men for the elders to select from. And finally, in the grimmest and most important context of all, in only six countries of one hundred and twenty-one do contemporary males live longer than females.

What children find easy to learn and enjoy learning reflects the biogrammar with which we are concerned. It is the starting point for any efforts at assimilating what (and how) we teach children with what they are and need.

Let us take two simple and contrasting examples. One cannot stop children from learning language. They assimilate language as they breathe air. Child language, as we now know, is not simply a poor imitation of adult speech; the child takes the raw material of the adult language as it is presented to him and uses it in consistent ways based on a simple grammatical scheme to make two- and three-word sentences.[20] He does this eagerly and easily unless he is actively prevented. He does not need to be taught; indeed, he demands and provokes the stimuli he needs for fresh information with which to work. His skill grows in a measurable way as his "language-acquisition device" takes in and puts out more complex structures. And in all this the child delights. Grammar is not for him the crabbed misery that ruins warm summer afternoons, but a thing to be reveled in and played with, to show off and romp about in. It is the pleasurable exercise of a skill that is essential to his survival. All he needs are encouragement, security, and input. He will do the rest. But at the same time as he is putting forth his first two-word sentences, the adult world is trying to "train" him to control his bladder and sphincter. While his speech is allowed to pour forth, his feces and urine are being ruthlessly held back. This is something for which the biogrammar, as we have seen, has no inbuilt rule; it must, in consequence, be culturally imposed.

The child will learn to control his excretory activity, but not without resistance, pain, and possible psychic damage. It is clear that much less damage is done if he is not "trained" early but left, as is the case in many so-called primitive cultures, until he can walk about.[21] Then he can easily imitate adult defecation postures and habits. Among many hunting tribes, for example, the infant is allowed to do as he pleases until such time as he can toddle. At this point an older sister will simply take him to the edge of the camp, gently and without fuss. Since our early ancestors lived out in the open and were actively nomadic, this was less of a problem for them than for later dwellers in permanent sites. There was no selection, obviously, for easy learning of early sphincter control, as there was for easy learning of early word control. The one is pleasurable, the other traumatic; the one emanates from the biogram, the other is an imposition on it. (There is one very important instruction in the wiring as far as excretion is concerned: when men are mortally afraid, their bodies automatically react in various ways, one of the more important being defecation and urination. Colloquial language recognizes this: a man is "scared shitless." This instruction is very ancient and is found in all mammals. Its explanation is very simple: the animal is preparing for flight and so gets rid of unwanted body weight, just as a fleeing bomber drops its unused load. This impulse is phylogenetically so deep that no learning is needed; its role in survival is too important to be left to that.)

To deal with the need for education in huge populations organized

on a national scale is to confront the same dilemma posed by
political and economic organization: whatever the evolutionary
demands and needs of the organism, the demands of the social system require bureaucratic organization, which of its very nature must
thwart the evolutionary thrust of the creature it controls. It may be
that the animal has been wired in terms of particular principles—
to learn certain things at certain times in certain ways. But because
of its sheer numbers of students and the complexity of the demands
made upon it, the educational system cannot be predicated on these
principles. It may also be, of course, that the system is organized in
ignorance of these facts and could be modified to meet them in some
degree. Perhaps this is the best we can hope for.

It is easy enough to blame school systems for rampant short-
comings, but we should first ask ourselves whether or not we are
asking too much of the schools in the first place. Young primates and
young hunters alike undertake their learning in the intimate surroundings of the kinship group into which they were born. They
learn things that are directly relevant to them and their relatives.
They have, throughout their evolution, learned to learn from role
models essentially parental and siblinglike. The transfer of knowledge
is only a part of this learning and cannot be separated as a process
from the context of learning in general. What we do with the institution of schools is to split off the inculcation of knowledge and hand
it over to specialists. This is curious enough. But even more curiously,
we proceed to hand more and more of the "familial" or "kinship"
functions—but not all of them—over to the schools as well. Then, when
the school, presented with this uneven package of demands, neither
educates the children well nor socializes them to our satisfaction, we
grumble and blame the teachers, the system, the government, or
anyone but ourselves. Parents who demand that sex education should
not be taught in schools may well have a point—if only we could
be confident that these same parents would not also treat it as a
taboo subject at home. We regard the teacher as *in loco parentis*
when it suits us to load him with responsibilities we do not want.
But we are quick to remind him that he is not a parent when he tries
to take this responsibility seriously in areas we consider "parental"
rather than purely "instructional." That this confuses a little hunting
primate trying precariously to speak his behavioral language to
people who talk different kinds of language themselves should not
surprise us. How could he ever learn his spoken language if only

nouns were spoken at home and verbs somewhere else, while the proper place to learn adjectives and adverbs was constantly in dispute?

We have already indicated the importance of security in stimulating and encouraging learning. What effect has it upon a child to move out of the home environment into one which—with the trend to larger and larger schools in the name of some (probably spurious) efficiency—may well be relatively far from his home, and will be composed of large numbers of unfamiliar persons? Of course, children survive such situations, and many even thrive on precisely that separation that we are questioning. But for the culture as a whole, the effects upon children's views of reality and of learning may be substantial, and even stimulate the constant rhetorical barrage erected to discuss the concept of "relevance" and its implication for school activities. The political and moral bases of the decision are clear: what is less clear is what, for example, "busing"—which is an exacerbation of this trend—does to the child's expectation of school and his attitude to home. Such a plan seems topsy-turvy; to overcome inequalities determined by affluent adults' unwillingness to share their resources and their sense of well-being with the poor and disadvantaged, the children of all these groups are urged at school into alliances of aliens to their own homes and to their own patterns of life. Cunning zoning regulations—in 1971 declared constitutional by the United States Supreme Court—enforce de-facto apartheid in various communities with racially and economically heterogeneous groups. The well-meaning assumption is that what parents cannot solve with equity and providence, children must solve by propinquity and by learning ways of relating to others which their parents are afraid to try, and which—if the children learn them well, as many no doubt do—will make them moral strangers to their parents. The question "What did you learn in school today?" comes to imply an answer tinged with rebuke at the strange antipathies of one's most familiar people, one's parents.

It would be foolish to emphasize this point at the cost of denying validity to all efforts to achieve equality of spirit and option in communities. But when educational systems are assumed to be the critical levers for changing morally and socially abhorred situations, children become condemned to soldiering in a war they never made and that they themselves cannot win. That the world they enter as adults may have the appearance or reality of improvement over the one they joined as children is a related but also another question. It is related, because educational systems are closely linked to all others in the society. But precisely because they become tools of social change, they are forced to perform very different functions from those that are demanded of them by their clients—the children. The basic biogrammar of instruction and initiation was not set up by natural selection to effect political changes in complex societies, but to let children know *how things are* in the world around them. This knowledge begins in the most intimate sphere and then allows them to apprehend first how they must behave in social situations, and then in those involving technical skills. Put another way: educational action has always been intensely conservative, concerned with integrating the child into the group. Our proposition is that it works best when it is conservative, because this is how the animal is geared. This is not political conservatism that we are talking about—a child can be socialized into a radical group—but, rather, temperamental conservatism, the conservatism of a system geared to the child's understanding of the continuities between the events of his life rather than their discontinuity of frank and conscious opposition. An educational system that teaches a child to survive in, and cope with, the ghetto where he lives is more successful *as an educational system* than one that fails to teach him to live securely and successfully in the disintegrated society of white suburbia with which he has no identification and to which he may not even aspire. The argument becomes immensely precarious if it is interpreted to mean that residents of ghettos should be trained like the slaves of yore to live happily and easily in their slums. Our point is exactly the reverse. The answer to the problems posed by the existence of ghettos is the abolition of ghettos. The answer to the difficulties placed in the way of ghetto residents' achievement of professional competence, economic integrity, and social pleasure is not to shift the children of ghettos into established environments where they must compete in an intense and irremediably stressful way. The answer is to revise notions of what constitutes competence, who decides who shall be accepted and advanced, who is allowed to set the community's standards, and finally, why it should be taken for granted that a child skilled at living in a complex and demanding ghetto should be held to require contact with the suburbs of Princeton and Burnt Oak in order to improve his talents and advance his prospects. Driving little children around in buses from place to place to permit them some contact with people different from their parents is a measure only of adult despair and communal disarray. This may be the only way poor schools can get more tax money—by having the children of the rich and powerful compelled to go to them. In such a case—and if the simple strategy of private schooling were unavailable—a mixture of children for socially desirable purposes is defensible as an expedient of transition. Education and directed social change are not the same thing, given the creatures children are and the problems they face. The social direction may "take," and future assistant professors, "apparatchniks," cadre leaders, and managers of debt-collection agencies will pop smoothly from the system like biscuits. But it may not take; the discontinuity between what children were promised was reality and what they see around them when the awkward chrysalis of school colors is shed may lead to cynicism and dismay.

We are pointing here to an unprimate and unhunter separation of home, school, and community. We have instanced a case in which the noneducational needs of the community have dictated the location and nature of schooling. We do not need to document the conflict between school and home; the problem is multiplied in our multi-community society, where a child may go through a very successful education (in the strictly adaptational sense of the term) in a restricted community, only to find that he has to apply this painfully won success in a totally different setting. Our child has been trained as a hunter and then rudely presented with a plow. Any educational system that, like our own, is essentially a system of selection rather than instruction, is faced with this problem. Whether schools are used as melting pots for immigrants or as an escalator for the socially mobile, they are promoting discontinuity and widening the gaps between themselves, home, and society; and this is the root of the problem.[22] Learning, like life, has ceased to be all of a piece and all of a purpose. The creature has been wired to learn in security, in familiar surroundings, from peers who will be lifelong companions and from elders who must be followed first and cared for later. He is wired to learn with an expectation of continuity in personnel and relevance of what is learned to what is done. It is hard to see anywhere in modern society where this wholistic, basic, biological process is operating. Perhaps it cannot, but we should at least be aware of how near to behavioral gibberish we are, and reserve our wonder for the courage of the young who tolerate as well as they do the uncouth grammar of their elders.

The fragmentation of the educational process puts considerable burdens on that figure of fun and awe, the teacher. His role deserves some consideration, since his specialized function is a truly human innovation. His function seems obvious to us, but it is not in any sense "given" in nature. His emergence is related, of course, to the growth of specialized knowledge; the first teachers, as such, were probably shamans who taught their successors; the first apprentice was probably the sorcerer's apprentice.[23] These magicians were specialists in traditional knowledge for its own sake—the myths of the tribe, and "useful arts" such as healing and divination: all things outside the normal primate repertoire. His modern successor is still expected to be something of a magician, and while in one sense he is unnatural, in another, at least as far as human life is concerned, he is inevitable. In his role as instructor he is an extension of the forebrain. In his role as controller he amplifies its functions just as the spear-thrower lengthens the hunter's arm. In his twin duties of instructing the child and molding his behavior, the good teacher can be very effective in the right setting.

Two utterly simple biological characteristics are in his favor: he is old and he is big. (If he is very big he has a good chance of becoming a principal.[24]) From at least the younger and smaller pupils he, or she, can therefore expect deference and attention. But to get these, he must naturally fulfill the conditions for them that lie in the old primate biogram waiting to be tapped. Given that set instruction is the pattern, the teacher can command the attention of the pupils if he combines the qualities of a successful dominant primate—authority with protection and credibility. The play group of young baboons always had with it an older male who did not interfere unless there was danger from outside the group or the threat of violence from within. But the moment he interfered, he was deferred to. The young animals liked to be near the dominant males, especially in times of danger. If the teacher can exhibit the right qualities, he should also be able to spark off the right reactions of deference and attention. A combination of impressive manner (however this is culturally defined), firmness, justice, and kindness will do the trick. But it is hard work, as every teacher knows. "Keeping the attention of the class" and "keeping them still" constitute two of the teacher's most difficult problems. Which raises a basic question about the whole pattern of "set instruction" and perhaps explains why, even with so much in his favor, the teacher often finds his job tiring and unrewarding.

The crux of the matter is very simple: dominance and attention are political devices, not instructional ones.[25] Children learn best when their attention is wholly on what they are doing rather than on the teacher. Attention to the teacher and all the neural and emotional processes that this involves may even interfere quite directly with learning. Dominance and attention are aspects of control rather than instruction, and while teachers must control as well as instruct, they run into trouble if they confuse the two. Good teachers know this very well, but they are often as constricted by the system as the children are. "Keeping still" is exactly what the young primate does not want to do. It cannot even learn very well by "keeping still." The teacher can use to advantage all the curiosity and exploratory urges of the child, but these are at their best when the child can move about to explore and manipulate—always in complete security and knowing that the adult is present to ensure justice. In forcing children to be still, the teacher may well abuse the energy that would be of most help to him in helping children to learn. He will get attention at the cost of curiosity, political control at the cost of instructional efficiency. And it is efficiency, not morals, that we are concerned with here. We are not asking whether the system is good or bad, but whether or not it can possibly do, given the methods it adopts, what it sets out to do. Schools always have to balance uneasily between discipline and learning; because they are bureaucratic institutions, they often decide in favor of discipline at the expense of learning. This may make them good political units, but it also makes them unfit teaching ones. Children who drop out are dropping out from the political, not the instructional system, although by the time they make this decision they may well be as confused as their teachers about the difference between the two.[26]

The teacher also has going for him both the child's delight in play and his propensity to learn through play. Again, the good teacher knows this. But again the system demands that work and play be segregated, and often denies play to punish a failure to work. Time segregated into work and play periods, and learning used as a vehicle of punishment, maximize control, but always at the expense of curiosity. It is like driving the car slowly with the brake firmly on: there is less danger of an accident, but one will not get very far—and do the car a lot of damage if one continues.

This is not to say that pure uninhibited play *for human children* is the only and best way for them to learn. We have to remember the forebrain and the hunting heritage. The teacher can utilize the incredible memory of the child and his long period of eager learning. He must instruct. The only question is what is the best way to instruct effectively. The answer, given the biogrammar, is that to guide the child's movement and curiosity toward whatever must be learned, to provide him with a model of learning activity oneself, and above all to provide him with the security to explore and find out, are infinitely more likely to work, since they tie in with the motives and propensities of the child himself, than dependence on dominance and attention structure. To make a simple equation, *guidance is to intellect what dominance is to initiation.* Education should be, at least in some respects, the expression of man's highest faculty—the free play of the intellect. Initiation is part of the political process and has to do with bringing restless youngsters into the hierarchical attention structure of the wider group. What is appropriate to the one process may be inimical to the other. But schools have always had to do both. Educational crises are often simply the outcome of the cross-cutting demands of the two pressures. Socrates was killed by the state because he saw the demands of intellect as superior to the claims of initiation.

Socrates' martyrdom symbolizes an important shift in formal attitudes to education. We know that educational systems perform both functions—teaching techniques and facts, and inspiring students with reverence for the community's ideology and attentive respect for the dictates of its leaders. Report cards, perhaps in most schools still may have two pages, one for "achievement in school" and the other for "Citizenship" or "Character" or even (in a stunning abuse of the English language) for "Behavior." The effect of "behavioral" failure in making "academic" failure more likely in school is known; it is hard to estimate how much this has to do with the assault on children's intellectual self-confidence. But a minimal prediction is that among primary-school children at least, the puzzling distinction upon which grown-ups insist between having skill and having "character," can lead only to progressive deterioration of the integrated skills, shared by all children in some measure and some way, for learning and for becoming more complexly sociable.

These are all old statements in an old battle about educational practice and ideals. Our concern here is with placing particular procedures in the context of what a relatively generous view of primate patterns of learning may help us see about the behavior of students and teachers. The amount of contention and the extent of the protestations of failure and alarm that surround the subject must encourage even an apparently oblique approach to what in many countries is one of the largest industries. It is now clear that there is a drastic relationship between early environment and experience, and what children can subsequently achieve in schools. One major study yielded that up to eighty percent of a child's ability to learn and perform was determined by the age of about four.[27] In other words, a tedious and oppressive four years at home will fix even a bright and energetic child at a level of performance that even a superior education can improve by little more than a margin of twenty percent. If his mother and father are themselves uninspired by the adventure of spending time with a child, if his house is unstimulating because it is poorly lit, because there are few objects with which he can play, because the emotional setup of the place denies him security or offers him no sense that what he can do himself and with friends is valuable and charming; if he is without effective role models and harassed by frightened or abused adults, the child will be very substantially set for life in a mold less generous than he might otherwise encompass and less demanding than he might otherwise crave. Yet this is very low-level human learning—and very high-level primate learning—that is involved; if so much is determined so early, it is not only necessary but urgent to attend to the biological infrastructure of even such a sophisticated and cerebral business as educating the young and allowing the old some confidence and pleasure in what they pass on to their offspring.

A prime example of how biological reality has been replaced by educational and political theory may be seen in how schools and teachers treat the chief biological difference—the sexual difference. Sex differences are also social differences. They are real, not just fictions of malevolent planners and bigoted patriarchs (though such types are nonetheless sprightly and active in this regard). The same point can be made with dual relevance for the educational system. Marion Levy, Jr., has noted that for the past two or three generations North Americans have been doing something very fundamental that no other community has ever done—using women teachers to discipline and instruct boys.[28] Historically and typically, where girls were educated at all, males and females were separated. We have already noted the major differences in the learning problems, options, and experiences of male and female primates. It is prudent to consider the possibility that similar distinctions apply—again with variation and convergence—to the human form of primate life.

To begin with, we can restate Patricia Sexton's argument about the feminized male—that creature who is successful in, and a product of, a school system largely staffed by females and in which female rather than male characteristics are rewarded.[29] For one thing, girls mature earlier than boys, who are thus at a constant disadvantage, since all statistical weighting is based on age, and since, in the name of equality, sex differences are not regarded as suitable to take into account in giving reward and threatening sanction.[30] In general boys are more physically active and wider-ranging than girls, yet much is made in schools of the strange virtue of keeping still, sitting in proper rows, moving about in orderly fashion, going like nuns to lunch and prisoners to games. Boys are more aggressive than girls, yet schools reward those who listen carefully, are obedient to rules, do not disturb either their teachers or their classes, and who cause minimal disruption of the other students. Boys who act more like girls than like other boys are more likely than their rambunctious and headstrong friends to succeed in the system.

The point of the educational system is to prepare people to assume adult roles in whatever community they inhabit. Historically, programs of formal education were geared to produce skilled adult males to fill the dominant roles. When coeducation developed, it was reasonably enough thought invidious and discriminatory for girls to learn different things from boys just because they were girls, and so, in many places an identity between male and female educational patterns became the rule rather than the exception. As a consequence, in many schools and colleges, certainly in Euro-America, there are only minor differences between what boys and girls learn. However, the crux of the dilemma is that, after the expensive and demanding exercise of learning things that males traditionally learned—but in ways more "feminized" than before—we find that female participation in those groups and activities for which they have in theory been trained is extremely low. Again, the sexual structure of occupations has changed very little over sixty years, despite extraordinary increases in the absolute and relative numbers of educated females.[31]

What does this mean? And why does it happen? The fact that education has made surprisingly little difference does not constitute a recommendation that females should learn only typing, baby care, and airline-hostessing. Why, then, this major discontinuity, which is financially expensive on one hand—because so much of the community's wealth is devoted to education, and perhaps one-third to one-half of this is used by females; and psychologically expensive on the other— because so relatively few women get to use or at least do use those skills that they patiently and hopefully acquired.

Perhaps the most obvious feature of what happened to educational systems under coeducation was that girls learned what boys had always learned, but boys did not also learn what girls had learned— however informally and casually. Also, school systems increased in size, and this required more taxes and more teachers. From having been a largely male occupation, teaching became largely female, at the lower levels particularly.[32] A woman is far more likely to be a third-grade teacher than a high-school and a college and university instructor. Female help is usually cheaper than male, though there is no evidence that it is worth less; this was clearly a reason for the sexual shift in the teaching corps. But there may have been another and possibly more interesting ethological basis for this change: grown men have nothing helpful to say to little girls in the context of the school. Or, rather, what they do have to tell little girls, both the men themselves and their communities at large may regard with less than enthusiasm.

In one sense this is a spurious argument, since teachers can in theory teach anyone equally well. But education is not just about knowledge and technical skill; it is also about initiation. What may be involved in much of the confusion and urgency surrounding educational thinking is a blurring of the lines, not only between education and initiation in general, but between male and female initiation and education. Among the other primates and among most humans still, female learning is especially relevant to childbearing and domestic roles, male learning to the groups in which they will one day find themselves as politicians, defenders, monitors, hunters, thinkers, etc. What was taught and by whom, and what was learned and by whom, were related to these clear visions of the future which the young could have and which the old could portray.

But once again, as with busing schoolchildren, we have pressured the educational system to make some changes that remain maladapted to the communities in which the schools exist. So parents will send a daughter to college and rebuke her silently or openly if she does not marry, or if her notion of her sexual experience does not include the proper summary—in their view—of the female pattern: husband, children, home, and local sacred perfection. Girls will do well in school and yet be mocked if they are or feel or want to be plain and not very active with the opposite sex. There remains the widespread folk myth that beautiful females must be stupid or that brilliant ones must be cheerless, bluestocking quasi-males. One need not append more details to the unhappy catalog. But its upshot is: that the system is predicated on the notion that what males do is superior to what females do, because that is how it once was, and still is, in terms of prestige and payment, and that at the same time males and females— throughout the educational life cycle—are the same. Our suggestion is that this becomes a fraudulent imposition on females, because their primate and sexual realities are denied as they seek mature participation in the major system of social opportunity in their community. And because in any breeding system, what one sex loses, the other loses too: directly and indirectly, the males with whom they have to spend this educational time are equally deprived. It is worth exploring what males also lose in a system purporting to be for their advantage and edification.

It would be too simple, but not untrue, to say that the boy loses early in the game because he is expected to behave like a girl, while the girl loses later in the game because she is expected to behave like a boy. In any case, whatever might be glossed over in the stages of sexual immaturity cannot be overlooked when puberty makes boys and girls more sharply diverge. In evolutionary terms, this is the period when girls enter almost immediately into motherhood and the female tasks of the division of labor, and when boys begin the intensive period of testing and proving their newfound manhood. Whether among primates or hunters, this is a period when the boys are in close and ambivalent contact with men, and when the men are testing the boys, and when both have little use for women, and even sex is often banned.

Perhaps it makes no difference that boys and girls are at school together before puberty; latency seems to be a period when sexual differences are suspended so that the child can learn skills. This may be the whole point of the much-discussed latency period. If Oedipal hostilities were not suspended for a while, no one would learn multiplication tables. But in the postlatency phase the whole thing erupts again. This is when the boys begin their physical or at least symbolic peripheralization. They may, like our Crow Indians, have to go off alone to the edges of their known world to suffer alone and mutilate themselves until they receive a vision of manhood. They may, like young BaVenda in southern Africa, go into lengthy initiation schools where they will be generously helped along by their elders.[33] It may be that they will simply be drafted into military service and trained in esoteric or useful knowledge, and what used to be known in less squeamish days as "manly arts" or even "male sympathies." Whatever the method, the males go through their apprenticeship at this period and learn the delicate and often painful—but presumably, their community hopes, rewarding—art of identifying with the society of the men. This is an ancient system of behavior—not in its specific forms, but in the underlying necessities. All this we know. And yet, in the name of sexual equality, we make girls behave as if they too were creatures of the transitory periphery, of the staggeringly increased testosterone, of the hostility and truculence to the older male, of the keen, impatient desire to be men.

Of course, even though girls' boarding schools are usually direct imitations of boys', and sororities of fraternities, girls' team sports modeled on boys', and even girls' clothing based on a ludicrously boyish pattern, it is hard even for imperceptive adults to push the analogy too far. Coeducation, particularly at the college level, means that both sides give something up in the quest for a common way of living. The end result is that many of the sheer initiatory functions of education get blurred. College—and the same is true of high school —becomes more and more an arena of courtship and less and less gladiatorial. Thus, while girls are trying, at a period of their lives when courtship is uppermost in their repertoire, to master knowledge in a way meant for boys, boys, who should be mastering the arts of maleness, are more and more pulled into a female pattern of behavior.

This may very well be a good thing, according to some standards of values held by those who would like to see differences between the sexes in behavior, life style, work, and even clothing and personal appearance reduced to nothing. The old joe-college type, with his sports, fraternities, panty raids, beer drinking, stag movies, and dirty jokes, is certainly now altogether a figure of fun. Nor is the Vassar beauty who cannot wait to pack her suitcase to get to Princeton for the weekend less ludicrous. But it may not be that simple: educational practice, if it is to achieve truly equal treatment, may well have to realize again that equality does not mean sameness. To pretend that boys and girls between fifteen and twenty-one-plus are really substitutable the one for the other is to deny not only obvious biological realities but the whole course of evolution. At least, if we are to tamper with the set of instructions that determine critically different paths for males and females, we should be aware of what we are doing. The case for allowing girls access to the means of higher education is certainly unarguable. The question is how and when, not why.

This raises the whole question of the phasing of education. One of the problems of "set instruction" for grade-schoolers was that the infant computers were being fed adult programs. We were putting in the wrong information in the wrong way—or, at best, the right information in the wrong way. We insist on trying to program the turbulent organisms of young adults of both sexes as if they were rational middle-aged scholars. This is the same mistake that was made with the grade-school children, and should be explored a little further.

We have seen the pressure in various kind of communities for the initiation of young males, and the apparently clear compliance of the initiates. They must feel that they are being initiated into something worthwhile, and if only because they do not know any other, into a company of worthwhile men. What happens, though, when it is no longer clear (a) that males are being initiated at all, (b) what they are being initiated into and with whom, and (c) that initiation is a real certification and the recognizable beginning of adult life? Young males in many cultures dominated by occupational choice, political and ethnic diversity, and a socially secular ideology can no longer enjoy the clarity that would allow them to aspire without ambiguity to an honorable place in their groups. High-school graduation? University graduation? Bar mitzvah? A driver's license? Being able to drink legally in public? Some of these involve tests, and some just becoming old enough. Our notion is that the drama, dedication, belief in their elders, and certainty about the value of their hard experience are considerably diminished by the feminized system within which many males are raised, and in terms of which their commitments to their community must be expressed. Much of the change results quite plainly from the fact that we are no longer hunters, and that many if not most jobs lack any evident majesty, any clear mandate and autonomy, even any opportunity to exercise those physical skills so important to adolescent males. In some communities the issues are more sharply drawn. Among the Iroquois near Montreal, the culture of the warrior found an apt and profitable translation into the dangerous and demanding work of rigging steel on skyscrapers. To this day Iroquois Indians create the structures within which admen and bookkeepers puzzle away over bits of paper.[34] Or among the boys of Hull and Newfoundland, where the male role is deep-sea fishing, the choice is easy: the only real thing men do is fish, so the boys fish too.[35] Even though trawler fishing is highly risky and not especially munificent, the recruits to the trade continue to come from among the sons of those who know it best—with all its dangers and inequities.

This is not to recommend some stunning ceremony which will cap the program of self-improvement, deferred gratification, and growing social commitment implied in many initiatory schemes. If anything, it is the mindless and parochial certainty of well-initiated politicians and generals in most countries of the world that threaten the peace of neighbors and the affable routines of those who pay for politicians' schemes and for generals' tools for the serious games of war. Nonetheless, the absence of such markers of initiation has its effect. Being male means essentially doing male things. If males are prevented from doing these things—some of which are deep in the wiring system—there remains the grim possibility that they will be unable to perform effectively their functions of protection, provision, and even procreation.

The problem becomes more acute when we appreciate that both males and females mature sexually earlier and earlier, but are compelled to stay in schools longer and longer to achieve that measure of certification that will permit them contact with whatever hopeful national myth about life style they seek to have. It may take a highly trained physicist or geographer thirty years to nab the doctorate, and then perhaps seven or eight more while he is scrutinized by calculating superiors who will decide at last whether he can join their little tribe, permanently, with tenure. In many communities a man is born, initiated, becomes a warrior, adviser, father, leader, and is dead by thirty-eight. In more "advanced" societies it may even happen that at thirty-eight a man has his first job giving him the security and sense of place that his age-mate in a poorer place has enjoyed from the time his voice was fully low and his beard marked him as a boy no longer. Small wonder that as the young become better informed about the acts of their elders, they insist on some symmetry between the ideals they have been taught for almost two decades of their lives and the realities they see around them that deny these ideals and make the managers of reality seem utterly crass and empty. Perhaps the managers are fools, thieves, incompetents, and liars— even to themselves. Perhaps not. But the ire of the young and the outrage of the old are perhaps more sanely seen to result from the lack of any acceptable contact between them.

Our life cycles have a predictable and rhythmical pattern that cause us on the one hand to put forth energy of a particular kind in a particular way and on the other hand to seek information and interaction of a certain kind in certain ways. The energy, interaction, and information that we both express and desire change over time in shape and substance; what is appropriate for one phase is inappropriate, or even detrimental, for another. The optimal conditions for learning when we are very young are astonishingly different from optimal learning conditions when we are young adults. The one phase demands security, the other risk. But what we want to learn and how we want to learn differ as much as the means whereby we learn. As we move into adulthood, we again change in both input and output; perhaps we forget the stresses of our youth as we mold the world of the young in our adult image. The behavioral rhythm of this life cycle, like the body which literally embodies it, is the end product of many millions of years of primate evolution, and several million of hominid hunting. The whole series of behavioral changes is as careful an adaptation to savanna life as the ankle bone and the buttocks are. Working from the general primate base, nature has produced a creature whose learning patterns, over its lifetime, have been mapped as carefully as the instincts of lower animals. We cannot assume that the demands of technology, bureaucracy, or ideology can go on redrawing this map without the risk of our losing our way completely.

7.

GOOD
GROOMING

ATTENTION TO RELATIVELY sophisticated forms of social life may deny us insight into deep structures of community life that are so important to us we can hardly perceive them. Here we want to indicate how the despair, pain, and anxiety of our concerns about health and death are closely tied in to our social performances, to our recreations and our gossip, to our play and our jovial use of spans of time. The people bending over an operating table are performing a stringent special act that is nonetheless as embedded in the same deep-structural system as the act of circling a roulette wheel in the community of gamblers. The husband and wife exposing their privacies and the particular dilemma of their marriage to a psychiatrist have just taken one step further in a process that began at a dinner party of close friends where they spoke for the first time of the circumstances which vexed them. The doctor's manner beside the bed and the lover's on it both affirm efforts to bestow some gift on another person; both intimacies are possible only in the context of some etiquette about permissible forms of giving and taking. The patient family doctor, the Sinhalese monk, and the sinewy lifeguard at a plush Riviera hotel are all part of the free-masonry of intervention in other people's lives—through the use of what we call medical skill, the invocation of what we call the super-natural, or the encouragement of what we call pleasure.

177

These various activities and processes look different to us largely because our category systems insist that they are. In the same way that we separate play from work and insist that all activity be categorized in either/or fashion, we segregate recreation from medication (the one is play and the other work, of course) without ever seeing the continuity of motive and activity between them. The bridge lies in "grooming." But not grooming in the narrow sense of simply picking parasites from the fur and skin of another animal. Man certainly performs this useful function. But he also trades in symbolic parasites and grooms symbolic fur. Grooming for him is the whole range of social activities that have to do with the well-being and being well of the community. This includes a great deal of seemingly nonpragmatic recreational activity and the whole body of charitable, caretaking, medicinal, and social-welfare services that communities erect for the sustenance of the weak and the insurance of the strong.

We are the only animal with hospitals, the only animal with psychiatrists, the only animal with an extremely complex way of feeding skillfully the experience of the past into managing the health and mortality of the animals of the present and the future. We are our own veterinarians.

Yet these patterns build on some generalized primate processes that can be identified. What primatologists barbarously call "epimiletic" behavior is a common feature of higher mammalian existence. It is care-giving and caretaking activity—a specialized form of reciprocity and a generalized way of building and maintaining links to the body social. All cultures have ways of relating private needs for health and psychological security to the apparatus of the community, to its resources of time, compassion, and skill. In Europe and North America—which are ambivalent indeed about the luxury of personal grooming behavior—the medical profession is able to perform grooming acts and ceremonies in the careful privacy of its offices and the bizarre hotel-hospitals in which the distraught are placed under the care of the inept. The medical profession nonetheless must remain our final spongy buffer against the animal fact of mortality. For to whom else can individuals turn when the tissue of expectations of further and better life is clearly rotting like the skin and bones on which these expectations are so elaborately based? In many other cultures medicine refers to magic; "medicine," the word, even means magic the process. But in our culture it has become confused with efficacious science. Science or not, it is a system to which we make pleas and demands when the programmed ways of preserving the body against the intrusions of the world fail. They fail either because the world has created new intrusions and hazards quite unanticipated by evolution— for example, silicosis and other pollutions—or because the expectations of any further life the symbol-making animal can contrive painfully outrun his ability to repair his own disease without the knowledgeable intervention of others.

As our evolution did not prepare us for some of the afflictions we have awarded ourselves, it may also have given us varieties of shape and action that once were useful but that now we reject. We tend to assume that mental illness is the result of the pressures of civilization on our "instinctive" life. It is probably the reverse. Most so-called mental illnesses are adaptive behaviors very useful to a hunting animal. But they are simply out of place in civilization, and so they are called crazy. And yet some mental attitudes—such as chronic and blinkered acquisitiveness—*are* products of civilization and are not called pathological.[1]

Caretaking as a general activity occurs in many forms among primates. We have seen it in operation between mother and child, between the young and the older females of the troop, between the young of the play group and the guardian older males, and between any two animals—mates, consorts, siblings, parents and children, bonded males —that groom each other for mutual comfort and cleanliness. The greatest amount of caretaking goes on between mother and child, but at the same time, the whole troop spends many hours in mutual grooming.[2] The overt purpose of this careful picking over of the fur of other animals is the removal of lice and ticks and other foreign matter. Animals that spend a lot of time alone are often in bad condition with unhealed wounds and patchy fur, apparently from lack of grooming. The "well-groomed" animal is usually a superior one. Good health means high status, because of the amount of grooming available as much as the high intake of favorable foods. Young infants also are greatly in demand for grooming, which is clearly to their advantage. Consort pairs groom each other incessantly, males groom one another as long as they belong to the exclusive central club, while peripherals perform their own mutual grooming—usually not as extensive. Caretaking is a social activity of a very integrative kind, and even though its overt function is the health of the community, a measure of who grooms who, when, where, and how much would almost be a measure of the structure of the whole social system. Outside of eating and sleeping, grooming takes up more time than any primate activity—far more than sex, for example.

But this social, reciprocal, health-promoting, caretaking behavior stops short of real medicine. We can consider it more useful in some ways than our own medical notions, since it is essentially preventive in its function: it is concerned with keeping up the general level of community health. But what it does not do is to care for the animal that is sick or wounded, except indirectly. A wound will heal faster if parasites are removed through grooming and the wound consequently kept clean. But an animal that is persistently sick and handicapped becomes a liability to the group, as there is no skill or even motivation to preserve it. Eventually it drops behind and dies or is picked off by predators. If it is a dominant animal it is rapidly and ruthlessly usurped. Healthy animals will help keep one another healthy, but the truly disabled animals will go to the wall.

Nevertheless, the fairly constant level of careful attention that these animals are paying to the welfare of others in a host of different ways is impressive. The basic caretaking program is there, embedded in social signals and social relations; it took humans to turn it into clinics and charities, into shamans and surgeons, into schemes for public welfare and private recuperation. Just as we specialized to develop the teacher, we created the specialist in grooming. Surrounding this specialism is an enormous complicated body of myth, truth, expectation, and resentment. The process and what accompanies it invite further examination.

Medicine, like economics, is a human creation cradled in a primate program. Like economics, it is dependent on the basal idea of reciprocity, of giving and receiving. In the small early human hunting community, membership was its own insurance policy. In return for contributing one's life and efforts to the group, one expected protection and care in times of trouble. The group in turn had nothing to gain by losing a member, and would bend its efforts to keep him alive. It thus actively intervened in the selective process—hence the genetic composition of the group—by refusing to let nature take its course. This intervention is a remarkable breakthrough in evolutionary history— as remarkable as the breakthrough from breeding systems to kinship systems or from ecologies to economies, and perhaps more far-reaching than either in its consequences. The old primate caretaking pattern moved from a system of preventive medicine to curative medicine: the group did not give up the ghost, or the body, once it was in disrepair, but turned all the caretaking attention at its primate disposal onto the sick member. It must be remembered that primate caretaking is embedded in social relationships—indeed, it is both a cause and an expression of them. In small human groups it was the same, and is the same today: the health and recovery of the members who are sick is a function of the whole network of social relationships. The sick person is not just restored to health, but to a place in society, a place jeopardized by his sickness in the first place, reconfirmed by his reentry in the second. And in reconfirming him in his physical and social health, the group reconfirms its own social and spiritual health.

That this group concern with the sick member came about as a result of the transition to hunting should be obvious. Hunters were precious, as were women, who were the mothers of future hunters. In the same way that a man ensured his economic position by culturally patterned "generosity," he ensured his health by standing by sick relatives and affines. When he was sick they would stand by him in turn. It was part of the network of obligations and counterobligations in which kin were enmeshed. But it was not simply ruthless self-interest that promoted this caretaking activity. Man had foresight. He knew he was going to die.

Despite tales of the happy hunting ground in the sky, most hunting peoples essentially see the next world as rather gray and colorless. Happiness and reward are in this life, and no one wants to end it prematurely.[3] In another man's potential death one sees one's own; in confirming the power to spare and lengthen an individual life, members of a group confirm their power to extend their own. In the hunting group more than any other, no man is an island, and every man's death diminishes the survivors in a real as well as a symbolic sense.

But the symbolism is real. A case of sickness and death is a reminder of the fragility not only of the individual but also of the group, and each individual knows that he cannot exist without the group. Even in other species, sheer natural selection has operated to produce what has been dubbed the "genetics of altruism": one can calculate when it pays, genetically, for any one animal in a population to sacrifice itself for the others—and patterns of behavior have evolved that ensure that the appropriate animal will do so.[4] Humans go further: not only do members sacrifice themselves, but they cooperate to give time and effort in restoring sick members to health. Genetically this is enormously important, since it means that selection for sheer physical health is not uppermost in the selective process. Individuals with brain power but weak bodies, for example, could be succored and preserved, and could eventually breed. Variation in the gene pool (other than that to do with physical abilities) could be preserved and passed on. This was definitive in an animal that was to depend more on brains than on brawn to survive. The intervention of medicine has often been cited as an example of man "going against" natural selection by cultural means. But, as usual, it is nothing of the sort. What it does is to preserve a greater range of variation in the species and help those to survive who are needed by the species in its growing dependence on intelligence, inquisitiveness, and social invention. True, it does this at the cost of preserving some deleterious specimens, but there is a gain and a cost in all genetic balance. It is not clear always, in any case, that congenital "illnesses" are deleterious, except to the people who suffer them. Epileptics may be great leaders, and someone with leukemia may be a genius. Social groups may need these, as they need people with certain emotional and artistic skills, capacities for love and poetry, entertainment and clowning, or anything to enrich and expand the life of the animal that put its money on the cerebral cortex rather than on fangs and speed in the struggle for survival. In other words, it was a biological necessity, not an intrusion into biology, that every effort be made to preserve every member.[5] If emotions of aggression are easy to arouse in man, so are emotions of pity, mercy, charity, self-sacrifice, empathy, and the desire to help those in need—to preserve the lives of allies as much as to take the lives of enemies. The pleasure we take in ministering to the sick is as much part of our biogram as the pleasure we take in the destruction of those who seek to destroy us.

All this is at the physical level, but the group and the individual are faced also with the *knowledge* of their potential extinction and so have to handle not only the problem of mortality but also the problem of immortality. The symbolizing animal has to guard against the fact of death not only on the physical but also on the spiritual level. In its earliest manifestations, medical practice cared about the soul as much as the body; indeed, it did not see a distinction between the two. Sickness and soul loss are often equated; to restore a man's health is to restore his soul.[6] Our ancestors, and their contemporary analogues, would be baffled by the concept of psychosomatic medicine.[7] This can be a concept only for people who began by making a distinction between mind and body, between a person and a disease that is something alien. The doctrine "cure the patient, not the disease" would not be a revolutionary medical slogan to a hunter, but a statement of normal practice. The medicine man dealt with the patient as a whole person in a familiar social setting, a person with spiritual problems expressing themselves in bodily discomfort, a person who needed restoring to wholeness and to a place in a society jeopardized by his disequilibrium.[8]

Medicine arose as a biological necessity, and with it a set of emotions and responses that are still with us. It arose as a group response to threats to group existence and to equilibrium within the group. It arose as an attempt to restore the whole patient to health and proper social functioning in society. Many so-called "primitive" healing systems retain these features but lack the technology to make their practices effective in a wide range of illnesses; our own system has perfected medical technology but in the process has lost touch with the behavioral setting in which medicine evolved and in which it is most satisfying to patient and practitioner alike. In the same way that our economies have produced material wealth but alienated men, our medical systems offer physical health but create strangely disturbed and dissatisfied people whose resentment of doctors and the medical professions in general seem to increase almost in accord with the advances, not to say cost, of technical skill.

It may be instructive to review some ways in which contemporary medical practice may reflect and inhibit the caretaking enthusiasms we do have. Bureaucracy forced people to relate to one another as instruments of a higher purpose, and not as individuals. The bureaucratization of mercy is even more difficult for the creature to tolerate. Particularly so when the individual is ill, fearful, and confused about the pains in his body or the distortions in his understanding of his social world. It is unnecessary to talk about the large, poorly staffed, and overworked urban hospitals in which individuals are treated with minimal effectiveness, humor, and affection. Of course, arms get bandaged, legs set, babies born, and ulcers cut away. It would be irresponsible to claim that these services are less than adequate because they are unaccompanied by the intimate contacts between patient and nurses and doctors that help locate the patient in a structure of dignity and feeling.

But this can be set beside the Greek ideal of the hospital as the place with the best food, the finest furnishings and paintings, and the most skilled musicians and comedians. It is not the healthy, but the sick who most vitally needed such agreeable and re-creative stimuli; and the resources the community had were most beneficially and sanely used in helping them ease their personal disarray and feel encouraged by this display of their community's careful concern.

In a labor-intensive activity such as medical care, people's time becomes valuable indeed, and thus attractive to economizing administrators. Nonetheless—as judicious and sensitive doctors and administrators know—such economies may be false, particularly in light of the fact that roughly half of all patients suffer from psychological rather than clearly defined physiological or structural difficulties. There is now a wealth of detail and analysis of the subjugation of individual patterns and autonomies to the demands of "total institutions," of which hospitals are perhaps the most obviously self-defeating kind. How many patients have been sent to the hospital for rest and removal from daily stresses only to be awakened routinely at six A.M. because that is when the departing night-shift nurses traditionally take the temperatures of patients whose breakfasts will not arrive for two hours? How many patients, resentful because they are weak, are treated as idiotic incompetents by members of hospital staffs who see personal and intellectual ineptitude as necessary accompaniments to illness? How many patients—even in as socially committed a scheme as the National Health Service of England—will not know, when they anticipate an operation, who the human being will be who will cut into their bodies, perhaps save them, or perhaps be the final agent of a death from which their consciousness will be hidden by drugs? How many patients must wait for half-days and whole days on clinic benches because there is no system for saving the time of ill people? In how many hospitals can patients make an even limited choice of foods they wish to eat, even though it is clear how important a link food is to the sense of well-being?[9]

Such a list could go on and on and still avoid discussing those cruelties and that outright cynicism which characterizes so many treatment centers that questions must be raised about the overall suitability of formalized places for recovery from illness. These are symptoms of the larger situation. Like a car being garaged for servicing, a patient is removed from a community and from a pattern of life, and forbidden explicitly and by implication to engage in the web of contacts that could reassure him and hearten his kin and friends with the prospect of his return to health. At a time when he most needs his community's support (whatever the community may be), he is taken away from it. This is only an example of the point that what is most efficient technically may be most unsound biologically. There is a double loss here, a loss to the patient and to the community to which he belongs. Curing is no longer a concern of the community for the member, and through its concern for the member, a statement of its faith in itself.

Consider an alternative approach to healing: the Negritos of northern Luzon in the Philippines live in small bands where the members all know one another intimately. When a Negrito is sick for any reason, he is put into a trance and observed and encouraged by the whole group. In the trance he overcomes the demon causing the illness, and demands a song and dance of it. Once out of the trance, he sings the song and performs the dance for the rest of his people. They learn these from him and sing and dance with him. His song and dance become part of the repertoire of the band—part of their recreational, religious, and aesthetic life. Through his illness he contributes to his culture, which he has made a participant in his illness.[10] The whole thing is therefore a community affair, public and ceremonial. Or take a healing ceremony of the Cochiti Indians in New Mexico. If a person has a persistent illness, the Cochiti put him through an adoption ceremony whereby he becomes a member of the clans of ceremonial mother and father—a man and wife chosen for the occasion. They wash his head and give him food and gifts and new names in the presence of his own clanspeople. He is then welcomed into the new clans by his adopted relatives, and when these clans in turn cure other people, he will go along and participate.[11]

In both these cases—and many like them could be cited from tribes around the world—the cure is *built into* the culture. In the case of the Negritos there is total participation, and the patient is made to contribute to the tribal repertoire; in the case of the Cochiti the patient is strengthened in his social allegiances: the clans—key elements in the social structure—become the means of restoring health by restoring the patient to a fuller role in the society and demanding his continued participation in the sociomedicinal system. Nothing less than the combined social and technical-supernatural resources of the community are brought to bear on this vital issue; and no possible source of comfort, encouragement, and knowledge of the patient's needs and style is overlooked in this enterprise of improvement.[12]

Of course, all this energy may not cure broken bones and perforated appendixes. And, most importantly, as far as the danger of unexpected death is concerned, the blandishments of rich cultures will be lost on infants in the first year. It is a plain fact that the life expectancy is higher in just those communities whose medical schemes we have seemed to see in such a gloomy light. Nonetheless, even members of poor cultures, once they reach puberty, stand almost as good a chance of a sixty-year life span as an American or Swede. The average is weighted heavily by the many infants who cannot survive; given their relative poverty of modern medical goods and savvy, the longevity of adult Bushmen, Australian aborigines, and Congolese raises some provocative questions.

The point is not the focus of our argument for nothing: a great discovery of so-called modern medicine was that a very considerable proportion—some physicians estimate anywhere from one-third to two-thirds, though these figures are mercurial—of the illness which they are asked to treat is significantly related, on the one hand, to social and economic stresses, and, on the other, to private anxieties and circumstances. Psychosomatic medicine is simply a reencounter of what technologically primitive people—and possibly even primates—know when they see bodily afflictions as expressions of spiritual distress or of malignancy in the web of social contacts. The perversion of supernatural power—essentially a social power—to individual and antisocial ends is called witchcraft. This implies that the normal functioning of the social network has broken down, that mistrust and suspicion, deceit and accusation, have taken over from reciprocity and mutuality. Accusations of witchcraft, as social anthropologists have shown so admirably, always reflect breakdowns in social relationships and in turn cause further breakdowns.[13] That the fear of witchcraft can also cause actual illness and even death is well enough known; that is why "cures" for witchcraft are often as concerned with restoring the whole community to health as they are with responding to the needs of the allegedly bewitched individual.[14]

This may seem strange to us. But the principle is the same here as in much of our own socially generated stress-disease. In some way or other the society ceases to be satisfying to the participant; he feels it as a series of pressures and unworkable demands rather than as a source of pleasure in participation. His body responds physiologically like an animal afraid and about to flee; this feeling, without release in actual flight, leads to physical breakdown.[15] The web of social contacts becomes not a home but a trap, and there are no longer any witches to blame. The harried executive with his ulcer and the nervous house-

wife with her migraine are as much victims of social breakdown as
their counterparts in Congolese compounds or Haitian villages dying
from the fear of the conspiracy of evil at work against them.

Illness is a social, not an individual, fact. Sickness in the body
social and sickness in the individual body are closely related. The
primitive tribe that sees an increase in illnesses as a signal that something is wrong with the society is going directly to the heart of the
matter. When it musters the community to restore the social structure
to a healthy state and the sick individual to his former social participation, it is showing an unconscious insight into an evolutionary truth
now more than half-forgotten. Communal grooming and communal
health are inseparably intertwined.

This point can be crystallized by looking no further than at the
various manifestations of the role of the doctor—a creature as critical
to the medical breakthrough as the teacher was to the educational
revolution. Very small hunting and gathering bands often do not have
any kind of medical specialization. As with the Negritos, the whole
band musters to help a sick person, unless his near kin have a special
responsibility for him. At a slightly higher level of sophistication the
world's first specialist appears—the medicine man. Medicine, despite
the alluring claims of other specialisms, is undoubtedly the oldest profession in the world. But since at this stage we had not begun to make
inviolable categorical distinctions between the individual and society
and between soul and body, the doctor had to have much more in his
repertoire than first-aid skills. He was the preserver of esoteric knowledge about the supernatural, the repository of practical skills in healing, the diviner of personal fortune, and the prognosticator of social
misfortune. He was often the only contact with the other world and
the only guarantee, over and above the strength and skill of the warriors themselves, of victory in war. In his diagnosis of personal and
social ills he started with an expert knowledge of the patient and of the
social relationships of his little world. He was the world's first sociologist, and in his exploration of dreams and the significance of small
events, the world's first psychiatrist. His custody of the supernatural
made him the world's first priest, master of ceremonies, and even
manager of the weather and the timing of the hunt. For his services
he often received very considerable gifts.[16]

All these items in his "primitive" doctor's bag were seen as connected
the one with the other, and all tied in with the health and happiness
of the people in his care. He was the first professional groomer.

Discussions of the crisis in modern medicine are probably equaled in frequency and intensity by worried examinations of the crisis of the modern family, whatever that is. The crisis of medicine is far more clear-cut, however. The problems the doctor faces are definable. We are not primarily concerned here with what is known in the trade as the "delivery system" of medicine (as if medicine were like letters or bread) and the various public and private devices for paying for medical service. Nor do we question the right of all members of the community to enjoy a standard of medical care commensurate with that community's wealth and skill. Nor do we wish to assign blame to participants in the medical interaction, but rather to try to define what is happening in this interaction.

And what is not happening. We have suggested that the doctor has traditionally been a person concerned with relating his technical knowledge about the body and its processes to his knowledge of the patient and the patient's psychosocial reality. For nearly all the time there have been human doctors this has been the pattern that substantially prevailed. But because of our astonishing technological increments and an even more astonishing set of metaphysical beliefs based on the mind-body distinction, we have come to separate the treatment of the disease from the broad understanding of its host; we have come to see doctors as experts in the servicing of subsections of bodies. This shift is neatly revealed in the word that now describes where the doctor meets his patient—"office"; it used to be "surgery." Like many university professors, whose traditional "studies" have now become "offices" too, the doctor is part of the bureaucratization of human encounter. He gains status among his colleagues by specializing, not generalizing. From his patients he gets money for doing one thing quickly and well.

But while he gains control over time in a new way, and certainly control over a vast amount of specialized information and technique, it is possible that he loses much of what the doctor has always had going for him—a place in a deeply rooted pattern of mutual grooming in which information and social commitment were virtually inextricable, and in which the willingness of the patient to yield to the skill and magic of the doctor was balanced by the doctor's own participation in a system of meaning beyond the pragmatic. Just as the teacher, if he or she is lucky, can tap "programs" for teaching and for learning that must be deep in an animal that needs so much knowledge and understanding, so the doctor can make use of the urge to groom and be groomed that marks all the primates and that in some human forms is the symptom of our greatest artistry and wisdom. But as the teacher is often prevented from using the resource that is rightfully his by overorganized, overpopulated, and underenjoyable school bureaucracies, so the doctor is forced by the notions of status that modern doctors have, by the methods of his payment, and by the trend to the special and the particular, to lose the vital ingredient of the patient's will to recover and his confidence in the higher meaning of the doctor's life and ethic.[17]

Efforts are always being made to overcome the formal rigidity of the system and to return to the warmth and equability of the traditional scheme. Even when a patient is sent to a specialist, it is customary for the specialist to take a rather lengthy and elaborate case history, which he may never consult. He is making a grooming gesture; he is seeking to assert an interest in the patient's whole being, not just his ear or femur or liver or episodic acne. Even the most imperiously esoteric practitioner cannot retain patients without some chitchat, some exchange of feeling, and some assertion of his personal commitment to the special version of the patient's problem. But if the patient is cunning or suspicious, he may test his doctor out next visit, to see what he recalls, to probe the doctor's memory of the poignant moment of revelation of the crisis and its meaning. Good doctors remember. The point is simply that a successful doctor has too many patients with too many statuses, indecisions, social relations, and private complexities ever to remember even a portion of these.

Competent doctors should treat just as many people as need them. The logic of our argument in its simplest form is that there should be more of them. Our concern is with the effectiveness of many contemporary medical arrangements for solving the broader problems of social affiliation and personal welfare; as primates and humans we have in other times and places solved them in ways far simpler and—so we propose—more likely to enhance the group's welfare as well as the patient's health.

This problem of social affiliation is not unknown to those concerned with broader aspects of health care, and a variety of practitioners and techniques have been developed to try to cope with this and other problems outlined here. Public health workers, nurses, psychiatric case workers, social workers, recreation directors, school nurses, and so on all augment the basic medical role of restoring the health of damaged organisms. (Psychiatry is a special matter and will be discussed shortly.) Obviously there are many possible approaches to managing communal health. But two trying problems have emerged, the first sociological, the second ethological. One of the characteristics of occupational groups in virtually any society is that they try to improve the standing they have in public esteem and the amount of control they exercise over their work and who is eligible to do it. The proof of the change from "occupation" to "profession" is that the state licenses only members of a profession to perform the services it claims it alone can provide—such as doctors, dentists, and lawyers—and that these services are so clear-cut that they permit an exact decision about the mandate to offer them. This same process is visible in the medical field, where customarily it takes longer and longer to become a more and more specialized member of the "grooming team"; this naturally affects the commitment of practitioners as well as their income and status. The net effect is a proliferation of precisely the problems that the creation of these additional specialties was meant to solve—to overcome the loss of the small-scale family-doctored community, and to provide compassion over the life cycle instead of a technique of the moment.[18]

This leads directly to the second, the ethological, difficulty, that a person in distress can be sent on a Kafkaesque adventure within a bureaucracy founded, ironically, on the belief in mercy. Yet he may find that in the interests of professional integrity and organizational efficiency, his special personal crisis becomes routine. His problems become the work load of a functionary and not the ardent business of someone whose commitment to a solution is as intense as his own anxiety.

We have fragmented the doctor's role, split it up among a host of specialists, not all of whom are medical: the priest, the troubleshooter, the teacher, the psychiatrist, and many others all have little pieces of the doctor's role in their repertoire. Yet we still demand all these things of the physician himself. The old small-town family doctor in many ways embodied them: he was the wise man of his community who knew its troubles and its weak spots, who was there to listen and advise, to patch up lives as well as limbs. As any such practitioner would be the first to assert—although not perhaps in so many words— he spends most of his time in nonmedical grooming activity. But this is perhaps the basic issue: in our perspective it *is* medical grooming that he is doing. He is close to his evolutionary roots and is satisfying a need that comes directly from the evolutionary demands of the community he serves as a genuinely concerned participant.

In the crowded urban communities with which we have so many difficulties, and increasingly in many entire countries, this no longer holds. A devoutly personal activity becomes more and more impersonal as the cross-currents of demands increase. The high status accorded specialization and the feeling that general practice is "amateurish," the increasing pressures on the time of doctors, the complexities of modern medicine, and the relatively low monetary rewards of the twenty-four-hour-on-call, house-visiting family physician, all combine to push even doctors otherwise inclined in the direction of emulating business "efficiency." A doctor wants to be like any other businessman, to have appointments and business hours, to go home from "work" and not have to worry about patients, but have his "life" to himself, and to draw the appropriate rewards. He is responding to a system overload with a form of withdrawal. Undoubtedly this is a natural strategy for the individual doctor, but it leaves the mass of anxious patients without the kind of shamanistic support that they need and now have to shop for, literally, in a dozen different places.

The shaman often had to have a vision to be "called" to the life of a doctor. We ourselves echo this in referring to medicine, teaching, and the priesthood as "callings" or vocations—the giving of a whole life to something because of an inner feeling or need. Now, in all these spheres the sense of vocation is being lost. They are all becoming "jobs." The practitioners increasingly resist the emotional demands for nurture that are made on them, and ask that they have the same privileges as other people in other jobs. In this context it becomes more understandable why so many pills are prescribed to patients to pep them up, tranquilize them, put them to sleep, make them indifferent to pain, make them lose weight or gain it. On one level these gifts of pills are sensible enough and overt in what they do. On another, they represent a continuation of the grooming process, even though the groomer is not physically near; a month's supply of pills begins to compensate for the ten-minute interview, which was all the practitioner could give. Of course, this is one reason why placebos work effectively as often as they do. Perhaps it is less the power of suggestion than the memory of encounter that gives pills of sugar such efficacy. And it is also understandable why doctor and patient are together forced to enter into a conspiracy based on the taking of drugs—to create even by artificial means the continued contact that their relationship may really need but can only symbolically achieve.

Again, an evolutionary perspective might alter our view of the nature of mental as well as physical illness. Already we have established that the psychosomatic approach—as well as notions of community care of the mentally ill—is compatible with an evolutionary perspective.[19] But what of mental illness itself? Let us not beg the question of what is normal and abnormal in behavior; in fact, let us avoid absolutist definitions of psychic health and ill health.[20] When behavior is looked at objectively, all that is obvious is a range of variation. Like all other natural features of natural populations, this variation will fall along a normal curve. Take aggressivity: at one extreme there will be people who revel in violence and enjoy killing and bloodshed, at the other people of immense timidity and passivity who could not under any circumstances be provoked to violence. In the middle there is the vast bulk of people who are capable of some violence but most of the time not particularly aroused to it. Take compulsiveness: at one end there are the "compulsive neurotics" who are meticulous to a fault and to whom orderliness is an end in itself; at the other there are the happy-go-lucky, totally unorganized folk; and in the middle, again, the vast majority, who have some compulsions, some degree of disorder, and, all in all, a working mixture of the two. Clearly societies are geared in their general day-to-day operations to the inclinations and abilities of the many; they have to be. But social circumstances will determine whether any of the extremes on any dimension are stigmatized as useless or rewarded as valuable. It is the same with natural selection itself: most of the time the extremes will be wiped out, but there will come times when selective pressures favor the odd-men-out, and these survive to change the structure of the gene pool and eventually the characteristics of the species. All we can say as good zoologists is that in all spheres of behavior variation exists, and that the same kinds of variation occur in all human populations. It is improper, therefore, to take moral positions and label any behavior good or bad; the proper procedure is to ask what the range of variation seems to be *for*.[21] What contingencies does nature have in mind in producing the particular kinds of variations that she does? (Whether these are learned or innate is beside the point, both because the dichotomy is unreal and because, as we have argued, if variations occur so regularly, there must be a statistically predictable propensity for learning them.)

In assuming that mental "illnesses" might have adaptive functions, we are not so far from Freud, to whom neuroses were essentially adaptive pieces of behavior. He, however, saw them only as adaptive

in the life of the individual, not the species. The problem with neuroses
was that while they might have been useful at their inception, they
certainly were not in future years. The proposition here is to put
behavior that falls at either end of the curve into social perspective by
seeing it as part of the normal variation in a population—as normal as
variations in height, speed, strength, intelligence, or any other feature.
Extremely high intelligence, for example, is "abnormal," and people so
endowed often cannot function very well in society. But they can solve
chess problems faster than computers, and so society eventually finds
a use for them. When people occur for whom we can find no use at
all, we call them lunatics and lock them away. But their seemingly
abnormal behavior may have once had a function that we can no longer
recognize because our circumstances have changed. Conversely, chronic
acquisitiveness would have been positively harmful in hunting societies,
and chronically acquisitive people would have been ostracized. In our
own society it is considered a "healthy" motive, and the man who gives
away all he earns is promptly suspected to be a nut. Thus, the end
of the curve that is favored has shifted.

Let us take an obvious example of how this process can work even
over short spans of time. Our maximum-security prisons and prison
hospitals are full of homicidal maniacs—compulsive killers. Many of
them have multiple and "senseless" killings to their credit. Some we
kill in turn, others we declare insane and lock up for life. These are
men who enjoy killing for its own sake, who are fascinated by the
business of death, who get a strange fulfillment from the act of murder.
Loose in society, they are a menace, and we are right to put them
away. But in every society the dedicated killer crops up, and it takes
no great imagination to see how useful he would be in times of trouble.
A man who will give himself wholly over to the killing life with dedication and even pleasure is just the man to send against the enemy
on raids—which are essentially murder expeditions. In our own time he
is the perfect commando, marine, green beret, or whatever. Among the
Crow Indians there was a society called the Crazy Dogs, or Those-
born-to-die. These were young men dedicated to fight to the death and
never move away from the enemy. To this end they would stake themselves into the ground with thongs tied through their back muscles and
face the enemy. They were reckless and lawless and were allowed all
kinds of privilege and indulgence. On the night before a battle or raid,
the Crazy Dogs would wreck the camp and rape the women—with
impunity, because the next day some of them would surely die. They

were among the most honored men of their community. The same is true of our own commandos, who receive medals and honors for acts that, performed on their own people in peacetime, would land them in the security wings of mental hospitals. These killers are always with us, but whether or not they become our greatest heroes or our criminal lunatics depends on which end of the curve we decide to reward. They are always with us, because if there is a curve of aggressivity, there must be someone at the violent end of it. A society of such men is clearly impossible, but a proportion of them is clearly useful, as is a proportion of cunning cowards.

The example of compulsion neuroses is much the same. The overly compulsive person can be useful in certain tasks requiring superfine ordering and routine repetitiveness. He is, for example, an excellent ritualist; Freud in fact noted the similarity of religious ritual to the compulsive acts of the neurotic patient.[22] Insofar as compulsion is a part of most religious ritual, and insofar as such ritual became a growing part of the hunter's adaptive repertoire, the relationship may be more than simply analogous. Once, we may have even needed our compulsive neurotics to keep the universe turning over in a proper and orderly fashion.

We mentioned that epilepsy is a very ancient and subtle form of behavior, probably deriving from mammalian escape techniques. Epileptics have two valuable traits: they go easily into trances, and they have to exercise great self-control.[23] On the one hand their trance behavior could well have been important in ritual and healing; on the other, their excessive self-control often makes them tough and effective leaders—with the added advantage that their occasional seizures are viewed by many peoples as cases of possession by God or the gods, and hence enhance the spiritual authority of leadership.

But what of true states of schizophrenia? What of delusions, paranoia, manic-depression, catatonia? Again, they crop up everywhere, and again they often serve very important functions. Christ would no doubt be diagnosed today as suffering from paranoid delusions (talking to God, destroying the world, etc.),[24] while Joan of Arc with her voices would not be burned, but bureaucratically incarcerated for life for her own good. But their "delusions" helped them to complete almost impossibly difficult tasks requiring more than the usual quota of heroism and dedication. In our hunting past, such requirements cannot have been uncommon, and a proportion of people with such "delusions"— with immediate and confident contact with the other world, for example—would have been more than useful and well worth the minor costs. We ourselves do not seem to mind paranoid delusions of grandeur in our leaders; it is only when they occur in "inappropriate" people—like assistant professors and busboys—that we send for the strait-jackets.

The roots of these mental-behavioral adaptations may go very deep. The origins of grandiose delusions, for example, may lie in the comportment of dominant animals under stress; a form of megalomania would have helped to make a convincing show of really dominant behavior. On the other hand, deep withdrawal symptoms may have characterized chronically subservient animals trying to stay out of trouble. Similarly, manic phases may have coincided with sudden rises in the hierarchy and the energy necessary to complete and maintain these, and depressive phases with equally sudden changes downward.[25] Sociologists have noted how sudden changes in status (in either direction) affect mental illness and especially suicide in contemporary human society.[26] In fairly small hunting groups it must have been much easier to find roles for all variant forms of behavior exhibited by the members. In our own huge societies the lack of fit between an individual's behavior and the roles available to him is often glaring, and so we have to put out of the way those whose behavior is "inappropriate" to their station. Our own failure to allow any honorable role to the homosexual contrasts miserably with the place he was accorded in the most manly of human cultures, the Plains Indians. That we have nothing to equal their *berdache* is a constant reproach to the tyranny of our norm.

And not content with harassing homosexuals and otherwise insisting on production norms of "adjustment," "personality," and "citizenship" from young and old alike, we are now employing our skill in making drugs to normalize the behavior of those who are found to be different. Some educators decry the growth of drug use among students yet also give drugs such as dexedrine and other stimulants to so-called slow learners. Persons who are nervy and abrupt are tranquilized because their sharpness impedes their smoothness. Truck drivers and business-men gulp pep pills to maintain a pace of output set by the hardiest in their groups. Athletes stung by fear of competing poorly stimulate their central nervous systems before games, and shy people are encouraged to take a formidable martini before a social meeting to ease the transition from privacy to extroversion. Whole societies become corrupted by the tyranny of the normal curve, especially in sexual activity, and by the psychologists and other engineers of life who buy their single-minded theory of social value in the narrow marketplace of high competitiveness. In the name of demos, the focal democratic principle of the preciousness of human variation becomes a coercive principle of exploitation of those whose most grievous error was to have been born in a less populous segment of the normal curve than someone else.

The essential point here is that natural groups are systems. The fast need the slow, the brilliant require the context of the steady, the big are burly only among the small. The "central tendency" in biological patterns still depends on what or who is *not* moderate or modish. Nothing is gained by laughing at midgets.

If humans are clever and provident enough to take care of one another when they are clearly ill, they are also sufficiently subtle and foresightful to amuse one another when they are well. The other side of the currency of grooming is play, recreation, social work, much of psychiatry, and the host of informal actions that all humans everywhere daily undertake to come into contact with friends, colleagues, and various arts and insights. In England when an automobile has an engine running because it will begin moving shortly, it is said to be "ticking over." Much of what Americans call "hanging around" is ticking-over behavior—that activity which keeps the body social in trim, cements social bonds, informs people about the character, strengths, and weaknesses of their friends and co-workers; provides artistic and dramatic rendition of forms of social life; and, in general, permits the community to be in shape to cope with crises and to celebrate triumph.

Medical grooming ensures that physical bodies are healthy so that when called upon they can go into action on behalf of the community. What we can loosely call "social grooming" keeps the members in psychological trim, keeps their engines ticking over in readiness for activity. Sometimes this is obvious. A good deal of competitive sport is indulged in not only for physical fitness, which is a by-product, but for the avowedly spiritual qualities it promotes—team spirit, loyalty, subservience of the individual to the team, strict observance of rules, fair play, etc. The first sociologist to give this overt recognition was the Duke of Wellington, whó observed that the battle of Waterloo was won on the playing fields of Eton—it was a commonplace of imperialistic English rhetoric that the Union Jack flew over every Rugby scrum. But perhaps it is not so obvious that gossip and gambling may well play equally important roles and that the seriousness with which these are pursued may be as justifiable as the training regime of an Olympic sprinter.

All of this is intensely social. The isolated animal of any gregarious species—and in particular the higher mammalian species—even if well fed and healthy, soon becomes morose and miserable if he lacks the contact with his kind for very long. We are attuned to interaction with our fellows. They keep us ticking over and alive. Symbolic human interchange has little to do with the passage of information, except in the very broadest sense. It has to do with *keeping up the interaction,* and with subtleties such as asserting or discovering status differences and maintaining in-group/out-group distinctions.

Play and learning are closely related, and the relationship promotes both general competence and social cohesion. As anyone who observes children at play will know, they take their efforts very seriously indeed. As they should, because there is much they must learn about the world, themselves, and about one another. Adult play is part of a more general grooming pattern, with functions for whole communities, comparable to child's play for the individual children. We know that children *must* play, and even the most unscintillating puritan schoolmaster will allot some miserable bit of time to his charges, if only to permit him a break in his own routine. But what does adult play mean, and why do we play? Why *do* we play poker and bridge, and bet on which horse runs faster than some other? Why do we scream our heads off when the hero scores a goal and pull our breath in sharply when the dancer takes a leap as beautiful as it is improbable? Why do we spend hours curling our hair and determining lapel shapes and producing overmuch overrich food for guests at feasts? Why do we believe that "talking things over" helps solve problems? Why is gossip so important?

All these seemingly unpragmatic pieces of behavior help to keep up the psychological tone of the community so that it is ready for really pragmatic action. They seek as well to reaffirm the psychological health of the members and of the social relationships in which they participate. Let us take some apparently unrelated areas of behavior. Gambling is a universal male activity.[27] Females indulge in it less, and usually imitate male forms when they do. In many hunting groups gambling is the most common leisure-time activity. Sometimes these are games of pure chance, sometimes they involve skill. Whatever their form, they involve a fascination with doing chance one better, with beating the odds. The more they become games of skill, the more

analogous they become to true hunting situations, in which the calculation of odds is always important. Among the Hadza of East Africa a
man or a group of men will go into the bush with poisoned arrows and
perhaps hit an animal at a distance. The poison works slowly; the
animal has to be tracked, killed, and then carried home. The men
return to the base camp and try to persuade other men to join them
in the tracking, which needs at least half a dozen hands to be successful. The men in the camp have to assess the odds: Will the expedition
be worth it? How reliable are the original hunters? How good are their
arrows? How long will it take to get the animal? Would they be better
employed going off and looking for an animal of their own? What are
the conditions in that part of the country where the animal was hit?
What, in sum, are the odds for and against success?[28] This is only
one kind of assessment of odds that hunters face. In the actual hunt
itself they must be calculating all the time. The experienced hunter,
like the experienced gambler, begins to see regularities and patterns;
he learns how to play for all it is worth whatever hand nature and his
own skill deal to him. A younger player is more reckless, but he learns
by experience when it is not worth making a large bet on a long shot,
and how to play shrewdly from a poor position.

It should not surprise us that men are fascinated by gambling. They
are always trying to reduce risk, to make a chancy experience more
certain, to beat the long odds. All over the world, in cultures otherwise
almost totally diverse, men gamble and engage one another in mara-
thon games of skill and chance. Along with pornography and drinking, it is the most nearly universal form of male ticking-over behavior.
It is just as important to the modern businessman as it was to his
hunting ancestor, since chance and odds are the order of the day in
the stock market as much as in the veld. A group of businessmen discussing whether or not to make a tricky deal are directly analogous to
the Hadza and their problem with the wounded animal in the bush.
Even men who no longer face the uncertainties of the universe in quite
the same way as their Paleolithic ancestors still find in gambling a
re-creation of that truly primitive thrill in pitting oneself against
opponents and trying to beat the laws of chance in order to make a
"killing."[29] Gambling is one of the more spectacular pieces of ticking-
over behavior.

There is a social gamble too in gambling. One also assesses one's
partners and fellow gamblers in the process. One becomes familiar with
their idiosyncrasies and weaknesses, their strengths and occasional
strokes of brilliance and stupidity. A great deal about a man comes

out when he gambles, as does a great deal about his colleagues. In the
sharing of time, tension, and the remarkably repetitive and (to out-
siders) tedious banter, there develops also a commitment to the little
group, its unique patterns, and its role in the histories of its members.
This is predictable, of course. But if we see such gambling as a ritual
way of intensifying the bonds that must come into play, we can understand why people who could be otherwise occupied sit about grunting
about cards, dice, and pebbles, groaning about their misfortune and
the luck of others, whooping about their skill in anticipating the laws
of chance and the error of an opponent—but also making more coherent a group that will have to act soon, and act well and with
mutual ease.

Now, in cultures such as Europe and North America, this may not
apply at all, because the people may be different from the people they
gamble with. An Italian accountant may work with Jews and Puerto
Ricans but play poker with Italians. A doctor may play cards with
his friends from high school who are not now of his social class. An
Ashanti civil servant will seek Ashanti kin rather than Ewe bureaucrats
for his game. But the fact remains that an overall orientation is being
expressed and stimulated by this exposure to significant males. Though
the gambling may have no overt function, the implicit grooming is
reward enough even for men who do not work together but who may
nonetheless turn to one another in times of personal crisis—for brief
loans, for advice about a wife or child, for evaluation of the merits
of changing jobs or selling a house and moving to an apartment instead. Or, just for company, just to "hang around," to feel a warmth
and support and some assurance that the five people or two or three
all share commitment to the destiny of any troubled member and are
happy to stand by, express opinion, and offer skill. Such ideas may
appear strange within the context of cultures in which friendship between males is often awkward unless formalized, and suspicious unless
clearly and aggressively "masculine." The exchange of tenderness and
the assertion of rich commitment between men are problems often
solved by participating as spectators at sports and occasionally as
drinking comrades at bars and pubs.[30]

Male primates groom one another as a function of their dominance
relations, and to maintain the overall tone of their essentially political
relationships. The same applies to human male bonding, and to the
forms of grooming such as games, conversation, and hanging around.
When businessmen take each other to lunches, when construction
workers share the task of buying a sixpack of beer, or when English

telephone repairmen heat water for a communal tea, they are all performing inessential actions—apparently inessential, that is—that elaborate the bonds between them, and put into richer and more humane context the work they have to do together.

If gambling and other forms of emotional and skillful interaction keep the men in trim for male activities, what happens among females? Of course, females gamble sometimes, and men gossip a lot, but each sex seems to have specialized in bringing its own particular grooming activity to the status of a high art. Few would dispute that women excel at gossiping. This area of intense interaction has been relatively neglected by sociologists and left to the brilliance of some social novelists. But recently social anthropologists have produced a variety of theories about the ritual functions of gossip in delineating in-group from out-group ("if we gossip with you, you are 'in' ") and passing out information.[31] Gossip does these things and more, but there are more general, underlying characteristics. The incessant attempts by female primates, for example, to groom newborn babies and infants not their own, and the constant interest shown in these young, is matched in the symbolic animal by the intensity of interest and talk that surrounds babies, new babies especially, and the whole absorbing task of raising children. In the seemingly endless, and to male ears repetitive, chatter that goes on among women regarding their offspring, not only is information passed, and not only are in-group practices confirmed, but a massive and encyclopedic confidence is built up in the gossipers. Deviants are mulled over and condemned, excellence is praised; but again, above all, there is sheer interaction between those currently concerned with this crucial task, those who have been concerned and are eager to pass on knowledge and retain some place around the infantile focus of attention, and those who will be concerned and who will almost unconsciously pick up attitudes and information that they will trade and use in turn.

Gossip is not only about babies, it is about morals. Gossip in the popular sense refers to accounts of scandalous behavior, to what the English charmingly call "goings-on." It preserves a rather tight morality among the female block of any local social system by subjecting the minutiae of behavior to exacting, horrified, and fascinated scrutiny. It is often thought of as a divisive force in society, but it is probably just the opposite, since it serves to unite the women into a common system of values and then maintain these. Gossip differs from simple conversation in that it deals essentially with standards and values, and their maintenance and abrogation. Through gossip the

gossipers constantly reassure one another of their own worth and contrast this with the wickedness of those gossiped about. Again, this
could scarcely be called a pragmatic activity; men who would cheerfully spend an evening playing poker would likely condemn it as a
silly waste of time. But gossip serves exactly the same grooming functions for the women as poker for the men. All concerned are servicing
one another in highly symbolic ways: they are keeping their morale in
trim, they are preserving and reinforcing the system of social relationships to which they are committed, and above all they are ticking
over—maintaining their emotional engines in states of readiness for
action by the constant tune-up of social interaction with their fellows.

What applies to males with males, and females with females of
course extends to the two together. As gossip is to ladies and gambling
to gentlemen, flirting is to both together. This is the great erotic
tune-up, the encounter that keeps active the enthusiasm for sex and
the confidence to engage in it.[32] We are not concerned here with the
strategic man or woman who exploits sexual skill for deliberate gain
of money or clear advancement, but with the pair next to each other
at a dinner party or opposite each other on a train or at coffee after
work. Flirting goes on all the time—whenever a male and female of
suitable age, style, habit, etc., happen to be in proximity. There are
gestures of courtliness or strategic avoidance, there are ploys; we know
even that when males see attractive females their pupils dilate on a
purely automatic basis (this suggests the depth of the responses involved). Flirting is the first stage of the courtship pattern, which can
lead in its complex turn to sexual intercourse and to what follows or
does not follow that. Flirting may embarrass some people, outrage
wives and husbands, cause disruption in the routines of men and
women, lend intrigue to parties and danger to rendezvous. There can
be little doubt that the presence of attractive males and females in an
office or factory or hospital or anywhere will have an effect on the
overall level of intensity and sense of pleasure of the people involved.
A handsome electrician or a beautiful laboratory analyst may indeed
interfere with patterns of work; but the switchboard operator will
enjoy the contact with the man who repairs the board, and the doctor
will find it entertaining and vitalizing to fetch a report from the lab.
Some media industries—television and advertising, for example—deliberately employ pretty girls in preference to others. These industries
depend on a constant level of creative productivity from the males—
on keeping up their level of creative tension—and the pretty girls, far
from distracting the men, act as a spur to their pride and a source of

excitement to their imaginations. All cultures flirt; indeed, there seem to be universal patterns of flirting associated with eye contact, lowering of the eyes, averting the head, glancing sideways, giggling, raising the eyebrows, etc. Again, this is not the real thing, but it is a constant state of readiness for the real thing, and perhaps the most obvious of all ticking-over mechanisms.

There is much in common between the covey of males on the street-corner watching girls pass by, the adolescent girls' screeching like some novel beasts when a pop star makes an appearance, and the suddenly enraptured wife and someone else's husband conferring elaborately at a party. What they all share is a commitment to the pleasure of a special form of grooming that, in turn, is tied to an always urgent pattern of sexual exchange, intrigue, and blandishment.

Psychiatry has been mentioned here as a symbolic grooming phenomenon. It is also an example of one of the many junctions between "medical" and "social" grooming. Psychiatry involves a subtle combination of flirting, gambling, and gossip with overtones of the supernatural. The old medicine man knew this very well when he threw bones to divine the "illness," but based much of his diagnosis of witchcraft on what he knew from gossip about the patient. With the fragmentation of the doctor's role and the abdication of communal involvement in curing, the old business of "hearing out" the patient's complaints about his abuses and troubles has passed over to these specialists in "mental" events. Even the boldest psychiatrists, however, do not claim to "cure" many people, but they do "help" them by enabling them to understand themselves better. One extreme school of "nondirective" therapists claims that it is best to do this by letting the patient reach his own understanding through talk, with a minimum of interference.[33] The cynical critics of this method ask why, then, a psychiatrist is any more use than a best friend. Perhaps this is the point. The psychiatrist is a very skilled best friend, one trained in a very special kind of friendship. In primates, friendship is, as we know, expressed by grooming. When in our species the symbolic mental equipment becomes tangled, infected, and painful, it needs grooming just as much as the fur of a baboon. The psychiatrist helps us to pick over the messy details of our confused and unhappy lives and to reorder them in some more satisfactory way. But he is only a more refined version of talking-it-over-with-a-friend. In this world of specialists he replaces some of the functions of the medicine men, of the elders of the tribe, of kin and companions, of confessors, of people who are there to listen with sympathy and to guide from experience. He concentrates in himself a whole range of caretaking and even caring activities that were once more diffuse. This may explain both his relative success and his elusive sense of failure, for like the hospital and the specialty clinic, he treats the patient outside of his milieu. Unlike the medicine man, he does not belong to the intimate society in which the patient finds both the source and the cure of his trouble.

Psychiatric skills and their derivatives can, however, be applied in social contexts, as they have been in family therapy, encounter sessions, and in a wide variety of enterprises of psychiatric social workers, recreationists, and others concerned with assimilating the confusions and fears of lonely individuals into the resilience and interest that come from groups. This can become bizarre, as with commercial encounter groups in which strangers off a street come together to experience some contact with other people, the spontaneity of which is equaled only by its spuriousness as a real factor in their lives. And it becomes dangerous when such superficial contacts come to replace the more trying and involving links between people that long-term contacts based on gossip, fun, religion, and games may stimulate.

There are many other modes of solution to these problems of keeping the body social in trim. Perhaps the most influential theory about the functions of religion, Émile Durkheim's, comes to precisely this conclusion about the social meaning of religion and what it does: it is a highly ritualized, repetitive, and satisfyingly communal rendition of man-nature, man-god, and man-man relationships.[34] Since there are no gods and no supernatural, the business of coping with these nonexistent matters must relate to some real earthly human problems. So must drama, opera, and works of artistic fantasy—all so clearly important to the understanding of man's extensions of himself and his delicate use of these extensions to reach other people either in truth or in fact. If poets are the unacknowledged legislators of mankind, it is because they greet people at this level of supersocial encounter— encounters extrapolated from those around us, and attuned more acutely to beauties and miseries a jump too far away for aldermen and merchants, princes and physicians. This is grooming radically far away from the stroking of faces and quiet muttering of contented creatures. And yet the acts of reading and writing, of hearing music and humming it to someone, of planting an interesting garden, and wandering contentedly around it, are gestures of persons to persons. They are gestures made and received to serve needs as focal and primitive as the form these gestures take is remarkable and colorfully unexpected.

8.

THE
NOBLE
SAVAGE

For centuries—probably for the whole of its existence—the species has deplored violence and taken steps to protect itself from the worst ravages of violence. But it has accepted it as part of the natural world in the way that it has accepted sex. Both urges have been at once glorified and vilified, and yet both the urge to kill and the urge to copulate have been accepted as inevitable. The question has been how to utilize or contain them according to one's aims. However, both were part of the package of original sin and therefore of human nature. Properly used, both were virtuous; improperly used, both were noxious. Legal fornication for the production of legitimate offspring was good, while inconsequential sexual pleasure outside marriage was bad; violence in the service of a legitimate cause such as religion or national defense was good, violence in the service of individual gain was bad—and so on. But no one doubted that sex and violence were "natural." For that reason, it was argued, we had to have stern religious and moral codes backed up by authority, even force to make sure that both these propensities were used legitimately. If individuals, or communities, or nations were sufficiently pious and strict, they might just be able to keep these dangerous propensities under control—and even end up "good." But the goodness thus achieved would proceed from their conquest of a natural tendency to be violent and promiscuous. And the goodness would not consist in being nonsexual or nonviolent, but in being sexual and violent in socially approved ways. Beasts, this philosophy maintained, could not achieve goodness, since they lacked souls. They could simply act out their sex and aggression without restraint. Only man, with his divine moral sense, could overcome his animal nature and perfect himself.

This essentially "medieval" view is interesting, since it accepts that there is a "beastly" part of man that makes him one with the rest of animal nature. In this respect he does not differ from the beasts. Where he differs is in his capacity to manipulate this animality in the service of symbols. His soul—or later his reason—could work on the animal part of him, tame it, and put it to uses determined by human will and conscious intention. About the time of the Romantic Movement in Europe, a new view of man arose that proposed a radical departure from this conception of human nature.[1] Man became different from the animals not only in that he had a mind and consciousness but also in that he lacked the basic animal nature that, in the medieval view, linked him to the rest of the mammalian universe. In this new view man was born without evil propensities. These were learned as a result of living in evil and corrupt societies. It therefore became possible, this philosophy went on to maintain, not just to contain and manipulate the animal wickedness of man (since this did not exist), but to eliminate all human violence by not teaching evil to people in the first place—by getting rid of the corrupt societies that spawned violence, terror, and subjection. (The same argument was not applied to sex, but then no one wanted to be rid of sex altogether, so the problem did not arise.)

Two world wars, hundreds of local wars, and millions upon millions of deaths by violence later,[2] many of us stubbornly cling to this view: that we can end violence by changing circumstances. Since violence is learned, we can simply stop teaching it—remove all the provocations to it—and men will then be the good and peaceful beings that they are by nature. Those who still cling to the medieval notion are likely to find themselves condemned as evil men who argue that violence is inevitable and thus encourage it.

At the risk of joining the ranks of the condemned, we argue that the medieval view is intellectually more satisfactory, scientifically more accurate, and pragmatically more sensible. It is also more humane, and in the long run less likely to push the species to the verge of annihilation than appealing delusions about human perfectibility.

It is easy to see how the view of man as basically good but cor-
ruptible could be transformed into the view of man as basically blank
but teachable. The culturalists vary in their estimation of man's innate
goodness, but mostly they are opposed to anything that suggests innate-
ness at all and therefore see man as faced with two alternatives:
either he can teach goodness, cooperation, etc., or he can teach wickedness, violence, etc. Since all human behavior is, in this view, learned,
violence as well as love must be learned; it must be impressed upon
the tabula rasa.

There is no question that both violence and love are indeed learned.
But they are learned as language is learned—easily. In our own terms,
violence and love are learned easily because we are wired to learn
them; because they have both been essential to survival, and so mutation and natural selection have produced a creature which will readily
learn both in the same way as it will readily learn languages and rules.
The potential for all this is there in the animal, and its large forebrain gives it the ability to shape and discipline these propensities to
its own symbolically determined uses. This is both our problem and
our opportunity: we are easily turned on by violence, but we can in
consequence do something about the switches; we can try to turn ourselves on less. To rid ourselves of violent potential altogether, however, while it may seem superficially attractive, is possibly dangerous.
There are times when men need violence to do right.

This is really very embarrassing. No one, except a few psychopaths
and some strange adventurers in other people's suffering, wants to
create violence and damage other people. It is embarrassing simply
because we return to violence again and again. Which is less dignified:
To be a cultural animal and yet consistently produce such appalling
cultures that they inevitably lead us to war? Or to be a violent animal
and disrupt our otherwise congenial and helpful cultures because we
have a taste for blood and a zest for mayhem?

We are both; we do both; we must fear both. A punch-up at a
bar can wreck a nose, a friendship, and leave a wide wake of gossip
and regret. A lovers' quarrel or a family feud can lead to pain and
even death; most homicides are between people who know each other
well. Intimacy, not distance, stimulates the murderer. These are always
desperate rips in the social fabric. We are rightly intrigued by the
trials of murderers and the circumstances of their awful dramas. But
these are little tragedies for modern communities. The big ones are
precisely those in which our cultural skills and our organizational

structures are most directly involved—when we make up gangs and rumble one another; when we give wealth to policemen to oppress ghettos and discipline the poor; and most spectacularly when we use our vast techniques with machinery and with people to conduct wars and to kill the others, whomever we culturally decide these evil others are.

It is a relatively modern conceit to assert that man is peaceful until he proves otherwise. In our enthusiasm for progress and our success in achieving forms of wealth and welfare, we have become committed to perfectibility and aspire to its wellsprings as ardently as at least one of our ancestors sailed after the fountain of youth. And yet we do fight; we always have fought, though most of the time we do not fight but tend our fields and flocks. Kings have always had barons to marshal foot soldiers; parliaments have always sought the power to raise armies; Russian communists came to power through violence; to protect their people and interests a state that was to wither away supported a vast militia that was in theory unnecessary. In constitutional terms, Americans were to be free to pursue liberty and happiness—even equality—and to carry guns and raise armies in small states. This grievously benign self-image has led to Guatemalas, Vietnams, and a stack of pious treaties. Switzerland is a neutral country whose male citizens train in the military three weeks each year. A thoughtless general ordering his troops toward Zurich and the Matterhorn would find the country a costly conquest. Neutral Sweden, the tough mecca of skilled optimists, has airplane factories carved into mountains, and troops who (with well-schooled Irish forces too) spent months in effortful schemes to bring peace to the Congo. The very day the French surrendered, in 1940, the Resistance became the official violent opposition, and some years later collaborators were shot and only their families grieved—if they did. In 1945 Japanese were fried like smelts by atomic rays, and just a generation later, some Japanese argued seriously for a proper military force again. Alleged to have a racial memory, a gene for war, the conquered Germans are urged by their allies to pull their warlike weight; the German army is once again the largest in Western Europe. The peaceful Indians swoop on Goa and contend with Pakistanis and Chinese for bits of remote territory. Boiling oil is dropped from parapets, and then napalm from airplanes. Women and children are still lined up and shot and pushed into graves. Only their names—if they have any—differ from the people who have died in the same way before; the insignia on the uniforms of their slaughterers are the only things that have changed.

The claim that we would live at peace if only there were no causes for war is a legitimate claim, but as pungent and provident a comment about reality as the affirmation that without disease there need be no hospitals. There is disease, there are hospitals; there is violence, and there are wars. We have saved millions because we accept that disease is real. We kill millions because we decide that we are good and the enemy is evil. In our rage at warriors we too easily fail to recall that they are human too.

Humanity has not changed; it goes on doing with more ruthless efficiency what it has been doing for the whole of its existence. But perhaps because of this, and because we now face the prospect of complete destruction for the species, we desperately maintain that this cannot be inevitable, that men are not in some deep way irrevocably committed to violence. If we accept that they are, and given the instruments of violence at their command, there is no hope for us. Indeed, it does seem to many that there is no longer hope of restraining or containing violence. The Pax Britannica and the Pax Romanum are things of the past. We cannot depend on superpowers using their instruments of violence to keep the peace of the world—if this is ever what they really did. Nor can we depend on "rules of war," for in atomic wars there are no rules, only unequivocal results.

Many of our intellectuals rush to quell our fears by telling us that *theoretically* none of this has to happen, that violence is not part of human nature, that it occurs only because of evil intentions and circumstances that we can eradicate.[3] They are the Christian Scientists of sociology; and they have not as yet solved the paradox: if we are not by nature violent creatures, why do we seem inevitably to create situations that lead to violence? If it is in our natures constantly to provoke violence in what is an essentially nonviolent organism, then we cannot win, however we play the game. The preliminary answer is clear: we are creatures who are by nature easily aroused to violence, we easily learn it, and we are wired to create situations in which the arousal and learning readily take place and in which violence becomes a necessity.

We have not talked about the "problem of aggression." This is because there is no problem of aggression, despite the gallons of printer's ink that have been used in discussing it.[4] Aggression in the human species is the same as aggression in any other animal species.[5] It springs

from the same causes and subserves the same functions. It is a necessary force in the evolutionary processes taking place in any sexually
reproducing species. There has to be competition in order for natural
selection to occur. One animal has to strive to outdo another for
nest sites, territory, food, mates, dominance, so that selection can take
place. Selection can of course favor timidity where a species is oriented
toward camouflage or hiding and fleeing behavior; only inspection of
the behavior of a species can tell us which way the pendulum has
swung. In the successful and gregarious higher mammals (among
others) it has swung decidedly in favor of aggression, and there is no
warrant, and above all no evidence, to suggest that the human species
is an exception. That a species is characterized by aggression does not
mean that its members do not cooperate and are never helpful or
loyal or loving—quite the contrary. Aggression is an essential component of these virtues, and ethologists have argued very cogently that
we should view it as a constructive motive, a positive force acting
for the benefit of a species.[6] Only when this positive force spills over
into violence does it threaten internal order and survival. Even then,
violence against predators can be seen as another constructive device.
There is a delicate balance to be achieved here; ethological studies
have brought out brilliantly how various animal populations manage
it. There must be sufficient aggression between members of the same
species in the same population to ensure that selection takes place and
various subfunctions are served; this must be contained—usually by
the process of "ritualization"—so that it does not develop into internal
violence and destroy the population; violent opposition to threats from
without the population must nevertheless be fostered.[7] Nonviolent
aggression within, and violent opposition on the outside, have constantly to be balanced in any human society: members must be capable
of violence in order to preserve its integrity, but toward one another
they should be nonviolently competitive.

Even this nonviolent competition will work only once it has become
clear to the participants that violence will *not* work, or, alternatively,
once violence *has* worked. Take our cousins the baboons: their intricate
social system, with its hierarchies and coalitions, etc., is maintained
by "ritualized" activities of threat and submission that rarely break
out into open violence. But they do break out on occasion, and savage
injuries can be inflicted. The savagery is contained because they know
it will not work; that is, the subdominants will not risk open violence
against their superiors because they know they would lose. The show-

ing of the canines will lead the subdominant to turn and present. But this same subordinate animal is one that survived because *he did not provoke the alpha males to savagery in the first place.* When the young males come to maturity and start to challenge the older males, many end up dead or badly wounded. There is no question that if they could they would indeed kill their elders and take over the leadership and the females. Equally, their elders and betters would cheerfully dispose of them if they really became a menace. But the balance is struck somewhere between these two extremes. Some old males disappear through natural death, or as a result of an ouster by coalitions of other-wise subdominant males. Some young males die or leave the band. Those that remain settle down to an "understanding," in which a reminder of the real facts of the situation—through threats and appeasements—is enough to preserve a stable structure. But the violence is there, and it is real. When leopards or lions or Ethiopian village dogs attack the troop, the violence is directed outward with spectacular success. The young males will be the first to turn their violent attention to the predator, while the alpha males come out from the center of the troop to tackle him.[8]

It is very important to bear these facts in mind in any discussion about the "ritualization" of aggression among animals, and to com-pare them gloomily with our own failures. In some ways, our own attempts at ritualization are just as impressive in view of the greater potential for destruction that we have evolved. Therein lies the crux of the issue. If the baboons were equipped with hand grenades (which they could probably learn to use quite easily), then there would not be many baboons left in Africa. The reason the baboons survive and flourish is that it is really very difficult for them to kill one another. Given the means, they would undoubtedly use them. The average young baboon, driven by primal urges to dominate and copulate, does not have the long-term interests of his species at the forefront of his imagination, and would not hesitate to try anything at his disposal to subdue his unwanted and tyrannical elders. With their territorial rivalries and competition for ranges, troops of baboons or prides of lions can be easily imagined wiping one another out—*if they had the means.* As George Schaller has remarked, if a lion strays onto the territory of another lion pride, then the only ritualization at its dis-posal is to run like hell.

Aggression and violence occur in animal societies and do not differ in kind from their human counterpart. Man has no *special* killer instinct that makes him different from the baboon.[9] Nor has he lost his powers of ritualization. He has simply handed himself a whole heap of problems for those by now familiar reasons: his forebrain and his artifacts. It was these that turned his primate power struggles into human politics, his primate ecologies into human economies, and his primate violence into human wars. Wars and organized killing, with the imperial component of conquest, arrive on the scene when the tool was perfected into the weapon, and the expanding and convoluting brain was able to cope with organization on the one hand, and with categories of friend and foe on the other. The latter is the most important leap after the advent of weapons. For animals these categories are fixed by nature, but for men they are capable of everchanging definition and redefinition. The human peril is only specifically human for the same reason that human politics and art and economics and religion are human. Man added no new genetic qualities and lost no old ones in the areas of aggression and violence. He is still the angry and conciliatory primate; he still strives to dominate and outdo rivals; he still resorts to bloody combat to gain his ends—in all this he is no different. But he adds the human dimension—tools and language; if you like, weapons and concepts. This is his problem here as in any other sphere, since it gives him the opportunity either to use his primate violence to his advantage or to work it to his own pain and destruction. About the violence he has no choice, any more than his ancestors and relatives had; about the use of the violence and its constraint he has all the possibilities of choice laid at his feet by his peculiar evolution.

Since we are primates and do have hand grenades, it is amazing that we molest one another so little and kill so rarely. One baboon troop cannot destroy another, because most of the losers will solve the problem with that ancient ritual, flight, in aid of which adrenalin like some super-overdrive is instantly brought into the system.[10] We secrete adrenalin too, but have other ways of coping with fights that build on animal rituals and become human artifacts. Just as the young baboon knows better than to step right up to the dominant male and demand he resign, so most humans have contrived ways of managing the antipathies they feel within their own communities. Though we are constantly in a state of aggression against at least some persons, we are rarely in a state of real violence against even one or two for long enough to harm them physically. When we do such harm, commonly there is some remand for this, some policeman-person to stop it, and some judge-person to ponder its implication for the people involved and for their community. There is no community so convinced of the normality and perhaps healthfulness of human violence that it permits murderers to wander about unmarked and unguarded.

But there are few communities without soldiers—without a group of people trained to kill. When they return from battle with blood in their histories, they are given honors and rewards—the very opposite of the isolation, bitterness, and often death incurred by the local strangler.

Why? What in the human biogrammar allows us this inconsistency? How indeed can we manage this special symbolic enterprise of defining enemies and friends and judging murder and heroism accordingly? A brief glance back at the biogrammar helps explain. We have seen that in the basic system of the human animal, young males are always in the situation of expressing enough energy, initiative, and skill to win the approval of their more powerful elders, but not so much that these same supportive elders will turn against them out of fear or out of custom and propriety masking fear. The male career involves sexual skill with females and social skill with males, and in both these areas a measure of tact and consent is always part of the mix along with zest and competence. An important way in which young males have related traditionally—and in many places still relate—to the dominant males in their communities is reflected in one simple, crude fact: war is not a human action but a male action; war is not a human problem but a male problem.[11]

Only males governed, only males hunted, and out of this lopsided sexual fact emerged another: only males cooperated to fight. The relentless and harassing initiations that young males received, and receive, stimulated loyalty to the group and willingness to defend it. When to this strong structure was added the heavy refinement of what the new cerebral cortex could do, we acquired war. Only an animal with brain enough to think of empires and try to manage them could conceive of war. Only an animal so wedded to the truths inside his skull could travel many miles and expend endless, precious calories and hours and artifacts to destroy others. Only an animal smart enough to build laboratories could be skilled enough to build bombs. Only a hunting primate could want to as much as the arsenals of the world suggest they do.

Perhaps the argument can be sketched more boldly with a simple prediction. So long as the use of nuclear weapons could be banned for one year, if all the menial and mighty military posts in the world were taken over by women, there would be no war. Of course, this is an unrealistic surmise, because for this to happen politics would have to change markedly, along with the control of force. But were we to continue this unfortunately frivolous proposition, we could well find that all the elaborately pious ritual, all the quietly insane military rigmaroles, all the puzzling hauteur of admirals huffing about their autonomy and their advancement, and finally all the energetic killing of the troops at the front would be radically changed. An army of women would be more intimate, less presumptuous about the outside world, more realistic, occasionally more vicious in small doses, but never initiating the vast episodes of poisoning that the wars of men are now and have been.

The very improbability of this ever happening is a measure of its foreignness to the biogrammar. It is the young males who practice throwing balls and spears endlessly, who play mock warfare in their games, who are excited by the rituals of military performance from which females are normally exempted (even where they are not, such as in Israel and Vietnam, they are never used on the front lines). Women may fight bitterly and with effect when their homes or home-land is being attacked. But they do not leave the home territory to fight on someone else's. They do not fly the fighter planes and steer the submarines (though of course they can). They do not become steeled marines or legionnaires lusty for agonized encounter. They do not huddle with the other generals and commanders in the head-quarters tent. They are the military sex of last resort.

However, *organized predatory violence* has always been a male monopoly, whether practiced against game animals or those enemy humans defined as "not-men" (and hence also a kind of prey animal). This is the important step in the move toward human warfare. It is not that man (or rather *men*) in the course of his evolution either learned to be a killer or lost his capacity to ritualize. He always was a killer—he still ritualizes. What he learned was the use of weapons, the predatory skill, and above all the organization of predation in male bands. He built into his biogram a whole set of satisfactions that did not have to do with killing as such, but with enjoying dangerous and status-enhancing activity in the company of other males.

Our armed and belligerent young primates in the evolving hunting groups were as status-conscious as their primate ancestors. The evolving human society solved this potentially dangerous situation by making status within the community of males dependent on success in conflict with males of other communities. The bands of young initiates, having forged their bonds, turn their status striving outward, to achieve success in war and/or hunting: a young Masai must kill a lion; a New Guinea Highlander must bring back a human head; a young Crow had to kill a buffalo and bring home a scalp.[12]

At this very primitive level there is not—nor was there ever—much of what we would recognize as "war." The history of our international violence has been, for more than ninety percent of the time, a history of raid and skirmish.[13] The actual violence took up much less time than the elaborate male rituals of violence, of preparation and celebration. In many cases there was nothing obvious to fight about. Men did not need justifications for their activities beyond the activities themselves. Sometimes "real" causes could be assumed—disputes over territory, hunting rights, water holes, women, real or imagined insults to tribal honor. But for the most part, enemies were what were traditionally defined as such. No Shoshone needed any "real" cause for fighting the Sioux: they existed to be fought. A great deal of this fighting was highly ritualized so that the men could get the maximum satisfaction from their sense of danger and exercise of courage, while neither side lost too many lives. Of course, this could all get out of hand, but so could the ritualization of animal fighting. The showing of courage and skill and the braving of dangers were more important than the wholesale slaughter of the enemy. The evolution of our fighting skills and motivations has been in this small-scale context, closely linked to male-group activities and needs. Hunters do not conquer one another, although they may occasionally displace one another. What they do is prey upon one another in a way controlled, or "ritualized," by customary modes of small-scale fighting. It was the recent agricultural leap backward that gave rise to that markedly human institution, the war of conquest.[14]

There is no advantage in conquest for hunters. There is a limit to the amount of territory any hunting band can exploit, and hunters have little use for slaves, who would simply be more mouths to feed.[15] But our agriculturist with his burgeoning populations and his toilsome work in the fields is open to temptation. He carries over into his radically altered and potentially large-scale operation all the motives and satisfactions of the warrior-hunter. He adds to these the possibilities of conquest and enslavement, simply because these are to his obvious advantage if he can pull them off. The combination of the ancient traits embedded in male hunting and male vanity with the new advantages so obvious in conquest and material gain was, and remains, explosive.[16]

As societies grew and became more complex, local and sectional interests came into conflict, and internal violence became common. Man had little precedent for dealing with communities above fifty or sixty people. Within these small communities, order was a face-to-face matter; violence would have been directed against one's kin and friends and intimate allies and acquaintances. It was relatively easily controlled at this level. The only precedent for larger-scale organization was the "treaty"—a relationship with other bands of the same language group, or other bands of a common territory. These treaties were usually sealed with marriages. They were relationships between equals, as with nations. Once classes, estates, castes, professions, baronies, and satrapies came into existence, all technically within one national framework, even this old precedent could not operate, since these were not equals and were engaged in exploitative relationships the one with the other. The possibility therefore was opened that one section of a technically united society would come to define another as essentially a different tribe—a group of "not-men," or a kind of game animal to be preyed upon.[17] And between such groups it was harder to "ritualize" violence, since real issues were at stake. Peasant rebels were not interested in counting coups on their oppressors in order to prove their manhood and improve their status with their fellows; they wanted bread for their children. Thus sectionalism within societies and conquest and booty between them became the issues into which all the male energy of the warrior-hunter heritage was poured. This has been our history, and there is nothing remarkable or strange about it. It needs no *special* explanation in terms of our innate wickedness and desire to kill and torture, or our innate goodness and fall from grace through the inability to give ourselves a better deal. It is an inevitable outcome of our primate heritage and our weapon-bearing, hunting past, with the addition to these of dense settlement and huge numbers.[18]

Why a pattern should continue to emerge even though conditions for it are unpromising is related to the simple fact that males will still be males. The intervening variable between individual interest in violence and the actual violence of a group is the male bond. The reason we could confidently assert that female warriors would be remarkably less dangerous to the species in general is that females do not bond in a warlike way. They do not create the structures, they do not maintain the continuities, and they do not stimulate the emotions and loyalties among each other that are essential for the sustained conduct of stressful violent enterprise. But males do. Put a bunch of males together long enough, and once they establish some hierarchy and etiquette they will begin to seek some external focus for their interest—something to change, to master, to construct, to destroy—to leave a mark of the special existence of this special group of men. They do this to relate to one another—looking together outside the group focuses the loyalties inside. As any cheap politician knows, shake a bayonet at the outside threat and reap immediate political advantage. In the more local context, under most circumstances the best proof or symptom of the internal strength of a group of males is its keenness to affirm its own reality against the resistances of the outside. Its failure to do so, and repel attack, will be seen widely as a proof of weakness and hence of unimportance.

They do this not because they are evil (though they may become so), nor because they are insecure (though they may be), nor because they are greedy and rapacious (though they may be), but because they are stone-age hunters with stone-age emotions and ways of interacting. They have all the enthusiasms of the hunting primate, but with few of the circumstances in which this reality can be reflected. So they create their own realities: they make up teams; they set up businesses and political parties; they form secret societies and cabals for and against the government; they set up regiments; they make up fantasies about honor and dignity; they turn their enemies into "not-men"—into prey. They generate forms of automatic loyalty and complete dedication that can spread the Jesuitical message of the Church Militant and also send screaming jets to a foreign country. All a country needs is a couple of dozen males who take their fantasies about their own omnipotence so seriously that they spend money, kill people, and even commit Abraham's presumptuous conceit of sacrificing their sons to voices of grandeur they think they hear.

We have immodestly elected to discuss the world's two most severe problems, overpopulation and war. One problem results from the urgency of male-female bonding, and we will come to that shortly. The other is the consequence of male bonding, and is just about as biological, just about as cultural, as elaborately real and yet fantasy-filled as thoughts of love and acts of sex. Once upon a time an animal

developed battle skills, ways of controlling interpersonal and inter-
group hostility on a small scale. War was part of the quintessential
male career. It allowed men to do the things many apparently love:
dress up in glorious garb festooned with primitive indices of rank;
exercise physical skills and a talent for ordering and for obeying;
protect the community by sharpening their toughness and their talents
at comprehending their enemy; seek out and kill and ritually praise
the animals that gave them meat and part of their spiritual estate.

War was controlled ritually. It was controlled also because to kill
meant to look clearly at the whites of their eyes and to smell the fear
of a man being beaten. Killing was done in small groups, and—as they
do still—warriors fought in terms of their clan, their fraternity, their
platoon. Battle cries could be heard and drums banged and war
dances jumped. There were no memos from abroad and no ridiculous
flying generals and ward bosses pouncing down to pronounce on matters of which they could have only indirect knowledge. But it is
precisely symbolic knowledge that makes our world go around. It stimulates our yarns about overkills, endless missile or other gaps, and en-
courages us to distrust those who talk of peace and disarmament
because we know our own imaginative capacity to prepare destruction
well enough to fear them. At the same time, symbolic knowledge is, and
can be, the instrument for peace and reciprocity. Meanwhile, the most
dangerous weapon the soldier has is the cerebral cortex under his hat.[19]

The imperial tendency had its roots in the devices that were used
to hold together groups of early humans that would have otherwise
drifted apart. Baboon troops split up when they are too large, and
become wholly separate entities, potentially in conflict with one another. Human hunting groups can split, but because they speak the
same language, worship the same ancestors, claim descent from the
same mythical animal, reckon to have come from the same hole in
the ground, they remain attached. The attachment is not necessarily
to other people as individuals, but to other people as sharers of the
same symbols. I do not owe hospitality and loyalty and protection
to you because you are my neighbor and always have been, but because we are both attached to a common symbol, because we are both
members of the Emu totem, or speakers of the Sioux language, or
serve the same flag, or owe allegiance to the same constitution, or acknowledge the same God.

This great evolutionary change of gear—from attachment to people
to attachment to symbols—was necessary to take the species over the

crucial divide between horde-living primate and tribe-living man. But what was a useful device for integration at the tribal level became a source of monstrous divisiveness for the species as a whole. In pre-symbolic days, conflict was by definition realistic, but now we can create our own conflicts out of any material at hand.

By the very nature of this process, groups are defined as in conflict. Systems of ideas, attitudes, beliefs, and values can differ profoundly, and if *our* system is to be legitimate, then *yours* must be illegitimate and very easily seen as a threat. In this conflict of symbols, be they nationalistic, religious, linguistic, class, ethnic, or whatever, the truly human skills evolved for local-level person-to-person living can play little part, although we constantly attempt to utilize them. But the controls that we must institute—the ritualizations that we must invent —to deal with gargantuan clashes of arms between coalitions of nations, or Christians and Muslims, or the proletariat and the forces of capitalist oppression, or the third world and imperialism, etc., are something of a different order from the ritualizations and controls that constrained our evolving warrior ancestors for all those millions of years. The new controls have to be, like the causes of the conflicts, highly symbolic. What this means is that controls on large-scale violence in large-scale society are dependent on the fragile reed of human inventiveness. The conduct of modern war is not at all the same as the conduct of war as we have been evolved to pursue and control it. It has become part of the apparatus of the bureaucratically organized market economy, in which decisions are made in arbitrary and technocratic ways. At the same time, it is still being fought and organized by groups of males acting under all the commands of an ancient aesthetic of battle which has little to do with the rhetorical issues politicians mouth in justi-fication.

The human animal is hoist on its own cerebral petard. The brain that was good enough to produce the skilled hunter who excelled and found satisfaction in his male-group predatory activities was also good enough to produce huge empires, noble causes to die for, vast armies, and megadeath. With all these at his disposal, he goes on behaving as if he were still a hunter-warrior, in a war party, on a raid for scalps, glory, and honor among equals. It is obvious to anyone that all the pomp and panoply of war, which may have served splen-didly to boost the morale of a war party, is completely ridiculous when the outcome is not a few scalps and a feather in the war bonnet, but the annihilation of the species. Yet men do not seem to know what else to do except go through these archaic paces. The aesthetic of the male war ritual is self-perpetuating. When it becomes associated with immensely powerful industrial and financial forces whose prosperity depend upon a high level of military expenditure, the temptations for the more fantasy-ridden and more inflated leaders to spend public money on "defense" become, apparently, unbearable. It comes to seem crass weakness and patriotic indecency to refuse requests from militarists whose schemes are limitless and whose ability to create immediate and ever-present dangers would challenge a corps of gifted poets. It is rather as if a group of attractive and aggressively alluring young females were suddenly put to room and board in a seminary. The mere fact of their existence would disturb the young seminarians carefully intent on their devotion and the moral craft they want to have. Have soldiers around, and they will quickly bond with entrepreneurs and politicians. They will make smooth and plausible speeches to a public impressed by their willingness to serve and even die, and by their eagerness to withstand those forces of the untrustworthy enemy they have so prudently understood. If you have a Pentagon, you will use it, and it you.[20]

Nonetheless, there *are* military machines, and it is a plain fact that weak countries have been invaded by others that have cultivated warfare and paid the cost of guns. Whoever started the escalation, whatever the original or recurrent causes of any potential conflict are, why communities decide to spend astonishing sums of money and life cycles of energy on the military—all this is in a deep sense beside the biological point, which is that a more or less large group of male organisms is primed and equipped to fight some other group, and will receive honor and benefit from so doing.

This remains an agonized question for all persons whose disposition is to peace and to the gentle resolution of human differences. What does one do or think to do about the reality of the use of force and the stubborn recurrence of episodes of violence? How can a reply be framed to the proposal that only powerful countries are proof against attack; that to rely on the goodwill of powerful neighbors is charming but hopeless and indeed perilous? Is it in fact possible any longer for a community to be without serious means of self-protection—which must by definition involve people who can hit and hurt, and some apparatus for destruction?

The evidence is discouraging for pacifists. There is no need to go once again into the dismal war record of the species even in its advanced state of allegedly reasoned modernity. That warlikeness seems to bear little relationship to the forms of society must dismay those who see in internal changes the basis for external affability. Peace-loving Communist Russia? Peace-loving Capitalist United States? Peace-loving Maoist China? Peace-loving Peru? Peace-loving Israel? Peace-loving Lebanon? Peace-loving France? Peace-loving Nigeria? Peace-lovers all, and all adulterous with a soldier. From the melancholy, slovenly cruelty of the South American general torturing his opponents, to the glow-eyed, self-declared emancipators in Washington, to the compactly cunning guerrillas in Southeast Asia, there is some pact with force, some decision of first or last resort about the need for specialists in hostility. Of course, after the war there will certainly be peace, and it is often best to declare war to make peace. Yes, goes the familiar wretched promise, this is a limited action, a bit of healthy surgery, a maneuver, really. Do not become alarmed, we are your leaders, prudent, aware, deep, men of peace whom our generals salute with gratitude and respect. The peasants may mass at monuments, may demonstrate, even the barons may grumble because there is a shortage of good harness and their hunting fields are used for training. The young may rebel against the press gang or the draft board, and fathers and mothers may connive to buy their sons out of the danger of having to serve. In international organizations, yards of words will be spun out in the air. And yet the hopeless logic regularly wins out, of warriors caught in structures built like corporations to expand indefinitely, appropriating as much wealth as possible.

We are not concerned with the causes of armed conflict. It has as many causes and justifications as it has instances. To those who fight them, all wars are just wars. We are concerned with the weight of evidence that indicates that groups of men banded together in some interest will readily resort to violence against other groups of men who are seen as opposed to that interest. The interest itself does not seem to matter: violence can serve any master. The answer seems to be, in our evolutionary perspective, that we are a naturally aggressive species easily aroused to violence; that we have invented the means to practice violence effectively on a large scale; that our cultural systems constantly provoke us to violence; that these systems always contain groups of males whose proclivity is violent; that within the last few thousand years of human history, violence has been taken out of its small-scale evolutionary context; that there are few evolutionary precedents for the control of violence on the scale on which it now occurs. The atavistic stimuli to violence still exist, but the means of ritualizing violence that evolved in the small-scale skirmishing days of our ancestors simply cannot operate in the huge, complex, and heavily armed international society of today.

The answer, if there is an answer, lies in the medieval attitude to violence. Left to their own devices, people will fight—or, rather, men will fight. They will make love *and* war. This may not stem from a basic killer instinct, but the end product is certainly the same. That it is not a basic drive seeking expression gives us some slender hope. We may not be able to get rid of violence by refusing to teach it, but we can contain and constrain it by ritualization, by agreement, by threat of greater violence, or by supernatural sanction. We cannot depend on any "natural" controls to operate here: they work only on that small scale we have irrevocably abandoned. And even they do not get rid of violence; they utilize and contain it. And that is what we must do. We must recognize our proclivity for it, our readiness to use it, our excitement in its exercise, our sense of its possible rewards. Given this recognition, we must seek to control it—without any very sanguine notions about getting rid of it altogether—by creating circumstances in which it will not be learned. The circumstances in which it is learned are our human circumstances, and these are a million times amplified by the events of the recent past—the past few thousand years, that is.

There is no great mystery about all this. The facts are clear. The problem is practical, not intellectual. The challenge is to deal with the literal, the obvious, by actually dealing with it, not by wishing it away. It would indeed be better if it were not so, but it is so, and we must try to make it better.

If war is the most public activity, lovemaking is the most private. What was once universally acclaimed for its long-run usefulness for the human group—that it gave us another member and established yet more firmly our hold on our earth and on our future—has now in some places at least become an ardor fraught with ambiguity and a form of creativity increasingly maligned by those who claim to speak for the species' future. What is essentially at issue is the extraordinary burgeoning of human population in this century, and the inevitable problems of housing, feeding, organizing, educating, healing, and living together that accompany this quantitative prosperity. The noble savage constrains his freedom and distorts his experience as much in enthusiastic sexual congress as in bitter acrimony and war.

Just as with hunting-become-war, population-expansion-become-explosion results from old urgencies and from strong and explicit programs. At puberty the human male and female change radically; they are now physically able to reproduce. The source of the population crisis is that people enjoy sexual intercourse and what precedes it. Copulation control is as much the issue as population control. It is surprising that so much of the emphasis in the search for solutions to this problem has been on the chemical and technical tools of contraception and not on the pattern of behavior that makes these necessary. For though means of contraception are now rather widely available (few women in North America of whatever class and education need become pregnant if that is not their clear intention), reproductive rates remain sufficiently high to make us wonder why once again human will fails while physical process perfectly succeeds. It is laughable to claim that those same women accused of wanton and rococo patronage of drugstore makeup counters are incapable of crossing over the aisle to the section where contraceptives are readily available. And males who concern themselves with moon rocketry, tubeless tires, and the horsepower of Fords are in a strong position to understand the nature of the condom, and of *coitus interruptus*.

The same people who say that man has no biological patterns of consequence, no innate propensities, no behavioral relationship to the other primates, are also realistically exercised about the growth of population—clearly a biological matter that must have some connection to our lives as animals. The facts, any way they are looked at, are all too clear. The human species cannot go on reproducing itself at the present rate, because soon there will not be enough food, or air, or room to maneuver. Finally the simple bodily heat our expanded masses will produce will literally cook us like some horribly superior nuclear device.[21] Because the expansion is geometric, not arithmetic, and because our medical skill keeps us alive longer and longer, and because for both nutritional and ethological reasons puberty widely occurs earlier and earlier, we are faced with a genuine and frontally personal crisis to which everyone who makes a child contributes. To have to think of the birth of a baby as an aspect of the pollution problem is gruesome, but realistic. Yet, so far, few of the warnings given and few of the predictions of dire consequences have very much affected how men and women comport themselves. As with violence, to which we are easily stimulated, however miserable the outcome, so we are intrigued and cajoled by the quiet private encounters an animal once learned to find agreeable and essential, but which now become an antisocial act. How private sexual acts can be antisocial in the animal world—where reproductive success is the criterion of fitness in the struggle for survival—repays our scrutiny.

We are perhaps back in the medieval situation: we see violence and sex as dangerous to us, and rightly, and we seek to control them without thinking that we can or should eliminate them. While we may, with some justification, toy with the idea of eliminating violence, we do not think of eliminating sex. Yet these are closely associated functions in human physiology, and the arousal and control of sex and aggression are intimately linked in the brain and in the glandular and nervous systems.[22] It may well be, therefore, that they are equally intimately linked as social phenomena. It is not simply that men fight over women (in fact, they fight much less over women than over property, for instance), but that the consequences of sex—more and more people—may in themselves be potent stimuli to violence. Not only may they stimulate violence, but, more importantly, they may change the condition of violence so that controls break down. If the species is living in dispersed bands with plenty of room for maneuvers, violence will occur. But it will itself be dispersed and sporadic, and related rather to the internal status structure of the band than to conquest or genocide. This we have established. But begin to fill in the intervening spaces with more and more people, and violence spills over onto them and envelops them. Hunters need space and will fight for it. Those who take up the valuable hunting territory will be destroyed. This rarely happens with hunters, because they manage, and managed for all that tediously familiar ninety-nine percent of our history, to keep their populations down to sizes that were in keeping with their hunting ecologies.[23] There was, besides, always somewhere else to go. And, like Schaller's lions, in the face of implacable and unbeatable harassment, one could always run like hell. Little hunting bands on the move from Siberia—perhaps about six of them—eventually populated the whole American continent.[24] Small crews of brown-skinned people from Southeast Asia filled up the islands of the Pacific. And so on. But once areas were filled, they proceeded, with the advent of agriculture and settlement, to become fuller and fuller, and soon there was nowhere else to go. Violence in these complex new circumstances continued, but it was now more difficult to contain. Dispersed rivals clash at intervals, then go away to lick wounds, celebrate or mourn, and prepare to try again. It all has a nice rhythm, a predictability, a control. But when potential rivals are living on top of one another all the time, they cannot play these games. The provocations to violence are constant, and the enemy is always there. He will go away only if he is killed, and there is often a great deal of killing to be done. Even if he is killed, he will be quickly replaced as human population continues to grow. It is endless.

It is often argued that sheer numbers, that density itself, is a cause or even *the* cause of constant armed violence in man.[25] This is only a half-truth. Man was violent *before* he had dense populations. What the dense populations do is to make the ancient means of organizing violence impossible—to change the stakes completely. We no longer wish to score off our enemies, but either to get rid of them to make way for ourselves or to conquer them so that we can use them for our purposes.

Density is not a basic *cause* of violence, but it remains a possibility —some would say a distinct probability—that density has its own pathological consequences, which, benignly enough, reduce the very density that causes them. For animal populations one can work out a "critical population density"—a figure above which it is dangerous for the population to rise without risk of social breakdown and subsequent drastic loss of numbers.[26] This ultimately has the effect of keeping the population in balance with its resources, but resources themselves do not seem the prime cause of the breakdowns. Populations with ample food, shelter, light, etc., will nevertheless crack up if the numbers rise above a certain point. This is because animals have space needs, social needs. They need a certain amount of space in which to perform their natural functions, and without this space these functions cannot be performed. If they are crowded, their sociospatial system breaks down, with the result that many die or remain unborn. Mothers will kill their young or neglect them until they starve to death. Animals low in the hierarchy will be arrested in constant submission and starve. Strong animals will kill one another in frantic fights. Pregnant females will abort or absorb the eggs back into the uterus. Disease will spread easily, and some animals will die "spontaneously," apparently from stress.[27]

The likenesses of animal to human breakdown in dense conditions are obvious and do not have to be challenged. But with humans the matter is more complex. Again, it does not seem to be sheer density— not density as such—that causes the pathologies. It is the conditions of density. There may be some features of density that inevitably give rise to stress, but it seems that it is not large numbers but the way the large numbers live and are organized that counts. We may have psychological difficulties dealing with large numbers, but we can deal with them more easily if they are crowded into luxury apartments than if they are herded into tenements. The inhabitants of the luxury apartments in overcrowded Manhattan can get out, move around a lot, and take long holidays in the Bahamas or on yachts. The apartment is simply a home base for a ranging life that can be quite satisfactory. The tenement dweller in Harlem is trapped physically and socially. There is nowhere for him to go. His adaptability is remarkable, but not infinite. Physically, socially, mentally, at some point he will crack, or withdraw, or revolt. And his revolt will often seem to the luxury-apartment dweller or the suburbanite to be of that random, destructive kind that afflicts the overtaxed society of animals. Density, plus social and physical constraint, seems to be the condition for social pathology in human communities. This follows from the failures of political and economic systems. It is not so much that slum dwellers are denied space, although this is important, as that they are denied participation. The denial of space is only a symptom of the denial of the right to participate. Given all the space in the world, men will revolt and resort to violence if they are too severely peripheralized for too long by too few.[28]

If we cannot use population pressure as an alibi for our violent propensities, there is still the dreadful truth that this very pressure increases the incidence and extent of violence and multiplies its consequences so that it embraces women and children and the old and innocent. While congregation may not be a novel and root cause of violence, dispersion would certainly help in the process of containing it.

The dispersed hunters are plugged into nature in a very profound and direct way. What the naturalist Wynne-Edwards has called "conventionalized competition" seems to be a prerequisite for population control in animal societies.[29] Uncontrolled violence would be damaging and would ultimately wipe the species out. But if the violence is "conventionalized"—or "ritualized"—it has the effect of spreading animals over a wide area. The animals so dispersed will guard and maintain territories on which they will breed. Those that do not obtain territories will not breed. This is one way of helping to keep numbers and resources in balance. It has been argued that social life in the world of animate things has its origin in the conventionalizing of competition for space. Human hunters are really only rather efficient predatory animals. They do what the lion and the panther do, only they do it with better brains and with tools and cultural adaptation. Thus they were able to spread to many more ecological niches than any of their predatory competitors—but they stayed within the scheme. They were hunting animals engaged in conventionalized competition, and they were consequently dispersed, and their numbers were never out of balance with their resources.[30] Exactly how this operates is not the concern here; it is still a matter of academic dispute. What is important is that at this level we were still part of the natural scheme of things, of which ritualized violence was a necessary part. It is *this* that changed with the advent of agriculture, pastoralism, and settlement, and the successive explosions of numbers that now threaten to double the population of the globe every thirty years. About ten thousand years ago we cut adrift from nature with a vengeance; if our violence now seems unnatural, it is not because it is alien to us but because we have drastically changed the scenario.

This raises the whole issue of the role of "territoriality" in human violence, about which so much has been written. That territoriality is closely connected with population control on the one hand, and with the conventionalizing of violence on the other, is obvious enough. Whether or not the defense of territory depends on an "instinct" common to man and animals is another point. In some species there seems to be a deeply programmed quality; in others there seems to be a contingency on circumstances. Many primates do not become "territorial" unless they are literally pushed for space. Hunting animals often do not defend specific areas, but have overlapping "ranges." There are many variations on this theme, and it does not really need a uniform instinct to explain what happens; the fact is obvious that no two animals can occupy the same space. Where space has a value for the animals, they will compete for it as for anything else. In this sense man is a territorial animal as much as any other, and he will accordingly fight over territory. But he will fight over so many other things as well. A piece of the earth's surface can become one of the things to which a group of humans express deep emotional commitment, but so can a language, a religion, a flag, or a way of life. It is hard to disentangle these things. When a people seem to be fighting for territory—in driving off an invader, for example—what they are probably really fighting is the prospect of domination. If an animal loses its territory, it loses its place in the breeding system, and perhaps even its life. A conquered people do not in the same sense "lose" their territory, but they do lose control over their own lives. Nevertheless, a man's defense of his home, and a people's of their homeland, are acts of the same order as an animal's defense of its piece of ground. Many of the same basic animal processes are brought into play. The analogy breaks down in the identification of human *property* with animal territory. The animal's defense of its space is absolute in the sense that if it loses this, it is finished. The same is sometimes true of human territory in the strict sense, and people will fight tenaciously for their farms, hunting grounds, and sacred places. But human property in general, including real estate and even parts of national entities, has the other essential feature that makes it truly human: it can be exchanged. Men will fight to defend and expand their property. Fights over women in primitive societies are mostly fights over women as property. They have nothing to do with fights over territory as such.[31]

While humans do have fights over territory that are equivalent to animal conflicts, their fights over property and over other focuses of symbolic attachment such as nationality or religion are not so readily equatable. These have much more to do with the preservation of autonomy and control over one's own life, both personal and national, than with the defense of a patch of earth.

What overcrowding and overpopulation do is to restrict this autonomy more and more—this sense of having some control over a personal life and fate. One is literally and metaphorically restricted. Huge populations require ever more efficient and impersonal bureaucracies, and the number of positions of dominance open to males does not increase in proportion. The cabinet in America is not much bigger now in a country of two hundred million than it was at the time of the Revolution, when there were only four million. And there is still only one President. Males live longer—one cause of population increase, of course—and continue to occupy positions of power, while generations turn over beneath them in increasing impotence.[32] What is lost in all this is the hunter's sense of his own power and responsibility and his immediate participation in the society on which he depends and which in a real sense depends on him. It is *autonomy* that is threatened by numbers and that results in frustration and an ever-ready tendency to resort to violent solutions: one thing that easily turns this animal on to violence is to cramp its style.

Here, once again, we encounter a gross and tragic paradox. One of the most direct and real ways people have to gain an outright sense of their own significance, and of their elaborate connection with their community and its future, is by having children. The widespread difficulty the species encounters in limiting population by conscious and technical means reflects an underlying unit of the biogrammar that is immensely persuasive, highly energized, and a source of special, long-term satisfactions. It is more than sentimentality to assert that the pleasures and provocations of motherhood and fatherhood are everywhere known by most adult men and women. That there may be disillusion and hardship for some from having children underlines the force of the pattern that urges people to undertake the responsibility, nonetheless. From an innocent perspective, it is altogether astonishing that so many people will either consciously or with less clear intention embark on the expensive and demanding career of parenthood. Why should members of even materialist cultures agree to devote their future and comfort to unborn organisms that will give little of formal value in return, except—what? Pleasure? A sense of personal continuity? An offering to one's parents? A re-creation of youth? Insurance of continued control of one's property? To cement a marriage or stimulate an as yet uncontracted one?

All such reasons may apply. But the simplest one is that the program is there, from puberty. All communities offer a sense of joy and accomplishment to parents of newborns. Infants and children themselves are extremely attractive organisms most of the time (as they are throughout the primate species). Having babies confirms adulthood in a strangely conclusive way. And finally—until this generation—conceiving and bearing a child was a deeply constructive affirmation of social ties and the continuity of the species. Even where contraceptive information is widespread, many babies are born. It may be claimed that the techniques are too complex and expensive and that men and women do not understand their meaning. Undoubtedly this is partly true, but the reduction in birth rates resulting from the pill is sufficiently small to force us to conclude that, for whatever reasons they do so, humans want to have children, enjoy having them, and seem intent on having them, despite options and blandishments to the contrary. For example, it is estimated that between a quarter and a third of North American babies are conceived out of wedlock—against law, against custom, against economic self-interest of many of the persons involved, and with little "going for" the pregnancy apart from its role in uniting a couple and its effective meaning for the life cycles of the parents.

This is not to overlook the effect of contraception and particularly abortion on reducing populations, particularly in Eastern Europe and

Japan. Where it is crowded, people have fewer children than where there is ample space for movement and play. Safe and easy legal abortion permits a conscious decision about having a child at a time when there are relatively disturbing and unpleasant hormonal changes reaching their peak in the female's body, and when the full consequences of having a first or another child become more pronounced.

Ever since Malthus, the clear consciousness of overpopulation as a problem has haunted human beings. The problem has burgeoned, until it is now staggering and beginning to approach a point of no return. The nub of the matter is that reproduction is private. For all intents and purposes, it is the consequence of an uncontrollable behavior. To have few children, people will have to decide to; and so far, the outlook for such voluntary restriction on the global scale which is necessary is unpromising. For one thing, it is not only individuals who will make their decisions in their own terms, but also governments.[33] Many governments currently support high birth rates by tax advantages and other perquisites because they are committed to a pattern of economic growth to some extent dependent on an expanding population. For another, governments always concern themselves with supplying their economies with labor—preferably native-born. For example, curious as it may seem to those who find that country already crowded enough, the Japanese government has been contemplating ways of encouraging births to fill its long-term manpower needs, since the effects of contraceptive and abortion practices have been so marked.[34] For decades France has sought to stimulate higher birth rates, and so have some Eastern European countries.[35] A worldwide birth-rate policy will be no easier to achieve than a worldwide policy of governing violence, or pollution, or the equitable distribution of wealth.

We can appreciate the problems on the international scale. What about the national? How can governments disinduce people from taking part in an enjoyable and fulfilling procedure? One answer lies in levying taxes with advantages for those who do not have children instead of for those who do. But as children are already expensive enough to parents, it is not clear that this will work. Must societies wait until the lives of adults are so cramped and ugly that it will seem merciless to bring children into the world? This may happen too late—the reproductive pattern is that uncritical and that strong.

The grimmest alternative unites population growth and violence. Faced with the mounting problems of controlling ever-greater numbers, states will have to exercise more and more rigid control over behavior. They have done this before with less justification, but as numbers lead us toward chaos and anarchy, unflinching control of even the most intimate details of lives will become more and more commonplace. The techniques exist; they need only to be applied.[36] The techniques will be applied in the name of saving humanity from itself, but we all know what happens when men achieve the kind of absolute power that such altruistic ends confer. It is too much part of the political biogrammar that power is an end in itself for us ever to trust the mandarins to act indefinitely as unselfish trustees of the public good. To control us for our own sakes, to save us from ourselves, is simply in the long run to control us for the sake of controlling us. It is only another means of putting power into the hands of a few. And when the ranks of the peripheralized become inordinately swollen, the fangs of the dominants will be lengthened and sharpened in proportion. They will not abandon violence—it is not their way; they will seek to monopolize it. And should we therefore seek to abandon violence in our turn? It is a hard question to answer for all who deplore armed and bloody conflict of any kind, and yet who are not willing to abandon human dignity.[37]

Such is the stark focus that must inevitably expose the two biological facts central to all natural process: living and dying. Who gets born and why, and who loses life and why, must preoccupy anyone interested in the species as a whole and not only in its local versions. In one way or another it seems likely that some human beings will have to try to urge many others to have only some children, or fewer children, or even none. Can this be done? Infanticide is miserable to contemplate. It is not even clear which would involve more administrative chicanery and simple human inequity—enforced celibacy, or celibacy stimulated by education. It is possible that people will accept the sanity of requiring licenses to conceive, just as there commonly are certificates of marriage. Yet this runs directly opposite to widespread feelings of all peripheralized persons that there is already too much adjudication by others of people's lives.

It is not likely that the conditions under which people now live will tend toward greater autonomy, more participation, and more provident encounter with cooperative, not antagonistic, fellow humans. It is also unlikely, given our experience so far, that administrative and political managers will yield any of their power to their clients. Precisely here the threat or reality of violence may have some meaning—when it is directed against a power structure by those who claim a more generous mandate for power and a more attractive structure with which to use this power in a wider interest. This was the bet the followers of George Washington, Padraig Pearse, Lenin, Castro, Bolívar, and Tito made. Communities may win or lose this often desperate and seemingly quixotic bet on energy and will against structure and the certainty of power. But it may be idle to ignore the forces potentially generated by the human wish to maintain at least some of the major conditions of being human in a situation in which these conditions threaten to become so scarce as to force some members of our species to live in ways that render them very much less than human.

In "Political Nature" we related the political system and the breeding system in primates and explored their role in the control of violence. We saw how in man these two systems became separated. In this chapter we have come around again to looking at the direct and potentially disastrous relationship between the political and reproductive systems of contemporary man. It would be a joyless anticlimax if man's extraordinary trajectory through the scheme of nature should come full circle to the principle that only the elite may breed.

9.

THE
CITY
OF MAN

OUR AIM HAS been to put a lot of well-known facts into a new focus—
or a not-so-new focus if our claim to be in the Darwinian tradition is
correct. We have tried to look at fairly general features of social structure and process that are true for all human societies as end products
of the evolution of social behavior in our species. Building on those
general features that we hold in common with our nearest relatives
(and some more distant, for that matter), we have examined the consequences for the biology of behavior that followed from the hunting
revolution and the transition to humanity. What we have examined
is the transition from the simple life to the symbol life. But in progress-
ing to those vast structures of symbol and fantasy that we call human
cultures, man retained much of his primate heritage. The old primate
brain was not lost, it was augmented. The old primate behavior was
not abandoned but rechanneled, amplified, and supplemented by the
rapidly expanding hunting forebrain. The end result is a creature that
actively demands certain inputs and actively puts out certain energies
involving the other creatures in its social universe. What we have
tried to do is to locate these various basic inputs and outputs, for they
form the skeleton of the human social biogrammar. This presents a
very different picture of human social behavior from the one offered
by cultural anthropology, behaviorist psychology, or instinct theory.

We neither posit specific instincts in man, nor do we see the human infant as a tabula rasa. We see certain human institutions as inevitable, since they follow from the interactions between creatures who are wired to learn certain things, to expend certain energies, and to respond to certain stimuli in ways that have been built into them by the peculiar evolutionary history of the species. If our perspective has any merit, it is that it focuses on these basic grammatical processes that unite mankind into a body of people all speaking the same behavioral language. Social science heretofore has tended to be obsessed with dialect differences, and has even denied that the dialects are linked into one language. While it is perfectly true that the speakers of different dialects often have great difficulty in communicating, it is also true that they are in some very profound way speaking the *same* language. It is this basic unity that we are interested in, and it is the basic categories and processes of the universal behavioral grammar of the species that we have been exploring. An important philosophical outcome of this kind of inquiry is a reassertion of the fundamental unity of mankind, and a natural basis for a theory of "natural" rights. The rights of man are not cultural inventions but statements about the nature of the creature. Men are not simply the creatures of culture, they are the creatures that create culture, because that is the kind of creature they are. But this is jumping ahead.

What are the limits of our approach? On the one hand it appears grandiose to seem to be mapping out huge schemes for the total understanding of human behavior; on the other, it appears simple to reduce human behavior to a few economical principles. Again, the grammatical analogy might help. Any outline of the grammar of a language is at one and the same time more comprehensive and more simple than any actual lengthy expression of the language in prose or poetry. The outline goes beyond any particular expression of the language by providing the rules it is necessary to observe in order to produce more expressions; but on the other hand it cannot, in and of itself, produce the expression nor predict any future expressions. This is precisely the limitation of our approach. We can point out the very general rules that must be observed if behavior is to be "human." We can also point out what will happen if these rules are abrogated or distorted. We cannot predict how the rules will be applied or distorted in any particular case, or how eloquently or clumsily their expression in actual behavior will emerge. No grammar can predict what people will actually say; only a close attention to their literary and oral traditions, their style and manner of speech, and the ethnography of their speech habits will allow us anywhere near our goal. Even if our aim is not prediction but "understanding," a grammar is of limited help. One must know French grammar in order to read Balzac, but this knowledge alone does not guarantee that one will "understand" Balzac in the fullest and widest sense. Thus, detailed analyses of historical events and cultural patterns are very necessary to a full understanding of human social behavior. Our approach does not mean to usurp these at all. All we would argue is that if one wants to learn a language one had better start by knowing the grammar.

Our problem as analysts of our own behavior is like that of speakers who deal with their own language. Students of English literature who speak English anyway do not need to learn English grammar in order to understand the symbolism of Ulysses or the unconscious origins of Shakespeare's Hamlet. If they wanted to follow out the philosophical development of Goethe's ideas, however, they would have to master German grammar. Our own social scientists take the grammar of human behavior very much for granted, since they are humans and they behave. When they come to deal with other species, it is a different matter: the grammar becomes important and cannot be taken for granted. We have treated our own behavior as if it were that of another species, as if it were an alien grammar whose code has to be cracked. At the moment, researchers move uncomfortably close to the Japanese scholar who is interested in the role of word rhythms and symbols in Nabokov but who does not know English. Or even to the serious Nabokov student who does not understand Nabokov's native language. Our concern is with the point of departure and not the meaning of the exploration and its consequence. Anyway, much of the work on human behavior now uses some notion of biogrammar, but it is an inadequate one that harshly separates man from the natural circumstances that envelop him, and from the specifically human portion of his primate history.

It would be stupid and cheerless to demand a unanimous approach and an affection for a new orthodoxy. The form of this biosociological explanatory exercise is relatively underdeveloped; what we have tried to do is create an opportunity for more precise and organized analysis of propositions that appear to flow legitimately and helpfully from well-tested work in the natural sciences. Finally, it is evident that facts can be interpreted in a variety of ways, and while we are willing to stand by the structure of our argument and the components with which we have made it, we are and must be strategically skeptical of any closure of these matters and of a set of *dicta* so self-supporting that critique of one invalidates all and evaluation of the set condemns the components.

More than one grammar can account for the actual speech of any linguistic community. Grammars based too heavily on Latin models, it has been shown, often turn out to be totally inadequate to describe economically the facts of very unlatinate languages. Alternative kinds of grammar exist for describing the actual speech of English speakers. We have suggested that the grammars of behavior based on learning theory or enculturation are not as adequate, not as comprehensive, not as economical as a grammar based on the biological nature of man. The proof of the pudding lies in its eating. The better the grammar, the easier it is to understand the language. The adequacy of a biobehavioral grammar should, once it gets beyond the sketchy stage it is in at the moment, enable people to understand their own social behavior better and hence to become better speakers, or at least to understand the limits of their capacity: they may well be trying to say too much too quickly. There is ample material for both optimists and pessimists. For the former a better knowledge of human nature may lead us to become better and more sensitive humans; for the latter this knowledge can only confirm that in some areas at least people have lapsed into irreversible behavioral gibberish.

There is also room for maneuver for both conservatives and radicals. Our perspective justifies neither one nor the other, but it can provide material for both. No attempt at a scientific assessment of human possibilities and limits justifies any moral position, since ideologies select from among the range of these possibilities those they wish to conserve or those they wish to change. Conservatives may be very foolish in trying to retain certain features on the grounds that they are part of "human nature" when they are clearly nothing of the kind. This was the fault of Social Darwinism and laissez-faire. Unbridled competition with no mitigating redistributive and communal grooming system is not an expression of human nature. But on the other hand radicals may be just as foolish in trying to make drastic alterations in something that should be rechanneled or molded gently because it does indeed reflect a basic propensity. It may even be that radicals are not radical enough, since their grasp of reality is colored by the traditional visions of the future they so ardently espouse. If our analysis of male-female differences is at all correct, then the greater participation of women in national life will not come about within the framework of the system as it stands. The realities of male-female interaction will simply get in the way. It may need something much more drastic like laws that compel boards of directors to have female members, or female quotas in legislatures, before the greater participation that would obviously be to everyone's benefit could be effected. On the other hand, radicals are undoubtedly right to suggest that war machines are a primary cause of wars, and that by dismantling these we would go a long way toward cutting down on warfare. They are right, but for reasons they may not be aware of.

We could proceed to list an elaborate series of policy proposals that could follow from the analyses we have made. But we do not regard this as either our responsibility or our particular competence. To state the matter as citizens, we see our function as part of the preliminary process of diagnosis and analysis. In this sense we are biological Fabians—committed to understanding biological infrastructure as a basis for social change, just as English Fabians were devoted to comprehending the factual realities of English society. Only such introductory social-scientific work, they knew, would permit social reforms to be undertaken with information in hand, and with some confidence that desirable innovations would have a predictable effect on social circumstances that had been clearly described.

This is not a particularly glamorous position to adopt, nor is it immediately exciting to those who would seek instant alteration of social conditions and rapid redress of obvious historical wrongs and inefficiencies. Some of these may be possible indeed. But our own confrontation with the data and theory of natural science in conjunction with what is known about human social life and how humans behave urges us to insist on the need for a tutored and probing knowledge of the range of options available to ambitious reformers. Paradoxically, the experience of researching and writing this book has committed us to the position that radical social changes will be within our grasp only if we first know the shape of the conservatism of the species and build on this with more than hope and ardor.

For humans alone among all the species on earth are able to organize themselves consciously against their own extinction. We are our own conservationists as well as our own veterinarians. And this should push home the point that what is proposed here is not a kind of determinism, any more than the law of gravity is a kind of determinism. To those who think that the law of gravity interferes with their freedom, there is nothing to say. To most sensible people this law is simply something that has to be taken into account in dealing with the world, like the second law of thermodynamics. If we ignore the famous second law, we will waste a lot of time trying to make perpetual-motion machines and other useless devices. In the behavioral sphere we may be ignoring laws just as fundamental. Our ability to ignore them illustrates the lack of determinism involved. We are not here proposing that man *must* behave in certain ways, but only that he is programmed *to* behave in certain ways. If he chooses to behave otherwise, then he must do so with as much hope of success as those who ignore the basic physical laws. Man conquered the physical world not by insisting that he could *outdo* nature but by finding out exactly what it was he could *do with* nature. Our modest suggestion is that the same demanding principle should be applied to our attempts at social transformations.

At this point we must consciously cross the boundary between scientific analysis and moral judgment. We can begin with another animal's situation—the chicken. Much of the world's chicken population lives in batteries—in highly mechanized assembly lines in which the sole concern is for the production of eggs and edible chickens. The creatures are bred to suit some market need or other—for more breast meat, smaller beaks and legs, faster laying cycles, and so on. But the behavior of the chicken is of no concern to anyone except insofar as it abets or hinders the process of production and of making profits. The unfortunate animals remain chickens, of course, but their behavior is not chicken behavior in the broad sense, and their view of the entire matter is perhaps reflected in the precautions necessary to prevent their flight from the specialized conditions under which they live.

The analogy with humans is all too clear. Humans can be made to live in battery-farm conditions, and to some observers either prison life or city life or Hong Kong life or the rat race or what have you are merely disguised versions of the miserable chickens' circumstance. Whatever one's response to this lament, the point remains that the limiting conditions of what can be done to human beings in the name of some theory or some power structure or some experiment are not settled; there are always innovators and tyrants with exotic mandates who claim some special view of what life should be like. The whole argument has been that while human potential for change and for being coerced by power and symbol is enormous, nonetheless there remain certain regularities in our needs: even astronauts have to defecate, and even blind children smile at people.

Perhaps our most profound confusion is that in precivilized conditions what were simply human needs, in postcivilized conditions became human rights. In dealing with our hunting evolution, we have documented at length what these needs are: needs for space to move about in; for a share of the communal kill; for participation in the predatory activity of the whole group; for a chance to rise in status through merit; for an opportunity to take risks; for the means to make deals and alliances; for exploration and novelty when young; for a sense of security derived from close association with the mother; for education geared to the realities of the life cycle; for accurate knowledge of the environment; for a chance to be brave and prove oneself; for a place at the triumph feast; for an acknowledgment of individual worth; for children and the caring for them and the protection and security that accompany this; for recreation and free use of the imagination; for support in times of stress; and above all the intense need to contribute with dignity to the community of which one is part.

These and more are the basic behavioral needs of the creature. They should not be things it has to claim and justify, any more than it has to claim and justify its right to breathe, or the chicken has to justify its right to peck, the hawk to swoop. We do not ask whether the cock has a right to crow; we accept that crowing is what the cock does. To prevent it from crowing is to take away something that is intrinsic to being a cock. The same is true, for example, of the so-called "right to work" in human societies, or the "right to vote." It is heartless to claim that these are abstract symbolic things that must be justified on the basis of divine intent or rational political theory; they are statements about what it is to be a human being: that a human being is the kind of animal that, of its very nature, contributes its labor to the group and participates in the conduct of the group's affairs. The "right" to a minimum wage, for example, or to adequate and inexpensive medical care, or to an education, or to a free and creative use of the intellect, is simply a "right" to behave in a way that is intrinsic to being human; it needs no more justification than the crowing of the cock.

By the same token, however, we cannot expect Utopias. It is as natural to man to create hierarchies, to attach himself to symbolic causes, to attempt to dominate and coerce others, to resort to violence either systematic or lunatic, to assert, to connive, to seduce, to exploit. The only possible Utopia, in our perspective, would lie in a return to a simple hunting existence. But this is impossible. We have crossed the divide in terms of population alone. Our societies of the future will be places that will have to deal with the continuing tension between the needs of a hunting primate on the one hand, and the conditions it has created for itself on the other—conditions that often work to negate the very needs that move it in the first place. Neither the state nor bureaucracy will wither away, and we are not evolved to cope with either. Nor were we evolved to cope with violence in the context in which it now manifests itself. But this new context is one with which we are stuck, and it is this with which we have to deal. Utopian idealism can only help to make the misery more unbearable by deluding us into thinking that we can, by simple acts of will and rational activity, make either a different creature out of man, or wish away the tensions that emanate from his premature leap into civilization. The reality is difficult enough to cope with, but we cannot begin to cope with it until we accept it as real. Utopias may be as careless in their treatment of the basic needs of the species as the real societies they implicitly or explicitly reproach and reject. It is difficult to envisage the possibility of human society without violence, disease, selfishness, oppression, and injustice. These are as much a part of human life as their opposites— love, health, altruism, and fair dealing. Many different social systems and sets of cultural beliefs are compatible in some degree with the range of human needs—even systems that may be repulsive to the tender-minded or obnoxious to the tough.

The insights gained from the evolutionary, species-wide perspective do not lead to Utopia or any very sanguine and comforting forecasts about the future of mankind. But it is our belief that they leave us less helpless in the long run. Without this perspective we are not tackling reality but only our own cultural versions of reality—and often just our conceit about what reality should be. With this perspective we should be in a position to assess what the problems really are, and to tackle them with a knowledge of how they came to be problems in the first place. Most of our problems with crime, economics, political unrest, the revolt of youth, the disaffection of women, the clash of races, are behavioral problems. They have to do with the constraints and distortions of behavior that we create, or, to be kind, that are created by the almost impossibly difficult context into which we are trying to fit our evolved human behavior. The behavior is in many cases clearly wrong for the context, and in other cases the context can only twist, fragment, and frustrate the behavior. We hear ourselves speak our own behavioral language through a set of amplifiers and loudspeakers that deafen us to our own words and garble our grammar. As long as we know the grammar, we can at least try to retune the instruments.

If there is any hope or confidence in the future of man, it resides in the lie this perspective gives to the dismal theories of culturalists of whatever school. If man were indeed a blank slate for his culture to write on at will whatever perverse message it chose, we would be in even greater peril than we appear to be. Our capacity to produce hideous cultures is immense, and we indulge it with a grotesque fondness. But time and time again men stand up and say no to their cultures in the name of humanity. And even if their versions of this humanity may differ the one from the other, there are enough common elements to suggest that enough men have an inkling of the grammar to demand that we speak properly. If the culturalists were correct, men would be wholly brainwashed by their cultures. Nevertheless, men keep asserting, by violence if necessary, those very basic needs that are part of the evolved repertoire of our behavior. Men do not need to learn or to be taught that slavery and exploitation are inhuman. They know they are. And they know this because they are human themselves, and they understand what it is to be dehumanized.

The Renaissance was a time of splendid and delicate contortion that we now admire and praise as the beginning of personality, of perspective, of a devotion to the protection an individual must have from the maelstrom of community. But it robbed humans of something to which some quick mention has already been made in this book— a sense of the ordered likelihood of evil and connivance and the absolute requirement for a special supervisory abstraction to assimilate the diverse human energies and turbulences in any place. God commanded, and in their lights kings, doges, princes, popes, cardinals, and sundry chiefs interpreted this improbable scheme first to support their palaces and even finally to ensure the persistence of their Genevans, Kumasians, Bangkokians, or Pekingese. At least in Europe, God could rule, and a host of squalid well-placed entrepreneurs tax-farm in his name. Out of the intimacy of empires no bigger than a Paris *arrondissement* or Philadelphia ward they established some theory of feudal order—almost primate in its certainty—of the necessity of human variation and the community of all those who served the God nobody had seen.

No such generous God interested in our welfare and interpreted by understandably enthusiastic divine-right kings and cardinals can help a species driven to distraction by its success in breeding, holding its nose against the rot of the mounds of products it tastes and drops away, and warmly expending millions of dollars every year on supersonic shields and spears and date-line-crossing missiles. Spaceship earth is on its own; so are its humans. Like hereditary shareholders in some golden corporation, we all have a piece of the remarkable genetic action, a touch of the wealth that the ages of testing, evolution, and defeat have laid by against good times and hard times. It may be stupid to assert these are especially bad times and that our credit with the natural order must be more carefully used than ever. This was the alarm of Greeks and Romans; Jeremiah gave the passion a name; Luther, Napoleon, and Hitler all threatened the old and good order with remarkable catastrophe. But these were parochial radicals—all believers in some preposterous charmless pomp about superior religions, superior classes, superior races, superior nations, even superior individuals. It is not the extermination of a class, religion, race, or nation that we face, but the possible extermination of the species. If the universal megalopolis that we are building for ourselves can no longer find its unity as the City of God, then it must find it as the City of Man. That in this city there may not be room or enthusiasm for a crying baby or an uncertain senile man is a violation of the glory of the prince and a rebuking disharmony for the melody of the poet. No one can make city walls out of paper theory, or even metal spikes, and no one can utterly destroy with ease the intimate affections and thoughtful providence of mothers and fathers and friends and children, even of pet dogs, even for familiar streets and places. No suave formula can entertain the citizens and ensure survival, and no special machine can proof us against disrepair. A stubborn million-year-old animal pushes its big-brained head above the litter of pieces and contrivances and stares with some new confusion at the other bigbrains across the way, in the other dump. Once before they joined to make a little empire. Again that stamina for encounter and that tenderness about the movements in the tribe are necessary, if only that swollen brain can contrive a method to harmonize all the massive schemes and affirm the absolute value of intimacies no more extensive than the reach of an unarmed arm.

NOTES

Books and articles are referred to by name of author and date of publication. Thus, Hull 1943 refers to the bibliography entry: Hull, C. L. 1943. *Principles of Behavior*. New York: Appleton, Century. References to books are to the edition actually consulted.

1. BEGINNING BIOGRAMMAR

1. Works by Darwin: Darwin 1859; 1871; 1873. For modern reviews: De Beer 1968; Roberts and Harrison 1959. General views of Darwinism: Barnett 1958; Eiseley 1958. Darwinism and the social sciences: Banton 1961. An anthropological approach: Alland 1967.
2. On adaptation: Williams 1966.
3. Striding walk: Napier 1967.
4. On concept of "species specific" behavior: Hinde and Tinbergen 1958; Tinbergen 1963.
5. Animal communication systems: Critchley 1958; Haldane 1955; Marler 1967; Sebeok 1965; Tinbergen 1962. On animal communication and human languages: Hockett 1958; 1959.
6. On primate threat gestures: Wickler 1967.
7. Herring gulls: Tinbergen 1953b.
8. Hamadryas: Kummer 1967; 1968.
9. Human gift giving: Mauss 1925.
10. Chimpanzees: Goodall 1968.

11. "Biogram" coined by: Count 1958-1959. Developed further in: Count 1958; 1967.
12. For a development of this argument (on which the chapter is partly based): Fox 1970a. *See also:* Dillon ed. 1971.
13. On physical continuity: Clark 1950.
14. Behavior and speciation: Romer 1958.
15. Bipedalism: Napier 1964.
16. Evolution of brain and behavior: Hassler and Stephen 1966; MacLean 1964; Roe and Simpson 1958, part II. *See also:* Penfield and Rasmussen 1950.
17. Anatomical evolution generally: Campbell 1966; Napier 1970; Pfeiffer 1969. For a comparative social ethological perspective: Crook 1970.
18. The "culturalist" position (attacked by Ardrey 1970 as "environmentalism") is echoed in most of the official pronouncements and textbooks of cultural anthropology and sociology. For examples from anthropology: Boas 1948; Bock 1969; Kaplan 1965; Kroeber 1917; 1952 (a partial retraction); Murdock 1945; White 1948; 1949; 1959. For criticism: Opler 1964. For an extended and perceptive review: Bidney 1953. For review of political aspects: Bressler 1968; Tiger 1970c. For a sociologist's view of the innate: Ginsburg 1964 (1921). Definitions of culture: Kroeber and Kluckhohn 1952. The nature-culture distinction: Lévi-Strauss 1949; Malinowski 1944. Conditioning, reinforcement, behaviorism: Hull 1943; Pavlov 1927; Skinner 1953; Watson 1930.
19. Chomsky 1965; 1966; 1968. Lenneberg 1967.
20. On instinct: Barnett 1967; Bowlby 1969, vol. 1, part II; Lorenz 1965; Schiller 1957; Thorpe 1956; Tinbergen 1951. On human instincts: Crombie 1965; Fletcher 1957. An elaboration of instinct theory regarding man: McDougall 1908. On the demise of instinct theory: Beach 1950; 1955. On the ideological aspects: Pastore 1949.
21. Needs and functional prerequisites: Aberle *et al.* 1950; Malinowski 1944.
22. Relations between older and younger males: Nissen 1961. Initiation: Tiger 1969, chap. 6.
23. Evolution and natural selection: Fisher 1958; Huxley 1963; Simpson 1950; 1953; Smith 1958; Tax 1960.
24. Evolution of behavior: Fox 1967b; Freedman 1968; Gavan 1955; Lorenz 1950; 1958; 1965; Roe and Simpson 1958; Simons 1962; Tinbergen 1960a; 1960b; 1964; 1965. Classic paper: Huxley 1914. On "ethology" as the science of the evolution of behavior: Eibl-Eibesfeldt 1968; 1970; Eibl-Eibesfeldt and Kramer 1958; Freedman 1965; Hess 1962; Hinde 1959; 1966; Huxley 1963; Roeder 1963; Thorpe 1956; Tinbergen 1953a; 1955; 1963. For criticism: Lehrman 1953; Schneirla 1956. For a defense: Lorenz 1965; 1969. *See also:* Hebb and Thompson 1954; Klopfer and Hailman 1967; Scott 1958.
25. Genetic code: Crick 1962.
26. Life cycle: Bonner 1965.
27. Brains producing culture: Keith 1948; Kroeber 1948 (1923), chap. 2.

28. Criticisms of this position: Geertz 1965; Howell 1964; Washburn and Howell 1960.
29. Toolmaking and use by early man: Dart 1957; 1959; Lancaster 1968; Napier 1962; Oakley 1950; 1957; 1961.
30. Tool use in chimpanzees: Goodall 1964.
31. Tools and brain evolution: Washburn 1959; 1960. For a critique of brain size as a criterion of advance: Holloway 1966. For another view: Caspari 1963. For evolution of specific areas of brain: Kotchetkova 1960.
32. On hunting as a selection pressure: Ardrey 1961; Dart 1953; 1958; 1959; Read 1920. For another view: Jolly 1970.
33. Speech and evolution: Hockett and Ascher 1964; Lancaster 1968.
34. Speculations on selection pressures affecting the evolution of primate and early human behavior: Bartholomew and Birdsell 1953; Crook and Gartlan 1966; Etkin 1954; Kortland and Kooij 1963; Shultz 1961.
35. Evolution of rule-obeying behavior: Waddington 1961.
36. Habits and instincts: Russell and Russell 1961.
37. Culture as selection pressure: Garn 1964.
38. Culture as aspect of human biology: Dobzhansky 1962; Simpson 1966.
39. For a bold and prophetic statement of a similar viewpoint to the one argued here, and one that contradicted the prevalent culturalist stand: Wissler 1916; 1923. For some relevant modern statements: Chapple 1970; Freedman 1967; Freeman 1966; Haldane 1956; Hallowell 1950; 1956; 1960; 1962. For a review of some of the issues: Callan 1970.
40. On possible antiquity of hominid line: Leakey 1967: Pilbeam 1967; Simons 1964; 1965. For another view setting a later date: Sarich 1968; Wilson and Sarich 1969.
41. On antiquity of known hominids: Clark 1970; Howell 1969; Rheinhold 1971. On *Australopithecinae:* Broom 1949; Broom and Schepers 1946; Clark 1967; Robinson 1964.
42. *Homo erectus:* Howells 1966.
43. For good general reviews: Washburn 1965; 1968; Washburn and Jay 1968.
44. On "newer" and "older" parts of brain: MacLean 1962; 1964; 1967.
45. Selection for immunity to epidemics: Livingstone 1960.
46. On conflicts between older and newer parts: Koestler 1967.

2. POLITICAL NATURE

1. Ant and insect societies: Kettlewell 1965; Richard 1953; Schneirla 1941.
2. Social organization of animals generally: Allee 1958; Eisenberg 1966; Etkin 1964.
3. Competition, pair-formation, territory, and breeding: Wynne-Edwards 1962.
4. Formation of systems through persisting dominance relationships: Chance and Jolly 1970; Tiger 1970a.

5. Major sources on primate social behavior: Altmann 1965; 1967; Carpenter 1964; DeVore 1965b; Hall 1965b; Imanishi 1960; 1963; Jay 1968; Morris 1967; Southwick 1963. General information on primates: Napier and Napier 1967.
6. Savanna primates and human evolution: DeVore and Washburn 1963; Jay 1968; Washburn and DeVore 1961. An alternative view: Reynolds 1966a; 1968.
7. Sex as basic bond: Sahlins 1959; 1960. Based on: Zuckerman 1932. Critique: Lancaster and Lee 1965.
8. Red deer: Darling 1937.
9. Effect of high-ranking mothers on rank of offspring: Kaufman 1966; 1967; Kawai 1965; Kawamura 1965; Koford 1963b; Koyama 1967; Sade 1965; 1967.
10. Care of infants by males: Itani 1963.
11. Watchfulness and attention: Chance 1967.
12. Dominance and breeding: Chance 1962b; Chance and Mead 1953; DeVore 1965; Ginsburg 1968.
13. Hunting transition: Lee and DeVore 1968. *See also:* note 32 in Chapter 1.
14. Fission in primate groups: Furuya 1969; Koford 1963a.
15. Size of hunting populations: Birdsell 1953; 1957; 1958.
16. On King Ismail: Barbour 1965.
17. Types of political domination: Weber 1947. Discussion of Weber: Bendix 1960.
18. On despotism: Wittfogel 1957.
19. Disraeli on aristocracy: Blake 1966.
20. Rebellion and feudalism: Gluckman 1954; 1955; 1963.
21. On badges of rank, etc.: Spencer 1876.
22. Stability of constitutional monarchies: Lipset 1959.
23. Visibility and democratic politics: Canetti 1962; Wallas 1948.
24. Political society as the integration of unequal organisms: Ardrey 1970; Masters 1968.
25. On prophets: Emmett 1956.
26. Weber on charisma: Gerth and Mills 1948.
27. Weber on charisma and biology: Weber 1947, p. 107. *See also:* Tiger 1966.
28. Critique of bureaucracy: Merton 1957.
29. Weber on bureaucracy: Gerth and Mills 1948.
30. On days of misrule, role reversal, etc.: Gluckman 1955; Leach 1961; Turner 1969.
31. Loyalty and orderliness in packs: Read 1920.
32. Breeding for different behavioral strains: Fuller and Thomson 1960; Hirsch 1967; Spuhler 1968.
33. "Trainability" and nervous system: Eysenck 1951. This is an extension of Pavlov's distinction between "hysterics" and "dysthymics," *see* Pavlov 1927; 1928.
34. Devonian lung fishes and conservatism of innovation: Romer 1958; 1959.
35. For a biological view of politics as a science: Somit 1968; Somit, Davies, and Schwartz (forthcoming).

3. BOND ISSUE ONE

1. Crow Indians: Lowie 1956.
2. On Kibbutz socialization: Spiro 1956; 1958. Kibbutz exogamy: Shepher 1971.
3. Bonding, aggression, and territory: Lorenz 1966.
4. Mother-child bond in mammals: Eisenberg 1966; Rheingold 1963.
5. Suckling and mother-child bond: Count 1967.
6. Mammalian nature of man: Hill 1957; LaBarre 1954.
7. On imprinting: Bateson 1966; Fabricius 1962; Hess 1958; 1964; Lorenz 1935; Moltz 1960; Salzen 1967. Critique: Klopfer 1965. Imprinting in humans: Ambrose 1969; Gray 1958; Hinde 1963. General discussion: Bowlby 1969, vol. 1, chap. 10.
8. Adverse effects of malnutrition on growth: Glass 1968b, part II; Zeman and Stamborough 1969.
9. Myelin and malnutrition: Chase, Dorsey, and McKhann 1967; Stock and Smythe 1963.
10. Effects of institutionalization on children: Bowlby 1951; Provence and Lipton 1962.
11. Psychoanalytic interpretations, see e.g.: Freud 1949; Horney 1945; Klein 1949.
12. For general treatments of separation: Ainsworth 1962; Bowlby 1953; 1958; 1960; 1961a; 1961b; 1963; 1969; Cassler 1961; Mead 1962.
13. On texture: Harlow 1958; 1959. On smell: Brill 1932; Kalogerakis 1963.
14. Social development in monkeys and apes: Hinde, Rowell, and Spencer-Booth 1964; Hinde and Spencer-Booth 1967; Mason 1965a; 1965b. Primate mothers and young: DeVore 1963; Harlow 1962a; Harlow, Harlow, and Hansen 1963; Harlow and Zimmerman 1959; Lawick-Goodall 1967a.
15. Effects of deprivation on sexual behavior: Harlow 1962b; Harlow and Harlow 1965.
16. Effects of deprivation on maternal behavior: Hansen 1966; Seay, Alexander, and Harlow 1964.
17. Effects of deprivation on primates generally: Griffin and Harlow 1966; Harlow and Harlow 1962; Kaufman and Rosenblum 1967a; Mason and Sponholz 1963; Nissen 1956; Seay, Hansen, and Harlow 1962. Critique: Meier 1965.
18. Mammalian mothers at parturition: Count 1967; Hediger 1955, chap. 7.
19. Exploration and curiosity in infants: Rheingold 1961; 1963.
20. Termination of bond: Kaufman and Rosenblum 1969.
21. Deer: Darling 1937.
22. Wolves: Mowat 1963; Murie 1944.
23. Hamadryas: Kummer 1968.
24. Gibbons: Carpenter 1940.
25. On family as a "natural" unit, see e.g.: Bell and Vogel 1960; Goode 1964; Murdock 1949; Westermarck 1903. On "pairing instinct": Morris 1967a; 1970.

26. For similar dissident views: Adams 1960; Bohannan 1963; Goodenough 1970; Linton 1936; Spiro 1954.
27. For a survey of patterns of attachment of males to mother-child units in man: Fox 1967a; 1970.
28. Examples of activation of brother-sister bond: deMoubray 1931; Gough 1959; 1961; Nakane 1963; Williamson 1962.
29. Examples of "sharing" between brother-sister and husband-wife ties: Eggan 1950; Malinowski 1929.
30. Examples of cooperative female households: Smith 1962; Smith 1956.
31. Kama sutra: Burton and Arbuthnot 1962 (1883). *See also:* Burton 1963 (1886).
32. On reproductive cycles in mammals and primates: Amoroso and Marshall 1960; Bullough 1961; Erickson 1967; Everett 1961; Harlow 1965b; Zuckerman 1930.
33. Savanna primate breeding systems: DeVore 1965a.
34. Smell as a sexual signal: Michael 1968; Michael and Keverne 1968.
35. Consort relationships: Reynolds 1970.
36. Desert baboons: Crook 1968; Kummer 1968.
37. Chimpanzees: Goodall 1965; Lawick-Goodall 1968; Reynolds 1965.
38. Gibbons: Carpenter 1940.
39. Carnivores and human evolution: Schaller and Lowther 1969.
40. Decline of hormonal control: Beach 1947; 1965; Ford and Beach 1952; Spuhler 1959.
41. *See* note 34.
42. On copulatory success in human and primate females: Michael 1970; Michael and Zumpe 1970; Udry and Morris 1968.
43. Female cycle generally: Dalton 1964; Moos 1969.
44. Smell sensitivity and cycle: LeMagnen 1950; 1953.
45. Hamburg 1968; Kopell 1969; Parker 1960.
46. Kopell 1969.
47. Dalton 1960b; 1964.
48. Dalton 1959; Janowsky *et al.* 1969.
49. Dalton 1960a; 1960c.
50. Pair bond and marriage: Morris 1970.
51. On courtship: Bastock 1967; Morris 1956.
52. Based on a personal communication from Dr. Kurt Freund.
53. For a development of the general argument: Fox 1967d; 1968.

4. BOND ISSUE TWO

1. Breeding systems and kinship systems: Fox 1971. *See also:* Darlington 1969.
2. Male-male bonds in general: Tiger 1969. Significance of male bonds in primates: Chance 1962a.
3. Hunting in primates: Dart 1963; Lawick-Goodall 1967b.
4. Cooperation in primates: Crook 1966. On male-female division of labor in hunters: Lee 1968. A recent general treatment of sex roles: Holter 1970.

5. Elimination of sexual competition: Sahlins 1960.
6. On exogamy and exchange of women: Chagnon 1968; Fox 1967a, chaps. 7 and 8; Lévi-Strauss 1949a; McLennan 1865; Needham 1962; Tylor 1888.
7. Shaka: Ritter 1955.
8. On topology and anthropology: Leach 1962, chap. 1. Topology as a science: Kuratowski 1962.
9. For an extended development of this argument: Fox 1971.
10. Crow wife abductions: Lowie 1956.
11. Hormones and sex behavior: Ball 1940; Beaman 1947; Harris 1964; Harris and Levine 1965; Levine 1966; Michael 1968; Money 1965; Witalen 1967; Young 1961; Young, Gay, and Phoenix 1964.
12. Sex-linked dominance: Duverger 1955; Goldberg 1968; Greenstein 1961; Murphy 1959; Royal Commission on the Status of Women 1970; Tiger 1970a; 1970b.
13. Formation of macaque groups: Vandenberg 1967.
14. Succession and control in matrilineal systems: Fox 1967a, chap. 4; Schneider and Gough 1961.
15. On the male conspiracy: Millett 1970. For comment, Tiger 1970d.
16. On limited female participation in public life: Dahlstrom 1967; Evans-Pritchard 1965; Mead and Kaplan 1965; Paulme 1964.
17. Female intellect: Maccoby 1970.
18. Political goals of feminist movements: Friedan 1963; Morgan 1970. Historical account of feminism: O'Neill 1967. *See also:* Bird 1968. For a complementary statement of male difficulties: Bednarik 1970. For a review of sex differences as reflected in reading matter: White 1970.
19. Primate females and newborn infants: Hinde 1965; Rowell, Hinde, and Spencer-Booth 1964.
20. Decrease of age at puberty: Tanner 1960.
21. Initiation for girls: Brown 1963.
22. Initiation for boys: Cohen 1964; Whiting *et al.* 1958.
23. Freud: Fox 1966; 1967b; Freud 1952.
24. On gerontocratic monopoly of females: Hart and Pilling 1960; Hiatt 1967; Goodale 1962; Nissen 1961.
25. Gangs: Thrasher 1936; Whyte 1943; Yablonsky 1964. Gangs and evolution: Davis 1962.
26. Inhibition of son-mother mating in primates: Sade 1968.
27. The literature on incest is vast. For some reviews: Aberle *et al.* 1959; Fox 1962; 1967a, chap. 2; Slater 1959.
28. As evidenced, for example, in the research of Kinsey and his associates: Kinsey, Pomeroy, and Martin 1948.

5. GIVE AND TAKE

1. On gifts and counter gifts—the basic insight on which this chapter is based: Mauss 1925.

2. On property: Engels 1905; based on Morgan 1877. Evolution of private property: Hobhouse 1913.
3. Territory and real estate: Ardrey 1966. Critique: Montagu 1968, especially Crook 1968. On territory generally: Carpenter 1958; Hediger 1962; Klopfer 1969.
4. Significance of food sharing: Laughlin 1968; Sahlins 1960. Hunting and food-sharing in carnivores: Kühme 1965; Shaller and Lowther 1969.
5. Paleolithic hunters: Howell and Clark 1963; Pericot 1962; Sollas 1924. Survey of hunting societies: Lee and DeVore 1968; Service 1966. On hunting and evolution *see* note 32 in Chapter 1.
6. On significance of tools *see* notes 29–31 in Chapter 1.
7. Social organization and evolution of hunting: Washburn and Lancaster 1968.
8. On exchange of females: Lévi-Strauss 1949. *See* note 6 in Chapter 4.
9. Emotions and evolution: Hamburg 1963; 1968.
10. Polygyny of hunting leaders: Laughlin 1968; Rose 1960; 1968.
11. Sanctions against "ungenerous" chiefs: Lévi-Strauss 1944.
12. Mauss 1925.
13. General characteristics of hunting economies: Lee 1966; 1968; Woodburn 1964.
14. Redistribution and reciprocity as basic principles: Polanyi 1967; Sahlins 1963a.
15. Deevey 1960a.
16. Origins of agriculture: Childe 1946. Critique: Binford and Binford 1968.
17. Domestication: Ucko and Dimbleby 1969.
18. Animals and man: Leeds and Vayda 1965.
19. Agricultural revolution: Braidwood 1960.
20. Agriculture and civilization: Adams 1966; Flannery 1965; MacNeish 1964.
21. Peasants generally: Redfield 1956; Wolf 1966.
22. Peasant marriages, *see* e.g.: Arensberg and Kimball 1968. Peasant economies: Firth and Yamey 1964.
23. Slavery: Nieboer 1900. Serfdom: Bloch 1961. Precapitalist economies generally: Marx 1964b.
24. Industrialization and its consequences: Disraeli 1845; Engels 1958.
25. Rapid social change and its consequences: Bock 1970; Leach 1967; Mead 1970. Also, on "hot" and "cold" societies: Lévi-Strauss 1966.
26. Marx on alienation: Marx 1964a; 1967; Marx and Engels 1948 (1888). Commentaries: Aron 1969; Axelos 1961; Wilson 1940. Alienation as a concept: Josephson and Josephson 1962; Kahler 1967; Pappenheim 1968.
27. Emergence of chiefs as redistributive centers: Fried 1967; Sahlins 1963b; Service 1965. Example of tribal system as redistributive: Maquet 1961.
28. Bantu: Schapera 1937.
29. Tribal economies generally: Dalton 1962; Forde and Douglas 1956; Nash 1966.
30. Pastoral economies: Darling 1955; Gulliver 1955.
31. Gardening and horticultural economies: Forde 1952.
32. Melanesian overseas "trading": Malinowski 1922; Uberoi 1962.

33. On New Guinea: Gardner and Heider 1968; Rappoport 1967; Salisbury 1962.
34. Lorenz 1956b.
35. Division of labor—classic work: Smith 1904 (1776).
36. Marx 1887.
37. Durkheim 1893.
38. Dehumanizing effects: Mayo 1945; Mumford 1934.
39. Effects of unemployment: Lebergott 1964.
40. On participation and its effects: Roethlesberger and Dixon 1939. On participation in industry: Blumberg 1968.
41. For "survival of fittest" arguments: Hofstadter 1944.
42. On eugenics: Pickens 1968.
43. On executives generally: Barnard 1954.
44. Early unions: Webb and Webb 1894.
45. Comparative economic systems: Schumpeter 1942.
46. Pervasiveness of division of labor by sex: Murdock 1937. On some causes: Brown 1970. Other aspects of sex differences: D'Andrade 1966.
47. On physiology of menstruation and behavioral effects *see* notes 43–49 in Chapter 3.
48. Astronauts: Tereshkova-Nikolayova 1970.
49. Female courtship behavior: Eibl-Eibesfeldt 1970. On pupil dilation and sexual interest: Hess 1965.
50. Sexual structure of occupations over time: Gross 1968; Wilensky 1968.
51. Economic rationality: Diesing 1950. Economic man: Chalk 1964; Gide 1930. General discussion: Parsons and Smelser 1956; Robbins 1932.
52. Exchange as fundamental: Blau 1964; Homans 1961.

6. THE BENIGN OPPRESSION

1. On the biology of learning: Harlow 1958b; Pribram 1969.
2. On brain and memory: Young 1965. On cortex and inhibition: Chance and Mead 1953; Fox 1967b; 1971.
3. Habits and instincts: Russell and Russell 1961.
4. Carnivore teaching: Mowat 1963.
5. For an example of learning without schooling: Opie and Opie 1961.
6. Learning failures: Holt 1964.
7. Criticism of formal education, *see* e.g.: Bruner 1966; Leonard 1968; Silberman 1970.
8. Security: Harlow 1959; 1962; Menzel 1963.
9. Curiosity: Butler 1954.
10. Fright: Freedman 1961.
11. On play in mammals: Beach 1945; Hediger 1955; Jewell and Loizos 1966; Welker 1961. Play in primates: Hinde and Spencer-Booth 1967; Loizos 1967; Welker 1956a; 1956b.
12. Goodall 1963.
13. Importance of peers: Hinde 1969.
14. Deprivation in macaques: Harlow 1965a.

15. Concept of "critical periods": Ambrose 1963; Caldwell 1962; Scott 1962.
16. General characteristics of education in primitive societies: Fortes 1938; Henry 1960; Levine 1963; Mayer 1970; Middleton 1970; Raum 1940; Read 1959.
17. Reviews of male initiation procedures: Cohen 1964; Eisenstadt 1955; Garfinkle 1956; Gluckman 1962; van Gennep 1909; Whiting 1958; Young 1965.
18. Testosterone at puberty: Hamburg 1970; Hamburg and Lunde 1966.
19. Female initiation: Brown 1963; Richards 1956.
20. Child language: Bellugi and Brown 1964; Braine 1963; Lenneberg 1967; Miller and Erwin 1964; Weir 1962.
21. Varieties of toilet training: Whiting and Child 1953.
22. Education and social mobility: Young 1958.
23. Education of sorcerers, *see* e.g.: Evans-Pritchard 1937.
24. Size and principals: Gross 1958.
25. Attention: Chance 1967.
26. Educational philosophies and schemes reflecting the nonformal approach: Becker 1967; Dewey 1916; Holt 1967; Kohl 1969; Montessori 1964; Neill 1960; Pettitt 1970.
27. Bloom *et al.* 1965.
28. Levy 1969.
29. Sexton 1969.
30. Sex differences in maturity: Tanner 1955.
31. Sex and occupation: Gross 1968; Wilensky 1968.
32. Teaching as a profession: Tropp 1957.
33. BaVenda: Stayt 1931.
34. Iroquois: Wilson 1960.
35. Hull: Tunstall 1962; Newfoundland: Faris 1966.

7. GOOD GROOMING

1. Acquisitiveness: Tawney 1921.
2. Grooming in primates: Sade 1965; Sparks 1967; Yerkes 1933.
3. Other world of hunters: Fox 1971.
4. Genetics of altruism: Hamilton 1963.
5. A precursor of this view: Kropotkin 1902.
6. Souls: Tylor 1870, vol. 2. Soul loss: Tax 1952.
7. Psychosomatic medicine: Grinker 1953; MacLean 1949.
8. Primitive medicine generally: Ackernecht 1942.
9. On social organization of hospitals generally: Bachmayer and Hartman 1943; Belknap 1956; Caudill 1958; Goffman 1961. On authority and power in hospitals: Cumming and Cumming 1956; Henry 1954; Parsons 1957; Rapoport and Rapoport 1957.
10. Negritos: Stewart 1954.
11. Cochiti: Fox 1964.
12. Primitive psychotherapy: Benedict and Jacks 1954; Kaplan and Johnson

1964; Kiev 1964; Leighton and Leighton 1941; Messing 1958; Wallace 1958.

13. Witchcraft accusations/confessions and social structure: Douglas 1970; Erstein 1959; Evans-Pritchard 1937; Gluckman 1955; Kitteridge 1929; Marwick 1965; Middleton and Winter 1963; Nash 1961; Turner 1957.

14. Death from witchcraft: Cannon 1942; Gillin 1948.

15. Physiology of flight and illness: Simeons 1960.

16. On medicine men, shamans, and divining: Evans-Pritchard 1937; Lévi-Strauss 1949a; Murphy 1964; Nadel 1946; Park 1938; Park 1963; Rasmussen 1929; Reichard 1939; Turner 1964.

17. Role of doctor: Henderson 1935; Parsons 1951b. In primitive society: Berndt 1964.

18. On professionalization: Abel-Smith 1964; Devereux and Weiner 1950.

19. Community care: Jones 1953.

20. On defining "health" and "normality": Devereux 1956; Foucault 1961. *See also:* Freeman 1965.

21. Psychiatric diagnosis as a "moral" judgment: Laing 1959; 1967. For a sociologist's view: Naegele 1970.

22. Religion and compulsion: Freud 1948–1950; 1952.

23. Trances: Bogorás 1904–1909; Lee 1967; 1968a.

24. Christ and paranoia: Schweitzer 1948.

25. Mental states and hierarchy: Price 1967.

26. Change of status and suicide: Durkheim 1951 (1897).

27. Gambling: Thomas 1906. Gambling and play: Huizinga 1949.

28. Hadza: Woodburn 1964.

29. On pitting oneself against environmental odds: Gould 1963.

30. Men in bars: Cavan 1966.

31. On gossip: Colson 1953; Gluckman 1963b; 1968; Paine 1967.

32. On flirting *see* note 49 in Chapter 5.

33. Nondirective therapy: Sullivan 1953; 1954.

34. Durkheim 1915.

8. THE NOBLE SAVAGE

1. Romantic view: Masters 1968; Russell 1945, Bk. III, part II.

2. Numbers of deaths by violence: Richardson 1960.

3. Nonviolent nature of man, *see* e.g.: Montagu 1968; Russell and Russell 1968—among many others.

4. On aggression: Bass 1961; Berkowitz 1962; Carthy and Ebling 1964; Scott 1958; Storr 1968. Frustration and aggression: Dollard *et al.* 1944. Critique: Berkowitz 1969; Tiger 1971.

5. Functions of aggression for animals: Collias 1944; Crook 1968; Eibl-Eibesfeldt 1961; Tinbergen 1936.

6. Aggression and bonds: Lorenz 1966.

7. Ritualization of aggression: Huxley 1966; Lorenz 1964; Tinbergen 1968.

8. On "real" aggression in baboons and other animals: Fisher 1964; Hall

1962; 1964; Matthews 1964; Washburn 1966; Washburn and Hamburg 1958.

9. On killer instincts: Ardrey 1961; Freeman 1964. Related arguments: Leakey 1967b; Trotter 1916.

10. Adrenalin and "fight and flight" response: Klopper 1964.

11. On war as male activity: Tiger 1969, chap. 7. Relation of individual to group aggression: Durbin and Bowlby 1939.

12. Status and war: Mishkin 1940.

13. Primitive warfare: Bohannan 1967; Gardner and Heider 1968; Newcomb 1950; Secoy 1953; Turney-High 1949; Vayda 1960; 1961.

14. Conquest and its consequences: Spencer 1896.

15. Slavery—lack of in hunters and expansion in agriculturalists: Hobhouse, Wheeler, and Ginsberg 1915.

16. Conquest and expansion among agriculturalists: Cook 1946; Otterbein 1967; Sahlins 1961; Vayda 1961.

17. Out-groups as "pseudo-species": Erikson 1966.

18. History and sociology of war generally: Andreski 1954; 1964; Davie 1929; Fried, Murphy, and Harris 1968; Wright 1942.

19. Psychology of men at war: Gray 1959.

20. Pentagon and economy: Rubinoff 1967.

21. Fremlin 1964.

22. Links between sex and aggression in brain: MacLean 1958; 1962; 1968— the latter a specific discussion of brain and violence. *See also:* Mark and Ervin 1970.

23. Population size and dispersion in hunters: Birdsell 1957; Carr-Saunders 1922.

24. Peopling of north America: Griffin 1960; Hopkins 1959.

25. Density as cause of violence, *see* e.g.: Russell and Russell 1968.

26. Density and social breakdown in animals: Calhoun 1962a; 1962b; Deevey 1960; Green and Evans 1940. In man: Leyhausen 1965.

27. Effects of stress: Barnett 1958; Barnett *et al.* 1960; Green and Larsen 1938.

28. Density and slums: Schorr 1966.

29. Wynne-Edwards 1962.

30. Population-resources balance: Christian 1970; Cragg and Pirie 1955; Lack 1954; Stott 1962; Wynne-Edwards 1964. In human populations: Thompson 1970. Critique: Douglas 1966.

31. On territory and property *see* note 3 in Chapter 5.

32. Restriction of top positions: Bednarik 1970. Constancy of numbers in cabinets: Parkinson 1957.

33. Population policy and its effectiveness: Davis 1967.

34. Japanese policy and abortion: Coyle 1959.

35. European policy: Class 1940.

36. Techniques of terror: Lowenthal 1946; Kogon 1950.

37. Numbers and power: Davis 1954.

BIBLIOGRAPHY

ABEL-SMITH, B.
  1964 *The Hospitals, 1800–1948; A Study in Social Administration in England and Wales*. Cambridge, Mass.: Harvard Univ. Press.
ABERLE, D.F.; COHEN, A.K.; DAVIS, A.K.; LEVY, M.J.; SUTTON, F.X.
  1950 The Functional Prerequisites of a Society. *Ethics* 60: 100–111.
ABERLE, D.F., *et al.*
  1963 The Incest Taboo and the Mating Patterns of Animals. *Amer.
  Anthrop.* 65: 253–265.
ACKERKNECHT, E.H.
  1942 Problems of Primitive Medicine. *Bulletin of the Hist. of Med.* XI:
  503–521.
ADAMS, R.
  1966 *The Evolution of Urban Society: Early Mesopotamia and Pre-
  Hispanic Mexico*. Chicago: Aldine.
ADAMS, R.N.
  1960 An Inquiry into the Nature of the Family. Dole, G.E., and Carneiro,
  R.L. (eds.), *Essays in the Science of Society in Honor of Leslie A. White*.
  N.Y.: Thomas Y. Crowell.
AINSWORTH, M.D.
  1962 The Effects of Maternal Deprivation: A Review of Findings and
  Controversy in the Context of Research Strategy. *Deprivation of Mater-
  nal Care: A Reassessment of its Effects*. Public Health Papers (14),
  Geneva: W.H.O.

ALLAND, A.
  1967   *Evolution and Human Behavior.* N.Y.: Natural History Press.
ALLEE, W.C.
  1958   *The Social Life of Animals.* Boston: Beacon Press.
ALTMANN, S.A. (ed.)
  1965   *Japanese Monkeys: A Collection of Translations.* Atlanta: Altmann.
  1967   *Social Communication Among Primates.* Chicago: Univ. of Chicago
          Press.
AMBROSE, J.A.
  1963   The Concept of a Critical Period for the Development of Social
          Responsiveness. Foss, B. (ed.), *Determinants of Infant Behavior* 2. Lon-
          don: Methuen. N.Y.: John Wiley & Sons.
  1969   *Stimulation in Early Infancy.* N.Y.: Academic Press.
AMOROSO, E.C., and MARSHALL, F.H.A.
  1960   External Factors in Sexual Periodicity. Parkes, A.S. (ed.), *Marshall's
          Physiology of Reproduction* (3rd ed., vol. 1, part 2). London: Longmans.
ANDRESKI, S.
  1954   *Military Organization and Society.* London: Routledge and Kegan
          Paul.
  1964   Origins of War. Carthy, J.D., and Ebling, F.J. (eds.), *The Natural
          History of Aggression.* London: Academic Press.
ARDREY, R.
  1961   *African Genesis.* London: Collins.
  1966   *The Territorial Imperative.* N.Y.: Atheneum.
  1970   *The Social Contract.* N.Y.: Atheneum.
ARENSBERG, C., and KIMBALL, S.T.
  1968 (1940)   *Family and Community in Ireland.* Cambridge, Mass.: Har-
          vard Univ. Press.
ARON, R.
  1969   *Marxism and the Existentialists.* N.Y.: Harper & Row.
AXELOS, K.
  1961   *Marx, penseur de la technique de l'aliénation de l'homme à la con-
          quete du monde.* Paris: Editions de Minuit.
BACHMEYER, A.C., and HARTMAN, G. (eds.)
  1943   *The Hospital in Modern Society.* N.Y.: The Commonwealth
          Fund.
BALL, J.
  1940   The Effects of Testosterone on Sexual Behavior of Female Rats.
          J. Comp. Psychol. 29: 151–165.
BANTON, M. (ed.)
  1961   *Darwin and the Study of Society.* Chicago: Quadrangle Books.
BARBOUR, N.
  1965   *Morocco.* London: Thames and Hudson.
BARNARD, C.I.
  1954   *The Functions of the Executive.* Cambridge, Mass.: Harvard Univ.
          Press.
BARNETT, S.A.
  1958 (ed.)   *A Century of Darwin.* London: Heinemann.

1958   Physiological Effects of "Social Stress" in Wild Rats. The Adrenal
       Cortex. *J. Psychosomatic Res.* 3: 1–11.
1967   *"Instinct" and "Intelligence."* London: Macgibbon and Kee.
BARNETT, S.A., EATON, J.C., and MCCALLUM, H.M.
1960   Physiological Effects of "Social Stress" in Wild Rats, 2: Liver Gly-
       cogen and Blood Glucose. *J. Psychosomatic Res.* 4: 251–260.
BARTHOLOMEW, G.A., JR., and BIRDSELL, J.B.
1953   Ecology and the Protohominids. *Amer. Anthrop.* 55: 481–498.
BASTOCK, M.
1967   *Courtship: An Ethological Study.* London: Heinemann.
BATESON, P.P.G.
1966   The Characteristics and Context of Imprinting. *Biol. Rev.* 41: 177–
       220.
BEACH, F.A.
1945   Current Concepts of Play in Animals. *Amer. Nat.* 79: 523–541.
1947   Evolutionary Changes in the Physiological Control of Mating Be-
       havior in Mammals. *Psychol. Rev.* 54: 297–315.
1950   The Snark was a Boojum. *Amer. Psychol.* 5: 115–124.
1955   The Descent of Instinct. *Psych. Rev.* 62: 401–410.
BEACH, F.A. (ed.)
1965   *Sex and Behavior.* N.Y.: John Wiley & Sons.
BEAMAN, E.A.
1947   The Effect of the Male Hormone on Aggressive Behavior in Male
       Mice. *Physiol. Zool.* 20: 373–405.
BECKER, E.
1967   *Beyond Alienation.* N.Y.: George Braziller.
BEDNARIK, K.
1970   *The Male in Crisis.* N.Y.: Alfred A. Knopf.
BELKNAP, I.
1956   *Human Problems of a State Mental Hospital.* N.Y.: Blakiston Di-
       vision, McGraw-Hill.
BELL, N.W., and VOGEL, E.F. (eds.)
1960   *A Modern Introduction to the Family.* N.Y.: Free Press.
BELLUGI, U., and BROWN, R.
1964   The Acquisition of Language. *Monog. Soc. Res. Child Devel.* 29 (1).
BENDIX, R.
1960   *Max Weber: An Intellectual Portrait.* London: Heinemann.
BENEDICT, P.K., and JACKS, I.
1954   Mental Illness in Primitive Societies. *Psychiatry* 17: 377–389.
BERKOWITZ, L.
1962   *Aggression: A Social Psychological Analysis.* N.Y.: McGraw-Hill.
BERKOWITZ, L. (ed.)
1969   *Roots of Aggression.* N.Y.: Atherton Press.
BERNDT, C.H.
1964   The Role of Native Doctors in Aboriginal Australia. Kiev, A. (ed.),
       Magic, Faith, and Healing. Glencoe, Ill.: Free Press.
BIDNEY, D.
1953   *Theoretical Anthropology.* N.Y.: Columbia Univ. Press.

BINFORD, S.R., and BINFORD, L.R.
1968 *New Perspectives in Archeology.* Chicago: Aldine.
BIRD, C.
1968 *Born Female: The High Cost of Keeping Women Down.* N.Y.: David McKay.
BIRDSELL, J.B.
1953 Some Environmental and Cultural Factors Influencing the Structuring of Australian Aboriginal Populations. *Amer. Nat.* (Supplement, May–June).
1957 Some Population Problems Involving Pleistocene Man. *Cold Spring Harbor Symposia on Quantitative Biology* XXII.
1958 On Population Structure in Generalized Hunting and Collecting Populations. *Evolution* (June).
BLAKE, R.
1966 *Disraeli.* London: Eyre and Spottiswoode.
BLAU, P.M.
1964 *Exchange and Power in Social Life.* N.Y.: John Wiley & Sons.
BLISS, E.L. (ed.)
1962 *Roots of Behavior.* N.Y.: Harper and Bros.
BLOCH, M.
1961 *Feudal Society.* London: Routledge and Kegan Paul.
BLOOM, B.S.; DAVIS, A.; and HESS, R.D.
1965 *Compensatory Education for Cultural Deprivation.* N.Y.: Holt, Rinehart and Winston
BLUMBERG, P.
1968 *Industrial Democracy: The Sociology of Participation.* London: Constable.
BOAS, F.
1948 *Race, Language, and Culture.* N.Y.: Macmillan.
BOCK, P.K.
1969 *Modern Cultural Anthropology.* N.Y.: Alfred A. Knopf.
BOGORAS, W.
1904–1909 *The Chukchee.* Franz Boas (ed.), *The Jesup North Pacific Expedition* VII. Leyden: E.J. Brill.
BOHANNAN, P.
1963 *Social Anthropology.* N.Y.: Holt, Rinehart and Winston.
BOHANNAN, P. (ed.)
1967 *Law and Warfare: Studies in the Anthropology of Conflict.* N.Y.: Natural History Press.
BONNER, J.T.
1965 *Size and Cycle.* Princeton: Princeton Univ. Press.
BOWLBY, J.
1951 *Maternal Care and Mental Health.* Geneva: W.H.O.
1953 Some Pathological Processes Set in Train by Early Mother-Child Separation. *J. Mental Sci.* 99: 265–272.
1958 The Nature of the Child's Tie to His Mother. *Int. J. Psycho-Anal.* 41: 89–113.

1960   Grief and Mourning in Infancy and Early Childhood. *Psychoanalytic Study of the Child* 7: 82–94.
1961a   Separation Anxiety. *Int. J. Psycho-Anal.* 41: 89–113.
1961b   Separation Anxiety: A Critical Review of the Literature. *J. Child. Psychol. Psychiat.* 1: 251–269.
1963   Pathological Mourning and Childhood Mourning. *J. Amer. Psychoanal. Ass.* 11: 500–541.
1969   *Attachment and Loss: Volume 1 Attachment.* (International Psycho-Analytical Library no. 79). London: Hogarth Press and the Institute of Psycho-Analysis.

BRAIDWOOD, R.
1960   The Agricultural Revolution. *Scientific American* (Sept.).

BRAINE, M.D.S.
1963   The Ontogeny of English Phrase Structure: The First Phase. *Language* 39: 1–13.

BRESSLER, M.
1968   Sociology, Biology and Ideology. Glass, D. (ed.), *Genetics.* N.Y.: Rockefeller Univ. Press and Russell Sage Foundation.

BRILL, A.A.
1932   The Sense of Smell in the Neuroses and Psychoses. *Psychoanalytic Quarterly* 1: 7.

BROOM, R.
1949   The Ape-Men. *Scientific American* (Nov.).

BROOM R., and SCHEPERS, G.W.H.
1946   *The South African Fossil Ape-man: The Australopithecine.* Transvaal Museum Memoirs No. 2.

BROWN, J.
1963   A Cross-Cultural Study of Female Initiation Rites. *Amer. Anthrop.* 65: 837–853.
1970   A Note on the Division of Labor by Sex. *Amer. Anthrop.* 72: 1073–1078.

BRUNER, J.
1966   *Toward a Theory of Instruction.* N.Y.: W.W. Norton.

BULLOUGH, W.S.
1961   *Vertebrate Reproductive Cycles* (2nd ed.). London: Methuen.

BURTON, R.F., and ARBUTHNOT, F.F. (trans.)
1962 (orig. 1883)   *The Kama Sutra of Vatsyayana.* N.Y.: E.P. Dutton.

BURTON, R.F. (trans.)
1963 (orig. 1886)   *The Perfumed Garden of the Shaykh Nefzawa.* London: Spearman.

BUSS, A.
1961   *The Psychology of Aggression.* N.Y. and London: John Wiley & Sons.

BUTLER, R.A.
1954   Curiosity in Monkeys. *Scientific American* (Feb.).

CALDWELL, B.M.
1962   The Usefulness of the Critical Period Hypothesis in the Study of Filiative Behavior. *Merrill-Palmer Quarterly* 8: 229–242.

CALHOUN, J.B.
  1952 Social Aspects of Population Dynamics. *J. Mammalogy* 33: 139–59.
  1962a Population Density and Social Pathology. *Scientific American* (Feb.).
  1962b A "Behavioral Sink." Bliss, E.L. (ed.), *Roots of Behavior*. N.Y.: Harper and Bros.
CALLAN, H.
  1970 *Ethology and Society: Towards an Anthropological View*. Oxford: Clarendon Press.
CAMPBELL, B.G.
  1966 *Human Evolution: An Introduction to Man's Adaptations*. Chicago: Aldine.
CANETTI, E.
  1962 *Crowds and Power*. London: Gollancz.
CANNON, W.B.
  1942 Voodoo Death. *Amer. Anthrop*. XLIV: 169–181.
CARPENTER, C.R.
  1940 A Field Study in Siam of the Behavior and Social Relations of the Gibbon (*Hylobates Lar.*) *Comp. Psychol. Monog*. 16.
  1958 Territoriality: A Review of Concepts and Problems. Roe, A., and Simpson, G.G. (eds.), *Behavior and Evolution*. New Haven, Conn.: Yale Univ. Press.
  1964 *Naturalistic Behavior of Nonhuman Primates*. University Park: Penn. State Univ. Press.
CARR-SAUNDERS, A.M.
  1922 *The Population Problem: A Study in Human Evolution*. Oxford: Oxford Univ. Press.
CARTHY, J.D., and EBLING, F.J. (eds.)
  1964 *The Natural History of Aggression*. London: Academic Press.
CASLER, L.
  1961 Maternal Deprivation: A Critical Review of the Literature. *Monog. Soc. Res. Child Devel*. 26: 1–64.
CASPARI, E.
  1963 Selective Forces in the Evolution of Man. *Amer. Nat*. XCVII (892): 5–14.
CAUDILL, W.
  1958 *The Psychiatric Hospital as a Small Society*. Cambridge, Mass.: Harvard Univ. Press.
CAVAN, S.
  1966 *Liquor License: An Ethnography of Bar Behavior*. Chicago: Aldine.
CHAGNON, N.A.
  1968 *Yanomamo—The Fierce People*. N.Y.: Holt, Rinehart and Winston.
CHALK, A.F.
  1964 Economic Man. Gould, J., and Kolf, W. (eds.), *Dictionary of the Social Sciences*. N.Y.: Free Press.
CHANCE, M.R.A.
  1962a Nature and Special Features of the Instinctive Social Bond of Primates. Washburn, S.L. (ed.), *Social Life of Early Man*. London: Methuen.

1962b   Social Behaviour and Primate Evolution. Ashley Montagu, M.F. (ed.), *Culture and the Evolution of Man*. N.Y.: Oxford Univ. Press.
1967   Attention Structure as the Basis of Primate Rank Orders. *Man: The J.R.A.I.* 2 (4): 503–518.
CHANCE, M.R.A., and JOLLY, C.J.
1970   *Social Groups of Monkeys, Apes, and Men*. N.Y.: E.P. Dutton.
CHANCE, M.R.A., and MEAD, A.P.
1953   Social Behaviour and Primate Evolution. *Evolution: Symposium of the Society for Experimental Biology* 7. N.Y.: Jonathan Cape.
CHAPPLE, E.D.
1970   *Culture and Biological Man*. N.Y.: Holt, Rinehart and Winston.
CHASE, H.P.; DORSEY, J.; and McKHANN, G.M.
1967   The Effect of Malnutrition on the Synthesis of a Myelin Lipid. *Pediatrics* 40: 551–559.
CHILDE, V.G.
1946 (orig. 1942)   *What Happened in History?* N.Y.: Penguin.
CHOMSKY, N.
1965   *Aspects of the Theory of Syntax*. Cambridge, Mass.: MIT Press.
1966   *Cartesian Linguistics: A Chapter in the History of Rationalist Thought*. N.Y. and London: Harper & Row.
1968   *Language and Mind*. N.Y.: Harcourt, Brace and World.
CHRISTIAN, J.J.
1970   Social Subordination, Population Density and Mammalian Evolution. *Science* 168: 84–90.
CLARK, J.D.
1970   *The Prehistory of Africa*. N.Y. and Washington: Praeger.
CLARK, W.E. LE G.
1950   *History of the Primates: An Introduction to the Study of Fossil Man*. London: British Museum.
1955   *The Fossil Evidence for Human Evolution: An Introduction to the Study of Paleoanthropology*. Chicago: Univ. of Chicago Press.
1960   *The Antecedents of Man: An Introduction to the Evolution of the Primates*. Chicago: Quadrangle Books.
1967   *Man-Ape or Ape-Man?* N.Y.: Holt, Rinehart and Winston.
COHEN, Y.A.
1964   *The Transition from Childhood to Adolescence*. Chicago: Aldine.
COLLIAS, N.E.
1944   Aggressive Behavior Among Vertebrate Animals. *Physiol. Zool.* 17: 83–123.
COLSON, E.
1953   *The Makah Indians*. Manchester: Manchester Univ. Press.
COOK, S.F.
1946   Human Sacrifice and Warfare as Factors in the Demography of Pre-Colonial Mexico. *Human Biology* 18: 81–102.
COUNT, E.W.
1958   The Biological Basis of Human Sociality. *Amer. Anthrop.* 60: 1049–1085.

1958–1959   Eine Biologische Entwicklungsgeschichte der Menschlichen So-
zialität. *Homo* 9: 129–146; 10: 1–35, 65–92.
1967   The Lactation Complex: A Phylogenetic Consideration of the Mammalian Mother-Child Symbiosis, with Special Reference to Man. *Homo*
18 (1): 38–54.

COYLE, D.C.
1959   Japan's Population. *Population Bulletin* 15 (7): 119–136.

CRAGG, J.B., and PIRIE, N.W. (eds.)
1955   *The Numbers of Man and Animals.* Edinburgh: Oliver and Boyd.

CRICK, F.H.C.
1962   The Genetic Code. *Scientific American* (Oct.).

CRITCHLEY, M.
1958   Animal Communication. *Transactions of the Hunterian Society of
London* 16: 90–111.

CROMBIE, D.L.
1965   An Evolutionary Approach to Human Behavior. *J. Coll. Gen. Pract.*
12 (133).

CROOK, J.H.
1966   Cooperation in Primates. *Eugenics Review* 58 (2).
1968   Gelada Baboon Herd Structure and Movement. *Symp. Zool. Soc.
Lond.* 18: 237–258.
1968   The Nature and Function of Territorial Aggression. Montagu, A.
(ed.), *Man and Aggression*. N.Y.: Oxford Univ. Press.
1970   Social Organization and the Environment: Aspects of Contemporary
Social Ethology. *Animal Behavior* 18.

CROOK, J.H., and GARTLAN, J.S.
1966   Evolution of Primate Societies. *Nature,* London 210 (5042): 1200–
1203.

CUMMING, E., and CUMMING, J.
1956   The Locus of Power in a Large Mental Hospital. *Psychiatry* 19:
361–369.

DAHLSTROM, E. (ed.)
1967   *The Changing Roles of Men and Women.* London: Duckworth.

DALTON, G.
1962   Traditional Production in Primitive African Economies. *The Quarterly J. Economics* 76: 360–378.

DALTON, K.
1959   Menstruation and Acute Psychiatric Illness. *British Medical Journal*
1: 148–149.
1960a   The Effect of Menstruation on Schoolgirls' Weekly Work. *Brit.
Med. J.* (Jan).
1960b   Menstruation and Accidents. *Brit. Med. J.* 2.
1960c   Schoolgirls' Behaviour and Menstruation. *Brit. Med. J.* (Dec.).
1964a   The Influence of Menstruation on Health and Disease. *Proc. Royal
Soc. Med.* (57).
1964b   *The Pre-Menstrual Syndrome.* Springfield, Ill.: Charles Thomas.

D'ANDRADE, R.G.
1966   Sex Differences and Cultural Institutions. Maccoby, E. (ed.),

The Development of Sex Differences. Stanford: Stanford Univ. Press.
DARLING, F.
1937   *A Herd of Red Deer*. London: Oxford Univ. Press.
1955   Pastoralism in Relation to Populations of Men and Animals. Cragg,
J.B., and Pirie, N.W. (eds.), *The Numbers of Man and Animals*. Edinburgh: Oliver and Boyd.
DARLINGTON, C.D.
1969   *The Evolution of Man and Society*. London: George Allen and Unwin.
DART, R.A.
1953   The Predatory Transition from Ape to Man. *International Anthropological and Linguistic Review* 1 (4).
1957   The Osteodontokeratic Culture of Australopithecus Prometheus.
Memoir Transvaal Museum.
1958   The Minimal Bone-Breccia Content of Makapansgat and the Australopithecine Predatory Habit. *Amer. Anthrop.* 60 (5).
1959   *Adventures with the Missing Link*. N.Y.: Harper and Bros.
1963   Carnivorous Propensity of Baboons. *Symp. Zool. Soc. Lond.* 10:
49–56.
DARWIN, C.
1859   *The Origin of Species by Means of Natural Selection*. N.Y.: New
American Library (1958 edition).
1871   *The Descent of Man*. London: Murray.
1873   *The Expression of the Emotions in Man and Animals*. N.Y. Appleton-
Century-Crofts. (New edition—N.Y.: Philosophical Library, 1956; preface
by Margaret Mead.)
DAVIE, M.R.
1929   *The Evolution of War*. New Haven, Conn.: Yale Univ. Press.
DAVIS, D.E.
1962   An Inquiry into the Phylogeny of Gangs. Bliss, E.L. (ed.), *Roots of
Behavior*. N.Y.: Harper and Bros.
DAVIS, K.
1954   The Demographic Foundations of National Power. Berger, M.;
Abel, T.; and Page, C.H. (eds.), *Freedom and Control in Modern Soc.*
N.Y.: Van Nostrand.
1967   Population Policy: Will Current Programs Succeed? *Science* 158:
730–739.
DEBEER, G.
1968   Evolution by Natural Selection. Freed, M. (ed.), *Readings in Anthropology* 1. N.Y.: Thomas Y. Crowell.
DEEVEY, E.S.
1960a   The Human Population. *Scientific American* (Sept. 1960).
1960b   The Hare and the Haruspex: A Cautionary Tale. *The Yale Review*
(Winter 1960).
deMOUBRAY, G.A. DE C.
1931   *Matriarchy in the Malay Peninsula and Neighboring Countries*.
London: George Routledge and Sons.
DEVEREUX, G.
1956   Normal and Abnormal: The Key Problem of Psychiatric Anthro-

pology. *Some Uses of Anthropology: Theoretical and Applied*. Washington, D.C.: Anthrop. Soc. of Wash.

DEVEREUX, G., and WEINER, F.R.
1950   The Occupational Status of Nurses. *Amer. Sociolog. Rev.* 15: 628–634.

DEVORE, I.
1963   Mother-Infant Relations in Free-Ranging Baboons. Rheingold, H.L. (ed.), *Maternal Behavior in Mammals*. N.Y.: John Wiley & Sons.
1964   The Evolution of Social Life. Tax, S. (ed.), *Horizons of Anthropology*. Chicago: Aldine.
1965a Male Dominance and Mating Behavior in Baboons. Beach, F.A. (ed.), *Sex and Behavior*. N.Y.: John Wiley & Sons.

DEVORE, I. (ed.)
1965b *Primate Behavior: Field Studies of Monkeys and Apes*. N.Y.: Holt, Rinehart and Winston.

DEVORE, I., and WASHBURN, S.L.
1963   Baboon Ecology and Human Evolution. Howell, F.C., and Bourlière, F. (eds.), *African Ecology and Human Evolution*. N.Y.: Viking Fund Publications in Anthropology No. 33.

DEWEY, J.
1916   *Democracy and Education*. N.Y.: Macmillan.

DIESING, P.
1950   The Nature and Limitations of Economic Rationality. *Ethics* 61: 12–26.

DILLON, W. (ed.)
1971   *Man and Beast*. Washington, D.C.: Smithsonian Institution Press.

DISRAELI, B.
1845   *Sybil, or, The Two Nations* (3 vols.). Philadelphia: Colburn.

DOBZHANSKY, T.
1962   *Mankind Evolving; The Evolution of the Human Species*. New Haven, Conn.: Yale Univ. Press.

DOLLARD, J. et al.
1944   *Frustration and Aggression*. London: Routledge and Kegan Paul.

DOUGLAS, M.
1966   Population Control in Primitive Groups. *Brit. J. Sociol.*, p. 263.

DOUGLAS, M. (ed.)
1970   *Witchcraft Confessions and Accusations*. A.S.A. Monograph 9. London: Tavistock.

DUBOS, R.
1968   *So Human an Animal*. N.Y.: Charles Scribner's Sons.

DURBIN, E.F.M., and BOWLBY, J.
1939   *Personal Aggressiveness and War*. N.Y.: Columbia Univ. Press.

DURKHEIM, E.
1893   *De la Division du Travail Social*. Simpson, G. (trans.), *The Division of Labor in Society*. Glencoe, Ill.: Free Press. 1933.
1951 (orig. 1897)   *Suicide*. Spaulding, J., and Simpson, G. (trans.), Glencoe, Ill.: Free Press.

1915 *The Elementary Forms of the Religious Life.* Swain, J.W. (trans.). London: Allen and Unwin.
DUVERGER, M.
1955 *The Political Role of Women.* Paris: UNESCO.
EGGAN, F.
1950 *The Social Organization of the Western Pueblos.* Chicago: Univ. of Chicago Press.
EIBL-EIBESFELDT, I.
1961 The Fighting Behavior of Animals. *Scientific American* (Dec.).
1968 Ethological Perspectives on Primate Studies. Jay, P.C. (ed.), *Primates: Studies in Adaptation and Variability.* N.Y.: Holt, Rinehart and Winston.
1970 *Ethology.* N.Y.: Holt, Rinehart and Winston.
EIBL-EIBESFELDT, I., and KRAMER, S.
1958 Ethology, the Comparative Study of Animal Behavior. *Quart. Rev. Biol.* 33: 181–211.
EISELEY, L.C.
1958 *Darwin's Century: Evolution and the Men Who Discovered it.* Garden City, N.Y.: Doubleday.
EISENBERG, J.F.
1966 *The Social Organization of Mammals.* Handbuch der Zoologie 8: 1–92.
EISENSTADT, S.M.
1955 *From Generation to Generation.* Glencoe, Ill.: Free Press.
ELLIOTT, K.
1970 *The Family and Its Future.* London: J. and A. Churchill.
EMMETT, D.
1956 Prophets and Their Societies. *J. Royal Anthrop. Inst.* 86 (part 1): 13–24 (Jan.–June).
ENGELS, F.
1905 *Origins of the Family, Private Property, and the State.* Chicago: C.H. Kerr.
1958 (1892) *Condition of the Working Class in England.* Oxford: Blackwell.
EPSTEIN, S.
1959 A Sociological Analysis of Witch Beliefs in a Mysore Village. *The Eastern Anthropologist* 12 (4): 234–251.
ERIKSON, E.H.
1966 Ontogeny of Ritualization in Man. *Philosophical Transactions of the Royal Society of London B* 251: 337–349.
ERIKSON, L.B.
1967 Relationship of Sexual Receptivity to Menstrual Cycle in Adult Rhesus Monkeys. *Nature* 216: 299–301.
ETKIN, W.
1954 Social Behavior and the Evolution of Man's Mental Capacities. *Amer. Nat.* 88: 129–142.
ETKIN, W. (ed.)
1964 *Social Behavior and Organization Vertebrates.* Chicago and London: Univ. of Chicago Press.

EVANS-PRITCHARD, E.E.
  1937 *Witchcraft, Oracles, and Magic Among the Azande*. Oxford: Clarendon Press.
  1965 *The Position of Women in Primitive Societies*. N.Y.: Free Press.
EVERETT, J.W.
  1961 The Mammalian Female Reproductive Cycle and Its Controlling Mechanisms. Young, W.C. (ed.), *Sex and Internal Secretion*. Baltimore: Williams and Wilkens Co.
EYSENCK, H.J.
  1957 *Sense and Nonsense in Psychology*. Harmondsworth: Penguin.
FABRICIUS, E.
  1962 Some Aspects of Imprinting in Birds. *Symp. Zool. Soc. Lond.* 8: 139–148.
FARIS, J.C.
  1966 *Cat Harbour: A Newfoundland Fishing Settlement*. St. Johns, N.F.: Instit. of Social and Economic Research.
FIRTH, R.W., and YAMEY, B.S.
  1964 *Capital, Saving, and Credit in Peasant Society*. Chicago: Aldine.
FISHER, J.
  1964 Interspecific Aggression. Carthy, J.D., and Ebling, F.J. (eds.), *The Natural History of Aggression*. London: Academic Press.
FISHER, R.A.
  1958 *The Genetical Theory of Natural Selection*. N.Y.: Dover.
FLANNERY, K.
  1965 Ecology of Early Food Production in Mesopotamia. *Science* 147.
FLETCHER, R.
  1957 *Instinct in Man*. London: Allen and Unwin.
FORD, C.S., and BEACH, F.A.
  1952 *Patterns of Sexual Behaviour*. London: Eyre and Spottiswoode.
FORDE, D.
  1952 *Habitat, Economy and Society*. London: Methuen.
FORDE, D., and DOUGLAS, MARY
  1956 Primitive Economics. Shapiro, H.L. (ed.), *Man, Culture, and Society*. N.Y.: Oxford Univ. Press.
FORTES, M.
  1938 *Social and Psychological Aspects of Education in Taleland* (Supplement to *Africa* 11:4) London: Oxford Univ. Press.
FOSS, B.M. (ed.)
  1961–1969 *Determinants of Infant Behavior* I–IV. N.Y.: John Wiley & Sons.
FOUCAULT, M.
  1961 *L'Histoire de la Folie*. Paris: Plon [*Madness and Civilization*, Howard, R. (trans.), N.Y.: Pantheon 1965].
FOX, R.
  1962 Sibling Incest. *Brit. J. Sociol.* 13: 128–150.
  1964 Witchcraft and Clanship in Cochiti Therapy. Kiev, A. (ed.), *Magic, Faith, and Healing*. Glencoe, Ill.: Free Press.

1966   *Totem and Taboo* Reconsidered. Leach, E.R. (ed.), *The Structural Study of Myth and Totemism*. (A.S.A. Monograph No. 5) London: Tavistock.

1967a   *Kinship and Marriage: An Anthropological Perspective*. London and Baltimore: Penguin.

1967b   In the Beginning: Aspects of Hominid Behavioural Evolution. *Man: The J.R.A.I.* 2 (3): 415–433.

1967c   Human Mating Patterns in Ethological Perspective. *Animals* (July).

1968   The Evolution of Human Sexual Behavior. *The New York Times Magazine* (March 24), pp. 32–33, 79–97.

1970a   Comparative Family Patterns. Elliott, K. (ed.), *The Family and Its Future*. London: J. and A. Churchill.

1970b   The Cultural Animal. *Information Sur Les Sciences Sociales* (UNESCO) 9 (1): 7–25. Also in: Dillon, W. (ed.), *Man and Beast*. Smithsonian Inst. Press, 1971.

1972   Sexual Selection and the Evolution of Human Kinship Systems. Campbell, B. (ed.), *Sexual Selection and the Descent of Man*. Chicago: Aldine.

1972   North America. *Historia Religionum*. Leiden: E.J. Brill.

FREEDMAN, D.G.

1961   The Infant's Fear of Strangers and the Flight Response. *J. Child. Psychol. Psychiat.* 1: 242–248.

1964   Smiling in Blind Infants and the Issue of Innate Versus Acquired. *J. Child. Psychol. Psychiat.* 5: 171–184.

1965   An Ethological Approach to the Genetic Study of Human Behavior. Vandenberg, S.G. (ed.), *Method and Goals in Human Behavior Genetics*. N.Y.: Academic Press.

1967   A Biological View of Man's Social Behavior. Etkin, W. (ed.), *Social Behavior From Fish To Man*. Chicago: Univ. of Chicago Press.

1968   An Evolutionary Framework for Behavioral Research. Vandenberg, S.G. (ed.), *Progress in Human Behavior Genetics*. Baltimore: Johns Hopkins Press.

FREEMAN, D.

1964   Human Aggression in Anthropological Perspective. Carthy, J.D., and Ebling, F.J. (eds.), *The Natural History of Aggression*. London and N.Y.: Academic Press.

1965   Anthropology, Psychiatry and the Doctrine of Cultural Relativism. *Man* 65: 59.

1966   Social Anthropology and the Scientific Study of Human Behavior. *Man: The J.R.A.I.* 1 (2): 330–342.

FREMLIN, J.H.

1964   How Many People Can The World Support? *New Scientist* 415: 285–287.

FREUD, A.

1949   Certain Types and Stages of Social Maladjustment. Eissler, K.R. (ed.), *Searchlights on Delinquency*. N.Y.: International Universities Press.

FREUD, S.
  1948–1950 Obsessive Acts and Religious Practices. *Collected Papers* II.
  London: Hogarth Press and the Institute of Psychoanalysis.
  1952 *Totem and Taboo.* Strachey, J. (trans.). N.Y.: W.W. Norton.
FRIED, M.
  1967 *The Evolution of Political Society.* N.Y.: Random House.
FRIED, M.; HARRIS, M.; and MURPHY, R. (eds.)
  1968 *War: The Anthropology of Armed Conflict and Aggression.* Garden
  City, N.Y.: Natural History Press.
FRIEDAN, B.
  1963 *The Feminine Mystique.* N.Y.: W.W. Norton.
FULLER, J.L., and THOMPSON, W.R.
  1960 *Behavior Genetics.* N.Y.: John Wiley & Sons.
FURUYA, Y.
  1969 On The Fission of Troops of Japanese Monkeys: II. General View of
  Troop Fission of Japanese Monkeys. *Primates* 10 (1): 47–69.
GARDNER, R., and HEIDER, K.G.
  1968 *Gardens of War.* N.Y.: Random House.
GARFINKLE, H.
  1956 Conditions of Successful Degradation Ceremonies. *Amer. J. Sociol.*
  61 (5).
GARN, S.M. (ed.)
  1964 *Culture and the Direction of Human Evolution.* Detroit, Mich.:
  Wayne State Univ.
GAVAN, J.A. (ed.)
  1955 *The Non-Human Primates and Human Evolution.* Detroit, Mich.:
  Wayne State Univ.
GEERTZ, C.
  1965 The Transition to Humanity. Tax, S. (ed.), *Horizons of Anthropology.*
  London: Allen and Unwin.
GENNEP, A. VAN
  1909 *Les Rites de Passage.* Paris: Nourry. [*Rites of Passage.* Vizedom,
  M.B., and Caffee, G.L. (trans.); Univ. of Chicago Press.]
GERTH, H.H., and MILLS, C.W. (eds.)
  1948 *From Max Weber: Essays on Sociology.* London: Routledge and
  Kegan Paul.
GIDE, C.
  1930 Economic Man. *Encyclopedia of the Social Sciences.* N.Y.: Mac-
  millan.
GILLIN, J.
  1948 Magical Fright. *Psychiatry* XI: 387–400.
GINSBURG, B.E.
  1968 Breeding Structure and Social Behavior of Mammals: A Servo-
  Mechanism for Avoidance of Panmixia. Glass, D.C. (ed.), *Genetics.* N.Y.:
  Rockefeller Univ. Press and Russell Sage Foundation.
GINSBURG, M.
  1964 (orig. 1921) *The Psychology of Society.* London: Methuen.

GLASS, D.
1940   *Population Policies and Movements in Europe.* Oxford: Clarendon
Press.
GLASS, D.G. (ed.)
1968a   *Biology and Behavior: Genetics.* N.Y.: Rockefeller Univ. Press and
Russell Sage Foundation.
1968b   *Biology and Behavior: Environmental Influences.* N.Y.: Rockefeller
Univ. Press and Russell Sage Foundation.
GLUCKMAN, M.
1954   *Rituals of Rebellion in South-East Africa.* Manchester: Manchester
Univ. Press.
1955   *Custom and Conflict in Africa.* Oxford: Basil Blackwell.
1963a   *Order and Rebellion in Tribal Africa.* N.Y.: Free Press.
1963b   Gossip and Scandal. *Current Anthrop.* 4: 307–315.
1968   Psychological, Sociological and Anthropological Explanations of
Witchcraft and Gossip: A Clarification. *Man: The J.R.A.I.* 3 (1): 20–34.
GLUCKMAN, M. (ed.)
1962   *Essays on the Ritual of Social Relations.* Manchester: Manchester
Univ. Press.
GOFFMAN, E.
1961   *Asylums.* Garden City, N.Y.: Anchor.
GOLDBERG, P.
1968   Are Women Prejudiced Against Women? *Transaction* (April).
GOODALE, J.
1962   Marriage Contracts Among the Tiwi. *Ethnology* 1 (4): 452–465.
GOODALL, J.
1963   Feeding Behavior of Wild Chimpanzees: A Preliminary Report.
Symp. Zool. Soc. Lond. 10: 39–48.
1964   Tool-Using and Aimed Throwing in a Community of Free-Living
Chimpanzees. *Nature* 201: 1264–1266.
1965   Chimpanzees of the Gombe Stream Reserve. DeVore, I. (ed.), *Primate Behavior.* N.Y.: Holt, Rinehart and Winston.
GOODE, W.J.
1964   *The Family.* Englewood Cliffs, N.J.: Prentice-Hall.
GOODENOUGH, W.H.
1970   *Description and Comparison in Cultural Anthropology.* Chicago:
Aldine.
GOUGH, K.
1959   The Nayars and the Definition of Marriage. *J. Royal Anthrop. Inst.*
89: 23–34.
1961   Nayar: Central Kerala. Schneider, D.M., and Gough, K. (eds.),
Matrilineal Kinship. Berkeley and L.A.: Univ. of California Press.
GOULD, P.R.
1963   Man Against His Environment: A Game Theoretic Framework.
Annals of the Assoc. of Amer. Geographers 53: 290–297.
GRASSÉ, P. (ed.)
1956   *L'Instinct dans le Comportement des Animaux et de l'Homme.* Paris:
Massero et Cie.

GRAY, J.G.
  1959 The Warriors. N.Y.: Harcourt, Brace.
GRAY, P.H.
  1958 Theory and Evidence of Imprinting in Human Infants. J. Psychol.
    46: 155–166.
GREEN, R.G., and LARSEN, C.L.
  1938 A Description of Shock Disease in the Snowshoe Hare. Amer. J. of
    Hygiene 28: 1087–1093.
GREEN, R.G., and EVANS, C.A.
  1940 Studies on a Population Cycle of Snowshoe Hares on Lake Alexander
    Area. J. of Wildlife Management 4: 220–238, 267–278, 347–358.
GREENSTEIN, F.
  1961 Sex-Related Political Differences in Childhood. J. Polit. 23: 2.
GRIFFIN, J.B.
  1960 Some Prehistoric Connections Between Siberia and America. Science,
    pp. 801–812.
GRIFFIN, G.A., and HARLOW, H.F.
  1966 Effects of Three Months of Total Social Deprivation on Social Adjust-
    ment and Learning in the Rhesus Monkey. Child Development 37:
    533–548.
GRINKER, R.R.
  1953 Psychosomatic Research. N.Y.: W.W. Norton.
GROSS, E.
  1968 Plus ça Change. . . . ? The Sexual Structure of Occupations Over
    Time. Social Problems 16: 198–208.
GROSS, N. et al.
  1958 Explorations in Role Analysis: Studies of the School Superintendency
    Role. N.Y.: John Wiley & Sons.
GULLIVER, P.
  1955 The Family Herds: A Study of Two Pastoral Tribes in East Africa,
    the Jie and Turkana. London: Routledge and Kegan Paul.
HALDANE, J.B.S.
  1955 Animal Communication and the Origin of Human Language. Sci.
    Progr. 40: 385–401.
  1956 The Argument from Animals to Men: An Examination of its Validity
    for Anthropology. J. Royal Anthrop. Inst. 86: 1–14.
HALL, K.R.L.
  1962 Sexual, Derived Social, and Agonistic Behavior Patterns in the Wild
    Chacma Baboon, Papio Ursinus. Proc. Zool. Soc. Lond. 139: 284–327.
  1964 Aggression in Monkey and Ape Societies. Carthy, J.D., and Ebling,
    F.J. (eds.), The Natural History of Aggression. N.Y.: Academic Press.
  1965 Social Organization of the Old-World Monkey and Apes. Symp. Zool.
    Soc. Lond. 14: 265–289.
HALLOWELL, A.I.
  1950 Personality Structure and the Evolution of Man. Amer. Anthrop. 52.
  1956 The Structural and Functional Dimensions of a Human Existence.
    Quart. Rev. Biol. 31: 88–101.

1960   Self, Society and Culture in Phylogenetic Perspective. Tax, S. (ed.), *Evolution of Man: Evolution After Darwin* II. Chicago: Univ. of Chicago Press.
1962   The Protocultural Foundations of Human Adaptation. Washburn, S.L. (ed.), *Social Life of Early Man.* London: Methuen.

HAMBURG, D.A.
1963   Emotions in Perspective of Human Evolution. Knapp, P. (ed.), *Expression of the Emotions in Man.* N.Y.: International Universities Press.
1968   Evolution of Emotional Responses: Evidence From Recent Research on Non-Human Primates. *Science and Psychology* 12.
1970   Recent Research on Hormonal Regulations of Aggressive Behavior. Paper presented at: UNESCO Expert meetings on the implications of recent scientific research on the understanding of human aggressiveness. Paris, May 1970.

HAMBURG, D.A., and LUNDE, D.
1966   Sex Hormones and the Development of Sex Differences in Human Behavior. Maccoby, E. (ed.), *The Development of Sex Differences.* Stanford: Stanford Univ. Press.

HAMBURG, D.A. et al.
1968   Studies of Distress in the Menstrual Cycle and the Postpartum Period. Michael, R.P. (ed.), *Endocrinology and Human Behaviour.* London: Oxford.

HAMILTON, W.D.
1963   The Evolution of Altruistic Behavior. *Amer. Nat.* 97: 354–356.

HANSEN, E.W.
1966   The Development of Maternal and Infant Behavior in the Rhesus Monkey. *Behavior* 27: 107–149.

HARLOW, H.F.
1958a   The Nature of Love. *Amer. Psychol.* 13: 673–685.
1958b   The Evolution of Learning. Roe, A., and Simpson, G.G. (eds.), *Behavior and Evolution.* New Haven, Conn.: Yale Univ. Press.
1959a   Basic Social Capacity of Primates. Spuhler, J.N. (ed.), *The Evolution of Man's Capacity for Culture.* Detroit, Mich.: Wayne State Univ. Press.
1959b   Love in Infant Monkeys. *Scientific American* (June).
1962a   Development of Affection in Primates. Bliss, E.L. (ed.), *Roots of Behavior.* N.Y.: Harper and Bros.
1962b   The Heterosexual Affectional System in Monkeys. *Amer. Psychol.* 17 (1): 1–9.
1965a   Total Social Isolation: Effects on Macaque Monkey Behavior. *Science* 148: 666.
1965b   Sexual Behavior in the Rhesus Monkey. Beach, F.A. (ed.), *Sex and Behavior.* N.Y.: John Wiley & Sons.

HARLOW, H.F., and HARLOW, M.K.
1962   Social Deprivation in Monkeys. *Scientific American* (Nov.).

HARLOW, H.F., and HARLOW, M.K.
1965   The Affectional Systems. Schrier. A.M.; Harlow, H.F.; and Stollnitz,

F. (eds.), *Behavior of Non-Human Primates* II. N.Y.: Academic Press.

HARLOW, H.F., HARLOW, M.K., and HANSEN, E.W.
1963   The Maternal Affectional System of Rhesus Monkeys. Rheingold, H.L. (ed.), *Maternal Behavior in Mammals*. N.Y.: John Wiley & Sons

HARLOW, H.F., and ZIMMERMAN, R.R.
1959   Affectional Responses in the Infant Monkey. *Science* 130: 421.

HARRIS, G.W.
1964   Sex Hormones, Brain Development, and Brain Function. *Endocrinology* 74: 627–651.

HARRIS, G.W., and LEVINE, S.
1965   Sexual Differentiation of the Brain and its Experimental Control. *J. Physiol.* 181: 379–400.

HART, C.W.M., and PILLING, A.R.
1960   *The Tiwi of Northern Australia*. N.Y.: Holt, Rinehart and Winston

HASSLER, R. and STEPHAN, H.
1966   *Evolution of the Forebrain*. Stuttgart: Georg Thieme Verlag.

HEBB, D.O., and THOMPSON, W.N.
1954   The Social Significance of Animal Studies. Lindzey, G. (ed.), *Handbook of Social Psychology* I. Reading, Mass.: Addison-Wesley.

HEDIGER, H.P.
1955   *Studies of the Psychology and Behavior of Captive Animals in Zoos and Circuses*. London: Butterworths.
1962   The Evolution of Territorial Behavior. Washburn, S.L. (ed.), *Social Life of Early Man*. London: Methuen.

HENDERSON, L.J.
1935   The Patient and Physician as a Social System. *New England J. Med.* 212: 819–823.

HENRY, J.
1954   The Formal Structure of a Psychiatric Hospital. *Psychiatry* 17: 139–151.
1960   A Cross-Cultural Outline of Education. *Current Anthrop.* I (4): 267–304.

HESS, E.H.
1958   Imprinting in Animals. *Scientific American* (March).
1962   Ethology: An Approach Toward the Complete Analysis of Behavior. Brown, R. (ed.), *New Directions in Psychology*. N.Y.: Holt, Rinehart and Winston.
1964   Imprinting in Birds. *Science* 146: 1128–1139.
1965   Attitude and Pupil Size. *Scientific American* 212: 46–54.

HIATT, L.R.
1967   Authority and Reciprocity in Australian Aboriginal Marriage Arrangements. *Mankind* 6 (10): 468–475.

HILL, O.W.C.
1957   *Man as an Animal*. London: Hutchinson.

HINDE, R.A.
1959   Some Recent Trends in Ethology. Koch, S. (ed.), *Psychology: A Study of a Science* 2. N.Y.: McGraw-Hill.

1963   The Nature of Imprinting. Foss, B.M. (ed.), *Determinants of Infant Behavior* 2. London: Methuen and N.Y.: John Wiley & Sons.

1965   Rhesus Monkey Aunts. Foss, B.M. (ed.), *Determinants of Infant Behavior* 3. London: Methuen and N.Y.: John Wiley & Sons.

1966   *Animal Behavior.* N.Y.: McGraw-Hill.

1969   Influence of Social Companions and of Temporary Separation on Mother-Infant Relations in Rhesus Monkeys. Foss, B.M. (ed.), *Determinants of Infant Behavior* IV.

HINDE, R.A.; ROWELL, T.E.; and SPENCER-BOOTH, Y.

1964   Behavior of Socially Living Rhesus Monkeys in Their First Six Months. *Proc. Zool. Soc. Lond.* 143: 609–649.

HINDE, R.A., and SPENCER-BOOTH, Y.

1967   The Behavior of Socially Living Rhesus Monkeys in Their First Two and a Half Years. *Anim. Behav.* 15: 169–196.

HINDE, R.A., and TINBERGEN, N.

1958   The Comparative Study of Species Specific Behavior. Roe, A., and Simpson, G.G. (eds.), *Behavior and Evolution.* New Haven, Conn.: Yale Univ. Press.

HIRSCH, J. (ed.)

1967   Behavior-Genetic Analysis. N.Y.: McGraw-Hill.

HOBHOUSE, L.T.

1913   The Historical Evolution of Property in Fact and in Idea. Hobhouse, L.T. (ed.), *Property: Its Duties and Rights.* London: Macmillan.

HOBHOUSE, L.T.; WHEELER, G.C.; and GINSBERG, M.

1915   *The Material Culture and Social Institutions of the Simpler Peoples.* London: Chapman and Hall.

HOCKETT, C.F.

1958   *A Modern Course in Linguistics.* N.Y.: Macmillan.

1959   Animal "Language" and Human Languages. Spuhler, J.N. (ed.), *The Evolution of Man's Capacity for Culture.* Detroit, Mich.: Wayne State Univ. Press.

HOCKETT, C.P., and ASCHER, R.

1964   The Human Revolution. *Current Anthrop.* 5: 135–147.

HOFSTADTER, R.

1944   *Social Darwinism in America.* Philadelphia, Penn.: Univ. of Penn. Press.

HOLLOWAY, R.

1966   Cranial Capacity, Neural Reorganization, and Hominid Evolution: A Search for more Suitable Parameters. *Amer. Anthrop.* 68: 103–121.

HOLT, J.

1964   *How Children Fail.* N.Y.: Pitman.

1967   *How Children Learn.* N.Y.: Pitman.

HOLTER, H.

1970   *Sex Roles and Social Structure.* Oslo: Universitetsforlaset.

HOMANS, G.C.

1961   *Social Behavior: Its Elementary Forms.* N.Y.: Harcourt, Brace and World.

HOPKINS, D.M.
  1959 *The Bering Land Bridge.* Stanford: Stanford Univ. Press.
HORNEY, K.
  1945 *The Neurotic Personality of our Time.* N.Y.: W.W. Norton.
HOWELL, F.C.
  1964 The Hominization Process. Tax, S. (ed.), *Horizons of Anthropology.* Chicago: Aldine.
  1969 Remains of Hominidae from Pliocene/Pleistocene Formations in The Lower Omo Basin, Ethiopia. *Nature, London* 223 (5212): 1234–1239.
HOWELL, F.C., and BOURLIÈRE, F. (eds.)
  1964 *African Ecology and Human Evolution.* London: Methuen.
HOWELL, F.C., and CLARK, J.D.
  1963 Acheulean Hunter-Gatherers of Sub-Saharan Africa. Howell, F.C., and Bourlière, F. (eds.), *African Ecology and Human Evolution.* Chicago: Aldine.
HOWELLS, W.W.
  1966 Homo Erectus. *Scientific American* (Nov.).
HUIZINGA, J.
  1949 *Homo Ludens: A Study of the Play-Element in Culture.* London: Int'l Library of Sociology and Social Reconstruction.
HULL, C.L.
  1943 *Principles of Behavior.* N.Y.: Appleton, Century.
HUXLEY, J.S.
  1914 The Courtship Habits of the Great Crested Grebe (*Podiceps cristatus*); with an addition to the Theory of Sexual Selection. *Proc. Zool. Soc. Lond.* (1914), 491–562.
  1963a *Evolution: The Modern Synthesis* (2nd ed.). London: Allen and Unwin.
  1963b Lorenzian Ethology. *Zeitschrift fur Tierpsychologie* 20: 402–409.
HUXLEY, J. (ed.)
  1966 Ritualization in Man and Animals. *Philosophical Transactions of the Royal Society of London B,* 251.
IMANISHI, K.
  1960 Social Organization of Sub-Human Primates in Their Natural Habitat. *Current Anthrop.* 1: 393–407.
  1963 Social Behavior in Japanese Monkeys, *Macaca fuscata.* Southwick, C.H. (ed.), *Primate Social Behavior.* Princeton: Van Nostrand.
ITANI, J.
  1963 Paternal Care in the Wild Japanese Monkey, *Macaca fuscata.* Southwick, C.H. (ed.), *Primate Social Behavior.* Princeton: Van Nostrand.
JANOWSKY, D.S.; GORNEY, R.; CASTELNUOVO-TEDESCO, P.; and STONE, C.B.
  1969 Pre-Menstrual Increases in Psychiatric Hospital Admission Rates. *Amer. J. of Obstetrics and Gynecology* 103: 189–191.
JAY, P.
  1968a Primate Field Studies and Human Evolution. Jay, P. (ed.), *Primates.* N.Y.: Holt, Rinehart and Winston.

1968b   *Primates: Studies in Adaptation and Variability.* N.Y.: Holt, Rinehart and Winston.
JEWELL, P.A., and LOIZOS, C.
1966   *Play, Exploration and Territory in Mammals.* (Symp. Zool. Soc.
Lond. No. 18) London: Academic Press.
JOLLY, C.J.
1970   The Seed-Eaters: A New Model of Hominid Differentiation Based
on a Baboon Analogy. *Man: The J.R.A.I.* 5 (1): 5–26.
JONES, M.
1953   *The Therapeutic Community.* N.Y.: Basic Books.
JOSEPHSON, E., and JOSEPHSON, M.
1962   *Man Alone: Alienation in Modern Society.* N.Y.: Dell.
KAHLER, E.
1967 (orig. 1957)   *The Tower and the Abyss.* N.Y.: Viking.
KALOGERAKIS, M.G.
1963   The Role of Olfaction in Sexual Development. *Psychosomatic Medicine* XXV (5).
KAPLAN, B., and JOHNSON, D.
1964   The Social Meaning of Navaho Psychopathology and Psychotherapy.
Kiev, A. (ed.), *Magic, Faith, and Healing.* Glencoe, Ill.: Free Press.
KAPLAN, D.
1965   The Superorganic: Science or Metaphysics. *Amer. Anthrop.* 67 (4):
958–974.
KAUFMAN, I.C., and ROSENBLUM, L.A.
1967a   Depression in Infant Monkeys Separated From Their Mothers.
Science 155: 1030–1031.
1969   The Waning of the Mother-Infant Bond in Two Species of Macaque.
Foss, P.M. (ed.), *Determinants of Infant Behavior* IV. London: Methuen.
KAUFMANN, J.H.
1967   Social Relations of Adult Males in a Free-Ranging Band of Rhesus
Monkeys. Altmann, S.A. (ed.), *Social Communication Among Primates.*
Chicago: Univ. of Chicago Press.
1966   Social Relations of Infant Rhesus Monkeys and Their Mothers in
a Free-Ranging Band. *Zoologica* 51: 17–28.
KAWAI, M.
1965   On the System of Social Ranks in a Natural Troop of Japanese
Monkeys: (1) Basic Rank and Dependent Rank. Altmann, S.A. (ed.),
Japanese Monkeys. Atlanta, Ga.: Altmann.
KAWAMURA, S.
1965   Matriarchal Social Ranks in the Minoo-B Troop: A Study of the
Rank System of Japanese Monkeys. Altmann, S.A. (ed.), *Japanese Mon-
keys.* Atlanta, Ga.: Altmann.
KEITH, A.
1948   *A New Theory of Human Evolution.* London: Watts.
KETTLEWELL, H.B.D.
1965   Insect Survival and Selection for Pattern. *Science* 148: 1290–1296.
KIEV, A.
1964   *Magic, Faith, and Healing.* Glencoe, Ill.: Free Press.

KINSEY, A.C.; POMEROY, W.B.; and MARTIN, C.E.
  1948   *Sexual Behavior in the Human Male.* Philadelphia, Penn. W.B.
  Saunders.
KITTREDGE, G.L.
  1929   *Witchcraft in Old and New England.* Cambridge, Mass.: Harvard
  Univ.
KLEIN, M.
  1949   *The Psycho-Analysis of Children.* London: Hogarth Press.
KLOPFER, P.H.
  1965   Imprinting: A Reassessment. *Science* 147: 302–303.
  1969   *Habitats and Territories: A Study of the Use of Space by Animals.*
  N.Y.: Basic Books.
KLOPFER, P.H., and HAILMAN, J.P.
  1967   *An Introduction to Animal Behavior.* Englewood Cliffs, N.J.: Prentice-Hall.
KLOPPER, A.
  1964   Physiological Background to Aggression. Carthy, J.D., and Ebling,
  F.J. (eds.), *The Natural History of Aggression.* London: Academic Press.
KNAPP, P.H. (ed.)
  1963   *Expression of the Emotions in Man.* N.Y.: International Universities Press.
KOESTLER, A.
  1967   *The Ghost in the Machine.* London: Hutchinson.
KOFORD, C.B.
  1963a Group Relations in an Island Colony of Rhesus Monkeys. Southwick, C.H. (ed.), 1963. *Primate Social Behavior.* Princeton: Van Nostrand.
  1963b Rank of Mothers and Sons in Bands of Rhesus Monkeys. *Science*
  141: 356–357.
KOGON, E.
  1950   *The Theory and Practice of Hell.* N.Y.: Farrar.
KOHL, H.
  1969   *The Open Classroom.* N.Y.: Vintage.
KOPELL, B.S. *et al.*
  1969   Variations in Some Measures of Arousal During the Menstrual
  Cycle. *J. Nervous and Mental Disease* 148 (2): 180–187.
KORTLANDT, A., and KOOIJ, M.
  1963   Protohominid Behaviour in Primates. *Symp. Zool. Soc. Lond.* 10:
  61–88.
KOTCHETKOVA, V.I.
  1960   L'evolution des regions specifiquement humaines de l'écorce cere-
  brale chez les Hominides. *Proc. 6th Int. Cong. Anthrop. and Ethnol.
  Sci. Paris* 1: 623–630.
KOYAMA, N.
  1967   On Dominance Rank and Kinship of a Wild Japanese Monkey
  Troop in Arashiyama. *Primates* 8 (3): 189–216.
KROEBER, A.L.
  1917   The Superorganic. *Amer. Anthrop.* 19: 163–213. Also in: *The Nature
  of Culture.* Chicago: Univ. of Chicago Press, 1952.

1948 (1923) *Anthropology.* N.Y.: Harcourt, Brace.
KROEBER, A.L., and KLUCKHOHN, C.
1952 Culture: A Critical Review of Concepts and Definitions. *Papers of the Peabody Museum of American Archeology and Ethnology* 47 (1). Cambridge, Mass.: Harvard Univ. Press.
KROPOTKIN, P.
1902 *Mutual Aid.* London: Heinemann.
KUHME, W.
1965 Communal Food Distribution and Division of Labor in African Hunting Dogs. *Nature, London* 205: 443–444.
KUMMER, H.
1967 Tripartite Relations in Hamadryas Baboons. Altmann, S.A. (ed.), *Social Communication Among Primates.* Chicago and London: Univ. of Chicago Press.
1968 *Social Organization of Hamadryas Baboons.* Chicago: Univ. of Chicago Press.
KURATOWSKI, K.
1962 *Introduction to Set Theory and Topology.* London: Pergamon and Reading, Mass.: Addison-Wesley.
LABARRE, W.
1954 *The Human Animal.* Chicago: Univ. of Chicago Press.
LACK, D.
1954 *The Natural Regulation of Animal Numbers.* Oxford: Clarendon Press.
LAING, R.D.
1959 *The Divided Self.* London: Tavistock.
1967 *The Politics of Experience.* N.Y.: Ballantine.
LANCASTER, J.
1968a Primate Communication Systems and the Emergence of Human Language. Jay, P. (ed.), *Primates: Studies in Adaptation and Variability.* N.Y.: Holt, Rinehart and Winston.
1968b On the Evolution of Tool-Using Behavior. *Amer. Anthrop.* 70: 56–66.
LANCASTER, J.B., and LEE, R.B.
1965 The Annual Reproductive Cycle in Monkeys and Apes. DeVore, I. (ed.), *Primate Behavior.* N.Y.: Holt, Rinehart and Winston.
LAUGHLIN, W.S.
1968 Hunting: An Integrating Biobehavior System and Its Evolutionary Importance. Lee, R.B., and DeVore, I. (eds.), *Man the Hunter.* Chicago: Aldine.
LAWICK-GOODALL, J. VAN
1967a Mother-Offspring Relationships in Free-Ranging Chimpanzees. Morris, D. (ed.), *Primate Ethology.* London: Weidenfelt and Nicolson.
1967b *My Friends, The Wild Chimpanzees.* National Geographic Society.
1968 The Behavior of Free-Living Chimpanzees in the Gombe Stream Reserve. *Anim. Behav. Monog.,* vol. 1, part 3.
LEACH, E.R.
1961 Time and False Noses. *Rethinking Anthropology.* London School of

Economics Monographs on Social Anthropology (22). London: Athlone Press.

1967   *A Runaway World?* London: B.B.C.

LEAKEY, L.S.B.

1967a   An Early Miocene Member of Hominidae. *Nature* (Jan. 14).

1967b   Development of Aggression as a Factor in Early Human and Pre-Human Evolution. Clemente, C.D., and Lindsley, D.B. (eds.), *Aggression and Defense.* Berkeley and L.A.: Univ. of California Press.

LEBERGOTT, S. (ed.)

1964   *Men Without Work.* Englewood Cliffs, N.J.: Prentice-Hall.

LEE, R.B.

1966   ! Kung Bushman Subsistence: An Input-Output Analysis. Damas, D. (ed.), *Ecological Essays: Proceedings of the Conference on Cultural Ecology, National Museum of Canada.*

1967   Trance Cure of the ! Kung Bushmen. *Natural History* (Nov.), pp. 30–37.

1968a   Sociology of the ! Kung Bushman Trance Performances. Prince, R.H. (ed.), *Trance and Possession States.* Montreal: R.M. Bucke Memorial Soc.

1968b   What Hunters Do For a Living, or How To Make Out in Scarce Resources. Lee, R.B., and DeVore, I. (eds.), *Man The Hunter.* Chicago: Aldine.

LEE, R.B., and DEVORE, I. (eds.)

1968   *Man The Hunter.* Chicago: Aldine.

LEEDS, A., and VAYDA, A.P. (eds.)

1965   *Man, Culture, and Animals: The Role of Animals in Human Ecological Adjustments.* Amer. Assoc. for the Advancement of Science (78).

LEHRMANN, D.S.

1953   A Critique of Konrad Lorenz's Theory of Instinctive Behavior. *Quart. Rev. Biol.* 28: 337–363.

LEIGHTON, A.H., and LEIGHTON, D.C.

1941   Elements of Psychotherapy in Navaho Religion. *Psychiatry* IV: 515–524.

LEMAGNEN, J.

1950   Physiologie des sensations: Nouvelles données sur la Phénomène de l'Exaltolide. *Compt. Rend.* 230: 1103.

1953   L'olfaction: le fonctionnement olfactif et son intervention dans les régulations psychophysiologiques. *J. Physiol.* (Paris) 45: 285.

LENNEBERG, E.H.

1967   *Biological Foundations of Language.* N.Y.: John Wiley & Sons.

LEONARD, G.B.

1968   *Education and Ecstasy.* N.Y.: Delta.

LEVINE, R.A.

1963   Child Rearing in Sub-Saharan Africa: An Interim Report. *Bulletin of the Menninger Clinic* 27 (5): 245–256.

LEVINE, S.

1966   Sex Differences in the Brain. *Scientific American* (April).

LÉVI-STRAUSS, C.

1944   The Social and Psychological Aspects of Chieftainship in a Primitive

Tribe: The Nambikwara. *Trans. of the New York Acad. of Sciences* (series 2, vol. VII, no. 1).

1949a   Le Sorcier et sa Magie. *Les Temps Modernes,* 4 annee, No. 41. (Reprinted in *Anthropologie Structurale.* Paris: Plon.)

1949b   *Les Structures Élémentaires de la Parenté.* Paris: Presses Universitaires de France.

1966   The Scope of Anthropology. *Current Anthrop.* (April).

1969   *The Elementary Structures of Kinship.* Bell, J.H., and Von Sturmer, J.R. (trans.); Needham, R. (trans. and ed.), Boston: Beacon Press.

LEVY, M.J.

1969   Kinship Contexts and Some Human Universals, Past and Future: A Set of Hypotheses. *Amer. Sociol.* 4 (1).

LEYHAUSEN, P.

1965   The Sane Community: A Density Problem? *Discovery* (Sept.).

LINTON, R.

1936   *The Study of Man.* N.Y.: Appleton, Century.

LIPSET, S.

1959   *Political Man.* London. Heinemann.

LIVINGSTONE, F.B.

1960   Natural Selection, Disease, and Ongoing Evolution, as Illustrated by the ABO Blood Groups. Lasker, G.W. (ed.), *The Processes of Ongoing Evolution.* Detroit, Mich.: Wayne State Univ. Press.

LOIZOS, C.

1967   Play Behavior in Higher Primates: A Review. Morris, D. (ed.), *Primate Ethology.* Chicago: Aldine.

LORENZ, K.

1935   Companionship in Bird Life: Fellow Members of the Species as Releasers of Social Behavior. Schiller, C. (ed.), *Instinctive Behavior.* N.Y.: International Universities Press (1957).

1950   The Comparative Method in Studying Innate Behavior Patterns. *Physiological Mechanisms in Animal Behavior.* (Sympos. Soc. Exp. Biol. No. 4) N.Y.: Academic Press.

1956a   The Objectivistic Theory of Instinct. Grassé, P. (ed.), *L'Instinct dans le Comportement des Animaux et de l'Homme.* Paris: Masson et Cie.

1956b   Plays and Vacuum Activities. Grassé, P. (ed.), *L'Instinct dans le Comportement des Animaux et de l'Homme.* Paris: Masson et Cie.

1958   The Evolution of Behavior. *Scientific American* (Dec.).

1964   Ritualized Fighting. Carthy, J.D., and Ebling, F.J. (eds.), *The Natural History of Aggression.* London and N.Y.: Academic Press.

1965   *Evolution and Modification of Behavior.* Chicago: Univ. of Chicago Press.

1966   *On Aggression.* London: Methuen.

1969   Innate Bases of Learning. Pribram, K.H. (ed.), *On the Biology of Learning.* N.Y.: Harcourt, Brace and World.

LOWENTHAL, L.

1946   Terror's Atomization of Man. *Commentary* 1 (3).

LOWIE, R.H.

1956   *The Crow Indians.* N.Y.: Holt, Rinehart and Winston.

MACCOBY, E. (ed.)

1966   *The Development of Sex Differences.* Stanford: Stanford Univ. Press.
1970   Feminine Intellect and the Demands of Science. *Impact of Science on Society* 20: 1. U.N.E.S.C.O.

MACLEAN, P.D.

1949   Psychosomatic Disease and the "Visceral Brain." *Psychosom. Med.* 11: 338–353.
1958   The Limbic System with Respect to Self-Preservation and the Preservation of the Species. *J. Nervous and Mental Disease* 127: 1–11.
1962   New Findings Relevant to the Evolution of Psychosexual Functions of the Brain. *J. Nervous and Mental Disease* 135 (4): 289–301.
1964   Man and His Animal Brains. *Modern Medicine* (Feb. 3).
1967   The Brain in Relation to Empathy and Medical Education. *J. Nervous and Mental Disease* 144 (5).
1968   Alternative Neural Pathways to Violence. Ng, L. (ed.), *Alternatives to Violence.* N.Y.: Time-Life Books.

MACNEISH, R.S.

1964   The Origins of New World Civilization. *Scientific American* (Nov.).

MALINOWSKI, B.

1922   *Argonauts of the Western Pacific.* London: Geo. Routledge and Sons.
1929   *The Sexual Life of Savages.* London: Geo. Routledge and Sons.
1944   *A Scientific Theory of Culture and other Essays.* Chapel Hill, N.C.: Univ. of North Carolina Press.

MALTHUS, T.R.

1798   *An Essay on the Principle of Population.* London: J. Johnson.

MANDEL, J.

1967   The Menstrual Cycle and Suicide. *J. Amer. Med. Ass.* (May).

MAQUET, J.

1961   *The Premise of Inequality in Ruanda.* London: Oxford Univ. Press.

MARK, V.H., and ERVIN, F.R.

1970   *Violence and the Brain.* N.Y.: Harper & Row.

MARLER, P.

1967   Animal Communication Signals. *Science* 157: 769–773.

MARWICK, M.G.

1965   *Sorcery in its Social Setting.* Manchester: Manchester Univ. Press.

MARX, K.

1887   *Capital: A Critical Analysis of Capitalist Production.* [3rd German ed., trans. by Moore, S., and Aveling, E.] London: S. Sonnenschein, Lowrey and Co.
1964a   *Early Writings.* N.Y.: McGraw-Hill.
1964b   *Pre-Capitalist Economic Formations.* London: Lawrence and Wishart.
1967   *Writings of the Young Marx on Philosophy and Society.* Garden City, N.Y.: Doubleday.

MARX, K., and ENGELS, F.

1948   (orig. 1888) *Communist Manifesto, Socialist Landmark.* (Original text plus a new appreciation written for the Labour Party by H.J. Laski) London: Allen and Unwin.

MASON, W.A.
  1965a Determinants of Social Behavior in Young Chimpanzees. Schrier,
    A.M.; Harlow, H.; and Stollnitz, F. (eds.), *Behavior of Nonhuman Pri-
    mates*. N.Y. and London: Academic Press.
  1965b The Social Development of Monkeys and Apes. DeVore, I. (ed.),
    Primate Behavior. N.Y. and London: Holt, Rinehart and Winston.
MASON, W.A., and SPONHOLZ, R.R.
  1963 Behavior of Rhesus Monkeys Raised in Isolation. *J. Psychiat. Res.*
    1: 299–306.
MASTERS, R.D.
  1968 *The Political Philosophy of Rousseau*. Princeton: Princeton Univ.
    Press.
MATTHEWS, H.L.
  1964 Overt Fighting in Mammals. Carthy, J.D., and Ebling, F.J. (eds.),
    The Natural History of Aggression. London: Academic Press.
MAUSS, M.
  1925 Essai sur le don. *Année Sociologique* N.S.1 [*The Gift*, Cunnison,
    I.G. (trans.), London: Cohen and West 1954].
MAYER, P. (ed.)
  1970 *Socialization: The Approach From Social Anthropology*. (A.S.A.
    Monographs in Social Anthropology 8) London: Tavistock.
MAYO, E.
  1945 *The Social Problems of an Industrial Civilization*. Cambridge, Mass.:
    Harvard Univ. Press.
MAYR, E.
  1963 *Animal Species and Evolution*. Cambridge, Mass.: Harvard Univ.
    Press.
McDOUGALL, W.
  1908 *Social Psychology*. London: Methuen.
McLENNAN, J.F.
  1865 *Primitive Marriage*. London: Black.
MEAD, M.
  1962 A Cultural Anthropologist's Approach to Maternal Deprivation.
    Deprivation of Maternal Care: A Reassessment of its Effects. Public
    Health Papers (14). Geneva: W.H.O.
  1970 *Culture and Commitment*. Garden City, N.Y.: Natural History
    Press.
MEAD, M., and KAPLAN, F.B. (eds.)
  1965 *American Women: The Report of the President's Commission on the
    Status of Women*. N.Y.: Charles Scribner's Sons.
MEIER, G.W.
  1965 Other Data on the Effects of Social Isolation During Rearing Upon
    Adult Reproductive Behavior in the Rhesus Monkey (*Macaca mulatta*).
    Anim. Behav. 13: 228–231.
MENZEL, E.W., JR.
  1963 The Effects of Cumulative Experience on Responses to Novel Ob-
    jects in Young Isolation-Reared Chimpanzees. *Behavior* 21: 1–12.

MERTON, R.K.
1957 Bureaucratic Structure and Personality. *Social Theory and Social Structure*. Glencoe, Ill.: Free Press.

MESSING, S.D.
1958 Group Therapy and Social Status in the Zar Cult of Ethiopia. *Amer. Anthrop.* 60 (6): 1120–1126.

MICHAEL, R.P.
1968 *Endocrinology and Human Behavior*. London: Oxford Univ. Press.

MICHAEL, R.P., and KEVERNE, E.B.
1968 Pheromones in the Communication of Sexual Status in Primates. *Nature, London* 218: 746–749.

MICHAEL, R.P., and ZUMPE, D.
1970 Rhythmic Changes in the Copulatory Frequency of Rhesus Monkeys (*Macaca mulatta*) in Relation to the Menstrual Cycle and a Comparison with the Human Cycle. *J. Reproduction and Fertility* 21: 199–201.

MIDDLETON, J. (ed.)
1970 *From Child to Adult; Studies in the Anthropology of Education*. N.Y.: Natural History Press.

MIDDLETON, J., and WINTER, E.H. (eds.)
1963 *Witchcraft and Sorcery in East Africa*. London: Routledge and Kegan Paul.

MILLER, W., and ERVIN, S.
1964 The Development of Grammar in Child Language. *Monog. Soc. Res. Child Devel.* 29: 9–33.

MILLET, K.
1970 *Sexual Politics*. Garden City, N.Y.: Doubleday.

MISHKIN, B.
1940 Rank and Warfare Among the Plains Indians. *American Ethnological Society Monograph*.

MOLTZ, H.
1960 Imprinting: Empirical Basis and Theoretical Significance. *Psychology Bulletin* 57: 291–314.

MONEY, J.
1965 Psychosexual Differentiation. *Sex Research: New Developments*. N.Y.: Holt, Rinehart and Winston.
1965 *Sex Research: New Developments*. N.Y.: Holt, Rinehart and Winston.

MONTAGU, M.F.A.
1957 *The Reproductive Development of the Female*. N.Y.: Julian Press.

MONTAGU, A. (ed.)
1962 *Culture and the Evolution of Man*. Oxford Univ. Press.
1968 *Man and Aggression*. N.Y.: Oxford Univ. Press.

MONTESSORI, M.
1964 *The Montessori Method*. N.Y.: Schocken.

MOOS, R.R.H.
1969 Typology of Menstrual Cycle Symptoms. *Amer. J. of Obstetrics and Gynecology* 103 (3): 390–402.

MORGAN, L.H.
1877 *Ancient Society*. N.Y.: H. Holt.

MORGAN, R. (ed.)
1970   *Sisterhood is Powerful*. N.Y.: Random House.
MORRIS, D.
1956   The Function and Causation of Courtship Ceremonies. Grassé, P.
       (ed.), *L'Instinct dans le Comportement des Animaux et de l'Homme*.
       Paris: Masson et Cie.
1967   *The Naked Ape*. London: Constable.
1970   *The Human Zoo*. N.Y.: McGraw-Hill.
MORRIS, D. (ed.)
1967   *Primate Ethology*. London: Weidenfeld and Nicolson.
MOWAT, F.
1963   *Never Cry Wolf*. Boston: Little, Brown.
MUMFORD, L.
1934   *Technics and Civilization*. N.Y.: Harcourt, Brace and World.
MURDOCK, G.P.
1937   Comparative Data on the Division of Labor by Sex. *Social Forces*
       15 (4): 551–553.
1945   The Common Denominator of Cultures. Linton, R. (ed.), *The Sci-
       ence of Man in the World Crisis*. N.Y.: Columbia Univ. Press.
1949   *Social Structure*. N.Y.: Macmillan Press.
MURIE, A.
1944   The Wolves of Mount McKinley. *U.S. Department of Interior,
       Fauna Series* (5): 1–238.
MURPHY, J.M.
1964   Psychotherapeutic Aspects of Shamanism on St. Lawrence Island,
       Alaska. Kiev, A. (ed.), *Magic, Faith, and Healing*. Glencoe, Ill.: Free
       Press.
MURPHY, R.F.
1959   Social Structure and Sex Antagonism. *Southwest. J. Anthrop.* 15 (1).
NADEL, S.F.
1946   A Study of Shamanism in the Nuba Mountains. *J. Royal Anthrop.
       Inst.* LXXVI: 25–37.
NAEGELE, K.D.
1970   *Health and Healing*. San Francisco: Jossey-Bass.
NAKANE, C.
1963   The Nayar Family in a Disintegrating Matrilineal System. Mogey, J.
       (ed.), *Family and Marriage*. International Studies in Sociol. and Soc.
       Anthrop. 1. Leiden: E.J. Brill.
NAPIER, J.
1962   The Evolution of the Hand. *Scientific American* (Dec.).
1964   The Evolution of Bipedal Walking in the Hominids. *Arch. Biol.* 75.
       Suppl., pp. 673–708.
1967   The Antiquity of Human Walking. *Scientific American* (April).
1970   *The Roots of Mankind*. Washington, D.C.: Smithsonian Institution
       Press.
NAPIER, J.R., and NAPIER, P.H.
1967   *A Handbook of Living Primates*. London and N.Y.: Academic
       Press.

NASH, M.
   1961 Witchcraft as Social Process in a Tzeltal Community. *America Indigena* 20: 121–126.
   1966 *Primitive and Peasant Economic Systems*. San Francisco: Chandler Publ.
NEEDHAM, R.
   1962 *Structure and Sentiment*. Chicago: Univ. of Chicago Press.
NEILL, A.S.
   1960 *Summerhill: A Radical Approach to Child Rearing*. N.Y.: Hart.
NEWCOMB, W.W.
   1950 A Re-Examination of the Causes of Plains Warfare. *Amer. Anthrop.* 317–329.
NIEBOER, H.J.
   1900 *Slavery as an Industrial System: Ethnological Researches*. The Hague: Martinus Nijhoff.
NISSEN, H.W.
   1956 Individuality in Behavior of Chimpanzees. *Amer. Anthrop.* 58: 407–413.
NISSEN, I.
   1961 *Absolute Monogamy*. Oslo: Aschehoug.
OAKLEY, K.P.
   1950 *Man the Tool-Maker*. London: British Museum.
   1957 Tools Makyth Man. *Antiquity* 31: 199–209. Also in: *Annual Report, Smithsonian Institution* 1958: 431–445.
   1962 On Man's Use of Fire, with comments on tool-making and hunting. Washburn, S.L. (ed.), *Social Life of Early Man*. London: Methuen.
O'NEILL, W.L.
   1967 *Everyone Was Brave: The Rise and Fall of Feminism in America*. Chicago: Quadrangle.
OPIE, I., and OPIE, P.
   1961 *The Lore and Language of School Children*. Oxford: Clarendon Press.
OPLER, M.E.
   1964 The Human Being in Culture Theory. *Amer. Anthrop.* 66 (3): 507–528.
OTTERBEIN, K.F.
   1967 The Evolution of Zulu Warfare. Bohannan, P. (ed.), *Law and Warfare*. N.Y.: Natural History Press.
PAINE, R.
   1967 What is Gossip About: An Alternative Hypothesis. *Man: The J.R.A.I.* 2: 278–285.
PAPPENHEIM, F.
   1968 *The Alienation of Modern Man; An Interpretation Based on Marx and Tönnies*. N.Y.: Modern Reader Paperbacks.
PARK, G.K.
   1963 Divination and Its Social Context. *J. Royal Anthrop. Inst.* 93 (2).
PARK, W.Z.
   1938 *Shamanism in Western North America*. Evanston, Ill.: Univ. of Illinois.

PARKER, A.S.
1960   Premenstrual Tension Syndrome. *Medical Clinic of North America*, No. 44 (March).
PARKINSON, C.N.
1957   *Parkinson's Law*. Boston: Houghton Mifflin.
PARSONS, T.
1951a   *The Social System*. N.Y.: Free Press.
1951b   Illness and the Role of the Physician: A Sociological Perspective. *Amer. J. Orthopsychiatry* 21: 452–460.
1957   The Mental Hospital as a Type of Organization. Greenblatt, M.; Levinson, D.J.; and Williams, R.H. (eds.), *The Patient and the Mental Hospital*. Glencoe, Ill.: Free Press.
PARSONS, T., and SMELSER, N.
1956   *Economy and Society*. Glencoe, Ill.: Free Press.
PASTORE, N.
1949   *The Nature-Nurture Controversy*. N.Y.: King's Crown Press.
PAULME, D. (ed.)
1964   *Women of Tropical Africa*. Berkeley: Univ. of California Press.
PAVLOV, I.P.
1927   *Conditioned Reflexes*. London: Oxford Univ. Press.
1928   *Lectures on Conditioned Reflexes*. London: Lawrence and Wishart.
PENFIELD, W., and RASMUSSEN, T.
1950   *The Cerebral Cortex of Man*. N.Y.: Macmillan.
PERICOT, L.
1962   The Social Life of Paleolithic Hunters as Shown by Levantine Art. Washburn, S.L. (ed.), *Social Life of Early Man*. London: Methuen.
PETTITT, G.A.
1970   *Prisoners of Culture*. N.Y.: Charles Scribner's Sons.
PFEIFFER, J.
1969   *The Emergence of Man*. N.Y.: Harper & Row.
PICKENS, D.K.
1968   *Eugenics and the Progressives*. N.Y.: Vanderbilt Univ. Press.
PILBEAM, D.R.
1967   Man's Earliest Ancestors. *Science J*. 3 (2).
POLANYI, K. *et al*.
1957   *Trade and Markets in Early Empires*. Glencoe, Ill.: Free Press.
PRIBRAM, K.H. (ed.)
1969   *On the Biology of Learning*. N.Y.: Harcourt, Brace and World.
PRICE, J.
1967   The Dominance Hierarchy and the Evolution of Mental Illness. *The Lancet* (July 29), pp. 243–246.
PROVENCE, S., and LIPTON, R.C.
1962   *Infants in Institutions*. London: Bailey and Swinfen. N.Y.: Internat'l Universities Press.
RAPOPORT, R.N., and RAPOPORT, R.S.
1957   "Democratization" and Authority in a Therapeutic Community. *Behavioral Science* 2: 128–133.

RAPPOPORT, R.A.
1967   Pigs for the Ancestors. New Haven, Conn.: Yale Univ. Press.
RASMUSSEN, K.
1929   Report of the Fifth Thule Expedition, 1921–24 VII (1). Intellectual
       Culture of the Iglulik Eskimos. Copenhagen: Gyldendalske Boghandel,
       Nordisk Forlag.
RAUM, O.F.
1940   A Chaga Childhood. London: Oxford Univ. Press.
READ, C.
1920   The Origin of Man and His Superstitions. Cambridge: Cambridge
       Univ. Press.
READ, M.
1959   Children of Their Fathers: Growing Up Among the Ngoni of Nyasa-
       land. London: Methuen.
REDFIELD, R.
1956   Peasant Society and Culture. Chicago: Univ. of Chicago Press.
REICHARD, G.
1939   A Navaho Medicine Man: Sand Paintings and Legends of Miguelito.
       N.Y.: J.J. Augustin.
REINHOLD, R.
1971   Bone Traces Man Back 5 Million Years. The New York Times
       (Feb. 19).
REYNOLDS, V.
1965   Budongo: A Forest and Its Chimpanzees. London: Methuen and Co.
1966a Open Groups in Hominid Evolution. Man: The J.R.A.I. 1 (4):
       441–452.
1968   Kinship and the Family in Monkeys, Apes and Man. Man: The
       J.R.A.I. 3 (2): 209–223.
1970   Roles and Role Change in Monkey Society: the Consort Relationship
       of Rhesus Monkeys. Man: The J.R.A.I. 5 (3): 449–465.
RHEINGOLD, H.L.
1961   The Effect of Environmental Stimulation Upon Social and Explora-
       tory Behavior in the Human Infant. Foss, B.M. (ed.), Determinants of
       Infant Behavior 1. N.Y.: John Wiley & Sons.
1963a Controlling the Infant's Exploratory Behaviour. Foss, B.M. (ed.),
       Determinants of Infant Behavior 2. N.Y.: John Wiley & Sons.
1963b Maternal Behavior in Mammals. N.Y.: John Wiley & Sons.
RICHARDS, A.I.
1956   Chisungu: A Girls' Initiation Ceremony Among the Bemba of North-
       ern Rhodesia. London: Faber and Faber.
RICHARDS, O.W.
1953   The Social Insects. London: Macdonald.
RICHARDSON, L.F.
1960   Statistics of Deadly Quarrels. London: Stevens and Sons.
RITTER, A.E.
1955   Shaka Zulu. N.Y.: G.P. Putnam's Sons.

ROBBINS, L.
1932   *An Essay on the Nature and Significance of Economic Science.* London: Macmillan.
ROBERTS, D.F., and HARRISON, G.A.
1959   *Natural Selection in Human Populations.* N.Y.: Pergamon Press.
ROBINSON, J.T.
1964   Adaptive Radiation in the Australopithecines and the Origin of Man. Howell, F.C., and Bourlière, F. (eds.), *African Ecology and Human Evolution.* London: Methuen.
ROE, A., and SIMPSON, G.G. (eds.)
1958   *Behavior and Evolution.* New Haven, Conn.: Yale Univ. Press.
ROEDER, K.D.
1963   Ethology and Neurophysiology. *Zeitschrift fur Tierpsychologie* 20: 434–440.
ROETHLESBERGER, F.J., and DIXON, W.J.
1939   *Management and the Worker.* Cambridge, Mass.: Harvard Univ. Press.
ROMER, A.S.
1958   Phylogeny and Behavior with Special Reference to Vertebrate Evolution. Roe, A., and Simpson, G.G. (eds.), *Behavior and Evolution.* New Haven, Conn.: Yale Univ. Press.
1959   *The Vertebrate Story.* Chicago: Univ. of Chicago Press.
ROSE, F.G.G.
1960   *Classification of Kin, Age-Structure and Marriage among the Groote Eylandt Aborigines: A Study in Method and a Theory of Australian Kinship.* Berlin: Akademie-Verlag. London: Pergamon Press.
1968   Australian Marriage, Land-Owning Groups and Initiations. Lee, R.B., and DeVore, I. (eds.), *Man The Hunter.* Chicago: Aldine.
ROWELL, T.E.; HINDE, R.A.; and SPENCER-BOOTH, Y.
1964   "Aunt"—Infant Interaction in Captive Rhesus Monkeys. *J. Anim. Behav.* 12: 219–226.
ROYAL COMMISSION ON THE STATUS OF WOMEN
1970   Participation of Women in Public Life. *Report of the Royal Commission on the Status of Women.* Ottawa: Information Canada.
RUBINOFF, C.
1967   *Pornography of Power.* N.Y.: Quadrangle Books.
RUSSELL, B.
1945   *A History of Western Philosophy.* N.Y.: Simon and Schuster.
RUSSELL, W.M.S., and RUSSELL, C.
1961   *Human Behaviour.* London: Andre Deutch.
1968   *Violence, Monkeys and Man.* London: Macmillan.
SADE, D.S.
1965   Some aspects of Parent-Offspring and Sibling Relations in a Group of Rhesus Monkeys, with a Discussion of Grooming. *Amer. J. Phys. Anthrop.* 23: 1–17.
1967   Determinants of Dominance in a Group of Free-Ranging Rhesus

Monkeys. Altmann, S.A. (ed.), *Social Communication among Primates.* Chicago: Univ. of Chicago Press.

1968   Inhibition of Son-Mother Mating Among Free-Ranging Rhesus Monkeys. *Science and Psychoanalysis* 12: 18–37.

SAHLINS, M.D.

1959   The Social Life of Monkeys, Apes, and Primitive Man. Spuhler, J.H. (ed.), *The Evolution of Man's Capacity for Culture.* Detroit, Mich.: Wayne State Univ. Press.

1960   The Origin of Society. *Scientific American* 203: 76–86.

1961   The Segmentary Lineage: An Organization of Predatory Expansion. *Amer. Anthrop.* 63: 322–345.

1963a   On the Sociology of Primitive Exchange. Banton, M. (ed.), *The Relevance for Models for Social Anthropology.* A.S.A. Monograph No. 1. London: Tavistock.

1963b   Poor Man, Rich Man, Big Man, Chief: Political Types in Melanesia and Polynesia. *Comp. Studies Soc. Hist.* 5: 285–303.

SALISBURY, R.

1962   *From Stone to Steel.* Cambridge: Cambridge Univ. Press.

SALZEN, E.A.

1967   Imprinting in Birds and Primates. *Behavior* 28: 232–254.

SARICH, V.M.

1968   The Origin of the Hominids: An Immunological Approach. Washburn, S.L., and Jay, P. (eds.), *Perspectives on Human Evolution* 1. N.Y.: Holt, Rinehart and Winston.

SCHALLER, G., and LOWTHER, G.

1969   The Relevance of Carnivore Behavior to the Study of Early Hominids. *Southwest. J. Anthrop.* 25: 307–341.

SCHAPERA, I. (ed.)

1937   *The Bantu-Speaking Tribes of South Africa.* London: Geo. Routledge and Sons.

SCHILLER, C.H. (ed.)

1957   *Instinctive Behavior.* N.Y.: International Universities Press.

SCHNEIDER, D., and GOUGH, K.

1961   *Matrilineal Kinship.* Berkeley and L.A.: Univ. of California Press.

SCHNEIRLA, T.C.

1941   Social Organization in Insects, as Related to Individual Function. *Psychol. Rev.* 48: 465–486.

1956   Interrelationships of the "Innate" and the "Acquired" in Instinctive Behavior. Grassé, P. (ed.), *L'Instinct dans le Comportement des Animaux et de L'Homme.* Paris: Masson et Cie.

SCHORR, A.L.

1966   *Slums and Social Insecurity.* Washington, D.C.: U.S. Dept. of H.E.W. Research, Report No. 1.

SCHRIER, A.M.; HARLOW, H.F.; and STOLLNITZ, F. (eds.)

1965   *Behavior of Nonhuman Primates: Modern Research Trends* 1 and 2. N.Y. and London: Academic Press.

SCHULTZ, A.H.
  1961   Some Factors Influencing the Social Life of Primates in General and
         of Early Man in Particular. Washburn, S.L. (ed.), *Social Life of Early
         Man*. London: Methuen.
SCHUMPETER, J.A.
  1942   *Capitalism, Socialism and Democracy*. N.Y.: Harper and Bros.
SCHWEITZER, A.
  1948 (1913 orig.)   *The Psychiatric Study of Jesus*. Boston: Beacon.
SCOTT, J.P.
  1958   *Aggression*. Chicago: Univ. of Chicago Press.
  1958   *Animal Behavior*. Chicago: Univ. of Chicago Press.
  1962   Critical Periods in Behavioral Development. *Science* 138: 949–
         958.
SEAY, B.; HANSEN, E.; and HARLOW, H.F.
  1962   Mother-Infant Separation in Monkeys. *J. Child. Psychol. Psychiat.*
         3: 123–132.
SEAY, B.; ALEXANDER, B.K.; and HARLOW, H.F.
  1964   Maternal Behavior of Socially Deprived Rhesus Monkeys. *J. Abnorm.
         Soc. Psychol.* 69: 345.
SEBEOK, T.A.
  1965   Animal Communication. *Science* 147: 1006–1014.
SECOY, F.R.
  1953   Changing Military Patterns on the Great Plains. *Monog. Amer.
         Ethnol. Soc.* (21).
SERVICE, E.R.
  1965   *Primitive Social Organization*. N.Y.: Random House.
  1966   *The Hunters*. Englewood Cliffs, N.J.: Prentice-Hall.
SEXTON, P.C.
  1969   *The Feminized Male*. N.Y.: Random House.
SHEPHER, J.
  1971   *Voluntary Imposition of Incest and Exogamic Restrictions in Second
         Generation Kibbutz Adults*. Ph.D. Thesis, Rutgers University, Dept. of
         Anthropology.
SILBERMAN, C.E.
  1970   *Crisis in the Classroom*. N.Y.: Random House.
SIMEONS, A.T.W.
  1960   *Man's Presumptuous Brain*. N.Y.: E.P. Dutton.
SIMONS, E.L.
  1962   Fossil Evidence Relating to the Early Evolution of Primate Behavior.
         Annals of the N.Y. Academy of Science 102 (2).
  1964   The Early Relatives of Man. *Scientific American* (July).
  1965   New Fossil Apes for Egypt and the Initial Differentiation of the
         Hominoidea. *Nature* 205.
SIMPSON, G.G.
  1950   *The Meaning of Evolution*. New Haven, Conn.: Yale Univ. Press.
  1953   *The Major Features of Evolution*. N.Y.: Columbia Univ. Press.
  1966   The Biological Nature of Man. *Science* 152: 472–478.

SKINNER, B.F.
1953   *Science and Human Behavior.* N.Y.: Macmillan.
SLATER, M.K.
1959   Ecological Factors in the Origin of Incest. *Amer. Anthrop.* 61: 1042–1059.
SLUCKIN, W.
1965   *Imprinting and Early Learning.* London: Methuen and Chicago: Aldine.
SMITH, A.
1904 (1776)   *Wealth of Nations.* London: Methuen.
SMITH, J.M.
1958   *Theory of Evolution.* Harmandsworth: Penguin.
SMITH, M.G.
1962   *West Indian Family Structures.* St. Louis: Washington Univ. Press.
SMITH, R.T.
1956   *The Negro Family in British Guiana.* London: Routledge and Kegan Paul.
SOLLAS, W.J.
1924   *Ancient Hunters.* London: Macmillan.
SOMIT, A.
1968   Toward a More Biologically Oriented Political Science: Ethology and Psychopharmacology. *Midwest J. of Political Science* 12 (4): 550–567 (Nov.).
SOMIT, A.; DAVIES, J.C.; and SCHWARTZ, D.C.
(in press)   *Biology and Politics.* Chicago: Aldine.
SOUTHWICK, C.H. (ed.)
1963   *Primate Social Behavior.* Princeton: D. Van Nostrand.
SPARKS, J.
1967   Allogrooming in Primates. Morris, D. (ed.), *Primate Ethology.* Chicago: Aldine.
SPENCER, H.
1876   *Ceremonial Institutions.* (Part 4 of *Principles of Sociology*) London: Williams and Norgate.
SPIRO, M.E.
1954   Is the Family Universal? *Amer. Anthrop.* 56: 839–846.
1956   *Kibbutz: Venture in Utopia.* Cambridge, Mass.: Harvard Univ. Press.
1958   *Children of the Kibbutz.* Cambridge, Mass.: Harvard Univ. Press.
SPUHLER, J.N.
1959   Somatic Paths to Culture. Spuhler, J.N. (ed.), *The Evolution of Man's Capacity for Culture.* Detroit, Mich.: Wayne State Univ. Press.
SPUHLER, J.N. (ed.)
1959   *The Evolution of Man's Capacity for Culture.* Detroit, Mich.: Wayne State Univ. Press.
1968   *Genetic Diversity and Human Behavior.* Chicago: Aldine.
STAYT, H.A.
1931   *The BaVenda.* London: Oxford Univ. Press.

STEWART, K.
  1954 *Pygmies and Dream Giants.* N.Y.: W.W. Norton.
STOCK, M.B., and SMYTHE, P.M.
  1963 Does Undernutrition during Infancy Inhibit Brain Growth and Subsequent Intellectual Development? *Archives of Disease in Childhood* 38: 546.
STORR, A.
  1968 *Human Aggression.* London: Penguin Press.
STOTT, D.H.
  1962 Cultural and Natural Checks on Population Growth. Montagu, M.F.A. (ed.), *Culture and the Evolution of Man.* N.Y.: Oxford Univ. Press.
STOUFFER, S. *et al.*
  1949 *The American Soldier.* Princeton: Princeton Univ. Press.
SULLIVAN, H.S.
  1953 *The Interpersonality Theory of Psychiatry.* Perry, H.S., and Gawel, M.L. (eds.), N.Y.: W.W. Norton.
  1954 *The Psychiatric Interview.* Perry, H.S., and Gawel, M.L. (eds.), N.Y.: W.W. Norton.
TANNER, J.
  1955 *Growth at Adolescence.* Oxford: Blackwell.
TANNER, J. (ed.)
  1960 *Human Growth.* (Symposium for the Society for the Study of Human Biology, No. 3) Oxford: Pergamon Press.
TAWNEY, R.H.
  1921 *The Acquisitive Society.* London: G. Bell and Sons.
TAX, S. (ed.)
  1952 *Indian Tribes of Aboriginal America.* Chicago: Univ. of Chicago Press.
  1960 *Evolution After Darwin.* (3 vols.) Chicago: Univ. of Chicago Press.
TERESHKOVA-NIKOLAYEVA, VALENTINA
  1970 Women in Space. *Impact of Science on Society* UNESCO 20 (1) (Jan.–March).
THOMAS, W.I.
  1906 The Gaming Interest. *Amer. J. Sociol.,* pp. 750–756.
THOMPSON, L.
  1970 A Self-regulating System of Human Population Control. *Proc. N.Y. Academy of Sciences,* pp. 262–270.
THORPE, W.H.
  1956 *Learning and Instinct in Animals.* London: Methuen.
  1956 Ethology as a New Branch of Biology. McGill, T.E. (ed.), *Readings in Animal Behavior,* 1965. N.Y.: Holt, Rinehart and Winston.
THRASHER, F.M.
  1936 *The Gang.* Chicago: Univ. of Chicago Press.
TIGER, L.
  1966 Bureaucracy and Charisma in Ghana. *J. of Asian and African Studies* 1 (1).

1969   *Men in Groups*. N.Y.: Random House.
1970a   Dominance in Human Societies. *Annual Review of Ecology and Systematics* 1 (1).
1970b   The Possible Biological Origins of Sexual Discrimination. *Impact of Science on Society* 20 (1): 29–44.
1970c   Biological Fabianism. *Canadian Forum.* 50: 112–117.
(in press)   Introduction, *International Social Science Journal* (Issue reporting Meeting of Experts on Human Aggressiveness, U.N.E.S.C.O., Paris, May 1970).
TIGER, L., and Fox, R.
1966   The Zoological Perspective in Social Science. *Man: The J.R.A.I.* 1 (1): 75–81.
TINBERGEN, N.
1936   The Function of Sexual Fighting in Birds; and the Problems of the Origin of Territory. *Bird Banding* 7: 1–8.
1951   *The Study of Instinct*. Oxford: Clarendon Press.
1953a   *Social Behavior in Animals*. N.Y.: John Wiley & Sons.
1953b   *The Herring Gull's World*. London: Methuen.
1955   Psychology and Ethology as Supplementary Parts of a Science of Behavior. Schaffner, B. (ed.), *Group Processes*. (Transactions of the First Conference) N.Y.: Josiah Macy, Jr., Foundation.
1960a   The Evolution of Behavior in Gulls. *Scientific American* (Dec.).
1960b   Behavior, Systematics, and Natural Selection. Tax, S. (ed.), *Evolution after Darwin: Volume 1 The Evolution of Life*. Chicago: Univ. of Chicago Press.
1962   The Evolution of Animal Communication—A Critical Examination of Methods. *Symp. Zool. Soc. Lond.* 8: 1–6.
1963   On the Aims and Methods of Ethology. *Zeitschrift fur Tierpsychologie* 20: 410–433.
1964   The Evolution of Signaling Devices. Etkin, W. (ed.), *Social Behavior and Organization Among Vertebrates*. Chicago and London: Univ. of Chicago Press.
1965   Behavior and Natural Selection. Moore, J.A. (ed.), *Ideas in Modern Biology*. N.Y.: Natural History Press.
1968   On War and Peace in Animals and Man. *Science* 160: 1411–1418.
TOFFLER, A.
1970   *Future Shock*. N.Y.: Random House.
TROPP, A.
1957   *The Schoolteachers*. London: Heinemann.
TROTTER, W.
1916   *Instincts of the Herd in Peace and War*. London: E. Benn.
TUNSTALL, J.
1962   *The Fishermen*. London: MacGibbon and Kee.
TURNER, V.
1957   *Schism and Continuity in an African Society*. Manchester: Manchester Univ. Press.
1964   An Ndembu Doctor in Practice. Kiev, A. (ed.), *Magic, Faith, and Healing*. Glencoe, Ill.: Free Press.

1969   *The Ritual Process*. Chicago: Aldine.
TURNEY-HIGH, H.H.
   1949   *Primitive War: Its Practice and Concepts*. Columbia, S.C.: Univ.
   of South Carolina Press.
TYLOR, E.B.
   1870   *Primitive Culture*. London: John Murray.
   1888   On a Method of Investigating the Development of Institutions.
   J. Royal Anthrop. Inst. 18.
UBEROI, J.S.
   1962   *Politics of the Kula Ring*. Manchester: Manchester Univ. Press.
UCKO, P.J., and DIMBLEBY, G.W. (eds.)
   1969   *The Domestication and Exploitation of Plants and Animals*. Chicago:
   Aldine and London: Gerald Duckworth.
UDRY, J.R., and MORRIS, N.M.
   1968   Distribution of Coitus in the. Menstrual Cycle. *Nature, London*,
   220: 593–596.
VANDENBERGH, J.G.
   1967   The Development of Social Structure in Free-Ranging Rhesus Monkeys. *Behavior* 29: 179–194.
VAYDA, A.P.
   1960   Maori Warfare. *Polynesian Society Maori Monograph* (2). Wellington: Polynesian Soc.
   1961   Expansion and Warfare Among Swidden Agriculturalists. *Amer.
   Anthrop*. 63: 346–358.
VAYDA, A.P., and LEEDS, A.
   1961   Anthropology and the Study of War. *Anthropologica* (n.s.), 3: 131–
   133.
WADDINGTON, C.H.
   1961   *The Ethical Animal*. N.Y.: Atheneum.
WALLACE, A.F.C.
   1958   Dreams and Wishes of the Soul: A Type of Psychoanalytic Theory
   Among the Seventeenth Century Iroquois. *Amer. Anthrop*. 60 (2): 234–
   248.
WALLAS, G.
   1948 (orig. 1908)   *Human Nature in Politics*. London: Constable.
WASHBURN, S.L.
   1959   Speculations on the Inter-relations of the History of Tools and
   Biological Evolution. Spuhler, J.N. (ed.), *The Evolution of Man's Capacity
   for Culture*. Detroit, Mich.: Wayne State Univ. Press.
   1960   Tools and Human Evolution. *Scientific American* (Sept. 1960).
   1961 (ed.)   *Social Life of Early Man*. Viking Fund Publs. in Anthropology
   (3). N.Y.: Wenner-Gren Foundation for Anthropological Research.
   1965   An Ape's Eye View of Human Evolution. DeVore, P.I. (ed.), *The
   Origin of Man*. N.Y.: Wenner-Gren Foundation.
   1966   Conflict in Primate Society. *Conflict in Society*. London: Ciba Foundation, J. and A. Churchill.
   1968a   *Behavior and the Origin of Man*. Rockefeller Univ. Review (Jan.–
   Feb.), pp. 10–19.

1968b *The Study of Human Evolution.* Eugene, Oregon: Oregon State System of Higher Education.

WASHBURN, S.L., and DEVORE, I.
1961 The Social Life of Baboons. *Scientific American* (June).

WASHBURN, S.L., and HAMBURG, D.A.
1968 Aggressive Behavior in Old World Monkeys and Apes. Jay, P. (ed.), *Primates: Studies on Adaptation and Variability.* N.Y.: Holt, Rinehart and Winston.

WASHBURN, S.L., and HOWELL, F.C.
1960 Human Evolution and Culture. Tax, S. (ed.), *Evolution After Darwin: Volume 2 The Evolution of Man.* Chicago: Univ. of Chicago Press.

WASHBURN, S.L., and JAY, P.C. (eds.)
1968 *Perspectives on Human Evolution* 1. N.Y.: Holt, Rinehart and Winston.

WASHBURN, S.L., and LANCASTER, C.S.
1968 The Evolution of Hunting. Lee, R.B., and DeVore, I. (eds.), *Man The Hunter.* Chicago: Aldine.

WATSON, J.B.
1930 *Behaviorism.* Chicago: Univ. of Chicago Press.

WEBB, S., and WEBB, B.
1894 *History of Trade Unionism.* London: Longmans, Green and Co.

WEBER, M.
1947 *Theory of Social and Economic Organization.* Glencoe, Ill.: Free Press.

WEIR, R.H.
1962 *Language in the Crib.* The Hague: Martar.

WELKER, W.I.
1956a Some Determinants of Play and Exploration in Chimpanzees. *J. Comp. Physiol. Psychol.* 49: 84–89.

1956b Effects of Age and Experience on Play and Exploration of Young Chimpanzees. *J. Comp. Physiol. Psychol.* 49: 223–226.

1961 An Analysis of Play and Exploratory Behavior in Animals. Fiske and Maddi (eds.), *Functions of Varied Experience.* Homewood, Ill.: Dorsey Press.

WESTERMARCK, E.
1903 *History of Human Marriage.* N.Y.: St. Martin's Press.

WHITE, C.L.
1970 *Women's Magazines 1693–1968.* London: Michael Joseph.

WHITE, L.A.
1948 Man's Control Over Civilization: An Anthropocentric Illusion. *Scientific Monthly* 66: 235–247.

1949 *The Science of Culture.* N.Y.: Farrar, Straus and Co.

1959 *The Evolution of Culture.* N.Y.: McGraw-Hill.

WHITING, J.W.M., and CHILD, I.
1953 *Child Training and Personality.* New Haven, Conn.: Yale Univ. Press.

WHITING, J.W.M.; KLUCKHOHN, R.; and ANTHONY, A.S.
1958 The Function of Male Initiation Ceremonies at Puberty. Maccoby, E.E. *et al.* (eds.), *Readings in Social Psychology.* N.Y.: Henry Holt.

WHYTE, W.F.
  1943 Street-Corner Society. Chicago: Univ. of Chicago Press.
WICKLER, W.
  1967 Socio-Sexual Signals and Their Intra-Specific Imitation Among Primates. Morris, D. (ed.), Primate Ethology. London: Weidenfeld and Nicolson.
WILENSKY, H.L.
  1968 Women's Work: Economic Growth, Ideology, Structure. Industrial Relations 7: 235–258.
WILLIAMS, G.C.
  1966 Adaptation and Natural Selection. Princeton: Princeton Univ. Press.
WILLIAMSON, K.
  1962 Changes in the Marriage System of the Okrika Ijo. Africa 32: 53–60.
WILSON, A.C., and SARICH, U.M.
  1969 A Molecular Time Scale for Human Evolution. Proc. Nat. Acad. of Sciences (U.S.A.) 63: 4.
WILSON, E.
  1940 To the Finland Station. N.Y.: Harcourt, Brace and Co.
  1960 Apologies to the Iroquois. N.Y.: Farrar, Straus and Cudahy.
WISSLER, C.
  1916 Psychological and Historical Interpretations of Culture. Science 43: 193–201.
  1923 Man and Culture. N.Y.: Crowell.
WITALEN, R.E. (ed.)
  1967 Hormones and Behavior. Princeton: D. Van Nostrand Co.
WITTFOGEL, K.
  1957 Oriental Despotism. New Haven, Conn.: Yale Univ. Press.
WOLF, E.
  1966 Peasants. Englewood Cliffs, N.J.: Prentice-Hall.
WOODBURN, J.C.
  1964 The Social Organization of the Hadza of North Tanzania. Ph.D. Thesis, Cambridge University, Dept. of Anthropology.
WRIGHT, Q.
  1942 A Study of War. (2 vols.). Chicago: Univ. of Chicago Press.
WYNNE-EDWARDS, V.C.
  1962 Animal Dispersion in Relation to Social Behavior. N.Y.: Hafner.
  1964 Population Control in Animals. Scientific American (Aug.).
YABLONSKY, L.
  1964 The Violent Gang. Harmondsworth: Penguin.
YERKES, R.M.
  1933 Genetic Aspects of Grooming, a Socially Important Primate Behavior Pattern. J. Social Psychology IV: 3–25.
YOUNG, F.
  1965 Initiation Ceremonies: A Cross-Cultural Study of Status Dramatization. N.Y.: Bobbs-Merrill.
YOUNG, J.Z.
  1965 The Organization of a Memory System. Proc. Royal Soc. 163B (Nov. 23, 1965).

YOUNG, M.
   1958   *The Rise of the Meritocracy, 1870–2033.* London: Thames and Hudson.
YOUNG, W.C.
   1961   *Sex and Internal Secretions* (2 vols.). Baltimore: Williams and Wilkens, Co.
YOUNG, W.C.; GAY, R.W.; and PHOENIX, C.H.
   1964   Hormones and Sexual Behavior. *Science* 143 (3603): 212–218.
ZEMAN, F.J., and STANBROUGH, E.C.
   1969   Effect of Maternal Protein Deficiency on Cellular Development in the Fetal Rat. *J. Nutrition* 99: 274–282.
ZUCKERMAN, S.
   1930   The Menstrual Cycle of the Primates. *Proc. Zool. Soc.*, pp. 691–754.
   1932   *The Social Life of Monkeys and Apes.* London: Routledge and Kegan Paul.

INDEX

Special Publication No 30

High Temperature Chemistry of Inorganic and Ceramic Materials

Keele University, September, 1976

The Proceedings of a Conference organized jointly by the Inorganic Chemicals Group of the Industrial Division of The Chemical Society and the Basic Science Section of the British Ceramic Society

Edited by
F. P. Glasser, University of Aberdeen
and
P. E. Potter, A.E.R.E., Harwell

The Chemical Society
Burlington House, London, W1V OBN

Printed in Great Britain by Henry Ling Ltd., a subsidiary of
John Wright and Sons Ltd., at the Dorset Press, Dorchester

Foreword

The papers included in this Special Publication of the Chemical Society were presented and discussed at a Symposium held at Keele University on 8th and 9th September 1976. The meeting was under the joint auspices of the Society's Inorganic Chemicals Group, a subject group of its Industrial Division, and the Basic Science Section of the British Ceramic Society.

The objective of the organizers was to bring together scientists and technologists, from both industry and the academic world, whose interests lay in the high-temperature chemistry (defined as above 1000 K) of non-metal systems. The scope was thus relevant not only to ceramists, but also to an increasing number of chemists working in high-temperature fields. It became apparent at the Symposium that a high proportion of participants as well as speakers were in fact members of the Societies, and it is perhaps surprising that this was the first meeting in which the two bodies had joined with each other. It is hoped that similar symposia may be held from time to time.

In addition to recording our thanks to the authors we should like to express our deep appreciation for the hard work and devotion of the two conveners, Dr. F. P. Glasser and Dr. P. E. Potter, who also undertook the editing of this publication, and to the head office staff of the British Ceramic Society who handled the local organization of this successful symposium.

D. T. Livey,
Chairman,
Basic Science Section,
British Ceramic Society.

R. Thompson,
Chairman,
Inorganic Chemicals Group,
The Chemical Society.

Introduction

The main objective of the conference was to review scientific and technological developments in inorganic and ceramic processes at temperatures above 1000 K, and to provide a critical guide to the selection and use of inorganic materials, including ceramics, in high temperature industrial processes.

The papers cover topics which are directly relevant to many processes used in diverse technologies such as in the ceramics, glass, steel and nuclear industries.

Aspects of ceramic studies are considerations of chemical corrosion of ceramic materials, where it is shown that in many cases the corrosion resistance of a refractory material is determined by the presence and properties of minor phases present. The behaviour of ceramic metarials in the presence of fluxes is discussed.

A whole complexity of high-temperature inorganic chemistry is revealed in a review of stable colorants. Calcia- and magnesia-stabilized zirconia electrolytes are described: these find practical application in the determination of oxygen levels in steel melts.

Complex equilibria in the $CaO-MgO-TiO_2-SiO_2$ system are presented: these will be of use to the extractive metallurgist in the exploitation of titania-containing iron ore. Kinetic aspects of iron and steel production are discussed in papers on slag—metal reactions and on the reduction of liquid iron ore by solid carbon; although the thermodynamics of these reactions are now comparatively well understood, the kinetics of such reactions still require study in order to optimize these metallurgical extraction processes. The kinetics of the desulphurization of pig-iron using a magnesium-impregnated coke is a further example of a recent kinetic study.

Materials are required to withstand more and more severe conditions and such an example is the use of stainless steel in a sodium-cooled fast breeder nuclear reactor; some detailed studies of the thermodynamics and phase equilibria of the sodium—chromium—oxygen and sodium—iron—oxygen systems are presented, together with similar studies of the Cs—Cr—O system. These data help evaluate container materials for nuclear fuel elements and explain their corrosion by fission products. A further example is a paper describing the application of thermodynamic principles to the production of uranium—plutonium oxide and carbide nuclear fuels.

An essential requirement for the optimization of any process is the provision of critically assessed thermodynamic data together with rapid manipulation. This is illustrated by the description of a thermodynamic data bank together with examples of its application to specific problems. An example of comprehensive application of thermodynamic data is provided by an assessment of the sulphur cycle in waste gases leaving a flat-glass manufacturing furnace.

The use of chemical vapour deposition reactions is described both for the deposition of amorphous boron coatings on metals and also for the fabrication of bodies of boron nitride.

Whilst silicon nitride is well known for its potential for use in gas turbines and other high-temperature engineering applications, the phase compositions of these materials are as yet, incompletely understood. A review of phase relationships in the silicon—aluminium—oxygen—nitrogen system (the so-called SIALONS) is given. It is apparent that these nitrogen ceramics provide many challenging opportunities for technological and fundamental studies.

A comprehensive review of the influence of heat treatment on the reactivity of carbons and graphite, a topic which is of great significance to the use of carbon as a reductant in many metallurgical and ceramic processes, is also included.

If there are future shortages of rutile, fluoride routes can be used for the beneficiation of ilmenite to produce titanium dioxide.

The papers included in this volume thus span a wide range of chemistry, both with respect to the range of substances studied and the relevant body of theory used to explain the results obtained. For this diversity as well as for the practical approach adopted in many of the papers, the editors make no apology. The aim of the conference was to review the current position of developments in high-temperature chemistry and in our view this was achieved. The papers reflect the developments in the field. It is the hope of the editors that this volume will provide a stimulus for further studies leading to the development of new materials and to improvements in existing materials. Moreover process optimization is increasingly a challenging area of research for the high-temperature chemist but one which is fraught with difficulty. With the increasing cost of energy and the increased unease about future supplies of energy, its production, application and conservation have assumed new importance. Many essential processes must, of necessity, be carried out at high temperatures. Nevertheless, there exists much scope both for the improvement of existing processes and the development of alternative technologies. A common theme linking many of the papers on process optimization was the need to assume a basic model for the process which was amenable to treatment using a thermodynamic or kinetic model, or one incorporating both approaches. The difficulties inherent in this arise when one realizes how often the basic thermodynamic values, or the relevant body of phase equilibrium data, are known only very imperfectly at the outset. Therefore an important part of most of the investigations was to obtain or improve the basic data. With respect to kinetic data, obtaining these was invariably an integral part of the investigation. Not surprisingly, therefore, process optimization is a somewhat uncertain and time-consuming task. Considerable judgement and feel for the subject are required in order to achieve models likely to yield reasonable predictions. We are thus led inescapably back to the inadequacies of the basic thermophysical data on high temperature reactions. There exists a serious possibility that, without concentrated efforts being made to add to and improve our knowledge in these areas, vital data for the solution of even the current generation of technological problems will not be available when required.

F. P. Glasser

P. E. Potter

Contents

The Resistance of Ceramics to Chemical Corrosion

By D. J. FISHER

The British Ceramic Research Association, Queens Road, Penkhull, Stoke-on-Trent, ST4 7LQ

Introduction

Corrosion is usually defined as chemical or electrochemical reaction between a solid material and its environment, resulting in deterioration of the appearance and the properties of the material. Such reactions are normally slow and result from prolonged contact, such as in the rusting of iron; however, slow corrosion under normal conditions may proceed rapidly when temperatures and pressures are increased.

Structural materials can be classified into metals, ceramics, and organic-based compounds. The term 'corrosion' is most frequently used to describe the deterioration of metals, which is always oxidizing in nature, but can equally well be used for the other classes, where both oxidizing and reducing reactions can take place. Here we are concerned with the use of ceramics in corrosive environments, and especially their use at high temperatures, where the organics are ruled out and metals frequently have severe limitations.

The use of clay-based ceramics at high temperatures has been standard practice for many years, and the advantages and limitations of these materials are fairly well understood. More recently a new class of ceramics, which are predominantly single-phase compounds, have been developed. This class has been variously defined as 'engineering ceramics', 'special ceramics', or 'technical ceramics', although no fully satisfactory term exists. The field covered is wide, including most pure metal oxides, mixed oxides, nitrides, carbides, borides, and silicides. However, most of the more promising materials have now been developed and several are in production. Their importance stems from combinations of favourable mechanical, thermal, electrical, and chemical properties. For the chemical and associated industries the last-mentioned are the most interesting, as it is necessary to know which of these new materials can be employed to advantage in the handling of reactive substances in processes.

The most common corrosive environments are mineral acids and alkalis at low temperatures, and glass, molten salts and vapours, and reactive gases at higher temperatures. More specialized types such as steel-making slags present their own difficulties, but will not be considered here. By considering the thermodynamic and kinetic aspects of possible reaction between the ceramic and its environment it is often possible to predict which material would be most suitable for a particular application, and hence to eliminate the need for an extensive series of trials. In this review a range of single-phase ceramics will be considered, and their theoretically likely reactions related where possible to those obtained under service conditions.

1

Thermodynamic and Kinetic Aspects of Corrosion

Introduction. The most important property to be considered in the prediction of chemical reactions is the free energy of formation of the reactants and products. In the case of high-temperature corrosion, a comparison of the free energies of formation at the operating temperature of the material and the potential product formed from interaction with its environment will be informative in predicting whether corrosion will occur. For example, molten lithium at 500 °C is an extremely corrosive medium. By considering the free energies of formation of some common refractory oxides and relating them to that of lithium oxide, an indication can be obtained as to whether the reaction

$$MO + 2Li = Li_2O + M$$

will be thermodynamically favourable. Some relevant free energies are listed in Table 1.[1] Thus the free energy change in the above equation favours the reduction of the oxide by lithium when M = Si or Al but not when M = Mg. This is

Table 1 *Free energy of formation of various metal oxides at* 500 °C

Compound	$-\Delta G^\circ$/kcal per gram atom oxygen
SiO_2	88.2
Al_2O_3	112.8
Li_2O	119.1
MgO	123.7

confirmed by the results obtained in practice; silica refractories are rapidly corroded, alumina less so, and magnesia under certain conditions not at all. In the case of magnesia, there is a very small change of free energy in the reaction, and it can be seen from the relationship:

$$\Delta G = -RT\ln K_p$$

that the equilibrium constant K_p is such that a reasonable concentration of all species exists; hence some attack occurs. A further example of this effect of the equilibrium constant on high-temperature reactions is given below.

The free energies of formation of reactants and products give a guideline to whether or not chemical corrosion of materials will take place. However, reactions which are theoretically probable may sometimes not take place; in this case the reaction kinetics are influencing the corrosion rate. This is the point at which the texture and porosity of the ceramic become crucially important; the reaction rate may depend on the surface area available, which in turn will be related to the porosity of the article, or the reaction may be inhibited by the formation of a protective layer. Frequently also in high-temperature reactions the partial pressures of gases, either as reactants or products, can influence the reaction kinetics.

Examples of the Factors influencing the Corrosion Rate. The following section illustrates generally how the fundamental principles outlined above affect be-

---

[1] D. R. Stalls, *Janaf Thermochemical Tables*, PB168370–1, U.S. Dept. of Commerce.

haviour in practice; subsequent sections consider individual ceramics in more detail.

Corrosion of non-oxide ceramics in air at high temperatures is a good general example of how kinetics can inhibit reactions. Silicon nitride (Si_3N_4) is thermodynamically unstable in air and is oxidized according to the equation:

$$Si_3N_4 + 3O_2 = 3SiO_2 + 2N_2$$
$$\Delta G^\circ = -59.4 \text{ kcal per gram atom oxygen at } 700\,^\circ C.$$

In practice, the above reaction takes place rapidly at first, resulting in a film of silica being formed over the nitride. This silica film then inhibits further attack, in a similar way to the oxide film formed on aluminium when it is attacked by strong mineral acids. Horton[2] has studied the oxidation rate and attributed the controlling process to diffusion of oxygen through the silica film. In a similar way, boron-containing ceramics such as the nitride and the carbide are protected by a film of boric oxide, although this is much less effective because of its volatility.

Alumina (Al_2O_3) is the only aluminium oxide stable at room temperature, and hence at low temperatures does not undergo any oxidizing or reducing reactions. However, at high temperatures the volatile species AlO and Al_2O have been detected, and in a reducing environment their formation is possible. When alumina is heated with carbon, the reaction

$$2C + Al_2O_3 = 2CO + Al_2O$$

is a possibility. The free energy change is +49.5 kcal mol^{-1} and therefore thermodynamics would indicate that the reaction will not occur, but the position of equilibrium at a particular temperature will depend also on the partial pressures of the products. As the free energy is related to the equilibrium constant by

$$\Delta G^\circ = -RT \ln Kp$$

the partial pressure of Al_2O vapour at a given temperature can be calculated, and it can be demonstrated that this pressure becomes appreciable above 1600 $^\circ C$; hence corrosion of alumina will occur.

A good example of high-temperature corrosion occurs in furnaces containing sulphur compounds.[3] Most refractories contain high proportions of alumina and silica, and these two materials differ strongly in their corrosion resistance to sulphur. Under reducing conditions a sulphide will be the principal reaction product, and it can be shown by thermodynamics that the formation of silicon sulphide gas is much more likely than that of aluminium sulphide. However, in oxidizing conditions the reverse is true, due to the comparative stability of aluminium sulphate. Thus either high-alumina or high-silica refractories can be suitable for handling sulphur compounds, under reducing or oxidizing conditions, respectively.

In a review of the chemical properties of refractories, Carniglia[4] pointed out that in the majority of cases, the refractories are not thermodynamically stable

[2] R. M. Horton, *J. Amer. Ceram. Soc.,* 1969, **52**, 121.
[3] C. B. Alcock, *Ceramics in Severe Environments,* 1970, Materials Science Research (Plenum Press), Vol. 5, p. 6.
[4] R. Carniglia, *Chemical and Mechanical Behaviour of Inorganic Materials,* (Wiley, 1968), p. 172.

in their corrosive service environments, and their development has been largely a matter of erecting kinetic barriers to deteriorative changes that are ultimately inevitable. This was illustrated by reference to glass-tank refractories where corrosion occurs more rapidly on a downward-facing surface, because the rate of reaction was influenced by trapped gas bubbles in the glass melt which act as sites where reaction can be initiated. It is thought that the trapped bubble acts as a 'turbulence generator', stirring high concentrations of alkali into the film between it and the brick and hence causing greater corrosion. In this way, altering the reactant concentration has led to a change in the kinetics so that the thermodynamically favourable attack of the brick by the glass can proceed.

Performance of Some Special Ceramics in Corrosive Environments
Oxides. Alumina (Al_2O_3) was the first of these materials to find widespread application in industry and is still the only one produced on a tonnage basis. High-alumina ceramics contain over 85% Al_2O_3, the balance being oxides such as lime, magnesia, and silica which form a small amount of a glassy phase after firing. This is done mainly to lower the firing temperature, and hence lower the cost. Alumina bodies have high strengths and good wear resistance and their use

Table 2 *Resistance to corrosion in some common environments of the leading technical ceramics*

Ceramic material	Resistance to corrosion by acids and acidic gases	Resistance to corrosion by alkaline liquids and gases	Resistance to corrosion by molten metals
Alumina	Good	Fairly good	Good
Magnesia	Poor	Good	Good
Beryllia	Fair	Poor	Good
Zirconia	Fairly good	Good	Good
Thoria	Poor	Good	Good
Titania	Good	Poor	Fair
Chromic oxide	Poor	Poor	Poor
Tin oxide	Fair	Poor	Poor
Silica	Good	Poor	Fair
Silicon carbide	Good	Fair	Fair
Silicon nitride	Good	Fair	Good
Boron nitride	Fair	Good	Good
Boron carbide	Good	Fair	No information
Titanium carbide	Poor	Poor	,,
Titanium nitride	Fair	Fair	,,
Chemical stoneware	Good	Fair	,,
Chemical porcelain	Good	Fairly good	,,

in the chemical industry is widespread. The acid resistance is good, except to strong phosphoric acids, and can be optimized in a 95% alumina body by using magnesia rather than lime as a glass-forming agent with silica.[5] Strong hydrofluoric acid will attack the glass in debased bodies, and thus very pure alumina is necessary for prolonged exposures. Prolonged exposure to strong alkalis results in slight deterioration, which becomes more pronounced as the alumina content

[5] G. Richards, Royal Worcester Industrial Ceramics Ltd., private communication.

of the body is decreased. As no higher or lower oxides exist in solid form the material is strongly resistant to both oxidizing and reducing gases; pure hydrogen causes discolouration and the ceramic may even become black, but without any structural damage. The colour change is thought to be due either to very small changes in stoicheiometry or to the reduction of transition-metal oxide impurities. Many metals can be melted in alumina vessels although the poor thermal shock resistance is a disadvantage.

High-alumina ceramics are commercially available from several British manufacturers and various fabrication routes can be used, leading to a wide range of component shapes.

Magnesia (MgO) is not now produced as an impervious predominantly single-phase body, except in experimental quantities. However, large quantities of porous refractory bricks with high magnesia contents are used in steel-making. Its acid resistance is poor and all but very high-purity dense bodies ($> 99\%$ MgO) are slowly attacked by water. These high-purity ceramics have good resistance to alkalis and are used experimentally in handling molten alkali metals, and highly alkaline oxides. Magnesia crucibles are used in metal melting because of this good corrosion resistance and despite a comparatively high vapour pressure in vacuum.

Beryllia (BeO) ceramics are available in limited quantities for predominantly electrical applications. Resistance to corrosion by strong acids and alkalis is not good, and the use becomes hazardous because of the highly toxic beryllium solutions that may be formed as reaction products. Beryllia ceramics react with water vapour at high temperatures, again leading to toxic vapours as by-products.

Zirconia (ZrO_2) has been extensively developed both as a porous refractory-type body and as a dense material, but is as yet not commercially available. Because of a volume change associated with a reversible phase-change at $1100\,^{\circ}C$, zirconia ceramics have to be 'stabilized' in the cubic form by adding a small amount of a doping oxide such as CaO, MgO, or Y_2O_3; these form cubic solid solutions. Lime-stabilized zirconia ceramics, which are the most usually studied, dissolve in concentrated acids; this may be due to preferential attack on the lime and it would be interesting to know if alternative stabilizers decrease this attack. Zirconia fibre, considered below, is stabilized by yttria, and good acid and alkali resistance has been claimed. The low-temperature resistance to alkalis is said to be good but attack would be expected at higher temperatures, especially as calcium zirconate ($CaZrO_3$), incidentally a ceramic material in its own right, can be formed as low as $600\,^{\circ}C$. The large negative free energy of formation of zirconia from its elements indicates that the stability to many molten metals is good, and zirconia crucibles have been employed in vacuum melting of metals; the combination of high corrosion resistance, thermal shock resistance, and low vapour pressure make it the most suitable of the pure oxide ceramics for this application. Similarly, zirconia nozzles have been used in a process for continuous casting of copper.

Thoria (ThO_2) ceramics are also available now only in experimental quantities although in the past commercial production has been tried. The radioactivity (β-particle emitter) of thoria has been a factor inhibiting more widespread use of this material, although the amount of emission is comparatively small. It is the most refractory oxide available, with a melting point of 3000 °C, and consequently could find more widespread applications where extremely high temperatures are required. However, acids will attack thoria ceramics comparatively readily. This poor acid resistance is compensated for, as with magnesia, by extremely good resistance to molten alkaline fluxes and molten alkali metals. Thoria is completely inert to molten lithium and sodium, and consequently a thoria-based conducting ceramic has been developed for use in an oxygen meter operating in molten sodium; other applications could be in specialized metal melting where the corrosion resistance will be excellent, poor thermal shock properties being the drawback here. Both thoria and zirconia can be used for kiln furniture in firing reactive materials such as titanates; high cost has tended to eliminate commercial use of thoria.

Titania (TiO_2) ceramics are used as electrical components where high permittivity and low dielectric losses are needed. Non-stoicheiometry can be induced in titania by firing in reducing conditions or by adding small amounts of doping oxides (or by both). This produces a conducting material with high dielectric loss. They have not found any important applications at high temperatures or in corrosive environments, with the exception of an experimental refining process for rutile ores. Although titania is comparatively cheap, it does not offer any advantages over alumina in chemical resistance, and is far inferior mechanically.

Chromium oxide (Cr_2O_3) has been prepared as a pure oxide ceramic, mainly for low-friction bearing applications. Its chemical resistance to acids and alkalis is poor; the principal use of chrome in the ceramic industry is in the form of refractory magnesium chromite ($MgCr_2O_4$) bricks. Pure magnesium chromite ceramics have good thermal shock resistance and are inert at high temperatures; they have been suggested as catalyst carriers.

Tin oxide (SnO_2) has recently found an application as a dense sintered ceramic in the glass industry.[6] It is used as an electrode in the electric melting of lead-containing glasses. The electric melting process is now predominant because of the low release of toxic lead oxide from the glass surface. Tin oxide ceramics have good electrical conductivity at the relevant temperature, are very resistant to corrosion by molten glass, and also do not have any tendency to impart undesirable colours to the melt. Electrodes up to 50 kg in weight have been produced from tin oxide by isostatic pressing and sintering.

Oxide Fibre Materials. Both alumina and zirconia are now available in the form of ceramic fibre. This type of material was originally developed as an aluminosilicate fibre formed from molten china clay; the pure oxide fibres now developed have the advantage of higher melting points and hence operating temperatures, and greater resistance to chemical attack. Alumina fibres can be used up to 1600 °C, and are resistant to acids, alkalis, and reducing atmospheres. Zirconia fibres have less good acid resistance but will tolerate exposure to boiling mineral acids for short periods. Hot phosphoric acid will rapidly attack it. Zirconia fibre additionally has good resistance to molten alkali metal chlorides and carbonates at temperatures up to 700 °C. Both types of fibre are used in a wide variety of furnace applications.

[6] B. Jackson, Dyson Group Research Laboratory, private communication.

In the ceramics industry, alumina fibre insulation has been used in glost-firing kilns where alumino-silicate fibres had been attacked by alkalis; this resistance to alkaline corrosion is also of use in applications in the glass industry, where alkali can attack conventional refractories as already described. Both types of fibre have been used as a filtration medium for hot gases, where chemical inertness is important. In addition to these specific uses of oxide fibres in corrosive environments, alumino-silicate fibres have many long-established uses in the chemical industry, including catalyst supports, high-temperature insulation in gas pipelines, and as stress relief at joints in welded pipes.

Silica (SiO_2) ceramics fall into two categories: impervious glassy silica (which may be non-transparent), and sintered fused silica. Both forms have good resistance to acids at low temperatures, with the exception of hydrofluoric, which dissolves them at room temperature. At higher temperatures, water vapour diffuses into the vitreous material forming silicon–hydroxyl (Si–OH) groups which disrupt the Si–O network and cause corrosion. The solubility of water in vitreous silica has been shown to be proportional to the square root of the vapour pressure, and is unaffected by temperature and impurities above 900 °C. Phosphoric acid will also attack silica at high temperatures with formation of the volatile silicyl phosphate.

Silica ceramics are more stable to acids than to alkalis, which attack them to form soluble metal silicates. Silica has found extensive application in the chemical industry as apparatus and plant in corrosive environments. It is used as packing material for cooling towers in which acid vapours are condensed, and as a heat exchanger for use in contact with acids. In the semiconductor industry, high-purity silica vessels are used for the formation of single-crystal silicon and silicon-doped materials. Reducing atmospheres and vacuum do not normally affect silica vessels, although hydrogen can slowly diffuse into the structure in a similar way to that described for water vapour.

Sintered fused silica ceramics are made by melting high-purity quartz and fabricating the resultant powder by pressing, casting, or plastic forming techniques. Sintered silica of high porosity is used as a material for preformed cores in investment casting, and the alkaline solubility is employed to remove the core from the cast metal product. The stability to molten metals is fairly good and the thermal shock resistance excellent. Iron, steel, and nickel–chrome alloys can be cast around silica cores to form complex shapes; titanium cannot as it reduces the silica to silicon. Sintered fused silica has also been used in the steel and non-ferrous metals industry for nozzles in continuous casting processes, and for the linings of chemical reaction vessels; it is, for example, resistant up to 500 °C to corrosion by chlorine gas.

Non-oxides. Non-oxide ceramics are a comparatively recent development, and include nitrides, carbides, and borides. Other classes of compound such as the silicides and phosphides have more specialized electrical applications and will not be considered here.

The two most widely available non-oxide ceramics are silicon nitride (Si_3N_4) and silicon carbide, (SiC), and both have been the subject of large-scale research and development in recent years, principally for proposed applications in high-temperature engines. By comparison with these engineering and refractory requirements the use in the chemical industry has been small; however, the chemical reactions likely to occur in service in turbines have been extensively studied.

Silicon carbide is available as a reaction-sintered or hot-pressed material. The sintered material is porous and comparatively weak; the reaction-sintered is stronger but contains free silicon; the hot-pressed is the strongest, densest, most expensive form. All forms have excellent resistance to all acids, with the exception of the reaction-bonded material where the silicon will dissolve in HF. This material has, however, found application in the chemical industry for use as seals in pumps handling other mineral acids,[7] where its strength and abrasion resistance are useful. The shafts of ships' cargo pumps have been fitted with silicon carbide sleeves, which have been proved effective in combating erosion and corrosion.

Silicon carbide is soluble in fused alkalis, where reaction is presumably initiated by solution of the surface silica layer in alkali; the silicate is soluble and thus progressive attack can continue. However, reaction is very slow on very high purity SiC. The attack of molten salts and gaseous impurities present in fuels has been considered by Singhal[8] and is considered below under silicon nitride. Arendt[9] observed slow corrosion of silicon carbide by molten alkali halide mixes; the rate-controlling process was thought to be either the oxidation rate of the ceramic, or the solution of silica in the melt; the lower corrosion rates than in fused alkalis are consistent with the less electropositive nature of the melt. Reaction-sintered silicon carbide has been used in chemical plant at temperatures up to 1400 °C, and in atmospheres containing such corrosive gases as SO_2.

Silicon nitride is currently the most extensively studied non-oxide ceramic material. It is available as hot-pressed impervious material or as a reaction sintered, micro-porous, body. The properties of the hot-pressed material are generally superior but it is far more expensive. The oxidation resistance of silicon nitride has already been mentioned; as in silicon carbide, the coherent protective coating of silica makes the material usable at temperatures up to 1500 °C.

Silicon nitride is not a very stable material according to thermodynamics, a fact which can be illustrated by the smell of ammonia which comes from the fine unprocessed powder. At high temperatures in service the protective silica coating prevents any attack by water vapour which would otherwise proceed according to the equation:

$$Si_3N_4 + 6H_2O = 3SiO_2 + 4NH_3$$

Silicon nitride is resistant to all acids except hydrofluoric which will react to form the tetrafluoride:

[7] R. W. D'Eye and J. V. Shennan, *Keram. Z.,* 1970, **22**, 752.
[8] S. B. Singhal, *Proceedings of the 1974 Conference on Gas Turbine Materials in the Marine Environment,* 1975, Columbus, Ohio, Metals and Ceramics Information Centre, Report MCIC 75–27, p. 369.
[9] R. Arendt, *Electrochemical Society Extended Abstracts,* May 1975, Abs. 274.

$$Si_3N_4 + 12HF = 3SiF_4 + 4NH_3$$

Strong alkalis may corrode silicon nitride in a similar way to the carbide by dissolution of the surface silica, but little information is available on this. Alkali metals form silicides when heated in contact with the nitride.

The good thermal and mechanical properties of silicon nitride have led to consideration of its use in metal melting; it is not wetted by the majority of metals and many of the less electropositive ones can be successfully melted, although titanium may again be an exception. Slag attack tests have been carried out to ascertain suitability for use in steelmaking, but it appears that metal oxides at high temperatures frequently form silicides and silicates with evolution of nitrogen. Silicon nitride has been shown to be incompatible with nickel oxide at 1200 °C,[10] forming nickel silicate in oxidizing environments and silicide in reducing ones. Metal oxide attack has also been demonstrated by the difficulty of forming a suitable glaze for porous silicon nitride ceramics; in all cases other than very thin layers the glaze layer is disrupted by nitrogen bubbles.

Neither silicon nitride nor carbide is significantly corroded by sulphur vapour or sulphur compounds, which is important in the gas turbine and engine applications because of sulphur impurities in the fuel. Singhal[8] also showed that in a marine environment where sodium sulphate can be formed from brine and sulphur, the amount of attack on the ceramics is low above 1000 °C. At lower temperatures the free energy change is favourable for the reaction:

$$Na_2SO_4 + SiO_2 \rightarrow Na_2SiO_3 + SO_3 \quad (SiO_2 \text{ from } Si_3N_4 \text{ surface})$$

and so some slight attack could be expected during the cooling cycle. The same work also demonstrated that the ceramics were compatible at high temperatures with vanadium compounds present as fuel impurities.

'Sialons' are a range of compounds in the Si–Al–O–N system, which are being developed. The principal advantages over silicon nitride are improved oxidation resistance and ease of fabrication.

Boron nitride (BN) in its normal hexagonal crystal form is a soft white material, with a structure closely akin to graphite. It is formed by hot-pressing and has the advantage of being readily machined into complex shapes. The oxidation resistance is fairly good up to 900 °C, but at higher temperatures the boric oxide coating volatilizes and the oxidation rate increases. It is used in seals and gaskets and other applications where thermal shock and corrosion resistance are more important than mechanical strength. Boron nitride dissolves in strong acids but is said to be stable to alkalis.[11] It has good lubricating properties and can be employed in the form of a coating on other ceramics or on metals to prevent corrosion or sticking. An example of the use of boron nitride as a gasket is in a proposed process in which ferric chloride vapour at 700 °C must be handled.[12]

In oxidizing atmospheres BN can be used up to temperatures between 800 and 1000 °C, depending on the purity. Many commercially available materials use a small amount of boric oxide or acid as a sintering aid; and this tends to

[10] D. B. Binns and D. J. Fisher, B.Ceram.R.A., 1973.
[11] Carborundum Co. (U.K.), Rainford, Lancs. Product literature on boron nitride ceramics.
[12] British Steel Corporation, private communication.

limit temperatures of use by volatilization. In inert or reducing atmospheres BN can be used up to 2750 °C.[11] It is used as a material for the vacuum melting of metals, where its good non-wetting properties outweigh its poor mechanical strength. Aluminium, silicon, and copper can be melted in BN vessels. The good resistance to alkalis is exploited in glass melting, where BN ceramics can be used for glass-forming tools; they are inert to molten alkali halide salts, lithium borate, and most commercial glasses under reducing conditions. Boron nitride crucibles have also been recommended for the melting of cryolite (Na_3AlF_6) and for gallium arsenide semiconductors.

Boron carbide (B_4C), in contrast to the hexagonal form of the nitride is a strong, hard ceramic material, second only to diamond in hardness. Its principal applications are as an abrasive, in shot blast nozzles, in nuclear reactors, and as ceramic armour; as hot-pressing is the only means of fabrication, the shapes that can be produced are severely restricted. Little information is available about chemical corrosion of boron carbide or its use in severe environments. It is unaffected by all mineral acids but dissolves in fused alkalis. Boron carbide would appear to offer great potential in cases where small parts are required to survive extremes of both abrasive conditions and corrosion.

Titanium forms a stable carbide and nitride which have been considered for various high-temperature applications. The carbide is stable in air to 1200 °C for short periods, and can be coated with glass to improve performance in longer cycles. Its stability to acids and alkalis is fairly poor, and most applications derive from its metal-like properties, such as electrical conductivity. The nitride is much less stable in oxidizing atmospheres, but has a greater corrosion resistance to acids and alkalis. Crucibles have been made from titanium nitride for experimental fusions of reactive metals such as cerium and beryllium; a composite TiN–TiC crucible was reported to be applicable for the melting of titanium and zirconium.[13]

Tungsten carbides are familiar materials used in abrasives such as grinding media and tool tips. It is oxidized above 700 °C, but can be used above this temperature in nitrogen. It is stable to all acids except a nitric–hydrofluoric mixture. Tungsten carbide is used for abrasion resistant components in chemical plant; the bonding metal phase may be corroded by acids and can be protected by a titanium nitride film.

One more non-oxide material of interest in these contexts is zirconium diboride (ZrB_2). This ceramic has good oxidation resistance for a non-oxide and by alloying it with mixtures of graphite and silicon carbide further improvement can be made. Such mixtures are commercially available in hot-pressed pieces; they have been tried in experimental steel-making and suggested[14] as a pump component for molten metals.

Chemical Stoneware and Clay-based Materials. Chemical stoneware and chemical porcelain are the most widely used ceramic bodies in the chemical industry. Both are clay-based materials formed by conventional ceramic processing techniques such as slip-casting, extrusion, and plastic forming as in whiteware. They

[13] Austrian P. 193 141 (1957).
[14] J. H. Chesters, *Refractories, Production and Properties*, (1973), 383.

are designed for use in handling corrosive liquids, especially mineral acids, at low or moderate temperatures. Chemical porcelain is usually recommended where thermal shock and moderately high temperatures are encountered; it has an alumina–silica ratio of approximately 1 : 1, compared with 1 : 2 or higher in chemical stoneware. Both types are impervious to liquids, owing to the large percentage of vitreous phase formed during firing. They are unattacked by all acids, excepting hydrofluoric (which attacks all silica-containing materials), but including phosphoric. Strong hot caustic alkalis or fused alkalis will attack both porcelain and stoneware; it would be expected that attack on the former would be slower. A more alkaline-resistant body has been proposed[15] containing forsterite and barium silicates. Most items of ware are glazed for ease of cleaning although the body is as resistant as the glaze to its surroundings. The ceramics find a large variety of applications in the chemical industry, including distillation and cooling towers, filtration media, connecting pipework, reaction vessels including tanks and troughs, acid-resistant floors and working surfaces, and pump components. It is probably true to say that this material is the first to be considered when a need arises for corrosion-resistant material in the chemical industry, because of its cheapness and ready availability. The oxide and non-oxide ceramics described above come into their own when for various reasons the particular requirements cannot be met by more conventional materials.

Conclusions

The technical ceramics discussed above are now often being considered for components operating at high temperatures in corrosive environments. Frequently the chemical properties of the material are not the first consideration, the use of ceramics being determined by favourable thermal or mechanical properties. This review has attempted to indicate the factors causing high-temperature chemical corrosion and to present the known data for each of the more common new ceramics. Much work remains to be done, particularly on the chemical reactions of the non-oxide materials.

The author would like to thank many of the U.K. technical-ceramic manufacturers for helpful information, Mr. P. Popper, Head of the Special Ceramics Division, B.Ceram.R.A., for useful comments and discussion, and Mr. A. Dinsdale, Director of Research, B.Ceram.R.A., for permission to publish this paper.

[15] E. Gugel, *Ber.Deut.Keram.Ges.*, 1966, **43**, 587.

Stable Colorants for High Temperatures

By N. C. WILDBLOOD

Blythe Colours Limited, Cresswell, Stoke-on-Trent

Introduction

The manufacture of stable colorants for use at high temperatures is a small specialized part of the inorganic chemical industry. The manufacture uses chemical processes at high temperature in order to produce such colorants. The manufacturers of such products mainly serve the ceramic industry. From these three facts one can see that an area where the ceramic and chemical industries are so closely interlinked is an entirely apposite choice for this conference.

The Need for Colour. One may start this survey in the world of Nature. The rules and principles that are familiar from our knowledge of that world will be found completely paralleled in the world of artificial things. In Nature colour is: (a) Decoration—as an attraction principally for sexual reasons; (b) camouflage —to hide animals and plants; (c) alarming or warning—red blood, black clouds, and the whole array of animal visual signals together with its opposite:—(d) calming or soothing; (e) distinguishing—for example to assist animals in selecting their foods. Colorants have been artificially supplied to man-made articles since earliest times to meet these same five purposes.

The Colorant-supplying Industry Today

One method of discussing the industry and the types of colorant used is by reference to the weight and value supplied. For our present purposes, the U.K. statistical data on the supply of colorants can be transformed into two sections, namely organic dyestuffs and pigments and inorganic pigments.

Organic Dyestuffs and Pigments. This section includes natural products like cochineal, and the much more numerous manufactured products. Examples include carbon black, azo dyes, and phthalocyanine pigments. These products generally meet most needs of the textile, printing, paint, plastic, and foodstuffs industries. Their maximum operating temperature is at least as high as the breakdown temperature of the material coloured—up to about 200 °C. In the U.K. the published data show three sub-divisions for production and value for 1975: dyestuffs, 43 000 tonnes worth £109 million; pigments, 11 530 tonnes worth £33 million; and carbon black, 217 000 tonnes worth £28 million.

Inorganic Pigments. This section can also be sub-divided. Just as carbon black shows by weight the greatest amount in the organic section, so titanium white (TiO_2) shows the greatest weight in the inorganic section and is by far and away the leader. It is needed not only for white but for the production of all the pastel shades in conjunction with the dyestuffs and pigments of the organic section. It could be argued that being colourless it is not a colorant but any

12

survey of colorants must include it. The figures for 1975 are 157 690 tonnes worth £58 million.

The next most manufactured colorant is actually red lead at about 20 000 tonnes, but of this only a small part is made for its pigmentary properties so it may be disregarded.

Another group is the natural mineral colours, principally iron oxides, providing a range of colorants from orange to brown. The 1975 figures are 16 617 tonnes worth £1.6 million.

Synthetic mineral colours include lead chromates and molybdates, which provide yellow to maroon shades, and the large group of precipitated iron oxides such as ferrite yellows. The 1975 figures are 16 327 tonnes worth £13 million.

The inorganic colorants noted so far are principally used for colouring purposes in the paint and stoving enamel industries. The 'ceramic colour' subdivision, as its name implies, covers products originally intended for use in the ceramic industry, where resistance to high processing temperatures is essential. This is the group of products with which it is now proposed to deal in more detail, although statistically it is only a small fraction of the total colorant industry. The 1975 figures are 3424 tonnes worth £8.2 million, out of a total of 466 000 tonnes worth £250 million.

Development of Ceramic Colours

Phase I. Research and development activity has been described as being split into 'push' work and 'pull' work. Experience shows that 'pull' work where the project is actively pulled into production and sale by market demand is much more likely to succeed than 'push' work where the impetus is generated in the research laboratory.

It was ever thus. In ancient Egypt there was keen demand for colorants to stand the temperatures of the ceramic firing process—usually between 900 and 1200 K. This demand was met initially by the use of iron earths and copper compounds. Iron produced shades from yellow to green and brown, whilst copper produced turquoise, blue, and green. These shades remained the mainstay of high-temperature colorants during the early Chinese periods up to about A.D. 1200. Later Chinese workers introduced cuprous (red) oxide, yellow lead antimoniate, cobalt silicate blue, and manganese silicate, which gave a purplish brown shade.

European progress was slow during the period up to 1700 but tin oxide (SnO_2) was introduced to Europe as a white colour by the Moors and colloidal gold was known as a pink colour in glass and pottery from 1580 onwards. From 1750 progress was more rapid as chemistry replaced alchemy and new materials became available. Chromium oxide (Cr_2O_3) came into use as a green colour in 1802 in France and was used with alumina to produce a pale pink at a slightly later date. In England chromium salts were 'mordanted' on to tin oxide in the presence of fluorspar and the resultant bright 'English pink' was introduced *ca.* 1820. Further colorants were produced in all countries until, by 1920, what one might call the traditional palette was virtually complete.

Process Methods. During the long development period up to 1920 the manufacturers of ceramic articles mostly produced their own colouring materials. Each one bought his own colouring oxides, often in impure form, and then 'stabilized' them by calcination through the pottery kilns on the factory. This process included the admixture to the colouring oxides of a range of 'developing' and 'stabilizing' and 'fluxing' materials. Thus formulae of the day indicate additions of silica, of felspar, of glass, of lead borate, of clay, and many other available white materials.

The period from 1800 to 1920 was a time when the secret formula book was part of the assets of any ceramic factory. Problems arose when the colour maker died, and sometimes the secret of his special blue or green pigment died with him.

Towards the end of the nineteenth century a number of trading houses started which specialized in the manufacture of the required colorants. Over the years they gradually improved the strength and stability of the available products. By reason of serving a wider market they could offer a wider range. By the end of the Second World War the majority of the world's temperature-resistant colours were supplied by them. In-house manufacture by pottery makers had virtually ceased.

Phase II. A new phase of improvement and development came with the concentration of ceramic colour production in a handful of specialist manufacturers in each of the Western countries. Competition to produce stronger and more stable shades was fierce. The traditional colorants were reinvestigated, processed by new techniques, and little by little improved in strength, in purity of shade, and in stability at their use temperature. New raw materials were tested as they became available to see if they could be processed to produce new and better products.

During this period tin oxide was processed with antimony oxide to produce a blue-grey colorant and with vanadium oxide to produce a more heat-stable yellow than the old lead antimoniate compositions. Titanium dioxide was found to act as a stable base with which to form an orange colour with antimony and chromium oxides and a bright yellow with antimony and nickel oxide. A stable pink colour was produced from alumina and manganese oxide, whilst alumina with molybdenum oxide was found to yield a useful greyish product.

Perhaps the greatest leap forward came with the discovery in 1944 in the U.S.A. that zirconium oxide (ZrO_2) and silica (SiO_2) could be recombined into zirconium silicate at surprisingly low temperatures in the presence of vanadium and fluorine to produce a beautiful bright turquoise colour. This was a totally unexpected result and sparked off interest in the strange mechanism of the process. Every element in the Periodic Table was examined to see if it would react similarly. Stranger even than the first reaction was the discovery that the rare earth praseodymium could act exactly like vanadium but in this case the result was canary yellow. Further work has led to the production of a stable reddish coral product when iron is substituted for vanadium. These three bases, vanadium turquoise, praseodymium yellow, and iron coral, are now market leaders in the high-temperature colour range. They were unknown thirty years ago.

The Ceramic Environment
Before proceeding to a discussion of the chemistry of the colorant-making pro-

cesses it is useful to look briefly at the conditions of heat and chemical attack which ceramic colours have to withstand, and then at the terminology used in the industry.

All ceramic colours must withstand heat for one or more extended periods. Usual temperatures range from 700 to 1600 K and time periods from 1 to 12 hours. Colorants may be mixed with the siliceous body material or with a glassy material used as a coating for the siliceous material. Table 1 summarizes the range of heat resistances and attacking conditions, and also shows some typical terminology of the industry.

Table 1

Temperature	Environment	Name	Use
700–900 °C	Molten lead borosilicate glass	enamel or overglaze colours	tableware
900–1060 °C	Molten lead borosilicate glass or alkali borosilicate glass	low-temperature glaze stains, underglaze colours	tableware, tiles
950–1160 °C	Siliceous bodies	body stains	tableware, fancies
1100–1350 °C	Molten alkali/lime silica glasses	glaze stains	tableware, tiles, sanitary-ware
1400–1700 °C	Lime/silica glasses, also with reducing atmosphere	high-temperature glaze stains	porcelain, insulators, specials

Thus if one considers the colorant in a typical piece of coloured sanitary-ware it must withstand a steady heating up to about 1250 °C over perhaps 15 hours, followed by a similar cooling period, and at the same time the attack of the molten glass for 5 or 6 hours. It must also be added in a finely divided form so as to impart a smooth and strong coloration to the finished piece.

In the case of a 'body stain', attack by mobile liquid glass is less important: the high temperature and reaction between the colorant and the material of the solid body may lead to degradation. However, it is common practice, having stained and fired the body, to coat it with a glass and to refire it, so that some liquid glass attack may occur in the second firing.

Classification of Ceramic Colorants

It follows from the above that the colorant should either dissolve in the siliceous glass and permanently make it coloured, or it should be insoluble in the glass or body. There is a third group consisting of colorants which dissolve in the glass at high temperatures but reprecipitate on cooling.

Examples of the first group are the simple oxides of copper, iron, manganese, and cobalt. The mechanism of the colouring effects of such oxides has been explained in detail by Weyl.[1] In principle they form coloured silicates and the fired glass is a continuous single phase.

[1] W. A. Weyl, *Coloured Glasses,* (Society for Glass Technology, Sheffield, 1959).

The second group depend for their effect on the basic particle being to some degree resistant to the attack of the molten glass or silica environment of the body material. Such materials include: alumina, tin oxide, antimony oxide, arsenic oxide, zirconium oxide, zirconium silicate, spinels, titanium dioxide, and silicon carbide. The colorant may be compounded with this type of base or protected by it or in the case of the spinels be self coloured.

The degree of solubility depends on the particle size and reactivity of the colorant, the dissolving power of the specific solvent (glaze or body) for that colorant, and the degree of heat applied and the time of such heating. As the last two factors are outside the control of the colorant manufacturer, it is to the first two parameters that his main attention is turned. He uses processes of heating and grinding to increase the stability of his products.

The third group of products may actually dissolve completely in the molten glass but can be caused to reprecipitate on cooling. An example is the precipitation of cadmium sulphide and cadmium sulphoselenides by annealing appropriate glass compositions. Cadmium sulphide was first introduced to ceramics in the early twentieth century. A bright canary yellow colour, it is well known to schoolboys from its occurrence in Group II of the Qualitative Analysis programme. It was later found that if selenium were admixed with it then cadmium sulphide—cadmium selenide solid solutions could be formed giving a complete range of shades from canary yellow through scarlet to a deep maroon with increasing selenium content. Owing to the attractive shades a very considerable effort has been applied to this group of colorants with a view to improving their normally poor heat stability.

These three groups of high-temperature colorants have been classified by Evans,[2] to whom Table 2 is due.

Processing Techniques

It has been shown that all ceramic colorants must withstand high temperatures and an aggressive environment. A supplier must also be able to provide two other qualities in addition to the normal commercial ones of price and rapid availability: these are *reproducibility* and *diversity*. Users of ceramic colours require their supplies to remain constant in colouring effect over hundreds of deliveries extending up to 15 years. In extreme cases products which give an identical result to those purchased up to 50 years ago may be needed. Order quantities may vary from 1 kilo up to 10 tonnes or more.

The second quality, diversity, is in effect the opposite of the world trend for product rationalization. Each user requires his finished products to be subtly different from those of his competitors. Coloration is an obvious choice to show difference so that in any given year many thousands of different shades have to be produced.

The logic of the basic colorant producing process owes very little to science and a great deal more to common sense and experience.

It has been seen that the product must withstand great heat in service. It would therefore seem entirely logical to apply great heat to it in the making process so that any changes which heat might cause to it are caused to happen and the colour is 'stabilized' or 'fixed'.

[2] W. D. J. Evans, *Trans. Brit. Ceram. Soc.,* 1968, **67,** 397.

Table 2

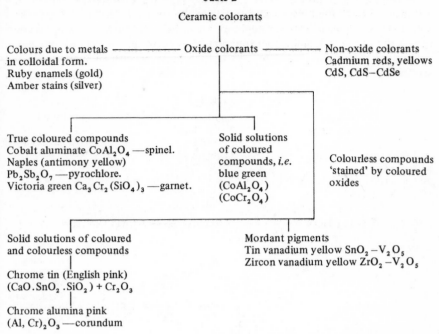

Ceramic colorants

Colours due to metals in colloidal form. Ruby enamels (gold) Amber stains (silver) — Oxide colorants — Non-oxide colorants Cadmium reds, yellows CdS, $CdS-CdSe$

True coloured compounds Cobalt aluminate $CoAl_2O_4$ —spinel. Naples (antimony yellow) $Pb_2Sb_2O_7$ —pyrochlore. Victoria green $Ca_3Cr_2(SiO_4)_3$ —garnet.

Solid solutions of coloured compounds, *i.e.* blue green $(CoAl_2O_4)$ $(CoCr_2O_4)$

Colourless compounds 'stained' by coloured oxides

Solid solutions of coloured and colourless compounds

Chrome tin (English pink) $(CaO.SnO_2.SiO_2) + Cr_2O_3$

Chrome alumina pink $(Al, Cr)_2O_3$ —corundum

Mordant pigments Tin vanadium yellow $SnO_2-V_2O_5$ Zircon vanadium yellow $ZrO_2-V_2O_5$

Secondly, it must withstand the aggressive environment of glazes and siliceous materials. So these materials are frequently mixed with the basic colorant and the whole is calcined together, again to stabilize or promote to completion the reactions which will later happen in service. Certain of these additives may serve to promote colour strength, or may in fact serve to protect the colorant.

We have therefore a high-temperature calcination process which is generally carried out between 600 and 1600 K, dependent on the individual product. Before calcination, intimate mixing of the ingredients is essential. Again, the degree of this mixing depends on the individual reaction, and the individual elements may need to be present in a size range from submicron to as coarse as 1 mm.

Unfortunately the calcination process itself promotes rapid grain growth in non-fusible mixes or even the production of an amorphous solid mass of coloured glass when components have melted together. Thus the calcined material has practically always to be crushed and then finely ground before being sold. It is at this stage that chemistry gives way to physics. The colouring power of an opaque pigment is very dependent on its grain size and on the particle size distribution. Yet, as has been shown previously, these tiny particles must withstand a range of aggressive environments in service. There is therefore an optimum balance point and the grinding process needs to be highly controlled. The colour tone produced will be completely dependent on the particle size and its distribution following Mie theory and its extensions.

In the case of 'solution' colours where the glass will dissolve the colorant and a transparent coloured glass will result then the finer the particle, the quicker it will dissolve. Typical 'solution' colours are cobalt silicate blue, copper colours (green and turquoise), and amber tones based on ferric and manganese oxides.

Table 3 shows the general process outline together with ancillary needs and services.

Table 3

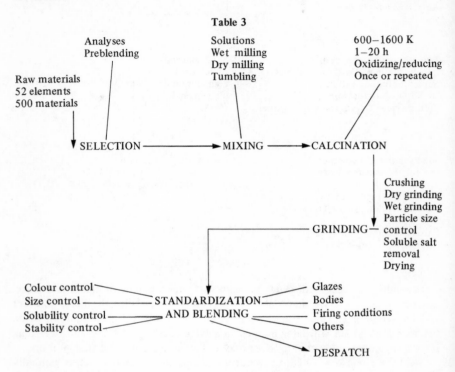

Modern Developments

There are a finite number of elements in the Periodic Table. The natural chromophoric elements available have all been investigated. All likely combinations of chromophores with natural heat-resistant oxide bases have probably been checked. Thus development is concentrated on: (a) developing improved versions of existing products; (b) producing durable synthetic bases that will incorporate chromophores; (c) increasing the stability of unstable chromophores; (d) preparing optimum versions of colorants for single purpose problems.

Improved Products. These may be classified as stronger, brighter, cleaner, cheaper, or of modified shade. Many improvements have been made and may be expected to continue to be made by the technique of second-order additions. Thus indium and yttrium oxides have been shown to be effective at low concentrations in the solid-state reaction of vanadium oxide with zirconium oxide to make stronger and more orange yellow colours. Cerium has been found to provide a similar effect with the centuries-old Naples yellow (lead antimoniate).

Beryllium oxide, although not used because of its high toxicity, has been shown to provide brighter chrome green pigments.

Synthetic Bases. Zirconium silicate, 'Zircosil' is a plentiful, insoluble and refractory base. In a finely ground form it has displaced both tin oxide and antimony oxide as a white opacifier in the ceramic environment. It is, however, so unreactive that it is virtually impossible to use it as a base to 'absorb' a chromophore. The temperature at which zirconium and silica combine to form $ZrSiO_4$ is normally in excess of 1400 K. During the 1940's it was discovered in the U.S.A. not only that this recombination temperature could not only be reduced to about 800 K in the presence of fluorine and vanadium oxide but also that a proportion of the chromophore was incorporated into the zirconium silicate crystal lattice. The resultant product was a very stable, clean and strong turquoise blue, useful in all the usual ceramic environments.

During the past 30 years similar techniques have been shown to work with praseodymium to give a bright yellow and with iron compounds to provide a pinkish red.

The mechanism of these processes has been extensively investigated. Perhaps the most elegant explanation has been by Eppler.[3] According to this theory there are three principal reactions:

$$SiO_2 + 4XF \rightarrow SiF_4 + 2X_2O$$
$$SiF_4 + O_2 + ZrO_2 \rightarrow ZrSiO_4 + 2F_2$$
$$2F_2 + SiO_2 \rightarrow SiF_4 + O_2$$

The fluoride recycles many times in the reaction mix and effectively carries the SiO_2 to the zirconium oxide. In practice the operation is carried out in closed vessels which increases the effectiveness. In a further development it has been shown that $ZrSiO_4$ itself can be broken down by alkali and then recombined *in situ* by the presence of fluoride and chromophore.

Increasing the Stability of Known Chromophores. A novel application of the zirconia and silica combination reaction has recently been reported. In this technique the well-known cadmium sulphide—selenide has been incorporated into a combining zirconia and silica reaction. Normally the cadmium colours will start to decompose in a glassy environment at about 600 K. Continuous development work has raised this to over 1000 K, and the latest claim is for ceramic use temperatures up to 1300 K.

Pigments for Single Purposes. For the most part, pigments which are used at temperatures over 1000 K have a ceramic history. There are additionally certain products which are highly heat-stable but have only limited ceramic use as they are not very glaze resistant. Examples of these products are colorants based on titanium dioxide and containing cobalt (blue) nickel (yellow), and chromium (orange). It is likely that there will be further advances on these specialized lines.

Special Non-ceramic Purposes for High-temperature Colorants

Because of their original purpose the ceramic colours find a useful outlet in the

[3] R. A. Eppler, *J. Amer. Ceram. Soc.*, 1970, **53**, 453; *Ind. Eng. Chem., Prod. Res. Develop.*, 1971, **10**, 3.

plastics field, especially where permanence is required and high processing temperatures are used. Few organic pigments are of value over 300 K and, as the plastics industry develops products of greater heat resistance, ceramic-type colorants are found waiting, as it were, to meet their needs.

The cement industry, with its problems of alkali attack, also finds use for stable ceramic pigments, most of which will withstand both strong alkalis and strong acids.

In the higher temperature ranges the ceramic colours are widely used for identification purposes in the metal industry, fusible marks being used to indicate alloy types, heat treatments, and the like. In general, the ceramic colours outlast the metallic substrates in high-temperature situations. This feature has been made use of in fault-tracing in a number of areas. For example certain parts of aircraft engines, nuclear equipment, and space vehicles have been coloured with ceramic-based colours. After destruction on test it is still possible to identify parts by their colour which has resisted the action of high-temperature fire.

Summary

Any consideration of products for use at high temperatures should include the inorganic ceramic colours. These have been briefly reviewed and some of the more recent developments mentioned.

Although the weight produced is tiny compared with overall colorant production, the range of products is very wide. This breadth of range for a small output makes detailed scientific investigation uneconomic. Nevertheless development work continues steadily and the ceramic colour range is available for new applications as the need arises.

The Influence of Gases in Slag/Metal Reactions

By R. J. POMFRET, I. D. SOMMERVILLE and P. GRIEVESON

Department of Metallurgy, University of Strathclyde, Glasgow

Introduction

The most important metallurgical extraction processes, from the tonnage view-point, depend upon reactions involving slag/gas/metal systems. The thermo-dynamics of these reactions, especially for ferrous extraction processes, are fairly well established, but the kinetics of these systems have received considerably less attention. An understanding of the nature of the rate processes is of extreme importance for optimization of these reactions in the many extraction processes. This paper reviews several investigations of the influences of the gas phase on slag/metal reactions and illustrates them by application to some of our own results.

The presence of a gas in a slag/metal system can have three different effects: (i) the gas phase may cause a slag/gas foam or a slag/metal/gas emulsion; (ii) the evolution of gas bubbles and their passage through the slag/metal interface can cause enhanced mass transfer across the interface; or (iii) the gas phase can itself play a significant role in controlling the rate of the slag/metal reaction.

Foams and Emulsions

Gas/liquid foams can be formed between slag and evolved gases in processes such as open-hearth steelmaking, in which bubbles are thought to be evolved at the bottom of a metal pool then pass through the slag/metal interface into the slag. In the more vigorously stirred pneumatic steelmaking processes, it is more common to form an emulsion in which metallic drops are carried in the slag/gas system. The presence of the foam or emulsion may be either desirable or unde-sirable. In open-hearth steelmaking, where thermal energy for the process is passed by radiation from a flame and then by conduction through the slag layer to the metal, the presence of a foam acts as an insulator and leads to a rapid fall in temperature. Foams are therefore usually avoided in open-hearth steelmaking. On the other hand formation of an emulsion in basic oxygen steelmaking leads to an increase in slag/metal/gas contact and can lead to an increase in chemical reaction rate, but this must be balanced by the fact that the foam formation leads to a rapid increase in volume and can cause overflowing. It is therefore important to have some knowledge of the formation, stability, and properties of slag foams and their occurrence during metallurgical processes.

Much of the work on foams has been carried out at IRSID; Kozakevitch[1] and Trentini[2] have recently reviewed the roles of foams and emulsions in steel-making.

[1] P. Kozakevitch, *Open Hearth Proc. AIME*, 1969, **51**, 203.
[2] B. Trentini, *Trans. Met. Soc. AIME*, 1968, **242**, 2377.

The first consideration is which slag properties are of importance to the stability of the foam. If a true foam is formed it decays by liquid drainage, and an increase in viscosity will counteract this and increase foam life. Similarly an increase in viscosity will decrease bubble elimination by a mechanism governed by Stokes' Law. Solids suspended in the liquid, often caused by partial crystallization or retarded solution of a high-melting constituent, will enhance foam stability both by increasing the apparent viscosity and also by becoming attached to gas bubbles and preventing their separation. In addition, surface active elements are instrumental in stabilizing foams in liquids of low viscosity and are often found in metallurgical systems. Foam formation will also be enhanced by the supply of external energy; a high-energy gas supply will cause foaming in an otherwise non-foam-forming liquid.

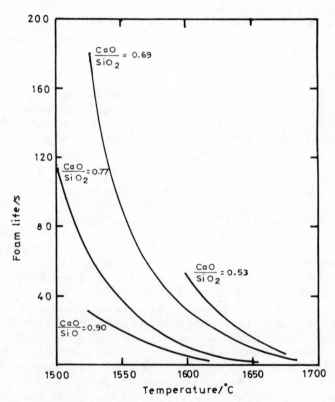

Figure 1 *Foam stability at constant* P_2O_5 *content and varying* CaO/SiO$_2$ *ratio (after Cooper and Kitchener[4])*

Kitchener and Cooper[3,4] have studied foam life of lime–silica slags by measuring the time taken for the foam to subside in a metal crucible, between two marks 4 cm apart, after the external foam-producing gas supply has been

[3] J. A. Kitchener and C. F. Cooper, *Quart. Rev.,* 1959, **13**, 71.
[4] C. F. Cooper and J. A. Kitchener, *J. Iron and Steel Inst.,* 1959, **193**, 48.

stopped. They found that lime—silica slags would not foam without an additional foam stabilizer. Small additions of P_2O_5 as calcium phosphate were made and these produced foams. The lives of foams containing 0.2 mole % P_2O_5 are shown in Figure 1; addition of more P_2O_5 was found to increase foam life further. It can be seen that foam life increased markedly with decreasing lime : silica ratio and with decreasing temperature. The effect of P_2O_5 is that of a surface-active agent, an observation supported by surface tension measurements in

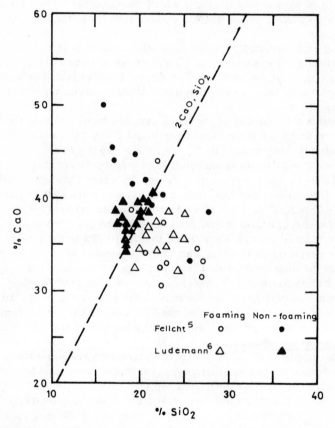

Figure 2 *Correlation between foaming of open-hearth slags and* CaO/SiO_2 *ratio (after Kozakevitch[1])*

which P_2O_5 was shown to be absorbed at the surface. The measured foam lives are, however, very small and demonstrate the necessity of a gas supply for foam formation in most metallurgical systems. They also studied the effect of Fe_2O_3 additions, and found that additions of Fe_2O_3 up to a concentration of about 1 mole % increased the foam life but that further additions led to a fall-off of the effect.

Fellcht[5] and Ludemann[6] have studied foam formation in open-hearth furnaces and have found a marked dependence upon slag composition (Figure 2)
and also upon the rate of carbon removal and hence of gas production. Foams
were more likely to form at high rates of gas production. These observations are
in line with the results outlined above. There seems to be no clear evidence as to
whether foams in the open-hearth furnace are stabilized by solid particles,
formed by partial slag precipitation, or by surface active elements. Kozakevitch
suggests it might be the latter and substantiates this by observing that foams can
be destroyed by addition of TiO_2, which decreases the surface tension, or by
using a smoky flame which will add carbon particles to the slag and reduce the
FeO content.

During basic oxygen steelmaking and other pneumatic processes the situation
is very different. The presence of a high-velocity gas stream leads to the formation of a slag/metal/gas emulsion. Turkdogan[7] has illustrated this using an argon
stream impinging on a water/oil system. Above a certain velocity an emulsion
can be seen to form.

A considerable amount of the metal bath can be carried into the slag emulsion as was demonstrated by Kozakevitch and Leroy[8] in a study of basic Besse-
mer emulsions. They found that 20–40 wt % of the slag could be metal particles
of between 1 and 16 mm in diameter. More recently Meyer *et al.*[9] made a study
of emulsions in basic oxygen steelmaking in which they quenched the slag
emitted through the tap hole of a basic oxygen furnace (BOF) usually after
about 8–10 min of the blow was quenched. As the tap hole was more than 10
feet above the quiescent metal pool surface, this provided clear evidence of
extensive foam formation. They found that up to 30% of the total metal charge
could be contained in the slag, and that the amount of metal in the slag decreased as the blow continued. Their most important observation was, however,
that the carbon content of the metal droplets was considerably below that in the
metal bath, demonstrating that the rate of decarburization of the droplets was
considerably faster than that of the metal bath by the gas stream. Similar results
have been quoted by Trentini.[2] The results of analysis of metal droplets from an
LD–AC vessel are given in Table 1. Both sets of workers also analysed for oxygen in the droplets but, whilst Meyer *et al.* reported oversaturation with oxygen
in many drops and proposed that oxygen can build up to such a level that homogeneous carbon monoxide nucleation can take place, the IRSID work shows no
evidence of oxygen saturation. It is clear from all the work on metal droplets in
slags that the composition is very different from that of the metal pool, suggest-
ing that reactions within the foam can be of prime importance in the process.

This has also been illustrated by Acheson and Hills[10] in a model study of the
BOF process. They used a model BOF with a pool of mercury amalgam to represent the metal, a mixture of water and glycerol to represent the slag, and a gas

 [5] K. Fellcht, *Met. Giessereitechnik*, 1955, **5**, 85.
 [6] K. F. Ludemann, *Met. Giessereitechnik*, 1955, **5**, 85.
 [7] E. T. Turkdogan, *Chem. Eng. Sci.*, 1966, **21**, 1133.
 [8] P. Kozakevitch and P. Leroy, *Rev. Met.*, 1954, **51**, 203.
 [9] H. W. Meyer *et al.*, *J. Metals*, July 1968, **20**, 35.
[10] R. Acheson and A. W. D. Hills, 'Physical Chemistry of Process Metallurgy; The Richard-
      son Conference', Institute of Mining and Metallurgy, London, 1974, p. 153.

jet of nitrogen/hydrogen chloride. The amalgam droplets created by the gas jet reacted with hydrogen chloride dissolved in the 'slag' layer to produce gas and form a dynamic emulsion. They compared rates measured in this experiment with those from single amalgam droplets. This led to a prediction that the rate of carbon removal should be constant for the majority of the blow and is controlled by the rate at which carbon monoxide bubbles can separate from the emulsion. During the later stages of the blow they predict that the foam will begin to subside and that the reaction rate will be controlled by mass transfer in the droplets. Their predicted carbon removal rates agreed well with those measured by Meyer *et al.*[9]

Table 1 *Analysis of metal droplets from LD emulsions (Analysis in* wt %)

From Trentini[2]

		>1 in	½–1 in	¼–½ in	<¼ in	Bath
C	Sample 1	0.380	0.322	0.285	0.225	0.610
	Sample 2	0.360	0.280	0.270	0.183	
P	Sample 1	0.014	0.006	0.005	>0.004	0.136
	Sample 2	0.028	0.012	0.007	0.005	
S	Sample 1	0.024	0.025	0.025	0.027	0.021
	Sample 2	0.023	0.025	0.025	0.032	

After Meyer *et al.*[9]

Measured wt % C *in drops*   *Calculated*

Size fraction (mesh)	% C	Bath C
28	0.30	3.04
48–100	0.60	
14	1.75	3.03
28	0.75	
48	0.82	
100	0.38	
14	1.53	3.04
28	1.05	
48–100	0.81	
6	2.08	3.11
14	0.61	
28	0.66	
48	0.65	
100	0.38	
14	0.55	3.76
28	0.33	
48	0.29	
100	0.22	
14	1.31	2.91
28	0.78	
48-100	0.47	
28	0.61	3.78
48-100	0.40	

It can therefore be seen that the presence of foams or emulsions is of great importance in pneumatic steelmaking, although the extent of reactions taking place within them, as opposed to directly between the gas jet and the metal, does not seem to be fully established. The metal particles blown into the emulsion will be those that have just been in contact with the impinging gas stream, and this may be why they are of different composition from the bulk metal. Very little work appears to have been done on the kinetics of reactions within foams in metallurgical systems and there would seem to be a need for an extension of such studies.

Bubble Stirring across Interfaces

Mass transfer across bubble-stirred interfaces has been the subject of considerable work by Richardson and co-workers[11-14] and has recently been reviewed by Robertson and Staples.[15] Subramanian and Richardson[12] used indium amalgams and aqueous solutions containing either mercurous acetate, ferric nitrate, or ferric chloride with additions of dextrose, glycerol, or poly(vinyl alcohol) to vary the viscosity. The interface was stirred by gas streams from a 1 mm orifice at up to 400 ml min^{-1}. Experimental conditions could be varied such that mass transport control could be in either the metal or the 'slag' phase. The empirical relationships (1) and (2) were obtained for the mass transfer coefficients, where k_{sl}

$$k_{sl} \propto \frac{\mu^{-(0.2-0.3)}}{D} \, f^{0.5} \, V_b^{0.42} \tag{1}$$

$$k_m \propto f^{0.32} \, V_b^{0.42} \tag{2}$$

and k_m are the mass transfer coefficients in the slag and the metal, respectively, μ is the viscosity, D the diffusion coefficient, f the bubble frequency, and V_b the bubble volume. This was extended by Brimacombe and Richardson[13] to the transfer of thallium across a bubble-stirred lead/molten salt interface, and they showed that the results were consistent with the room-temperature aqueous systems and that $k_m^2 \propto Df$ in the absence of interfacial turbulence.

Robertson and Staples demonstrated that these results can be correlated with the relationship (3)

$$k^2 = \frac{BDQ}{d^2_{cell}} \tag{3}$$

where B is a proportionality constant, Q is the volume flow rate of gas, and d_{cell} is the cell diameter. For metal depths greater than about 5 cm they found that for mass transport control in the metal $B \sim 120 \, cm^{-1}$ and for control in the slag $B \sim 50 \, cm^{-2}$. They also analysed the system using the mass transfer theories of Machlin[16] and of Davies[17] and found that both predicted the same form of empirical relationship.

[11] W. F. Porter, F. D. Richardson, and K. N. Subramanian, 'Heat and Mass Transfer in Process Metallurgy,' Institute of Mining and Metallurgy, London, 1967, p. 79.
[12] K. N. Subramanian and F. D. Richardson, *J. Iron and Steel Inst.*, 1968, **206**, 576.
[13] J. K. Brimacombe and F. D. Richardson, *Trans. Inst. Mining Met.*, 1971, **80**, C140.
[14] J. K. Brimacombe and F. D. Richardson, *Trans. Inst. Mining Met.*, 1973, **82**, C63.
[15] D. G. C. Robertson and B. B. Staples, 'Process Engineering of Pyrometallurgy', Institute of Mining and Metallurgy, London, 1974, p. 51.
[16] E. S. Machlin, *Trans. Amer. Inst. Mining Engineers*, 1960, **218**, 314.
[17] J. T. Davies, 'Turbulence Phenomena', Academic Press, New York, 1972.

This model of bubble-stirred mass transfer across a slag/metal interface has been used to illustrate the autocatalytic nature of the decarburization reaction in the open-hearth furnace. The rate of oxygen transfer from slag to metal and hence the rate of decarburization, $\dot{n}$, is given by equation (4) where A is the sur-

$$\dot{n} = kA \, (C_m - mC_{sl}) \qquad (4)$$

face area, C_m and C_{sl} are the concentrations of oxygen in the metal and slag, and m is the distribution coefficient. However, $\dot{n}/A \propto Q$, but, from equation (3), $k^2 \propto DQ$, giving the relationship (5), which demonstrates that a doubling of the

$$\dot{n} \propto DA \, (C_m - mC_{sl})^2 \qquad (5)$$

oxygen concentration will lead to a fourfold increase in the rate of decarburization.

This model will be applied to laboratory slag/metal kinetic studies below.

Interface Reaction Control in Slag/Metal Gas Reactions

In the preceding sections, the gas phase has been considered to be involved in the system solely in a physical manner. It has stirred the slag/metal interface and increased the mass transfer rate or it has been responsible for the creation of a foam or emulsion in the slag phase. In this section we will consider slag/metal systems in which the gas phase takes part in the interfacial chemical reaction and in which such a reaction is thought to be rate controlling.

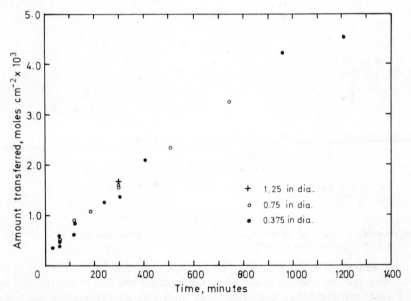

Figure 3 *Reduction rate of silica-saturated slags by carbon-saturated iron in graphite cruci-bles* at $1460\,^{\circ}\mathrm{C}$ *(Pomfret and Grieveson[18])*

[18] R. J. Pomfret and P. Grieveson, 'High Temperature Chemical Reaction Engineering', Institute of Chemical Engineers Symposium, No. 43, London, 1975.

The Reduction of Silica from Slags. Pomfret[18] has studied the reduction of silica from slags by carbon-saturated iron in graphite crucibles at 1460 °C. The slag used was silica-saturated $CaO-SiO_2-6\%$ MgO and the effects of crucible size, slag depth, small additions of calcium fluoride, and ambient atmosphere (carbon monoxide or argon) were investigated. The overall reaction can be written as (6),

$$(SiO_2) + 2\underline{C} = \underline{Si} + 2CO(g) \qquad (6)$$

(where the parentheses indicate a component in solution within the slag and underlining indicates a component in solution in molten iron), which can be split into two simpler reactions, (7) and (8). In general the results indicate a linear

$$(SiO_2) = \underline{Si} + 2\,\underline{O} \qquad (7)$$

$$2\underline{C} + 2\,\underline{O} = 2CO(g) \qquad (8)$$

increase of silicon content with time (Figure 3). The metal samples were sectioned horizontally for silicon analysis and silicon profiles were found in all cases. These profiles are as would be predicted by the solution of Fick's Second Law for a constant flux of silicon across the slag/metal interface and could not be accounted for by interfacial silicon equilibrium coupled with mass transport control in the metal. Typical gradients, together with the predicted gradients for $D_{Si} = 5 \times 10^{-5}$ cm^2 s^{-1}, are shown in Figure 4. Similar gradients were observed by Turkdogan *et al.*[19] in a similar study of silicon transfer.

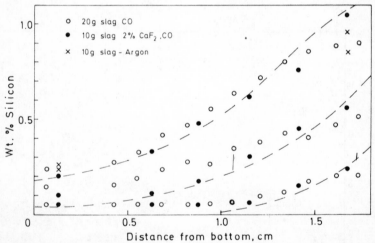

Figure 4 *Silicon gradients in metal samples reacted with silica saturated slags at* 1460 °C (*Pomfret and Grieveson*[18])

Increasing the slag depth led to an increase in the silicon transfer rate, whilst changing the crucible diameter led to no apparent increase in the transfer rate per unit slag/metal area, indicating that there was no dependence upon slag/crucible contact area. Similarly, additions of calcium fluoride or changing the ambient atmosphere from carbon monoxide to argon increased the transfer rate

[19] E. T. Turkdogan, P. Grieveson, and J. F. Beisler, *Trans. Met. Soc. AIME*, 1963, **227**, 1265.

(Figure 5). The only physical observation to be made is that use of an argon atmosphere caused slag wetting of the crucible whilst a carbon monoxide atmosphere did not. Similar observations on ambient atmosphere have also been made by Kawai *et al.*[20] The crucial point to note is that all these parameters had the same effect on silicon transfer rate; they all appear to increase it to the same value.

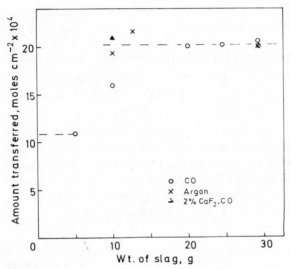

Figure 5 *The effect of slag depth, ambient atmosphere, and fluoride additions on the reduction of silica-saturated slags (Pomfret and Grieveson*[18]*)*

Turkdogan *et al.* and Rawling and Elliot[21] both explained their results as being chemical reaction controlled, and it is considered that Pomfret's results can be explained by the same mechanism. It is instructive, however, to compare these results with those of Schofield[22] on the reduction of silicate slags by graphite crucibles, and with the results of Schwerdtfeger[23] on the rate of reduction of solid silica spheres in a flowing carbon monoxide–carbon dioxide atmosphere.

Schofield measured the rate of carbon monoxide evolution from a sealed system containing silicate slag in a graphite crucible. Carbon monoxide was evolved by reaction (9). The silicon monoxide condensed from the gas phase just above

$$(SiO_2) + C = SiO(g) + CO(s) \qquad (9)$$

the crucible. He studied the effect of both temperature and ambient pressure and found that gas evolution rate was strongly dependent upon both. This cannot be explained by mass transport control within the slag but could be accounted for by mass transport in the gas.

[20] Y. Kawai, K. Mori, and M. Iguchi, *Trans. I.S.I. Japan*, 1972, **12**, 138.
[21] J. R. Rawling and J. F. Elliott, *Trans. Met. Soc. AIME*, 1965, **233**, 1539.
[22] J. G. Schofield, Ph.D Thesis, University of Strathclyde, 1966.
[23] K. Schwerdtfeger, *Trans. Met. Soc. AIME*, 1966, **236**, 1152.

However, the reduction rate can be compared with that found by Schwerdt-feger.[23] He found that at high gas velocities the reduction rate was independent of both flow and specimen diameter, and explained it in terms of chemical reaction control. He also observed that the rate of silicon monoxide formation was proportional to $p(CO)/p(CO_2)$. As the reduction rates measured by Schofield are comparable to those of Schwerdtfeger it is reasonable to test Schofield's results in terms of a chemical reaction controlled process.

Considering the stability of silica, the most likely slow step in the chemical reaction sequence is the reduction of the silica component to SiO, which is expressed as reaction (10), with the complementary reaction (11). Thus the relationships (12) and (13) can be derived, where θ is the number of available

$$|\ \ |_{slag} + (SiO_2) = SiO(g) + |O|_{adsorbed} \tag{10}$$

$$|O|_{adsorbed} + CO(g) = CO_2(g) + |\ \ |_{slag} \tag{11}$$

$$-dn(SiO_2)/dt = k_{10}(1-\theta)SiO_2 - k'_{10}p(SiO)\theta_O \tag{12}$$

$$dn(CO_2)/dt = k_{11}\theta_O p(CO) - k'_{11}p(CO_2)(1-\theta) \tag{13}$$

sites and θ_O the number of sites occupied by O atoms.

By substituting for θ_O in equation (12) and by considering the overall equilibrium, the relationship (14) is obtained, which gives (15) on integration:

$$-dn(SiO_2)/dt = k_{10}(1-\theta)SiO_2 - (SiO_2)_{eq} \tag{14}$$

$$-\log(SiO_2)_t/(SiO_2)_0 = k_{10}(1-\theta)t \tag{15}$$

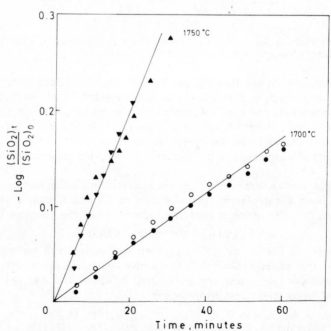

Figure 6 *Variation of* $\log (SiO_2)_t/(SiO_2)_0$ *with time for* $CaO-Al_2O_3-45\%$ SiO_2 *slag in graphite crucible at* 1 atm pressure *(after Schofield[22])*

where $(SiO_2)_t$ and $(SiO_2)_0$ represent the amount of silica in the slag at time $t = t$ and at time $t = 0$.

Figure 6 shows a plot of $\log (SiO_2)_t/(SiO_2)_0$ against time and the good straight line fit indicates that the assumed chemical reaction control mechanism is reasonable to describe the experimental results.

It then remains to consider the dependence of rate upon ambient pressure. The temperature dependence of the rate constant $k_{10}(1-\theta)$, obtained from plots like Figure 6, is shown in Figure 7 for three different ambient pressures. The lines have been drawn to be 0.6 apart on a logarithmetic scale, *i.e.* ×4 on a linear scale, and these give a good fit to the experimental rates. It is therefore apparent that the rate is inversely proportional to the square of the ambient carbon monoxide pressure.

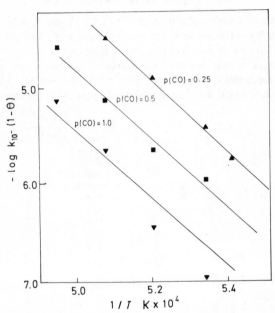

Figure 7 *Temperature variation of rate constants for various ambient pressures (after Scho-field[22])*

In a graphite crucible the carbon monoxide pressure is related to the carbon dioxide pressure by equation (17), where a_C is the surface activity of graphite.

$$CO_2(g) + C_{gr} = 2CO(g) \tag{16}$$

$$p(CO_2) = p^2(CO)/(a_C K_{16}) \tag{17}$$

The observed inverse dependence of reaction rate upon the square of the ambient pressure is therefore equivalent to an inverse dependence upon the carbon dioxide partial pressure $p(CO_2)$. In other systems a relationship of this form is usually an indication of strong surface absorption of that species and a retardation of surface reactions on the poisoned surface.

The surface activity, a_x, of any component, x, can be expressed in terms of the fraction of sites occupied, θ_x, as in equation (18). For a strongly absorbed

$$a_x = k_x \theta_x / (1 - \theta) \tag{18}$$

species $\theta_x \to 1.0$, and therefore in this case we can write equation (19). Substituting this value into equation (15) we obtain equation (20), and use of equation

$$(1 - \theta) = k_{CO_2} / [1/p(CO_2)] \tag{19}$$

(17) leads to equation (21), otherwise expressed as equation (22), which describes the observed dependence upon $p(CO)$.

$$-\log (SiO_2)_t / (SiO_2)_0 = k_{10} [k_{CO_2} / p(CO_2)] t \tag{20}$$

$$-\log (SiO_2)_t / (SiO_2)_0 = k_{10} k_{CO_2} a_C K_{16} / [1/p^2(CO)] t \tag{21}$$

$$-\log (SiO_2)t / (SiO_2)_0 = K[1/p^2(CO)] t \tag{22}$$

The temperature dependence of K is shown in Figure 8, with a result extrapolated from Schwerdtfeger and, for comparison, from the slag/metal studies of Kawai, Turkdogan et al., Pomfret and Grieveson, and Grimble, Ward, and Williams.[31] The close agreement of the values of the reduction rate would suggest that the mechanism for all the three reduction systems (solid silica/gas, liquid silicate slag/carbon, and liquid silicate slag/metal) is the same.

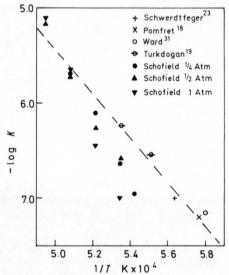

Figure 8 *Comparison of rate constants for the reduction of solid silica by* CO/CO_2 *(Schwerdtfeger[23]), liquid slag by carbon (Schofield[22]), and liquid slags by carbon-saturated iron (Pomfret and Grieveson[18], Turkdogan et al.[19], Kawai et al.[20], Grimble et al.[31])*

It is therefore reasonable to suggest that silica reduction from slags by molten iron is controlled by an interfacial reaction step similar to that proposed for Schofield's work, and that silicon may transfer from metal to slag as SiO by way of a gaseous layer. Turkdogan *et al.* have pointed out the importance of a surface gas layer, as in its absence they observed a marked decrease in the silicon transfer rate. Further experiments are in progress to study the effect of ambient pressure on this reaction in the hope that this will support the proposed mechanism. The argon atmosphere has been observed to change the slag/graphite/gas interfacial tension, and it is reasonable to suppose that it may also influence the slag/metal interface and affect gas bubble formation. Similarly, calcium fluoride is known to be a surface active addition to slags. The effect of slag height is not understood but may again affect the formation of gas bubbles.

The Reduction of Iron Oxide from Slags. Sommerville[24] has investigated the rate of iron oxide reduction from slags by carbon dissolved in liquid iron. The iron was contained within an alumina crucible whilst the slag was contained in an iron crucible. The reaction rate was monitored by measuring the amount of carbon monoxide evolved. The results of four typical experiments are shown in Figure 9. These feature a long linear reduction period in which the rate is apparently unaffected by the falling iron oxide content and then a relatively sharp cut-off in reaction rate at about 0.6 wt % FeO, a concentration considerably above that predicted by thermodynamic equilibrium for completion of reduction.

Attempts to explain these results in terms of mass transfer control in either slag or metal were unsuccessful, in particular, the long linear period being difficult to understand. Attention was then focused on the possibility of the rate

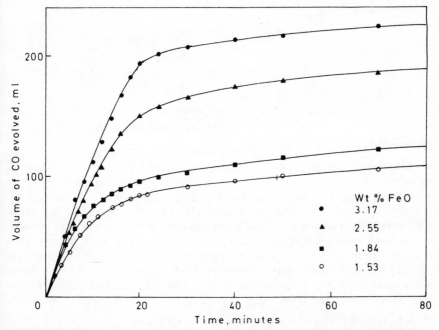

Figure 9 *Typical FeO reduction rate curves for 4% C in iron (after Sommerville[24])*

[24] I. D. Sommerville, P, Grieveson, and J. Taylor, Annual AIME Meeting, 1976.

being controlled by an interfacial chemical reaction, and the reaction which best fits the experimental results is the gaseous decarburization of iron, the rate of which has been shown to be independent of carbon content by Sain and Belton.[25] It is therefore envisaged that the metal surface quickly becomes covered with gas film bubbles, and that the reaction takes place through the gas phase. This concept is supported by the X-ray fluoroscopy observations of Hazledean and Davies,[26] who studied the decarburization of iron carbon droplets in slags. They reported that for a large period of the reaction time the metal droplets were surrounded by a gaseous halo and that this persisted when the droplet fell to the crucible bottom so that the metal and slag were separated by a gas film.

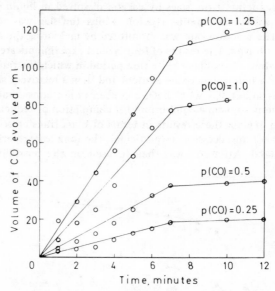

Figure 10 *The effect of ambient pressure on the reduction of* 2% FeO *slags by* 4% C *in iron (after Upadhya[27])*

Sommerville's work is being extended by Upadhya,[27] whose preliminary results indicate that the reaction rate is independent of the carbon content of the iron in the range 2–4 wt %C. He has also carried out work at different ambient pressures and finds a marked dependence upon pressure (Figure 10). Metal samples were also quenched at various times and some interesting observations were made. In all cases gas bubbles were observed on the surface when the metal was quenched from the fast reaction period (Figure 11), whilst specimens which had reached the slow second stage showed no trace of gas bubbles. These observations again show that gas is present at the metal–slag interface during the fast reduction period. The observation that there is a fast first stage of reduction

[25] D. R. Sain and G. R. Belton, to be published in *Metall. Trans.*
[26] E. W. Mulholland, G. S. F. Hazledean, and M. W. Davies, *J. Iron and Steel Inst.*, 1973, **211**, 632.
[27] K. Upadhya, unpublished work, University of Strathclyde.

followed by a slower second stage has also been made by Philbrook and Kirk-bride[28] and Tarby and Philbrook[29] in their studies of iron oxide reduction by carbon-saturated iron in graphite crucibles.

a.
Showing the presence of CO bubbles after 5 minutes.

b.
Showing the absence of CO bubbles after 15 minutes.

Figure 11 *The surface of quenched metal specimens for reduction of slag containing* 2% FeO *and* 4% C *iron at* 1 atm *pressure (Upadhya[27])*

It is therefore proposed that during the fast reduction period the overall reaction (23) takes place as the sum of two reactions (24) and (25) occurring

$$(FeO) + \underline{C} = Fe + CO(g) \tag{23}$$

at different sites. As these reactions are sequential they will be controlled by the slower one, and this is assumed to be (25).

$$\text{slag/gas} \quad (FeO) + CO(g) = Fe + CO_2(g) \tag{24}$$

$$\text{slag/metal} \quad CO_2(g) + \underline{C} = 2CO(g) \tag{25}$$

Values for the rate constant for reaction (25) are in good agreement with those of Sain and Belton,[25] which supports the view that this is the rate-controlling step. The value calculated from the present results is 2×10^{-2} mol min^{-1} cm^{-2}.

The onset of the slower reduction period and the rate-controlling step in this period are not yet fully understood for FeO reduction and are the subject of current work. During the reduction of PbO, however, a similar two stage reduction process occurs and the slow stage has been explained in terms of mass transport.

The Reduction of Nickel and Lead Oxides from Slags. The kinetics of the reduction of nickel and lead oxides in slags by carbon in iron have been investigated using the technique described above for iron oxide reduction. Experiments were made[32] with slags of various NiO and PbO contents and 2.2, 3.1, and 4.3%C in the metal.

The general pattern of results is similar to that observed for FeO, *i.e.* a period of virtually constant rate followed by a rapid fall-off to a very low rate (Figure

[28] W. O. Philbrook and L. D. Kirkbride, *Trans. Met. Soc. AIME*, 1956, **206**, 351.
[29] S. K. Tarby and W. D. Philbrook, *Trans. Met. Soc. AIME*, 1967, **239**, 1005.
[30] E. T. Turkdogan, *Trans. Inst. Mining Met.*, 1974, **83**, C67.
[31] M. Grimble, R. G. Ward, and D. J. Williams, *J. Iron and Steel Inst.*, 1965, **203**, 264.
[32] I. D. Sommerville, Ph.D. Thesis, University of Strathclyde.

12). Surprisingly, the CO evolution rate is equivalent for both PbO and NiO (Figure 13) and the initial reducible oxide content of the slag appears to have virtually no effect on the reduction rate. However, the initial carbon content has a noticeable effect on CO evolution rate, a linear dependence being found (Figure 14). This is in contrast to the FeO reduction results where the reduction rate was independent of carbon content.

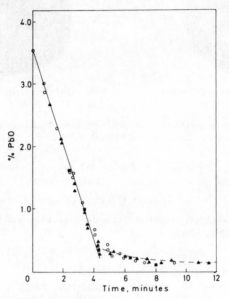

Figure 12 *The reduction of PbO by carbon in iron (Sommerville[32])*

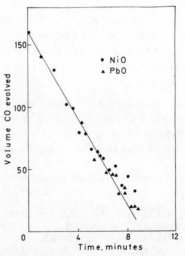

Figure 13 *Evolution of CO for NiO and PbO reduction (after Sommerville[32])*

For lead oxide the deceleration of reduction rate is observed at lead oxide contents considerably higher than would be expected for the approach to equilibrium. Because of the similarity in form to the results for FeO reduction it was considered reasonable to assume that gas bubbles were present at the interface in PbO and NiO reduction. In PbO reduction it was considered that the onset of the slow reduction step was related to the onset of mass transport control as the metal oxide content gets smaller.

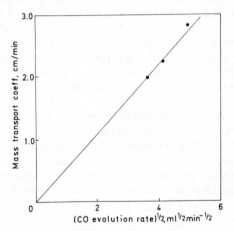

Figure 14 *Variation of CO evolution rate with carbon content (after Sommerville[32])*

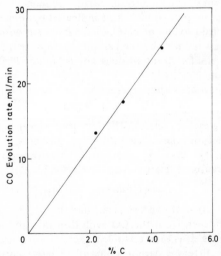

Figure 15 *Variation of mass transport coefficient with CO evolution rate (after Sommerville[32])*

Using an argument for mass transport in the slag similar to that applied to the open-hearth furnace (see above) equation (26) is obtained where C_{PbO} is the concentration and D_{PbO} the diffusion coefficient of PbO, respectively. If the

$$\frac{dC_{PbO}}{dt} \propto D_{PbO} \, A \, (C_{PbO}^{bulk})^2 \tag{26}$$

equilibrium interfacial concentration of PbO is taken to be zero, integration shows that if this concept holds, a plot of $1/C_{PbO}$ against t should be linear. All the data were plotted and the average value of k (mass transfer coefficient) was calculated. The predicted curve for mass transport control was then calculated and is shown as a dotted line in Figure 12. As can be seen this agrees very well with the experimental points. Furthermore, the calculated k's are proportional to $Q^{1/2}$ (Figure 15) as predicted by Robertson and Staples[15] for bubble-stirred interfaces. Therefore the PbO results are consistent with an initial fast transfer rate followed by a slow period controlled by mass transport. Furthermore, as the carbon content of the iron, and hence the initial CO evolution rate, is lowered, the PbO content is increased and mass transport becomes more important.

In the case of nickel oxide the reaction becomes very slow at an apparent NiO content far in excess of equilibrium. Study of the slags revealed the presence of solid nickel particles, indicating reduction within the slag. Furthermore, close investigation of the experimental results shows that a break occurred during the fast regime and the reaction subsequently became slower. The explanation of this would seem to be related to the exchange reaction (27) occurring

$$(NiO) + \underline{Fe} = \underline{Ni} + (FeO) \tag{27}$$

simultaneously with the reduction of NiO by the carbon reaction. This results in the oxygen being held in the slag as FeO not NiO, during the later stages of reduction. Experimental evidence to support this comes from analysis of the slags. This shows a virtual absence of nickel (as indicated by dimethylglyoxime), whereas the analysis of iron oxide indicates good agreement with the amount of oxide which had not been reduced by the carbon reaction, as indicated by the amount of CO evolved. A similar situation does not occur for PbO owing to the insolubility of lead in iron.

For the linear carbon reduction reaction the relationship (28) is found, where

$$dn_{NiO}/dt = k_c A_1 \tag{28}$$

A_1 is the area of gas/slag contact. The fact that nickel is found in the slag indicates that this reaction takes place in the slag, probably at the gas/slag interface. If we assume that the exchange reaction is mass transport controlled then we can use the mass transport relationships developed for PbO, that is equation (29),

$$dn_{NiO}/dt = k_m A_2 C_{NiO} \tag{29}$$

where A_2 is the slag/metal contact area, such that $A_1 + A_2 = $ Area of slag/metal contact; $k_c A_1$ is known from the CO evolution rate and $k_m A_2$ is known from the PbO experiments. It is then possible to solve for A_1 and A_2 from the experimental results for different carbon contents. These solutions allow the evaluation of the variation of NiO and FeO contents and comparison with experiment gives good agreement. Figure 16 shows these calculated curves.

For the fast carbon reaction the results are interpreted in terms of the postulate that gas bubbles are formed at the slag/metal interface and that the overall reaction (30) takes place as the sum of reactions (31) and (32). Unlike FeO re-

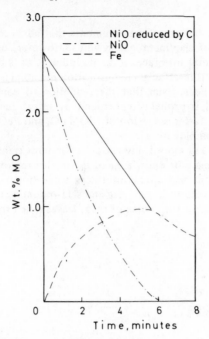

Figure 16 *Variation of* FeO *and* NiO *with time during the reduction of* NiO *from slags (after Sommerville[32])*

$$(MO) + \underline{C} = M + CO(g) \tag{30}$$
$$\text{gas–slag } (MO) + CO(g) = M + CO_2(g) \tag{31}$$
$$\text{gas–metal } CO_2(g) + \underline{C} = 2CO \tag{32}$$

duction, calculation of rate constants shows that gaseous decarburization cannot be rate controlling for either NiO or PbO since the rates are far lower than observed by Sain and Belton.[25] Therefore some slower reaction must be controlling. The likelihood of this can be seen by a consideration of the equilibrium $p(CO_2)$ values:

	FeO	NiO	PbO
K for reaction (30) at 1400 °C	0.26	24.0	133.0
Equilibrium $p(CO_2)/p(CO)$ for $a_{MO} = 0.03$	0.008	0.72	4.0

It is likely that it is the scarcity of CO_2 that makes the decarburization reaction rate-controlling for FeO.

Thus for NiO and PbO the rate-controlling reaction is most likely to be at the slag/gas interface. It is surprising that the reduction rate appears independent both of the nature and amount of reducible oxide (Figure 13). However, Upadhya[27] has recently shown that the rate is pressure-dependent, and since the rate also increases with increasing carbon in the iron, it seems probable that some adsorption or desorption step at the slag-gas interface is important, and is related to the slag composition instead of the reducible oxide content. Some preliminary results indicate that the rate increases with increasing slag bascity.

Conclusions

It can be seen from the preceding comments that advances have been made in our understanding of slag/metal/gas systems. However, our knowledge of the structure of slag—metal interfaces is in its infancy, as is the theoretical understanding of the various interfacial chemisorption phenomena.

Indications have been given that the reduction of complex anions, such as silicates, is slow and is probably controlled by interfacial kinetics. It has also been shown that the faster reduction of NiO, PbO, and FeO is controlled by gas/ liquid reactions at complex interfaces.

Whilst we understand empirically the effect on mass transfer of bubble stirring in very simple systems, our knowledge of the nucleation of gas bubbles in liquid slags and metals and at slag—metal interfaces is inadequate. There is also a growing indication that reactions in gas—slag and slag—metal systems may be coupled, and our ability to predict the course of these leaves much to be desired.

Phase Equilibria in the System CaO–MgO–TiO$_2$–SiO$_2$

By H. B. BELL, A. H. COOPER, Y. B. H. MANSOR and R. J. ROXBURGH

Department of Metallurgy, University of Strathclyde, Colville Building, North Portland Street, Glasgow G1 1XN

Introduction

Many large deposits of titania-containing iron ore occur but few have as yet been exploited as a source of iron. Small-scale plants are in operation in Canada, New Zealand, Norway, and South Africa, and in the latter two countries the deposits may also be exploited on account of their vanadium content. There are several possible ways of using these ores: by producing liquid metal and slag in a blast furnace or submerged arc furnace, or by a solid-state reduction process. The present work is part of an investigation of the liquid slags which will be produced in smelting and is concerned with the melting relations in the quaternary system CaO–MgO–TiO$_2$–SiO$_2$. From the point of view of the smelter the main interest is the liquidus temperature of the slags, but in order to represent these systematically the phase equilibria at the liquidus must also be known. In addition, if one wishes to recover titania from the slags the phase distribution and the state of combination of the TiO$_2$ must also be known. The high-temperature phase equilibria are also of interest in the choice of refractories for use with these slags.

The present report is concerned with four planes in the system, namely CT–M$_2$S–MT$_2$, CT–MT$_2$–MS, CT–M$_2$S–MS, and CT–MS–CTS.* The data on these systems are combined with previous data on the CaO–MgO–TiO$_2$,[1] MgO–TiO$_2$–SiO$_2$,[2] and CaO–SiO$_2$–TiO$_2$[3] systems to yield a phase diagram for part of the quaternary system. Compositions studied range from SiO$_2$ = 30–60 wt %, TiO$_2$ = 41–80 wt %, CaO = 0–41 wt % and MgO = 20–57 wt %. The data refer to the system at the oxygen pressure of air (0.21 atm) and the titanium is quadrivalent. Further work is necessary to find the effect on the system of lower oxygen pressures, and this will be important to understand fully the behaviour of the slags under smelting conditions.

Experimental Technique

This has been described in an earlier paper on the CaO–MgO–TiO$_2$ system and employed hot stage microscopy, quenching followed by X-ray diffraction, and both micro- and macro-DTA studies. The slags were prepared by melting the 'AnalaR' oxides in platinum crucibles using a high-temperature furnace. Primary phase identification was made in two ways: (i) by observation in the high-temperature microscope and (ii) by quenching the primary phase and identi-

---

* The following abbreviations are used. C = CaO, M = MgO, T = TiO$_2$, S = SiO$_2$. Thus CT = CaO,TiO$_2$ or CaTiO$_3$, etc.

[1] M. A. Rouf, A. H. Cooper, and H. B. Bell, *Trans. Brit. Ceram. Soc.*, 1969, **68**, 263.

[2] F. Massazza and E. Sirchia, *Chimica e Industria*, 1958, **40**, 460.

[3] R. C. De Vries, R. Roy, and E. F. Osborn, *J. Amer. Ceram. Soc.* 1955, **38**, 161.

fying it by *X*-ray powder diffraction. In this system which involves binary, ternary, and quaternary invariant points and in which many of the troughs have small temperature gradients, it is desirable to have as much information as possible in order to deduce the phase diagram. Over 1000 melts were made during this study.

Results and Discussion

Tie Lines for the System. The first stage in the investigation was to determine the solid-state tie lines. Berezhnoi[4] has published a diagram giving the tie lines in this system but his scheme is suspect for two reasons: (i) the stable tie line MT–CTS cuts the plane MS–CT–MT$_2$, which is supposed to be a ternary system; and (ii) there is a pentahedron shown *i.e.* TiO$_2$–MT$_2$–MS–SiO$_2$–CTS.

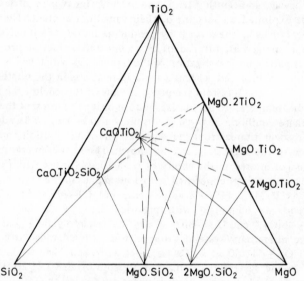

Figure 1 *Tie lines in the system* TiO$_2$–CaO,TiO$_2$–SiO$_2$–MgO

A number of appropriate compositions were prepared to resolve these anomalies: melts were slowly cooled in the furnace and subsequently annealed at 1000 °C. A crystallization on the tie line MS–TiO$_2$ showed that this phase combination was stable, in agreement with the results of Massazza and Sirchia.[2] A crystallization on the tie line CTS–MT showed that they are not a stable phase combination, but MT$_2$ and CTS were found to be a stable pair of phases and the existence of the tie line M$_2$S–MT$_2$ was confirmed. A melt whose composition lay at the intersection of the joins CT–MS and CTS–M$_2$S crystallized to yield CT and MS. This finding is in conflict with predictions made using free energy of formation data for CT, MS, M$_2$S, and CTS and would suggest that data for at least one of these compounds are incorrect. The thermodynamic data are possibly in conflict because they show MS + CT + MT$_2$ as being less stable than CTS + MT; the difference is, however, within the accuracy of the data.

[4] A. S. Berezhnoi *Ognepury*, 1950, **15**, 453.

The revised tie lines are shown in Figure 1 for the titania-rich side of the plane $CT-MgO-SiO_2$.

The $CT-M_2S-MT_2$ Plane. This plane was selected for study since the three compounds involved melted congruently and it was thought that the system would be relatively simple. Data were available for the $CT-MT_2$[1] and M_2S-MT_2[2] binaries but not for the $CT-M_2S$ binary. Data on the latter, as determined in this investigation, are included in Figure 2; it is a simple eutectic system with the eutectic (e_{11}) at $1480\,^{\circ}C$.

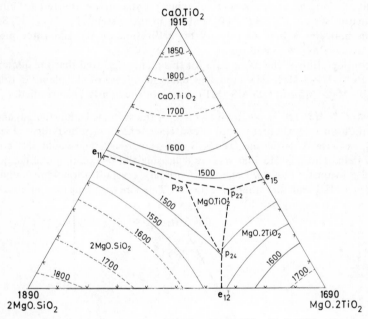

Figure 2 *Phase diagram of the system* $CaO,TiO_2 -2MgO,SiO_2 -MgO,2TiO_2$. *Concentrations are in weight per cent of* CaO,TiO_2, $2MgO,TiO_2$ *and* $MgO,2TiO_2$: *Temperatures are in* $^{\circ}C$

The convention used in lettering the various eutectic, peritectic, crossing, and piercing points in the system is to use the symbol e for eutectic points, r for peritectic points and p for piercing and crossing points. The first number in the suffix denotes if it is a binary (1), a ternary (2), or a quaternary (3) point. The second number denotes the actual point. Liquidus measurements were made on 75 different compositions within the ternary system but these did not disclose the existence of a ternary eutectic point; instead liquidus temperatures appeared to be relatively constant across the central regions of the diagram. The DTA results indicated that thermal arrests occurred at about $1350-1370\,^{\circ}C$ and about $1420\,^{\circ}C$, whereas the minimum liquidus temperature of the slags studied was about $1440\,^{\circ}C$. These results suggested that a quaternary peritectic reaction might occur and that contrary to expectations, the plane was pseudo-ternary.

Quenching experiments, supplemented by X-ray diffraction, were made on 44 slags having compositions selected to lie on liquidus plateau. These studies revealed an area of compositions within the diagram having MT as the primary phase. The area of primary crystallization of MT was delineated only approximately since a great many compositions would be required to fix its boundaries with any degree of certainty. Instead, it appeared more fruitful to study some of the contiguous planes to obtain a better picture of the phase relations. The diagram shown in Figure 2 was constructed from a consideration of the melting points, X-ray data from quenched melts, and DTA data, and also by taking into account the origins of the various piercing points curves, the ternary eutectic (e_{22}) in the system CT–MT–MT$_2$ and e_{21} in the system MT–MT$_2$–M$_2$S. The diagram indicates a field of primary crystallization of MT and three piercing points, namely p_{22}, p_{23}, and p_{24}.

A consideration of the phase data for this plane suggested that the quaternary volume CT–MT$_2$–M$_2$S–MS should be examined. Two of the planes in this system, CT–M$_2$S–MS and CT–MS–MT$_2$, have not previously been studied.

The Join CT–MS. This is common to three of the systems being studied, and the main question was whether or not it contained a field of primary crystallization of MS, because if it did the CT–M$_2$S–MS ternary system would also contain an MS field. The CT–MS join was studied using all the experimental techniques applied previously; only two regions of primary crystallization were found, one of liquid + M$_2$S and the other of liquid + CT. There was only one minimum on

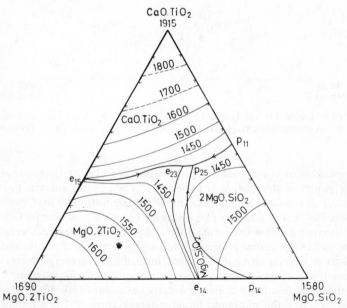

Figure 3 *Phase diagram of the system* CaO,TiO$_2$–MgO,2TiO$_2$–MgO,SiO$_2$. *Concentrations are in weight per cent of* CaO,TiO$_2$, MgO,2TiO$_2$ *and* MgO,SiO$_2$: *Temperatures are in* °C

the liquidus surface, the crossing point p_{11}, with composition and temperature as in Table 1. The liquidus temperatures can be read from Figure 3.

The Plane $CT-MT_2-MS$. Although the ternary invariant curve $L + MS + M_2S$ does not cross the join $CT-MS$ the situation is different in the $MgO-TiO_2-SiO_2$ plane where the curve crosses the MT_2-MS join. This was shown by Massazza and Sirchia[2] and was confirmed in the present work by finding p_{14}.

Table 1

Point	Ref.	Temp.	Phases involved	TiO_2	CaO	MgO	SiO_2
e_{11}		1480	$L + M_2S + CT$	30.6	21.4	27.4	20.6
e_{12}	2	1540	$L + M_2S + MT_2$	52.0		33.0	15.0
e_{13}	1,6	1620	$L + MT + MT_2$	72.3		27.7	
e_{14}	2	1444	$L + MT_2 + MS$	32.0		32.0	36.0
e_{15}	1	1460	$L + CT + MT_2$	71.5	16.5	12.0	
e_{16}		1300	$L + CTS + MS$	27.4	19.1	13.2	40.3
e_{17}	3	1375	$L + CTS + CT$	42.8	30.0		27.2
e_{18}	4	*ca.*1700	$L + CT + M$	not determined			
e_{19}	1	1590	$L + CT + M_2T$	54.5	20.8	24.7	
e_{110}	5	*ca.*1860	$L + M_2S + M$			64.0	36.0
r_{11}	1,6	1680	$L + M_2T + MT$	68.4		31.6	
r_{12}	5	1557	$L + M_2S + MS$			39.2	60.8
r_{13}	6	1740	$L + M + M_2T$	58.2		41.8	
p_{11}		1398	$L + CT + M_2S$	32.0	22.5	18.3	27.2
p_{12}	1	1500	$L + CT + M_2T$	64.0	20.6	15.4	
p_{13}	2	*ca.*1580	$L + M_2T + M_2S$	48.0		39.4	12.6
p_{14}	2	1510	$L + MS + M_2S$	16.0		36.0	48.0
p_{15}		1485	$L + MS + M_2S$	10.6	7.4	29.6	52.4
p_{16}	1	1660	$L + M_2T + M$	52.6	12.2	35.3	
p_{17}	5	*ca.*1700	$L + M + M_2S$	29.0		53.0	18.0
e_{21}	2	1520	$L + MT + MT_2 + M_2S$	52.6		34.4	13.0
e_{22}	1	1430	$L + MT + MT_2 + CT$	68.2	17.5	14.3	
e_{23}		1380	$L + CT + MT_2 + MS$	45.5	18.9	17.0	18.6
e_{24}	2	1440	$L + MT_2 + M_2S + MS$	34.6		32.2	33.2
e_{25}		1220	$L + CT + CTS + MS$	34.5	24.2	10.1	31.2
e_{26}	2	1390	$L + MT_2 + MS + T$	33.4		31.4	35.2
e_{27}			$L + CT + M_2S + M$	not determined			
e_{28}		<1590	$L + CT + M_2T + M$	not determined			
r_{21}	2	1540	$L + M_2T + MT + M_2S$	51.6		35.8	12.6
r_{22}	1	1470	$L + M_2T + MT + CT$	64.2	19.6	16.2	
r_{23}		1390+	$L + CT + MS + M_2S$	32.3	22.6	16.8	28.3
r_{24}	2	1580	$L + M_2T + M + M_2S$	43.6		43.8	12.6
p_{21}			$L + CT + M_2T + M_2S$	not determined			
p_{22}		*ca.*1430	$L + CT + MT_2 + MT$	61.6	15.6	17.2	5.6
p_{23}		1450	$L + CT + M_2S + MT$	50.5	16.9	21.5	11.1
p_{24}		1500	$L + M_2S + MT_2 + MT$	54.3	4.9	28.4	12.4
p_{25}		1390	$L + CT + MS + M_2S$	42.2	19.0	17.8	21.0
p_{26}			$L + CT + M + M_2S$	not determined			
p_{27}			$L + CT + M + M_2T$	not determined			
e_{31}		1370	$L + CT + MT_2 + MS + M_2S$	not located			
e_{32}			$L + CT + CTS + MS + MT_2$	not determined			
r_{31}		1450–1470	$L + CT + MT + M_2S + M_2T$	not determined			
r_{32}		1425	$L + CT + M_2S + MT_2 + MT$	not located			
r_{33}			$L + CT + M_2S + M_2T + M$	not determined			

An examination of a large number of compositions using the various techniques disclosed four primary phase fields in the $CT-MT_2-MS$ system. These fields were M_2S, MS, MT_2, and CT. There appeared to be two possibilities for the univariant curves, either one involving liquid $+ MS + CT$ or one involving liquid $+ M_2T + M_2S$. X-ray diffraction patterns obtained from quenched melts suggested that the former was correct. Nineteen sections of the diagram at constant mol fraction CT or MS or MT_2 were studied, and from these the diagram given in Figure 3 was constructed. This shows an invariant point e_{23} at 1380 $^{\circ}$C involving liquid $+ CT + MT_2 + MS$, and a piercing point p_{25} involving liquid $+ MS + M_2S + CT$. This plane is not a subsystem one. The data for the binary joins $CT-MT_2$ and MT_2-MS are those of Rouf et al.[1] and Massazza and Sirchia,[2] respectively.

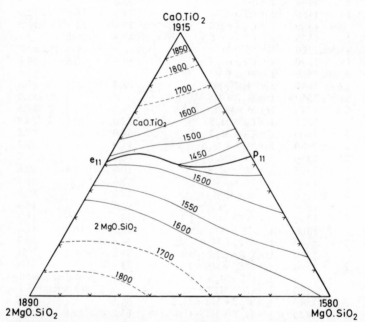

Figure 4 *Phase diagram of the system* $CaO,TiO_2-2MgO,SiO_2-MgO,SiO_2$. *Concentrations are in weight per cent of* CaO,TiO_2, $2MgO,SiO_2$ *and* MgO,SiO_2: *temperatures are in* $^{\circ}C$

The Plane $CT-M_2S-MS$. The data for the join $CT-MS$ had shown that there was no primary field of MS in this system. A series of sections with constant ratio of M_2S to MS and CT to MS were examined by the various experimental techniques. From the data obtained the diagram given in Figure 4 was constructed. This plane was also a pseudo-ternary one and shows a univariant curve involving liquid $+ CT + M_2S$ crossing the diagram from the eutectic point e_{11} on the $CT-M_2S$ binary to the crossing point p_{11} on the $CT-MS$ edge of the diagram. There is only a limited range of composition with liquidus temperatures below 1500 °C. The data for the join M$_2$S–MS was taken from Bowen and Anderson.[5]

The Plane CT–MS–CTS. The results for the CT–MS join showed that the primary field of crystallization of M$_2$S extended into the CT–MS–CTS plane, and a knowledge of this system is necessary to understand the phase relationships in the tetrahedron CT–MS–M$_2$S–MT$_2$.

The tie line MS–CTS was first examined using the various experimental techniques. The data obtained showed a crossing point p_{15}, where liquid + MS + M$_2$S were involved, and a eutectic e_{16} involving liquid + MS + CTS. The liquidus data for the system can be obtained from Figure 5.

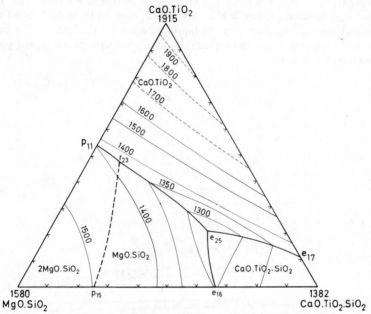

Figure 5 *Phase diagram of the system* CaO,TiO$_2$ –MgO,SiO$_2$ –CaO,TiO$_2$ SiO$_2$. *Concentrations are in weight per cent of* CaO,TiO$_2$, MgO,SiO$_2$, *and* CaO,TiO$_2$,SiO$_2$: *temperatures are in* °C

A series of 32 sections in the ternary system were studied at constant mol fractions of CT ranging from 10 to 50 mol % CT, at constant mol fractions of CTS ranging from 5 to 50 mol % CTS, and at constant mol fractions of MS ranging from 5 to 50 mol % MS. Considerable problems were encountered in locating the boundary between the primary phase field of M$_2$S and MS owing to the shallow temperature gradients in that part of the system. In addition, it is not easy to distinguish between MS and M$_2$S in the high-temperature microscope, and the X-ray quench technique was not as useful as in other

[5] N. L. Bowen and D. A. Anderson, *Amer. J. Sci.*, 1914, **37**, 487.
[6] F. Massazza and E. Sirchia, *Chimica e Industria*, 1958, **40**, 378.

regions of the system. In order to locate the boundary, the following considerations were taken into account in addition to the liquidus and X-ray data: (i) examination of compositions on the join CT–MS had shown no field of primary crystallization of MS; and (ii) a consideration of the temperatures of the various invariant points in the quaternary suggest that the four-phase equilibria liquid + MS + M_2S + CT (r_{23}) must occur above 1390 °C. It should be noted that in determining the temperatures of the various eutectic, peritectic, and piercing points, data from at least six different investigations involving several different experimental techniques had to be reconciled, and at best an uncertainty of ±10 °C should be expected.

The reaction point r_{23} involving liquid + M_2S + MS + CT and the trough involving liquid + M_2S + MS, i.e. r_{23} to p_{15}, are shown in Figure 5. The ternary eutectic e_{25}, involving liquid + MS + CT + CTS, was more easily located and is shown in Figure 5 together with the liquidus curves for the system. The compositions and temperatures of the various eutectic, peritectic, crossing, and piercing points are given in Table 1.

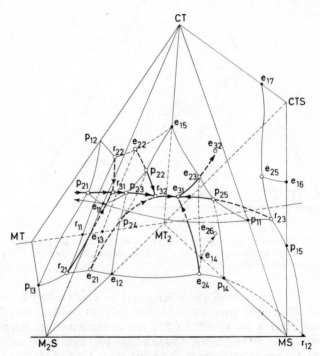

Figure 6 *Diagrammatic view of the phase relations in the phase volume* CaO,TiO$_2$ –MgO, TiO$_2$ –2MgO,SiO$_2$ –MgO,SiO$_2$ –CaO,TiO$_2$,SiO$_2$

The $CT–M_2S–MT_2–MS$ *Tetrahedron.* The data already discussed can be combined to give a picture of the phase relations in the tetrahedron CT–M_2S–MT_2–MS. This is complex in that (i) the primary phase volume of MT penetrates into the system, as has been shown earlier to occur on the $CT-M_2S-MT_2$ plane, and (ii) the primary phase volume of MS re-enters from the adjacent quaternary $CT-CTS-MS-MT_2$.

There are two quaternary invariant points in the system: r_{32}, which is a peritectic point, and e_{31}, a quaternary eutectic point. These are shown in Figure 6 and Table 1. The temperatures assigned to these points take into account DTA measurements as well as phase relations on the adjacent ternary planes. The exact liquid compositions at points r_{32} and e_{31} have not been determined.

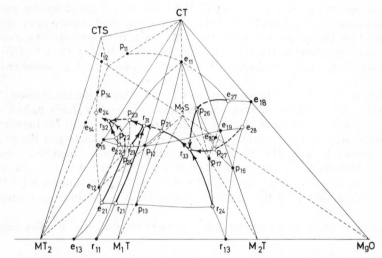

Figure 7 *Diagrammatic view of the phase relations in the phase volume* CaO,TiO_2-MgO, $SiO_2-MgO,2TiO_2-MgO-2MgO,SiO_2$

The tetrahedron $CT-M_2S-MT_2-MS$ cannot be considered without reference to the adjacent tetrahedra $CT-MT_2-MS-CTS$, $CT-MT-M_2S-MT_2$, $CT-MT-M_2T-M_2S$, and $CT-M_2T-M_2S-MgO$. It is on this basis that Figures 6 and 7 have been constructed. The various eutectic, peritectic, and piercing points are labelled in these Figures and their compositions and temperatures, where known, are given in Table 1. In Figure 7 the univariant curve liquid + CT + M_2T is shown as extending to e_{28} in the $CT-M_2T-MgO$ system, thereby giving rise to a eutectic point for this ternary sub-system, with the univariant curve liquid + M_2T + M re-entering this area to join e_{28} from r_{13}. This was indicated in previous work.[1] Although the triangle $CT-M_2S-MgO$ is unexplored, the invariant point e_{27} must be eutectic in nature since the present work has indicated only primary fields of CT and M_2S on the $CT-M_2S$ join.

Because of the position of r_{24} within the triangle $M_2S-MT-M_2T$, it has been assumed that r_{33} is a quaternary peritectic point for the tetrahedron $CT-M_2S-M_2T-MgO$. This gives rise to two piercing points in the plane $CT-M_2S-M_2T$, i.e. p_{26} and p_{27}. It is possible, although less likely, that r_{33} is a eutectic point lying on the MgO-rich side of the plane $CT-M_2S-M_2T$. If it were, it would give rise to two different piercing points, *i.e.* those for the quaternary univariant curves liquid $+ CT + M_2S + M_2T$ and liquid $+ M_2S + M_2T-MgO$, resulting in the plane $CT-M_2T-M_2S$ having one pseudo-ternary eutectic point and one piercing point.

Two planes bounding the system $CT-CTS-MS-MT_2$ have been studied (see Figure 6), *i.e.* $CT-CTS-MS$ and $CT-MT_2-MS$ but phase relations on the other two are not known.

The next tie line on the TiO_2- and SiO_2-rich side of the MT_2-MS join is $MS-T$, and e_{26} is the invariant point for the ternary system $MT_2-MS-TiO_2$. Thus the point e_{31} of the system $CT-M_2S-MS-MT_2$ is joined by the quaternary univariant curve liquid $+ MS + MT_2 + CT$ *via* e_{23} to the quaternary invariant point for the system $CT-CTS-MT_2-MS$ (e_{32}). It is possible that e_{32} could be a peritectic point in the $MT_2-TiO_2-CTS-MS$ or $MT_2-CTS-CT-TiO_2$ or $CTS-MS-SiO_2-TiO_2$ tetrahedron. A study of the join MT_2-CTS would resolve this.

There are as yet no data on the plane $CT-MT-M_2S$ of the tetrahedron $CT-M_2S-MT-MT_2$, but the information available for the other planes, particularly points r_{21} and r_{22}, suggests that the quaternary invariant point for the system $CT-M_2S-MT-M_2T$ is peritectic in nature, *i.e.* r_{31}. This would give rise to p_{21} in the plane $CT-M_2S-MT$. There is a possibility that there could be a eutectic point in the volume $CT-M_2S-MT-M_2T$, in which case the plane $CT-MT-M_2S$ would have three piercing points, liquid $+ MT + M_2T + M_2S$, liquid $+ MT + M_2T + CT$, and liquid $+ CT + MT + M_2S$, the latter being a pseudo-ternary eutectic point.

The most likely phase distribution is given in diagrammatic form in Figures 6 and 7.

The High-temperature Reduction of Liquid Iron Ore by Solid Carbon

By M. W. DAVIES, R. J. HAWKINS, and A. L. ROBSON

British Steel Corporation, Teesside Laboratories, PO Box 11, Grangetown, Middlesbrough, Cleveland, TS6 6UB

Introduction

The reduction of iron oxide from iron-bearing slags by carbon is a chemical reaction of obvious importance to the iron and steel industry. This reaction, in one form or another, plays an important part in most of the commercial methods of iron- and steel-making in use today, as well as forming the basis of a number of process developments which have been or are under consideration for commercial exploitation. One such development, being studied at the BSC's Teesside Laboratories, involves reducing liquid iron ore with coal in a rotating vessel.[1] The speed of rotation is such that the product iron is centrifuged to the walls of the reactor thus protecting the refractories from attack by the aggressive iron oxide slag.

The principal research is on the pilot plant scale, but in support of this activity mathematical simulation of the total process has assisted experimental design, aided our understanding of the effects of the more important variables, and assisted process optimization. In order to achieve accurate mathematical simulation, it is of course necessary to understand the nature of each of the process steps involved, for example, the mechanism of heat transfer, the fluid flow phenomena, and the chemical reaction regimes. This paper therefore gives an account of some of the laboratory-scale experimental work carried out in order to try to obtain an understanding of the reaction mechanisms involved in the reduction of liquid iron oxide-bearing slags by solid carbon.

Quite obviously, simulating on the laboratory scale the reaction of coal particles floating on a slag bed is very difficult, since the reaction area is not known and since the gaseous product can itself interrupt contact between the reacting phases. These difficulties are compounded by the problem of selecting a container material which does not alter the slag composition during the experiment because of slag attack. It was therefore decided to use the carbon reductant itself as the crucible: thus the slag remains free of contamination, and the geometry of the system is reasonably well known. Although it will be seen later that this last assertion requires clarification, by using the simple geometry it was hoped that application to the pilot plant system would be possible by adjustment of geometric parameters.

Previous Work

Despite the importance of the system, previous work on the reduction of iron

---

[1] D. A. Hawkes, 'Alternative Routes to Steel', The Iron and Steel Institute, London, 1971 p. 80.

oxide-containing slags by solid carbon is limited. Philbrook and Kirkbride[2] and Tarby and Philbrook[3] studied the reduction from slags containing less than 5% iron oxide in graphite crucibles at temperatures between 1400 and 1600 °C. The results were interpreted in terms of slag-phase mass transfer. Krainer, Beer, and Brandl,[4] using graphite and coke crucibles and a thermogravimetric balance, studied reduction of slag containing up to 60% iron oxide between 1300 and 1500 °C. Lime-containing slags were found to react more rapidly than those based on the binary $FeO-SiO_2$ system, and these authors concluded that the reduction reaction proceeds by two consecutive steps (1) and (2), with the

$$FeO + CO = Fe + CO_2 \qquad (1)$$

$$CO_2 + C = 2CO \qquad (2)$$

overall rate being controlled by the chemistry of reaction (1). Kondakov, Ryzhonkov, and Golenko[5] reduced liquid iron oxide in a graphite crucible in the temperature range 1450–1650 °C. The gasification of carbon was assumed to be the rate-determining step. Yershov and Popova[6] studied the reduction of a revolving graphite disc immersed in slag held in a zirconia crucible. At between 40 and 60% FeO, interface chemical kinetics was deduced to be the rate-determining step, but below 20% diffusion processes dominate. Additions of CaO to the slag resulted in an increase in reaction rate. Sugata, Sugiyama, and Kondo[7] used a similar technique, but used pure iron crucibles and confined their studies to somewhat lower temperatures. Throughout the concentration range studied (5–90% iron oxide), it was concluded that at high rotation speeds the rate was controlled by interface chemical reaction, but that at low rotation speeds the reaction was controlled by a mixed regime of chemistry and diffusion. Fay Fun[8] studied the reduction at temperatures around 1600 °C, using a graphite rod partially immersed in slag which was contained in a magnesia crucible. Large quantities of MgO were picked up by the slag making interpretation of results difficult. However, from the results obtained and those of other workers, Fay Fun concluded that neither the chemical rate of gasification of carbon nor gas-phase mass transfer could account for the observations. The importance of the gas evolution step was stressed, however, and this was underlined by the work of Shavrin and his co-workers[9,10] who, using an X-ray technique, observed the evolution of bubbles from a graphite sphere immersed in an iron oxide–lime–boric oxide slag.

[2] W. O. Philbrook and L. D. Kirkbride, *J. Metals,* 1956, **206**, 351.
[3] S. K. Tarby and W. O. Philbrook, *Trans. Met. Soc. AIME,* 1967, **239**, 1005.
[4] H. Krainer, H. P. Beer, and H. Brandl, *Techn. Mitt. Krupp Forsch.-Ber,* 1966, **24**, 139.
[5] V. V. Kondakov, D. I. Ryzhonkov, and D. M. Golenko, *Izvest. V.U.Z. Uchebn Chern., Met.,* 1969, **4**, 19.
[6] G. S. Yershov and E. A. Popova, *Izvest. Akad. Nauk S.S.S.R., Metally i Toplivo,* 1964, **1**, 32.
[7] M. Sugata, T. Sugiyama, and S. Kondo, *Trans. I.S.I. Japan,* 1974, **14**, 88.
[8] Fay Fun, *Met. Trans.,* 1970, **1**, 2537.
[9] S. V. Shavrin, I. I. Zakharov, and G. S. Kulikov, *Izvest. Akad. Nauk S.S.S.R., Metal. i gornoye delo,* 1964, **1**, 26.
[10] S. V. Shavrin and I. I. Zakharov, *Fiz. Khim Rasplav Shlakov,* 1970, 55.

Experimental

Two series of experiments have been carried out. Series I was designed to enable very careful measurements of the reduction rate to be made under conditions where the contact area between slag and crucible was kept approximately constant, and where the metallic iron product was not allowed to accumulate; hence it caused minimum interference with the principal reaction, that between solid carbon and slag. An account of the apparatus and procedure has been given previously[11] and will only be summarized here. Crucibles were either machined from electrode graphite or produced from coal by a hot-pressing technique. Binary $Fe_2O_3-SiO_2$ slags were prepared by mixing the required amounts of the pure powders which fused at the commencement of the reduction runs, whereas ternary slags were prepared by mixing Fe_2O_3 with a powder prepared from prefused $CaO-SiO_2$ mixtures. The reduction experiments were carried out in an apparatus heated by a 450 kHz high-frequency furnace using a graphite susceptor. An argon atmosphere was maintained in the apparatus and the temperature was measured by means of a Pt/Pt-Rh thermocouple in the base of the crucible. The course of the reduction process was followed by sampling the molten slag at intervals and analysing for iron.

Table 1 *Average reaction rates to 60% FeO (series I)*

Crucible Material	Weight ratio CaO : SiO$_2$	Reaction area/cm^2	Weight of slag/g	Temp/$^\circ$C	Average rate kg(FeO)m^{-2} s^{-1}
Graphite	0	47.5	100	1400	0.014
Graphite	0	50.8	120	1400	0.019
Graphite	0.1	52.4	120	1400	0.012
Graphite	0.6	55.7	120	1400	0.008
Graphite	0	10.2	20	1400	0.015
Coal	0	6.8	10	1400	0.015
Graphite	0	10.4	20	1450	0.031
Graphite	0.5	17.8	20	1450	0.018
Coal	0.5	8.0	10	1450	0.016
Graphite	0	10.5	20	1500	0.047

In order to prevent accumulation of iron, each experiment was carried out for a few minutes' duration only. The slag composition of the next experiment was adjusted to be equivalent to that measured for the final sample of the previous experiment. The slag composition range for the binary slag mixture varied between 97 and 60% Fe_2O_3, whilst for the ternary slag mixtures a range of 95 to 5% Fe_2O_3 with the CaO : SiO$_2$ ratios given in Table 1 was used. In this way a curve of iron oxide concentration against time was built up with the volume of the slag in the crucible remaining sensibly constant. The reaction area was taken to be that wetted by the slag: this could be observed visually at the end of each run.

The experiments in series II were carried out specifically to determine the effect of temperature on reduction rate over a very wide range of temperature,

[11] M. W. Davies, G. S. F. Hazeldean, and P. N. Smith, 'Physical Chemistry of Process Metallurgy: The Richardson Conference', The Institution of Mining and Metallurgy, 1974, p. 95.

the results of series I having indicated the importance of temperature variation as a guide to determining the mechanism of reduction. In series II, apart from the use of a W/W-Re thermocouple at the highest temperatures, the apparatus was much the same as series I. However, a simplified procedure was adopted. No attempt was made to prevent accumulation of product iron and the same slag was retained throughout each run. Consequently, the volume of slag could be expected to decrease due to removal of iron oxide. The only CaO : SiO$_2$ ratio used was 1 : 2 by weight, and the initial range of Fe$_2$O$_3$ compositions narrowed to between 60 and 30%. Because of the very high temperatures of the runs it was not found possible, as in series I, to heat the crucible and slag from the cold without incurring excessive reduction before the 'start' sample was taken. Consequently, the crucible was raised to a temperature somewhat in excess of the reaction temperature, the slag introduced and a 'start' sample taken when the reaction temperature was established. The degree of superheat required was determined by experience.

Results

In determining the reduction rates the slag samples were analysed for residual iron and the results expressed for convenience as %FeO. This convention, however, is not intended to imply that any assumptions have been made regarding the state of oxidation of iron in the slag.

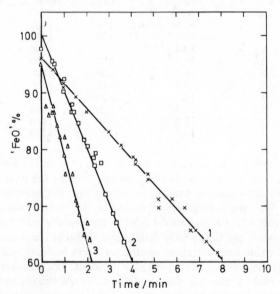

Figure 1 *Effect of temperature on the reduction of 'FeO'–SiO$_2$ slag in graphite crucibles. Line 1 represents 1400 °C. Line 2 represents 1450 °C. Line 3 represents 1500 °C*

Series I. The main features of the results obtained are given in Table 1 and illustrated in Figures 1–3 where %FeO is plotted against time. For those experiments involving binary FeO–SiO$_2$ slags there is a limit to the concentration ranges which are fully in the liquid region; at the experimental temperatures used, only the ternary slags could be examined down to low FeO concentrations. Consequently, it is difficult to determine for the binary slags whether a straight-line relationship or a first-order curve is applicable. For the ternary slags, however, a first-order fit seems reasonably appropriate over most of the concentration range in Figures 2 and 3. In Table 1 the rates quoted refer to the average rate above 60% FeO even for the ternary slags.

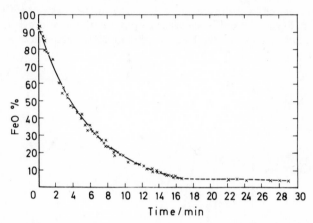

Figure 2 *Reduction of 'FeO'–CaO–SiO$_2$ slag at* 1450 °C *in small graphite crucibles*

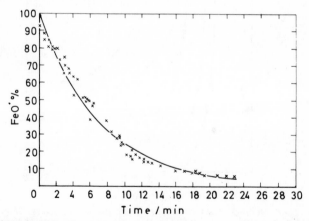

Figure 3 *Reduction of 'FeO'–CaO–SiO$_2$ slag at* 1450 °C *in small coal crucibles*

The use of two sizes of graphite crucibles having different contact surface area to slag volume ratios indicates that crucible size does not affect the rate when this is expressed in terms of mass per unit surface area of contact. Furthermore, the rates measured using coal do not differ significantly from those using graphite crucibles. There was, however, a significant difference between the surfaces of slags reduced in the two types of crucibles. In graphite, bubbles could be observed breaking the surface, whereas in coal the surface was apparently quiescent. Permeability tests showed that gas was not escaping through the walls and hence it has been concluded that the bubble size and frequency differ significantly in the two cases, coal crucibles generating a stream of tiny bubbles which are not visible when breaking the surface.

In contrast to the findings of other workers, CaO reduces the reaction rate under the conditions imposed in the present experimental arrangement.

The effect of temperature on the binary slag in the region 1400–1500 °C is illustrated in Figure 1, and an Arrhenius plot of the first-order rate constant calculated from these results leads to an apparent activation energy of 67 kcal mol^{-1}.

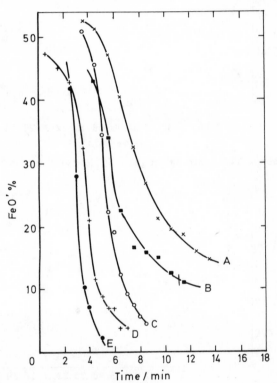

Figure 4 *Reduction of* 'FeO'–CaO–SiO$_2$ *slag at various temperatures. Line A represents* 1501 °C. *Line B represents* 1607 °C. *Line C represents* 1701 °C. *Line D represents* 1819 °C. *Line E represents* 1862 °C

Series II. This series covered the temperature range 1496–1862 °C, and examples of the reduction curves obtained are given in Figure 4. In contrast to series I, it was not possible to express the results in terms of reaction over a measured wetted area of the crucible since although attempts were made to assess the wetted area, no sensible correlation with rate of concentration change could be found. The longer experimental times used, leading to a diminution of slag weight with time and the progressive accumulation of iron may have contributed to an uncertainty in the surface area measurements, and hence to poor correlation with concentration changes. Attempts to obtain a reaction order by application of the rate equation (3), where dN/dt is the number of moles of iron oxide

$$\frac{1}{A}\ \frac{dN}{dt} = -k\,C^n \tag{3}$$

reacting per unit time, A the reaction area, and C the concentration of iron oxide in moles per unit volume, have led to n values varying between 0.8 and 2.5 both from run to run and within a given run. This result is perhaps not surprising since neither the surface area of the reaction nor the volume of the slag is known at any given time.

Close examination of the curves, however, has shown that all are characterized by an 'induction period' which in part reflects the uncertainty in the experimental procedure at the beginning of a run. Following this period the results can be reasonably represented by first-order plots derived from equation (3). As $C = N/V$, where V is the slag volume, we can write equation (4), which on

$$\frac{dN}{N} = -k\ \frac{A}{V}\ dt \tag{4}$$

integration yields equation (5), where a represents the number of moles (or

$$\ln \frac{a}{a-x} = k\frac{A}{V}t \tag{5}$$

weight) of iron oxide at zero time and $(a-x)$ at time t. While no theoretical justification has been found for this behaviour, after the induction period all the results are found to give straight lines when $\ln \frac{a}{a-x}$ is plotted against time. This is illustrated in Figure 5. Slags giving two consecutive straight lines began with

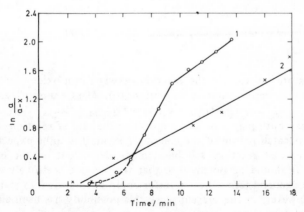

Figure 5 *Plot of* $\ln a/(a-x)$ *against time for slags containing 60% Fe$_2$O$_3$, and 30% Fe$_2$O$_3$ in the charge at 1500 °C. Line 1 represents slags containing 60% Fe$_2$O$_3$. Line 2 represents slags containing 30% Fe$_2$O$_3$*

60% Fe_2O_3 in the charge (although not all 60% Fe_2O_3 slags give two lines), while slags having 30% Fe_2O_3 in the charge gave only one straight line. Values of $k' = kA/V$ were calculated for all experiments (Table 2), and it was found that an Arrhenius plot (Figure 6) yielded two populations of points, representing on the one hand, the k_1' values for 60% Fe_2O_3 slags and on the other hand the k_2' values for the 60% Fe_2O_3 slags, together with the k_1' values for the 30% Fe_2O_3 slags. Apparent activation energies were 31 ± 13 and 36 ± 17 kcal mol^{-1} respectively.

Table 2 *Values of k' from series II experiments, all slags containing* CaO : SiO_2 *ratio of 1 : 2*

Charge weight/g	Initial % Fe_2O_3	Temp./°C	k_1'/min^{-1}	k_2'/min^{-1}
50	60	1496	0.300	—
50	30	1500	0.110	—
50	60	1501	0.340	0.150
100	30	1547	0.130	—
100	30	1549	0.100	—
50	60	1550	0.700	0.100
50	60	1561	0.350	0.120
50	60	1607	0.500	0.155
50	60	1615	0.390	—
50	60	1616	0.410	0.200
100	30	1620	0.238	—
100	30	1646	0.195	—
50	60	1650	0.380	0.210
50	60	1656	0.760	0.270
50	30	1671	0.243	—
100	30	1696	0.232	—
50	60	1701	1.000	—
50	60	1755	1.320	0.250
50	60	1801	0.800	—
50	60	1805	0.900	—
50	60	1819	0.624	—
50	60	1844	1.840	—
50	60	1852	1.750	—
50	60	1862	2.000	—

Discussion

Four phases are involved in the reaction between iron oxide-bearing slags and solid carbon as represented by equation (6). Mass transport and chemical

$$(FeO)_{slag} + C_{solid} = Fe_{liquid} + CO_{gas} \qquad (6)$$

processes may both play a part in controlling the rate of reaction, and because of the complicated nature of the reacting system, it is to be expected that the measured rates of reaction will be strongly dependent on the experimental conditions. It should be noted, too, that the reaction is strongly endothermic and hence in general terms, heat transfer could be important in maintaining the reaction. However, in the present work this possibility has been eliminated by experimental design.

Simultaneous contact of three phases can only be achieved along a line, and reaction subject to this geometric constraint would be expected to be slow. For example, for reaction around the periphery of CO bubbles only 0.1 mm diameter in contact with carbon at the slag–carbon interface, the oxidation rate of carbon needs to be about one million times greater than its known value to account for observed reaction rates. It seems reasonable therefore to consider two-phase contact only as being important, where there is an ample area for interaction. There are six areas of two-phase contact, and it is instructive to examine the chemical reactions taking place at these interfaces, as well as the transport of reactants to them, in relation to the results of both the present experimental study and those carried out by other workers. In this way some understanding of the more important processes determining the overall reaction rate can be obtained.

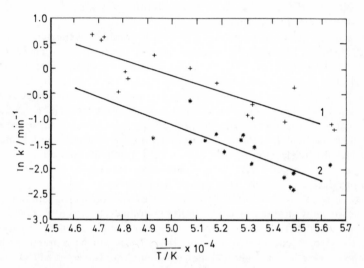

Figure 6 *Arrhenius plot for series II experiments. Line 1 represents k'_1 values for slags containing 60% Fe_2O_3. Line 2 represents k'_2 values for slags containing 60% Fe_2O_3 and k'_1 values for slags containing 30% Fe_2O_3*

At the slag–carbon interface, oxygen can adsorb on the carbon surface, as in equation (7), where C_f represents a free site and $C(O)$ an adsorbed oxygen. This

$$O^{2-} + C_f = C(O) + 2e \qquad (7)$$

is followed by rearrangement to give adsorbed CO. To maintain electroneutrality, ferrous ions will be reduced to iron by reaction (8). Reaction by this route can

$$Fe^{2+} + 2e = Fe \qquad (8)$$

continue until all the surface sites are filled and, to proceed further, free sites must be regenerated by CO desorption. This process requires the presence of a gas phase, but the extensive porosity of carbon coupled with the poor wetability by slag should ensure that the nucleation of carbon monoxide is not rate-limiting. For instance, when $a_C = a_{FeO} = 1$, the overpressure of CO is 3×10^3 atm, and pores as small as 60 Å diameter can act as growth sites (assuming a slag–carbon contact angle of $140°$ and a surface tension of 570 dyn cm^{-1}). When a CO bubble reaches a critical size it can break away from its site and move across the carbon surface. In so doing, larger areas of the carbon surface are exposed, and adsorbed CO can desorb into the bubble. There is experimental evidence that small bubbles move freely over carbon surfaces. Taking the measured rates of reaction for 'FeO'–SiO_2 slags with carbon crucibles, at $1500\,°C$ the rate of desorption of CO should be 9.5 cm^3 CO s^{-1} per cm^2 of slag–crucible contact. Measured rates of carbon gasification controlled by CO desorption are about 3.7 cm^3 CO s^{-1} per unit area of carbon at this temperature. Thus, 2.5 cm^2 of slag–carbon contact per cm^2 of crucible are required. This is easily met since, for example, a slag with a surface tension of about 500 dyn cm^{-1} and a contact angle of $140°$ at 1 atm pressure will fill all cavities of diameter greater than 15 μm.

On the other hand, different types of carbon would be expected to differ in their gasification behaviour,[12] whether this is controlled by adsorption of oxygen or desorption of CO, since the number of active sites will differ. Although iron is known to catalyse the adsorption step[13] this should still be so because the catalyst will not alter the relative numbers of active sites available. Both the present experimental results and those of other workers[4,7,14] indicate that at high iron oxide contents, the rate of slag reduction is unaffected by the nature of the carbon. This evidence, together with the expectation that once iron has nucleated, the electron-transfer reaction (5) producing metallic iron is likely to be very fast, suggests that the chemical processes taking place at the slag–carbon interface are unlikely to be rate controlling.

X-Ray studies[10] of carbon spheres immersed in iron oxide-containing slags have shown only limited and intermittent contact between slag and either carbon or metal; an almost continuous gas film forms around the carbon. It is therefore worth considering whether the process can be represented by the simultaneous reactions (1) and (2) and whether either transport of CO and CO_2 across the gas film, or one of the reaction sequences at the gas–metal or gas–slag interface is contributing to the overall control.

In the case of gas transport, the molar rate of production of CO_2, which is equal to the production rate of iron, is given at the gas–slag interface by

$$\dot{N}_{CO_2} = \frac{CD_{CO_2-CO}}{\delta} \, [p(CO_2)^s - p(CO_2)^b] \qquad (9)$$

equation (9) and its rate of destruction at the gas–carbon interface by

$$\dot{N}'_{CO_2} = \frac{CD_{CO_2-CO}}{\delta'} \, \ln \frac{1 + p(CO_2)^b}{1 + p(CO_2)^c} \qquad (10)$$

equation (10) where C is the molar concentration, D_{CO2-CO} is the diffusivity of CO_2 in CO, δ and δ' are boundary layer thicknesses, $p(CO_2)^b$ is the partial pressure of CO_2 in the bulk of the gas, $p(CO_2)^s$ in equilibrium with the slag, and

[12] E. T. Turkdogan and J. V. Vinters, *Carbon,* 1970, 8, 39.
[13] P. L. Walker, M. Shelef, and R. A. Anderson, Chemistry and Physics of Carbon', Edward Arnold, London, 1968, Vol. 4, p. 287.
[14] B. A. Kukhtin, G. A. Toporishchev, O. A. Esin, and V. N. Boronenkov, *Izvest. V.U.Z. Tsvetnaya Metallurgiya,* 1971, 2, 45.

$p(CO_2)^c$ in equilibrium with carbon. As $p(CO_2)^c \ll 1$ and by assuming $\delta = \delta'$ and that D_{CO_2-CO} is proportional to $T^{0.8}$ where T is the absolute temperature,[15] equation (11) can be derived. The experimental results obtained in series

$$\dot{N}_{CO_2} = \dot{N}_{Fe} = b\, T^{0.8}\, [p(CO_2)^s - p(CO_2)^b] \qquad (11)$$

I at 1500 °C can be used to derive a value of b and this in turn used to calculate reaction rates at higher temperatures. The results of the calculation are shown in Figure 7, and indicate that not only are lower rates predicted than extrapolated values obtained from series I, but also that a negative temperature coefficient is predicted. This follows because the increase in diffusivity with temperature is insufficient to overcome the decrease in driving force brought about by the decrease in CO_2 partial pressure in equilibrium with the slag. As a further check on the prediction of a negative temperature coefficient, the carbon gasification rates measured by Day *et al.*[16] using high oxygen flows, but under conditions where gas diffusion control was operative, were used as by Walker *et al.*[17] to derive corresponding rates for CO_2-CO mixtures. Figure 7 shows the iron production rate calculated on the assumption that the carbon gasification reaction (2) is the slow step and with the CO : CO_2 ratio calculated for equation (1) as the driving force. The turbulence in the fast-moving gas is obviously much higher than in the slag—carbon system, and it is therefore not surprising that the

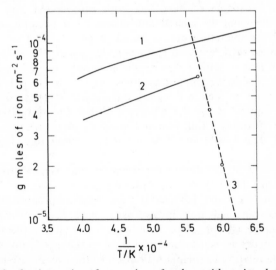

Figure 7 *Rate of reduction to iron for reaction of carbon with an iron-bearing slag versus (temperature)⁻¹. Line 1 represents rates predicted by carbon gasification. Line 2 represents rates predicted by equation (11). Line 3 represents experimental rates determined from series 1 experiments*

[15] J. Szekeley and N. J. Themelis, 'Rate Phenomena in Process Metallurgy', Wiley, New York, 1971.
[16] R. J. Day, P. L. Walker, and C. C. Wright, 'Industrial Carbon and Graphite', Society of Chemical Industry, London, 1958, p. 348.
[17] P. L. Walker, F. Rusinko, and L. G. Austin, *Adv. Catalysis*, 1959, **11**, 133.

results calculated using Day's work are higher than those measured in series I. However, a negative temperature coefficient is again predicted. As this is at variance with the measured results in series II, it must be concluded that gas-phase mass transfer does not contribute to the overall rate-controlling process.

It is also improbable that chemical reaction at the gas–carbon interface is contributing to overall rate control. The similarity in results between graphite and coal crucibles virtually eliminates as a significant factor any of the carbon gasification steps, since different types of carbon are known to gasify at different rates. Similarly, that chemical reactions at the gas–slag interface are not important can be inferred from the work of Sugata *et al.*,[7] who found that reduction by CO of iron oxide-containing slags was very much slower than reduction by solid carbon. In the present work the gas passed upwards through a slag foam out of contact with carbon, yet the CO_2 content in the effluent gas was too small to be measured, thus indicating that the CO–slag reaction is probably slow. Grieveson *et al.*[18] studied the reduction of pure iron oxide by CO and showed that liquid-phase mass transport controlled the reaction, concluding that mass transfer must play a part in determining the rate of a reduction process proceeding by way of CO.

The reaction steps given above assume that iron, once formed, plays no further part in the reduction process except that of an inert product or catalyst. However, iron is capable of dissolving both carbon and iron oxide, and, in either way, influencing the overall rate process. For example, it is possible to speculate that the induction period found in series II is a result of the time necessary to make sufficient iron to sustain the reaction at a reasonable rate. It will be recalled that in series I the crucible and contents were heated from room temperature thus allowing ample time for some iron to form. It is unlikely that the carbon dissolution step will significantly affect slag–carbon kinetics. This contention is supported by the observation that the metal wets the carbon crucible surface forming a thin film and many droplets giving an adequate area for dissolution. The dissolution of carbon is also known to be very fast: Olsson, Koump, and Perzak[19] showed that mass transport of carbon in the metal controlled the rate of dissolution for Reynolds numbers up to 18 000 in the temperature range 1470–1640 °C. Reaction between slag and liquid iron will result in increased iron and dissolved oxygen. Further progress of the reduction process by this route will now involve reaction between dissolved oxygen and carbon to produce CO or CO_2. Thus chemical steps at the metal–slag and metal–gas interfaces as well as transport through the metal and slag phases must be considered in relation to their contribution to the overall rate process.

Adsorption at the metal–slag interface is clearly an essential step in the transport of oxygen to the metal–gas interface where it can react with carbon. Unfortunately, little is known about the kinetics of such an adsorption process and so its overall importance cannot be assessed. On the other hand, transport through the metal phase is not considered to be significant since it can be cal-

[18] P. Grieveson and E. T. Turkdogan, *Trans. Met. Soc. AIME*, 1964, **230**, 1609.
[19] R. G. Olsson, V. Koump, and T. F. Perzak, *Trans. Met. Soc. AIME*, 1966, **236**, 426.

culated that with a value of 3×10^{-2} cm s^{-1} for the mass transfer coefficient[20] for both [C] and [O], the measured rates of reaction can be accounted for if only 1–3% of the carbon surface is covered by iron. Experimental observations suggest that coverage is much greater than this. Further evidence comes from Krainer's work[4] where droplets embedded in slag showed no evidence of surface decarburization.

The process of desorbing CO from the metal into the gas phase could be important to the overall kinetics since, as oxygen is known to be surface active, its very presence can reduce the number of sites available for adsorbed CO to form from the carbon and oxygen in solution. King *et al.*[21] found that at low carbon concentrations, the process is controlled by the rate of formation of adsorbed CO. Thus in the reaction sequence (12) and (13) reaction (12) is

$$[C] + [O] \rightarrow (CO)_{ads} \tag{12}$$

$$(CO)_{ads} \rightleftharpoons CO_{gas} \tag{13}$$

rate-controlling. Sugata *et al.*[7] found, under conditions where slag-phase mass transport did not contribute to rate control, that the rate was proportional to iron oxide activity. Provided that equilibrium is established between slag and metal with respect to oxygen, equations (14) and (15) will hold, where f_O is

$$(FeO)_{slag} \rightleftharpoons Fe + [O]_{metal} \tag{14}$$

$$[O] = \frac{K \, a_{FeO}}{f_O} \tag{15}$$

the activity coefficient of oxygen. Thus $[O] \, \alpha \, a_{FeO}$ from which it follows that, provided carbon is in excess of oxygen in the metal phase, the rate of reaction (12) is proportional to the activity of iron oxide in the slag. This argument of course implies that the oxygen adsorption step at the slag–metal interface does not interfere with oxygen transport in any way and that the source of carbon is the metal [reaction (12)] not the gas. The presence of small metal droplets in the body of the slag, both in the series II experiments of this work and in that of Krainer[4] provides additional evidence for the importance of the chemistry of the metal–gas interface. These droplets probably arise when, because of the slow CO desorption step, CO overpressures build up in the metal films, sometimes leading to explosive nucleation of CO.

The final process to be considered is that of transport through the slag phase to the slag–metal or slag–carbon interface. This will be influenced by stirring, either induced naturally by the escaping gas bubbles or created artificially by rotating the carbon.[7,14] Although Fay Fun[8] suggests that mass transport in the slag phase cannot be important because bubble stirring is so vigorous, there is little doubt from the work of Sugata *et al.*[7] and Kukhtin *et al.*[14] that mass transport is important when the carbon is either stationary or slowly rotating.

[20] L. Tiberg, *Jernkont. Ann.*, 1960, **144**, 757.
[21] T. B. King, R. A. Karasev, and P. Dastur, 'Heterogeneous Kinetics at Elevated Temperatures' Plenum Press, New York, 1970, p. 409.

For a bubble-stirred system it might be expected that the mass transfer coefficient would be proportional to the rate of release of bubbles leading to an equation of the form (16),[22],[23] where $\dot{n}/A$ is the molar flux of oxygen, D_O its

$$\dot{n}/A \; \alpha \, D_O \; (KC_{sl} - C_m)^2 \tag{16}$$

diffusion coefficient in the slag, C_{sl} and C_m its concentration in slag and metal, respectively, and K an equilibrium constant. Shavrin *et al.*[10] claim that this equation adequately describes the behaviour of stationary graphite spheres in borate slags containing 5–15% FeO Shurygin *et al.*[24] found second-order kinetics for 2–9% FeO in calcium aluminosilicate slags with a stationary graphite disc. Fay Fun, although dismissing mass transport, also found second-order behaviour between 1.5 and 15% FeO, and 1.8 order between 15 and 40% FeO in $CaO-FeO-SiO_2$ slags. In the present work in series I (the well-controlled experiments) first-order kinetics were found, but the measurement technique was such that gross changes in the system were not allowed to occur during the experiments. The measured rates were significantly lower than those found by other workers, and the virtual absence of a vigorously boiling metal film and reacting metal droplets probably means that the overall stirring effect was less, such that bubble-stirred regime necessary to give second-order kinetics was not present. First-order kinetics would still be obtained with gentle stirring since the mass transport in the slag phase would be controlled by concentration gradients.

From the above discussion, it is clear that no unequivocal conclusions can be drawn regarding the overall rate-controlling process, although it seems probable that in the system studied both chemical steps and slag-phase mass transport contribute. Of the chemical steps, it is tentatively concluded that the process of desorption of CO from metal into gas has the largest effect on the overall rate process. It seems possible also that the existence of two populations of points in the Arrhenius plot for series II (Figure 6) is a result of the two rate-controlling processes differing in their contributions depending upon the iron oxide concentration.

The authors wish to thank Mr. T. Gare, who was responsible for the series I experiments; and Mr. K. G. Bain, who carried out the series II experiments and contributed to many lively discussions.

[22] F. D. Richardson, 'Physical Chemistry of Melts in Metallurgy', Academic Press, New York, 1974. Vol. 2, p. 516.

[23] E. T. Turkdogan, *Minerals Sci. Eng.*, 1976, 8, 85.

[24] P. M. Shurygin, V. N. Boronenkov, B. I. Kryuk, and V. V. Revelstsov, *Izvest. V.U.Z. Chern. Met.*, 1965, 8, 23.

The Chemical Changes occurring during the Cooling of Hot Gases from Flat Glass Furnaces

By B. J. KIRKBRIDE

Pilkington Brothers Limited, Research and Development Laboratories, Lathom, Ormskirk, Lancs L40 5UF

Introduction

'Flat glass' is a soda—lime—silicate glass of approximate composition (wt %): SiO_2 72%, Na_2O 12%, (CaO + MgO) 14%, together with small amounts of Al_2O_3 and K_2O. It is the material used for the manufacture of such articles as windows in buildings and windscreens in cars. The molten glass is made by heating together the raw materials: sand (SiO_2), limestone ($CaCO_3$), dolomite ($CaCO_3 MgCO_3$), soda ash (Na_2CO_3), and saltcake (Na_2SO_4). The glass is generally manufactured in large regenerative furnaces in which the raw materials are melted by burning either oil or natural gas just above the surface of the raw materials and the partly formed glass melt. Furnace crown temperatures can reach $1550-1600\,^{\circ}C$. The melting process leads both to entrainment of some of the raw materials in the combustion gases and to volatilization of some of the components from the raw material and from the melt.

Table 1 *The waste gas composition from a gas-fired flat glass furnace*

	Volume %	Amount/mol vol^{-1}
H_2O	13.3	83.4
CO_2	8.6	53.5
O_2	5.2	32.7
N_2	72.7	454.3
SO_2	1.6×10^{-2}	10^{-1}
Total Na (as NaOH)	8.3×10^{-3}	5.2×10^{-2}
Total Cl (as HCl)	4.0×10^{-3}	2.5×10^{-2}
Total		624.6

The hot waste gases leave the furnace and enter the regenerator system at about $1500\,^{\circ}C$ and cool both on passage through the heat recovery system and through the flue and chimney system downstream of this. The volatile material in the gas stream condenses at some stage during the cooling process and deposits material on the walls of the gas passages. These deposits affect the heat transfer in the system and can lead to blockage of the passages. Both the hot vapour and hot condensed material can cause corrosion of the refractories in the furnace and regenerator system. To be able to control these processes it is useful to understand the chemistry of the hot waste gases.

A detailed mass balance on the furnace gives an estimate of the analysis of the waste gas on an elemental basis, and the general correctness of this is confirmed by careful sampling of the gas leaving the furnace at the regenerator top. A typical analysis of the gas from a gas-fired furnace is shown in Table 1. Other materials lost from the furnace, such as SiO_2, Al_2O_3, and CaO, are presumed to be involatile and their loss presumed to be as particulate matter entrained in the gas. Such techniques only give the elemental analysis of the gas although the results are frequently reported for convenience in terms of oxides. Perhaps because of this there is a tendency to assume that the molecular species actually present in the gas are these oxides. The other extreme assumption is that all the sodium in the gas is present as sodium sulphate because it is this material which is found most frequently in the deposits from the cooled gas.

The aim of this paper is to present, as a limiting case, the chemical thermo-dynamic calculation of the equilibrium molecular composition of the gas as it leaves the furnace and the chemical changes which might be expected to occur as the gas cools leading to the condensation of one or more species. Similar exercises have been carried out for both pulverized coal-fired and oil-fired steam-raising plants where the concern has been the fouling and corrosion of superheater tubes,[1,2] and a related area has been an investigation of the formation of deposits on turbine blades, particularly in marine engines.[3,4] The method adopted here is similar to the ones used in the quoted works and is based on that of Kandiner and Brinkley.[5]

Sodium Sulphate

The thermodynamic properties of sodium sulphate are such an important element in the analysis of the system that a discussion of the available infor-mation is apposite. JANAF Thermochemical Tables[6] quote values for the properties of the solid and liquid phases, which have been used henceforward, but give no information on the vapour. The data quoted in the literature for the vapour pressure of sodium sulphate are summarized graphically in Figure 1, the limits of the lines indicating the temperature range quoted by the author. As can be seen, the quoted values span three or four orders of magnitude at a given temperature and the gradients of the lines give heats of vaporization lying between 20 and 80 kcal mol^{-1}.

Three types of method have been used by the various authors to produce these data: (i) 'calculation' based on a semi-empirical rule;[7,8] (ii) transpiration methods;[9,10,14,15] and (iii) the Knudsen effusion method.[11,12,13] The results

[1] R. H. Ball and H. C. Patel, *Trans. A.S.M.E., J. Eng. Power*, Paper No. 60–WA182, 1960.
[2] W. D. Halstead and E. Raask, *J. Inst. Fuel*, 1969, 42, 344.
[3] M. A. DeCrescente and N. S. Bornstein, *Corrosion*, 1968, 24, 127.
[4] J. G. Tschinkel, *Corrosion*, 1972, 28, 161.
[5] H. J. Kandiner and S. R. Brinkley, *Ind. and Eng. Chem.*, 1950, 42, 850.
[6] D. R. Stull and H. Prophet (editors), 'JANAF Thermochemical Tables', U.S. Dept of Commerce, Second Edition, 1971.
[7] G. Eyber, *Glastechn. Ber.*, 1960, 33, 283.
[8] E. Terres, *Brennstoff Chem.*, 1954, 33, 225.
[9] H. Liander and H. Olsson, *IVA*, 1937, 4, 145.
[10] R. Brückner, *Glastechn. Ber.*, 1962, 35, 93.

under heading (i) do not agree between themselves and are at variance with the experimental results both in magnitude and gradient. The experimentally based results fall into two broad groups determined both by method and temperature range. The Knudsen effusion work has been carried out below or close to the melting point (884 °C) of the sulphate and gives results generally higher than the extrapolated values of the results of the transpiration method which have been carried out at higher temperatures on the molten salt.

One of the problems with sodium sulphate is the extent to which the vapour is dissociated. This is well discussed by Cubicciotti and Keneshea.[14] Sodium sulphate vaporizes congruently, that is the vapour and condensed phase have the

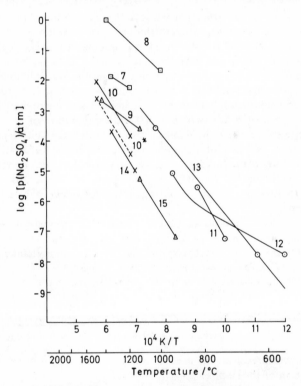

Figure 1 *Literature data for the vapour pressure of sodium sulphate plotted as* log *(vapour pressure/*atm*) against reciprocal of the absolute temperature. The reference numbers of the sources of information are given on the lines. The symbols indicate the method of determination:* □ *semi-empirical calculation,* ○ *Knudsen effusion,* △ *transpiration in air,* × *transpiration in nitrogen.* 10* *represents the results of ref. 10 recalculated to 'plateau' flow conditions*

[11] C. Kröger and J. Stratmann, *Glastechn. Ber.,* 1961, **34**, 311.
[12] D. G. Powell and P. A. H. Wyatt, *J. Chem. Soc. (A),* 1971, 3614.
[13] Ref. 2, Figure 4.
[14] D. Cubicciotti and F. J. Keneshea, *High Temp. Sci.,* 1972, **4**, 32.
[15] R. E. Fryxell, C. A. Trythall, and R. J. Perkins, *Corrosion,* 1973, **29**, 423.

same stoicheiometric composition. Thus one can write equation (1) and define

$$Na_2SO_4 \text{ (s or l)} \rightarrow Na_2SO_4 \text{ (g)} \tag{1}$$

a vapour pressure $p(Na_2SO_4)$ of Na_2SO_4 above the condensed phase. The $Na_2SO_4(g)$ can dissociate in the vapour phase, likely processes being reactions (2)–(4), and, if the atmosphere is damp, reaction (5). The presence of oxygen

$$Na_2SO_4 \text{ (g)} \rightarrow 2Na(g) + SO_2(g) + O_2(g) \tag{2}$$

$$Na_2SO_4 \text{ (g)} \rightarrow Na_2O(g) + SO_2(g) + {}^1/_2O_2(g) \tag{3}$$

$$Na_2SO_4 \text{ (g)} \rightarrow 2NaO(g) + SO_2(g) \tag{4}$$

$$Na_2SO_4(g) + H_2O(g) \rightarrow 2NaOH(g) + SO_2(g) + {}^1/_2O_2(g) \tag{5}$$

or sulphur dioxide in the atmosphere above the solid or liquid phase will inhibit the decomposition processes, whereas the presence of water will favour it, and consequently the material transfer from the condensed phase will depend upon the composition of the atmosphere above it.

The degree of the problem can be illustrated from the available thermodynamic data which allow the equilibrium pressures of the dissociation products above the condensed sodium sulphate to be calculated. Table 2 summarizes these calculated partial pressures for two cases: (i) the vaporization of sodium sulphate into dry nitrogen, and (ii) the vaporization into nitrogen containing 1% water vapour, the total pressure of the system being maintained at 1 atm. The table also contains values for $p(Na_2SO_4)$ taken from Cubicciotti and Keneshea. As can be seen the undissociated Na_2SO_4 only accounts for about 20% of the total pressure of sodium species in dry nitrogen and for between 1 and 10% in the damp nitrogen.

In a 'weight loss' method of vapour pressure determination, which covers both transpiration and Knudsen effusion methods, the reported vapour pressure could be at least three quantities: (a) the true thermodynamic equilibrium pressure of $Na_2SO_4(g)$ above the condensed phase, $p(Na_2SO_4)$; (b) the total pressure of all the sodium species in the gas phase above the melt, Σp or Σp^*, where

$$\Sigma p = p(Na_2SO_4) + p(Na) + p(Na_2O) + p(NaO) + p(NaOH)$$

$$\Sigma p^* = 2p(Na_2SO_4) + p(Na) + 2p(Na_2O) + p(NaO) + p(NaOH)$$

(c) the total pressure of all the species above the condensed phase arising from the vaporization of the sulphate, p_{tot}:

$$p_{tot} = \Sigma p + p(O_2) + p(SO_2) + p(SO_3)$$

Which of these is reported depends in detail upon the method, the carrier gas, and the degree to which the results are corrected. Only Cubicciotti and Keneshea make a detailed allowance for the effects of dissociation and compare the effects of using nitrogen and an SO_2-O_2 mixture as carrier gases. Brückner[10] used nitrogen, air, and an SO_2-O_2 mixture as carrier gases, but extrapolated his transpiration results to zero flow rate. The validity of this is questionable (see, for example, p.170 of ref. 16). There are sufficient data to recalculate his results

[16] O. Kubaschewski, E. L. Evans, and C. B. Alcock, 'Metallurgical Thermochemistry', Pergamon Press, Fourth Edition, 1967.

Table 2 *The equilibrium pressures of sodium sulphate dissociation products*

(a) *In dry nitrogen, total pressure 1 atm*

T/K	$p(Na)/atm$	$p(Na_2O)/atm$	$p(NaO)/atm$	$p(SO_2)/atm$	$p(O_2)/atm$	$p(Na_2SO_4)/atm$	$\Sigma p/atm$	p_{tot}/atm	$\dfrac{p(Na_2SO_4)}{\Sigma p}$ %
1000	5.5×10^{-10}	2.4×10^{-18}	7.41×10^{-16}	2.75×10^{-10}	2.75×10^{-10}	2.08×10^{-10}	7.58×10^{-10}	1.31×10^{-9}	27.4
1200	2.88×10^{-7}	6.03×10^{-14}	6.46×10^{-12}	1.44×10^{-7}	1.44×10^{-7}	8.09×10^{-8}	3.69×10^{-7}	6.57×10^{-7}	21.9
1500	1.12×10^{-4}	1.70×10^{-9}	5.50×10^{-8}	5.60×10^{-5}	5.60×10^{-5}	3.15×10^{-5}	1.43×10^{-4}	2.55×10^{-4}	22.0
1800	6.08×10^{-3}	1.26×10^{-6}	2.00×10^{-5}	3.04×10^{-3}	3.04×10^{-3}	1.68×10^{-3}	7.76×10^{-3}	1.38×10^{-2}	21.6

(b) *In nitrogen containing 1% water, total pressure 1 atm*

T/K	$p(Na)/atm$	$p(SO_2)/atm$	$p(O_2)/atm$	$p(NaOH)/atm$	$p(Na_2SO_4)/atm$	$\Sigma p/atm$	p_{tot}/atm	$\dfrac{p(Na_2SO_4)}{\Sigma p}$ %
1000	6.2×10^{-11}	3.4×10^{-8}	1.7×10^{-8}	6.8×10^{-8}	2.08×10^{-10}	6.8×10^{-8}	1.19×10^{-7}	0.3
1200	1.5×10^{-8}	3.8×10^{-6}	1.9×10^{-6}	7.6×10^{-6}	8.09×10^{-8}	7.7×10^{-6}	1.34×10^{-5}	1.0
1500	2.1×10^{-5}	4.3×10^{-4}	2.2×10^{-4}	8.5×10^{-4}	3.15×10^{-5}	9.0×10^{-4}	1.55×10^{-3}	3.5
1800	2.8×10^{-3}	9.0×10^{-3}	5.1×10^{-3}	1.5×10^{-2}	1.68×10^{-3}	2.0×10^{-2}	3.41×10^{-2}	8.4

in nitrogen and air taking the values from the plateau of the curve of apparent pressure against flow rate. The accuracy is not very good but the results are quite consistent with those of Cubicciotti, and with those of Fryxell et al.,[15] who used air as the carrier. Cubicciotti and Keneshea report their best line for the vapour pressure as $\log[p(Na_2SO_4)/atm] = (5.858 \pm 0.15) - (15540 \pm 380)/T$ in the temperature range 1400–1625 K, giving $\Delta H_{vap} = 70.9 \pm 1.8$ kcal mol^{-1}, and $\Delta S_{vap} = 26.6 \pm 0.7$ cal mol^{-1} K^{-1}. Fryxell et al. give log $[p(Na_2SO_4)/atm]$ $= (6.04 \pm 0.55) - (15866 \pm 765)/T$ in the temperature range 1230–1480 K, giving $\Delta H_{vap} = 72.6$ kcal mol^{-1} and $\Delta S_{vap} = 27.6$ cal mol^{-1} K^{-1}.

The Knudsen effusion data all extrapolate to give values for the molten sulphate at least an order of magnitude higher than the transpiration results. The discrepancy cannot be explained by the high vacuum conditions used in the effusion method as the extent of dissociation of the vapour should be the same as in a dry nitrogen atmosphere at the same temperature. The discrepancies of the effusion data between themselves lead to doubts about their accuracy.

It would be more satisfactory if results from the two methods agreed. However, there are a group of three independent transpiration determinations in the temperature range of interest which are consistent and which must be taken as giving the best available value for $p(Na_2SO_4)$. The results of Cubicciotti and Keneshea have been used with the temperature range widened to cover the range 1200–1750 K, encompassing the temperature limits of all three sets. Using this vapour pressure equation the values of log K_p quoted in JANAF Tables for $Na_2SO_4(l)$ have been extended to the vapour phase using the relationship (6).

$$\log K_p (Na_2SO_4, g) = \log K_p (Na_2SO_4, l) + \log p(Na_2SO_4) \qquad (6)$$

Basis of Calculation of Equilibrium Gas Composition

The significant elements in the waste gas are the minority elements sodium, sulphur, and chlorine. The species containing these elements which have been considered as being possibly present in the waste gas are:

Containing sodium: NaO, Na_2O, NaOH, NaCl, Na_2CO_3, Na_2SO_4, Na
Containing sulphur: SO_2, SO_3, Na_2SO_4
Containing chlorine: HCl, NaCl

In view of the relatively high oxygen content of the gas more reduced sulphur compounds were not considered. Calculation showed that the amounts of elemental sodium and of disodium oxide (Na_2O) in a gas containing over 10% water are negligibly small.

The amounts of the other species present at equilibrium within the temperature range 1000–1800 K are calculated as follows: (a) assume initially that all the sodium, sulphur, and chlorine are present as NaOH, SO_2, and HCl (the 'primary' species); (b) write equations expressing the formation of the other possible compounds ('secondary' species) from these primary species and evaluate the equilibrium constants for these reactions within the temperature range from the available thermodynamic information (summarized in Table 3a); (c) write the mass balance equations for the minority species allowing for the possibility of condensation of Na_2SO_4, Na_2CO_3, and NCl (Table 3b). the amounts of the majority species are so large as to be essentially constant;

(d) solve simultaneously the equilibrium and mass balance equations with the constraints that the amounts of Na_2SO_4, Na_2CO_3, and NaCl in the gas cannot exceed the concentrations given by the saturated vapour pressures of the compounds at the temperature of calculation. The vapour pressure data used are given in Table 3c.

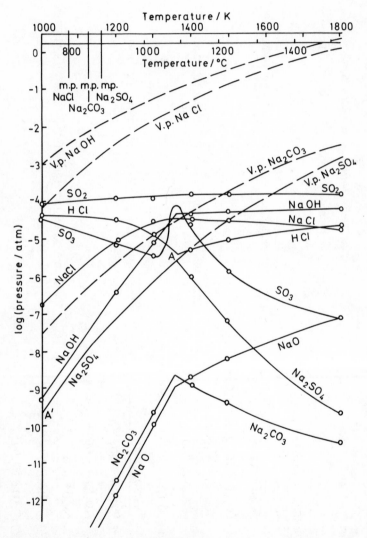

Figure 2 *The equilibrium pressure of materials in the waste gas from a gas-fired flat glass furnace. The solid lines represent the variation of* log (pressure/atm) *with temperatures of the indicated species. The broken lines indicate the variation of* log (vapour pressure/atm) *with temperature of the pure compounds. The gas is saturated with* Na_2SO_4 *in the range* A–A'

Table 3 Thermodynamic data used in waste-gas equilibrium calculation

(a) Reactions

Equilibrium equations

			Equilibrium constant at temperature/K			
Reactions	1000	1200	1300	1400	1500	1800
(1) $NaOH(g) + HCl(g) \rightarrow NaCl(g) + H_2O(g)$ $K_1 = \dfrac{n_{NaCl}\, n_{H_2O}}{n_{NaOH}\, n_{HCl}}$	1.05×10^6	9.38×10^4	3.72×10^4	1.65×10^4	8.28×10^3	1.64×10^3
(2) $2NaOH(g) + CO_2(g) \rightarrow Na_2CO_3(g) + H_2O(g)$ $K_2 = \dfrac{n_{Na_2CO_3}\, n_{H_2O}\,(n)}{(n_{NaOH})^2\, n_{CO_2}}$	1.02×10^4	3.52×10^1	4.90×10^0	9.77×10^{-1}	2.51×10^{-1}	1.28×10^{-2}
(3) $2NaOH(g) + SO_2(g) + {}^1/_2\,O_2(g) \rightarrow Na_2SO_4(g) + H_2O(g)$ $K_3 = \dfrac{n_{Na_2SO_4}\, n_{H_2O}\,(n)^{3/2}}{(n_{NaOH})^2\, n_{SO_2}\,(n_{O_2})^{1/2}}$	1.77×10^{14}	2.84×10^9	5.62×10^7	1.64×10^6	8.93×10^4	1.19×10^2
(4) $NaOH(g) + {}^1/_4\,O_2(g) \rightarrow NaO(g) + {}^1/_2\,H_2O(g)$ $K_4 = \dfrac{n_{NaO}\,(n_{H_2O})^{1/2}\,(n)^{-1/4}}{n_{NaOH}\,(n_{O_2})^{1/4}}$	7.88×10^{-8}	2.66×10^{-6}	1.03×10^{-5}	3.28×10^{-5}	8.98×10^{-5}	9.47×10^{-4}
(5) $SO_2(g) + {}^1/_2\,O_2(g) \rightarrow SO_3(g)$ $K_5 = \dfrac{n_{SO_3}\,(n)^{1/2}}{n_{SO_2}\,(n_{O_2})^{1/2}}$	1.82×10^0	2.59×10^{-1}	1.23×10^{-1}	6.52×10^{-2}	3.80×10^{-2}	1.06×10^{-2}

(b) *Mass balance equations*

$q_{NaOH} = n_{NaOH} + n_{NaCl} + 2n_{Na_2SO_4} + 2n_{Na_2CO_3} + D_{NaCl} + 2D_{Na_2SO_4} + 2D_{Na_2CO_3}$

$q_{SO_2} = n_{SO_2} + n_{SO_3} + n_{Na_2SO_4} + D_{Na_2SO_4}$

$q_{HCl} = n_{HCl} + n_{NaCl} + D_{NaCl}$

(c) *Vapour Pressure Data*

		Ref.	Vapour pressure/atm at temperature/K					
			1000	1200	1300	1400	1500	1800
NaOH	$\log P = \dfrac{-7.520}{T} + 4.55$	16	1.07×10^{-3}	1.92×10^{-2}	5.82×10^{-2}	1.51×10^{-1}	3.44×10^{-1}	2.35
NaCl	$\log P = \dfrac{-11.530}{T} - 3.48 \log T + 17.89$	16	6.74×10^{-5}	3.69×10^{-3}	1.53×10^{-2}	8.49×10^{-2}	1.41×10^{-1}	1.43
Na_2SO_4	$\log P = \dfrac{-1.554 \times 10^4}{T} + 5.86$	14	2.09×10^{-10}	8.32×10^{-8}	8.13×10^{-7}	5.74×10^{-6}	3.16×10^{-5}	1.70×10^{-3}
Na_2CO_3	$\log P = \dfrac{-1.15 \times 10^4}{T} + 3.96$	11	2.88×10^{-8}	2.40×10^{-6}	1.29×10^{-5}	5.56×10^{-5}	1.95×10^{-4}	3.71×10^{-3}

Nomenclature

n_i = equilibrium amount of species i in system. (n) = total number of moles in system at equilibrium.

q_j = total number of moles of 'primary species' j in system initially. D_k = equilibrium amount of species k condensed.

Results and Discussion

The results of the calculation of the equilibrium partial pressures of the chemical species present in the gas of overall composition given in Table 1 are illustrated in Figure 2. This Figure and Figure 3 show how the distribution of the available sodium in the system varies with the temperature; Figure 3 also illustrates the variation in the amount of sodium which has condensed as sodium sulphate.

From the graphs it can be seen that at the highest temperature (1800 K) virtually all the sodium is present as either NaOH (79%) or NaCl (21%). The amount present as Na_2SO_4 is $3.4 \times 10^{-4}\%$ and there is even less Na_2CO_3. NaO accounts for about $10^{-1}\%$ of the sodium content of the gas.

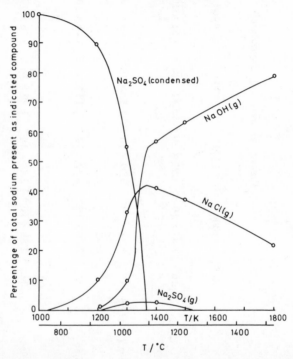

Figure 3 *The distribution of sodium between different compounds in the waste gas from a gas-fired flat glass furnace*

As the gas cools both sodium sulphate and sodium carbonate are formed increasingly by reactions (2) and (3) (Table 3). At 1400 K the concentration of Na_2SO_4 has increased by a factor of 10^4 but nevertheless it only accounts for 2.4% of the sodium. At a slightly lower temperature (point A in Figure 2, $T \sim$ 1360 K) the concentration of Na_2SO_4 has risen to a level at which the gas is just saturated with Na_2SO_4. On further cooling below this temperature the concentration of Na_2SO_4 follows the vapour pressure curve AA' and increasing amounts of sulphate condense, as can be seen in Figure 3. By 1200 K 90% of the sodium originally in the gas has condensed as sulphate, and by 1000 K virtually 100%.

The condensation of the sodium sulphate reduces the total amount of sodium in the gas phase and thus brings about sharp reductions in the concentrations of NaOH and Na_2CO_3 and a more gradual reduction in the NaCl concentration as the temperature falls. The NaO concentration decreases with temperature before the onset of sulphate condensation. This decrease, together with that due to the overall removal of sodium from the gas phase by condensation, reduces its concentration to a negligible amount.

It is worth re-emphasizing that the molecule Na_2SO_4 is always a minor component of the gas phase. That sodium sulphate is deposited from the cooling gas is due to a combination of two factors: (i) the increasing stability of the Na_2SO_4 molecule in the gas as the temperature falls, and (ii) the fact that sodium sulphate has the lowest vapour pressure of the sodium-containing compounds present in the system. The major sodium-containing compound in the gas phase at temperatures above the sodium sulphate saturation temperature is NaOH, as Figure 3 illustrates.

Effect of Variation in SO_2 *Concentration.* As can be seen from equation (3) (Table 3a) an atomic ratio of S : Na of 1 : 2 just provides sufficient sulphur to deposit all the sodium as Na_2SO_4. The calculation to date has been based on a S : Na ratio of approximately 2 : 1, a four-fold excess of sulphur over sodium. The sulphur content of the waste gas can be appreciably greater than this if the furnace is oil-fired and can be less in a gas-fired furnace if the sodium sulphate content of the raw material is lowered.

Calculation shows that an increase in the proportion of SO_2 by a factor of 10 from $q_{SO_2} = 10^{-1}$ to 1.0, that is a change in vol % SO_2 from 1.6×10^{-2} to 1.6×10^{-1}, which encompasses the change from gas to oil firing, does not affect the situation appreciably. The amount of Na_2SO_4 in the gas is generally increased by a factor of 10 at the expense of the NaOH, and this leads to an increase in the temperature of condensation of Na_2SO_4 of about 50 K; the larger excess of sulphur over sodium generally ensures that at a given temperature a larger proportion of the sodium has condensed as sulphate.

Reduction of the sulphur content of the gas by a factor of 10 lowers the S : Na ratio to 1 : 5, and there is now insufficient sulphur to deposit all the sodium as sulphate. The effect of this on the chemistry of the system can be seen in Figure 4. The broken lines labelled III illustrate the situation with $q_{SO_2} = 10^{-2}$. Despite the reduction in sulphur content it is still sodium sulphate which first condenses, but at a lower temperature (point C, Figure 4), and this is also the case if the sulphur is reduced to 1/100th of the base figure ($SO_2 = 10^{-3}$, point D, Figure 4). However, because of the sulphur limitation the maximum amounts of sodium which can be removed as condensed sulphate are 38.5 and 3.85% respectively. The remaining sodium is likely to be deposited as sodium carbonate.

The sodium carbonate concentration in the gas rises as the temperature falls but less rapidly than that of the sodium sulphate. At temperatures above the condensation temperature of the sulphate the carbonate concentration is virtually independent of the SO_2 concentration. With the onset of Na_2SO_4 condensation the sodium content of the gas falls, and with it the Na_2CO_3 concentration (lines A'–A' and B'–B'). In case III, where there is insufficient sulphur to deposit all the sodium, the reduction in sodium content of the gas is less marked, and whilst it slows down the rise in Na_2CO_3 concentration the saturation concentration of Na_2CO_3 is reached at some temperature just above 1000 K (*ca.* 1020 K, point C' in Figure 4).

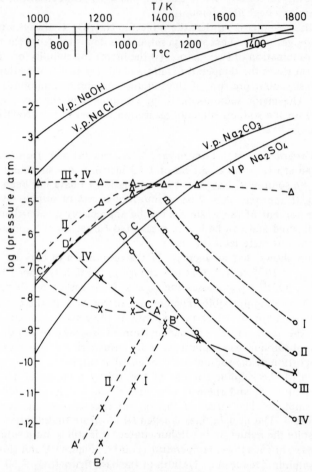

Figure 4 *The effect of sulphur content on the equilibrium pressure of sodium compounds in the waste gas. The solid lines represent the variation of* log (*vapour pressure*/atm) *with temperature of the four compounds. The broken lines represent the variation of* log (*pressure*/atm) *with temperature of three sodium compounds:* △ NaCl, ○ Na_2SO_4, *and* × Na_2CO_3 *at four concentrations of* SO_2 I = 1.0, II = 10^{-1}, III = 10^{-2}, *and* IV = 10^{-3} mol vol^{-1} *of* SO_2

The amount of sodium sulphate deposited decreases as the sulphur content decreases, and thus the amount of sodium remaining in the gas at a given temperature increases, and with it the Na_2CO_3 concentration. Because of this the deposition temperature of the sodium carbonate rises. In case IV ($SO_2 = 10^{-3}$) the sodium carbonate deposits at 1100 K (point D'). If there is no sulphur at all in the gas there will be no deposit of Na_2SO_4, and the first material to deposit as the gas cools will be Na_2CO_3. This will also occur at a temperature very close to D'.

Where the sulphur content is low, the NaCl concentration remains practically constant as the temperature falls (dotted line, Figure 4); the formation and deposition of sulphate and carbonate are at the expense of the NaOH in the gas. By extrapolation of the NaCl vapour pressure curve to temperatures below 1000 K it is clear from Figure 4 that sodium chloride itself will also condense at about 980 K. When the temperature has dropped to 800 K more than 99% of the chloride in the gas has condensed as NaCl, and this deposited NaCl accounts for 47% of the total sodium.

There is marked contrast with higher concentrations of SO_2, I and II; when there is excess SO_2, the NaCl concentration remains fairly constant until there is a marked drop in the total sodium content due to Na_2SO_4 deposition. Thereafter a combination of reactions (1) and (3), namely reaction (7), decomposes

$$2NaCl(g) + SO_2(g) + \tfrac{1}{2}O_2(g) + H_2O(g) \rightarrow Na_2SO_4(l) + 2HCl(g) \qquad (7)$$

the NaCl with deposition of the sodium as sulphate and evolution of the chloride as HCl in the waste gas. Hence where there is excess SO_2 the chloride in the waste gas is emitted with the waste gas as HCl; where there is insufficient SO_2 to react with all the sodium in the waste gas the chloride condenses as NaCl and there is no HCl emission.

The variations of the composition and condensation temperature of the deposits with SO_2 concentration are summarized as a bar chart in Figure 5, in which the amounts deposited within 50 K temperature intervals are plotted against temperature. Comparison of Figures 5(a) and 5(b) illustrates the difference between the situations with an excess and with a deficiency of SO_2.

Effect of Variation in Sodium Content of Gas. In assessing the effect of a variation in SO_2 concentration the total concentration of sodium compounds in the gas has been kept constant. The effect of reducing the sodium content of the gas at a fixed SO_2 level can be summarized as follows. (i) At temperatures above the condensation temperature the main effect is a reduction in the concentration of the sodium-containing compounds in the gas approximately proportional to the reduction in total sodium concentration, with the exception of NaCl whose change in concentration is much less sensitive to change in total sodium concentration. (ii) The deposition temperature of the Na_2SO_4 is decreased because of the lower Na_2SO_4 concentration at a given temperature, but the change is quite small, being only about 30 K for a reduction in total sodium content of 25%. (iii) If there is an excess of sulphur over sodium then the total amount of Na_2SO_4 condensed is reduced by exactly the amount of the reduction in sodium content of the gas; if there is an excess of sodium over sulphur the total amount of Na_2SO_4 condensed is unchanged but the amounts of Na_2CO_3 and NaCl condensed are reduced. In fact in the situation illustrated by line III in Figure 4 ($SO_4 = 10^{-2}$) a reduction of the total sodium content by 25%

leads to the condensation of a reduced amount of NaCl but to no condensation of Na_2CO_3, the Na_2CO_3 concentration never reaching saturation.

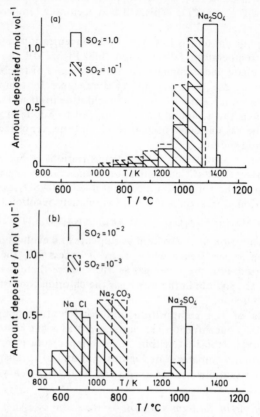

Figure 5 *The relative amounts of material condensing from waste gas within 50 K temperature intervals. Diagram (a) shows the effect of a ten-fold change of SO_2 concentration when there is an excess of S over Na in the gas. Diagram (b) shows the different situation at two SO_2 levels at which there is an excess of Na over S in the gas*

The influence of the S : Na ratio is a notable feature of the chemistry of the hot gas. When there is an excess of sulphur over sodium the chemical changes are dominated by the condensation of Na_2SO_4 and the ultimate conversion of all sodium compounds into the condensed sulphate as the temperature falls. However, when there is an excess of sodium over sulphur the chemistry also depends upon the relative amount of chlorine present. If the excess of sodium over sulphur is stoicheiometrically greater than the chlorine content of the gas then the chlorine effectively forms a 'sodium chloride' subsystem which is not greatly influenced by the chemical changes occurring in the other subsystem formed by the remaining sodium and available sulphur. The $NaCl-H_2O$ equilibrium given by equation (1) in Table 3, *i.e.* reaction (8), is relatively independent of

$$NaOH(g) + HCl(g) \rightarrow NaCl(g) + H_2O(g) \qquad (8)$$

temperature, and the NaCl concentration remains fairly constant until the gas becomes saturated with NaCl (see for example the line for NaCl at $SO_2 = 10^{-2}$ in Figure 4). Thus at low SO_2 levels one can distinguish between an effect of the reduction in sodium content alone, which leads to changes in the amounts of sodium carbonate and chloride deposited as discussed above, and a reduction of the 'sodium chloride' content, *i.e.* a reduction of sodium content and an equivalent reduction in chlorine content. The only effect of a reduction in 'sodium chloride' content at low SO_2 levels is on the sodium chloride subsystem and results in a reduction both of the amount of chloride deposited and of its deposition temperature, the amounts of sodium sulphate and carbonate being virtually unchanged.

Summary

The equilibrium composition of the waste gases leaving a flat glass furnace has been calculated at a number of temperatures in the range 1000–1800 K using tabulated high-temperature thermodynamic data together with data for $Na_2SO_4(g)$ based on an assessment of the literature values for the vapour pressure of sodium sulphate. The calculation shows that at temperatures above that at which material first condenses from the gas the vast majority ($> 95\%$) of the sodium present in the gas is as NaOH(g) and NaCl(g). This is so whether the furnace is fired by oil or by gas. $Na_2SO_4(g)$ is always a minor component of the gas phase. Nevertheless it is sodium sulphate which first condenses from the cooling gas owing to a combination of two factors, (a) the increasing stability of the $Na_2SO_4(g)$ molecule as the temperature falls and (b) the fact that sodium sulphate has the lowest vapour pressure of the sodium-containing compounds present in the system.

With a stoicheiometric excess of sulphur over sodium in the waste gas, the condition normally found even in a gas-fired furnace, all the sodium in the waste gas should condense as sulphate. With an excess of sodium over sulphur all the sulphur should condense as sodium sulphate, the excess sodium condensing at lower temperatures as sodium carbonate and chloride. With 'excess sodium' the NaCl component of the gas is little affected by the condensation of other sodium compounds and its concentration remains fairly constant until the gas temperature falls to the point at which the NaCl(g) concentration just exceeds the vapour pressure and sodium chloride condenses. With 'excess sulphur' the NaCl(g) along with other sodium compounds is converted into condensed sodium sulphate and the chlorine leaves the system as gaseous HCl.

This paper is published with the permission of the Directors of Pilkington Brothers Limited and Dr. D. S. Oliver, Director of Group Research and Development.

The Application of Thermochemical Principles to the Production of Nuclear Fuel Materials

By G. R. CHILTON

RDL Windscale and Calder Works, Seascale, Cumbria

Introduction

Ceramic fuels are now dominating nuclear power programmes throughout the world. Uranium dioxide is the current choice for thermal reactors, whether water-cooled or gas-cooled. Solid solutions of urania–plutonia (with compositions in the range 20–30% Pu) are the preferred fast reactor fuels. Of possible advanced fast reactor fuels, considerable interest is being shown in the mixed uranium–plutonium monocarbides, while uranium monocarbide is under consideration for the breeder blanket as an alternative to uranium dioxide.

The manufacture of these fast reactor fuels offers several examples of the application of thermochemical principles to achieve the desired fuel composition. In oxide fuel solid solutions of urania–plutonia can exist over a wide range of plutonium concentrations and oxygen : metal ratios. It has been established that oxides with an oxygen to metal (O/M) ratio (M = U+Pu) near or a little below 2.00 have the most suitable properties to minimize the chemical and physical interactions with the stainless steel cladding which are the important life-limiting processes leading to rupture of the cladding and failure of the fuel element. Unfortunately, complicating factors make it difficult to establish an ideal initial fuel stoicheiometry. Not only does oxygen re-distribute radially owing to temperature gradients in the pile, but also the average O/M ratio of the fuel rises steadily during irradiation because the oxygen created during fission of the heavy atoms is not taken up completely by the fission product elements. Thus the problem for the fuel fabricator is to be able to produce a range of oxide fuels of precisely controlled stoicheiometry ranging from the minimum possible (O/M ratio 1.85 in $U_{0.7}Pu_{0.3}$ oxide) through near-stoicheiometric levels to hyperstoicheiometric fuels which are required for small-scale irradiation and materials property testing.

For monocarbides, the optimum stoicheiometry is again difficult to establish; recommended compositions range from stoicheiometric monocarbide to those containing over 30% of the M_2C_3 phase. In this case, precise control of stoicheiometry is achieved using basic thermochemical data to predict the conditions for the conversion of oxide into carbide and the formation of CO.

Oxide Fuels

Fast reactor oxide core fuel is manufactured in the form of either sintered pellets or granules which are contained in stainless steel cladding to form the fuel 'pin' or fuel 'rod'. The fabrication process for these oxide fuels closely follows established ceramic manufacturing processes, the essential stages being calcination followed by ball-milling of the raw powder, binder addition, and granulation into free-flowing agglomerates. This material is either pressed into pellets which are then sintered, or classified and used for the production of sintered granules. The organic binder, usually added to aid granulation and pressing, is removed by a low-temperature treatment in CO_2 prior to sintering at temperatures between 1500 and 1650 °C. It is at this last sintering stage that the stoicheiometry of the oxide has to be adjusted by making use of the oxidizing or reducing potential of the sintering atmosphere.

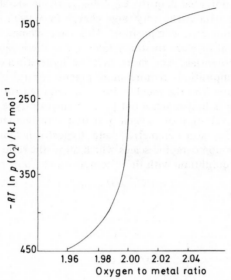

Figure 1 *Oxygen potentials for* $U_{0.75}Pu_{0.25}$ *oxides at* 1550 °C

For the control of stoicheiometry the fuel manufacturer relies on the oxygen potential data for the mixed oxide. These data are required over the whole range of temperatures to which the oxide is exposed during sintering. Extensive data for the U–O system are available.[1-3] For the urania–plutonia system the data are more sparse. Markin and McIver[4] measured the oxygen potentials of U–Pu oxides up to 1150 °C using an EMF technique. More recently these measurements have been extended to the higher temperatures for both the hyperstoicheiometric oxide[5] and the hypostoicheiometric oxide.[6,8] At lower temperatures ($<$ 1150

[1] R. J. Bones and T. L. Markin, *UKAEA Reports*, AERE-R4042 (1962), AERE-R4178 (1962) Part II, AERE-R5560 (1967).

[2] R. J. Bones, T. L. Markin, and V. J. Wheeler, *J. Inorg. Nuclear Chem.*, 1968, **30**, 807

[3] V. J. Wheeler, *J. Nuclear Materials*, 1971, **39**, 315

[4] T. L. Markin and E. J. McIver, 'Plutonium, 1965', Chapman and Hall, London, 1967, p. 845

[5] G. R. Chilton and I. A. Kirkham, 'Proceedings of the 5th International Conference on Plutonium and Other Actinides, 1975', North Holland, Amsterdam, 1976.

[6] R. E. Woodley, HEDL-TME 72-85

[7] N. A. Javed and J. T. A. Roberts, ANL-7901

[8] M. Tetenbaum, 'Thermodynamics of Nuclear Materials, 1974', IAEA, Vienna, 1975, Vol. II, p. 305

°C), Markin and McIver found that the oxygen potential data were identical for U–Pu oxides, containing between 10 and 30% plutonium, when plotted in terms of uranium valency in the hyperstoicheiometric region and plutonium valency in the hypostoicheiometric region. At higher temperatures this simple relationship breaks down and a knowledge of the oxygen potential associated with oxides of each particular composition is required for precise control of the stoicheiometry.

Typical oxygen potential data for $U_{0.75}Pu_{0.25}$ oxide are shown in Figure 1. A feature of these data is the very large change in oxygen potential on either side of the stoicheiometric composition. This large change simplifies the production of oxides at or close to stoicheiometry, as these can exist over a wide range of oxygen potentials. The more extreme hyperstoicheiometric or hypostoicheiometric compositions require more precise control of oxygen potential in their manufacture. The thermochemical data required for the production of these compositions is best represented by an Ellingham-type diagram shown in Figure 2. Here the variation of oxygen potential with temperature is shown for hyperstoicheiometric, stoicheiometric, and hypostoicheiometric oxides. The figure also includes nomographic scales which allow the ratio of CO to CO_2 and of H_2 to H_2O, in equilibrium with these compositions, to be read directly at any temperature.

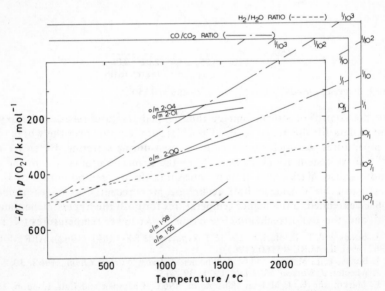

Figure 2 *Oxygen potentials for* $U_{0.75}Pu_{0.25}$ *oxides and* H_2–H_2O, CO–CO_2 *mixtures*

Hyperstoicheiometric Oxides. Oxygen potentials of around 200 kJ mol^{-1} O_2 are required for the production of hyperstoicheiometric oxides at sintering temperatures of 1500–1650 °C. Examination of Figure 2 shows that oxygen potentials of this level are produced by CO–CO_2 mixtures in the range 1/10 to

1/1. These can be estimated directly from the nomographs or calculated precisely from standard thermochemical data. The alternative gas system $H_2 - H_2O$ is unattractive since the main component is steam, which would create many practical difficulties if it were to be used as a furnace sintering atmosphere. A mixture of CO and CO_2 is therefore preferable. The progress of the oxidation in a batch furnace is monitored by measurement of the oxygen potential of the $CO-CO_2$ gas as it leaves the furnace, using a calcia-stabilized zirconia EMF cell.

As the oxide cools after sintering, the oxygen potential of the oxide deviates from that of the sintering atmosphere (Figure 2). This can result in significant loss of oxygen to the $CO-CO_2$ and a final stoicheiometry lower than intended. In practice the desired stoicheiometry attained at the sintering temperature does not significantly alter, provided that cooling occurs in a *static* atmosphere; although this equilibrates with the oxide, no significant change in composition occurs.

Stoicheiometric Oxides. Problems associated with the fabrication of the stoiche-iometric oxides are reduced since the large range of oxygen potentials over which the oxide is stable allows more latitude in choice of sintering atmosphere. Pure hydrogen can be used for urania since, at normal sintering temperatures, the oxide cannot be reduced significantly below the stoicheiometric composition. In the U-Pu oxide system stoicheiometric compositions probably exist over the range $-250 \pm 20 \, \text{kJ mol}^{-1}$ O_2 at sintering temperatures. Oxygen potentials of this level are produced by CO : CO_2 ratios ranging from $\sim 4 : 1$ to $1 : 2$. Alternatively, this level of oxygen potential can be produced by dilution of water-saturated hydrogen with an inert gas, usually argon.

As with the hyperstoicheiometric oxide the adjustment to stoicheiometric composition can be monitored using an EMF cell during the sintering operation. The wide range of oxygen potentials over which the stoicheiometric oxide is stable allows the cooling part of the sintering cycle to be carried out in the same atmosphere as was used for adjustment of the stoicheiometry at sintering temperature.

Hypostoicheiometric Oxides. The oxygen potential of the furnace gas which is required for the production of these compositions can be produced using either hydrogen or hydrogen diluted to a safe limit with argon. The safety requirements for the operation of sintering furnaces for urania-plutonia preclude the use of undiluted hydrogen in all except the smallest furnaces and then only with ade-quate safety precautions and carefully monitored conditions. The use of diluted hydrogen means that the speed of reduction potential at a given flow rate is reduced in direct proportion to the dilution.

To obtain significant reduction of the oxide, atmospheres with lower oxygen potentials than the equilibrium potential are used and the flow rate, time, throughput rate, and temperature balanced to give the correct O/M ratio.

The kinetics of this reduction process are much simpler than those of the oxidation process where surface reactions limit the oxidation rate. Lay[9] found that at low temperatures (up to 1100 °C) the reduction rate was limited by the

[9] K. W. Lay *J. Amer. Ceram. Soc.*, 1970, **30**, 369

oxygen diffusion rate. Lindemer and Bradley[10] found that at higher tempera-tures, normally encountered in sintering, reduction was controlled by the hydrogen flow rate. Assuming that the H_2 : H_2O ratio of the gas in the furnace was in equilibrium with the instantaneous stoicheiometry of the oxide, they calculated a theoretical reduction rate by integrating the incremental times required to accomplish a stepwise reduction. For this calculation they used an extrapolation of the early low-temperature oxygen potential data. The equation for the reduction time (t) was expressed as equation (1), where N = mols of oxide,

$$t = 11.208 \frac{Nx}{f_{H_2}} \int_{4}^{V_{Pu}} H \, d(V_{Pu}) \tag{1}$$

f_{H_2} = hydrogen flow in l/unit time, x = Pu: (U + Pu) ratio, V_{Pu} = valency state of the Pu in the reduced oxide, and H = H_2 : H_2O ratio existing during the incremental reduction. The integral term was evaluated for temperatures up to 1727 °C and plutonium valencies between 3.95 and 3.00.

The differences between the calculated and observed reduction rates were attributed to errors in extrapolation of the low-temperature data. However, by using recently obtained and probably more accurate values of the oxygen poten-tials at high temperatures, these differences have been considerably reduced.

In practice the use of an equation based on thermochemical data helps the fuel manufacturer to select a combination of reduction temperature, time, and flow rate of reducing gas that is compatible with furnace operation.

Carbide Fuels

Mixed uranium and plutonium carbide ceramic materials, used as nuclear fuels, are seldom in the form of pure monocarbides but can contain second phases of higher carbides M_2C_3 and MC_2, as well as significant quantities of oxygen held in solid solution in the monocarbide phase. A true two-phase mixture of the monoxycarbide with free oxide is under investigation in the U.K.: it is intended as the fuel in a sodium-bonded fuel pin design, that is a fuel pin in which liquid sodium provides an efficient heat transfer medium between fuel and the stainless steel clad. Whatever composition is used, the quantity of second phase must be carefully controlled and the formation of free uranium—plutonium metal must be avoided.

To make high-density carbide pellets or granules, a low-density 'coke' is first prepared by the carbothermic reduction of the oxide using elemental carbon under vacuum or flowing gas conditions. The product is comminuted in a high-energy vibro mill to produce a sinterable powder which is subsequently granu-lated and then either classified into the correct size range and sintered into granules for direct vibro compaction into fuel pins or pressed into pellets and sintered.

An alternative 'single stage' route exists for the manufacture of monocarbide granules where an intimate blend of oxide and carbon in granular form reacts and is sintered in one operation. This route has the advantage of avoiding the intermediate comminution and regranulation stage necessary for carbide powder,

[10] T. B. Lindemer and R. A. Bradley, *J. Nuclear Materials*, 1971, **41**, 293

but has the disadvantage that the granules produced are of a lower density than that achieved in the two-stage process.

Two of the main problems associated with the manufacture of monocarbides are (i) control of reaction rate and (ii) composition control. The former is of particular importance to the manufacture of 'single stage' monocarbides where the aim is to ensure the completion of the carbothermic reduction process before sintering commences, in order to obtain the most dense product. The final composition of the monocarbide is determined by the initial oxide to carbon ratio and the extent of reaction. If the process is stopped too early the product contains excess free oxide and higher carbides and will not be stable in the nuclear reactor. If the reaction goes too far, under certain circumstances, free uranium–plutonium metal can be formed which could be very detrimental to the fuel performance.

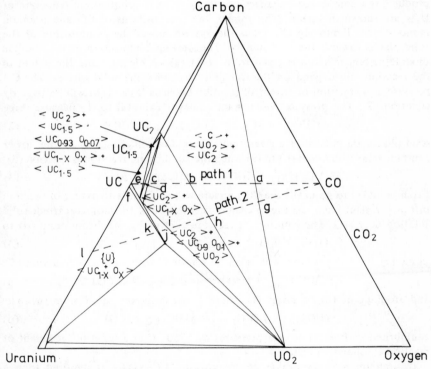

Figure 3 *The* U–C–O *phase diagram at* 1300 – 1750 °C

Control of the extent of reaction and reaction rate are both closely associated with changes in the carbon monoxide overpressure in the reaction vessel. Ainsley *et al.*[11] studied the effect of carbon monoxide overpressure on reaction rate. Relative to the rate at zero pressure, a CO pressure 0.1 of the equilibrium value

[11] R. Ainsley, B. R. Harder, N. Hodge, R. G. Sowden, D. B. White, and D. C. Wood, 'New Nuclear Materials including non-metallic fuels', IAEA, Vienna, 1963, p. 349

halved the reaction rate while at a CO pressure 0.5 the equilibrium value the rate was reduced by 0.9.

Thermochemical data enable the calculation of the CO equilibrium pressures for the various reactions in the temperature range of interest for fuel manufacture. By adjustment of the CO overpressure and temperature the various stages in the production of carbides can be monitored and controlled. This is discussed in the following section where the use of thermochemical data to achieve the desired reaction rate and composition is demonstrated for the production of uranium monocarbide and uranium monoxycarbide, using the data reviewed and analysed by Potter.[12] The introduction of plutonium into the U–C–O system produces a more complex reaction but the same broad principles apply.

Figure 3 shows the equilibrium phase fields for the U–C–O system between 1300 and 1750 °C. If uranium monocarbide (UC) is required as the ultimate product, the composition changes occurring during carbothermic reduction of UO_2 are shown in Figure 3 by joining the compositions of CO and uranium monocarbide. Removing CO from the system moves the composition of the solid phases towards the U–C binary. The starting composition of the uranium dioxide/carbon mixture is given by a point (a) on Figure 3 and the extent of the reaction will depend on the CO pressure above the solid phases. The CO pressure as a function of extent of reaction between (a) and (b) will be given by equation (2). The pressure will remain constant from (a) to (b) because three

$$<UO_2> + 4<C> \rightleftharpoons [UC_2]_{UO_2} + 2(CO)* \qquad (2)$$

solid phases are present at a given temperature but will change to another lower constant value from point (b) to (c) when the equilibrium reaction is reaction (3).

$$3[UC_2]_{UO_2} + <UO_2> \rightleftharpoons 4[UC]_{UO} + 2(CO) \qquad (3)$$

From point (c) to point (d) the CO pressure will decrease with extent of reaction in this bivariant region as the oxygen concentration of the monoxycarbide solid solution decreases. The equilibrium reaction is given by (4). From point (d) to

$$[UO]_{UC} + 2[UC_2]_{UO_2} \rightleftharpoons 3[UC]_{UO} + (CO) \qquad (4)$$

point (e) the CO pressure will again be constant with extent of reaction (5),

$$5[UC_2]_{UO_2} + [UO]_{UC} \rightleftharpoons 6<UC_{1.5}> + (CO) \qquad (5)$$

and from point (e) to point (f), there is the bivariant equilibrium (6). The

$$[UO]_{UC} + 4<UC_{1.5}> \rightleftharpoons 5[UC]_{UO} + (CO) \qquad (6)$$

equilibrium carbon monoxide pressures at 1750 °C as a function of extent of reaction are shown in Figure 4.

If uranium monoxycarbide of composition $UC_{0.7}O_{0.3}$ is required then a starting composition of $C + UO_2$ corresponding to point (g) on reaction path 2 in Figure 3 is taken. The reaction paths cross the same phase field until point (i) is reached and from point (i) to point (j) the bivariant region U monoxycarbide + UO_2 is traversed. Here the equilibrium reaction is (7). The CO pressure will

---

[12] P. E. Potter, *J. Nuclear Materials*, 1972, **42**, 1

*Symbols: < > solid state; { } liquid state; [ ] dissolved state, suffix denotes solvent; ( ) gaseous state.

$$[UC]_{UO} + 2<UO_2> \rightleftharpoons 3[UO]_{UC} + CO \qquad (7)$$

decrease as the oxygen content of the monoxycarbide increases, and further decrease as the single-phase region (j) to (k) is traversed. At (k) the bivariant region U metal + U monoxycarbide is reached; here the CO pressure will decrease as the oxygen content of the monoxycarbide decreases from point (k) to point (l). This equilibrium is given by (8). CO equilibrium pressures for this

$$[UC]_{UO} + [UO]_{UC} \rightleftharpoons U + (CO) \qquad (8)$$

reaction path are shown on Figure 4. In the last phase field between (k) and (l) the reaction path deviates from the line joining the points representing CO to the initial C + UO_2 composition since the uranium vapour pressure exceeds the CO pressure. At lower temperatures as the extent of reaction approaches 100%, however, the contribution to the gas phase by uranium atoms is lower.

These equilibrium CO pressure data may be applied to fuel manufacture in the following ways. In the production of carbides and oxycarbides, two reduction environments are available: vacuum and purged atmosphere. The levels of CO overpressure attainable in each of these environments differ greatly. In the purge furnace the oxide–carbon mixture reacts in a rapidly flowing inert gas which sweeps away the CO formed. The minimum CO overpressure under these conditions depends on flow rate; in practice a minimum of $\sim 10^{-3}$ atm is probable. Reduction of flow rate increases the CO overpressure. Using the data provided in Figure 4 it can be seen that at 1750 °C, it is feasible to make uranium monocarbide containing little oxygen in the purge furnace. The production of uranium monoxycarbide, however, would be incomplete at 1750 °C, the reaction stopping as it approaches (j) on the reaction path.

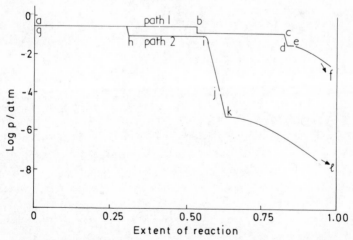

Figure 4   CO *pressure as a function of extent of reaction for the* U–C–O *system at* 1750 °C

At lower temperatures the equilibrium CO pressure is considerably reduced. At 1400 °C the CO equilibrium pressure for the reaction in the phase field of equation (2) is reduced to 3.2 × 10^{-3} atm and in that of equation (3) to

1.6 X 10^{-3} atm. Under these conditions it is just feasible to carry out reactions (2) and (3) in the purge furnace, and the composition (c) on Figure 3 is attained. Beyond this point higher temperatures are required to complete the reaction in this environment.

In vacuum systems very low CO overpressures (less than 10^{-6} atm) are attainable and considerable control of the reaction conditions can be obtained by throttling the vacuum system, thereby increasing the carbon monoxide overpressure. At 1750 °C the production of compositions in the monoxycarbide-free metal phase field are readily obtainable. At lower temperatures, around 1400 °C. complete reaction is feasible.[11] When dense UC is made by a single-stage process, complete reaction is required before extensive sintering can occur. The oxide–carbon mixtures first react at low temperatures (1400 °C) and at a pressure just below the equilibrium pressure, until reactions (2) and (3) are complete [point (c) on Figure 3]. At this point the pressure in the system begins to fall and the final reaction is completed by reducing the pressure in the reaction chamber to less than 1 X 10^{-5} atm.

The above examples illustrate the application of thermochemical principles to ceramic fuel fabrication routes now being developed on a large scale. Development and modification of these routes would require further applications of these principles.

Establishment of the basic thermochemical data helps towards a proper understanding of the processes occurring and ultimately allows the operating conditions of a full-scale preparation or sintering process to be specified with confidence.

Refractories in the Presence of Fluxes

By L. R. BARRETT

Ceramics Laboratories, Imperial College, London SW7

Introduction

A 'flux' is used to lower the temperature of fusion of a substance or mixture in which it is present or to which it is added. The term has fallen out of use in scientific circles in ceramics but the function remains, for example, the presence of alkalis in clays or borax added to ceramics to dissolve a colouring oxide at high temperatures in a kiln. Calcium fluoride is used as a flux for metallurgical processes but as a refractory container in the reduction of uranium fluoride to uranium[1] (Figure 1). Flux implies flowing, for example the flowing of metals such as in soldering, brazing, and welding where the flux keeps the metal surface clean by dissolving the oxide film which would be formed in the air. In pottery bodies (using felspar as flux) the flux enters into the body itself, conferring strength and impermeability and also into the glaze and coloured decoration. The flux permits a satisfactory degree of bonding to be achieved at comparatively modest temperatures, generally in the range 700–1250 °C.

Figure 1 *Calcium fluoride crucibles for uranium production, (the tallest measures 21 inches)*[1]

[1] P. Rado, in 'Special Ceramics', ed. P. Popper, Haywood, London, 1960, p. 237.

In pottery the flux acts at elevated temperature but is needed in the body at room temperatures (when it is essentially glassy but brittle). However, a different action is expected of the flux in liquid-phase sintering. Pure, micron-sized powders suitably pressed together can be sintered to strong, low porosity bodies, an example would be alumina, but the presence of a liquid-phase at the sintering temperature helps speed the reaction.

Extending the idea of reactive sintering to the use of a large ratio of flux to crystals, large, nearly perfect single crystals can be grown. Finally, the word 'flux' can also include the use of easily deformable substances to facilitate hot-pressing (LiF, MgO).

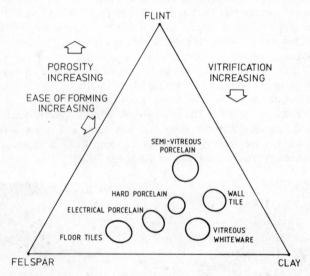

Figure 2 *Compositions of whiteware bodies on a triaxial diagram*

Fluxes in Pottery

Most pottery bodies can be visualized as consisting of three substituents; silica (flint), clays, and felspar. These can be represented either on a raw material triaxial diagram (Figure 2) or, within limits, on a phase equilibrium diagram such as that showing mullite, silica, and leucite ($K_2O.Al_2O_3.4SiO_2$), (Figure 3)[2]. One of the advantages of these bodies is their tolerance to minor changes in composition. If the temperature of firing increases a little, more silica dissolves which raises the viscosity of the liquid-phase. Therefore the body remains resistant to deformation although the proportion of liquid increases as the firing temperature rises. The lower-temperature bodies are more porous (up to 30% by volume) and reaction is far from complete, the silica being present as a filler. Even isotropic cristobalite can be distinguished from felspathic glass by its lower refractive index.

[2] W. D. Kingery, H. K. Bowen, and D. R. Uhlmann, 'Introduction to Ceramics', 2nd ed., Wiley, New York, 1976, p. 533.

The foregoing considerations have ignored the well-known observation of Mellor that 'ceramics is the study of arrested reactions'. This is particularly true of ceramic ware which is heat-treated to the point of customer acceptance. The question, 'how far does a particular reaction proceed in a given time?' must therefore be answered. In the past this has been approached rather empirically. Meyer[3] and Shelton[4], following previous work, studied the maturing of triaxial whiteware bodies particularly as regards heating rate, soaking time, and temperature. Starting with the Arrhenius equation, assuming the vitrification process to be a chemical reaction, some cumbrous expressions were derived which may be presented on a single chart (Figure 4). In this if A_{Σ}, corresponding to a certain degree of vitrification of the body, is known, other heat treatments productive of the same degree of vitrification can be deduced.

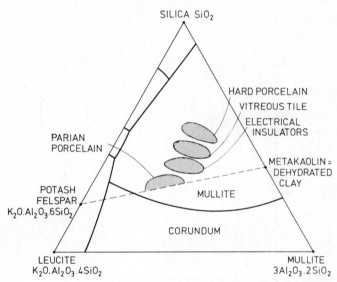

Figure 3 *Areas of triaxial whiteware composition shown on the silica–leucite–mullite phase equilibrium diagram*[2]

The decoration of glass and glazed pottery with colours, whilst not as old as the potter's craft, is lost in the mists of antiquity. Window glass in our great medieval cathedrals was self-coloured and painted. The painter's 'black flux' was a dark brown substance[5] made from iron and copper scale with green and blue lead glass as the flux. The colouring agents for the glasses were the same as those used today. Gentle heat treatment caused the paint to adhere to the glass, which was supported on lime on an iron plate and the whole fired in a oven fueled with beechwood.

[3] W. W. Meyer, *J. Amer. Ceram. Soc.*, 1938, **21**, 75.
[4] G. R. Shelton and W. W. Meyer, *J. Amer. Ceram. Soc.*, 1938, **21**, 371.
[5] F. Hermann, 'Painting on glass and porcelain' 2nd ed., translated by C. Salter, Scott Greenwood, London, 1897.

In porcelain painting the colour suffuses into the glaze, whereas in glass painting vitrifiable metallic colours are employed which are fused only on to the surface. In both classes the pigments are separate from the flux. It seems that the flux of a glassy nature may merely encapsulate the colouring oxide, as in the case of iron oxide, or it may react with it, as with copper and cobalt, to produce the colour.

Liquid-phase Sintering

In systems with a small amount of liquid-phase, typical of vitrifying ceramic

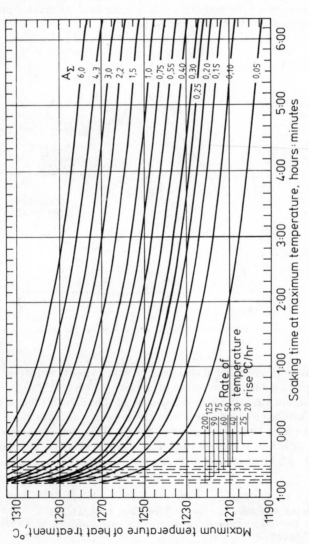

Figure 4 *Meyer's heat-treatment chart for felspathic bodies*

bodies, it has been shown by White and co-workers[6] that the rate of sintering is much greater than when liquid is absent. Thus, when 10% of the MgO—CaO—Al_2O_3 eutectic liquid was mixed with 90% of pure MgO, the sintering rate was increased 20-fold, but the mechanism of the process seems to have been unchanged since the apparent activation energy of the process was unchanged at about 175 kJ mol^{-1} which is characteristic of magnesia single phase sintering.

Most of the work carried out on sintering in the presence of a liquid-phase has been on the addition of relatively large (> 10%) fractions of liquid.[7] With such an appreciable amount of liquid present the process can be considered to occur in two stages: (i) the rearrangement of the solid particles in the liquid matrix to give a more dense body, (ii) solution of the solid at the point of contact, followed by reprecipitation. There is increased solubility at the points of contact due to the surface tension forces between the particles.

With small additions of liquid the effect of the rearrangement process will be minor compared with the solution—precipitation process and the rate controlling factor should be the diffusion of ions to the neck.

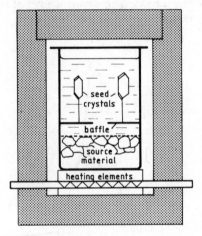

Figure 5 *Fluxed-melt growth techniques*[11]

Where appreciable quantities of liquid are present as in the firing of, for example, china, porcelain and engineering brick, processes generally similar to the dissolution of refractory crystals and glasses in slags and melts will occur. The hydrodynamic conditions will be less well defined but it may be reasonably inferred that when a felspathic (silicate) melt is dissolving silica the process will be diffusion controlled. Experimental studies of the dissolution of quartz have been handicapped because quartz cracks readily in the melt. The problem of cracking of quartz by immersion in a melt was overcome by Kreider and Cooper[8]

[6] P. W. Clark, J. H. Cannon, and J. White, *Trans. Brit. Ceram. Soc.,* 1953, **52**, 1.
[7] W. D. Kingery 'Sintering into Presence of a Liquid Phase' in 'Kinetics of High Temperature Processes', ed. W. D. Kingery, Wiley, New York, 1959, p. 187.
[8] K. G. Kreider and A. R. Cooper, *Glass Technol.,* 1967, **8**, 71.

by using very small (1 mm) spheres; these were shown to dissolve in sodium silicate by a diffusion controlled process. The solution of alumina in many silicate melts has also been shown to be diffusion controlled[9] as was the solution of silica glasses in vanadate melts.[10]

Fluxed-melt Preparation of Single Crystals

White has given a good general account of crystal growth techniques.[11] Figure 5 shows the procedures. A molten salt is used as the solvent. It should be non-volatile and readily removable by washing in water at the end of the growth run. It is essential that the solvent does not react irreversibly with the solute. Contamination by the solvent can be reduced by using a common ion for example $BaTiO_3$ is grown in $BaCl_2$ and $PbTiO_3$ in PbO. Crystallization is initiated by slow cooling in the vicinity of a seed crystal until growth begins. Some of the advantages of flux growth are: (i) the crystals are of good quality; (ii) refractory crystals can be grown at low temperatures; (iii) solid solution crystals can be grown in a controllable manner; (iv) doping agents can be homogeneously incorporated.

A recent book on this subject is recommended;[12] it is particularly good on the topic of refractory metals as resistors and containers.

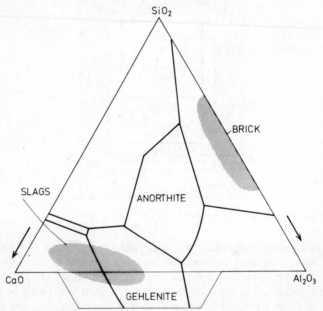

Figure 6 *Phase diagram of a part of the system* $CaO-Al_2O_3-SiO_2$ *showing the field of anorthite lying between typical blast-furnace slag and brick compositions*[13]

[9] (a) L. Reed, Ph.D. Thesis, University of London, 1952; (b) L. Reed, and L. R. Barrett, *Trans. Brit. Ceram. Soc.*, 1955, **54**, 671; *ibid.*, 1964, **63**, 509.
[10] M. Safdar, Ph.D. Thesis, University of London, 1961.
[11] E. A. D. White, *Hilger J.*, 1964, 8, 61; *ibid.*, 1965, 9, 3.
[12] D. Elwell and H. J. Scheel, 'Crystal Growth from High Temperature Solutions', Academic Press, London, 1975.

Liquid in Refractories at High Temperature

Good factual introductions to this subject are to be found in several studies. [13,14] The reaction of alumino–silicate refractories as used in blast-furnace linings were studied by Hugill. Minerals were identified in the cold bricks by petrological methods and some very fine serial micro-graphs produced. The lime-rich metallurgical slags used in the process lead to the formation of anorthite ($CaO.Al_2O_3$. $2SiO_2$) a phase intermediate in composition between blast-furnace slags and the siliceous or mullitic bricks (Figure 6). Cockbain and Johnson[14] studied the liquids in chrome–magnesite (25–55% MgO) and magnesite–chrome (55–80% MgO) bricks in the roofs of open-hearth furnaces (Figure 7). They found merwinite ($3CaO.MgO.2SiO_2$) and monticellite ($CaO.MgO.SiO_2$). Several views were formed on the action of the fluxes accumulated behind the hot-face at a temperature of some 1500–1600 °C but it is noteworthy that a roof at Bilston,

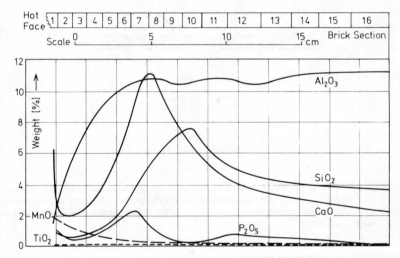

Figure 7 *Distribution of fluxes in used chrome–magnesite bricks*[14]

Staffordshire, very robustly constructed but never allowed to fluctuate more than 100–200 °C in temperature, had a phenomenal life of 2205 heatings and the hot-face was preserved intact. Conventional charging with cold scrap would bring the temperature of the hot-face down to 1000 °C and it is now possible to conclude that this might well have contributed to the 'slabbing' or peeling of the hot-face arising from the stresses set up by mismatch between the properties (for example thermal expansion) of the brick and of the flux-rich zones.

Examination in the laboratory of used bricks from the Bilston roof by Richardson and colleagues lead to the concept of a 'direct-bonded' chrome–

[13] W. Hugill and A. T. Green, 'First Report on Refractory Materials', Iron and Steel Institute Special Report No. 26, 1939, p. 295.
[14] A. G. Cockbain and W. Johnson, *Trans. Brit. Ceram. Soc.*, 1958, 57, 511.

magnesite brick[15,16]. The load-bearing characteristics of the nose of the brick were still very good, which could be explained if the flux had been removed from the points of contact between the periclase and spinel grains to ball up in the interstices. Chesters[17] reported the manufacture of a brick containing large chrome crystals, low silica to minimize flux content, and given a thermal history similar to that of the Bilston hot-face brick by firing it to the highest attainable temperature. The resulting brick performed well in use. Thus the first 'direct-bonding', that is, periclase-to-spinel intergrowth was achieved. Later, it was shown that the development of direct bonding was accompanied by a marked increase in hot tensile strength.[18]

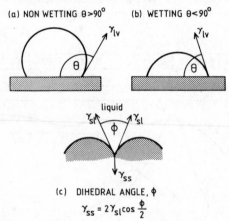

Figure 8 *(a), (b) Section through liquid drop on surface of a solid showing non-wetting (a) and wetting (b). (c) Section through two solid grains which are in contact with each other and with a liquid, showing relationship between dihedral angle ϕ and surface tensions*[19]

Wetting of Refractories by Fluxes

Two questions need to be answered when considering the factors which control the wetting of refractories by liquids: (i) What is the condition that the liquid-phase should be retained in the interstices between the solid grains? (ii) Assuming it is retained, what are the conditions that determine whether it will penetrate between the grains or form discrete globules?[19] [Figure 8(a), (b), (c)].

The angle (Θ) between the drop of liquid and the flat solid on which it rests must be less than $90°$. This is also the condition for liquid to rise in a capillary. The value of Θ, when equilibrium is established is in turn determined by the relation (1), where γ_{SV} is the surface energy of the solid, γ_{LV} is that of the

15   G. R. Rigby and H. M. Richardson, *Trans. Brit. Ceram. Soc.,* 1957, **56**, 23.
16   H. M. Richardson, *Refractories J.,* 1959, **35**, 119.
17   J. H. Chesters, 'Refractories for Iron- and Steel-Making, The Metals Society, London, 1974, p. 237.
18   W. F. Ford, A. Hayhurst, and J. White, *Trans. Brit. Ceram. Soc.,* 1961, **60**, 581.
19   J. White, *Refractories J.,* 1963, **39**, 126.

$$\gamma_{SV} = \gamma_{SL} + \gamma_{LV} \cos\Theta \qquad (1)$$

liquid, and γ_{SL} is that of the solid–liquid interface.

The answer to the second question is provided by Figure 8c which shows a section through two grains which are in contact with each other and with the liquid phase. In this case the condition for equilibrium is given in equation (2)

$$\gamma_{SS} = 2\gamma_{SL} \cos\frac{\phi}{2} \qquad (2)$$

where γ_{SS} is the energy of the interface, that is the grain-boundary between the two grains and ϕ is the dihedral angle at which the solid surfaces intersect. The condition for complete penetration, which is that ϕ should be zero, is given in equation (3) when $\gamma_{SS} < 2\gamma_{SL}$ complete penetration will not occur and ϕ will

$$\frac{\gamma_{SS}}{\gamma_{SL}} > 2 \qquad (3)$$

increase that is the penetrating tendency will decrease as γ_{SS}/γ_{SL} decreases.

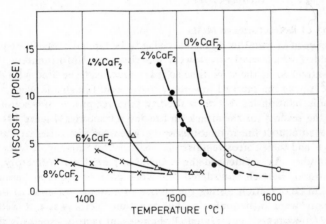

Figure 9 *The effect of fluorides on slag viscosities*[22]

The dihedral angle found by van Vlack[20] for cristobalite compacts quenched from 1550 °C, was 55°, whilst Buist has found similar values for mullite compacts so that these two classes, for example, silica and mullite bricks, may be said to be direct bonded. This fits the observation that liquid drains from certain high alumina bricks on heating to 1700 °C. It is frequently necessary to take elaborate precautions to ensure that wetting occurs. Thus, to achieve good adherence in the vitreous enamelling of steel, iron, cobalt, and nickel need to be present, cobalt in the ground coat (often with added manganese) and nickel as a coating of nickel oxide on the metal. This is achieved by dipping the metal into

[20] L. H. van Vlack, *J. Amer. Ceram. Soc.*, 1960, **43**, 140.

nickel sulphate solution after first pickling with acid and washing. In making metal-ceramic seals, molybdenum and manganese are frequently incorporated[21] to facilitate wetting and adherence.

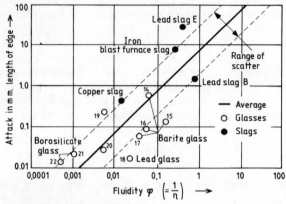

Figure 10 *Slag attack—viscosity curves*[23]

Dissolution of Refractories in Melts

It has long been known that to enable a slag to be tapped easily fluorspar (CaF_2) can be added which markedly lowers the viscosity. Unfortunately the refractories are attacked at the same time so it is a practice to be used with discretion. Figure 9[22] shows the marked lowered experienced. Endell and Wens,[23] showed a monatonic relationship between fluidity (the reciprocal of viscosity) of the melt and the severity of the attack on fireclay refractories (Figure 10). Hartman also found an almost linear relationship between the viscosities of $CaO-SiO_2-Al_2O_3$ slags and their corrosive power as measured by Salmang. It was recognized that the fluidity also influenced the removal of particles of refractory, a process termed erosion. Bartsch considered this work open to criticism because (i) the slag alters in composition during the course of a static test and (ii) the heating arrangements were inadequate so that the time factor was not well defined. Endell and co-workers[24] considered all the relevant factors, especially the hydrodynamic conditions, and concluded that, 'one of the most important factors governing such attack is the diffusion coefficient of the dissolved material in the slag. The extraordinary rapid increase of slag attack with increasing temperature is the result of the combined influence of increasing solubility, fluidity and diffusivity'. These remarks remain true and still constitute a good guide to this complicated subject, though these authors were not able to quantify satisfactorily the data at their disposal. The present author benefited from these earlier works and, being convinced that too many factors were allowed free play,

[21]   L. Reed and R. C. McCrae, *Bull. Amer. Ceram. Soc.,* 1965, **44**, 12.
[22]   P. Kozakevitch, discussed in, F. D. Richardson, 'Physical Chemistry of Melts in Metallurgy', Academic Press, London, 1974, pp. 108–110.
[23]   K. Endell and C. Wens discussed in J. R. Rait, *Bull. Brit. Refract. Assoc.,* 1939, **50**, 139.
[24]   K. Endell, R. Fehling, and R. Kley, *J. Amer. Ceram. Soc.,* 1939, **22**, 105.

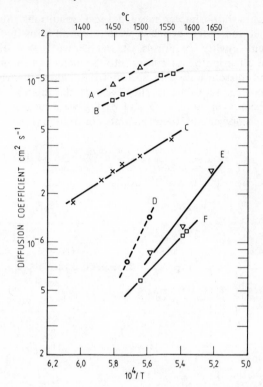

Figure 11 *Diffusion coefficients of* CaO (A, B, C) *and* Al_2O_3 (D, E, F) *in lime–alumina–silica melts* [9a,26]

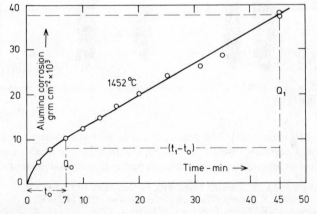

Figure 12 *Build up of boundary layer in diffusion controlled process* [9b]

directed researches into simpler more defined conditions. Single crystals of corundum, spinel and, later, periclase were dissolved in melts formulated with analytical reagent quality chemicals. It was shown[25] that diffusion control operated by the diffusion of refractory into the melts and energies of activation of viscosity and dissolution were shown to fit when the viscosities of the appropriate lime slags saturated as they were at the interface were used. The diffusion coefficients of both CaO and Al_2O_3 were measured and the latter shown to be much slower and, therefore, rate controlling (Figure 11).[9a, 26]

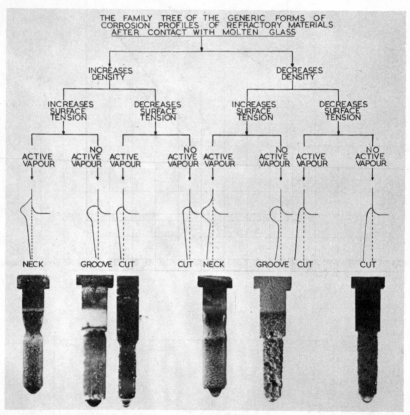

Figure 13 *Corrosion profiles of refractory materials after contact with molten glass in the finger test*[30]

Similar diffusion controlled reactions occur with dissolution of spinel (MgO, Al_2O_3)[27] and periclase (MgO)[28] in $Na_2Si_2O_5$. In regard to MgO a contrary view, that surface or chemical control was important, was first advanced[27] but on

[25] N. McCallum and L. R. Barrett, *Trans. Brit. Ceram. Soc.,* 1952, **51**, 523.
[26] D. Barham and L. R. Barrett, *Trans. Brit. Ceram. Soc.,* 1968, **67**, 49.
[27] A. G. Thomas, Ph.D. Thesis, University of London, 1955.
[28] H. K. Park, Ph.D. Thesis, University of London, 1976.

insufficient evidence. The criteria for the two modes of dissolution[29] are: (i) Diffusion through a boundary layer (melt saturated at interface)—stirring enhances the rate by reducing the thickness of the boundary layer and surface features, for example, fine pores, grooves, and grain boundaries play no part. (ii) Reaction at the refractory surface (no saturated surface layer)—stirring has no effect on the rate of dissolution and surface features, for example, crystal orientation, porosity, are important in controlling the rate. Figure 12 shows data for Al_2O_3.

During the time that this laboratory work was in progress, of which the above is a much truncated account, interesting work was being done by Griffith and colleagues. An example is given in Figure 13[30] which shows the contour of the refractory (left-hand side curve) and glass level (right-hand side curve). For many years to come specific experimentation will be necessary but theoretical studies will be gradually assimilated.

The author thanks Mr. P. Rado and Worcester Royal Porcelain Co. Ltd. for the use of the photograph of calcium fluoride crucibles (Figure 1).

[29] D. Barham, L. R. Barrett, F. A. Faruqi, H. K. Park, Paper presented to 'Microstructure of Ceramics' meeting, Oxford 1975, organized by the British Ceramic and Mineralogical Societies.

[30] E. Vago and C. F. Smith, 'Proc. 7th Intern. Congr. Glass'. Paper No. 62, Brussels, 1965.

Some Effects of Heat-treatment in the Range 1000–3000 K on Porosity and Reactivity in Carbons and Graphites

By B. McENANEY and M. A. WILLIS

School of Materials Science, University of Bath, BA2 7AY

Introduction

This paper is a broad highly selective review of two related aspects of the behaviour of carbons and graphites, namely the changes in porosity and in reactivity to oxidizing gases as a function of heat-treatment in the range 1000–3000 K. Reference is made to more detailed reviews of several topics which are touched on but not dealt with in detail. The chief concern is with physico-chemical aspects, but the technical significance of several points will be indicated where appropriate.

The Structure of Carbons and Graphites. The words 'carbon' and 'graphite' are used not only to describe the element and its allotrope but also as generic terms for a wide range of carbonaceous materials of natural and artificial origin. The diversity of form and methods of manufacture of some technically important carbons and graphites may be appreciated by reference to Table 1, which is by no means comprehensive. Accounts of the production and properties of these materials are given in the references cited in Table 1.[1—6]

Although it is possible to produce highly oriented pyrolytic graphite with some properties which approach those of ideal crystalline graphite,[7] the vast majority of carbons have less perfect structures. X-Ray diffraction analysis shows that the majority of manufactured graphites consist of microcrystalline graphitic regions in an essentially amorphous matrix. The mean basal plane dimension, L_a, and the crystallite thickness, L_c, may be determined from X-ray diffraction. Except for some carbons which have been heat-treated to ∼ 3000 K or subjected to catalytic graphitization at lower temperatures, there is no ordered stacking sequence of graphitic planes within the crystallites, such a structure being termed 'turbostratic.' The degree of graphitic character varies widely depending upon factors such as the nature of the organic precursor and the thermal history of the material. The influences of such factors on the structure revealed by X-ray diffraction has been reviewed by Hutcheon.[8]

1. C. L. Mantell, 'Carbon and Graphite Handbook', Interscience, New York, 1968.
2. J. M. Hutcheon, 'Modern Aspects of Graphite Technology', ed. L. C. F. Blackman, Academic Press, London, 1970, p. 49.
3. J. C. Bokros, *Chem. and Phys. Carbon,* 1969, **5**, 1.
4. W. H. Smith and D. M. Leeds, 'Modern Materials, Advances in Development and Application', ed. B. W. Gonser, Academic Press, New York, 1970, Vol. 7, p. 139.
5. P. J. Goodhew, A. J. Clarke, and J. E. Bailey, *Mater. Sci. Eng.,* 1975, **17**, 3.
6. G. M. Jenkins and K. Kawamura, 'Polymeric Carbons—Carbon fibre, glass and char', Cambridge University Press, 1976.
7. A. W. Moore, *Chem. and Phys. Carbon*, 1973, **11**, 69.
8. J. M. Hutcheon, ref. 2, p.l.

More recently, high-resolution electron microscopy (HREM) has shown promise in refining the model of the structure of carbons and graphites.[9] It has been suggested[10] that the amorphous regions in a glassy carbon consist of randomly distorted, graphitic layers in intertwined, ribbon-like arrays which are continuous with the more perfect microcrystalline regions (Figure 1). This implies that the 'amorphous' regions of carbons are more organized than was hitherto supposed. In agreement with this view, a recent re-examination[11] of X-ray reflections of a glassy carbon previously attributed to disorganized carbon suggests that they result from low-angle X-ray scattering from pores.

Table 1 *Some technically important carbons and graphites*

Material	Examples of organic precursor	Method of manufacture	Ref.
Metallurgical coke	coal	carbonization in retorts	1
Electrode graphites Nuclear graphites Refractory carbons and graphites	(i) petroleum coke filler (ii) coal tar pitch binder	(i) mixing (ii) extrusion (iii) baking (iv) graphitization (v) machining	1, 2
Carbon blacks	hydrocarbon gases	incomplete combustion	1
Pyrolytic carbons and graphites	hydrocarbon gases	thermal decomposition at 1500 – 3000 K	3, 4
Carbon fibres	polyacrylonitrile or cellulose fibres	closely controlled heat-treatment	5
Glassy carbons	phenolic resins		6

The Carbonization Process. The ability of carbons from solid precursors to develop graphitic character depends principally upon the nature of the carbonization process. Carbonization processes consist of two stages: the primary carbonization, which occurs at temperatures up to $\sim$ 800 K, and the secondary carbonization, which occurs mainly in the range 800–1300 K, but may continue to higher temperatures. Primary carbonization involves the breakdown of the organic precursor which results both in the expulsion of volatile products as tars and gases and, simultaneously, in condensation reactions to yield polynuclear aromatic compounds. In secondary carbonization the polynuclear aromatic compounds condense to form a carbon residue by elimination of peripheral hydrogen atoms and aliphatic side-chains. The evolution of gases, mainly

[9] L. L. Ban, in 'Surface and Defect Properties of Solids', ed. M. W. Roberts and J. M. Thomas (Specialist Periodical Reports), Chemical Society, London, 1972, Vol. 1, p. 54.
[10] G. M. Jenkins, K. Kawamura, and L. L. Ban, *Proc. Roy. Soc.*, 1972, **A327**, 501.
[11] S. Bose and R. M. Bragg, 'Preprints of 2nd Carbon Conference, Baden-Baden' Deutsche Keramische Gesellschaft, 1976, p. 205.

hydrogen and methane, increases and unpaired electrons are trapped in the condensed ring structures. The chemistry of the carbonization process has been reviewed in detail by Fitzer *et al.*[12]

If a plastic state occurs during primary carbonization, it is found that anisotropic droplets may separate from the fluid mass. The droplets are called 'the mesophase' and contain highly oriented, polynuclear, aromatic molecules; these droplets coalesce to form the optically anisotropic flow lines often seen in cokes. It has been proposed[13] that the molecules lie parallel to the equatorial axis of the droplet with distortion at the edges due to surface effects. This morphology is similar to some conventional nematic liquid crystals, although the formation of the mesophase appears to have no exact parallel in other known liquid crystal systems.

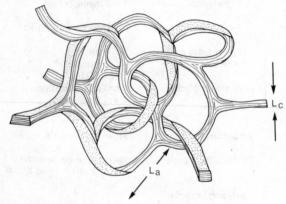

Figure 1 *A model for the structure of a glassy carbon*[10]

The significance of the mesophase lies in its relevance to the subsequent course of graphitization. Extensive graphitization of carbons occurs only if the carbonizing mass passes through a plastic state during which coalesced mesophase is formed. It appears that the mesophase is important in the development of nuclei from which the graphitic microcrystals can grow upon heat-treatment. Carbons produced in this way are called 'soft' or 'graphitizing' carbons. White[14] has shown that materials such as needle-cokes have structures which would be expected if disclinations, which exist in conventional liquid crystals, also exist in the mesophase.

If there is no plastic zone on carbonization, either because the precursor is heavily cross-linked (*e.g.* a thermoset resin) or because cross-links develop during carbonization, then the amount of graphitic character developed on heat-treatment is small; such carbons are termed 'hard' or 'non-graphitizing' carbons.

The Graphitization Process. The transition from carbonization to graphitization is a continuous one which varies widely with starting material. For graphitizing

[12] E. Fitzer, K. Mueller, and W. Schaefer, *Chem. and Phys. Carbon,* 1971, 7, 237.
[13] J. D. Brooks and G. H. Taylor, *Chem. and Phys. Carbon,* 1968, 4, 243.
[14] J. L. White, *Progr. Solid State Chem.,* 1974, 9, 59.

carbons the basal plane dimension, L_a, increases progressively to ~ 70 nm on heating to ~ 3000 K; L_c values vary more widely and lie in the range $15-17$ nm at 3000 K. These changes are accompanied by a decrease in interlayer spacing from the turbostratic value of 0.344 nm towards the graphitic value (0.335 nm).[8]

The study of the kinetics of graphitization is experimentally difficult and it is not surprising that a unanimous view of the process has not emerged. The classical view due to Franklin[15] is that the degree of graphitization is determined by temperature rather than time at a given temperature. This implies that the process of graphitization has a spectrum of activation energies which increase with the degree of graphitization. However, more recently, Fischbach[16] has proposed that the transformation of carbons to graphites is a thermally activated process having a single activation energy. Given sufficient time, the process may proceed to completion at a given temperature with no evidence for imperfect, limiting structures. Pacault and co-workers[17] also concluded that graphitization is a time-dependent transformation with a single activation energy, but they have also reported evidence for two- or three-stage isothermal transformations. Details of the annealing mechanisms are not well understood. Fischbach infers that self-diffusion of carbon atoms by a vacancy mechanism parallel to basal planes is the dominant process.

The changes which occur upon heat-treatment of non-graphitizing carbons are poorly understood. The diffusion mechanisms *via* point defects which lead to the improvement of the structure of graphitizing carbons cannot bring about the substantial three-dimensional ordering which is necessary in such disordered materials. Franklin[15] found evidence for localized graphitization in non-graphitizing carbons which she attributed to a stress-induced transformation. Nucleation and growth do not occur to a significant extent during graphitization. Evidently, it is the nucleation and growth of the mesophase during carbonization ($T \sim 700$ K) which is significant in determining the course of subsequent graphitization. This is a very important point in connection with the fabrication of graphite bodies which has only been fully appreciated relatively recently. Clearly, the quality of a graphite product depends upon correctly specified fillers and binders as well as close control of the graphitization process.

Porosity in Carbons and Graphites

There have been very many studies of the development of porosity during carbonization and graphitization. The most widely used techniques are density determinations in gases and liquids, including liquid metals. The determination of heats of wetting of carbons by liquids, adsorption from solution and small-angle X-ray scattering have also been used; an extensive review of these techniques was edited by Bond.[18] Surface areas may be determined by gas adsorption using the classical BET method. Total pore volumes may be obtained from measurements of the densities of carbons and graphites in helium and mercury.

[15]   R. E. Franklin, *Acta Cryst.*, 1950, **3**, 107; *Proc. Roy. Soc.*, 1951, **A209**, 196.
[16]   D. B. Fischbach, *Chem. and Phys. Carbon*, 1971, **7**, 1.
[17]   A. Pacault, *Chem. and Phys. Carbon*, 1971, **7**, 107.
[18]   'Porous Carbon Solids', ed. R. L. Bond, Academic Press, London, 1967.

Porosity in Non-graphitizing Carbons. Non-graphitizing carbons have surface areas in the range 200–500 m^2 g^{-1}, whereas graphitizing carbons have very much smaller surface areas, in the range 0.25–0.50 m^2 g^{-1}. Examination of the pore size distribution in a variety of non-graphitizing carbons by Dubinin and co-workers[19] has revealed a trimodal distribution rather than a continuous one, ranging from pores of molecular dimensions to pores visible to the naked eye. The three types of pores are termed (i) macropores, those visible in the optical microscope, (ii) micropores, those less than ~ 3 nm in size, and (iii) an intermediate size range of transitional or mesopores with dimensions in the range ~ 3 to ~ 200 nm. Of these pore types, micropores make the greatest contribution to the total surface area.

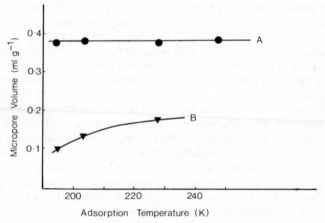

Figure 2 *The effect of activated diffusion upon the micropore volume of carbons. Carbon A, a wide-pore carbon; carbon B, a fine-pore carbon*[23]

The microporous nature of non-graphitizing carbons greatly complicates the interpretation of adsorption and density measurements, since the dimensions of the pores or of the pore entrances are commensurate with the dimensions of the penetrating molecule. The validity of the BET equation when applied to microporous materials has been questioned. Active carbons have been produced with surface areas of ~ 4000 m^2 g^{-1} when determined by the BET method;[20] this is an unrealistically high figure. Barrer[21] has suggested that the term 'monolayer equivalent area' be used to emphasize the notional nature of the surface area. An alternative approach developed by Dubinin and Radushkevich[22] is to determine the micropore volume from gas adsorption using a development of the Polanyi Potential Theory.

[19] M. M. Dubinin, *Chem. and Phys. Carbon,* 1966, **2**, 51.
[20] T. G. Lamond and H. Marsh, *Carbon,* 1964, **1**, 293.
[21] R. M. Barrer, 'Structure and Properties of Porous Materials', Butterworth, London, 1958, pp. 6, 53.
[22] M. M. Dubinin and L. V. Radushkevich, *Doklady Akad. Nauk. S.S.R.,* 1947, **55**, 331.

Activated diffusion effects and the related phenomenon of molecular sieve action are commonly observed in microporous carbons. The former effect is illustrated in Figure 2, which shows the micropore volume of two active carbons determined by adsorption of carbon dioxide at different temperatures.[23] Carbon A contains pores whose dimensions are greater than the kinetic diameter of the adsorbate molecule. Consequently, the micropores are freely accessible to the adsorbate molecule at all temperatures and the micropore volume is independent of temperature. Carbon B contains finer pores with dimensions comparable with the dimensions of the carbon dioxide molecule and diffusion into the pores is an activated process. As the temperature of the adsorbate is lowered, the proportion of molecules having the requisite energy to penetrate micropores is reduced and consequently the micropore volume apparently decreases with temperature.

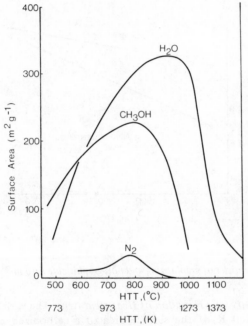

Figure 3 *The effect of heat-treatment on the surface area of a carbonized coal*[33]

Density or adsorption measurements using 'molecular probes', that is penetrant molecules of different molecular diameters, provide a means of obtaining micropore size distributions.[24-26] Meso- and macro-pore size distributions are

[23] B. McEnaney and N. G. Dovaston, *Carbon*, 1975, **13**, 515.
[24] J. J. Kipling and B. McEnaney, 'Proceedings 2nd Conference on Carbon and Graphite', Society for Chemical Industry, London, 1966, p. 380.
[25] B. McEnaney, *J. C. S. Faraday I*, 1974, **70**, 84.
[26] D. H. T. Spencer, ref. 18, p. 87.

108   *B. McEnaney and M. A. Willis*

determined by analysis of adsorption hysteresis[27] and mercury porosimetry.[28] Adsorption of molecules with similar size but with different shapes has been used to establish that micropore entrances are slit-shaped, possibly due to the presence of turbostratic platelets in the carbon.[29,30] The presence of slit-shaped pores suggests that carbon-based molecular sieves may find application in the petroleum industry for separation of straight-chain and branch-chain hydrocarbons.[31]

Porosity in Graphitizing Carbons. The low surface areas found for graphitizing carbons signify a low porosity which is mainly associated with macropores, resulting from the persistence of bubble structure from the plastic stage of carbonization. The helium density of graphitized carbons is often about 5% below the theoretical value for graphite, signifying the presence of closed porosity; this has been attributed to micro-cleavages in basal planes resulting from the relief of thermal stresses created on cooling from the graphitizing temperature.[32]

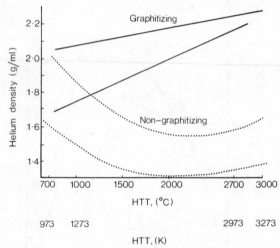

Figure 4 *Helium densities of graphitizing and non-graphitizing carbons*[34]

Changes in Porosity as a Function of Heat-treatment. The variation with carbonization to ∼ 1400 K of the surface area of a carbonized coal measured by adsorption of water and methyl alcohol vapours at 391 K and nitrogen at 77 K is shown in Figure 3.[33] The very low surface area accessible to nitrogen at 77 K indicates an activated diffusion effect. There is also evidence of molecular sieve

[27] J. W. Sutherland, ref 18, p. 2.
[28] G. F. Hewitt, ref 18, p. 203.
[29] J. R. Dacey and D. G. Thomas, *Trans. Faraday Soc.,* 1954, **50**, 740.
[30] T. G. Lamond, J. E. Metcalfe, jun., and P. L. Walker, jun., *Carbon,* 1965, **3**, 59.
[31] R. B. Mason and P. E. Eberley, jun., U.S. P., 3 222 412 (1965).
[32] S. Mrozowski 'Proceedings 1st and 2nd Carbon Conference, Buffalo', Pergamon, New York, 1957, p. 31.
[33] P. Chiche, S. Durif, and S. Pregermain, *J. Chim. phys.,* 1963, **60**, 825.

action between methyl alcohol and water vapour which increases with increasing heat-treatment temperature (HTT). This suggests that the reduction in surface area at HTT $> \sim 1100$ K is associated with a narrowing of micropores or micropore entrances.

Kipling and co-workers[34] studied changes in porosity of a range of graphitizing and non-graphitizing polymer carbons on heat-treatment to 3273 K; changes in helium density are shown in Figure 4. The helium densities of graphitizing carbons increased progressively with HTT approaching the density of graphite.

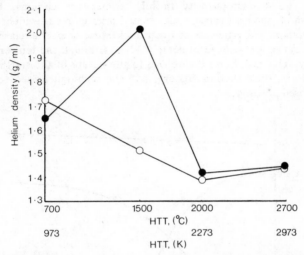

Figure 5 *Helium densities of a cellulose carbon at 298 and 573 K*[35] *Open circles, 298 K; closed circles, 573 K.*

The decrease in helium densities for non-graphitizing carbons is associated with the formation of micropores which are closed to helium. This effect is illustrated by the helium densities of a non-graphitizing cellulose carbon determined at 298 and 573 K (Figure 5).[35] The difference in densities found for the 973 K carbon results from adsorption in micropores at 298 K. The very much higher densities found at 573 K for the 1733 K carbon is attributed to an activated diffusion effect for helium at 298 K. The fall in helium densities for the 2273 K and 2973 K carbons suggests that substantial porosity becomes closed to helium at 573 K.

Broadly similar conclusions were reached by Greenhalgh and co-workers[36] in a study of the influence of HTT upon porosity in a non-graphitizing poly-

[34] J. J. Kipling, J. N. Sherwood, P. V. Shooter, and N. R. Thompson, *Carbon,* 1964, **1,** 315, 321.

[35] J. J. Kipling, J. N. Sherwood, P. V. Shooter, N. R. Thompson, and R. N. Young, *Carbon,* 1966, **4,** 5.

[36] E. Greenhalgh, B. J. Miles, E. Redman, and S. A. Sharman, 'Proceedings 2nd Conference on Carbon and Graphite', Society for Chemical Industry, London, 1966, p. 405.

(vinylidene chloride) (PVDC) carbon and a graphitizing poly(vinyl chloride) (PVC) carbon. Considerable open porosity was found in PVDC carbon upon heat-treatment to 2073 K. A drastic reduction in open porosity occurred at higher HTT with evidence of closed porosity in the 2773 K PVDC carbon. Over the HTT range studied, open and closed porosity were not detected in PVC carbons with the techniques employed in this work. Evidence that surface homogeneity increased with HTT was found from stepped krypton isotherms on 2273 K PVDC carbon and 2773 K PVC carbon.

Thus for non-graphitizing carbons, it appears that the predominant effect of heat-treatment is a reduction in open micropore volume and the production of appreciable closed microporosity in high-temperature carbons. The process of conversion of open micropores into closed micropores is evidenced by molecular sieve action. A drastic loss of open microporosity over a relatively narrow temperature range is a feature of some studies, although the temperature range varies widely. This variation may be due to the nature of the starting materials for the carbons, their thermal history, and the techniques used to determine open and closed porosity.

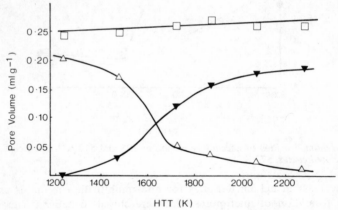

Figure 6 *Pore volumes of a non-graphitizing carbon as a function of heat-treatment*[23] *□ Total pore volume, △ open micropore volume, ▼ closed micropore volume.*

'Sintering' Processes in Carbons and Graphites. The results of a recent study[23] of the development of porosity in a non-graphitizing carbon are shown in Figure 6; pore volumes were determined by carbon dioxide adsorption and from mercury densities. The results show a progressive conversion of open micropores into closed micropores with little change in the total pore volume. Thus there is no evidence for loss of porosity by 'sintering'. The density of many non-graphitizing carbons decreases on heat-treatment (see Figure 4), and in a recent study of density changes in glassy carbon, such decreases were attributed primarily to volume expansion resulting from internal pressure generated within closed porosity by desorption and continued pyrolysis.[37]

[37] D. B. Fischbach, 'Preprints of 2nd Carbon Conference, Baden-Baden', Deutsche Keramische Gesellschaft, 1976, p. 185.

Presumably, sintering mechanisms involving diffusion and grain growth do not occur in non-graphitizing carbons because of the absence of substantial numbers of microcrystalline nuclei. In contrast, Kipling and co-workers[34] found that in graphitizing carbons a small amount of closed porosity was converted into open porosity with increase in HTT (Table 2). This process is consistent with the elimination of voids between near-parallel crystallites as graphitization proceeds and may therefore be regarded as similar to a sintering mechanism involving grain growth with elimination of small pores at grain boundaries. An assessment of the extent to which porosity changes in carbons and graphites compare with those found in other ceramic materials is a subject which is worthy of investigation.

Table 2 *Variation of open pore volume and closed pore volume for a poly(vinyl chloride) carbon*[34]

Heat-treatment temperature /K	Open pore volume/ml g^{-1}	Closed pore volume/ml g^{-1}
973	0.055	0.096
2273	0.079	0.023
2973	0.100	0.010
3273	0.146	0.000

Reaction of Carbons and Graphites with Oxidizing Gases

The study of the gasification of carbons and graphites by oxidizing gases such as oxygen, steam, and carbon dioxide is an immense field of both technological and fundamental interest. The gas reactions of carbons and graphites are of great importance in conventional and nuclear power generation, in metallurgical and chemical processes, in fuel gas production, and in rocket technology. Although among the most widely studied of solid–gas reactions, there is still dispute concerning the mechanisms of reaction and disagreement on kinetic data throughout the literature. An extended account of the literature will not be attempted here since a number of comprehensive reviews are already available.[38–41] Instead some of the factors underlying the occurrence of conflicting data in the literature will be discussed, together with an account of the generally accepted mechanisms of reaction at temperatures greater than 1000 K.

Factors affecting the Rate of Reaction. It has been shown many times that the carbon surface is energetically heterogeneous. In addition, as the reaction proceeds, the surface is continually changing as carbon atoms are removed into the gas phase. The overall reaction mechanism consists of diffusional steps and a number of chemical steps which govern the intrinsic chemical rate. It is only

[38] P. L. Walker, jun., F. Rusinko, and L. G. Austin, *Adv. Catalysis*, 1959, **11**, 133.
[39] C. G. von Fredersdorff and M. A. Elliott, 'Chemistry of Coal Utilisation', (Supplementary Volume), ed. H. H. Lowry, Wiley, New York, 1963, p. 892.
[40] S. Ergun and H. Menster, *Chem. and Phys. Carbon*, 1966, **1**, 203.
[41] J. B. Lewis, 'Modern Aspects of Graphite Technology', ed. L. C. F. Blackman, Academic Press, New York, 1970, p. 129.

possible to observe the true chemical reaction rate when the retarding effects of reactant and product diffusion have been eliminated. The considerations have been neatly summarized for the case of porous carbon solids by Wicke.[42] In order to ensure that the intrinsic chemical rate of reaction is being investigated, small samples of fine particle size and fast gas flows are employed in kinetic studies at high temperatures; alternatively, very low pressures are employed.

The reactivity of a given carbon is structure-dependent by virtue of the fact that attack by an oxidizing gas occurs primarily at carbon atoms situated at the edges of graphitic planes, and in the so-called amorphous regions; attack on the basal planes is very slow.[43,44] The preferential attack of amorphous or disorganized parts of the structure has been shown by Arnell and Barss[45] and is apparent in the opening of pore entrances in the early stages of gasification as restrictions and blockages are selectively removed.[46] Thus, all other factors being equal, highly graphitic material of large crystallite size will exhibit a lower reactivity than a relatively amorphous carbon. In well-ordered graphites additional active centres for oxidation are provided by grain boundaries, dislocations, vacancies, and other imperfections in graphite lattice. Localized attack resulting in the formation of etch pits visible under the optical microscope[47,48] has been attributed to the presence of such defects.

The concept of active sites is central to any discussion of reactivity of carbons. Active sites exist at those surface features which are preferentially attacked by oxidizing gas. The surface chemical reactions involve chemisorption of the oxidizing gas, surface rearrangement, and desorption of product gas. That chemisorption occurs primarily at certain sites on the carbon surface has been shown by many workers. For example, Loebenstein and Deitz[49] found oxygen to chemisorb on less than 6% of the total surface of four carbons. The reaction rate during high-temperature oxidation depends on the formation and removal rates of the surface complexes, and upon the number and extent of coverage of active sites (not all those available may be participating in the reaction at any one time).

The presence of heteroelements or impurities in the carbon can exert a most important influence upon the reactivity of the carbon. The extensive literature on the catalysis of gas-carbon reactions has been reviewed.[50] Almost any inorganic impurity, whether added deliberately or occurring incidentally, can affect the rate of oxidation and the rate may be accelerated or retarded. The

[42] E. Wicke, 'Proceedings 5th Symposium on Combustion', Rheinhold, New York, 1955, p. 245.
[43] G. R. Hennig, 'Proceedings 2nd Conference on Carbon and Graphite', Society for Chemical Industry, London, 1966, p. 109.
[44] G. R. Hennig, 'Proceedings 5th Conference on Carbon', Pergamon, New York, 1962, Vol. 1, p. 143.
[45] J. C. Arnell and W. M. Barss, *Canad. J. Research,* 1948, **26A,** 236.
[46] B. McEnaney and C. J. Weedon, 'Proceedings 3rd Conference on Carbon and Graphite', Society for Chemical Industry, London, 1971, p. 207.
[47] J. M. Thomas, *Chem. and Phys. Carbon,* 1966, **1,** 121.
[48] G. R. Hennig, *Science,* 1965, **147,** 733.
[49] W. Loebenstein and V. R. Deitz, *J. Phys. Chem.,* 1955, **59,** 481.
[50] P. L. Walker, jun., M. Shelef, and R. A. Anderson, *Chem. and Phys. Carbon,* 1968, **4,** 287.

chemical state of the catalyst, not only before addition but at the conditions prevailing during gasification, is of vital importance; metallic salts may to some extent be reduced to the metal. The physical state of the catalyst is also important, since the effects on reactivity are functions of the location of the impurity in the carbon matrix and the extent of interaction of the impurity with the matrix. Addition of discrete particles of impurity would thus be expected to exert an influence on reactivity different from solution impregnation.

In contrast to the extensive literature on the catalytic effects of metallic additions and impurities, very limited data are available on the effects of residual oxygen and hydrogen on carbon reactivity. Both are generally present because carbons are derived from pyrolysed organic compounds, the amounts depending upon the maximum HTT. The total oxygen content is evolved as oxides of carbon and water generally well below 1500 K, but hydrogen is considerably more difficult to remove. Hydrogen evolution only commences above 900 K, and Puri and Bansal[51] estimated that 30–40% of the combined hydrogen is still retained in carbon blacks at a heat-treatment temperature of 1470 K. Significant amounts (about 40 p.p.m.) can still be measured in cokes and graphites treated to near 3200 K.[52] The effect of this chemically combined oxygen and hydrogen on carbon reactivity is unclear.

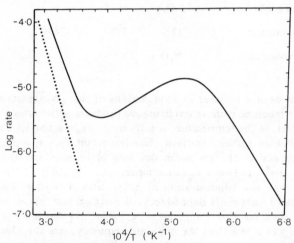

Figure 7 *Rates of reaction of a pyrolytic graphite with CO_2. Full line, reaction rate; broken line, vaporization rate*

It has been shown many times that product gases strongly retard the gasification rate, for example carbon monoxide retards the carbon–carbon dioxide reaction and hydrogen retards the carbon–steam reaction.[53] Other gaseous impurities in the oxidizing gas can have a marked effect on the rate of reaction.

51 B. R. Puri and R. C. Bansal, *Carbon*, 1964, **1**, 451.
52 R. T. Meyer, A. W. Lynch, J. M. Freese, M. C. Smith, and R. J. Imprescia, *Carbon*, 1973 **11**, 258.
53 F. J. Long and K. W. Sykes, *Proc. Roy. Soc.*, 1948, A193, 377.

Recent studies show that in high-purity systems even trace amounts of hydrogen can seriously retard the reaction of graphite with carbon dioxide.[54]

Reaction at High Temperatures. Early studies on reaction[55-56] of carbons and gases at high temperatures were carried out on carbon filaments at low pressures. Developments in rocket technology in the 1960's prompted work using high pressures and fast gas flows.[57-59] It is pleasing to note that closely similar results were obtained in both types of experiment. A typical curve of the variation in reaction rate with reaction temperature in the range 1000–3000 K is shown in Figure 7.[58] The rate rises to a maximum and then falls to a minimum before rising once more as the temperature approaches 3000 K. This most unusual type of behaviour is found quite generally for a variety of carbons, graphites, and oxidizing gases; some typical values of the temperatures at which maximum and minimum rates occur are given in Table 3.

Table 3 *Rate maxima and minima in some gas–carbon reactions*

Substrate	Gas	T_{max}/K	T_{min}/K	Ref.
Pyrocarbon	CO_2	1375	1825	60
Reactor graphite	O_2	1875	—	56
Vitreous carbon	CO_2	2200	2800	59
Pyrographite edge	H_2O	2500	—	59

There have been a number of explanations of this phenomenon. Duval[55,60] proposed that reaction with an oxidizing gas produces active sites on the surface of a carbon, but, if the temperature is sufficiently high, active sites may become de-activated before further reaction. The important factors are therefore the collision frequency of the gas molecules with active sites and the rate of de-activation of sites. At low reaction temperatures (~ 1000 K) the rate of de-activation is low, the concentration of active sites rises to a stationary-state, and the normal (Arrhenius) dependency of reaction rate upon temperature is observed. At high reaction temperatures (~ 2000 K) the lifetime of a newly created active site is less than the collision frequency, and the concentration of active sites approaches the level in the unoxidized material; in consequence the reactivity falls. Duval proposed that de-activation is associated with closure of micro-cleavages in the graphitic planes. This accords with the generally accepted

[54] M. Shelef and P. L. Walker, jun., *Carbon,* 1967, **5**, 93.
[55] X. Duval, *Ann. Chim. Phys.,* 1955, **10**, 903.
[56] J. Nagle and R. F. Strickland-Constable, 'Proceedings 5th Conference on Carbon', Pergamon, New York, 1961, Vol. 1, p. 154.
[57] J. R. Walls and R. F. Strickland-Constable, *Carbon,* 1964, **1**, 333.
[58] I. R. Ladd and P. N. Walsh, *Carbon,* 1966, **4**, 539.
[59] J. C. Lewis, I. J. Floyd, and F. C. Cowland, 'Proceedings 3rd Conference on Carbon and Graphite', Society for Chemical Industry, London, 1971, p. 282.
[60] P. Wehrer, X. Duval, and R. Sauvageot, *Carbon,* 1974, **12**, 71.

view of the mechanism of graphitization and is also consistent with studies of graphitization which show that the presence of an oxidizing gas can catalyse the graphitization process.[26]

Strickland-Constable[56,57] proposed a two-site mechanism involving reactive sites (type A), and less-reactive sites (type B) which are produced by annealing of type A sites. As the reaction temperature increases, the proportion of type B sites increases and so the reactivity falls. By ascribing empirical values to the parameters of the model, the variation of rate with heat-treatment temperature was accounted for. Although there are important differences in the two theories, both ascribe the decline in reactivity to de-activation of the surface resulting from enhanced surface mobility at higher temperatures.

Another explanation has been advanced by Khaustovich,[61] who attributes the decrease in reaction rate to a reduction in the BET surface area which occurs upon heat-treatment. This explanation has not found general acceptance; it is the area of active sites and not the BET area which is likely to be significant. However, Duval and co-workers[60] concede that measurements of change in surface area during reaction are required before further consideration can be given to the phenomenon.

The increase in reactivity which occurs at temperatures above 2600 K is generally attributed to effects related to the vaporization of graphite. Vaporization rates are generally lower than reaction rates but show a similar temperature-dependence (Figure 7). At such temperatures, homogeneous reactions in the boundary layer possibly involving dissociated gas molecules[62] become increasingly important. It has been proposed[58] that such reactions may enhance the rate of vaporization by reducing the concentration of volatile carbon species in the boundary layer. Other workers[59] have suggested that vaporization increases surface reactivity by creating free valencies. Golovina and Kotova[63] observed that carbon is consumed from the interior of particles at temperatures greater than 2000 K. This is attributed to diffusion of carbon atoms under the influence of temperature and concentration gradients imposed by the reaction. It is clear that there is a great deal of scope for further work in the study of gas–carbon reactions at high temperatures.

[61] G. P. Khaustovich, *Zhur. fiz. Khim.*, 1968, **42**, 1646, 1684 (*Russ. J. Phys. Chem.*, 1968, **42**, 862, 882).
[62] M. D. Gray and G. M. Kimber, *Nature*, 1967, **214**, 797.
[63] E. S. Golovina and L. L. Kotova, *Carbon*, 1968, **6**, 637.

The Liquid Metal–Oxygen Probe as a Ceramic System

By C. B. ALCOCK

Department of Metallurgy and Materials Science, University of Toronto, Toronto, Ontario, Canada M5S 1A4

Introduction

The high temperature measurement of the thermodynamic properties of oxide systems, and of solutions of oxygen in liquid metals and alloys, was given considerable impetus in 1958 by the publication by Kiukkola and Wagner[1] of the results of their studies using a solid electrolyte in a high-temperature oxygen concentration cell. The measurements involved electrodes, in pellet form, made of metal–metal oxide powder mixtures, pressed on either side of a pellet of calcia-stabilized zirconia which functioned as an electrolyte. The cell

$$Ni-NiO \ / \ electrolyte \ / \ Fe-FeO$$

which was amongst those studied in the pioneering research has an e.m.f. given by the thermodynamic equation (1), where p_{O_2} and p'_{O_2} are the dissociation

$$E = \frac{RT}{4F} \ln \frac{p_{O_2}}{p'_{O_2}} \tag{1}$$

pressures of a nickel–nickel oxide and an iron–ferrous oxide mixture at the temperature T, R is the gas constant, and F is the Faraday constant. In order to carry out the measurements in the temperature range $700-1000\,^{\circ}C$ the cell was placed in the even zone of a furnace and held at a constant temperature during a measurement, electrical contact between the cell and a potentiometer which was at room temperature being made by way of platinum leads. The cell atmosphere was a chemically inert stream of argon. The cell functions quantitatively as an electrochemical device because the zirconia pellet has a high conductivity for oxygen ions, the conduction by positive holes and defect electrons being of negligible importance over a wide range of temperature and oxygen partial pressure. This material can therefore be described as having unit transference number for oxygen ions, under these experimental conditions, and is a solid electrolyte.

The electrolyte studied by Kiukkola and Wagner was zirconia-based, but solid solutions based on thoria which also have a high electrical conductivity due to oxygen ion migration were soon afterwards established as potential electrolytes.[2] Numerous measurements over a wide range of electrode systems followed swiftly and continuously in the wake of these first studies. A number of metal–metal oxide mixtures were used as electrodes,[3] and metal alloys mixed with the oxide powder of the metal having the greater oxygen affinity,[4] oxygen dissolved

[1] K. Kiukkola and C. Wagner, *J. Electrochem. Soc.*, 1957, **104**, 308.
[2] H. Peters and H. H. Möbius, *Z. Phys. Chem. (Leipzig)*, 1958, **209**, 298.
[3] B. C. H. Steele, and C. B. Alcock, *Trans. A.I.M.E.*, 1967, **233**, 1359.
[4] R. A. Rapp and F. Maak, *Acta Met.*, 1962, **10**, 63.

in low melting metals such as tin and lead,[5,6] and gaseous mixtures having defined equilibrium oxygen pressure at a given temperature[7] have since been used as electrodes in high temperature cells of this kind. Table I shows typical systems which have since been studied by the use of this technique. In each cell, both electrodes must establish well-defined oxygen activities at the electrode—electrolyte interfaces, and have no chemical effects on the composition of the electrolyte material. The characteristic oxygen potential of each electrode must be applied at only one face of the electrolyte, there must be complete separation of the two electrodes, and a chemically inert electrical contact of relatively low resistance must be made between each electrode and a potential-measuring device which is at room temperature.

TABLE I - Some systems which have been established by the use of solid electrolyte galvanic cells

Metal - metal oxide electrodes (Potential reference systems)

Fe-FeO , Ni-NiO , Co-CoO, Cu-Cu$_2$O , In-In$_2$O$_3$,, Ga-Ga$_2$O$_3$,

Ge-GeO$_2$, Sn-SnO$_2$, Pb-PbO , Ta-Ta$_2$O$_5$, Cr-Cr$_2$O$_3$, Mo-MoO$_2$,

Mn-MnO .

Oxygen solutions in liquid metals and alloys

O-Fe , Cu+Fe , Co+Fe , Ni+Fe

O-Cu , Cu+Sn , Cu+Pb , Cu+Ag , Cu+In, Cu+Ga , Cu+Ge

O-Ag , Ag+Pb

O-Pb , Pb+Sn

O-Sn , O-Ni , O-Co , O-Na

Non-stoichiometric oxides

MoO$_{2\pm x}$, UO$_{2+x}$, FeO$_{1+x}$, TiO$_{2-x}$, NbO$_{2-x}$, PuO$_{2-x}$

and Magnéli phases in Ti$_n$O$_{2n-1}$ and V$_n$O$_{2n-1}$.

Solid alloys

Cu+Ni , Cu+Au , Cu+Pt , Cu+Pd , Fe+Ni , Fe+Cr, Fe+Pd, Fe+Pt ,

Fe+Au , Co+Au , Co+Mo , Co+Nb , Ni+Pd , Ni+Pt .

Such a promising research tool was bound to conjure up schemes for application on the industrial scale, and to date the two most significant fields of use in plant operations have been as oxygen sensors for gases and as oxygen probes for metallurgical production. The limitations to success on these two applications have largely centred around the physical and chemical properties of the materials forming the high-temperature cells, and the degree to which the potential industrial application could be approximated to the customary laboratory environment.

The production device which is to be used as a liquid metal—oxygen probe is an assembly of components each of which must have the appropriate intrinsic

[5] C. B. Alcock and T. N. Belford, *Trans. Faraday Soc.*, 1964, **60**, 822.
[6] T. N. Belford and C. B. Alcock, *Trans Faraday Soc.*, 1964, **61**, 443.
[7] R. Littlewood, *Steel Times*, 1964, **189**, 423.

properties as well as being chemically compatible with the other components of the probe under service conditions. It is this mutual interdependence of the functioning of each component that must be stressed in describing the oxygen probe as 'a ceramic system'. The phrase is used in its engineering sense to describe a collection of materials and objects so assembled and interacting as to perform a specified operation under specified physical circumstances and for a designated period of time. This definition must be clearly and qualitatively differentiated from the physicochemical definition of a system as 'a part of the universe which is separated for study'. In the engineering context a system must be designed to achieve a specified result, and the system which fails to carry out a specified task has failed, and is of no practical interest until suitably modified.

The major use of the oxygen probe in the steel industry which is foreseen at present is for the determination of the oxygen level in the liquid metal at the end of the refining stage, so that the appropriate aluminium addition may be made during casting to de-oxidize the metal and to control the 'rimming' action. This is the technical jargon for the evolution of carbon monoxide during the cooling of the liquid metal to the solid state. The de-oxidation reaction (2),

$$2[Al]_{Fe} + 3[O]_{Fe} \rightarrow Al_2O_3 \tag{2}$$

where $[\ ]_{Fe}$ represents a substance dissolved in liquid iron, may be assumed for calculation purposes to go practically to completion but the final level of oxygen in the melts is usually about $1-10$ p.p.m., which indicates some failure to reach complete thermodynamic equilibrium. The measurement must obviously be made on the liquid steel before casting, and so the apparatus must function at $1600\,^{\circ}C$, $70\,^{\circ}C$ above the melting point of iron.

Because of the extreme temperatures involved, and because measurements are normally made on large quantities of liquid steel during the refining stage, the trend in design of an oxygen probe for steelmaking has been in the direction of a short period of immersion of the probe, in order to reduce contact time for the operator. This, in turn, has meant that the probe must undergo extremely rapid temperature changes during immersion and therefore to the normal problems of chemical compatibility which are part of the probe designer's concern, must be added consideration of thermal shock resistance.

Laboratory Systems

Let us first consider a typical laboratory apparatus which functions under ideal circumstances, and yields results which can be corroborated by other experimental techniques. The apparatus used by Belford and Alcock to measure oxygen in solution in liquid lead[5] incorporated a commercial magnesia-stabilized zirconia crucible as a container for the liquid metal and as an electrolyte (Figure 1). The crucible was closed with an alumina lid, and so the liquid metal was well separated from the nickel–nickel oxide electrode placed on the outside of the bottom of the crucible. One of the major experimental problems in the temperature range $510-700\,^{\circ}C$ was the choice of an inert, electrically conducting, material which could be used to contact the liquid metal electrode. Following the experiments of Richardson and Webb,[8] iridium metal was used

[8] F. D. Richardson and L. E. Webb, *Trans. I.M.M.*, 1954–55, **64**, 529.

and this functioned satisfactorily over many days of experimentation. In a subsequent study of oxygen in liquid tin in the same temperature range[6] osmium was used as an electrical contact to the liquid metal, and a thoria–yttria solid solution crucible was used as a container. Subsequently Richardson and Diaz[9] and other workers have found that cermets of molybdenum with ZrO_2, Al_2O_3, or Cr_2O_3 can give satisfactory service under moderately oxidizing conditions, such as those prevailing in liquid copper containing a solution of oxygen up to one atomic percent at $1200\,^\circ C$.

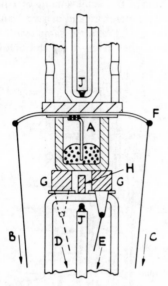

Figure 1 *Cell assembly.* A: *electrolyte crucible containing* Pb *and* Ir *probe;* B *and* C: *leads to electrometer and coulometric circuit via silica bollards;* D *and* E: *leads to earth and coulometric circuit, respectively, via silica bollards;* F: Pt *foil;* G: *semicircular metal + metal oxide pellets:* H: *alumina spacer;* J: *thermocouples*

The choice of an electronically conducting contact to the liquid metal is a very difficult one because the chosen material must be chemically compatible both with the liquid metal and with the oxygen potential which is generated by the oxygen dissolved in the metal. At high temperatures it is not only important to consider the possible formation of condensed oxides at the contact–liquid metal interface but volatile oxides such as PtO_2, RhO_2, MoO_3, and WO_3 whose formation can lead to oxygen loss from the liquid metal phase at the interface. Providing the measurements are to be made on a large metal bath this can be a relatively unimportant effect.

The electrical conductivities of the cermets are somewhat lower than that of platinum metal, and indeed, as long as the conductivity is reasonably high when compared with the electrolyte conductivity even semiconducting oxides may be

---

[9] C. M. Diaz and F. D. Richardson, in 'EMF measurements in high temperature systems', ed. C. B. Alcock, Inst. of Mining and Metallurgy, London, p. 29.

used as electronic contacts. Thus ZnO has been used with some limited success as a contact material to liquid tin containing oxygen.[10]

In most of these and subsequent laboratory studies of liquid metal–oxygen solutions, either a crucible or a tube made out of the solid electrolyte has played an important role. An apparatus which was used for the study of sodium–oxygen solutions[11] in which a thoria-yttria tube was employed is shown in Figure 2. Because of the thermal shock sensitivity of these ceramic configurations, the apparatus is normally allowed to reach the experimental temperature during a heating cycle of several hours. The achievement of equilibrium is only assumed when the e.m.f. at a given temperature and oxygen content can be held constant to within a few millivolts at most, and the same result can be achieved when the chosen temperature is approached from above and below.

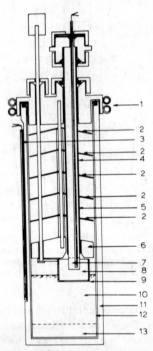

Figure 2 *Apparatus used in the study of the unsaturated sodium solutions. 1. Cooling coil: 2. Nickel fins; 3. Wall thermocouple measuring temperature of sodium pool; 4. MgO tube; 5. Electrolyte tube; 6. Thick nickel cover plate; 7. Sn–SnO$_2$ reference electrode; 8. Unsaturated sodium sample; 9. Nickel cup; 10. Sodium pool equilibrated with* Ta; *11. Outer stainless-steel jacket; 12. Inner nickel jacket; 13. Tantalum powder*

Relatively accurate information now exists for oxygen solutions in many liquid metals. These have been obtained either by e.m.f. techniques or by gas equilibration. In a few cases both techniques have been employed and the con-

[10] G. Petot-Evans, R. Farbi, and C. Petot, *J. Chem. Thermodynamics*, 1975, **7**, 1131.
[11] C. B. Alcock and G. P. Stavropoulos, *Canad. Met. Quart.*, 1971, **10**, 257.

cordance of the results decreases as the experimental temperature increases above 1000 °C. The scatter in the results for tin, copper, and liquid iron reflects the increase in the magnitude of the experimental task as steelmaking temperatures are approached. In Table II are the results which are now available, together with the heats of formation of the lower oxide of each metal. It follows that the oxygen potentials of the metal–metal oxide systems indicate the levels of oxygen potential at which we must work for the study of each metallic solvent.

TABLE II - Thermodynamics of oxygen solutions in liquid metals and the corresponding oxides

Metal	$\Delta \bar{G}_{\frac{1}{2}O_2}$ for $\frac{1}{2}O_2 \rightarrow [O]$ cal.	ΔH°_{298} oxide,cal/g. atom of oxygen
Silver	$-3,400 + 1.2T$	$-7,300$ Ag_2O
Nickel	$-18,000 - 1.6T$	$-57,500$ NiO
Cobalt	$-20,000 - 1.8T$	$-57,000$ CoO
Copper	$-20,300 + 1.5T$	$-40,000$ Cu_2O
Iron	$-27,900 - 3.0T$	$-63,200$ FeO
Lead	$-28,500 + 3.4T$	$-52,400$ PbO
Germanium	$-39,000 + 3.5T$	$-61,000$ GeO_2
Tin	$-43,900 + 6.6T$	$-69,300$ SnO_2
Indium	$-51,400 + 8.1T$	$-73,800$ In_2O_3
Gallium	$-52,700 + 6.5T$	$-86,300$ Ga_2O_3
Sodium	$-87,000 + 18.8T$	$-100,000$ Na_2O

In each case, the oxide quoted is in equilibrium with the saturated solution of oxygen in the liquid metal.

The limitations due to the properties of the electrolyte systems which we have at present can be brought out by considering the electrical conduction properties of these systems in relation to the oxygen potentials and temperatures which it would be desirable to study. The container material was changed from stabilized zirconia to thoria-yttria in these first two laboratory studies of oxygen in solution in liquid lead and tin because of the greater stability and hence much lower oxygen potential of the oxygen–tin system.

Two experimental techniques have been used principally to determine the range of oxygen potentials and temperature over which these two electrolytic solids function satisfactorily. By electrical conductivity measurements[12,13] it has been shown that the zirconia-based electrolytes are principally electrolytic from oxygen pressures of 1 atm down to about 10^{-12} atm at 1000 °C and the thoria-based electrolytes from about 10^{-6} down to 10^{-30} atm (Figure 3). If these results are combined with the Ellingham diagram for oxide formation, it can be shown that the zirconia electrolytes function down to iron–FeO on the stability scale, and the thoria electrolytes down to sodium–Na_2O and chromium–Cr_2O_3.

[12] H. Schmalzried, *Z. Phys. Chem.*, 1963, **38**, 87.
[13] M. F. Lasker and R. A. Rapp, *Z. Phys. Chem.*, 1966, **49**, 198.

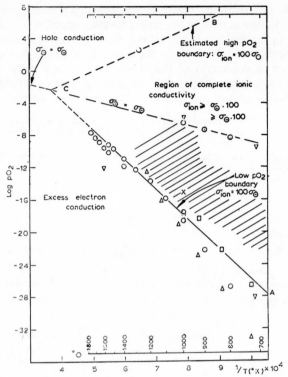

Figure 3 *Temperature and oxygen pressure conditions for purely ionic conduction in calcia-stabilized zirconia*

The second technique which has been used for the determination of the ionic transference number at temperatures up to 1000 °C employs electrochemical cells with electrodes of known, selected oxygen potentials. The e.m.f. is given by the general form of equation (3), where t_i is the electrochemical transference

$$E = \frac{RT}{4F} \int_{p_{O_2}}^{p'_{O_2}} t_i \, d\ln p_{O_2} \qquad (3)$$

number of oxygen ions in the electrolyte.

The remaining and less frequently used technique for the determination of oxygen ion transference numbers is the 'blocking' electrode method, in which a cell of the type

gold electrode | solid electrolyte | metal–metal oxide

is polarized, and the partial defect electron conductivities are calculated from the steady-state conductivity, *e.g.* equation (4), where σ_+^o is the conductivity due

$$I_\infty = \frac{RT}{FL} \left\{ \sigma_+^o \, [1 - \exp(-V)] + \sigma_+^o \, [\exp(V) - 1] \right\} \qquad (4)$$

to positive holes, $V = EF/RT$, and L is the specimen length. When excess electrons contribute to the conductivity only, equation (5) is obtained, where σ_-^o is the conductivity due to electrons. The values of σ_+^o and σ_-^o in these equations

$$I_\infty = \frac{RT}{FL}\left\{\sigma_-^o\ [1-\exp(-V)] + \sigma_-^o\ [\exp(V) - 1]\right\} \tag{5}$$

are obtained by plotting $I_\infty/[1-\exp(-V)]$ (LF/RT) against $\exp(V)$ and extrapolating to zero value of the applied potential E.[14]

Although the thoria-based electrolytes would thus appear to be superior at the low oxygen potentials which are reached during steel de-oxidation, they are not used commercially because of the radioactivity hazard which would be associated with their manufacture and use.

Pilot Plant Studies

The equipment which was developed for the laboratory studies made use of small metal samples of a few grams only in an electrochemical cell which functioned at a well determined temperature. In turning to the pilot plant scale of operations we must now consider measurements with liquid metal samples of 100–500 lbs, and this change of scale brings about a complete change in experimental procedure. Because of environmental considerations, the operator now is able to approach the hot metal phase only very briefly, yet during this time the measurements must be carried out, and the oxygen probe must be brought up to thermal equilibrium with the liquid metal in the relatively short times available, and hence the change to the 'probe' technique. Because of the thermal shock which is associated with bringing the probe up to thermal equilibrium with liquid steel at 1600 °C, the crucible or tube design of the laboratory study has been replaced with a pellet of electrolyte sealed into a quartz or Vycor tube for the basic component of the pilot plant scale probe. The joining procedure for these components can either be flame-sealing or cementing. In the former there are many attendant problems of manufacture which influence the design of the final system, but this technique is more convenient for industrial assembly methods. The reason quartz has been chosen as the separating component between the liquid metal on one side of the electrolyte pellet and the reference electrode on the other side, is not because of its thermal shock resistance, but because at steelmaking temperatures, *i.e.* 1600 °C, quartz softens, and the peripheral strains induced when a quartz tube is sealed at one end to an electrolyte pellet, are annealed out very quickly. Secondly, quartz, being transparent, permits rapid radiative heat transfer from the hot liquid metal to the (initially) cold reference electrode which is held within the tube. The cell can thus reach thermal equilibrium a matter of a few seconds after immersion.

The choice of electrolyte material is directed towards the zirconia systems because of the absence of toxicity of the powdered material from which the electrolyte pellets are to be made, and the choice of a particular electrolyte seems to be between zirconia with calcia or magnesia stabilization for large scale production.

The phase diagrams for the $CaO-ZrO_2$ and $MgO-ZrO_2$ systems (Figures 4 and 5) show that in both cases the monoclinic–tetragonal crystal structure of

[14] J. W. Patterson, E. C. Bogren, and R. A. Rapp, *J. Electrochem. Soc.*, 1967, **114**, 752.

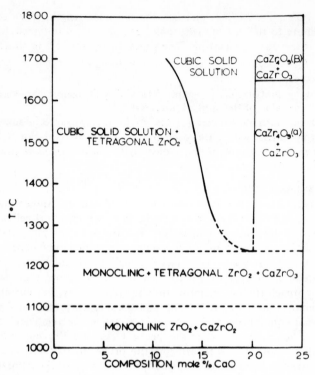

Figure 4 *A region of the* CaO−ZrO$_2$ *phase diagram*

pure ZrO$_2$ is transformed into a fluorite (CaF$_2$) structure on solid solution formation. Compounds of the type CaO,ZrO$_2$ can be formed at high alkaline earth
oxide content, but we will focus on the terminal ZrO$_2$-rich solid solution for this
discussion.

One immediately obvious difference between these two phase diagrams is
the existence of a phase transformation in the MgO−ZrO$_2$ system at around
1400 °C, below which the fluorite solid solution reverts to the tetragonal modification of ZrO$_2$ together with pure MgO. Above this temperature a 10 mole percent solid solution in ZrO$_2$ will function as a solid electrolyte, and below the
transformation temperature the system is a semiconductor with a predominating
electronic partial conductivity. Because this transformation occurs relatively
slowly below about 1100 °C, electrolytes based on MgO−ZrO$_2$ have functioned
satisfactorily in the low temperature range, even although islands of semiconducting material gradually form within the electrolyte sample owing to transformation during the measurements. Providing that the regions of semiconductor are
well separated from one another by grains of electrolytic material, a cell can still
function satisfactorily. Needless to say, the phase diagram suggests that the MgO−
ZrO$_2$ system will function as an electrolyte at steelmaking temperatures.

There is another drawback of a chemical nature to the use of calcia-stabilized
zirconia for a steelmaking probe incorporating a quartz tube. This is that there is

a very strong interaction between CaO and SiO$_2$ and so the quartz tube tends to 'leach' out the calcium oxide from the electrolyte during the flame sealing process, leaving a layer of semiconducting ZrO$_2$-rich material around the periphery of the electrolyte pellet. Magnesium oxide has a much lower affinity for silica than does CaO, and hence this leaching effect during flame sealing is much less marked with MgO–ZrO$_2$ electrolytes.

Ideally one should take advantage of the respective merits of MgO and CaO as additions to zirconia to form solid electrolytes and in this way it is possible by appropriate synthesis and heat treatment to make MgO–CaO–ZrO$_2$ solid electrolytes of a desired composition and structure.

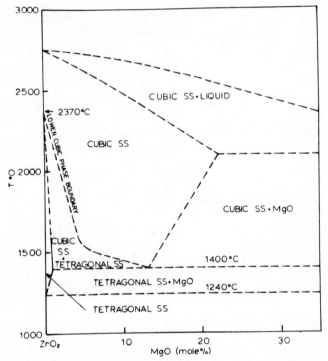

Figure 5 *A region of the* MgO–ZrO$_2$ *phase diagram*

The structural aspect seems to be of greatest significance in controlling the thermal shock resistance of the electrolytes. Because of the monotonic nature of the increase of the thermal expansion coefficient of calcia-stabilized zirconia, an electrolyte pellet made of this material is found to undergo considerable stress during a rapid change of temperature. This in turn leads to the propagation of micro-cracks and the brittle failure mode of behaviour which is characteristic of ceramic materials, and the electrolyte pellet is often shattered.

The propagation of micro-cracks can be reduced in one of two ways, both making use of a second 'phase' to absorb the crack propagation energy. A sample of fluorite-structure zirconia can be made to contain islands of tetragonal zirconia by choosing the appropriate composition in the two-phase region of the phase diagram for the CaO$-$ZrO$_2$ system, *e.g.* 5$-$10 mole percent CaO, and the mixture is referred to as 'partially stabilized' zirconia. Alternatively, this two-phase mixture may be achieved in the MgO$-$ZrO$_2$ system by controlled annealing for a limited period below the transformation temperature of 1400 °C. This second process produces a microstructure which is more readily controlled and hence is of a more reproducible behaviour, whereas the preparation of partially stabilized calcia$-$zirconia will have a phase distribution which is largely dependent on the particle size and sintering behaviour of the original powders.

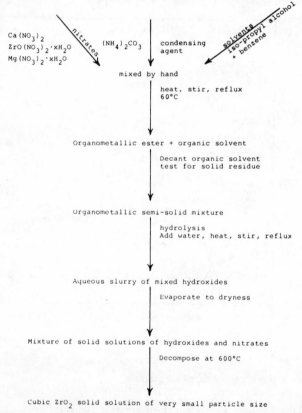

Figure 6 *Schematic diagram of the preparation of cubic zirconia solid solution using an organometallic compound*

An alternative 'phase' which sometimes prevents the propagation of cracks in ceramics is a well-distributed pore volume. This is usually found in a typical industrial product which results from sintering at a temperature which is too low to allow approach to theoretical density but which is sufficient to provide sufficient mechanical strength for handling and use in oxygen probes. Ceramographic examination of a number of successful commercially produced electrolyte pellets made for oxygen probes by sintering at the relatively low temperature for zirconia of 1600 °C shows a pore structure, which probably accounts for the resistance to thermal shock of these materials.

The understanding of the mechanical properties of these two-phase thermally tough materials requires a great deal of experimental study, and the preparation, reproducibly, of samples having a well-defined micro-structure is still a matter of empirical approach and requires very reproducible preparative techniques. The rather haphazard procedure of preparing oxide solid solutions from starting materials of separate oxide powders can be altogether eliminated by using organometallic compounds as starting points. The route which was used to make controlled electrolytes in the author's laboratory is shown in Figure 6, and several routes for other ceramic oxide systems have been described.[15] The material so produced is usually too fine for use in industry as a starting material and some considerable work must be done to discover how much pre-sintering can be achieved before the final shaping and sintering of the electrolyte pellet. Our studies indicated that pre-sintering at 1100 °C for about 24 h produced the best particles for shaping and sintering at 1600 °C for 8–12 h. A satisfactory and reproducible electrolyte could be produced by mixing calcium and magnesium ions in the fluorite-type zirconia phase by balancing the amounts of the cubic and non-cubic zirconia phases as well as the pore volume and distribution.

The Activity and Content of Oxygen in a Steel

In order to test an oxygen probe it is necessary to compare the measured e.m.f. and the oxygen contents of samples of the metal which are analysed by the more conventional inert gas-fusion analysis. Figure 7 shows pilot plant results for a 200 lb melt of liquid iron in which the oxygen content was reduced first of all by ferrosilicon and then by aluminium deoxidation. The agreement between the electrochemical and inert gas-fusion results is certainly satisfactory for industrial purposes in this instance, but a complication would arise if an alloy steel had been tested. This is because the cell provides information concerning the *activity* of oxygen whereas the analytical procedure yields the oxygen content. One of these may be calculated from the other providing that the activity coefficient of oxygen in the steel is known. When the solvent is almost pure liquid iron, the activity coefficient is practically constant over the whole solution range (0–0.22 wt % at 1600 °C). However, when alloying elements such as chromium, which have a stronger or much weaker affinity for oxygen, are introduced in substantial amounts, *i.e.* greater than a mole fraction of 0.1, the oxygen activity coefficient may alter drastically, depending on the alloying element.[16]

It follows that knowledge is required of the effects of alloying elements on the activity coefficient of oxygen dissolved in liquid iron before the relationship between the probe e.m.f. and the oxygen content can be established for any particular steel. The theoretical analysis and prediction of alloying element effects on the activity coefficient of oxygen in other metals besides iron is being carried on from the results of measurements made by the use of solid-state electrochemistry and conventional gas–liquid equilibrium studies, and some

[15] K. S. Mazdiyasni, C. T. Lynch, and J. S., Smith, *J. Amer. Ceram. Soc.,* 1966, **49**, 286.
[16] J. Chipman, *J. Iron Steel Inst.*, 1955, **180**, 97.

reasonably quantitative description can now be given. In an equation developed by Jacob and Alcock,[17] the activity coefficient of oxygen in a binary solvent A+B can be calculated, given a knowledge of the activity coefficient of oxygen in pure A and pure B and of the activity coefficients of the metals A and B in the ternary A+B+O alloy. The theory is based upon a mixture of the free electron model with the chemical bond approach and takes account of the repulsion of the conduction electrons from the metal atoms surrounding oxygen ions which are thought to be the dissolved species. This equation (6) can be shown to

$$\frac{1}{(\gamma_O^{A+B})^{1/4}} = X_A \frac{(\gamma_A^{A+B})^{1/2}}{(\gamma_O^A)^{1/4}} + X_B \frac{(\gamma_B^{A+B})^{1/2}}{(\gamma_O^B)^{1/4}} \qquad (6)$$

account for all of the experimental data which exist for the ternary metal–oxygen systems to a very good approximation.

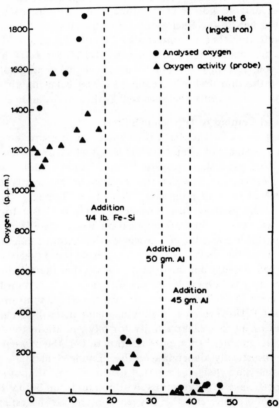

Figure 7 *Oxygen concentration changes with various additives.* (Abscissa : time/min)

The Long-term Measurement of Oxygen in Liquid Metals

The probes which are presently available at a reasonably well-developed stage of reliability are mainly only suited for a brief period of immersion in the liquid metal. Typical oxygen probes using oxygen–platinum as the reference electrode

[17] K. T. Jacob and C. B. Alcock, *Acta Met.*, 1972, **20**, 221.

and a calcia–zirconia electrolyte pellet sealed in quartz are destroyed by the melt between 5 and *ca.* 100 s after the initial thermal equilibration. There are many applications of the probe at temperatures above 1000 °C where it would be desirable to monitor the oxygen content for much longer periods, such as the monitoring of the metal stream during a continuous casting process, and we have succeeded on the laboratory and pilot plant scales in producing such an oxygen probe. The change introduced in this system by comparison with the 'normal' probes is that the measuring apparatus is no longer maintained at a constant temperature, but the reference electrode compartment is outside the liquid metal and at a different, but known, temperature. In such a non-isothermal probe, the e.m.f. is measured between a known oxygen partial pressure p_{O_2} at one temperature T_C and the unknown p'_{O_2} at a higher temperature T_H, that of the metal phase, and to a sufficiently good approximation equation (7) holds.

$$E = \frac{RT_C}{4F} \ln p_{O_2} - \frac{RT_H}{4F} \ln p'_{O_2} + a(T_H - T_C) \tag{7}$$

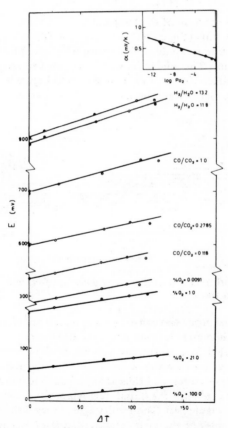

Figure 8 *The dependence of e.m.f. (E) on the temperature gradient (ΔT) and oxygen pressure (P_{O_2}) using a non-isothermal cell*

This equation is an approximation to the irreversible thermodynamic equation and involves irreversible terms such as the entropy of transport of oxygen ions within the electrolyte sample which spans the temperature gradient $T_H - T_C$ and α is the Seebeck coefficient of the electrolyte material.

To establish the fundamental basis for this new technique, the e.m.f.'s were measured in a twin cell arrangement in which oxygen passed down the inside of the calcia-zirconia tube which was maintained in a thermal gradient of 100 °C and various gas mixtures (oxygen + argon) or (carbon monoxide + carbon dioxide), flowed around the outside of the tube. Platinum contacts to each end of the tube, both inside and out, enabled measurements to be made of the non-isothermal e.m.f. for each of the gas mixtures against pure oxygen for a fixed temperature gradient at a number of average levels. The e.m.f. for a gas of fixed oxygen partial pressure over the temperature gradient is given by equation (8),

$$E = \frac{RT}{4F}(S^o_{T_H} - S^o_{T_C}) + a(T_H - T_C) \qquad (8)$$
$$\cong \beta(T_H - T_C)$$

practically a linear function of the temperature.

Experimental results (Figure 8) show that the Seebeck coefficient, which in principle is a function not only of temperature but also of oxygen potential, can be assumed constant. The apparatus which was used to establish these results in the temperature range 1000–1300 °C is shown in Figure 9. Results which agree with this conclusion have been obtained at high temperatures by Fischer.[18]

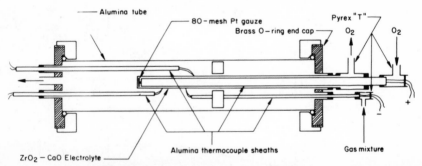

Figure 9 *The non-isothermal cell used to determine the effects of temperature gradient and oxygen potential on the e.m.f.*

A non-isothermal probe was constructed using this principle, in which a calcia–zirconia rod was immersed at one end in a 200 lb melt of liquid iron and the other end was sealed in a jacket through which air was passed at a controlled flow rate. Electrical contact was established with the rod inside the jacket at three different temperatures, and thus at any given time results were obtained for three temperature gradients, the liquid steel temperature being the high temperature in each case (Figure 10). The results agreed very well with those calculated from analysed samples of the melt. The oxygen level was again varied by ferro-

[18] W. Fischer, *Z. Naturforsch.*, 1967, **22a**, 1575.

silicon addition, and the probe followed the variation of the oxygen content of the inductively stirred melt practically instantaneously. The probe can therefore be used in all respects in an equivalent role as the isothermal probe, but the endurance of the non-isothermal probe in continuous contact with liquid steel is >3 h.

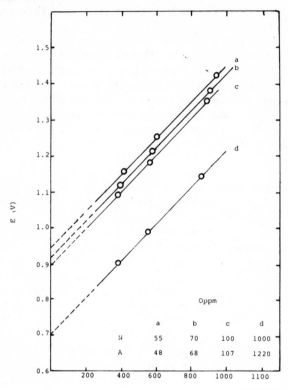

Figure 10 *The dependence of e.m.f. (E) on temperature gradient (ΔT) using a non-isother-mal probe immersed in liquid iron with different oxygen concentrations (N: nominal; A: analysed).*

The additional merit of the non-isothermal probe apart from its endurance in liquid steel is the simplicity of construction. The electrolyte rod which is immersed in the liquid metal at one end is one of the simplest structures to make and one at least sensitive to thermal shock; this is because the end which is immersed is free of constraint. The seal between the electrolyte rod and the jacket surrounding the reference electrode is outside the liquid metal and therefore can be run at a much lower temperature. The component which is now most likely to give rise to problems is the electronic contact to the metal, but we saw at the beginning of our consideration of the materials aspects of this problem, that many semiconducting materials and cermets whose suitability remains to be explored.

Conclusion

From the many aspects of the oxygen probe system which have been studied at the University of Toronto and from the results of our discussions with industrialists, it is concluded that there are four principal aspects aside from such commercial aspects as materials cost and patentability which are significant in the development of a new system such as the oxygen probe. These are collected in Figure 11.

The first of these is that since the instrument can only, theoretically, provide information of an intrinsically rather limited nature, that is to say the thermodynamic oxygen potential, there is a need for a substantial supporting data base. This consists in this example of information about the activity and activity coefficient of oxygen in solution in liquid metals and alloys and of the metal—metal oxide systems which can be used as reference electrodes, the chemical compatibility of electronic contact materials, and the electrical properties of potential electrolytes.

1. Basic ancillary data	Activity coefficients of oxygen in metals & alloys.
	Reference electrode thermodynamics.
	Corrosion-resistant electrode contact materials.
2. Fabrication procedure	Preparation routes for reproducible electrolytes.
	Sintering conditions applicable in volume production.
	Cost of production relative to value to user.
3. Field trials. To evaluate	Suitability to use by industrial labour force.
	Potential market volume in relation to changing industrial practice.
4. Continuing research to improve flexibility of application	New fabrication processes.
	New electrolyte properties.
	Second-generation devices.

Figure 11 *Aspects of development research for an oxygen probe*

Secondly, there are problems which relate to the ease of manufacture at a significant volume of production. The fabricating route must be simplified and tailored to the least complicated industrial processing so that prohibitively complex production facilities are not involved, the main exception being where the product cost will allow this.

Thirdly, the industrial value of the output of the device must be proven in the field, and consideration given to possible reduction in demand once preliminary trials have provided an empirical guide to future practice. If the use of a hundred probes provides a steel company with a sound operating procedure which no longer involves the use of a probe, then the future demand outlook will not be very encouraging to a probe manufacturer.

Fourthly, as in this case, an instrument such as the oxygen probe usually leads directly to the demand for a new type of equipment such as the long duration probe, and it is valuable when the production experience which has been gained in the first design can be made use of in the development of the second generation device. The same could not be said, for example, of an attempt to develop a sulphur or a nitrogen probe from the design data for an oxygen probe, because a similar input data base to that which supported the oxygen probe design has not been established for such developments.

The oxygen probe has come a long way in less than twenty years and much research and development has been expended in bringing us to the present stage, but we still wait to see just what the industrial importance of this device in the metal-making industry will finally turn out to be. High-temperature chemistry has certainly benefited from the effort whatever the outcome.

I would like to express my thanks for the efforts and co-operation of my colleagues past and present in the Electrochemical Sensors Group at the University of Toronto, and to the National Research Council of Canada for their invaluable financial support.

Phase Diagrams and Thermodynamic Studies of the Cs–Cr–O, Na–Cr–O and Na–Fe–O Systems and their Relationships to the Corrosion of Steels by Caesium and Sodium

By C. F. KNIGHTS and B. A. PHILLIPS

Materials Development Division, A.E.R.E. Harwell, Nr Didcot, Oxon

Introduction

Caesium is a major fission product of uranium–plutonium oxide fuel in nuclear reactors, and the oxygen potential of the fuel increases as fission proceeds. Since corrosion of the steel cladding creates associations of Cs, Cr, and oxygen,[1-5] the studies reported here of the ranges of Cs vapour pressures and oxygen potentials necessary for the stability of Cs–Cr–O compounds are relevant to an assessment of the integrity of the cladding.

The thermodynamic and phase studies of the Na–Cr–O and Na–Fe–O systems are relevant both to the corrosion by liquid sodium in sodium cooled reactors[6,7] and to the corrosion of heat exchangers by Na–Na$_2$O–NaOH mixtures arising from leaks of water into the sodium circuit.[8-12]

The thermodynamic studies presented in this paper are largely the work of the authors whilst the corrosion studies considered are drawn from the literature.

Experimental

The materials used in the preparative work were of the highest purity available. Cs (99.9%) and Cr$_2$O$_3$ (99.99% purity) were supplied by Koch Light Laboratories whilst 98% Na$_2$O (containing ~2% Na, Na$_2$O$_2$) and Cs$_2$CrO$_4$ (99.9%) were supplied by Ventron Corporation. Sodium (<5 p.p.m. oxygen) was obtained at Harwell by distillation of reactor grade sodium, and oxygen was taken from bulbs of spectroscopically pure gas. Air active materials were handled in an

1   J. E. Antill, K. A. Peakall, and E. F. Smart, *J. Nuclear Mater.*, 1975, **56**, 47.
2   W. Batey and K. Q. Bagley, *J. Brit. Nuclear Energy Soc.*, 1974, **13**, 49.
3   M. Aubert, D. Calais, and R. Le Beuze, *J. Nuclear Mater.*, 1976, **60**, 1.
4   P. Hofmann and O. Götzmann, International Atomic Energy Agency, Panel Proceedings, 1972, *IAEA-PL*-463/14.
5   R. W. Ohse and M. Schlehter, International Atomic Energy Agency, Panel Proceedings, 1972, *IAEA-PL*-463/18.
6   A. W. Thorley and C. Tyzack, *Liquid Alkali Metals*, (Conference Proceedings, British Nuclear Energy Society), 1973, 257.
7   B. H. Kolster, *J. Nuclear Mater.*, 1975, **55**, 155.
8   H. V. Chamberlain, *et al.*, USAEC Report, 1970, APDA-254;
9   W. T. Lee, USAEC Report, 1971, LMEC-70-21.
10 R. N. Newman and C. A. Smith, *J. Nuclear Mater.*, 1974, **52**, 173.
11 K. Buxton, A. Mackay, and K. Tregonning, *J. Brit. Nuclear Energy Soc.*, 1975, **14**, 77.
12 International Atomic Energy Agency, Study Group Meeting on Steam Generators for Liquid Metal Fast Breeder Reactors, Bensberg, Germany, Oct. 1974, IWGFR/1.

argon-filled glove box ($<$2 p.p.m. oxygen, $<$10 p.p.m. H_2O) and reactions were conducted in alumina or nickel crucibles in glass vacuum apparatus. Reaction products were identified by X-ray diffraction at room temperature using Cu/K_α radiation for Cr compounds and Co/K_α for Fe compounds.

Vapour pressure measurements in the range $10^{-9} - 10^{-4}$ atm were made in a Bendix 'time of flight' mass spectrometer with a Knudsen cell unit attachment enclosed in a glove box. Thoria liners were occasionally used in the nickel or stainless steel Knudsen cells (1 mm orifice). The Pt/Pt–13% Rh thermocouple calibrations were made in situ against the melting points of gallium, gold, and indium, and the heats of vaporization of gallium, copper, lead, caesium, and sodium were used to calibrate the mass spectrometer. Before and after each period of operation an internal machine calibration was made with the pure parent alkali metal.

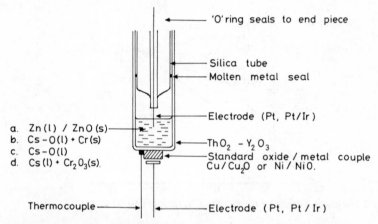

a. $Zn(l) \, / \, ZnO(s)$
b. $Cs-O(l) + Cr(s)$
c. $Cs-O(l)$
d. $Cs(l) + Cr_2O_3(s)$.

Labels in figure: 'O' ring seals to end piece; Silica tube; Molten metal seal; Electrode (Pt, Pt/Ir); $ThO_2 - Y_2O_3$; Standard oxide / metal couple Cu/Cu_2O or Ni/NiO; Thermocouple; Electrode (Pt, Pt / Ir)

Figure 1 *E.M.F. cell for liquid metal studies. The unit was supported in a pyrophyllite block under an atmosphere of argon contained in a silica tube. Couple (a) was used to check all operations. Systems (b), (c), and (d) were the phases examined*

Oxygen potential measurements in the Cs–Cr–O system were made with $ThO_2 - Y_2O_3$ and $ZrO_2 - Y_2O_3$ electrolytes. Studies of equilibria between all solid phases were made with these electrolytes in disc form in a cell essentially identical with that of Alcock and Stavropoulos,[13] each new electrolyte disc being checked for correct operation against a Cu, Cu_2O/Ni, NiO combination using the data of Flengas and Charette.[14] Liquid solutions were held within a $ThO_2-Y_2O_3$ tube ($ZrO_2-Y_2O_3$ tubes were not used because of severe corrosive attack by Cs–O liquids) with an arrangement shown schematically in Figure 1.[15] The correct functioning of the cell and initial e.m.f. values were checked satisfactorily against Ni/NiO and $Zn(l)/ZnO(s)$ using the data of Wilder.[16] The e.m.f. continually drifted away (for example 0.011 V in 18 min) due to corrosion of

[13] C. B. Alcock and G. P. Stavropoulos, *Canad. Metallurg. Quart. Trans.*, 1971, **10**, 257.
[14] S. N. Flengas and G. G. Charette, *J. Electrochem. Soc.*, 1968, **115**, 796.
[15] C. F. Knights and B. A. Phillips, to be published.
[16] T. C. Wilder, *Trans. Met. Soc. AIME*, 1969, **245**, 1370.

iridium or platinum contacts. Long term stability (days) was possible in Cs—O solutions between 3 and 17 atomic percent oxygen although outside this range the cell stability deteriorated.

The Cs—Cr—O System

The Cs—Cr—O phase diagram at 600–700 °C has tie lines radiating from Cr_2O_3 to the elements Cs and Cr and to the compounds $Cs_2Cr_2O_7$, Cs_2CrO_4, Cs_3CrO_4, and Cs_4CrO_4 (Figure 2). The last two ternary compounds have not been previously reported and the X-ray diffraction patterns will be published elsewhere.[15]

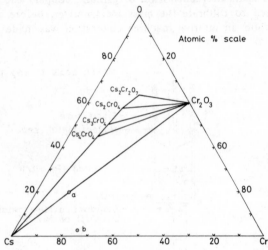

Figure 2 *The phase diagram of the* Cs—Cr—O *system* (~650 °C)

The oxygen potentials $(RT \ln p_{O_2})$ at 650 °C in liquid caesium resulting from the addition of Cr_2O_3 (point a, Figure 2) drifted from 8 to 16 kJ mol^{-1} O$_2$ less negative than the couple for $Cr(s)/Cr_2O_3(s)$ whilst those resulting from the addition of Cr to Cs + O (3.3 at % point b, Figure 2) drifted from 2 to 18 kJ mol^{-1} O$_2$ more negative. The initial values were those closest to the Cr/Cr_2O_3 potential. The subsequent drift to the much more distant values occurred in experiments lasting 12–48 h and could have been partially due to the observed preferential loss of Y_2O_3 (15 w/o → 12 w/o) from the electrolyte and the formation of a Cs—Th—Y—O deposit. These results, the consistency with the conclusions drawn from the Cs vapour pressure measurements (see later), and the fact that caesium liquid at 600 °C did not react noticeably with Cr_2O_3 in 16 h favours the existence of a stable Cr_2O_3—Cs(l) tie line rather than a tie between Cs_4CrO_4 and Cr.

Repeated attempts to prepare a compound of the composition $CsCrO_2$ by the two reactions below were unsuccessful.

$$\left.\begin{array}{l} Cs_2CO_3 + Cr_2O_3 \neq 2 \ 'CsCrO_2' + CO_2 \\ Cs_2CrO_4 + Cr \neq 2 \ 'CsCrO_2' \end{array}\right\} \ 600\text{--}800 \,°C$$

Table 1 *Experimental measurements in the Cs–Cr–O system*[a]

Phase field	$RT\ln(p_{Cs}/\text{atm})$ J(g atom Cs)$^{-1}$ (T/K)	$RT\ln(p_{O_2}/\text{atm})$ J(g mole O_2)$^{-1}$ (T/K)
	(1)	(2)
$Cs_2CrO_4(s)$ $Cs_3CrO_4(s)$ $Cr_2O_3(s)$	$-(163 \pm 9)10^3 + (91 \pm 11)T$ (750–950 K)	$(-520 \pm 84)10^3 + (190 \pm 90)T$ (870–1100 K)
	(3)	(4)
$Cs_3CrO_4(s)$ $Cs_4CrO_4(s)$ $Cr_2O_3(s)$	$-(107 \pm 9)10^3 + (84 \pm 7)T$ (500–680 K)	See Table 2
	(5)	(6)
$Cs_4CrO_4(s)$ $Cr_2O_3(s)$ $Cs(l)$	$-70000 + 73.7T$ (600–900 K) vapour pressure over pure Cs	$-(736 \pm 60)10^3 + (170 \pm 60)T$ (890–990 K)

(a) The $\pm$ error bands are linked: + to +, – to –.

Addition of Cs(l) to Cs_2CrO_4 (yellow) readily created the compound Cs_3CrO_4 (green, m.p. >1000 °C under pressure) and further addition created Cs_4CrO_4 (brown). Measurement of the Cs vapour pressures in equilibrium with the three-phase assemblages $(Cs_4CrO_4–Cs_3CrO_4–Cr_2O_3)$ and $(Cs_3CrO_4–Cr_2CrO_4–Cr_2O_3)$ together with the value of $\Delta G_f^\circ(Cs_4CrO_4)$—established from the e.m.f. cell data—permitted the calculation of ΔG_f° for Cs_3CrO_4 and Cs_2CrO_4 and, in turn, calculation of the oxygen potentials in these fields shown in Table 1 and Figure 3. Oxygen potentials calculated for the $Cs_3CrO_4–Cs_2CrO_4–Cr_2O_3$ assemblage lie in the middle of the range of oxygen potentials (±30 kJ at 650 °C) determined experimentally (Figure 3) and provide a valuable check of the data, as does the comparison of $\Delta G_f^\circ(Cs_2CrO_4)$ with the published data for Cs_2CrO_4 at 298 K (Table 2).

The position of the boundary shown in Figure 3 between the Cs_xCrO_4 compounds and the Cs–O liquid solutions (entirely liquid above 500 °C[15,17]) has

Table 2 *Thermodynamic values derived from data in Table 1*[a]

Compound	ΔG_f° from Cs(l), O_2 (gas), Cr(s) J(g mole)$^{-1}$ (T/K)	Comments (numbers refer to Table 1)
$Cs_2CrO_4(s)$	$-(1410 \pm 120)10^3 + (398 \pm 130)T$	from values (1) and (2)
$Cs_2CrO_4(s)$	$-(1430)10^3 + 375\ T$	$\Delta H_{f\,298}^\circ, S_{298}^\circ$ (ref. 27)
$Cs_3CrO_4(s)$	$-(1510 \pm 130)10^3 + (430 \pm 140)T$	from values (1) and (2)
$Cs_4CrO_4(s)$	$-(1550 \pm 140)10^3 + (440 \pm 140)T$	from values (1), (2), and (3)
$Cs_4CrO_4(s)$	$-(1480 \pm 90)10^3 + (340 \pm 100)T$	from (6)
$RT\ln p_{O_2}$ for $Cs_3CrO_4–Cs_4$	$-(680 \pm 100)10^3 + (215 \pm 130)T$	from ΔG_f° $Cs_3CrO_4(s)$ above
$CrO_4–Cr_2O_3$ phase field	$-(620 \pm 80)10^3 + (140 \pm 100)T$	from ΔG_f° Cs_4CrO_4 (6)

(a) The $\pm$ error bands are linked: + to +, – to –.

[17] R. P. Elliott, 'Constitution of Binary Alloys, First Supplement', McGraw Hill, 1965, p. 368.

been estimated assuming that the position of the boundary is close to that calculated at 500 °C from oxygen potential data in the Cs–O system[15] and the known value of ΔG_f° for $Cs_2O(s)$ at 490 °C.[18]

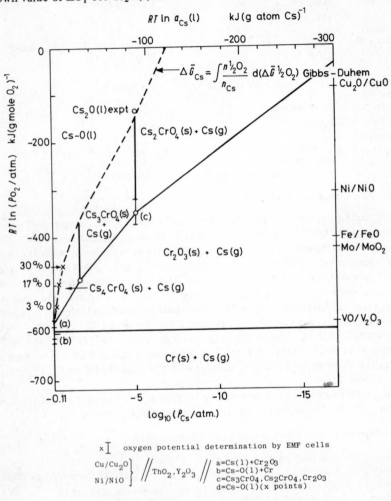

Figure 3 *Oxygen and caesium potential ranges at 650 °C for the stability of phases in the* Cs–Cr–O *system*

Corrosion of Steels by Caesium as a Function of Oxygen Potential[1–5]

The main source of the data on corrosion by caesium as a function of oxygen potential is the work of Antill *et al.*,[1] in which Cs was contained at the bottom of vertical, sealed, steel tubes with a variety of low-potential oxygen buffers

[18]   H. E. Flotow and D. W. Osbourne, *J. Chem. Thermodynamics*, 1974, **6**, 135.

(CuO/Cu$_2$O, Fe/FeO, Ni/NiO, Mo/MoO$_2$, and VO/V$_2$O$_3$) held at the top of the tube. The initial carbon dioxide atmosphere would have rapidly reacted with the Cs at 400–680 °C to give low CO$_2$ and CO pressures, and a Cs–O liquid. The Cs vapour over this liquid would have interacted, in the 200–2000 h of the experiments, with the oxygen source at 650–840 °C to form Cs–O liquid.

These thermodynamic conclusions are supported by experiment. First, a liquid phase had apparently been present in and around the alumina crucible containing the higher pressure oxygen sources. Secondly, in experiments at ⩾800 °C-with a Ni/NiO source, the tube surface showed evidence of liquid-phase formation with concomitant slagging. Thirdly, since the rate of mass transfer implied by the corrosion results cannot be achieved entirely by vapour phase transfer, Cs–O liquids are probably the prime means of mass transport.

The maximum rates of penetration of Type 316 steel by intergranular oxidation at 800 °C were measured optically. They decreased from 0.4 μm h^{-1} for Ni/NiO to 0.04 μm h^{-1} for Mo/MoO$_2$ and were undetectable (<0.02 μm h^{-1}) for VO/V$_2$O$_3$.

In the presence of Cr in the alloy and of Cs–O liquid in equilibrium with the higher oxygen potential sources Cs$_x$CrO$_4$ compounds should have formed. However, sectioning prior to metallographic examination would have removed these reactive phases and created surface voids. Such voids were indeed observed for Ni/NiO sources and less clearly for Fe/FeO sources. The surface oxide retained had Cs/Cr ratios in the range 0.07–0.4 for Ni/NiO, and 0.01–0.1 for Fe/FeO. The ratios decreased to 0.01–0.1 for Ni/NiO and 0.01–0.02 for Fe/FeO sources for internal oxide. Cs penetration was still detectable by ion probe analyses at concentrations of 10^{-2}–10^2 p.p.m. at depths several hundred microns greater than the oxide limit for Fe/FeO and Mo/MoO$_2$ buffers. Even these penetrations, however, were not observed for the VO/V$_2$O$_3$ buffer, implying that the threshold oxygen potential for attack by Cs–O liquid (Figure 3, dashed line) lies at a value between that for VO/V$_2$O$_3$ and Mo/MoO$_2$—a value consistent with the minimum oxygen potential required for the formation of Cs–Cr–O ternary compounds.

The Sodium–Chromium–Oxygen System

All the ternary compounds shown on the phase diagram (Figure 4) have been previously reported[19,20] and all but Na$_2$Cr$_2$O$_7$ have been shown to contain the chromium tetrahedrally co-ordinated by oxygen.[19] Na$_2$CrO$_3$ has been reported to occur[20] but probably does not exist.[21]

The existence of stable tie lines from NaCrO$_2$(s) to Cr$_2$O$_3$(s), Cr(s), Na(1), and Na$_2$O(s) and between the Na$_x$CrO$_4$ compounds (x = 2, 3, or 4) were suggested by experimental observations in the literature.[22,23] Confirmation of these tie lines,

[19] L. Lavielle and H. Kessler, *J. Electron Spectroscopy and Related Phenomena*, 1976, 8, 95.

[20] C. C. Addison and M. G. Barker, *J. Chem. Soc.*, 1965, 5534; *J. C. S. Dalton*, 1975, 2487.

[21] E. G. Van den Broek, P. J. Gellings, and H. Van Lith, *Inorg. Nuclear Chem. Letters*, 1975, **11**, 817; M. G. Barker and A. J. Hooper, *J. C. S. Dalton*, 1976, 1003.

[22] M. G. Barker and D. J. Wood, *J. Less Common Metals*, 1974, **35**, 315.

[23] M. G. Barker and D. J. Wood, Proc. 7th Internat. Symp. Reactivity of Solids, Bristol, 1972, (Ed. J. S. Anderson *et al.*), Chapman and Hall, London, 1972, 623.

Table 3 *Experimental measurements to date and derived standard free energies of formation of ternary compounds in the* Na–Cr–O *system*[a]

Phase field	Experimental data $RT\ln(p_{Na}/\text{atm})$ J(g atom Na)$^{-1}$	$RT\ln(p_{O_2}/\text{atm})$ J(g mole O$_2$)$^{-1}$	Derived data ΔG_f° J(g mole)$^{-1}$ for temp. range of expt. data[b] Phase	A[c]	B[c]
(i) NaCrO$_2$ Cr$_2$O$_3$ Cr	$-(226 \pm 5)10^3 + (109 \pm 9)T$ 510–1100 K, three samples	$-(749.9 \pm 7)10^3 + 170T$ from Cr/Cr$_2$O$_3$	NaCrO$_2$	(v) $-(876 \pm 18)10^3 + (194 \pm 9)T$ from (i) and ΔG_f°(Cr$_2$O$_3$)	(ix) $-(909.4 \pm 27)10^3 + (203 \pm 29)T$ from (ii), (x), and ΔG_f°(Na$_2$O)
(ii) NaCrO$_2$ Na$_4$CrO$_4$ Na$_2$O	$-(204 \pm 3)10^3 + (117 \pm 10)T$ 660–890 K, two samples	$-(414 \pm 16)10^3 + (147 \pm 10)T$ from (ii) and ΔG_f°(Na$_2$O)	Na$_4$CrO$_4$	(vi) $-(1601 \pm 25)10^3 + (437 \pm 19)T$ from (ii), (v), and ΔG_f°(Na$_2$O)	(x) $-(1635 \pm 20)10^3 + (446 \pm 19)T$ from (iii) and (xi)
(iii) NaCrO$_2$ Na$_4$CrO$_4$ Na$_3$CrO$_4$	$-(250 \pm 10)10^3 + (150 \pm 15)T$ 760–940 K, one sample	(iii) $-(274 \pm 65)10^3 + (48 \pm 66)T$ from (iii), (v), and (vi)[d] $-(377 \pm 80)10^3 + (75 \pm 32)T$ from (iii), (v), and (xi)	Na$_3$CrO$_4$	(vii) $-(1451 \pm 35)10^3 + (372 \pm 34)T$ from (iii) and (vi)	(xi) $-(1485 \pm 10)10^3 + (381 \pm 4)T$ from (iv) and (xii)
(iv) NaCrO$_2$ Na$_3$CrO$_4$ Na$_2$CrO$_4$	$-(259 \pm 5)10^3 + (129 \pm 3)T$ 900–1063 K, one sample	(iv) $-(256 \pm 45)10^3 + (90 \pm 40)T$ from (iv), (v), and (vii) $-(290 \pm 28)10^3 + (99 \pm 13)T$ from (iv), (v), and (xii)	Na$_2$CrO$_4$	(viii) $-(1291 \pm 40)10^3 + (328 \pm 37)T$ from (iv) and (vii)	(xii) $-(1325 \pm 5)10^3 + (337 \pm 1)T$ references 26–28

(a) The study is continuing: more samples are to be examined for measurements (ii), (iii), and (iv). (b) The data are derived directly from the experimental vapour pressure data using the literature data for Na(1) → Na(g), $\Delta G = +99730 - 85T$; ΔG_f°(Na$_2$O) $= -414800 + 137.6T(\pm 2 \text{ kJ})$,[24,25] ΔG_f°(Cr$_2O_3$) $= -1125000 + 255T(\pm 10 \text{ kJ})$,[25] in the temperature range 800–1000 K. (c) A, B: ΔG_f°'s derived from NaCrO$_2$ and Na$_2$CrO$_4$, respectively. The standard states in this range are Na(l), O$_2$ (g), Cr(s). (d) Very low ΔS_{O_2} implies that the best value for ΔG_{Na} in the NaCrO$_2$–Na$_4$CrO$_4$–Na$_3$CrO$_4$ field lies at the extreme of the error limit.

and the determination of the remaining phase boundaries are found in the X-ray and sodium vapour-pressure studies of the present work.

The thermodynamics of $Na_2O(s)$,[24,25] $Na_2CrO_4(s)$,[26-28] and Cr_2O_3,[25 b] are well established whilst for $NaCrO_2$, only $\Delta H^\circ_{f\,298K}$ was previously known.[29] A $\Delta G^\circ_{f\,298K}$ value seemed to be incorrect[30] and ΔG°_f at elevated temperatures had been only estimated from electromotive force experiments.[31,32] The difficulties associated with e.m.f. measurements in sodium led us to use mass spectrometry. Our results to date (Table 3) have been used to derive ΔG°_f as a function of temperature in the range 700–1100 K for $NaCrO_2$, Na_4CrO_4, Na_3CrO_4, and Na_2CrO_4 and, in turn, the stability of these compounds with respect to sodium vapour pressure and oxygen potential at 650 °C (Figure 5).

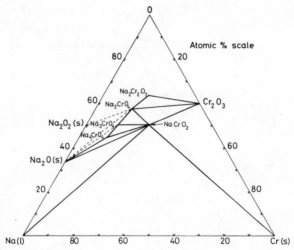

Figure 4 *The phase diagram of the* Na–Cr–O *system* (~650 °C)

Heating pure $NaCrO_2$ in a Knudsen cell with the intention of entering the $NaCrO_2$–Na_2CrO_4–Cr_2O_3 phase field did not result in the attainment of an equilibrium sodium pressure: the stainless steel Knudsen cell failed by corrosion at 860 °C while the sodium pressure was still decreasing. The final value recorded was 3×10^{-8} atm. These low sodium pressures imply high oxygen pressures, and

24 P. A. G. O'Hare, *J. Chem. Phys.*, 1972, **56**, 4513.
25 D. R. Stull and H. Prophet *et al.*, JANAF Thermochemical Tables NBRDS, NBS, 1970, 37; see also supplements in (a) *J. Phys. Chem. Ref. Data*, 1974, **3**, 311 and (b) 1975, **4**, 1.
26 L. G. Heppler, C. Moss, and T. Nelson, *J. Phys. Chem.*, 1960, **64**, 376.
27 J. Boerio and P. A. G. O'Hare, *J. Chem. Thermodynamics*, 1975, **7**, 1195.
28 L. Denielou, Y. Fournier *et al.*, *Compt. rend.*, 1971, **272**, C, 1855.
29 P. Gross, W. A. Gutteridge, and G. L. Wilson, *J. Chem. Soc.(A)*, 1970, 1908.
30 B. Jakuszewski and Z. Kozlowski, *Lodziensis Acta Chim.*, 1958, **3**, 5 (in English).
31 P. C. S. Wu, USAEC Report, 1972, IS-T-508.
32 E. Berkey and S. A. Jansson, 'Corrosion by Liquid Metals', ed. J. E. Draley and J. R. Weeks, Plenum Press, 1970, p. 479.

indeed a value of $\sim 10^{-4}$ atm at 500 °C was observed over a physical mixture of Na_2CrO_4, Cr_2O_3, and $NaCrO_2$. Although the oxygen release was not reversible it none the less was confirmation of the high oxygen pressures calculated for this region.

Corrosion of Chromium-containing Steels by Sodium

The thermodynamic data (Figure 5) emphasize the role of sodium chromite as the most important corrosion product encountered in sodium circuits containing oxygen. At 650 °C, it is formed in sodium containing $\geqslant 7$ p.p.m. O,[7] and can coexist with oxygen-saturated sodium[22] as well as sodium oxide at low sodium

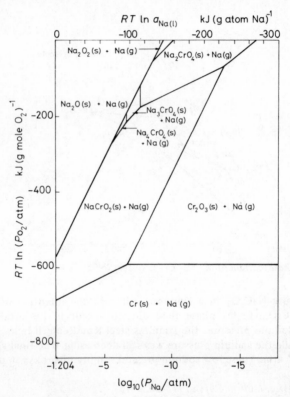

Figure 5 *Oxygen and sodium potential ranges at 650 °C for the stability of phases in the Na–Cr–O system*

pressures. No other ternary Na–Cr–O compound has been observed as a corrosion product in contact with liquid sodium. At less than ~ 7 p.p.m. O, however, the carbon activity in sodium circuits is normally sufficient for the dominant corrosion products of chromium-containing alloys to be $M_{23}C_6$ carbides containing $\sim 80\%$ Cr together with Fe, Ni, and Mn.[7]

Sodium chromite acts as a lubricant: it also reduces the rate of loss of nickel from the underlying steel[33] and holds small quantities of Al, Si, and Mn.[34] Therefore the conditions for its stability are of considerable importance.

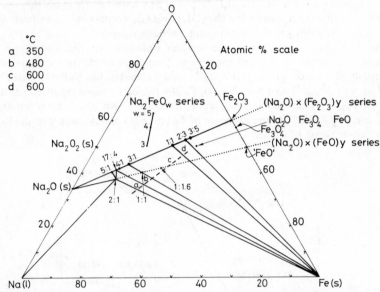

Figure 6 *A tentative phase diagram for the* Na–Fe–O *system* (350–600 °C)

The Na–Fe–O System

Much of the phase diagram for the Na–Fe–O system at 650 °C shown in Figure 6 is tentative. The existence of tie lines from Na_4FeO_3 to Fe and Na (the latter containing 1000 p.p.m. oxygen at 650 °C) has been well established,[22] though at 400 °C the ternary compound is unstable and the indicated tie is replaced by one between Na_2O and Fe.[35] In the present work *X*-ray diffraction indicated that loss of sodium gas caused an appropriate solid-phase assemblage to change its bulk composition along the dotted line (Figure 6). In the presence of iron, and as sodium was eliminated, the 17 : 4, 3 : 1, 1 : 1, and 2 : 3 compounds in the $(Na_2O)_x(Fe_2O_3)_y$ series[23,31,36-39] were progressively encountered. This is consistent with the work of Tschudy *et al.*,[38] who examined the reaction

[33] A. W. Thorley and C. Tyzack, 'Alkali Metal Coolants', Proc. Symp. IAEA, Vienna, 1966, 97.
[34] A. J. Hooper and S. B. Fisher, CEGB Report RD/B/N2804, 1973.
[35] C. C Addison, M. G. Barker, and A. J. Hooper, *J. C. S. Dalton*, 1972, 1017.
[36] M. Kh. Karapet'yants and M. K. Karapet'yants, 'Handbook of Thermodynamic Constants of Inorganic and Organic Compounds', Ann Arbor-Humphrey, 1970.
[37] L. B. Pankratz, D. W. Richardson, and J. M. Stuve, US Bureau of Mines, Report 1971, R1-7535.
[38] A. Hatterer, H. Kessler, and A. Tschudy, 'Liquid Alkali Metals', Conference Proceedings, British Nuclear Energy Society, 1973, p. 209.
[39] R. Collongues and J. Thery, *Compt. rend.*, 1960, **250**, 1070.

between $Fe_{1-x}O$ and Na_2O in vacuo at 800 °C. At the ratio (r) of Na_2O to $Fe_{1-x}O$ equal to unity, the products were iron and $(Na_2O)_3Fe_2O_3$; at $r = 2$, $(Na_2O)_5Fe_2O_3$, $(Na_2O)_2FeO$, and Fe were formed; at higher ratios, Na_2O remained unconsumed. Tschudy *et al.*,[38] were unable to prepare $(Na_2O)_2FeO$ pure from the oxides and Na_2O,FeO[31] was not observed. It is on this evidence that the tie line from iron to the $(Na_2O)_x(Fe_2O_3)_y$ compounds have been drawn. Recently a Na_2O,Fe_3O_4,FeO compound has been reported.[40]

We have yet to determine the sodium potentials in the system, and our present knowledge of the free energies of formation of the ternary compounds is restricted to $\Delta G^{\circ}_{f,T}(Na_2O)_4Fe_2O_3$,[37] and estimates for $NaFeO_2$ based upon $\Delta H^{\circ}_{f\,298}$ and S°_{298},[36] and for $(Na_2O)_xFeO(x = 1$ or $2)$ based upon e.m.f. data[31] and $\Delta H^{\circ}_{f\,298}$.[41] These data are plotted in Figure 7. An e.m.f. determination of ΔG°_f for Na_2O,FeO[31] in the presence of Fe and FeO seems suspect in the light of the phase diagram of Figure 6.

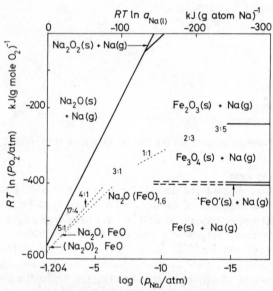

Figure 7 *Oxygen and sodium potential ranges at 650 °C for the stability of phases in the* $Na-Fe-O$ *system. Ratios refer to* x : y *for the series* $(Na_2O)_x(Fe_2O_3)_y$

Loss of Iron from Steels Exposed to Sodium

Since ternary $Na-Fe-O$ compounds have not been detected in fast reactor sodium circuits containing <10 p.p.m. oxygen, the loss of iron is attributed to the solubility of Fe in sodium. The rate of solution, however, at constant flow rate, temperature, and temperature gradient, is not insensitive to the oxygen

[40] J. Aubry, M. El Balkhi, and M. Zanne, 17th Seminaire de Thermodynamiqu and de Chemie Physique Metallurgiques, Enseeg-Irsid, Maizières lès Metz, 17/18th June 1976, PCM-RE 349, p. 50.
[41] P. Gross and G. L. Wilson, *J. Chem. Soc.* (A) 1970, 1013.

level. For pure iron the rate is proportional to the oxygen level to a power (n) of 2.1–2.3 [(O p.p.m.)^n] decreasing to $n = 2$ for a 2.25 Cr–1Mo steel, to $n = 1.5$ for M316 steel and $n = 1.3$ for Incoloy 800.[6] Since the formation of Na–Fe–O ternary compounds cannot be responsible for the loss, Na–Fe–O 'associations' stable at the surface of the metal[42] or in the sodium[7] have been invoked as a means of increasing the rate of solution of iron. The compounds stable at higher oxygen potentials and lower sodium pressures are still of interest; conditions favourable for their formation might occur by corrosion of heat exchangers by Na–Na$_2$O–NaOH mixtures, the latter forming from water leaks in the sodium circuit. In sodium hydroxide at 700–1000 °C the corrosion product of 2.25 Cr–1Mo steel is β–NaFeO$_2$.[10,43] In mixtures containing Na$_2$O, the corrosion product expected on the basis of Figure 7 would be one or more of the (Na$_2$O)$_x$ (Fe$_2$O$_3$)$_y$ compounds with $x > y$, while for mixtures containing liquid Na, it would be (Na$_2$O)$_2$FeO.

The authors are indebted to Dr. M. H. Rand for invaluable advice on thermodynamic aspects of the work and to Dr. M. G. Barker and Dr. A. J. Hooper for discussions in 1974 which led to working hypotheses for the Na–Cr–O and Na–Fe–O phase diagrams at the beginning of our studies of these systems. Dr. J. E. Antill has had a continuous involvement in the direction the studies have taken, and the authors are grateful for his critical and constructive comments on the work and on this paper.

[42] H. S. Isaacs and J. R. Weeks, 'Chemical Aspects of Corrosion and Mass Transfer in Liquid Sodium', Proc. AIME Symp., Detroit, Michigan, 19–20 October 1971, p. 1.
[43] C. F. Knights and R. Perkins, unpublished data.

The Application of Phase Equilibria and Thermodynamic Data to the Optimization of Amorphous Boron Coatings on different Metallic Substrates

By J. THEBAULT and R. NASLAIN

Laboratoire de Chimie du solide, Talence, France

C. BERNARD

L.T.P.C.M., Centre d'information thermodynamique, Domaine Universitaire, St. Martin d'Hères, France

Introduction

Fibres of amorphous boron are used as reinforcements in composite materials, and titanium is one of the metals currently used as a matrix for supporting boron fibres in composite materials intended for use at high temperatures. It is thus of interest to prepare diffusion couples of amorphous boron and titanium in order to study the nature of the chemical interaction which occurs at high temperatures. Amorphous boron is obtained by three methods: (i) evaporation under vacuum followed by condensation of the vapour on a cold substrate; (ii) the quenching of a liquid phase between two cooled plates, one of which is forced against the other; and (iii) by vapour deposition on a hot substrate. We have used the third method for two reasons: a diffusion couple forms between boron and metal by chemical interactions which occur spontaneously in the course of deposition, and it is the method which is used for the manufacture of boron fibres. Thus, one simulates the material structure and some of the chemical reactions which characterize the commercial product.

To obtain the chemical vapour deposition of boron one can use boranes which decompose giving amorphous boron at low temperatures (although there are certain difficulties with this method) or one can use BCl_3 or BBr_3. Because the usual industrial route employs a BCl_3-H_2 mixture, the thermodynamic properties of this gaseous mixture with respect to titanium have been studied in the temperature regions ($T \leqslant 1500$ K) appropriate to the formation of amorphous boron.

Conditions for the Deposition of Amorphous Boron on the Metallic Substrate

The classification presented by Bonetti et al.[1] is subdivided in terms of chemical compatibility between boron and metals and the feasibility of coating different substrates with boron. Titanium and its alloys are at the bottom of the series, apparently having little or no potential as substrates.

This is confirmed by our own experiments; the use of the technique for the deposition of amorphous boron on tantalum, molybdenum, and tungsten does

[1] R. Bonetti, D. Conte, and H. E. Hintermann, *Proc. 5th Internat. Conf. CVD, Electrochem. Soc.*, 1975, 495.

146

not give diffusion couples of boron and titanium of satisfactory quality. The morphology of the deposit obtained is irregular, the thickness is variable and its surface is broken into separate regions by deep cracks exposing the titanium. An analysis of the reactions for the reduction of the boron halides allows one to explain these results.

In the hypothetical case of an inert substrate, vapour deposition of boron is due mainly to the reduction of the halide by hydrogen on the hot substrate. This corresponds to the total reaction (1). In practice, boron deposition can be

$$2BX_3(g) + 3H_2(g) \rightarrow 2B(s) + 6HX(g) \qquad (1)$$

accompanied by some parasitic reactions due to the interactions between substrate and the gaseous phase, particularly at the beginning of the deposition. In this competition between two reductants, if the metal reacts with halide formation of the required diffusion couple will be difficult or even impossible. It is then of interest to see if a thermodynamic study can predict the most favourable experimental conditions.

Optimization of Boron Deposition on Titanium

We used a method of minimization of the total Gibbs free energy of the system to calculate thermodynamic equilibria.[2] For a given temperature, pressure, and initial composition of the gaseous mixture, one can calculate the partial pressures of each gas at equilibrium as well as the nature and quantity of the condensed phases. The only limitation is that one must have thermodynamic data for the species concerned. Gaseous species likely to be found at equilibrium are those present in the equilibria between a BCl_3–H_2 mixture and a heated substrate,[3,4] namely: H_2, H, Cl_2, Cl, B_2, B, HCl, BCl, BCl_2, BCl_3, BH, BH_2, BH_3, $BHCl_2$, B_2H_6, and $B_{10}H_{14}$. To these species the titanium halides TiCl, $TiCl_2$, $TiCl_3$, and $TiCl_4$ must be added, as well as the following condensed phases: Ti, B, TiB, TiB_2, and $TiCl_2$. Owing to the lack of thermodynamic data, BH_2Cl is not included but according to Carlton[3] it will be present in low quantities at equilibrium. The process has been broken down into successive steps illustrating the different biphasic equilibria possible in the system titanium–boron in order to simulate those which occur in practice. These equilibria are Ti–TiB, TiB–TiB_2, and TiB_2–B. It is reasonable to suppose that these steps follow in this order at the beginning of the reaction. The calculation of the corresponding equilibria has been carried out.

Initial Stage: Deposition of Titanium Monoboride

Interest is centred first on the study of the phenomena occurring in the intitial stages of deposition. While the titanium substrate is in chemical excess, the only phase likely to deposit is titanium monoboride. A study of the influence of the parameters of production on the quantity of BCl_3 reduced by titanium has been carried out in the regions of pressure, temperature, and composition usually

[2] C. Bernard, Y. Deniel, A. Jacquot, P. Vay, and M. Ducaroir. *J. Less Common Metals*, 1975, **40**, 165.

[3] H. E. Carlton, J. H. Oxley, E. H. Hall, and J. M. Blocker Jr., *Proc. 2nd Internat. Conf. CVD, Electrochem. Soc.*, 1970, 209.

[4] P. N. Walsh, *Proc. 4th Internat. Conf. CVD, Electrochem. Soc.*, 1973, 135.

used in chemical vapour deposition, namely at pressures varying from 0.1 to 10 atm, temperatures between 1300 and 1900 K, and mixture compositions of BCl_3-H_2 varying between 0.1 : 0.9 and 0.9 : 0.1. Table 1 shows how the equilibrium, expressed as the ratio of the number of moles of titanium monoboride to the sum of the number of moles of titanium halides, varies as a function of vapour composition and pressure. The fact that this ratio remains close to unity shows that reduction of BCl_3 is an essential requirement for deposition to occur on a titanium substrate.

Table 1 *Values of the ratio* $[TiB]_{eq} : [TiCl_x]$ *for different pressures and initial* BCl_3-H_2 *compositions at* 1300 K

mol. BCl_3 (init)	0.1	0.2	0.3	0.4	0.5	0.6	0.7	0.8	0.9
mol. H_2 (init)	0.9	0.8	0.7	0.6	0.5	0.4	0.3	0.2	0.1
$p = 0.1$ atm	1.004	1.004	1.004	1.005	1.005	—	—	—	1.007
$p = 1$ atm	1.015	1.015	1.017	1.018	1.019	1.020	1.021	1.022	1.022
$p = 3$ atm	1.020	1.022	1.024	1.026	1.028	—	—	—	0.910
$p = 10$ atm	1.028	—	—	—	—	—	—	—	—

To investigate this phenomenon a similar study has been carried out on the initial phase of boron deposition on tantalum and tungsten substrates. It is interesting to compare the behaviour of titanium with that of the metals usually used as substrates in the vapour deposition of boron. Tungsten is the most important as it is the substrate most often used to make commercial boron fibres. Because an excess of tantalum or tungsten is present, the deposited borides will

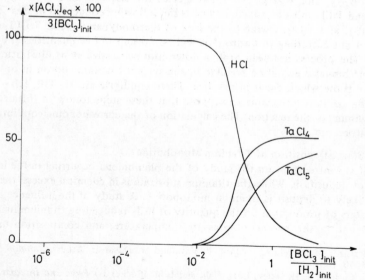

Figure 1 *Dependence of* $x[TaCl_x]_{eq} \times 100/3[BCl_3]_{init}$ *on* $[BCl_3]_{init}/[H_2]_{init}$ *for a tantalum substrate at* 1300 K *and* 1 atm

be, respectively, Ta_3B_2 and W_2B in the temperature range used. Thermodynamic functions for these two borides have been estimated.[5]

The percentage of BCl_3 either reduced by hydrogen to HCl or combined as metallic halides by the substrates is shown in Figures 1 and 2. The data are shown as functions of the dilution of BCl_3 in the initial gaseous mixture (1 mol H_2, $10^{-2}-10$ mol BCl_3, for 1300 K and 1 atm pressure). It appears that for the usual dilutions (for example, 1 mol H_2 to 0.1 mol BCl_3), reduction is due to hydrogen in the case of tungsten, but in the case of tantalum it is due partly to hydrogen and in a lesser degree to the substrate.

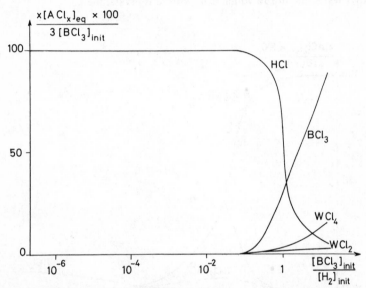

Figure 2 *Dependence of* $x[WCl_x]_{eq} \times 100/3[BCl_3]_{init}$ *on* $[BCl_3]_{init}/[H_2]_{init}$ *for a tungsten substrate at* 1300 K *and* 1 atm

These Figures can be divided into two regions; the region rich in BCl_3 where the reduction of boron halide is made by the metal substrate and the zone rich in hydrogen where this element is the reductant. From Figures 1 and 2 it seemed that the more reactive the metal is the more one must dilute the gaseous mixture in BCl_3 during the initial stages of reaction in order to avoid an excessive corrosion of the substrates.

The reaction with titanium has been restudied over a much wider concentration range using initial mixtures in the range $10^{-6}-10$ mol BCl_3 to 1 mol H_2. The curves in Figure 3 present the same characteristics as those for tantalum and tungsten. The zone where hydrogen is the only reducing agent with respect to BCl_3 only appears at dilutions greater than 10^{-5}. Thus, one can avoid the corrosion of titanium yet also obtain a deposit of boron using a gas containing about 10^{-5} mol BCl_3 to 1 mol of hydrogen.

[5]   J. Thebault, Thesis, Bordeaux, 1977.

The optimization of the temperature for this stage of the reaction is very desirable. In fact, the equilibrium is not much displaced as a function of temperature. For example, an increase of 200 K shifts the curves for a given reduced BCl_3 percentage only slightly in the direction of greater BCl_3 concentrations. This shift is marked by two asterisks in Figure 3, the upper marking the point of intersection at 1500 K of the curves for HCl and $TiCl_3$ and the lower corresponding to the $TiCl_2$ concentration. Because of the small gain expected to occur as a result of raising the temperature, the initial stages of the deposition should be carried out at 1300 K. It may also be noted that if the reaction temperature is in excess of 1500 K the boron which is deposited is crystalline.

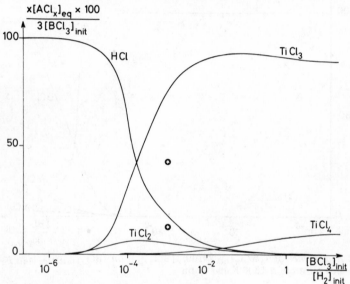

Figure 3 *Dependence of* $x[TiCl_x]_{eq} \times 100/3[BCl_3]_{init}$ *on* $[BCl_3]_{init}/[H_2]_{init}$ *for a titanium substrate at 1300 K and 1 atm. The asterisks show the position of the intercept of the curve relative to HCl and $TiCl_3$ at 1500 K, and the point having the same abscissa for the $TiCl_2$ curve (see text)*

Intermediate Step

The second stage of the reaction occurs after the substrate is covered by a monoboride. During this stage the reduction of BCl_3 results in the formation of titanium diboride. An analysis of this process can be carried out by introducing an excess of TiB into the equilibrium calculation. Figure 4 presents results obtained at 1300 K and 1 atm: it shows the percentages of BCl_3 reduced in this stage. Moreover, the region of the reduction of BCl_3 by hydrogen is enlarged compared with the initial stage. A gaseous mixture richer in BCl_3 (1 mol hydrogen to 10^{-3} mol BCl_3) than was used in the first stage (10^{-5} mol BCl_3) can be tolerated, assuring a greater rate of deposition and thereby limiting corrosion of the substrate.

Final Stage

When the titanium monoboride is covered by diboride, deposition of boron occurs; it is the main step in vapour deposition of boron on inert substrates. The

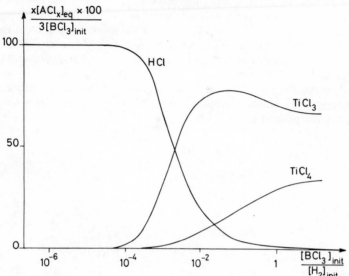

Figure 4 *Dependence of* $x[TiCl_x]_{eq} \times 100/3[BCl_3]_{init}$ *on* $[BCl_3]_{init}/[H_2]_{init}$ *for an excess of titanium monoboride at* 1300 K *and* 1 atm

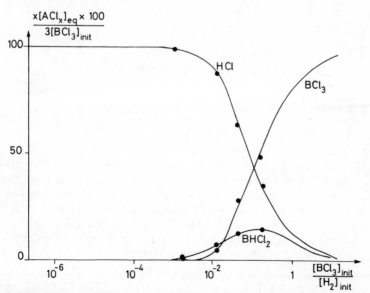

Figure 5 *Dependence of* $x[MCl_x]_{eq} \times 100/3[BCl_3]_{init}$ *on* $[BCl_3]_{init}/[H_2]_{init}$ *on a neutral subtrate* (TiB$_2$, TaB$_2$, WB$_2$, *or* B) *at* 1300 K *and* 1 atm. *The dots represent the results of Walsh*[4]

thermodynamic equilibrium appropriate to this stage has been studied and the results relative to the BCl_3 percentages reduced are presented in Figure 5. This Figure may also be divided into two regions but these do not have the same significance as before. At high BCl_3 dilutions a region of reduction of BCl_3 by hydrogen occurs but on the other hand, at BCl_3 concentrations higher than 10^{-1} mol per 1 mol hydrogen, boron trichloride is no longer totally consumed, and for this to be consumed the gases must be recycled. However, $BHCl_2$, an unstable compound, forms and is difficult to recover: therefore its formation must be minimized.

Walsh[4] studied the equilibrium between gaseous BCl_3-H_2 mixtures and elemental boron. Data points in Figure 5 show his results, which agree with values calculated in the present study.

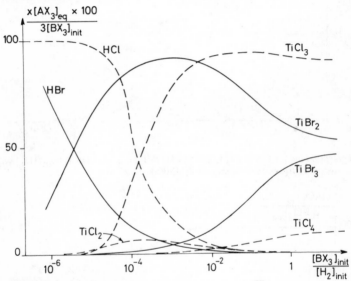

Figure 6 *Dependence of* $x[TiBr_x]_{eq} \times 100/3[BBr_3]_{init}$ *on* $[\overline{BBr_3}]_{init}/[H_2]_{init}$ *for a titanium substrate at* 1300 K *for* 1 atm. *The curves obtained for boron trichloride (Figure 3) are represented by dashed lines*

Mixtures of BBr_3 and Hydrogen

It follows from our calculations that a gas must be utilized, at least for the initial stage, having a low BCl_3 concentration (10^{-5} mol per mol hydrogen). This high degree of dilution is difficult to realize in practice. As BBr_3 is a source of much purer boron and is much more readily reduced by hydrogen than BCl_3,[6,7] the possibility of using BBr_3 to enhance the deposition of amorphous boron on titanium has been investigated. The initial phase of the deposit of monoboride in presence of an excess of titanium has been studied at 1300 K (1 atm pressure).

[6] R. Naslain, 'Preparative Methods in Solid State Chemistry', ed. P. Hagenmuller, Academic Press, New York, 1972, p. 439.

[7] R. Naslain, 'Boron and Refractory Borides', ed. V. I. Matkovich, Springer Verlag, in press): 'Crystal chemistry of boron and of some boron-rich phases; preparation of boron modifications'.

Figure 6 presents the results. In order to contrast the respective advantages of BBr_3 and BCl_3, results obtained previously for boron chloride have also been shown. The shape of the curves for the percentage of BBr_3 transformed is almost the same as that for the chlorides, but there is a shift of the curve towards the large dilutions of boron halides. Thus, far from improving the conditions of deposition, using BBr_3 favours corrosion of titanium substrates.

Experimental Technique for the Deposition of Boron on Titanium: the Initial Step

The details of the optimization of boron yield with respect to the temperature and composition of the initial gaseous mixtures, as well as of the minimization of $BHCl_2$ production during the latter stages of boron deposition, will be published elsewhere. We will describe here only the experimental conditions for the first stage of deposition.

The results obtained indicate the necessity of using a mixture of BCl_3 highly diluted by hydrogen in order to achieve a passivation of the substrate. It is very difficult to obtain a gaseous flow corresponding to a partial pressure of hydrogen of 760 mmHg and a partial pressure of BCl_3 of 10^{-2} mmHg. A method of achieving passivation was developed by trial and error. It works as follows:

(a) The substrate is heated at 1300 K in hydrogen then cooled under the same atmosphere; this traps a small concentration of hydrogen on the surface of titanium.

(b) At ambient temperature the substrate is swept for five minutes by a mixture of BCl_3–hydrogen of composition $BCl_3 : H_2 = 1.64$. Some boron trichloride is absorbed on the walls of the apparatus.

(c) Hydrogen is flushed through for 15 min at ambient temperature to eliminate most of the boron halides.

(d) The substrate is then heated to 1300 K for 7 min in the presence of hydrogen, which is thus doped with a trace of BCl_3 approximately in the BCl_3/H_2 ratio defined by the thermodynamic optimization (10^{-5}).

Following this passivation treatment, microscopic observation of the substrate shows it to consist of a uniform mat surface, black-grey in colour, composed of very fine grains of microcrystalline titanium borides. Some diffusion couples of amorphous boron and titanium of good quality have been obtained; they have permitted a detailed study of the chemical interaction phenomenon which occurs between the fibres of boron and titanium in composite materials.[8,9]

Conclusion

This work shows how in a multicomponent system a quantitative knowledge of the complex thermodynamic equilibrium allows one to optimize the conditions of deposition.

The authors would like to express their gratitude to Dr. P. E. Potter, A.E.R.E., Harwell, for his considerable help in the preparation of the English version of this paper.

[8] R. Naslain, J. Thebault, and R. Pailler, 'Chemical Compatibility in metal-boron composites', *Internat. Conf. on Composite Materials*, Geneva and Boston, 1975.

[9] J. Thebault, R. Pailler, G. Bontemps-Moley, M. Bourdeau, and R. Naslain, *J. Less Common Metals*, 1976, **47**, 221.

The Beneficiation of Ilmenite by Fluoride Routes

By N. C. CABELDU, J. H. MOSS, and A. WRIGHT

Chemistry Department, Teesside Polytechnic, Borough Road, Middlesbrough, Cleveland, TS1 3BA

Introduction

In recent years there has been considerable interest in the beneficiation of ilmenite to produce titanium(IV) oxide owing to possible shortages of rutile. Several beneficiation methods have been energetically investigated but there is little in the patent literature[1-4] concerning the beneficiation of ilmenite using fluorides. It is the aim of this paper to examine some possible high-temperature

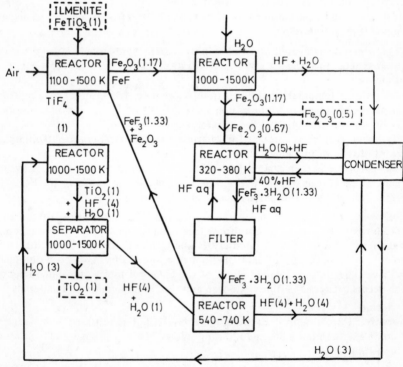

Figure 1 *The* FeF_3 *route for ilmenite beneficiation. The figures in parentheses refer to mole quantities of materials involved for one mole ilmenite,* $FeTiO_3$, *starting material*

[1] R. B. Jackson, D. H. Kelly, and R. V. Townsend; U.S. P., 2 900 233.
[2] S. S. Svendsen, U.S. P., 2 042 434.
[3] S. S. Svendsen, U.S. P., 2 042 435.
[4] G. L. Herwig, Austral. P., 428 758.

routes for the beneficiation of ilmenite using fluorides. Three principal routes have been examined. These are (i) the iron(III) fluoride route (Figure 1); (ii) the hydrofluoric acid route (Figure 2); and (iii) the ammonium fluoride route (Figure 3).

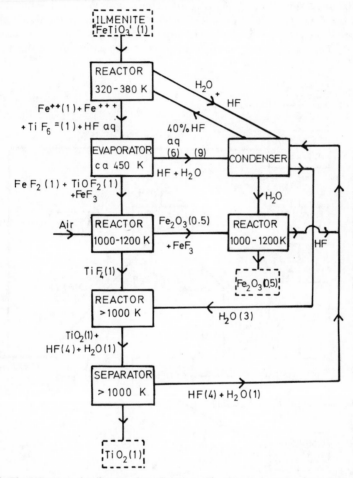

Figure 2 *The HF route for ilmenite beneficiation. The figures in parentheses refer to mole quantities of materials involved for one mole ilmenite, $FeTiO_3$, starting material*

Experimental

Western Mineral Sands (Australia) ilmenite was used for experiments, frequently after complete oxidation in air at 1200 K. The analysis is shown in Table 1. Some 95% of the particles had sizes between 75 and 350 μm. FeF_3,[5] VOF_3,[6] and MoO_2F_2[6] were prepared by previously reported methods. Other reagents

[5] R. Colton and J. H. Canterford, 'Halides of the First Row Transition Metals', Interscience, New York, 1969, Chapter 6, p. 272.
[6] N. C. Cabeldu, B. Leng, and J. H. Moss, *J. Fluorine Chem.*, 1975, **6**, 357.

were commercially available. Thermal analyses were carried out on Stanton T.R.1. or H.T.5. thermal balances, which were also used for small scale (50–1000 mg) isothermal studies. For larger scale reactions (1–100 g) or where volatile products were collected, reactions were carried out in heated nickel or aluminia tubes (length 1 m, internal diameter 4 cm). A slow stream of oxygen carried the volatile reaction products into a PTFE trap cooled in liquid nitrogen. The liquid oxygen condensed with the volatile products was allowed to evaporate off in an inert atmosphere box. Purification by sublimation was

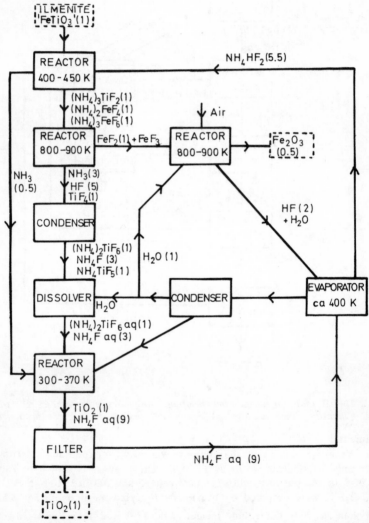

Figure 3 *The* NH_4HF_2 *for ilmenite beneficiation. The figures in parentheses refer to mole quantities of materials involved for one mole ilmenite,* $FeTiO_3$, *starting material*

carried out in copper equipment.[7] X-Ray diffraction traces were recorded on materials obtained from cooled reaction mixtures using a Siemens Type F diffractometer and copper $K\alpha$ radiation.

Table 1 *Analysis of ilmenite and beneficiated products figures in p.p.m.; fluoride products analysed after hydrolysis to the oxide*

Oxide	WMS* ilmenite	TiF_4 condensate	TiF_4 sublimate	Best stage decontamination factor†
Al_2O_3	7500	10	<8	1000
SiO_2	5000	<100	<100	>50
P_2O_5	100	<100	<100	>3
K_2O	100	5	<1	200
CaO	100	10	<1	50
V_2O_5	1500	60	<10	25 (75)
Cr_2O_3	300	1	<1	300
MnO	1500	6	<1	>2000
Fe_2O_3	441 000	300	<10	>2000
ZnO	300	20	<10	>15
As_2O_3	45	2	0.5	>20
ZrO_2	400	40	<3	>10
Nb_2O_5	1500	300	<80	12 (13)
MoO_3		60	20	4 (50)
SnO_2	38	1	<1	30
Sb_2O_3		10	<1	>10
Ta_2O_3		5	<1	>10
WO_3		8	<3	8
PbO	20	4	<1	>5
MgO	200	100	12	30

* Western Mineral Sands (Australia).
† Figures in brackets are the results of separate studies at higher concentrations.

Table 2 shows the results of isothermal reactions between oxidized ilmenite and FeF_3. To study the reaction of FeF_3 vapour with ilmenite, FeF_3 (0.1 g) was placed at the bottom of a 5 cm^3 platinum crucible. Above this was placed a 5 mm layer of CaF_2 or SnO_2 and above this last a layer of oxidized, finely ground ilmenite. The crucible and contents were heated at 1400 K for 3 h. Provided that the ilmenite layer was at least 8 mm thick, analysis indicated no loss of iron from the crucible, though in the absence of ilmenite FeF_3 was completely volatilized under these conditions. Table 3 records experiments on the steam hydrolysis of TiF_4. Fe_2O_3 (10 g) either precipitated, calcined, or the residues from the ilmenite–FeF_3 reaction, was treated with hot 20 or 40% aqueous HF (100 cm^3) for 3 h. In all cases FeF_3, $3H_2O$ was the only solid found after the reaction. Table 4 records experiments on the dehydration of $FeF_3,3H_2O$. Table 1 records analyses of ilmenite and the products of various stages of benefication. Table 5 gives the solid products of pyrolysis of ilmenite after dissolution in 40% aqueous HF. Table 6 gives the products of pyrolysis of

[7] N. C. Cabeldu, PhD Thesis, Teesside Polytechnic, 1974, p. 15.

ilmenite after dissolution in fused NH_4HF_2. Table 7 gives the products of reaction of aqueous TiF_4 with NH_3 at various pH.

Table 2 *Isothermal reactions of solid FeF_3 with oxidized ilmenite*

Temp./K	Ilmenite particle size/μm	% excess FeF_3	Time reaction/h	% Volatilization Ti
1220	75–150	2	1.5	93.5
1150	150–250	10	1.5	100
1150	150–250	5	2.0	98
1150	150–250	2	2.0	86
1150	<50	2	2.0	91
1150	<50*	2*	0.8	99.1

* The reactants were finely ground and pressed together.

Table 3 *Steam hydrolysis of TiF_4*

Temp./K	500	600	700	800	1000	1200
Solid products	$TiOF_2 + TiO_2$ (trace)	$TiOF_2 + TiO_2$ (minor)	$TiOF_2 + TiO_2$ (minor)	TiO_2	TiO_2	TiO_2

In all cases the anatase form of TiO_2 was found, except at 1200 K when there was also a little rutile.

Table 4 *Dehydration of $FeF_3,3H_2O$*

Dehydrating agent	Weight $FeF_3,3H_2O$ taken/g	Reaction conditions	Weight product/g	Residue analysis % theoretical F
HF anhydrous	34.0	300–870 K in 2h	23.6	>99
Vacuum	11.5	550 K (2h) then 620, 690, 750 K (1h each)	7.3	85
Dry air	11.6	300–770 K in 6h	7.7	82
40% aqueous HF vapour	10.7	540 K for 1.5h then to 740 K in 3h in dry air	11.0	95

Results and Discussion

The Iron(III) Fluoride Route. FeF_3 reacts with TiO_2 at 720–1000 K according to equation (1), but FeF_2 under similar conditions requires a higher temperature

$$4FeF_3 + 3TiO_2 = 2Fe_2O_3 + 3TiF_4 \qquad (1)$$

of 1220 K for complete reaction.[8] To reduce temperatures reactions were studied under oxidizing conditions, for convenience usually using preoxidized ilmenite. Reaction between FeF_3 and oxidized ilmenite was observed at 870 K but complete (> 99%) volatilization of the titanium was not observed below

[8] B. Leng and J. H. Moss, *J. Fluorine Chem.*, 1975, 5, 93.

1150 K. Complete reaction could be achieved at this temperature either by using a 10% excess of FeF_3 or by using only a 2% excess of FeF_3 and finely grinding and pressing the reactants. Above 1200 K FeF_3 showed significant volatility, and at 1400 K the vapour reacted rapidly and completely with ilmenite.

Table 5 *Air pyrolysis of the reaction product of ilmenite and* 40% HF

Temp./K	510	760	820	950	1270
Solid products	FeF_3, $TiOF_2$, FeF_2	FeF_3, $TiOF_2$, TiO_2	FeF_3, $TiOF_2$, FeOF	FeF_3,' α-and γ-Fe_2O_3	α-Fe_2O_3

In all cases the anatase form of TiO_2 was found.

Table 6 *Pyrolysis of the reaction product of oxidized ilmenite and fused* NH_4HF_2

Temp./K	300	670	830
Solid products under N_2	NH_4HF_2, $(NH_4)_3TiF_7$, $(NH_4)_3FeF_6$	NH_4FeF_4, FeF_3	FeF_3, FeF_2

Temp./K	670	870	1090
Solid products in air	NH_4FeF_4, FeF_3, $TiOF_2$	FeF_3, Fe_2O_3, TiO_2	FeF_3, Fe_2O_3

Table 7 *Products of the reaction of aqueous* TiF_4 *with aqueous* NH_3

pH	4	6	8	10
Solid products	NH_4TiOF_3	NH_4TiOF_3	TiO_2*	TiO_2*

* The TiO_2 only became crystalline on heating the product.

The steam hydrolysis of TiF_4 is thermodynamically favourable.[9] $TiOF_2$ is a possible product of this reaction, as well as TiO_2 [equations (2) and (3)].[10]

$$TiF_4 + H_2O \rightleftharpoons TiOF_2 + 2HF \tag{2}$$
$$TiF_4 + 2H_2O \rightleftharpoons TiO_2 + 4HF \tag{3}$$

If the free energies of conversion of oxides into fluorides are plotted against the temperature, as shown in Figure 4, a low hydrolysis temperature is found to favour formation of $TiOF_2$ which is then relatively difficult to hydrolyse to TiO_2.[11] There are two plausible processes for hydrolysis of TiF_4. The first, shown in Figure 5, operates above 1000 K and produces TiO_2 directly. The reaction equilibrium constant,[9] $\log K = 3.7 \pm 1.0$, which does not vary rapidly with temperature over the range 500–1500 K, indicates that for efficient ($> 99\%$) production of TiO_2 there must be a significant ($> 10\%$) concentration of steam in the product gases. The second process, shown in Figure 6, below

[9] O. Kubaschewski, E. L. Evans and C. B. Alcock, 'Metallurgical Thermochemistry' Pergamon, Oxford, 4th Edition, 1967, Table A, p. 304.
[10] A. Wright, PhD Thesis, Teesside Polytechnic, 1975, p. 34.
[11] J. H. Moss and A. Wright, *J. Fluorine Chem.*, 1975, 5, 163.

800 K produces $TiOF_2$ which is then pyrolysed above 900 K to produce TiO_2 and TiF_4,[11] the latter being recycled. The second process has the disadvantage of requiring two stages although it is easier to manipulate and utilizes steam more efficiently.

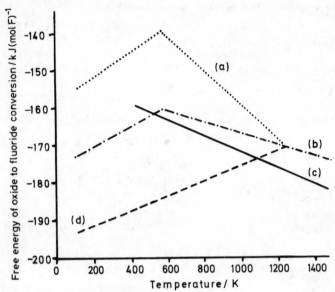

Figure 4 *Free-energy–temperature diagram for the conversion of titanium and hydrogen oxides into fluorides. (a)* $TiOF_2$ *into* TiF_4; *(b)* TiO_2 *into* TiF_4; *(c)* H_2O *into* HF; *(d)* TiO_2 *into* $TiOF_2$

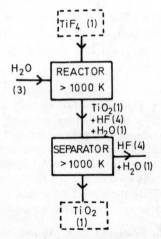

Figure 5 *The high-temperature route for hydrolysis of* TiF_4 *to* TiO_2. *The figures in parentheses refer to mole quantities involved for one mole of ilmenite,* $FeTiO_3$, *starting material*

Theoretically FeF_3 may be made by the action of HF gas on Fe_2O_3, but the reaction has not been observed. Hot 40% aqueous HF, however, attacks all forms of Fe_2O_3. $FeF_3,3H_2O$ is formed[5] according to equation (4) and is readily

$$Fe_2O_3 + 6HF + 3H_2O = 2FeF_3,3H_2O \tag{4}$$

separated as a moderately soluble solid. Dehydration to FeF_3 is theoretically favoured by low temperatures, as shown in Figure 7, but the reaction is then slow. Dehydration in air or vacuum only gives 80% anhydrous FeF_3 due to hydrolysis. It is possible to obtain 100% yields if the dehydration is carried out in anhydrous HF gas, though this would be difficult to provide in a simple process. Dehydration at 540 K in the vapour of 40% aqueous HF followed by air drying at higher temperatures gives 95% yields.

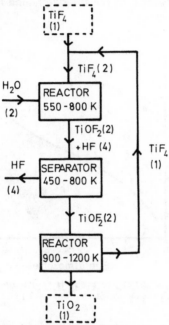

Figure 6 *The low-temperature route for hydrolysis of* TiF_4 *to* TiO_2. *The figures in parentheses refer to mole quantities of materials involved for one mole ilmenite,* $FeTiO_3$, *starting material*

The major impurity requiring removal in ilmenite beneficiation is iron. Fe_2O_3 is involatile, and at 1100 K FeF_3 has a low volatility so that at this temperature little iron volatilizes. At 1400 K FeF_3 is gaseous but reacts rapidly with ilmenite, so again little iron need be volatilized. FeF_3 impurity in TiF_4 may be efficiently removed by sublimation at 556 K. The behaviour of the minor impurities of ilmenite in the beneficiation process is of some importance as they can cause appreciable fluoride losses in recycling. Also pigmentary grade TiO_2 has very low levels of chemical impurities, and it is of interest to see whether a fluoride process can achieve this purity.

Most of the oxides of the impurities in ilmenite react with FeF_3 above 800 K; only SnO_2 and Cr_2O_3 do not react.[6] The appropriate free-energy–temperature graphs shown in Figure 8 indicate that this is as expected thermodynamically. Many of the impurity fluoride products have a low volatility at the reaction temperatures so the evolved gases are purer than the original ilmenite. The TiF_4 may be condensed to a solid at ambient temperatures leaving gaseous fluoride impurities behind. Sublimation of the TiF_4 effects a further substantial purification. Fluorides such as ZrF_4 which are sparingly volatile at the initial reaction temperatures are efficiently separated by sublimation. Fluorides volatilizing at temperatures fairly close to TiF_4, such as NbF_5, give separation factors similar to ratios of the vapour pressure of the pure fluorides, as shown in Figure 9. It seems probable that a TiO_2 of pigmentary purity could be made, though further work would be desirable. Most of the fluoride bound by the impurities may be recovered by steam hydrolysis.[12]

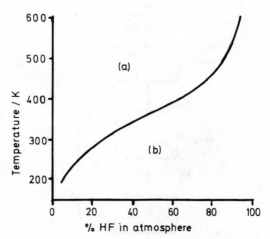

Figure 7 *Stability of* Fe_2O_3 *and* FeF_3 *phases in* $H_2O–HF$ *atmospheres at various temperatures.* (a) *Zone with* Fe_2O_3 *stable;* (b) *zone with* FeF_3 *stable*

The Hydrogen Fluoride Route. The reaction of HF acid with ilmenite and pyrolysis of the products to produce TiF_4 is covered in a patent,[1] the claimed chemistry of which is shown in Figure 10. Jackson and co-workers suggested that $FeTiF_6$ and $Fe_2(TiF_6)_3$ were produced from HF acid solutions and subsequently pyrolysed to volatilize TiF_4. However, on evaporating solutions of ilmenite in hydrofluoric acid we only obtained FeF_2 and a solid solution of FeF_3 in $TiOF_2$. Pyrolysis of these solids in dry air led first to oxidation of FeF_2 to FeF_3 and Fe_2O_3.[5] The $TiOF_2$ pyrolysed to TiO_2 and TiF_4 at 670–820 K. The TiO_2 reacted metathetically with the FeF_3 at 800–950 K[7] according to equation (1), volatilizing all the titanium.

[12] J. D. Rushmere and H. Mason, 'U.K.A.E.A. (Industrial Group) Report' 1959, SCS-R-392.

The pyrohydrolysis of TiF_4 can proceed by either of the two methods discussed for the FeF_3 route for ilmenite beneficiation. The behaviour of impurity elements is apparently similar in the two processes.

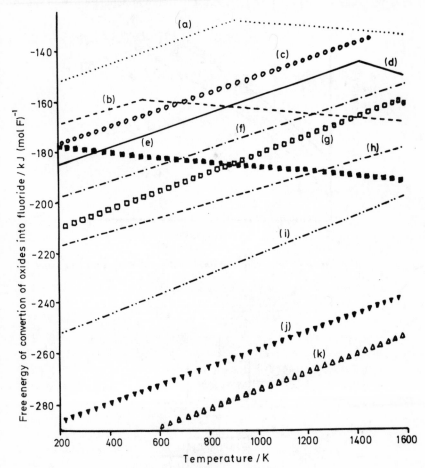

Figure 8 *Free-energy–temperature diagram for the conversion of some oxides into fluorides.*
(a) SnO_2 *into* SnF_4; (b) TiO_2 *into* TiF_4; (c) Cr_2O_3 *into* CrF_3; (d) Fe_2O_3 *into* FeF_3; (e) SiO_2 *into* SiF_4; (f) MnO *into* MnF_2; (g) Al_2O_3 *into* AlF_3; (h) PbO *into* PbF_2; (i) MgO *into* MgF_2; (j) CaO *into* CaF_2; (k) BaO *into* BaF_2

The HF process has fewer steps than the FeF_3 process, but obtaining solids from the HF solution is more difficult in the HF process than in the FeF_3 process owing to their greater solubility. Also, the solid products from the HF acid process contain more fluorine than is needed to convert all the titanium into TiF_4.

The Ammonium Hydrogen Difluoride Route. Three patents describe previous work on ilmenite beneficiation using NH_4HF_2. In one,[2] ilmenite was treated with ammonium fluorides at up to 700 K volatilizing 'titanium(IV) fluoride ammines' and leaving behind iron(II) fluoride. In another,[3] also by Svendsen, heating was only continued to 600 K and the titanium separated from the iron

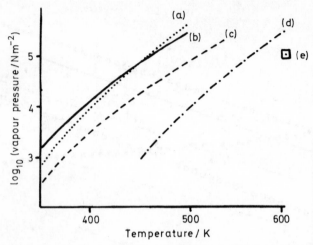

Figure 9 *Vapour pressures of some fluorides.* (a) $MoOF_4$; (b) WOF_4; (c) NbF_5 and TaF_5; (d) TiF_4; (e) SbF_3

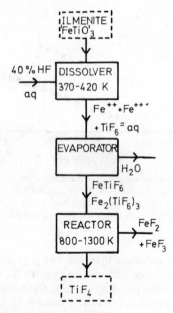

Figure 10 *Part of a U.S. patent for* TiF_4 *manufacture*[1]

by aqueous leaching. In both patents TiF_4 was obtained by treating solutions containing TiF_4 with ammonia, and fluoride was recovered by separate steps using sulphuric acid and ammonium sulphate. In the third, more recent patent,[4] the chemistry of which is shown in Figure 11, ilmenite is treated with molten NH_4HF_2 at 390—450 K and subsequently heated to 670 K. Further heating at 870—1170 K volatilized TiF_4, NH_3, and HF. TiO_2 was obtained by reaction of the TiF_4—NH_4F fluoride sublimate with steam at 420—520 K and HF from the FeF_3 in the process residues, also by steam hydrolysis. We found that the

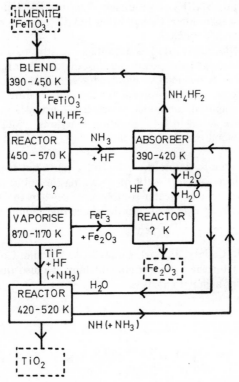

Figure 11 *Australian patent for a* NH_4HF_2 *ilmenite beneficiation route*[4]

solution of oxidized ilmenite in molten NH_4HF_2 after cooling gave, as solid phases, $(NH_4)_3FeF_6$ and a phase having the probable composition $(NH_4)_3 TiF_7$, though the exact composition was not established. Pyrolysis of these complex ammonium salts occurred according to the scheme shown in Table 6. Pyrolysis in air was more complex than in nitrogen, chiefly because the ammonia evolved was partly oxidized at higher temperatures to water which then hydrolysed some of the complex fluoro salts. The higher temperatures required in the air pyrolysis agree with those reported in the third patent as necessary for complete titanium volatilization.[4] Treatment of aqueous TiF_4 with ammonia precipitated amorphous TiO_2 above pH 8. The resultant aqueous NH_4F solutions regenerated NH_4HF_2 at 380–400 K. Impurity behaviour in the NH_4HF_2 process has not been examined, though excellent separations of titanium from iron are to be expected at the temperatures used.

Summary

All of the proposed fluoride routes for ilmenite beneficiation are chemically feasible. They give an efficient titanium recovery and a by-product Fe_2O_3 low in titanium. Fluoride losses are low. In all routes an extra purification stage of sublimation or distillation is feasible if desired.

As proposed, the NH_4HF_2 route differs from the HF and FeF_3 routes more than these do from each other, though other NH_4HF_2 routes more similar to the HF or FeF_3 routes are possible.[4]

The proposed NH_4HF_2 route has advantages relative to other fluoride routes of lower temperatures and the possible use of metals other than noble metals as containing materials. It has relative disadvantages of a considerably greater complexity, a probable greater requirement for low-temperature heat, and the need for an additional chemical, ammonia, which has substantial losses. The HF and FeF_3 routes involve novel high-temperature reactions, though the pyrohydrolysis of TiF_4 has some similarity to that of SiF_4, in which there is industrial interest.[13-16]

The HF route is more simple than the FeF_3 route but has slight relative disadvantages of an increased difficulty of obtaining the solids from HF solutions, owing to their considerably greater solubility, and when the solids are obtained they tend to contain an excess of fluorine above that required for the stoicheiometric formation of TiF_4 on pyrolysis.

We thank Teesside County Borough Council (A. W.) and Tioxide International Limited (N. C. C.) for the award of studentships. We also thank Tioxide International Limited for help with analyses.

[13] G. L. Flammert, Ger. P. 1 075 567.
[14] R. E. Driscoll, U.S. P., 3 661 519.
[15] G. L. DeCuir, U.S. P., 3 645 684.
[16] Z. G. Smirnova, N. Z. Nikitina, V. V. Illarianov, A. A. Mazlowskii, and J. Laukovics, *Zhur. prikl and Khim.* 1967, **40**, 1667.

The Preparation and Properties of Pyrolytic Boron Nitride

By N. J. ARCHER

Fulmer Research Institute Limited, Stoke Poges, Slough, SL2 4QD

Introduction

Pyrolytic boron nitride (PBN) is not a new material[1] but its increasing availability in the form of crucibles, tubes, and plates has made it an appropriate subject for review. PBN hardware (Figure 1) is now being grown on a regular basis by three laboratories in the world: the Carbon Products Division of the Union Carbide Corporation in the U.S.A., the Fulmer Components Division of Fulmer Research Institute Limited in the U.K. and a Russian laboratory.[2] The PBN produced by these laboratories is grown by chemical vapour deposition (CVD) and, although several other forms have been reported, they all produce PBN with a hexagonal structure and overall anisotropic properties. The properties of this PBN are quite different from those of the material produced by hot pressing. The differences are mainly due to the complete absence of any binder and the much increased degree of orientation amongst the PBN crystallites.

It is intended in this paper to bring together the available data on PBN in order to indicate the capabilities and limitations of the material.

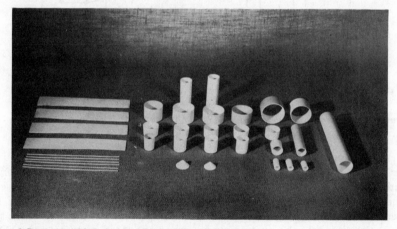

Figure 1 *Some typical shapes in pyrolytic boron nitride*

The Crystal Structure of Boron Nitride

Boron nitride is isoelectronic with carbon and therefore it is not surprising that it has two structures which are analogous with graphite and diamond. Only the

[1] V. M. Goldschmidt, *Norsk. geol. Tidsskr*, 1926, **9**, 258.
[2] 'Semiconductor Materials and Materials for Electronic Engineering', 1975, V/K Techsnabexport, Moscow G200, U.S.S.R.

hexagonal structure has been obtained by chemical vapour deposition. Cubic boron nitride is produced by a high-pressure synthesis similar to that used for synthetic diamond. Figure 2 shows the structure of boron nitride in which the boron and nitrogen atoms take alternate places in the hexagonal rings.[3] The B—N distance within the hexagonal layers is 1.45 Å, while between the layers it is 3.33 Å. The hexagonal structure of boron nitride is exactly similar to that of graphite except in the stacking of the layers. In boron nitride the hexagonal rings of atoms are packed directly on top of each other, whereas in graphite a form of close packing exists, in which half the atoms lie between the centres of the hexagonal rings in the adjacent layers. The X-ray data gave a theoretical density of 2.270 g cm^{-3} for hexagonal boron nitride, which is rather greater than that which is normally measured on macroscopic samples (normally between 2.0 and 2.2 g cm^{-3}). The discrepancy appears to be associated with packing faults similar to those observed in graphite.

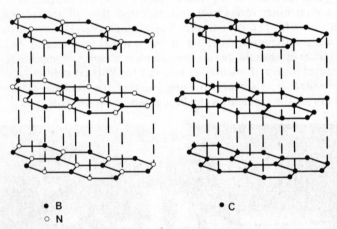

● B
○ N

Figure 2 *Crystal structures of graphite and boron nitride*

Chemical Vapour Deposition Routes to PBN

The technique of chemical vapour deposition, widely used to make high-temperature materials,[4] consists of causing a mixture of gaseous reagents to impinge on a heated surface where a reaction occurs to form the required material. The essential feature is that the product is not transported, but is grown at the substrate. Consequently the process can be carried out at temperatures much below the melting point or boiling point of the product and generally a very dense deposit of material is obtained. Also it is possible to grow materials in useful shapes such as tubes and crucibles by causing the reagent gases to flow around appropriately shaped moulds.

[3] R. S. Pease, *Acta Cryst.*, 1952, **5**, 356.
[4] C. F. Powell, J. H. Oxley, and J. M. Blocher, 'Vapour Deposition', John Wiley, New York, 1966.

Hexagonal boron nitride is a very stable and involatile compound and therefore almost any high-temperature reaction between compounds of boron and nitrogen tends to yield boron nitride. The compounds most usually employed as a source of boron are diborane, B_2H_6,[5] the boron halides, BX_3,[6,7] borazole, $B_3N_3H_6$,[8] and *B*-trichloroborazole, $B_3N_3H_3Cl_3$.[8] The last two compounds have the hexagonal structures shown in Figure 3 and are obviously suitable precursors for hexagonal boron nitride. Ammonia is the most usual source of nitrogen. Nitrogen itself has been used but it reacts very much more slowly than ammonia.[7] At temperatures greater than those indicated in reactions (1)–(3) the

$$B_2H_6 + 2NH_3 \xrightarrow{>500\,^\circ C} 2BN + 6H_2 \tag{1}$$

$$BCl_3 + NH_3 \xrightarrow{>1000\,^\circ C} BN + 3HCl \tag{2}$$

$$B_3N_3H_3Cl_3 \xrightarrow{>1300\,^\circ C} 3BN + 3HCl \tag{3}$$

only product is boron nitride, but at lower temperatures various side-reactions occur, leading to products which still contain some hydrogen.[9] Borazole gives a polymeric $(BNH)_x$ compound at 500 °C which is only converted into BN above 800 °C. Similarly *B*-trichloroborazole gives an unsatisfactory product at temperatures below 1300 °C.[8] The reaction between the boron halides and ammonia is complicated at temperatures below 1000 °C by an addition product.[6] The reaction between diborane and ammonia is most suitable for producing BN at temperatures in the range 700–1250 °C. Below 1000 °C it appears to yield amorphous BN, which is not very stable and which decomposes if subsequently heated above 1000 °C. However, diborane and ammonia above 1000 °C yield polycrystalline BN, which is much more stable.

The structure of PBN is very much related to the temperature at which it is formed. At temperatures below 1000 °C the product is amorphous, while at temperatures in the range 1000–1200 °C a polycrystalline structure starts to

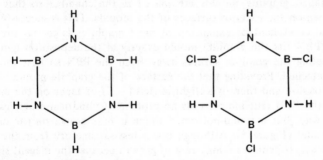

Figure 3 *Some precursors used in the chemical vapour deposition process for boron nitride*

[5] M. Hirayama and K. J. Shohns, *Electrochem. Soc.*, 1975, **122**, 1671.
[6] F. Meyer and R. Zappner, *Ber.*, 1921, **54**, 560.
[7] M. Basche, U.S. P. 3 152 006 (1964).
[8] R. Francis and E. R. Flint, U.S. Army Report WAL766.41/1 (1961).
[9] Gmelin's Handbuch der anorganischen Chemie, 8th edn., Verlag Chemie, Weinheim/Bergstrasse, No. 13 (1954).

develop which is believed to be turbostratic.[10] The B_3N_3 hexagons are packed in layers parallel to the substrate but otherwise their orientation is random. Above 1300 °C the hexagonal structure begins to develop an increasing degree of order, and highly ordered material with densities approaching the theoretical X-ray value of 2.270 g cm^{-3} are obtained at 1700–2100 °C. It is not practical to prepare BN at temperatures much in excess of 2100 °C because its dissociation pressure becomes significant. Boron nitride grown at temperatures above 1800 °C has very pronounced anisotropic properties, but material grown in the temperature range 1300–1700 °C has been reported to have an isotropic structure.[11]

The deposition pressure and the reactant flow rates also have an important influence on the properties of vapour-deposited boron nitride. Low pressures have been found to be important in avoiding the formation of powdery deposits. Pressures as low as 0.5 Torr have been used, although pressures in the range 5–50 Torr are more common.[8] It is also important to control the rate of deposition to achieve a high-density product. Control of deposition rate has been obtained both by restricting the flow of one reagent[8] and by dilution with an inert carrier gas.[7]

The CVD of Anisotropic Pyrolytic Boron Nitride

At Fulmer the CVD of PBN is carried out in large steel vacuum chambers. The basic system is illustrated in Figure 4. The reaction chamber components are graphite and are heated inductively by a water-cooled coil. It is supported on a graphite and nickel column which also acts as the reactant gas inlet to the chamber. The spent gases escape from the top of the reaction chamber into the outer steel chamber from which they are removed by continuous pumping. The temperature of the reaction chamber is measured optically along the gas inlet tube and also by means of thermocouples embedded in the outer susceptor.

All the inner surfaces of the reaction chamber become coated with PBN. Crucible-shaped graphite moulds are placed in the chamber so that crucibles can be grown on the exterior surfaces of the moulds. This is successful because the thermal coefficient of expansion of most graphites is greater than that of PBN. The PBN fits the graphite mould exactly at the deposition temperature, but on cooling the graphite shrinks away from the PBN so that the crucible becomes detached. Providing that the surface of the graphite mould is polished before deposition and there is a slight angle (1–2°) of taper on the mould, the release of the PBN crucible presents no problem. Cylindrical crucibles are best made this way, but a round-bottomed shape is best grown on the inside of a graphite mould (Figure 5). Although this is less satisfactory from the point of view of release, it achieves a high rate of growth because the reagent stream can be directed into the graphite mould. Small tubes (up to 25 mm) are readily made externally in the same way as crucibles. However, large tubes present a more difficult problem. When their diameter approaches that of the deposition chamber they must be made internally on a large graphite sleeve. The thermal mis-match

[10]   R. J. Patterson, R. D. Humphries, and R. R. Haberecht, 'Thin Films of Boron Nitride', National Electrochemical Society Meeting, Pittsburg, 1963.
[11]   A. Simpson and A. D. Stuckes, *J. Phys.(D)*, 1976, **9**, 621.

between the PBN and graphite on cooling is overcome by scoring the graphite sleeve so that it is the weaker component. On cooling, the boron nitride should rupture the graphite sleeve without suffering damage, but this is not always successful.

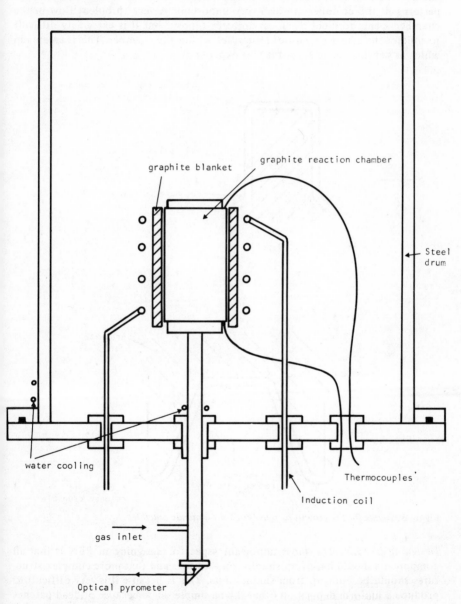

Figure 4 *Reaction chamber used for the chemical vapour deposition of boron nitride*

Flat plates of PBN can be grown by placing polished graphite plates in the reaction chamber. It is very important to minimize the stress in the deposit in order to obtain a plate which does not distort on release from the graphite.

The overall flow rates, the temperature and the pressure in the reaction chamber control the nature of the boron nitride which is produced, but the flow patterns in the chamber are also very important. A very turbulent flow in the chamber seems to yield the most uniform deposit, but it is extremely difficult to predict the effect of various structures within the chamber. This is an area in which as yet there is no substitute for experience.

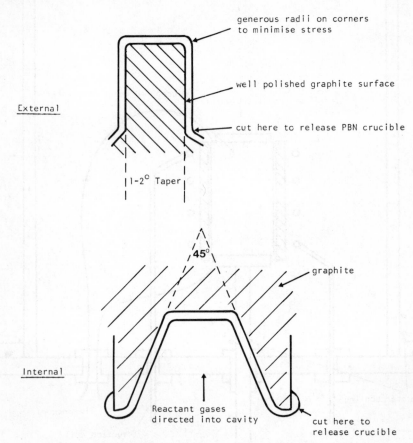

Figure 5 *Moulds for the growth of pyrolytic boron nitride crucibles*

Designing in PBN. The most important aspect of designing in PBN is that all components should have very simple cross-sections and that more complex structures should be built up from simple units. This is because it is very difficult to produce a uniform deposit on other than a simple shape because of dead patches in the gas flow and undesirable thickening at other points. It is also important that components should be designed in such a way that they can be released from the graphite moulds. In most cases a slight taper is required on the mould to obtain an easy release. All the shapes illustrated in Figure 6 can be easily made and many more complex arrangements can be built up from these units. It should be noted that the internal dimensions of the PBN components are most accurately controlled when the PBN is grown externally. By grinding the external dimensions of one PBN component it is possible to produce a sliding fit into another component.

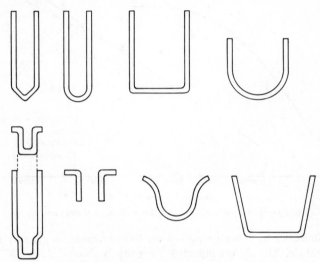

Figure 6 *Some shapes which can be grown in boron nitride*

The maximum size of crucible that can presently be grown externally at Fulmer is 40 mm in diameter by 40 mm in length. Larger sizes (up to 70 mm diameter) can be grown internally. These sizes are limited only by the present reaction chambers and there is no fundamental reason why larger crucibles should not be made. The largest plates which are presently being made at Fulmer are 150 × 25 × 1 mm. Again there is no basic reason why these sizes should not be increased.

The Physical Properties of PBN and their Relation to the Deposition Conditions
PBN can be produced under a wide range of conditions and, although the product in all cases is substantially the same from the chemical point of view, the detailed physical properties vary considerably.

Anisotropic PBN as grown by Fulmer and Union Carbide is slightly off-white, opaque material. It is not very hard and readily accepts a good polish. It has a slightly silky feel. It has a significant degree of flexibility when bent in the direction which allows the basal planes to slide over each other.

Density and X-ray Data. Pyrolytic boron nitride has a hexagonal unit cell with the following dimensions at 35 °C: $a = 2.50399 \pm 0.00005$ Å and $c = 6.6612 \pm$

0.0005 Å. This leads to a calculated density of 2.270 g cm^{-3} which should be compared with a density of 2.29 ± 0.03 g cm^{-3} obtained by the displacement method on the same sample of material. This sample had been recrystallized by heating at 2050 °C for a number of hours in a stream of nitrogen.[3]

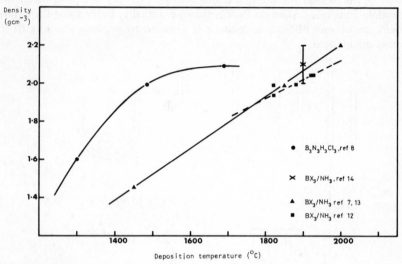

Figure 7 *Density of pyrolytic boron nitride as a function of temperature*

Various densities have been reported for boron nitride, in general increasing with temperature. The lowest reported[11] density is about 1.25 g cm^{-3} for isotropic PBN. At 1800 °C densities of about 2.05 g cm^{-3} are obtained for anisotropic PBN, and this continues to approach the X-ray density at higher temperatures. Unpublished results[12] at Fulmer have shown that although the physical density continues to increase over this range, the X-ray density is constant throughout, implying that there is a gradual improvement in the crystal packing. Figure 7 shows data collected from several sources[7,8,12,13,14] for anisotropic PBN, which indicate that different reagent mixtures yield a range of densities at temperatures between 1300 and 1500 °C, but that they all converge at higher temperatures. From the point of view of growing the maximum density material it is evident that a high temperature is preferable. However, the dissociation pressure of PBN begins to be significant at about 1900 °C and so the PBN begins to evaporate as rapidly as it is formed, resulting in an overall lowering of deposition rate. The calculated equilibrium pressures of nitrogen over PBN at temperatures in the range 1700–2000 °C are given in Table 1. PBN can be sublimed in one atmosphere of nitrogen at 2330 °C.[15] Also at these very high temperatures the

[12]   J. P. Theophilus, N. J. Archer, and C. Hayman, Fulmer Research Institute, Unpublished observations.
[13]   A. W. Moore, *Nature*, 1969, **221**, 1133.
[14]   'Boralloy' Data Sheet No. 713–204 EF, Carbon Products Division, Union Carbide Corporation, 270 Park Avenue, New York, NY10017.
[15]   JANAF, Thermochemical Tables.

reaction between boron nitride and graphite to give boron carbide becomes an additional problem.[13]

The density of PBN can be increased by high-temperature annealing. Moore[13] has demonstrated that the density of a sample increased from 2.20 to 2.23 g cm^{-3} on being heated at 2350 °C for 4.8 h. Apparently PBN does not recrystallize when subjected to a tensile deformation parallel to the basal plane of up to 1100 kg cm^{-2} at 2200 °C.[16] In this respect PBN behaves differently from pyrolytic graphite, which can be recrystallized under these conditions. However, compressive annealing perpendicular to the basal planes at a temperature in the range 2300−2400 °C results in a dramatic structural change in PBN.[13] The normal white opaque boron nitride is converted into a transparent form with much greater crystal orientation and close to theoretical density. Pressures of up to 1000 kg cm^{-2} are required for this transformation, and it is difficult to see how this technique could be applied to shapes other than flat plates or discs.

Table 1 *Dissociation pressure of PBN*

*Temp./*K	N_2 *pressure/*Torr
1900	1.8×10^{-2}
2000	8.7×10^{-2}
2100	3.6×10^{-1}
2200	1.3
2300	4.3

However, at Fulmer similar transparent material has actually been grown without the use of high pressure. As yet the conditions under which this occurs are not understood, but there is evidently the possibility of producing PBN in complex shapes thereby avoiding the geometric restrictions imposed by high-pressure annealing. Although PBN as grown at 1800−1900 °C is anisotropic, with the *c* axis of the hexagonal crystallites aligned preferentially perpendicular to the substrate surface, there is still a considerable spread about this orientation. An *X*-ray measure of this lack of alignment is the full width at half maximum intensity (FWHM) of the (022) orientation distribution function. This can be measured directly on rod-shaped specimens cut with the rod axis parallel to the deposition plane and mounted in such a way that the rod axis is perpendicular to the normal of the diffraction planes. The intensity of the (002) reflection can be plotted as a function of the rotation angle, ϕ, about the rod axis. The value $\Delta \phi$ FWHM (002) using copper $K\alpha$ radiation has been found to be 50−100 ° for PBN grown from BCl_3 and NH_3 at 1900 °C. Compressive annealing at 2300 °C reduces this to 2−3° with a corresponding increase in density.[13] In contrast, an isotropic form of PBN has been reported by the Raytheon Corporation and the British Ceramic Research Association (BCRA), in which there is no preferred orientation at all. This has been obtained at lower temperatures and has a much lower density (approximately 1.25 g cm^{-3}).[11]

Stress. The stress in CVD deposits is commonly ascribed to the development of cone-like structures growing perpendicular to the substrate surface. The struc-

[16] W. V. Kotlensky and H. E. Martens, *Nature*, 1962, **196**, 1090.

tures observed in boron nitride are similar to those observed in graphite. The cone structure is most pronounced at high growth rates. For example it becomes very pronounced at vapour pressures of about 4 Torr with *B*-trichloroborazole and vanishes almost entirely at pressures of around 0.1 Torr.[8] Stress levels are certainly higher in rapidly deposited material and also in material deposited at lower temperatures. Material deposited at temperatures above 1900 °C appears to exhibit least stress.

The combination of stress and the planar structure of PBN leads to failure by delamination. This mode of stress-relieving is particularly encountered at sharp corners, for example at the bottom edge of a parallel-sided crucible, and for this reason it is best to give corners as large a radius as possible. Narrow bore tubes also have a tendency to delaminate into a number of concentric tubes. Residual stress in crucibles makes itself apparent by a tendency to delaminate after repeated temperature cycling.

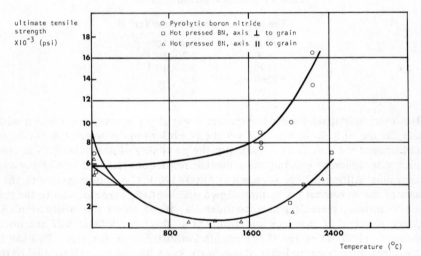

Figure 8 *Strength of pyrolitic boron nitride deposited at different temperatures*

Mechanical Strength. The ultimate tensile strength of PBN in the '*a*' direction (parallel to the basal planes) has been studied at a range of temperatures.[16] Figure 8 shows that it increases with temperature from 423 kg cm^{-2} at room temperatures to 1057 kg cm^{-2} at 2200 °C [14] Very few other materials have comparable hot strength. The compressive strength in the '*c*' direction is in excess of 1400 kg cm^{-2} at room temperature and about 300 kg cm^{-2} at 2200 °C, beyond which a structural change begins to occur. Young's modulus at room temperature, measured by compression in the '*c*' direction, is approximately 7 × 10^4 kg cm^{-2} and approximately 2 × 10^5 kg cm^{-2} in the '*a*' direction. In thin layers and narrow strips PBN is quite flexible, and in this respect it is quite unlike many ceramics.

There appear to be no published data on the hardness of boron nitride. It is very difficult to measure because the reflectivity of the material makes it impossible to see microscopic hardness indentations. PBN can be cut and machined by most types of tool, but it tends to blunt steel tools rather rapidly. Diamond and silicon carbide impregnated tools are better. Crucibles are best cut while still attached to their mandrels, while plates can easily be handled by sticking them to a steel plate. The surfaces of PBN plates can be ground flat and parallel by this method. The best results are obtained by grinding dry, but with high-speed cut-off wheels it is essential to cool the wheel with water.

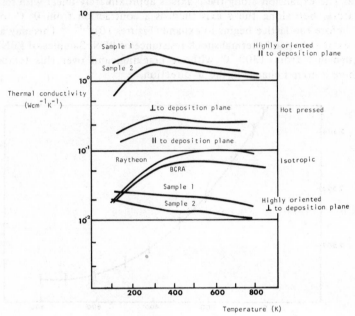

Figure 9 *Physical properties of pyrolytic boron nitride*

Thermal Properties. The thermal conductivity of highly oriented PBN is as good as metallic iron in the '*a*' direction. In this respect PBN is a very unusual material because it has good thermal conductivity combined with very poor electrical conductivity. The thermal conductivity of PBN in the '*a*' direction is 2.5 W cm^{-1} K^{-1} at 235 K, while its electrical resistivity is about 10^{15} ohm cm at the same temperature. Figure 9 shows the data obtained by Simpson and Stuckes[11,17] from a flash technique for measuring thermal diffusivity. The thermal conductivity for well-oriented PBN in the '*a*' direction is about a hundred times greater than in the '*c*' direction. Figure 9 also shows the thermal conductivity of hot-pressed boron nitride and isotropic PBN (provided by BCRA and Raytheon) which, although less than the conductivity in the '*a*' direction of PBN, is still very good for a ceramic. The only comparable ceramic material with

[17]   A. Simpson and A. D. Stuckes, *J. Phys.(C)*, 1971, **4**, 1710.

better thermal conductivity is hot-pressed beryllia. As there are no known toxi-city hazards associated with boron nitride, an increasing amount of hot-pressed boron nitride is being used in place of beryllia in thermally conducting insulators on high-power semiconductor devices. It is unfortunate that the orientation of CVD PBN is not very useful for this type of application, (the good direction of thermal conductivity is not perpendicular to the plane of the plates). However, rods cut from anisotropic PBN plate are used in microwave tubes and take advantage of the good thermal conductivity in the 'a' direction along the rod.

The thermal expansion behaviour of PBN is very similar to that of pyrolytic graphite. The expansion along the c axis is approximately linear with respect to temperature, but along the a axis there is a contraction from $0\,^{\circ}C$ to about $800\,^{\circ}C$ before the lattice begins to expand (Figures 10).[3,14,18] This may account for the extremely good thermal shock resistance of PBN. Samples of PBN can be water-quenched from $1300\,^{\circ}C$ without cracking, and over this temperature range there is no net change in the 'a' direction.

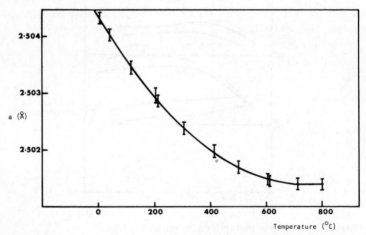

Figure 10 *Thermal expansion of boron nitride in the 'a' crystallographic direction*

The combination of good thermal shock resistance with high thermal conduc-tivity in the 'a' direction makes PBN an unusual crucible material. Because of the orientation of the 'a' direction parallel to the substrate, heat flows around the walls of the crucible much faster than through them. Consequently any local heating on the outside of the crucible is spread out as it is transmitted through the crucible walls thus avoiding local hot spots.

Electrical Properties. PBN is a good electrical insulator at high temperatures, particularly in the 'c' direction. It remains better than fused alumina up to about $1700\,^{\circ}C$.[14] PBN has been used as a support material in microwave tubes because it has stability at high temperatures, a dielectric constant which is

[18] B. Yates, N. J. Overy, and O. Pirgon, *Phil. Mag.*, 1975, **32**, 847.

largely independent of temperature, and a dielectric loss which remains low even at high temperature. Anisotropic boron nitride with a density of 2.10 g cm^{-3} has a dielectric constant of about 5 at room temperature[14] and the loss tangent is about 10^{-4} at 10^{10} Hz and $25\,^{\circ}$C.

Chemical Properties. PBN is chemically very inert. It is not attacked by most acids or acidic fused salts, although molten alkali attacks it to form a borate. Aqueous alkaline solutions will dissolve boron nitride over long periods.

Table 2 *Chemical resistance of PBN*

Environment	Temp./$^{\circ}C$	Duration of test	Result
Metals			
Ag	m.p.	brief	no attack, no wetting
Au	m.p.	several hours	no attack, no wetting
Al	m.p	several hours	no attack, no wetting
Si	m.p.	several hours	no attack, no wetting
Ge	m.p.	several hours	no attack, no wetting
Sn	m.p.	several hours	no attack, no wetting
Cu	m.p.	several hours	no attack, no wetting
Cd	m.p.	several hours	no attack, no wetting
Fe	m.p.	several hours	no attack, no wetting
Sb	m.p.	several hours	no attack, no wetting
Bi	m.p.	several hours	no attack, no wetting
In	m.p.	several hours	no attack, no wetting
As	m.p.	several hours	no attack, no wetting
SmCo$_5$	1500	several hours	no wetting, very resistant
GaAs	1500	several hours	no attack
InP/In	1500	several hours	some attack
NaOH	fused	—	decompose to form ammonia and sodium borate
Cryolite, Na$_3$AlF$_6$	fused	—	no attack, no wetting
Borosolicate glass	fused	—	no attack, no wetting
Lithium tetraborate	fused	1 h	wets PBN, but no attack
As$_2$O$_3$, HgO, CuO	—	—	reduced at high temperatures
H$_2$O	—	—	hydrolysis at $>100\,^{\circ}$C
HCl	aqueous	—	no attack
HF	aqueous	—	very slow attack
HNO$_3$	aqueous	—	no attack
H$_2$SO$_4$	aqueous	—	no attack
H$_2$SO$_4$/F	b.p.	—	dissolves PBN
Na$_2$HPO$_4$ (aqueous)	300	500 h	PBN dissolved
Organic solvents	—	—	no effect
Carbon	>2200	—	forms B$_4$C
Cl$_2$	>800	—	forms BCl$_3$
CO	>800	—	no effect

Molten metals generally do not wet boron nitride, and it is only attacked by those which form nitrides or borides which are more stable than BN itself. These include aluminium, but in practice PBN can be used as an evaporator crucible for aluminium because the rate of attack is acceptably low. Table 2 gives some of the environments in which PBN has been tested.

PBN has good oxidation resistance up to about 1300 °C, beyond which the rate of attack becomes significant (Figure 11). This is probably because it develops a skin of boron oxide which becomes volatile at about 1300 °C. A glassy skin of boron oxide can be seen on the surface of PBN which has been heated at 800 °C for 100–200 h. This skin can easily be removed by immersing the PBN in boiling water for a short period. High-density PBN is not affected at all by this treatment.

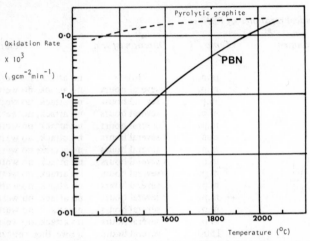

Figure 11 *Relative resistance to oxidation of graphite and pyrolytic boron nitride*

The chemical purity of PBN grown by CVD is extremely high. There is no evidence for non-stoicheiometry in boron nitride produced at temperatures above 1700 °C, although there is some evidence for the retention of hydrides at lower temperatures. One of the advantages of the CVD technique is its tendency not to transport impurities. The reagents transported into the hot zone are substantially pure, and the only impurities which will persist in the high-temperature region are those with very stable and non-volatile borides and nitrides. The total concentration of metallic impurity obtained in PBN at Fulmer is about 30 p.p.m. and this probably comes from the graphite supports. This low level of contamination makes PBN crucibles a valuable alternative to fused quartz for growing electronic materials. It does not appear to be possible to make vitreous carbon of this purity, and the only comparable graphite is Ringsdorf spectroscopic grade.

Conclusion

As a crucible material and as an electronic support material anisotropic boron nitride has some unique advantages. Its increasing use should improve the availability of the material and decrease its cost. This may make it possible to use PBN in a much wider range of analytical and similar applications where an inert and stable material is required.

Desulphurization of Molten Pig-iron by Magnesium

By M. H. RAND, T. D. A. KENNEDY, C. F. KNIGHTS, AND B. A. PARTRIDGE

AERE, Harwell, Didcot, Oxon.

Introduction

In the Galag process for the desulphurization of pig-iron by magnesium-impregnated coke, a charge of magnesium-coke, containing about 43 wt% Mg with average lump size of 65–140 mm, is plunged beneath the surface of the iron melt held in a ladle at about 1350 °C. The charge of material is held under the metal surface by a refractory-coated iron bell which, as shown in Figure 1, has holes in the sides for the release of the magnesium vapour evolved. The temperature of the coke rapidly rises to the boiling point of magnesium, and the magnesium vapour released through the bell holes forms bubbles which rise to the surface of the melt. During this movement the magnesium reacts with dissolved sulphur in the melt to form magnesium sulphide particles which are transferred to the melt surface and into a slag layer.

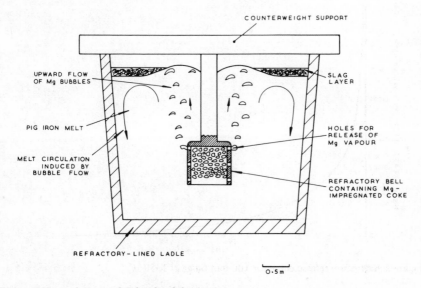

Figure 1 *The technique of Galag desulphurization*

The objective of the work described in this paper was to establish a quantitative model of the Galag operation so that a sound physical basis could be laid for the optimization and development of the technique.

181

The Physical Model

In order to formulate a quantitative description of the desulphurizing operation it is convenient to subdivide the process into four stages: (i) heat transfer to the coke lumps from the surrounding iron melt which governs the instantaneous rate of vapour evolution; (ii) release of vapour from the holes in the bell, and the formation of bubbles; (iii) mass transfer at the bubble boundaries, and reaction of the magnesium with dissolved sulphur in the melt; (iv) transfer of magnesium sulphide particles to the melt surface, and retention in the slag.

Heat Transfer and the Rate of Magnesium Evolution. Heat transfer conditions within the magnesium-coke charge inside the bell are complex; in the present model, as a first approximation to the real situation, the rate of magnesium evolution is calculated from the transient rate of heat conduction within a coke lump taken to be cylindrical in form, surrounded by a 'semi-infinite sea' of molten iron. At time zero, the cylinder is taken to be at 50 °C and to be immersed in molten iron which extends 100 mm outside the cylinder in all directions. Thereafter, the temperature of the iron is held constant at this boundary, but varies within it. After a few seconds, the vapour-filled pores of the coke act as a thermal barrier limiting the vaporization rate.

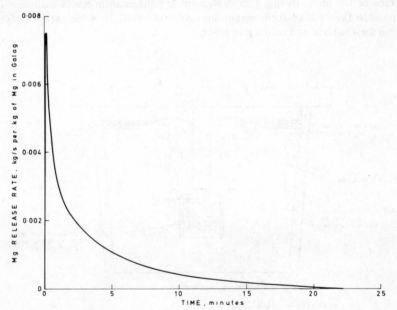

Figure 2 *Magnesium release curve for* 100 mm *Galag at* 1350 °C

The rate of heat transfer to the coke cylinder is obtained from a finite difference solution of the general transient heat conduction equation. Phase changes occurring in the magnesium are taken into account by appropriately increasing its specific heat over a discrete temperature interval around the melting and boiling points, the local conductivity being adjusted accordingly. Dimensional considerations indicate that a single release curve can be obtained for a given temperature by plotting $m_v d^2 m_{Mg}$ against t/d^2, where m_v = rate of release of Mg vapour, from the Galag cylinder (kg s^{-1}); m_{Mg} = original mass of Mg in the cylinder (kg); d = lump diameter (m); t = time (s).

A typical release curve (given as kg s^{-1} per kg Mg in the original Galag) is shown in Figure 2 for a 100 mm cylinder at 1350 °C. This general form of the release curve is in good agreement with plant observations. The calculations show that the release rate is very dependent on lump size and to a lesser extent on melt temperature.

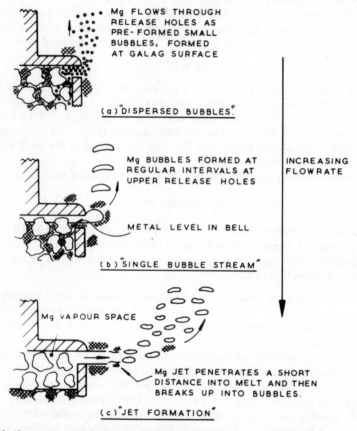

Figure 3 *Alternative models of vapour release from a bell*

Vapour Release from the Bell and Bubble Formation. Initial qualitative consideration suggested that magnesium vapour release from the bell might occur in one or more of the three modes shown in Figure 3, *i.e.* (i) as small dispersed bubbles which form at the surface of the Galag lumps and pass, without significant coalescence, through the bell holes and into the melt; (ii) as a more or less orderly succession of single bubbles formed at exit from the bell holes, or

(iii) as a continuous stream, or jet, which breaks up a short distance into the melt into a flow of bubbles.

Calculations strongly suggest that the rate of vapour flow through a hole is much higher than could be accommodated by a dispersed bubble flow, but is not high enough to lead to jet formation. It is concluded therefore that vapour release is characterized by the formation of comparatively large bubbles directly at the mouth of a bell hole. Moreover, pressure considerations indicate that only the holes at the highest level are operative, and that even these top holes or slots are partially melt-filled as shown in Figure 3b. Thus the volumetric flow-rate through individual holes is likely to be from 4 to $200 \, l \, s^{-1}$.

For flow rates up to $12 \, l \, s^{-1}$ measured bubble volumes in other systems obey the relation (1), where V_B = bubble volume at detachment from orifice (m^3) and Q = volumetric flowrate of gas ($m^3 \, s^{-1}$). Since the predicted peak flowrate

$$V_B \propto Q^{6/5} \tag{1}$$

of Mg vapour in a Galag application is a factor of ~20 higher than the highest value for which studies exist, further measurements on bubble formation have been carried out in the Harwell water tank at flow rates up to $100 \, l \, s^{-1}$ through a 50 mm release slot. The experiments confirmed the theoretical predictions that jet formation would not occur, and that the liquid level in the 'bell' would be depressed less than the diameter of the holes.

The experimentally determined relationship (2) has been used in the present model.

$$V_B = 0.3767 \, Q^{6/5} \tag{2}$$

Bubbles of the volume involved in a typical Galag operation ($0.4-40 \, l$) almost certainly have a spherical cap form with a subtended angle of $100°$, and rise at a velocity (U) $= \frac{2}{3} \sqrt{gR} \, (m \, s^{-1})$, where g = acceleration due to gravity ($m \, s^{-2}$) and R = radius of curvature of the spherical cap (m).

Desulphurizing Rate. At the high temperature involved in Galag treatments the basic chemical reaction between magnesium and sulphur in the melt is likely to be very fast, and it is assumed that mass transfer effects dominate the rate of desulphurization.

Although the solubility of magnesium in pure iron is quite low, the solubility in Fe–C alloys is appreciable and will play an important part in the mechanism of the process. Speer and Parlee[1] have shown that under the conditions of a typical Galag treatment ($p_{Mg} = 1.5$ atm, $T = 1350 \, °C$) the Mg solubility is about 0.5 wt%, roughly ten times greater than the normal maximum starting sulphur level. Since the diffusion coefficients of Mg and S in the melt will be similar, the greater driving force for Mg transfer will be dominant and the concentration profiles in the boundary layer around a bubble will be as shown in Figure 4. The reaction zone, in which chemical equilibrium is attained and MgS particles are formed, is, therefore, quite close to the outside of the boundary layer.

The application of Fick's law to this counter-diffusion problem shows that the process can be regarded as essentially one of magnesium dissolution (with

[1] M. C. Speer, A. D. Parlee, *AFS Cast Metal Res. J.*, 1972, 122

the driving force $[C_{Mg}]_B - [C_{Mg}]_M$), with a (small) enhancement due to sulphur diffusion into the boundary layer.

The mass transfer coefficient, k_L, is obtained from the work of Baird and Davidson,[2] who have analysed the problem of liquid-phase controlled gas absorption at the curved surface of a spherical cap bubble. The equation (3)

$$k_L = 1.934 \, g^{¼} \, D^{½} \, R^{-¼} \qquad (3)$$

may be deduced for a bubble of subtended angle $100°$ where D is the diffusion coefficient of the diffusing species in the liquid $(m^2 \, s^{-1})$.

Although the bulk of the magnesium transferred from the bubble reacts to form MgS, a proportion goes into solution in the melt. In evaluating this latter effect, it is assumed that the Mg–S solubility is maintained in the well-mixed bulk metal; a simple mass balance then apportions the transferred magnesium between reaction to MgS and dissolution.

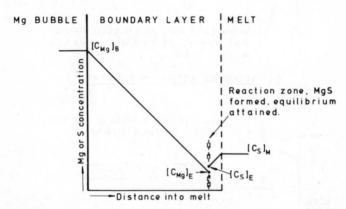

Figure 4 *Magnesium and sulphur concentration profiles in boundary layer around a rising bubble*

A difficulty now appears in the application of the model since the data involving the Mg–S solubility product (K_{SP}) are far from consistent.

There are two sets of direct measurement of this solubility product, by Speer and Parlee[1] who give values from 1×10^{-4} to 1×10^{-3} (wt %)^2, at $1260 \, °C$, and by Lavric and Marincek[3] whose values range from 6×10^{-5} to 1×10^{-4} at $1250–1350 \, °C$. However, these values are very much greater than those which can be derived from the well-defined thermodynamic data for MgS, and the dissolution of Mg and S in pig-iron, which indicate a value of about 2×10^{-6} (wt %)^2 with an uncertainty of a factor of 3 at $1250 \, °C$. In addition Duhem[4] has given a line for the temperature variation the solubility product with temperature which lies roughly midway between the directly determined and 'thermodynamic' values.

[2] M. H. I. Baird and J. F. Davidson, *Chem. Eng. Sci.*, 1962, **17**, 87
[3] B. Marincek, *Giesserei. Tech. Wiss. Beih, Giessereiw. Metallk.*, 1964, **16**, 185
[4] F. Dunhem, private communication

In view of this serious uncertainty in an important parameter, we have, in the subsequent analysis, determined the value of K_{SP} which brings the predictions of the model into agreement with plant observation for a given Galag treatment.

The quantitative assessment of the model then rests on the general consistency of the K_{SP} values so derived from a substantial number of well-documented plant runs.

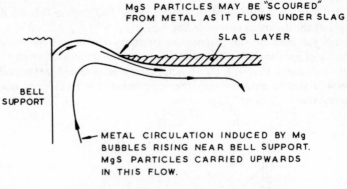

MgS PARTICLES MAY BE "SCOURED"
FROM METAL AS IT FLOWS UNDER SLAG

SLAG LAYER

BELL
SUPPORT

METAL CIRCULATION INDUCED BY Mg
BUBBLES RISING NEAR BELL SUPPORT.
MgS PARTICLES CARRIED UPWARDS
IN THIS FLOW.

(a)"SCOURING" ACTION OF SLAG LAYER.

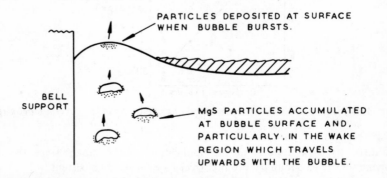

PARTICLES DEPOSITED AT SURFACE
WHEN BUBBLE BURSTS.

BELL
SUPPORT

MgS PARTICLES ACCUMULATED
AT BUBBLE SURFACE AND,
PARTICULARLY, IN THE WAKE
REGION WHICH TRAVELS
UPWARDS WITH THE BUBBLE.

(b)PARTICLES CARRIED AT BUBBLE SURFACES AND IN BUBBLE WAKES.

Figure 5 *Transfer of* MgS *particles to the melt surface*

Transfer of MgS *Particles to the Melt Surface.* The magnesium sulphide particles formed in the process are small (approximately 10 μm diam), and a mechanism other than simply buoyancy needs to be invoked to explain the effective separation observed during the relatively short period associated with a Galag treatment. The movement of the magnesium bubbles induces a circulation in the melt which is upwards in the vicinity of the bell, where the concentration of sulphide particles is greatest, and, as indicated in Figure 5a, the slag may exercise a 'scouring' action as the metal flows outwards under the surface layer.

It also seems possible that some of the sulphide particles are retained on formation, in the bubble boundaries by surface tension forces or are carried upwards in the bubble wakes as indicated in Figure 5b. Any bubbles disappearing due to complete reaction will deposit sulphide particles which may then be picked up by succeeding bubbles. If correct, this mechanism implies that 100% utilization of magnesium in the melt would be undesirable since it would leave no excess vapour to act as a sulphide carrier.

Assessment of the Model by Comparison with Plant Data

An assessment of the model has been made by comparing the predictions with

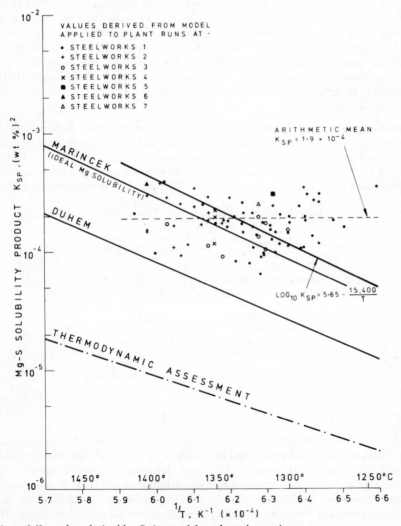

Figure 6 K_{SP} *values derived by fitting model to plant observations*

84 well-documented desulphurization runs which cover a variety of treatment situations, including the use of two bells in simultaneous or successive applications.

For each plant run, the value of K_{SP}, the magnesium sulphide solubility product, has been found which brings the final sulphur level predicted by the model into agreement with the observed result. The log K_{SP} values found in this way are plotted in Figure 6 as a function of $1/T$, together with three lines discussed in the paper. The fitted K_{SP} values fall within a broad band, consistent with a number of directly determined values.

Although a purely statistical assessment of the plant values would suggest that K_{SP} varies very little with temperature, we have preferred at the moment to put more weight on the fact that all the three derived lines suggest a marked increase in K_{SP} at higher temperatures. Two extreme cases have therefore been considered: (i) the heavy line, which is the line through the centre of gravity of the points with the same slope as the 'ideal solubility' curve, and (ii) the broken line, with K_{SP} independent of temperature. The first line is likely to underestimate the efficiency at temperatures above 1340 °C and the second to give an underestimate below 1340 °C.

Relationship Between Operating Parameters and Predicted Plant Performance

A particular advantage of the calculation model is that it may be used to assess the influence of the process variables on desulphurizing performance. A comparison of this assessment with the substantial body of practical experience may then be used as a basis for optimization and development of the technique.

Table 1 *Typical conditions for a Galag treatment*

Parameter	Typical Value	Range Encountered
Hot metal/tonne	250	—
Metal temperature/°C	1350	1300–1400
Initial sulphur conc./wt %	0·05	0·05–0·02
Galag application rate/kg per tonne	1·0	0·6 –1·4
Galag lump size/mm	100	65–140
Galag Mg content/wt %	43	40–43
No. of release holes per bell	10	6–14
Size of release hole/mm	64	50–110
Plunge depth, to holes/m	1·5	0·75–2·25
Plunge time/min	15	8–25

History of a Typical Application. Conditions representative of a typical Galag treatment are listed in Table 1, and the predicted progress of such an application is shown in Figure 7. It is seen that no desulphurization occurs for the first 30 s of the plunge, while the magnesium concentration in the melt is rising to the value in equilibrium with the initial sulphur concentration. Thereafter, the magnesium transferred from the rising bubbles is available for desulphurization. The early peak in the magnesium release rate results in a loss of magnesium (about

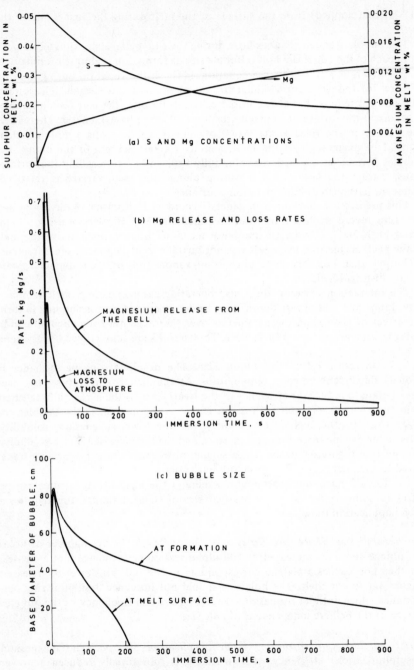

Figure 7 (a) *and* (b): *predicted progress of a typical desulphurizing run.* (c): *predicted bubble frequency and size during a typical desulphurizing run*

11% of that applied) from the surface of the melt during the first 3 min of the run.

The bubble frequency varies little during the run, being approximately 5 per s from each of the 10 release holes. Bubble size at formation is almost proportional to gas flowrate [$V_B \propto Q^{6/5}$, see equation (1)], so the variation during the run (Figure 7c) follows a form similar to that of the basic magnesium release rate. The model predicts that at the initial peak release rate, the magnesium bubbles breaking at the surface of the melt are about 80 cm in base diameter. Thereafter, the decline in the release rate leads to smaller bubbles giving a more efficient transfer of magnesium to the melt, and after about 3.5 min of the plunge the bubbles formed at the bell are being fully utilized before reaching the surface. Thus, during the last 11.5 min of the plunge the melt surface is relatively quiescent, although desulphurization continues.

This predicted behaviour is in general accord with the visual observations and cine-film record made during three treatments at BSC Hartlepool using 90 mm Galag at 1350 °C. Owing to the dense magnesia fume formed above the melt at the peak magnesium release, it was not possible to make precise measurements of bubble size, but very large pockets of vapour, up to 70 cm diameter, were clearly distinguished.

The interaction between the Galag operating parameters (*e.g.* melt temperature, lump size, and plunge depth) may be demonstrated by considering, in turn, the effect of changes in the parameters over the range normally encountered in Galag treatments and given in Table 1. These results are summarized briefly here.

Melt Temperature and Galag Lump Size. The desulphurizing performance is strongly dependent on melt temperature. At the higher temperatures two factors operate to reduce the efficiency of the treatment: (i) the magnesium released from the charge is transferred less efficiently to the melt since the bubbles are larger (due to the higher release rate) and the lower magnesium solubility reduces the driving force for mass transfer, and (ii) the increased Mg–S solubility product (see Figure 6) means that a smaller proportion of the magnesium transferred to the melt is available for desulphurization.

The loss of magnesium to the atmosphere at the higher temperatures can be offset to some extent by using a larger size of Galag, although this requires a longer application time.

Number and size of Release Holes and Plunge Depth. As the number of holes and plunge depth are increased, the desulphurization performance first increases, but then approaches a plateau corresponding to the full transfer of the released magnesium to the melt. The hole size should not influence desulphurizing performance, since until jet formation occurs, the size and frequency of the bubbles formed at the bell are independent of hole size.

Initial Sulphur Concentration, Galag Application Method. The magnesium (desulphurization) efficiency of a treatment is substantially reduced at lower initial sulphur levels in the melt. This effect follows directly from the solubility product relationship.

For a given application rate, there is a slight advantage if the Galag can be shared between two bells, used either in succession or simultaneously, rather than in a single plunge within one bell, due predominantly to the increased number of release holes available.

Conclusions

In summarizing the conclusions of the model we can say that the desulphurizing efficiency of the Galag technique is governed by two, largely independent, factors: (i) the efficiency with which the magnesium in the charge is transferred to the melt, and (ii) the extent to which the transferred magnesium is available for desulphurization.

The efficiency of magnesium transfer in the process is generally high (*i.e.* better than 85%), with appreciable amounts of magnesium being lost to the atmosphere only in treatments at 1400 °C or above.

Slag Equilibria and Sulphur Removal after Galag Treatment

The problem of sulphur removal from the ladle slag after the Galag treatment, and prior to steelmaking in an oxygen converter, is an important aspect of the desulphurizing process.

At present, converter operating practice demands the physical removal of the Galag slag in order to avoid substantial reversion of the sulphur which would normally occur during steelmaking, and any minor addition to, or simple modification of converter practice which allowed the sulphur to be removed chemically and thus to avoid this tiresome procedure would be very welcome.

Our analysis indicates that if the sulphur in the slag is kept predominantly as MgS, rather than being allowed to convert into CaS, contacting the slag with carbon dioxide could lead to appreciable transfer of sulphur to the gas phase [as $S_2(g)$ and $SO_2(g)$]. The quantities of carbon dioxide are not excessive— about 200 st m^3 of gas to remove 25 kg of sulphur from 100 tonnes of hot metal, assuming that 10% of the feed gas reacts.

In contemplating a CO_2 treatment of the slag while still in the ladle the important facts favouring the maintenance of a high MgS content of the slag are: (i) a low volume or high viscosity of the slag, and (ii) a minimum disturbance of the slag/hot metal interface.

For the situation in which the Galag slag is charged with the hot metal to the converter, sulphur release could be achieved only during the early stages of a blow before the Galag material becomes incorporated in the normal converter slag. Once incorporation is complete, however, substantial sulphur release to the gas phase is unlikely.

The authors would like to thank Mr F. J. Wallace and F. J. Ravault, Foseco International Ltd, for many stimulating discussions during this work, and Foseco International Ltd, for permission to publish this paper.

A Review of Phosphate-bonded Refractories

By J. E. CASSIDY

ICI Mond Division, PO Box 8, The Heath,
Runcorn, Cheshire, WA7 4QD

Introduction

In 1950 Kingery[1] wrote the first comprehensive study of phosphate bonding in refractories. It is interesting to note that Kingery quoted 43 references in his review article and covered the literature from 1902 to 1950, while in a recent review by Chvatal[2] 222 references were quoted covering the literature from 1965 to 1975: a book[3] has also been written on the subject.

Progress has been made in three major areas: (i) understanding the fundamental chemistry of the bonding processes; (ii) the development of new and more sophisticated phosphate bonds; (iii) the use of phosphate-bonded refractories. This paper is primarily concerned with the first two.

The Chemisty of Phosphate Bonds

Kingery stated that phosphate bonding is accomplished by three methods: (i) the reactions between siliceous materials and phosphoric acid; (ii) the reactions between oxides and phosphoric acid; (iii) the direct addition or formation of acid phosphates. These methods are still widely used, but in addition we have a variety of other bonding systems available in both liquid and solid form. These include ammonium phosphate,[4] chromium–aluminium phosphate,[5] alkali metaphosphates,[6] magnesium acid phosphates,[7] aluminium chlorophosphate hydrate,[8] and mixtures of aluminium phosphate hydrate and urea phosphate.[9]

Phosphoric acid and solutions of monoaluminium phosphate (MAP) are the most widely used and studied bonding agents.

New bonding agents have been developed to overcome problems associated with the use of liquid bonds in certain applications or with certain aggregates. Thus, the alkali polyphosphates are particularly useful in bonding basic aggregates; phosphoric acid or solutions of MAP tend to react too fast. Aluminium chlorophosphate hydrate (ACPH) is a dry powder developed especially for use in castable refractories. Its use overcomes problems associated with bond migration, bloating due to reaction with metallic iron, and the instability of some

[1] W. D. Kingery, *J. Amer. Ceram. Soc.,* 1950, **33,** 239.
[2] T. Chvatal, *Huttenpraxis,* 1975, 833.
[3] P. P. Budnikov and L. B. Khovoschavin, 'Refractory concretes with phosphate bindings', Moscow, 1971.
[4] H. H. Gregar and J. J. Reimer, U.S.P. 2 425 152.
[5] T. Chvatal, *Sprechsaal,* 1966, **99,** 903.
[6] J. E. Lyons, *Amer. Ceram. Soc. Bull.,* 1966, **45,** 1078.
[7] L. G. Sudkas, *Izvest. Akad. Nauk S.S.S.R., neorg. Materialy,* 1970, **6,** 932.
[8] J. D. Birchall and J. E. Cassidy, B.P. 1 322 724; B.P. 1 357 541.
[9] K. Diel, Ger.P. 2 412 474.

refractories on storage. It also introduces a novel concept in bonding inasmuch as its setting reactions do not require the formation of intermediate metaphosphate phases.

Mixtures of aluminium phosphate and urea phosphate were specifically developed that gave a dry powder bond: these overcame the problem of high hygroscopicity which is encountered when solid monoaluminium phosphate is used.

Phosphoric Acid. Phosphoric acid reacts with metal oxides and hydroxides at temperatures ranging from 20 to 200 $^\circ$C to form hard solid shapes. In practice, the most favoured are the amphoteric oxides, because they react at a controllable rate. Hardening systems based on H_3PO_4 and TiO_2, CaO, FeO, Fe_2O_3, NiO, ZnO, ZrO_2, MgO, Al_2O_3, and CrO_3 have been investigated.[10] The $H_3PO_4 - Al_2O_3$ system, and the mechanisms and phase transformations occurring therein, have been studied by many workers, and the phases formed by treating Al_2O_3 with H_3PO_4 or $Al(OH)_3$ and H_3PO_4 have been reported to be similar.[11] It is generally agreed that the process involves first the formation of acid phosphates of the type $Al(H_2PO_4)_3$ (see later). However, on subsequent heating and in the presence of excess Al_2O_3 the final bonding phase is almost certainly $AlPO_4$.

Direct calorimetric analysis (DCA) studies[12] on tabular alumina—phosphate acid have shown that the bonding reactions start at about 127 $^\circ$C. Most of the reactions occur over the temperature range 127–427 $^\circ$C and involve the formation of aluminium phosphates and possibly formation and melting of pyrophosphoric acid. At about 510 $^\circ$C a change in slope occurs that remains up to 732 $^\circ$C. Continuous changes in slope occur over the temperature range 732–1327 $^\circ$C, arising from the formation of aluminium phosphate bonding phases and phase transitions therein. It is suggested that this devitrification of the bond accounts for the fact that specimens fired to 1093 $^\circ$C have a lower strength than those fired to either 371 $^\circ$C or 815 $^\circ$C. These authors also confirmed that the addition of CrO_3 increases the thermal stability of the phosphate bond.

Sheets and co-workers[13] used phosphoric acid to make castable refractories (*i.e.*, compositions that set without firing). These authors introduced the concept of adding an inhibitor: Rodine 78, a complex amine, was used to reduce the phenomenon known as bloating which results from the reaction between phosphate and metallic iron. They found that it was not possible to get a cold set using mixtures of phosphoric acid with either alumina grog, fine reactive alumina, or hydrated alumina, but found that such compositions had to be dried. However, the addition of ammonium fluoride enabled a cold-setting mixture to be formed. Compositions based on zirconia, beryllia, mullite, and silicon carbide were also investigated. The properties of these materials were, not surprisingly, different from those based on pure alumina grogs. *This observation is most*

[10] S. L. Golynko-Vol'fson, M. M. Sychev, *et al.* 'Chemical Principles of the Technology and use of Phosphate Binders and Coatings', 1968.

[11] A. S. Yutina, Z. D. Zhukova, and S. V. Lysak, *Izvest. Akad. Nauk. S.S.S.R., neorg Materialy*, 1966, **2**, 1748.

[12] M. J. O'Hara, J. J. Duga, and H. D. Sheets, *Amer. Ceram. Soc. Bull.*, 1972, **51**, 590.

[13] H. D. Sheets, J. J. Bulloff, and W. H. Duckworth, *Brick and Clay Record*, 1958, **133**, 55.

important. It is impossible to make any general statement about the properties of phosphate bonds without specifying both the type of bond used and the composition and grading of the aggregate, particularly if one is to compare the relative properties of different binder systems.[14,15]

Although phosphoric acid is a good bonding agent for high-alumina refractories, ramming mixtures may experience premature hardening and loss of workability. This problem is associated with the formation of insoluble $AlPO_4$ hydrate. Sequestering agents such as 5-sulphosalicylic acid, acetylacetone, or dextrin[16] can be added to stabilize the mix: oxalic acid and citric acid can also be used.

Aluminium Acid Phosphates. The most important characteristic of a liquid binding agent is the acidity, which is defined as x, the molar $P_2O_5 : Al_2O_3$ ratio. It has been shown[17] that mixtures with $x < 3$ are metastable. Mixtures in which $x = 2.3$ throw down a deposit and harden on prolonged storage, and mixtures with $x < 2.3$ are even more unstable.

Typical commercial[18] products have $x \simeq 3$, and are about 50% w/w solutions of $Al(H_2PO_4)_3$. Studies on the phase changes that occur when such solutions are heated are numerous.[11,17,19-21] The most detailed studies have been carried out on a binder with $x = 2.28$. The results are summarized in Table 1.[12]

It must be remembered, however, that real refractory systems contain an excess of some reactive phase, such as Al_2O_3, ZrO_2, SiO_2, or SiC. Under these conditions solutions of aluminium phosphate bond in two ways: by acidic metaphosphate binding and by chemical (or reaction) bonding with the aggregate.

In the low to middle temperature range hydrogen-bonded polymers are formed, whereas at high temperatures condensation takes place giving rise to polymeric phosphates which are mostly glassy or amorphous. At still higher temperatures, the glassy phases begin to crystallize and phosphates begin to decompose thermally. Thus, Kolb[20] found that when pure $AlPO_4$ (cristobalite) was heated to about 1500 °C it began to decompose (see Table 2) liberating P_2O_5 and forming Al_2O_3.

Chemical bonding takes place when the acid phosphates react with weakly basic or amphoteric oxides. This results in the formation of crystalline orthophosphates as the bond.

[14] M. Palfreyman, *Amer. Ceram. Soc. Bull.*, 1970, **49**, 538.
[15] K. Fisher, *Proc. Brit Ceram. Soc. Fabrication Sciences*, 1969, **2**, 51.
[16] E. Eti and W. B. Hall, *Amer. Ceram. Soc. Bull.*, 1971, **50**, 604.
[17] I. L. Roshkoran, L. N. Kuzminskaya, and A. Kopeikin, *Izvest. Akad. Nauk S.S.S.R., neorg. Materialy*, 1966, **2**, 541.
[18] A. A. Christyakova, V. A. Sivkina, A. P. Kashovskaya, and V. I. Sadkov, *Izvest. Akad. Nauk. S.S.S.R., neorg. Materialy*, 1969, **5**, 1573.
[19] A. A. Christyakova, V. A. Sivkina, V. I. Sadkov, A. P. Kashovskaya, and L. G. Povysheva, *Izvest Akad. Nauk S.S.S.R., neorg Materialy*, 1969, **5**, 536.
[20] L. Kolb, *Sillikattechnik*, 1965, **16**, 160.
[21] V. A. Kopeikin, A. I. Kudryashova, L. N. Kuzminskaya, I. L. Rashkovan, and I. A. Tananaev, *Izvest. Akad. Nauk S.S.S.R., neorg Materialy*, 1967, **3**, 737.

Table 1 *Effect of Heat Treatment on Aluminium Acid Phosphate Binder*

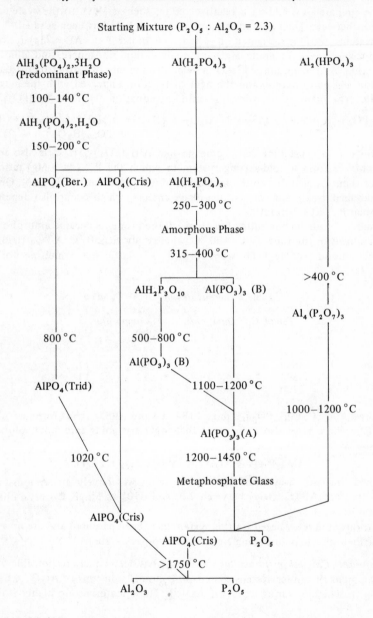

Starting Mixture (P_2O_5 : Al_2O_3 = 2.3)

$AlH_3(PO_4)_2,3H_2O$
(Predominant Phase)

$Al(H_2PO_4)_3$

$Al_2(HPO_4)_3$

100–140 °C

$AlH_3(PO_4)_2,H_2O$

150–200 °C

$AlPO_4$(Ber.) $AlPO_4$(Cris) $Al(H_2PO_4)_3$

250–300 °C

Amorphous Phase

315–400 °C

>400 °C

$AlH_2P_3O_{10}$ $Al(PO_3)_3$ (B)

$Al_4(P_2O_7)_3$

800 °C   500–800 °C

$Al(PO_3)_3$ (B)

$AlPO_4$(Trid)   1100–1200 °C   1000–1200 °C

$Al(PO_3)_3$(A)

1020 °C   1200–1450 °C

Metaphosphate Glass

$AlPO_4$(Cris)

$AlPO_4$(Cris) P_2O_5

>1750 °C

Al_2O_3 P_2O_5

Abbreviations: Ber = Berlinite, the quartz-like polymorph, tridymite (trid) and cristobalite (cris) are phases isostructural with the high-temperature polymorphs of SiO_2. Polymorphs of $Al(PO_3)_3$ are designated by letters A or B, following the notation of F. d'Yvoire, *Bull. Soc. chim. France*, 1962, 1237.

Cold-setting concretes[22] are usually formulated as two-pack systems. These can be prepared by adding a reactive oxide, such as MgO, to the system. The reaction between MgO and aluminium acid phosphate has been studied.[23] Various systems were investigated in which the molar P : (Al + Mg) ratio was varied using a reagent grade MgO, monoaluminium phosphate, and aluminium hydroxide. As the amount of MgO increased so the rate of setting increased The reaction was endothermic and the heat of reaction increased with the magnesia content. The main reaction is represented by equation (1). Thus $MgHPO_4,3H_2O$

$$Al(H_2PO_4)_3 + mMgO + (1-m/2) Al_2O_3 + kH_2O \rightarrow m(MgHPO_4,3H_2O) + (3-m)$$
$$(AlPO_4,nH_2O) \ (m \leqslant 2) \quad (1)$$

is formed as a crystalline salt: some gel-like $AlH_3(PO_4)_2,3H_2O$ is also found. Attempts to form a cold-setting system in which the P : (Al + Mg) ratio was greater than 1 failed due to the formation of water soluble $Mg(H_2PO_4)_2$. On subsequent heat treatment the various phase changes which occur also depend on the molar P : (Al + Mg) ratio.

Thus in bonds having ratios less than 1.0, the products became amorphous at temperatures in the range 200–400 $^{\circ}$C, whereas above 650 $^{\circ}$C, $AlPO_4$ (trid) and a small amount of $Mg_2P_2O_7$ were formed. The latter has a melting point of 1383 $^{\circ}$C.

Table 2 *Thermal stability of* $AlPO_4$ *in air*

Temp/$^{\circ}$C	Duration/h	Composition %	
		$AlPO_4$	Al_2O_3
1500	1	93.7	6.3
1650	1	86.8	13.2
1800	1	86.5	13.5
2200	not stated	—	100.0

Above 900 $^{\circ}$C, $Mg_3(PO_4)_2$ (m.p. 1184 $^{\circ}$C) and $AlPO_4$ (trid) form, as in reaction (2). There were also indications that MgO was going into solid solution in the $AlPO_4$.

$$3Mg_2P_2O_7 + Al_2O_3 = 2Mg_3(PO_4)_2 + 2AlPO_4 \quad (2)$$

When this ratio was equal to 1.0, the bond was largely amorphous except for a trace of $AlPO_4$ (trid) between 200 and 650 $^{\circ}$C. $Mg_2P_2O_7$ crystallizes at about 650 $^{\circ}$C.

Various concretes based on this system have been patented and are now commercially available in both single-pack and two-pack systems.[24-26]

Aluminium–Chromium Phosphate. Chvatal[5] has been largely responsible for the development of binder systems based on colloidal solutions of $Al_2O_3, xCr_2O_3, 3P_2O_5$ in which x varies from 0.1 to 1.0. These materials are highly stable in

[22] W. H. Gitzen, L. D. Hart, and G. Maczura, *Bull. Amer. Ceram. Soc.*, 1956, **35**, 217.
[23] J. Ando, J. Shinada, and C. Hiraoka, *Yogyo Kyokai Shi*, 1974, **82**, 644.
[24] C. R. Enoch, B.P. 1 032 146.
[25] C. R. Enoch, B.P. 1 311 198.
[26] Asahi Glass Co, Jap.P. 8 034 210.

water and develop condensed phosphates at a temperature of $200\,°C$ which remain glassy or amorphous up to $900\,°C$. These phosphates have good thermal stability. Chvatal's results have been confirmed by others.[12,27]

Alkali Polymetaphosphates. The use of alkali metaphosphates as a bond for refractory mortars was first investigated in 1947.[28] Sodium hexametaphosphate, $Na_6P_6O_{18}$, forms rubber-like polymers and yields high-strength mortars with fire clay aggregates. These materials are used in high-alumina refractory mortars and ramming mixtures, and as bonds for basic aggregates.

Sodium phosphate glasses may be represented as follows:

Polymers having average values of n from 6 to 21 can be prepared. The stability of the polymers to hydrolysis in aqueous media increases with n.

Foessel and Treffner[29] have reviewed the literature on the use of sodium polyphosphates in basic refractories. Very high hot-strengths (1500–2500 psi) can be achieved at $1500\,°C$ in magnesite and magnesite-chrome refractory brick. The most important factor governing the strength is the $CaO : (P_2O_5 + SiO_2)$ ratio. Venables and Treffner showed[30] that $CaNaPO_4$, sodium rhenanite, was present in the bonding phase.

Aluminium Chlorophosphate. A novel bonding material chemically related to aluminium phosphate was introduced during 1970: this is aluminium chlorophosphate hydrate.[8,31] It is a dry powder, readily soluble in water. It decomposes on heating directly to $AlPO_4$ without forming intermediate metaphosphates. It can be used in both heat-setting and cold-setting formulations (the latter by the addition of MgO to the mix). Recently it has been modified[32] to include a small proportion of an acetylenic alcohol condensate that enables the bond to be used in conjunction with aggregates containing metallic iron. The acetylenic alcohol retards reaction between HCl and Fe, thereby minimizing bloating. The simple thermal chemistry of ACPH enables the refractories to be heated rapidly without cracking or spalling.

[27] E. Eipeltaner and H. Hoffman, *Radex-Rundschau*, 1968, **1**, 31.
[28] P. G. Herold and J. F. Burst, *Missouri Univ. School of Mines and Met. Bull.*, 1947, **18**, 1.
[29] A. H. Foessel and W. S. Treffner, *Amer. Ceram. Soc. Bull.*, 1970, **49**, 652.
[30] C. L. Venables and W. S. Treffner, *Amer. Ceram. Soc. Bull.*, 1970, **49**, 660.
[31] J. E. Cassidy, B.P. 1 386 518.
[32] J. E. Cassidy and B. Schofield, B.P. 1 426 459.

Table 3 Typical physical properties of some commonly used and trial roof refractories

	Silica	85% Al$_2$O$_3$ fired	80–85% alumina phosph. bonded	96% Al$_2$O$_3$	High-fired mag-chrome	High strength magnesite
Porosity (%)	19–23	17–21	15–19	13–17	16–20	13.5–17.5
Pores						
More than 40 μm	0.4	0.5	0.1	0.7	1.0	1.3
More than 20 μm	1.1	2.0	0.5	3.6	5.2	3.7
Thermal expansion (%) 0–1000 °C	1.3	0.66	0.66	0.80	0.90	1,26
P.V.C.[a] after 2h at 1500 °C	Nil to +1.0	Nil to −0.7	+1.5 to +3.5	Nil	—	—
2h at 1600 °C	Nil to +1.0	Nil to −2.0	+1.0 to −3.0	Nil	Nil to +0.5	Nil
2h at 1700 °C	—	−1.0 to −3.0		−0.2	Nil to +0.5	−0.4 to −0.6
Thermal conductivity (mean temp. 900 °C)	12	11	11	18	17	36

(a) Permanent volume contraction

Table 4 Typical mechanical and chemical properties

	Silica	85% Al₂O₃ fired	80–85% alumina phosph. bonded	96% Al₂O₃ (tabular)	High-fired mag-chrome	High strength magnesite
MORᵃ/p.s.i.						
Room temp.	1300	1700	1200	3000	750	2650
1260 °C	1100	2000	600	1000	1600	2450
1400 °C	900	1000	350	600	1000	2400
1500 °C	—	—	—	—	500	2000
1600 °C	—	—	—	—	250	900
Creep in torsion/mR h⁻¹						
1300 °C	—	2–5	~100	—	6.5	0.7
1400 °C	0.7	41	—	7.5	25.0	2.5
1500 °C	—	—	—	—	—	5.0
Chem. analysis (%)						
SiO₂	96.5	8.5	11.0/8.2	2.70	1.9	1.7
TiO₂	0.1	2.7	2.7/2.6	0.04	—	—
Fe₂O₃	0.5	1.6	1.4/1.4	0.10	7.1	0.7
Al₂O₃	0.6	86.0	82.0/84.0	96.60	11.6	0.2
Cr₂O₃	—	—	—	—	13.0	—
CaO	1.7	0.4	0.3/0.3	0.02	1.0	2.9
MgO	0.1	0.1	0.2/0.2	0.02	65.0	94.3
Alkalis	0.15	0.2	0.3/0.3	0.30	—	—
P₂O₅	—	—	1.3/3.0	—	—	—
Cost/unit volume (silica = 1) of standard shapes	1.0	2.7	2.6	10.2	2.8	3.9

(a) Modulus of rupture

Other Acid Phosphates. Ammonium phosphate, $NH_4H_2PO_4$, has been shown to be a useful bond for basic aggregates.[33-37] Binders comprising both aluminium phosphate and ammonium or urea phosphate have also found use in heat-setting high-alumina compositions where a dry powder is required.[9]

Properties of Phosphate-bonded Refractories

Phosphate-bonded refractory bricks, mortars, ramming mixes, plastics, and cold-setting castables utilizing almost all the known refractory oxides and silicon carbide are now widely used. In general (i) they do not show 'weak' regions on heating, (ii) they have good refractoriness, (iii) they possess high abrasion resistance at elevated temperatures, and (iv) they have good slag resistance and melt repellancy. These desirable properties can only be achieved by the correct choice of phosphate bond and aggregate.

Unfired Refractory Bricks and Ramming Compositions. Phosphoric acid (and sometimes solutions of monoaluminium phosphate) are used to prepare the so-called unfired refractory bricks. Pressed bricks composed of high-alumina aggregates and containing 5–10% w/w of the phosphate bond require to be cured at only moderate temperatures. These products have high cold-crushing strength, accurate dimensions, and good slag and abrasion resistance. This combination of properties has made them acceptable for use in electric arc-furnace roofs.

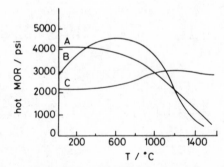

Figure 1 *Hot modulus of rupture of some tabular Al_2O_3 bodies fired at* 1700 °C. *Curve* A, *calcined* Al_2O_3: *curves* B *and* C, *calcined* Al_2O_3 *bonded with* H_3PO_4 *and* SiO_2, *respectively*

Palfreyman[14] has described the properties of a variety of high-alumina based pressed bricks bonded with phosphoric acid and compared them with similar products bonded either with calcined alumina or calcined alumina–silica mixtures. Some of the results are shown in Figure 1. It will be seen that the phosphate-bonded product has good strength at moderate temperatures. The phosphate-bonded product showed a lower hot strength than the others at

[33] P. A. Gilham-Dayton, *Trans. Brit. Ceram. Soc.,* 1963, **62,** 85.
[34] R. W. Limes, D. Ponzani, and E. Spirko, *Abs. Amer. Ceram. Soc. Bull.,* 1964, **43,** 201.
[35] R. W. Limes, *J. Metals,* 1965, **17,** 663.
[36] R. W. Limes and D. Ponzani, U.S.P. 3 285 758.
[37] B. Jackson and T. J. Partridge, *Trans. J. Brit. Ceram. Soc.,* 1973, **72,** 139.

temperatures above 1300 °C. Jackson and Partridge[37] compared the properties of various types of brick (including the phosphate-bonded, high-alumina type) for use in electric arc-furnace roofs. The physical, mechanical, and chemical properties are shown in Tables 3 and 4. These results show the phosphate-bonded product to have low porosity, high creep in tension, and good (but not the highest) hot modulus at temperatures above 1200 °C. These authors make the observation that in some furnaces these properties may impart slag resistance superior to that of the ceramic-bonded product. They also note that the addition of P_2O_5 reduced the refractoriness of bodies containing 80–85% Al_2O_3.

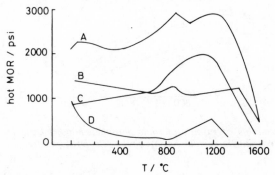

Figure 2 *Hot modulus of rupture of basic brick: data from ref. 29. Curve A, phosphate bonded: curve B, periclase curve C, direct bonded periclase-chrome spinel: curve D, chemically-bonded periclase-chrome spinel*

Phosphate-bonded refractories are often described as having good slag resistance. Povlovski has shown[38,39] that in the case of a refractory bonded with monoaluminium phosphate, the composition of the slag is an important consideration. Thus, Na_2O, K_2O, and PbO react with $AlPO_4$ and reduce refractoriness at temperatures above 800 °C: CuO and ZnO react above 1000 °C, MgO above 1300 °C and Fe_2O_3, NiO, and CaO above 1400 °C. Menjsakov[40] has shown that Al_2O_3 + H_3PO_4 ramming compositions are particularly resistant towards Fe_2O_3 slags at temperatures up to 1350 °C, although slag attack occurs when 2% MgO is present.

A systematic study of the resistance of phosphate-bonded refractory composition to metal infiltration has been carried out by Feldhus.[41] Others have shown[42,43] that the addition of P_2O_5 reduces the surface energy of the refractory so that it becomes poorly wetted by molten metals and slags. Phosphate-bonded compositions of this type are being used in Japan as linings for blast furnace runners and in ladles. Phosphate-bonded silicon carbide refractories are

[38] S. Povlovski, *Epitoayag*, 1965, **17**, 333.
[39] S. Povlovski, Proceedings of the 8th Silicon Conference, Budapest, 1966, p. 669.
[40] F. S. Menjsakov, *Ogneupory*, 1969, **1**, 35.
[41] H. G. Feldhus, *Giesserei-Praxis*, 1971, **2**, 1.
[42] W. H. Kreidl and H. G. Feldhus, *Sprechsaal*, 1971, **104**, 3.
[43] N. A. Batrakow, *et al.*, Studies of the Urals Polytech. Inst. Collective Volume 199 Sverdlowsk 102, 1971.

J. E. Cassidy

widely used in steam generating boilers.[44][46] Phosphoric acid, monoaluminium
phosphate, and even sodium polyphosphate have been used, but the aluminium
phosphate-containing compositions are claimed to be the best.

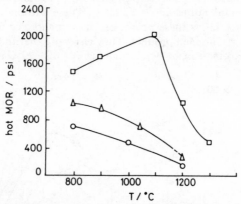

Figure 3 *Hot modulus of rupture of some phosphate-bonded castables. Squares, silicon
carbide: triangles, tabular* Al_2O_3 *: circles calculated bauxite*

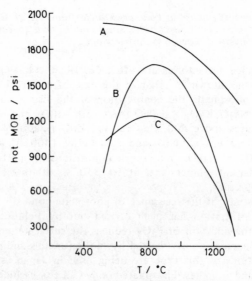

Figure 4 *Hot modulus of rupture of calcium aluminate castables (curve* A*) compared with
chrome-based and fireclay-based materials (curves* B *and* C, *respectively). The data
are taken from* Chem. Eng. Progr. 1970, **43**, 66

[44] Babcock-Bau (Oberhaussen), Report.
[45] A. W. Andrejcenko, U.S.S.R.P. 361 160.
[46] A. K. Karlitt, *et al.*, *Ogneupory*, 1975, **3**, 22.

Mention was made earlier of the use of sodium polyphosphates as bonds for the preparation of bricks. Figure 2 shows the hot modulus of rupture of a typical phosphate-bonded product. Compared with a burned periclase (MgO) refractory and either a direct or chemically bonded magnesium oxide—chrome spinel refractory, the phosphate-bonded product has superior properties.

Phosphate-bonded Castables. In recent years so-called 'cement free' phosphate-bonded castables have become available. These are either one-pack systems based on solid phosphate bonds such as ACPH, or two-pack systems containing liquid bonds (such as monoaluminium phosphate). They set in the cold by the reaction of the acid bond with MgO. The properties of these materials vary depending on the type and amount of bond used and the type and grading of the aggregate.

Some typical hot MOR results for some ACPH-bonded SiC, Al_2O_3 and a bauxite castable are shown in Figure 3. It is interesting to compare these with those of calcium aluminate products (Figure 4) and with the heat-set materials (Figure 1). If we look at the tabular alumina-based materials, it will be seen that all the materials show a fall-off in hot strength at temperatures above 800 °C. The rate at which strength decreases is greater with the MgO-containing materials than with the others. This type of material is used widely in chemical plant, and has been shown to be very effective in steel works applications such as in electric arc-furnace roofs.[47] Phosphate-bonded high-aluminas make effective patching materials for coal gasification reactors.[48]

Looking at Figure 3, it is interesting to note the difference in properties between the high-alumina products and silicon carbide. The modulus of the latter increases up to 1100 °C and then decreases. We believe this to be due to the formation of silicophosphates. The addition of silicon carbide to high-alumina, phosphate-bonded products certainly increases their hot strength.

Conclusion
Phosphate-bonded refractories are now in general use, and are the preferred materials for a number of applications. Many of the limiting problems encountered (bond migration, low shelf life, bloating, and low hot strength) are now being eliminated by the development of new bond systems and by proper choice of aggregate.

The author would like to thank the Research Director of ICI Mond Division for permission to publish this paper and to his colleagues in ICI for gathering much of the data.

[47] J. E. Cassidy, P. J. Whinyates, and E. H. Brooks, Paper presented at the Fall Meeting of the Amer. Ceram. Soc. (Ref. Div.) Bedford Springs, Oct. 1975.
[48] M. S. Crowley, *Ceram. Bull.*, 1975, **54**, 1072.

Sialons and Related Nitrogen Ceramics: their Crystal Chemistry, Phase Relationships, Properties and Industrial Potential

By K. H. JACK

Crystallography Laboratory, The University, Newcastle upon Tyne

Introduction

Silicon nitride is one of the special ceramics at present being developed for gas turbines and other high-temperature engineering applications. The present paper attempts to show that it is only the first of a very wide field of nitrogen ceramics.

In each of its structural modifications, α and β, Si_3N_4 is a covalent solid built up of SiN_4 tetrahedra joined in a three-dimensional network by sharing corners.

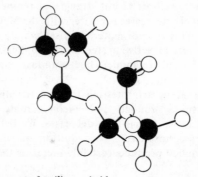

Figure 1 *The crystal structure of β-silicon nitride*

Indeed, the atomic arrangement of $\beta-Si_3N_4$ (see Figure 1) is the same as those of beryllium and zinc silicates. In all silicates the building unit is the $[SiO_4]^{4-}$ tetrahedron carrying four negative charges; these units may occur separately or in pairs, or may be joined together in chains or rings, in two-dimensional sheets or in three-dimensional networks. Aluminium plays a very special role in the silicates because the $[AlO_4]^{5-}$ tetrahedron—this time with five negative charges —is about the same size as $[SiO_4]^{4-}$ and can replace it in the chains, rings, sheets or networks, provided that the necessary charge or valency compensation is made elsewhere in the structure. For example, in the amphibole silicate tremolite, the tetrahedra are joined in double chains of composition $[Si_4O_{11}]^{6-}$ which are held together by Ca^{2+} and Mg^{2+} cations. However, considerable variations can occur in the chemical composition without changing the structure (see Figure 2).

The Sialons

By analogy with the silicates it was thought possible to replace N^{3-} in Si_3N_4 by O^{2-} if at the same time Si^{4+} was replaced by Al^{3+}. Charge compensation might also be feasible by introducing other metal atoms, and it was suggested[1] that a variety of new materials, vitreous as well as crystalline, could be built up with the $(Si,Al)(O,N)_4$ tetrahedron as a structural unit in the same way that the almost infinite range of mineral silicates is built up of $(Si,Al)O_4$ tetrahedra. In spite of these expectations, the first results of the reaction of silicon nitride with alumina by hot-pressing at $1700-2000\ °C$ were surprising (see Figure 3).[2] With mixtures containing up to about 70 wt% of alumina, the X-ray diffraction patterns of the products were identical with $\beta - Si_3N_4$, except that as Si$-$N was replaced by Al$-$O there was a small increase in the hexagonal unit-cell dimensions.

$$\text{Tremolite}$$
$$\text{amphibole double chain:} \left[Si_4O_{11}\right]^{\bar{6}}$$

$$(O,OH,F)_2^{2-4}(Ca,Na)_2^{2-4}(Na,K)_{2-0}^{2-0}(Mg,Fe)^2(Mg,Fe;Al,Fe)_4^{8-12}$$
$$\left[(Al,Si)_2Si_6O_{22}\right]^{\overline{12}-14}$$

$$(Ca_2Mg_5)^{14}\left[Si_8O_{22}\right]^{\overline{12}}(OH)_2^{\bar{2}}$$

Figure 2 *The chemical composition of tremolite*

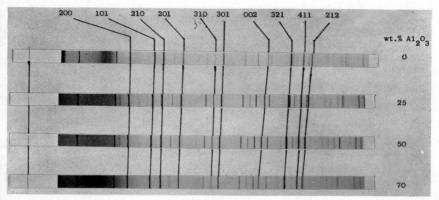

Figure 3 *X-ray photographs of β'-sialons prepared by reaction of Si_3N_4 and Al_2O_3 at $2000\ °C$*

The compositions shown in Figure 4 were considered for this 'β'—sialon' phase with the $\beta - Si_3N_4$ structure and it was concluded, on inadequate analytical evidence, that it was $Si_{6-0.75x}Al_{0.67x}O_xN_{8-x}$. Subsequent work at the

[1] S. Wild, P. Grieveson, and K. H. Jack, 'The Crystal Chemistry of Ceramic Phases in the Silicon—nitrogen—oxygen and Related Systems', 1968, Progress Report No. 1, Ministry of Defence Contract N/CP.61/9411/67/4B/MP 387. See 'Special Ceramics 5', ed. P. Popper, Brit. Ceram. Res. Assoc., Stoke-on Trent, 1972, p. 289.
[2] K. H. Jack and W. I. Wilson, *Nature*, 1972, **238**, 28.

Joseph Lucas Research Centre,[3] at the Max-Planck Institute in Stuttgart[4] and at Newcastle,[5] has shown this to be wrong, and in fact the composition is $Si_{6-z}Al_zO_zN_{8-z}$, with z varying from 0 to about 4. For each nitrogen atom in silicon nitride replaced by oxygen, one silicon is replaced by one aluminium.

$$\beta \quad Si_6^{24} N_8^{\overline{24}}$$
$$\downarrow_{l}'$$
$$\beta \quad Si_{6-0.75x}^{24-3x} Al_{0.67x}^{2x} O_x^{\overline{2x}} N_{8-x}^{\overline{24-3x}}$$
$$\searrow Al_{5.33}^{16} O_8^{\overline{16}} \equiv Al_2O_3$$

$$\beta \quad Si_6^{24} N_8^{\overline{24}}$$
$$\downarrow$$
$$\beta' \quad Si_{6-x}^{24-4x} Al_x^{3x} O_x^{\overline{2x}} N_{8-x}^{\overline{24-3x}}$$
$$\searrow Al_6^{18} N_2^{\overline{6}} O_6^{\overline{12}} \equiv Al_2O_3 \cdot AlN$$

Figure 4 *Possible compositions originally considered for β'-sialon*

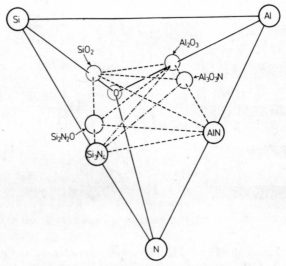

Figure 5 *The tetrahedral representation of the Si–Al–O–N system*

3   R. J. Lumby, B. North, and A. J. Taylor, 'Special Ceramics 6', Brit. Ceram. Res. Assoc., Stoke-on-Trent, 1975, p. 283.
4   L. J. Gauckler, H. L. Lukas, and G. Petzow, presented at the Second Powder Metallurgical Seminar at the Max-Planck-Institut, Stuttgart, 1974. See *J. Amer. Ceram. Soc.*, 1975, **58**, 346.
5   K. H. Jack, *J. Mater. Sci.*, 1976, **11**, 1135.

The Representation of the Si—Al—O—N *System.* The silicon—aluminium—oxygen—nitrogen system has four components and should be represented by a tetrahedron (Figure 5). However, if the elements have their normal valencies (Si^{IV}, Al^{III}, O^{II}, and N^{III}) then all possible solid compounds lie on an irregular quadrilateral plane, and if concentrations are expressed in equivalents, that is the corners of the tetrahedron are respectively $3Si^{12+}$, $4Al^{12+}$, $6O^{12-}$ and $4N^{12-}$, then these solid compounds all lie on a square plane (Figure 6). If, conventionally, Si_3N_4 is placed at the bottom left-hand corner of the square diagram, then any point within the latter represents a combination of 12 positive and 12 negative valencies. Distances from left to right represent replacement of silicon by its equivalent of aluminium and distances from bottom to top the replacement of nitrogen by oxygen. Figure 7 is the behaviour diagram for the Si—Al—O—N system at about 1750 °C. It is not claimed to be an equilibrium phase diagram in a thermodynamic sense, but recent calculations at the Ecole des Mines in Paris by Mocellin and Torre[6] suggest that it is at least self-consistent and compatible with equilibrium at one atmosphere.

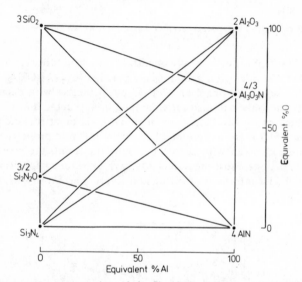

Figure 6 *The square representation of the* Si—Al—O—N *system using equivalent concentrations*

Si—Al—O—N Phase Relationships

Each phase in the 'sialon' system extends in a direction of constant metal : non-metal atom ratio (M : X) along which Si—N is replaced increasingly by Al—O. The homogeneity ranges perpendicular to this, that is in the direction parallel to the SiO_2—AlN join, are quite small and must be due, at least in part, to the similarities and differences in bond lengths: Si—N (1.75 Å) $\approx$ Al—O (1.75 Å), whereas Al—N (1.87 Å) $\neq$ Si—O (1.62 Å).

[6] A. Mocellin and J-P. Torre, private communication.

208

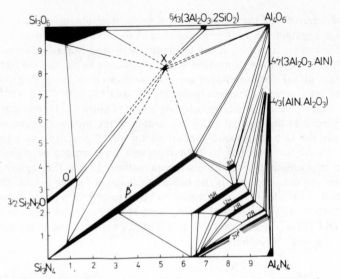

Figure 7 *The* $Si_3N_4 - AlN - Al_2O_3 - SiO_2$ *system, based on research at Newcastle*

The β'-phase. The β'-phase with the silicon nitride-type structure extends essentially along the 3M : 4X line with a homogeneity range $Si_{6-z}Al_zO_zN_{8-z}$, where z reaches a maximum exceeding 4 at 1700 °C but decreases with decreasing temperature. It is the only sialon so far examined in any detail and because, until recently, specimens usually contained other vitreous or crystalline phases (for example, X or 15R) it is not certain whether the intrinsic properties of β' have yet been evaluated. Even with such limitations the results are promising for a variety of applications. Most measurements have been on compositions containing about equal concentrations of silicon and aluminium, $Si_3Al_3O_3N_5$ with $z = 3$.

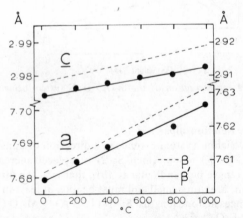

Figure 8 *Thermal expansion of β'-sialon ($z = 3$; full lines) compared with $\beta-Si_3N_4$ (dashed lines)*

Because of its structure, its physical and mechanical properties are similar to those of β-silicon nitride, but chemically it is closer to aluminium oxide. Thus (see Figure 8), its thermal expansion coefficient (2.7×10^{-6}) is less than that of $\beta-Si_3N_4$ (3.5×10^{-6}) and so its thermal shock properties are good: Figure 9 shows the test procedure. Oxidation resistance (see Figure 10) is better than for silicon nitride, probably because a coherent and protective layer of mullite is formed on the surface. Compatibility with molten metals is surprisingly good, and the buttons shown in Figure 11 were kept molten in sialon crucibles for 30 min—aluminium and copper at 1200 °C and pure iron and cast iron at 1600 °C; neither the metals nor the crucibles showed signs of attack. Larger scale tests made by Joseph Lucas Limited are shown by Figure 12.

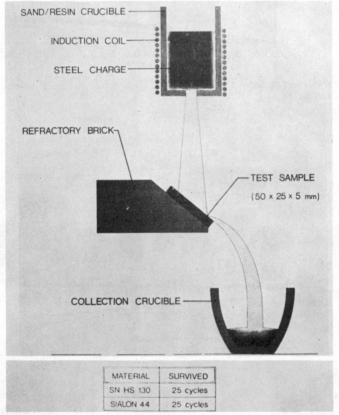

MATERIAL	SURVIVED
SN HS 130	25 cycles
SIALON 44	25 cycles

Figure 9 *Joseph Lucas Limited steel splash test*[7]

The use of sialons for holding and conveying molten metals, including steel, is perhaps more important—and more easily realized—than the very exacting applications for turbine blades.

[7] W. J. Arrol, 'Ceramics for High-Performance Applications'. Proceedings of the Second Army Materials Technology Conference at Hyannis, November 1973, Brook Hill, Chestnut Hill, Massachusetts, 1974, p. 729.

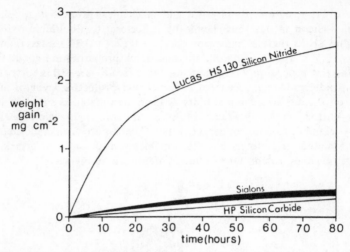

Figure 10 *Oxidation in flowing dry air at 1400 °C of silicon nitride, β′-sialon and silicon carbide*[7]

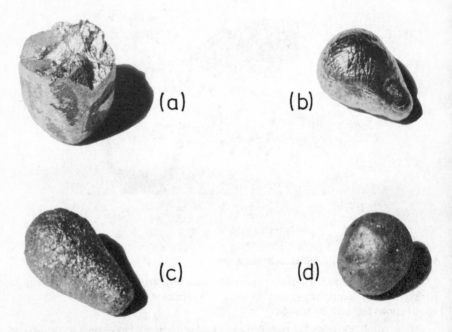

Figure 11 *Compatibility of sialon crucibles with molten metals: (a) aluminium; (b) copper; (c) pure iron; (d) cast iron*

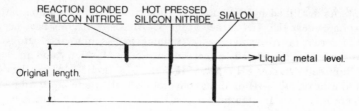

STEEL	TEMP °C	TIME mins	% Wt Loss		
			RBSN	HPSN	SIALON
MILD STEEL	1650	25	100	84	5
STAINLESS STEEL	1600	15	100	17	5

Figure 12 *Resistance of sialon and silicon nitride to attack by moletn steel. RBSN and HPSN are reaction-bonded and hot-pressed silicon nitride, respectively*[7]

One potential advantage of sialon over silicon nitride is in fabrication. The usual ceramic techniques of extrusion, pressing, and slip-casting can be used to produce shapes of the mixed components and then these can be fired to near-theoretical density in an inert atmosphere at about 1600 °C.

The O'-phase. The O'-phase with the structure of silicon oxynitride, Si_2N_2O, extends to a limited extent along the 2M : 3X line.

The X-phase. Originally this phase was designated as 'X' because its powder diffraction pattern could not be indexed; it was thought[2] to have a composition $SiAlO_2N$, but recent observations at Newcastle suggest $Si_2Al_3O_7N$. X-ray and electron diffraction patterns have been variously interpreted. For example, Drew and Lewis[8] have suggested a triclinic structure with the cell dimensions $a = 9.9$, $b = 9.7$, $c = 9.5$Å; $a = 109°$, $\beta = 95°$, $\gamma = 95°$. Gugel and co-workers[9] proposed an orthorhombic cell with $a = 7.85$, $b = 9.12$, $c = 7.965$Å. Neither these nor other suggestions are compatible with the X-ray data obtained from specimens of at least 95% purity prepared at Newcastle, and the unit cell has been determined[10] unequivocally as monoclinic with $a = 9.728$, $b = 8.404$, $c = 9.572$ Å; $\beta = 108.96°$. Although a full structure determination has not yet been completed, the description of X-phase as a 'nitrogen-mullite' is not too misleading.

Tetrahedral AlN-polytype Structures. Of the six uncharacterized phases first reported by Gauckler and co-workers,[4] the one which occurs most frequently is found as a minor phase in the hot-pressing of AlN-rich β' compositions. It was designated initially at Newcastle as 'Y' and occurs also in the Mg–Si–Al–O–N

[8] P. Drew and M. H. Lewis, *J. Mater. Sci.*, 1974, **9**, 1833.
[9] E. Gugel, I. Petzenhauser, and A. Fickel, *Powder Met. Int.*, 1975, **7**, 66.
[10] D. P. Thompson and K. H. Jack, to be published.

212 K. H. Jack

system.[11] As described by Roebuck and Thompson[12] the diffraction patterns of the six phases near the AlN corner of the Si−Al−O−N diagram have been interpreted in terms of AlN-polytypes containing excess non-metal atoms. Their structures are directly related to their compositions $M_m X_{m+1}$ and are described by the Ramsdell symbols 8H, 15R, 12H, 21R, 27R, and 2H. Along the c-dimension of the hexagonal (H) or rhombohedral (R) cells there are n double layers MX, where n is the Ramsdell numeral; $n_H = 2m$ and $n_\Gamma = 3m$. One layer in each block of m layers contains an extra non-metal atom X, that is it is an MX_2 layer. Near AlN the concentration of MX_2 layers is so small that they are too far apart for an ordered arrangement, and for M : X greater than about 9 : 10 an expanded AlN-type $2H^\delta$ structure is observed, the δ superscript indicating disorder in the widely spaced MX_2 layer sequence. Figure 13 shows the direct lattice image of the (001) planes of the 8H sialon polytype with interplanar spacing 23.3 Å. Details of these and numerous other polytypes occurring in the Si−Al−O−N and related systems are described by Roebuck and Thompson.[12]

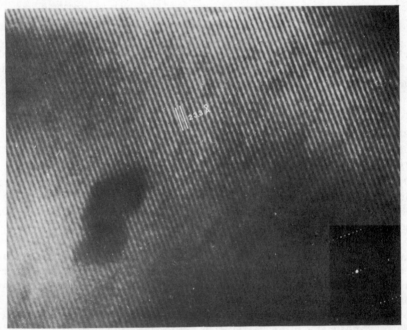

Figure 13 *Direct lattice image of (001) planes in the 8H sialon polytype with corresponding electron diffraction pattern;* $d_{(001)} = 23.3$Å

Sialon Preparation

There are many preparative routes for the production of sialons, and any particular composition can be made in a number of ways using different combinations of starting materials: Si_3N_4, AlN, Al_2O_3, SiO_2, Si_2N_2O, and so on. In

[11] A. Hendry, D. S. Perera, D. P. Thompson, and K. H. Jack, 'Special Ceramics 6', Brit. Ceram. Res. Assoc., Stoke-on-Trent, 1975, p. 321.
[12] P. H. A. Roebuck and D. P. Thompson, in this publication, p. 222

Japan,[13] satisfactory sialon ceramics are being made from volcanic ash—that is, impure silica—by heating it with aluminium powder in molecular nitrogen. Wild at the Polytechnic of Wales is making sialons by nitriding clays with ammonia,[14] and Cutler at the University of Utah is nitriding clay and carbon mixtures with molecular nitrogen. Instead of clays, we are using $SiO_2 - Al_2O_3$ mixtures prepared by gel-processing and supplied by the U.K.A.E.A., Harwell. The results are promising and the products are white—not black as is usually the case when sialons are prepared from commercially available silicon nitride.

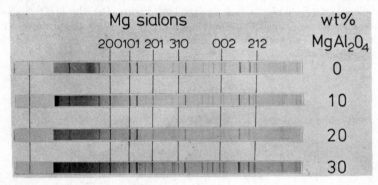

Figure 14 X-ray photographs of β'-magnesium sialons prepared by reaction of Si_3N_4 and $MgAl_2O_4$ at 1700 °C

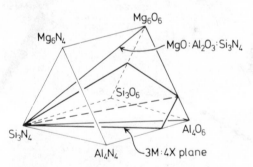

Figure 15 *Outline representation of the magnesium-sialon system showing the* 3M : 4X *plane cutting the sub-system plane* MgO : Al_2O_3 : Si_3N_4

Metal—Sialon Systems

Magnesium, manganese, lithium, and other metal—silicon nitrides and oxynitrides all have structures built up of MX_4 tetrahedra and can be regarded as orthorhombic superlattices of the hexagonal AlN-type atomic arrangement. Thus, it seemed likely that these metals could be incorporated into sialons. In early work[15] it

13 S. Umebayashi and K. Kobayashi, *Amer. Ceram. Soc. Bull.*, 1975, **54**, 534.
14 S. Wild, *J. Mater. Sci.*, 1976, **11**, 1972.
15 K. H. Jack, *Trans. J. Brit. Ceram. Soc.*, 1973, **72**, 376.

was shown that magnesium aluminium spinel ($MgAl_2O_4$) with a 3M : 4X atom ratio reacts with Si_3N_4 to give a β'-magnesium sialon (Figure 14). However, the complete representation of the Mg−Si−Al−O−N system is possible only by using a triangular prism diagram—Jänecke's prism (Figure 15).[16] The latter is based on the Si−Al−O−N square of Figure 7 with Mg in equivalent units along a third dimension. Again any point in the volume represents a combination of 12 positive and 12 negative valencies. Each of the phases of the basal square plane extends into the prism volume, generally along a plane of constant M : X ratio which cuts across other triangle planes representing pseudo-ternary systems, for example $6MgO:Si_3N_4:4AlN$. Conversely (see Figure 16), the $MgO−Si_3N_4−AlN$ section cuts across planes of constant M : X ratio and so shows very few extended single-phase regions except β'. In general, mixtures of α', X-phase, 12H, 15R, and nitrogen-spinel are observed.

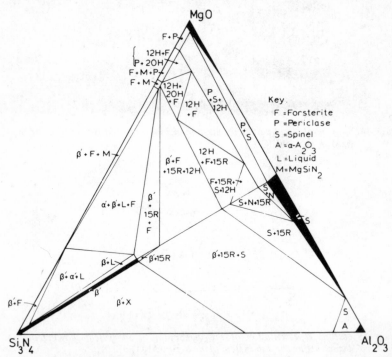

Figure 16 *The* $MgO−Si_3N_4−Al_2O_3$ *section of the* Mg−Si−Al−O−N *system at* 1800 °C

The 3M : 4X plane of the magnesium-sialon is important (Figure 17) because silicon nitride powder always contains about 5 wt % silica as a surface layer on the particles, and this prevents the production of a homogeneous single-phase material when the powder is hot-pressed using magnesium oxide as a 'flux'. From Figure 17 it can be seen that forsterite (Mg_2SiO_4) is soluble in β'-sialon, and so if appropriate amounts of Al_2O_3 and AlN are added to silicon nitride

[16] E. Jänecke, *Z. anorg. Chem.*, 1907, **53**, 319.

powder with just sufficient MgO to react with the surface silica, a homogeneous, single-phase β'-sialon can be obtained.

In the lithium-sialon system (Figure 18), as with magnesium, completely new phases occur as well as those which extend from the basic Si–Al–O–N behaviour diagram. In addition to α' and β' silicon nitride-type phases, β-eucryptite, spinel, and cristobalite (γ) structures occur, all containing nitrogen.

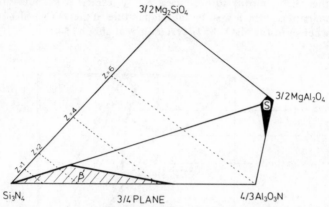

Figure 17 *The* 3M : 4X *plane of the* Mg–Si–Al–O–N *system at* 1800 °C

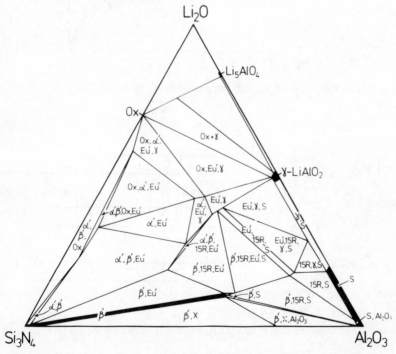

Figure 18 *The* Li_2O–Si_3N_4–Al_2O_3 *section of the* Li–Si–Al–O–N *system at* 1550°C

Yttrium Sialons

Yttrium sialons are important for two reasons. It was shown about three years ago[17] that much improved high-temperature strengths can be obtained by hot-pressing silicon nitride with yttria instead of magnesia and, more recently, that the highest strength ceramic so far obtained is with additions of yttria and alumina to silicon nitride. It was at first thought that yttria reacted with the silica on the silicon nitride to produce a highly refractory yttrium silicate as a grain boundary phase: the lowest liquid temperature in the $Y_2O_3-SiO_2$ system is 1660 °C, whereas in the $MgO-SiO_2$ system it is at about 1540 °C.

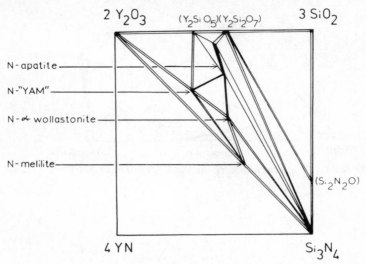

Figure 19 *The* $Y_2O_3-YN-Si_3N_4-SiO_2$ *section of the* Y–Si–Al–O–N *system at* 1600 °C

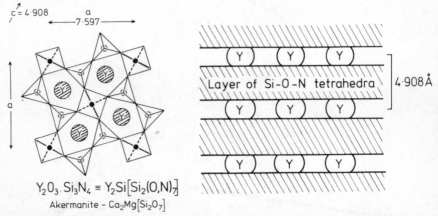

Figure 20 *(Left) Projection of* $Y_2Si[Si_2O_3N_4]$ *on* (001). *(Right) Projection of* $Y_2Si[Si_2O_3N_4]$ *on* (100)

17 G. E. Gazza, *J. Amer. Ceram. Soc.*, 1973, **56**, 662.

Since then, our investigations have given a $Y_2O_3-SiO_2-Si_3N_4$ phase diagram (see Figure 19) with four quarternary phases: N-melilite, $Y_2Si[Si_2O_3N_4]$; N-apatite, $(Y,Si,\square)_{10}[Si(O,N)_4]_6(O,N,\square)_2$, with a range of homogeneity; N-YAM, $2\,Y_2O_3,Si_2N_2O \equiv Y_4Si_2O_7N_2$ (J-phase); and N-a-wollastonite Y_2O_3, $Si_2N_2O \equiv 2YSiO_2N$ (H'-phase). The existence of the first three has been confirmed by laboratories in Japan and the U.S.A.

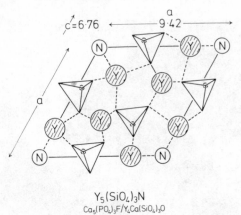

$Y_5(SiO_4)_3N$
$Ca_5(PO_4)_3F/Y_4Ca(SiO_4)_3O$

Figure 21 *Projection on* (001) *of one-half of the unit-cell of nitrogen yttrium apatite*

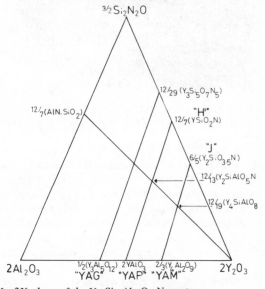

Figure 22 *The* 2M : 3X *plane of the* Y−Si−Al−O−N *system*

The N-melilite consists of sheets of Si−O−N tetrahedra stacked one on top of the other and held together by yttrium cations between them (Figure 20). It is isostructural with the melilite silicates akermanite $Ca_2Mg[Si_2O_7]$ and gehlenite

$Ca_2Al[AlSiO_7]$, and it forms with each of them a continuous series of solid solutions. Even the 50 : 50 intermediate compositions have melting points above 1600 °C so that appreciable amounts of Ca, Mg, Al, and other impurities in silicon nitride which would otherwise form a glass with a low softening temperature are accommodated in the structure without loss of refractoriness and creep resistance.

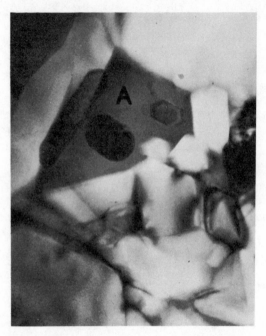

Figure 23 *Transmission electron micrograph of hot-pressed silicon nitride with amorphous (liquid) region 'A' from which has grown a well-defined hexagonal β-Si_3N_4 crystal* (× 20 000)

N-apatite (Figure 21) has an appreciable homogeneity range near (Y_4Si) $[Si_3O_{11}N]N$, and it is not yet known exactly where the nitrogen atoms are located. It was interesting to find nitrogen analogues of apatites because these are the structural materials of bones and teeth. It was subsequently learned that Lang and his colleagues at the University of Rennes were studying a series of lanthanide apatites, $(Ln,M)_5Si_3(O,N)_{13}$, in which there are up to four nitrogen atoms replacing four of the 13 oxygen atoms depending on the valency of the metal M.

The J-phase is isostructural with the yttrium aluminate 'YAM', and the H'-phase with the yttrium aluminate having a similar structure to α-wollastonite $Ca_3Si_3O_9$, where the units are three-membered rings of tetrahedra. These yttrium–silicon oxynitrides H' and J lie on the 2M : 3X plane of the yttrium–sialon system and form continuous series of solid solutions with the corresponding yttrium aluminates (Figure 22).

Yttria seems an ideal hot-pressing additive for silicon nitride. It reacts initially with the surface silica and a little Si_3N_4 to give a liquid which allows densification by liquid-phase sintering. As the reaction proceeds, the liquid combines with more Si_3N_4 to give one or more refractory bonding phases. These are all analogues of calcium aluminates or aluminosilicates and so can accommodate in a refractory solid solution those impurities which, with magnesium as an additive, would give a non-creep-resistant glass.

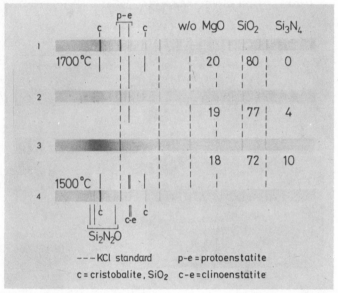

Figure 24 X-ray diffraction patterns of vitrified and devitrified products of the reaction of SiO_2, MgO, and Si_3N_4 at 1700 °C

Nitrogen Glasses

Finally, there are nitrogen glasses. The transmission micrograph (Figure 23) is from early work at Newcastle on hot-pressing silicon nitride with magnesium additive. The well-defined hexagonal crystal of silicon nitride has grown within the liquid region 'A', which on cooling forms a glass. This glass devitrifies on heat-treatment to give enstatite ($MgSiO_3$) and silicon oxynitride (Si_2N_2O). Clearly, the original high-temperature liquid and the glass that forms from it on cooling is not just a magnesium silicate—it must contain nitrogen. Samples of this Mg–Si–O–N glass have now been prepared both by hot-pressing and by pressureless heat-treatment at 1700 °C of mixtures of MgO, SiO_2, and Si_3N_4 in a boron nitride crucible. Without silicon nitride, mixtures of 20 wt % MgO : 80 wt % SiO_2 give enstatite and cristobalite but, quite remarkably, addition of 10 wt % Si_3N_4 to this same mix gives a completely vitreous product. The X-ray diffraction patterns and corresponding optical micrographs are shown in Figures 24 and 25. The glass contains about 6 at % N at a composition $Mg_{12}Si_{26}O_{56}N_6$ with a density of about 2.6 g cm^{-3}, and it devitrifies at 1500 °C to give cristobalite, enstatite, and silicon oxynitride.

Additions of Al_2O_3 extend the vitreous region, and although a systematic study has not yet been made, about 10 at % N has been introduced. In the Y–Si–Al–O–N system glasses have been prepared with up to 12 at % N at a composition $Y_{12}Si_{15}Al_{12}O_{49}N_{12}$. A sample with 9 at % N is transparent in thin section with a refractive index of 1.76, and it devitrifies after 16 h at 1200 °C to give β–$Y_2Si_2O_7$, yttrium aluminium garnet ($Y_3Al_5O_{12}$), and silicon oxynitride.

19 MgO : 77 SiO$_2$: 4 Si$_3$N$_4$ (wt%)

Partially vitrified

18 MgO : 72 SiO$_2$: 10 Si$_3$N$_4$ (wt%)

Glass

Above glass
devitrified

Figure 25 *Optical micrographs* ($\times$ 400) *of vitrified and devitrified products of the reaction of* SiO_2, MgO, *and* Si_3N_4 *at* 1700 °C

It is known that even small additions of nitrogen to oxide glasses increase the softening temperature, the viscosity, and the resistance to devitrification. Glasses with 10 at % N or more might be expected to have more unusual properties, and there is the prospect also of producing highly refractory glass ceramics.

Summary

'Sialons' are phases in the Si–Al–O–N and related systems and are comparable in variety and diversity with the mineral silicates. They are built up of one-, two-, and three-dimensional arrangements of $(Si,Al)(O,N)_4$ and $(Si,M)(O,N)_4$ tetrahedra in the same way that the fundamental structural unit in the silicates is the SiO_4 tetrahedron. For example, β'-sialon is isostructural with $\beta-Si_3N_4$ and has a range of homogeneity $Si_{6-z}Al_zO_zN_{8-z}$, where z varies from 0 to 4. With about equal concentrations of oxygen and nitrogen the material combines the physical and mechanical properties of silicon nitride with the chemical properties of alumina.

In addition to β', the sialons so far prepared include structure types based upon a-silicon nitride, silicon oxynitride, aluminium nitride and silicon carbide, eucryptite, spinel, melilite, apatite, wollastonite, and many others. They are being explored for their thermal, mechanical, chemical, and electrical properties.

Just as nitrogen replaces oxygen in the crystalline silicates, similar replacements in vitreous silicates gives sialon glasses and glass-ceramics containing up to ten atomic per cent nitrogen.

The field of sialons and related nitrogen materials is a very wide one. Not all are going to be useful as ceramics, but they offer almost unlimited prospects for technological development in other directions as well as providing some fascinating chemistry.

I thank all my colleagues, and particularly Dr. D. P. Thompson, for help in preparing this review of their work. Most of the research has been financed by Joseph Lucas Limited and the Wolfson Foundation.

Polytypes in the Si–Al–O–N and Related Systems

By P. H. A. ROEBUCK and D. P. THOMPSON

Crystallography Laboratory, The University, Newcastle upon Tyne

Introduction

The Si–Al–O–N system[1] is remarkable for the number and diversity of crystalline phases it contains. Six of these phases occur close to the aluminium nitride corner with ranges of homogeneity elongated along lines of constant metal : non-metal ratio of the type $M_m X_{m+1}$ where $4 \leqslant m \leqslant 10$.[2] An exactly antitypic series of compounds is observed in the Be–Si–O–N system,[3] extending from the 1M : 1X composition of the BeO–BeSiN$_2$ join to the 3M : 2X composition of β–Be$_3$N$_2$. Similar compounds are observed near the Mg$_3$N$_2$ corner of the Mg–Si–O–N system; again, the structures are determined by the metal : non-metal ratio.

The Si–Al–O–N Polytypes

Most of the phases in the Si–Al–O–N system show extended regions of homogeneity along lines of constant metal : non-metal ratio (Figure 1). Thus, along

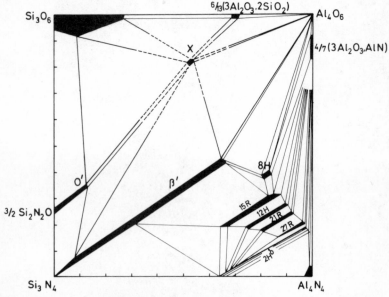

Figure 1 *The* Si$_3$N$_4$–AlN–Al$_2$O$_3$–SiO$_2$ *system*

[1] L. J. Gauckler, H. L. Lucas, and G. Petzow, *J. Amer. Ceram. Soc.*, 1975, **58**, 346.
[2] K. H. Jack, *J. Mater. Sci.*, 1976, **11**, 1135.
[3] D. P. Thompson, *J. Mater. Sci.*, 1976, **11**, 1377.

the 2M : 3X line, small amounts of alumina can be incorporated into the silicon oxynitride structure, and along the 3M : 4X line, equimolar quantities of alumina and aluminium nitride (Al_2O_3,AlN $\equiv$ Al_3O_3N) can be simultaneously incorporated into the β-silicon nitride structure to give a continuous solid solution extending up to a limiting composition of $Si_{1.5}Al_{4.5}O_{4.5}N_{3.5}$ at 1750 °C. Along lines of higher M : X ratio a series of crystallographically similar phases occur with structures based on that of aluminium nitride but differing in stacking sequence owing to the insertion of an extra non-metal atom at regular structural intervals.

Table 1 *Aluminium nitride polytypes in the* Si–Al–O–N *system*

M : X	Type	$a/\text{Å}$	$c/\text{Å}$	$c/n/\text{Å}$
4 : 5	8H	2.988	23.02	2.88
5 : 6	15R	3.010	41.81	2.79
6 : 7	12H	3.029	32.91	2.74
7 : 8	21R	3.048	57.19	2.72
9 : 10	27R	3.059	71.98	2.67
>9 : 10	$2H^{\delta}$	3.079	5.30	2.65
1 : 1	2H	3.114	4.986	2.49

The X-ray diffraction patterns of these polytype phases have been indexed on the basis of hexagonal or rhombohedral unit cells (Table 1) with very similar a parameters but widely differing c parameters. The number (n) of MX plus MX_2 layers in the c repeat distance is given by the l index of the first strong 00l reflection. A linear relationship exists between the mean layer separation, c/n, and the proportion of MX_2 layers in the stacking sequence (Figure 2). The slope and intercept of this line correspond to values of 2.49 Å for an MX layer separation (in good agreement with half the c repeat distance in aluminium nitride) and 4.01 Å

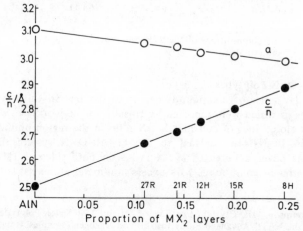

Figure 2 *Unit-cell dimensions for* Si–Al–O–N *polytypes plotted against* MX_2 *layer concentration*

for an MX_2 layer separation. Crystal structure determinations carried out on the 8H and 15R sialon polytypes[4] show that most of this increase in spacing is due to a layer of AlO_6 octahedra inserted halfway between each MX_2 layer. The octahedral layer introduces an . . ABC . . layer sequence into the otherwise . . ABAB . . metal stacking of a simple wurtzite structure. An even number of metal-atom layers between each . . ABC . . unit gives a rhombohedral unit cell and an odd number of layers results in a hexagonal structure. A cubic close-packed metal-atom arrangement of more than three consecutive layers, for example ABCA . . ., is never observed.

The range of sialon polytypes extends as far as 9M : 10X, but at higher ratios a disordered phase, $2H^\delta$, occurs in which the additional non-metal atoms are incorporated randomly as MX_2 layers in the MX wurtzite stacking sequence. The X-ray diffraction pattern of this phase is similar to that of aluminium nitride except that whereas $hk0$ reflections are sharp, all other reflections are broadened and shifted to higher d values. The M : X range for $2H^\delta$ is limited and a two-phase region $2H^\delta$ + AlN exists between about 10M : 11X and 1M : 1X.

Table 2 *Polytype phases in the* Be—Si—O—N *system*

Compound	Polytype	$a/\text{Å}$	$c/\text{Å}$	$c/n/\text{Å}$
$\beta-Be_3N_2$	4H	2.841	9.693	2.423
$Be_6O_3N_2$	15R	2.770	34.58	2.305
$Be_8O_5N_2$	21R	2.752	47.87	2.280
$Be_9O_6N_2{}^a$	27R	2.738	61.05	2.261
BeO	(2H)	2.698	4.375	2.187
$\beta-Be_3N_2$	4H	2.841	9.693	2.423
Be_7SiN_6	9R	2.861	21.520	2.391
Be_4SiN_4	8H	2.862	19.22	2.403
$Be_9Si_3N_{10}$	15R	2.857	36.32	2.421
$Be_5Si_2N_6$	12H	2.860	29.10	2.425
$Be_{11}Si_5N_{14}$	21R	2.860	50.98	2.428
$Be_6Si_3N_8{}^a$	27R	2.862	65.11	2.411
$BeSiN_2$	(2H)	2.880	4.687	2.343

(a) The compositions of the 27R polytypes are probably $M_{10}X_9$ and not M_9X_8.

The Be—Si—O—N Polytypes

A very similar series of compounds occurs in the Be—Si—O—N system, phase relationships in which were reported by Huseby and co-workers,[5] who observed new phases along lines of constant M : X ratio in the region bounded by BeO, $BeSiN_2$, and Be_3N_2. In contrast to the Si—Al—O—N system, Be—Si—O—N compositions cover a range of M : X ratios on both sides of 1M : 1X, but a polytypic series of compounds with excess non-metal atoms has so far not been observed.

[4] D. P. Thompson, 'The Crystal Structures of 8H and 15R Sialon Polytypes', paper presented at the NATO Advanced Study Institute on Nitrogen Ceramics, University of Kent, Canterbury, August 1976.

[5] J. C. Huseby, H. L. Lukas, and G. Petzow, *J. Amer. Ceram. Soc.*, 1975, **58**, 377.

The X-ray diffraction patterns of the Be–Si–O–N phases have been indexed by Thompson[3] in terms of layer structures with exactly the same Ramsdell symbols as the Si–Al–O–N polytypes (Table 2). More recently, in collaboration with Dr. L. J. Gauckler of the Max-Planck-Institut für Metallforschung, Stuttgart, Thompson has observed a 9R polytype at the M_4X_3 composition along the Si_3N_4–Be_3N_2 join. The 9R structure is that expected for a M_4X_3 composition, and extends the series through to the M_3X_2 composition of beryllium nitride. The high-temperature β-form of Be_3N_2 is itself a layer structure with a Ramsdell symbol 4H; the atomic arrangement[6,7] is completely consistent with that proposed for the higher Be–Si–O–N polytypes if, in fact, they are antitypes of the equivalent Si–Al–O–N phases.

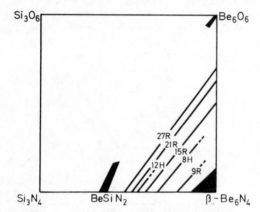

Figure 3 *Polytype phases in the* Si_3N_4–Be_3N_2–BeO–SiO_2 *system*

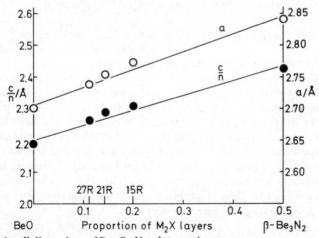

Figure 4 *Unit-cell dimensions of Be–O–N polytype phases*

[6] P. Eckerlin and A. Rabenau, *Z. anorg. Chem.*, 1960, **304**, 218.
[7] D. Hall, G. E. Gurr, and G. A. Jeffrey, *Z. anorg. Chem.*, 1969, **369**, 108.

The Be$-$Si$-$O$-$N and Si$-$Al$-$O$-$N polytypes are similar in other ways. A 2H$^\delta$ phase occurs in the Be$-$Si$-$O$-$N system at ratios less than 10M : 9X. The 16H polytype, which might be expected at 8M : 9X in Si$-$Al$-$O$-$N and at 9M : 8X in Be$-$Si$-$O$-$N, is absent on both systems. The ranges of homogeneity for the Be$-$Si$-$O$-$N polytypes are very extensive and for 27R, 21R, and 15R they extend over their full theoretical limits. Incomplete evidence suggests that the other polytypes may extend further than is indicated in Figure 3. When the *a* and *c/n* values are plotted against composition, there is a linear variation along the BeO$-$Be$_3$N$_2$ join (Figure 4) but no systematic variation along the BeSiN$_2-$Be$_3$N$_2$ join (Table 2). Thus, although for example the 27R polytype extends between the two joins BeO$-$Be$_3$N$_2$ and BeSiN$_2-$Be$_3$N$_2$, the atomic arrangement is probably not identical over its whole 10M : 9X range.

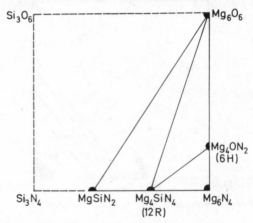

Figure 5 *Polytype phases in the* Si$_3$N$_4-$Mg$_3$N$_2-$MgO$-$SiO$_2$ *system*

Analogous polytype phases occur in the Al$_4$C$_3-$AlN system.[8,9] Four compounds have been observed, Al$_5$C$_3$N, Al$_6$C$_3$N$_2$, Al$_7$C$_3$N$_3$, and Al$_8$C$_3$N$_4$. Aluminium carbide has a 9R polytype structure with carbon atoms stacked in a sequence .. ABC BCA CAB ... Each group of three carbons is stacked in a cubic-packed manner and separated from the next group by a hexagonal stacking fault. The central carbon atom in each group is octahedrally co-ordinated by aluminium, whereas the other two are in tetrahedral co-ordination. The additional aluminium atom in the formula is accommodated by filling both tetrahedral sites in the layer at the break in cubic stacking. In the carbonitrides, the basic aluminium carbide structure is preserved, but additional layers of aluminium and nitrogen atoms stacked in a hexagonal wurtzite manner are included between the aluminium and carbon layers. The polytypes observed have Ramsdell symbols 8H, 15R, 12H, and 21R; higher polytypes may also exist.[8]

The Mg$-$Si$-$O$-$N Polytypes
In the systems discussed above, the kind of polytype observed depends only on

[8] G. A. Jeffrey and V. Y. Wu, *Acta Cryst.*, 1963, **16**, 559.
[9] G. A. Jeffrey and V. Y. Wu, *Acta Cryst.*, 1966, **20**, 538.

the metal : non-metal ratio. Thus, M_5X_6 or M_6X_5 always has a 15R structure. In the Mg–Si–O–N system (Figure 5), two polytype phases occur, 6H–Mg_4N_2O and 12R–Mg_4SiN_4. The different polytype designations arise because the non-metal stacking sequences contain blocks of three successive cubic close-

Table 3 *X-ray data for* 6H–Mg_4ON_2. *Unit cell: a =* 3.549, *c* = 15.991 A

hk l	d_{calc}	d_{obs}	I_{obs}
002	8.00	7.99	m
004	4.003	4.000	mw
100	3.073	3.075	ms
101	3.018	3.017	vs
006	2.667 ⎫	2.663	ms
103	2.663 ⎭		
104	2.437	2.437	s[a]
105	2.216	2.215	w
106	2.014	2.014	m
008	2.000	2.000	m
107	1.834	1.833	m
110	1.774	1.774	vs
112	1.732	1.733	vvw
114	1.622	1.622	vw
200	1.537	1.537	w
201	1.530	1.530	mw
203	1.476	1.476	m
204	1.434	1.433	mw
118	1.327	1.327	m
1012	1.223	1.223	mw

(*a*) Overlap with MgO

Table 4 *X-ray data for* 12R–Mg_4SiN_4. *Unit cell: a* = 3.442, *c* = 31.326 A

hk l	d_{calc}	d_{obs}	I_{obs}
003	10.44	10.37	m
009	3.481	3.481	w
101	2.967	2.968	s
012	2.927	2.927	m
104	2.786	2.787	ms
0012	2.611	2.609	m
107	2.481	2.480	m
018	2.372	2.372	w
1010	2.159	2.159	w
0015	2.088	2.088	mw
1013	1.874	1.874	mw
0114	1.789	1.790	w
110	1.721	1.721	ms
118	1.575	1.574	vw
0117	1.567	1.567	vw
027	1.414	1.414	w
1022	1.285	1.285	w

packed layers rather than the two observed in previous series. The stacking sequences are therefore .. ABCACB .. in the 6H polytype and .. ABCA CABC BCAB .. in the 12R polytype. Tables 3 and 4 list X-ray diffraction data for these compounds.

In contrast to Be—Si—O—N, no phases have been observed at M : X ratios other than 4M : 3X and 5M : 4X in the Mg—Si—O—N system. The two magnesium polytypes have a negligible range of composition and occur essentially at discrete points along the $MgO-Mg_3N_2$ and $Mg_3N_2-Si_3N_4$ joins. This is probably a result of the complete ordering (and hence a simple ratio between the two different kinds of metal atoms) which occurs when magnesium and silicon occupy tetrahedrally co-ordinated metal-atom sites, for example in oxide systems, in $MgSiN_2$,[10] and in $MgAlSiN_3$.[11]

Conclusion

The present study gives an indication of the wide range of occurrence of polytype phases in nitrogen ceramics. The picture is by no means complete and it is to be expected that additional phases will occur as the work is extended to other metal—silicon—aluminium—oxygen—nitrogen systems.

We are grateful to Professor K. H. Jack for discussion and encouragement and to Mr. D. S. Perera for carrying out much of the experimental work in the Mg—Si—O—N system. The research has been financed by Joseph Lucas Limited and the Wolfson Foundation.

[10] J. David, Y. Laurent, and J. Lang, *Bull. Soc. franç Mineral Crist.*, 1970, **93**, 153.
[11] D. S. Perera, 'Magnesium Sialons', PhD Thesis, University of Newcastle upon Tyne, September 1976.

The NPL Metallurgical and Inorganic Thermochemical Data Bank and its Applications

By G. P. JONES

Division of Chemical Standards, National Physical Laboratory, Teddington, Middlesex

Introduction

In the practice of materials sciences, many of the practical questions are: (i) is X stable in contact with Y? (ii) how much AB is formed from contact between BC and AC? (iii) what temperature causes appreciable loss (vaporization) of A when AB and CD are treated together? (iv) what causes substance S to lose its required properties above a given temperature?

Unfortunately, there is all too often no specific knowledge from which to obtain an answer, or else it is not possible (or economically practicable) to determine by chemical or instrumental analysis the identity and amount of the substances involved. However, if the example in question involves substances being held at moderately high temperatures, there is a reasonable prospect that equilibrium conditions can be approached, at least at interfaces. In such circumstances, information about a problem can often be obtained by the application of the principles of equilibrium thermodynamics.

Partial Neglect of Applied Thermodynamics

The application of thermodynamics as an analytical tool is not a new concept, and there are of course many materials scientists who would subscribe in principle to its application in the context of their specific problems. However, our experience is that many of them would not themselves seriously seek to apply thermodynamics practically. This points to the existence of certain deterents to the application of thermodynamics, which may perhaps be thought of as follows.

(i) Many would-be users shrink away from the subtleties of the subject, such as: what is the formal thermodynamic representation of a question, is the correct theory being invoked, is that theory applied correctly?

(ii) There are data problems: are these the appropriate data, are these data sufficiently accurate, and often, where are these data available?

(iii) There are numerical problems: is the arithmetic correct?

Limitations of Thermodynamic Data

To someone hoping to use thermodynamics to solve a problem, it may be surprising that in the late seventies in spite of the explosion in output of scientific publications in the late fifties and sixties, there should still be a shortage of reliable thermodynamic data on relatively commonplace materials. While this situation exists, there are unfortunate consequences. Data not available in major compilations have to be sought painstakingly in the literature. Even valuable compilations like the JANAF tables and the NBS 270 series of selected thermodynamic tables have omissions (for example, zinc compounds, and thermal properties above 298 K, respectively) and have certain other drawbacks, among which is that they are 'frozen' at the time of printing, with the consequence that any changes in values for key substances (such as those recommended by CODATA) are not easily incorporated in any reprint. The CODATA Task Group on Key Values for Thermodynamics has been gradually tackling the assessment and tabulation of the standard enthalpies of formation and standard entropies of key substances at 298.15 K, to provide an internationally agreed basis for key data on which the data for thermodynamically related substances are based.

Use of the Digital Computer in Data Manipulation

Fortunately, concurrent with the information explosion came the development and increasingly widespread application of the digital computer. It was eventually sufficiently advanced in capability to perform a number of different functions. These were (i) the storage of large amounts of mixed alphabetic and numeric data, (ii) the searching or scanning of the stored data at high speed, (iii) the identification and retrieval of stored information having 'labels' matching those in an input interrogation, (iv) the performance of even the most difficult arithmetical operations, singly or iteratively, upon one or more groups of data or data-sets, (v) the execution of these tasks by remote access in one machine and in one user-operation using real-time computing, and (vi) the extension of the scope of the computations by using an appropriate program requiring numerous simple responses from the user. The program not only gives scope for user-control within one of its sub-sections, but by subsequently looping back to branch-points gives the user repeated opportunity to select a subsection offering a different facility. With such facilities it is practicable for a computer to be used for scientific data-banking.

A data bank may be defined as a large collection of data, organized into a structured body which can be repeatedly consulted and manipulated (as well as updated) to provide reliable and labour-saving answers to varied and/or difficult interrogations.

The creation of such a data bank, given proper machine programming, both simplifies the correct application of thermodynamic principles for the user and also guarantees the numerical reliability of the calculation. All relevant data sets can (and ideally should) be already stored in the bank, and are then accessed and handled by program. The subject and the subsequent course of the calculation are directed in conversational mode by the user from a computer terminal. Human error is largely eliminated by automatic output of error warnings.

Function and Limitations of Data Bank

To be effective, the purpose of a data bank such as NPL's 'MTDATA' must be defined and restricted, to avoid the real danger of pointless expense in unnecessary data preparation, handling, and storage, as well as excessive program size and operating costs. NPL's program routines therefore focus on the familiar relationships shown in equations (1)–(4), where G is the Gibbs energy, H the

Inherent property for a single substance	Change in property upon reaction	
$G^{\ominus} = H^{\ominus} - TS^{\ominus}$	$\Delta G^{\ominus} = \Delta H^{\ominus} - T\Delta S^{\ominus}$	(1)
—	$\Delta G^{\ominus} = -RT \ln K_p$	(2)
$H_T^{\ominus} = H_{298}^{\ominus} + \int_{298}^{T} C_p^{\ominus} . dT$	$\Delta H_T^{\ominus} = \Delta H_{298}^{\ominus} + \int_{298}^{T} \Delta C_p^{\ominus} . dT$	(3)
$S_T^{\ominus} = S_{298}^{\ominus} + \int_{298}^{T} C_p^{\ominus}/T . dT$	$\Delta S_T^{\ominus} = \Delta S_{298}^{\ominus} + \int_{298}^{T} \Delta C_p^{\ominus}/T . dT$	(4)

enthalpy, S the entropy, C_p the heat capacity at constant pressure of one mole of the substance involved, and K_p is the equilibrium constant. The delta prefix is applied to changes in these quantities for a *system*, namely the changes which accompany the total conversion of reactants into products by a chemical reaction. When used here together with the suffix f, it means the change on formation from the elements, *e.g.* $\Delta_f H^{\ominus}$ is the standard enthalpy of formation. The superscript $^{\ominus}$ is used when these symbols are applied to substances (or reacting systems) in their thermodynamic standard state (*i.e.* the pure condensed phase or the gas at one atmosphere). The suffix 298 or T refers to the temperature in kelvins.

Inspection of these equations will reveal that a set of data for every substance involved, containing the values for standard enthalpy of formation $\Delta_f H_{298}^{\ominus}$ and standard entropy $S_{298}^{\ominus}$, together with expressions for the dependence upon temperature of the molar heat capacity $C_p^{\ominus}$, is sufficient to allow all of the above thermodynamic quantities to be calculated.

The task of data-assessment itself is a demanding one which requires time, effort, and skill. Though there is a perpetual requirement for data-banking of this type, it is not discussed in this paper. The NPL data bank 'MTDATA' currently contains more than 2000 carefully assessed data 'sets' (see below) drawn from NPL sources and others, including the compilations mentioned above. Some estimates are included where necessary. All banked data are in the form of completed data sets, so that properties at elevated temperatures may normally be calculated.

Data Representation and Formats

As already mentioned, the values of the standard molar enthalpy of formation and entropy at 298.15 K are stored for every substance represented in the bank. Calorie units are used throughout, as in the bulk of the world's thermodynamic literature, though calculation in joule units is equally provided for within the routines of MTDATA bank.

The molar heat capacity C_p is represented by equation (5), where a, b, c, d are

$$C_p = a + bT + cT^2 + dT^{-2} \tag{5}$$

stored coefficients and T is the thermodynamic temperature (Kelvin). The last two of these four coefficients may be thought of as introducing to the representation of an experimentally measured C_p, which might perhaps be roughly linear, terms which represent, respectively, any high-temperature or low-temperature curvature. The resultant expressions may be used for long or short temperature ranges, beginning at 298.15 K, as may be appropriate to represent accurately the known values for a given substance.

Each set of C_p coefficients is followed by its upper temperature limit of validity, then by a value for the enthalpy of transition to any further phase or state, and in that eventuality by another such line of data. When more than one set of coefficients is necessary for the accurate representation of heat capacity over a given temperature range, the enthalpy of transition between the notional ranges is naturally zero. The number of C_p ranges is a significant datum: it is filed preceding the C_p data themselves. However, C_p values derived from such equations, if used beyond the temperature range to which they apply, can sometimes be grossly inaccurate. The computer program therefore restricts the temperature range available to the user for calculation, from 298 K to an upper temperature set by the *lowest* of the upper limits applying to the set of substances which are the subject of calculation. However, the experienced user may with care override this restriction.

The 'label' used to identify each data set is the chemical formula of the substance which represents, suitably adapted to computer filing and other special

Data-set for Chlorine Gas

$Cl_2(g)$

Standard Enthalpy of Formation;	Standard Entropy;	No. of Equations to reach Upper Temp. Limit to C_p
$\Delta_f H^\circ_{298}$/cal mol^{-1}	S°_{298}/cal mol^{-1}	
0	53.29	2

Equation for C_p/cal mol^{-1} K^{-1}

$$a \quad +bT \quad +cT^2 \quad +dT^2$$

Coefficients of Equation				Upper Temperature for range	Enthalpy of Transition to to next range
a	b	c	d	/K	/cal
8.725	0.365E−3	−0.075E−6	−0.642E5	2000	0
7.045	0.950E−3	−0.084E−6	21.801E5	6000	0

Set of Coefficients as Filed in the Computer.

```
CL02.000(G)

0.0000E+00  5.3289E+01   2

8.7249E+00  3.6499E−04  −7.4999E−08  −6.4200E+04  2.0000E+03  0.0000E+0
7.0449E+00  9.4999E−04  −8.3999E−08   2.1801E+06  6.0000E+03  0.0000E+0
```

Figure 1 *Typical data set, containing formal label and normalized array of coefficients for chlorine gas*

purposes of the program. Since it is still far from usual to find computer terminals able to print lower case typescript, there exist obvious possibilities for confusion, *e.g.* between Co and CO, unless care is taken. In the NPL system these possibilities are avoided by representing all elements by two letters, those which are normally single being amended by repetition, *e.g.* O becomes OO.

To achieve rapid, positive and unique location of a data-set within its data file, the label for a compound is composed in strict alphabetical order, and each element symbol occurring in the label is quantified by a number in a filled five-digit field xx.xxx following it, which thus permits handling of data for non-stoicheiometric compounds. Figure 1 shows a typical data set.

Handling Filed Data

Although the total exactness of the labelling data-base within the computer files may seem to imply that the user must be equally rigid when defining the subject(s) of his enquiry, this is not so: the 'logical' capacity of the computer is able for file-search purposes to facilitate the user's enquiry. It will re-organize a non-standard label (if sufficiently definitive) into the standard file format. Further, since the computer can readily handle in one interaction the data coefficients representing the properties of several compounds, it is able to handle the calculation of the changes in molar thermodynamic quantities for a multi-component chemical reaction. For file-searching purposes, the computer handles *alphabetical* information, which here is always delimited from numerical data by enclosure within single quotation marks [see equation (6c)].

The NPL representation of an equation for a reaction is made entirely within these delimiters and uses negative and positive prefixes for the constituents of the left and right hand sides respectively. It must be terminated with a semicolon. The prefixes act as the separators and command operators used within the program.

If the thermal properties of a single substance are required, the input interrogation is in the form: '+ AA;'. The output tabulation lists the values of heat capacity, standard entropies and enthalpies, and Gibbs energy functions over the selected temperature range.

Thermodynamic States treated in 'MTDATA'

The states of the materials to which the data sets apply are denoted by suffixes to the formal or any simplified name. To date, four kinds of suffix are in use. Data banked with suffix (C) or (G) relate to pure substances in their standard condensed states or gaseous state, respectively. Data for the partial molar thermodynamic properties of substances (*i.e.* in their non-standard state) are banked for dilute solutions of condensed (A) and gaseous (D) elements in numerous metals, *i.e.* for their Alloyed or Dissolved state, respectively.

Calculations for reactions involving substances in the non-standard state are made in two stages, by using appropriate data for the reaction in the standard (pure) state, and 'adding' to that the data for the reaction by which the substance is converted from the non-standard into the standard state:

$$- AA(G) - BB(C) + AA\ BB(C) \qquad (6a)$$

$$- BB(A) + \qquad BB(C) \qquad (6b)$$

$$\overline{'- AA(G) - BB(A) + AA\ BB(C)'} \qquad (6c)$$

Of course, the conditions of solution of the solute have to be defined, and this is done in an input, on the line following the initiating equation, which identifies the solvent and gives the molar concentration, for each solute. (See example 2 and 3(a) below, and their respective figures.)

The banked data for dilute solution are those representing the properties of a solute in a given solvent over the concentration range zero to an upper limit, in which Henry's law is known to apply. In this region, the partial molar enthalpy $\overline{\Delta H}$ and partial molar (excess) entropy $\overline{\Delta S}$ of solution both remain constant, and the equation giving the Gibbs energy change per mole at a temperature T on converting from the standard into the non-standard state is therefore (taking account also of the effect of entropy of random mixing):

$$\overline{\Delta G} = \overline{\Delta H} - T(\overline{\Delta S} - R\log_e N) \qquad (7)$$

where N is the mole fraction of the solute.

Since in dilute solution the solute species is monatomic, whereas the standard state of the element concerned may not be, it is necessary also to bank a datum giving the relevant atomic ratio. An upper limit of concentration and upper and lower limits of temperature for which the partial molar quantities are valid are also banked.

Both the standard-state and dilute-solution data-sets thus exist in standard arrays. Therefore, once having entered an enquiry in the form of an equation, it is readily possible to specify a particular data set, whether in the first or any second input line which defines the equation, namely by its position in that line. Likewise, one specific datum within that set can be located by specifying its row and column number. The program therefore provides for temporary amendment of any datum on receiving as input four numbers serving as locator, followed by the temporary datum.

Using the Data Bank

Before describing the mechanics of access to the 'MTDATA' bank, it should first be emphasized that operation of the system by unqualified personnel wholly untrained in programming or computing can be undertaken after only a few minutes of instruction. Of course, some scientific direction is necessary to frame the particular 'enquiries', but as already emphasized, competence in thermodynamics is not required. On the other hand, professional thermodynamicists do themselves find 'MTDATA' a very useful tool.

A telephone and GPO Modem or acoustic coupler are used to gain access to the commercial time-sharing computer-bureau on which the data bank is currently housed. On supplying a valid bureau-password, the user will command RUN MTDATA, and after a confirmatory response will supply a password. Before inviting the user to type an equation, the system responds with a list summarizing program options, which is numbered 0–5. This reminds the user of the various discrete operations possible within the program, any of which may be selected at the conclusion of any various sub-sections of the program, in response to the output OPTION = ?. To date, the available options are: to proceed in the simplest manner (for unfamiliar users); to inspect the data; to amend temporarily the data ex-bank; to calculate using the data for selected temperatures; to initiate a wholly new enquiry; or to terminate the session.

As previously stated, the enquiry is usually entered in the form of an equation, which is permitted to contain up to 10 interacting components. If this equation refers to a dilute solution, by the use of suffix (A) for substances with condensed reference states or (D) for gaseous reference states, respectively, it provokes a request for the user to provide a second line for the 'equation'. This will formally define the solvent, and − if known − the relevant concentration, thus enabling the appropriate data file for dilute solutions to be read, and the standard and non-standard data sets to be combined.

In cases where reactions on pure substances involve gases, the final computer tabulation of the changes in principal thermodynamic properties is extended by automatic output of an extra column giving the appropriate values of equilibrium constant for the reaction.

For chemical reactions involving substances in dilute solution, the changes in thermodynamic properties (except C_p) are again tabulated normally in the output, provided all compositions are specified.

If one solute concentration is unspecified, these changes cannot be calculated: instead, the concentration of that solute is determined for the imposed supposition that $\Delta G = 0$, and tabulated as $\log_{10} N$, where N is the solute mol fraction. This quantity is in effect a 'saturation solubility'.

If more than one solute concentration is unspecified, the corresponding output is in effect the logarithm of a 'solubility product'.

Examples of Types of Application

A few examples to illustrate the very wide range of application of the 'MTDATA' bank are now given. For some of us, the illustrations which follow may offer an unfamiliar but helpful comment. They show how the bank can be variously of use to the chemist, the metallurgist, or the ceramist, to give information about or to explain certain aspects of materials behaviour.

Example 1: Chemical Processes

Titanium producers use two main routes for the extraction of titanium from ores and minerals: the sulphuric acid leaching of ilmenite, $Fe\,TiO_3$, or related compounds, and the chlorination of rutile, TiO_2. The process of chlorination of ilmenite has, however, generally been avoided, probably because of practical difficulties, but some considerations which might affect the chances that it could ever be successfully implemented are: (i) the extent to which titanium can be selectively chlorinated; (ii) the handling problem due to the presence of iron chlorides in the conversion plant, if chlorination were unselective; and (iii) the extra consumption and cost of chlorine in that case.

If chlorination were selective, the two main end-products leaving the converter would be gaseous titanium tetrachloride and an iron oxide. The extent to which these materials could undergo 'double decomposition', *i.e.* might be mutually unstable, is examined in the calculation shown in Figure 2. Here, the large negative value of DELTAG (ΔG) at all practical temperatures suggests (as do similar considerations involving the other iron chlorides) that the chlorination of ilmenite will not selectively produce $TiCl_4$(g) because iron chlorides will form preferentially, provided equilibrium is approached. The conclusion is drawn that treatment of ilmenite feeds by normal chlorination techniques will always be much more expensive than is the case with rutile feeds, even if (ii) above is manageable, because of the selectivity for iron.

THERMODYNAMIC FUNCTIONS

-3TICL4(G)-2FE2O03+3TIO02+2FE2CL6(G)

T K	DELTACP CAL/K MOL	DELTAS CAL/K MOL	DELTAH CAL/MOL	DELTAG CAL/MOL	LOG10KP
400.00	-0.919	-2.943	-47357	-46180	25.232
600.00	-8.089	-4.727	-48285	-45449	16.555
800.00	-14.377	-7.925	-50539	-44199	12.075
1000.00	-8.952	-11.583	-53816	-42233	9.230
1200.00	-2.877	-12.444	-54739	-39807	7.250

TRANSITIONS WITHIN REQUESTED TEMPERATURE RANGE
    950.000

Figure 2 *Stability of gaseous titanium chloride against iron oxide*

Example 2: Metallurgical Processes
The production of ferrochrome and of metallic chromium is achieved alumino-thermically. Figure 3 shows that at the given temperatures the changes in enthalpy and free energy for the given number of moles of reactants are each very negative, thus indicating why this method of production is effective. However, in production practice, a heat 'balance' has to be struck, so that sufficient heat is evolved on the reaction of aluminium with the metal oxides to melt the metallic

THERMODYNAMIC FUNCTIONS

-CR2O03-2AL+AL2O03+2CR

T K	DELTACP CAL/K MOL	DELTAS CAL/K MOL	DELTAH CAL/MOL	DELTAG CAL/MOL
300.00	-6.542	-9.481	-130012	-127168
400.00	-4.045	-10.977	-130526	-126136
2150.00	3.771	-11.500	-123369	-98644
2200.00	3.758	-11.414	-123181	-98071
2250.00	3.743	-11.329	-122994	-97502

TRANSITIONS WITHIN REQUESTED TEMPERATURE RANGE
    933.250   2130.000

Figure 3 *Aluminothermic production of chromium*

chromium, but with a controlled and limited excess temperature. To this end, some preheating may be necessary.

The end-temperature of the hypothetically adiabatic reaction is obtained by calculating the temperature which would be reached if the process were carried out isothermally at the starting temperature, and all the energy evolved were available to heat the reaction products.

THERMODYNAMIC FUNCTIONS

```
-AL2OO3+2AL(A)+1,5OO2(D)
       /CR,O.OO1//CR,O/

    T          LOG1O< (N(OO)$ 3.OO)> + LIMITS

 1850.00      -18.036          0.001
 1950.00      -16.210          0.001
 2050.00      -14.564          0.001
 2150.00      -11.632          0.005
 2250.00      -10.387          0.005

 TRANSITIONS WITHIN REQUESTED TEMPERATURE RANGE
 NONE
```

Figure 4 *Residual oxygen in aluminothermic chromium*

However, this view of the aluminothermic process is rather oversimplified. Thus in fact, molten chromium is readily able to *dissolve* metallic aluminium, which is then no longer at unit activity. Further, oxygen itself is perceptibly soluble in molten chromium. Within the time span of the reaction, little solution of chromia is thought likely to take place in solid alumina, although chromia too is soluble in both solid and liquid alumina, and to a lesser degree in aluminate slags. If the solution of chromia is neglected, it is clear that at completion of the exchange reaction, an equilibrium will be established between solid alumina and the solutes oxygen and aluminium in liquid solvent chromium. If we assume that a residual level of 0.1 mol% alloying aluminium in the chromium were intended and achieved, then given appropriate thermodynamic data, the equilibrium oxygen content in the chromium is calculable, and is given in Figure 4.

THERMODYNAMIC FUNCTIONS

```
-3MGOO-2AL+AL2OO3+3MG(A)
        /AL,O/

    T          LOG1O< (N(MG)$ 3.OO)> + LIMITS   | 100N[Mg]_Al /% |

 1000.00      -5.858          0.050              |      1.1       |
 1100.00      -5.284          0.050              |      1.7       |
 1200.00      -4.804          0.050              |      2.5       |
 1300.00      -4.395          0.050              |      3.4       |
 1400.00      -4.042          0.050              |      4.5       |

 TRANSITIONS WITHIN REQUESTED TEMPERATURE RANGE
 NONE
```

Figure 5 *Take-up of magnesium from magnesia by aluminium*

Note that the use of the suffix (A) [and equally (D)] in the original inter-rogating equation had automatically provoked a request for the solution conditions in a second line of the 'equation' which has been re-output at the head of the table. In the relevant position in this second line, the oxygen content of the chromium was left unstated by the use of 0 in the solution parameter /Cr,O/, and the 'MTDATA' program therefore calculates the oxygen content for the equilibrium (saturated) condition. The table shows that the oxygen content of the melt is perceptible. This content, if trapped as oxide on cooling, will clearly affect some properties of the chromium button.

Example 3(a): Stability of Refractory Materials against Foundry Metal

A foundry may need to melt aluminium when only a magnesia-lined furnace is available. Although simple considerations suggest that this is thermodynamically permissible, calculation indicates that in practice it would not be. The values given in Figure 5 show that some of the furnace aluminium can reduce magnesia from the refractory to metallic magnesium *in solution* in the remaining aluminium, *i.e.* at reduced activity, and that the reaction could proceed to a significant extent at normal furnace temperatures. Column 2 lists values of $\log_{10} N^3$[Mg], and the added figures (boxed) show them evaluated as mol% [Mg]. The potential pick-up of magnesium by the aluminium can be seen to be considerable. (Column 3 lists the upper limit of concentration of the solute for which the banked data, and therefore related output tabulations, are valid.)

THERMODYNAMIC FUNCTIONS

-MGCR2OO4-1.5OO2(G)+MGOO+2CROO3(G)

T K	DELTACP CAL/K MOL	DELTAS CAL/K MOL	DELTAH CAL/MOL	DELTAG CAL/MOL	LOG1OKP
1600.00	-6.818	26.114	116178	74396	-10.162
1700.00	-7.129	25.691	115481	71806	-9.231
1800.00	-7.445	25.275	114752	69258	-8.409
1900.00	-7.764	24.864	113992	66751	-7.678
2000.00	-8.087	24.457	113199	64285	-7.025
2100.00	-8.412	24.055	112374	61859	-6.438

TRANSITIONS WITHIN REQUESTED TEMPERATURE RANGE
NONE

Figure 6 *Volatilization of chrome from refractories*

Example 3(b): Stability of Refractory Materials in Unsuitable Atmospheres

If a chrome-magnesite refractory is used in an oxidizing atmosphere, oxidation of the chrome content of the refractory can occur, leading to losses by volatilization. Thus the equilibrium constants given in Figure 6 give an idea of the scale and temperature-dependence of oxidation loss fron the spinel $MgCr_2O_4$ in the form of the volatile chromium trioxide $CrO_3(g)$. It can be seen that at 1900 K in an atmosphere of substantially pure oxygen the logarithm of the equilibrium partial pressure of $CrO_3(g)$ is $-7.678/2$ or -3.839. This corresponds to more than 0.1 mmHg (*ca.* 13 Pa or $1.32.10^{-4}$ atm).

The long life of electric-resistance furnace heater-elements constructed from molybdenum disilicide $MoSi_2$ is well known. It results from the protection against further oxidation given to this substance by a coherent and relatively impervious sheathing largely of silica. However, it is less well realized that this high-temperature protection is entirely dependent on the presence of an atmosphere containing a sufficient partial pressure of oxygen, and that failure to provide sufficiently oxidizing conditions can cause $MoSi_2$ to lose completely its characteristic and marked oxidation resistance, and give rise to a known form of component failure.

The normal oxidation process for $MoSi_2$ in air is summarized in equation (8a). The principal oxidation product is the protective coating of silica; if any molybdenum does become oxidized it forms volatile MoO_3, which generally evaporates from the surface and contributes little to the oxidation resistance of this material. If the oxygen pressure is too low for the formation of SiO_2, the protective coating of silicide can be removed by the formation of SiO gaseous molecules as represented by equation (8b). Equation (8c) represents a reaction in which SiO gaseous molecules could be lost from an already oxidized silicide coating; such a reaction could again lead to thinning of the protective layer. These processes,

$$5/7 \; MoSi_2 + O_2(g) = SiO_2(c) + 1/7 \; Mo_5Si_3 \qquad (8a)$$

$$10/7 \; MoSi_2 + O_2(g) = 2 \; SiO(g) + 2/7 \; Mo_5Si_3 \qquad (8b)$$

$$5/7 \; MoSi_2 + SiO_2 = 2 \; SiO(g) + 1/7 \; Mo_5Si_3 \qquad (8c)$$

$$2 \; SiO(g) + O_2(g) = 2 \; SiO_2 \qquad (8d)$$

together with equation (8d), all take part in the general equilibrium which is attained in any given conditions. However, the extent of these reactions varies with temperature, and with the oxygen pressure in the ambient atmosphere. When (8b) is thermodynamically favoured relative to (8a), then

$$\Delta G(8b) < \Delta G(8a), \text{ and } \Delta G(8b) - \Delta G(8a) \; [= \Delta G(8c)] < 0$$

THERMODYNAMIC FUNCTIONS

-0.357MOSI2-0.5SIO02+0.071MO5SI3 + SIO0(G)

T K	DELTACP CAL/K MOL	DELTAS CAL/K MOL	DELTAH CAL/MOL	DELTAG CAL/MOL	LOG10KP
1600.00	-3.279	39.106	87507	24937	-3.406
1700.00	-3.332	38.906	87177	21036	-2.704
1800.00	-3.387	38.714	86841	17155	-2.083
1900.00	-3.445	38.529	86499	13293	-1.529
2000.00	-4.922	37.696	84845	9453	-1.033

TRANSITIONS WITHIN REQUESTED TEMPERATURE RANGE
   1995.000

Figure 7 *Calculation of stability regions for protective coatings on* $MoSi_2$ *(see text)*

Because of the above interrelationships, it is not necessary to calculate the various equilibrium conditions under which (8b) would predominate over (8a), for reaction (8c) is a more convenient indicator of this when $\Delta G = O$. The condition for reaction (8c) together with reaction (8d) defines the partial pressure of oxygen below which the gaseous oxidation process for $MoSi_2$ due to reaction (8a) will cease. Process (8c) is shown evaluated (for half-quantities) in Figure 7, where the partial pressure of SiO when $\Delta G(8c) = O$ is given by $\log K_p = \log p(SiO)$. The critical values of oxygen partial pressure in the ambient atmosphere below which reaction (8a) cannot occur and only reaction (8b) occurs, are given in Table 1 for temperatures of interest.

Table 1 *Retention of oxidation barrier on* $MoSi_2$

Initial partial pressure of oxygen in non-reacting atmosphere		Calculated maximum temperature for stable SiO_2
/log atm	/mmHg	/K
−1.334	35	2000
−1.5	24	1966
−1.830	11.24	1900
−2.0	7.6	1867
−2.384	3.14	1800
−2.5	2.4	1780
−3.0	0.76	1701
−3.005	0.75	1700
−3.5	0.24	1628
−3.707	0,15	1600

From Table 1 it can be inferred that if reaction (8b) occurs at about 1780 K ($\approx 1500\,^{\circ}C$) with the oxygen pressure given in Table 1 the equilibrium partial pressure of SiO could be as much as ≈ 5 mmHg, high enough to cause appreciable loss from the $MoSi_2$ substrate. Thus if for a given value of pressure or temperature in Table 1 the corresponding listed temperature were exceeded, or pressure not attained, then reaction (8b) would become dominant and silica would no longer be formed, and $MoSi_2$ would undergo early failure.

Conclusion

These example calculations, each of which can be executed without any delay in less than 5 min at a computer terminal, illustrate the utility and versatility of this multiple-interaction, computational, numerical NPL data bank. It is available to potential customers, either as a postal service, or on license for direct use, and enquiries are welcomed by the author.

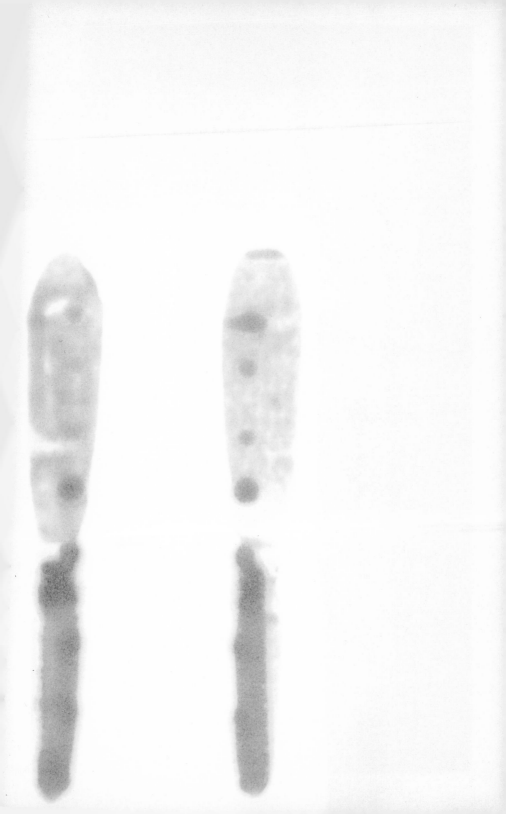